SOVEREIGNTY, STATEHOOD AND STATE RESPONSIBILITY

This collection of essays focuses on the following concepts: sovereignty (the unique, intangible and yet essential characteristic of States), statehood (what it means to be a State, and the process of acquiring or losing statehood) and State responsibility (the legal component of what being a State entails). The unifying theme is that they have always been and will in the future continue to form a crucial part of the foundations of public international law.

While many publications focus on new actors in international law such as international organisations, individuals, companies, NGOs and even humanity as a whole, this book offers a timely, thought-provoking and innovative reappraisal of the core actors on the international stage: States. It includes reflections on the interactions between States and non-State actors and on how increasing participation by and recognition of the latter within international law has impacted upon the role and attributes of statehood.

CHRISTINE CHINKIN is Professor of International Law at the London School of Economics and Political Science, a barrister, a member of Matrix Chambers and William Cook Global Law Professor at the University of Michigan.

FREYA BAETENS is Associate Professor of Law, Director of Studies and Head of the LUC Research Centre at Leiden University, the Netherlands; Visiting Professor at the World Trade Institute at Bern University, Switzerland; and Associate Lawyer with VVGB (Brussels Bar).

SOVEREIGNTY, STATEHOOD AND STATE RESPONSIBILITY

Essays in Honour of James Crawford

Edited by
CHRISTINE CHINKIN
and
FREYA BAETENS

CAMBRIDGE
UNIVERSITY PRESS

CAMBRIDGE
UNIVERSITY PRESS

University Printing House, Cambridge CB2 8BS, United Kingdom

Cambridge University Press is part of the University of Cambridge.

It furthers the University's mission by disseminating knowledge in the pursuit of education, learning and research at the highest international levels of excellence.

www.cambridge.org
Information on this title: www.cambridge.org/9781107044258

First published 2015

A catalogue record for this publication is available from the British Library

Library of Congress Cataloguing in Publication data
Sovereignty, statehood and state responsibility: essays in honour of James Crawford / edited by Christine Chinkin, Freya Baetens.
pages cm
Includes bibliographical references and index.
ISBN 978-1-107-04425-8 (hardback)
1. Sovereignty 2. State, The 3. Government liability. 4. International law.
I. Chinkin, C. M., editor. II. Baetens, Freya, editor. III. Crawford, James, 1948–, honouree.
KZ4034.S67 2014
341.26 – dc23 2014032233

ISBN 978-1-107-04425-8 Hardback

CONTENTS

List of contributors *page* viii
Editors' preface xi
James Crawford: the early years, by Ivan Shearer xiii
An Australian in England, by Philippe Sands xx
List of cases xxvi
List of domestic legislation xxxviii
List of treaties xli
List of resolutions xliv
List of other international instruments and reports xlvi

PART I **Sovereignty**

1 The war against cliché: dispatches from the international legal front 3
KAREN KNOP AND SUSAN MARKS

2 International law and the responsibility to protect 23
MICHAEL BYERS

3 Human rights beyond borders at the World Court 51
RALPH WILDE

4 Fragmentation, regime interaction and sovereignty 71
MARGARET A. YOUNG

5 The legitimacy of investment treaties: between Exit, Voice and James Crawford's quest for a more democratic international law 90
LLUÍS PARADELL TRIUS

6 Polar territorial and maritime sovereignty in the twenty-first century 110
DONALD R. ROTHWELL

7 An enquiry into the palimpsestic nature of territorial sovereignty in East Asia – with particular reference to the Senkaku/Diaoyudao question 126

KEUN-GWAN LEE

8 General legal characteristics of States: a view from the past of the Permanent Court of International Justice 144

OLE SPIERMANN

PART II **Statehood**

9 The Security Council and statehood 155

CHRISTINE CHINKIN

10 The dynamics of statehood in the practice of international and English courts 172

ALEXANDER ORAKHELASHVILI

11 How to recognise a State (and not): some practical considerations 192

TOM GRANT

12 An analysis of the 1969 Act of Free Choice in West Papua 209

THOMAS D. MUSGRAVE

13 Recognition of the State of Palestine: still too much too soon? 229

YAËL RONEN

14 The role of the *uti possidetis* principle in the resolution of maritime boundary disputes 248

SUZANNE LALONDE

15 Room for 'State continuity' in international law? A constitutionalist perspective 273

INETA ZIEMELE

PART III **State Responsibility**

16 Law-making in complex processes: the World Court and the modern law of State responsibility 287

CHRISTIAN J. TAMS

17 Defending individual ships from pirates: questions of State responsibility and immunity 307

DOUGLAS GUILFOYLE

18 Excessive collateral civilian casualties and military necessity: awkward crossroads in international humanitarian law between State responsibility and individual criminal liability 325

YUTAKA ARAI-TAKAHASHI

19 Third-party countermeasures: observations on a controversial concept 340

MARTIN DAWIDOWICZ

20 The Appellate Body's use of the Articles on State responsibility in *US – Anti-dumping and Countervailing Duties (China)* 363

ISABELLE VAN DAMME

21 The application of the rules on countermeasures in investment claims: visions and realities of international law as an open system 389

KATE PARLETT

22 The external relations of the European Union and its Member States: lessons from recent developments in the economic sphere 406

DAMIEN GERADIN

23 Invoking, establishing and remedying State responsibility in mixed multi-party disputes: lessons from Eurotunnel 421

FREYA BAETENS

Index 442

CONTRIBUTORS

YUTAKA ARAI-TAKAHASHI
Chair of International Law and International Human Rights Law (University of Kent at Brussels)

FREYA BAETENS
Associate Professor of Law (Leiden University), Visiting Professor (World Trade Institute, Bern University), Associate Lawyer (VVGB – Brussels Bar)

MICHAEL BYERS
Professor and Canada Research Chair in Global Politics and International Law (University of British Columbia)

CHRISTINE CHINKIN
Professor of International Law (London School of Economics and Political Science), Barrister (Matrix Chambers)

MARTIN DAWIDOWICZ
Departmental Lecturer in Public International Law (University of Oxford)

DAMIEN GERADIN
Professor of Competition Law and Economics (Tilburg University), Professor of Law (George Mason University School of Law), Partner (Covington & Burling LLP)

TOM GRANT
Senior research fellow (Wolfson College, University of Cambridge), Visiting Professor (Catholic University of Lille), National Fellow (Hoover Institution, Stanford University)

DOUGLAS GUILFOYLE
Reader in Law (University College London)

KAREN KNOP
Professor of Law (University of Toronto)

SUZANNE LALONDE
Professor of Law (University of Montréal)

KEUN-GWAN LEE
Professor of Law (Seoul University)

SUSAN MARKS
Professor of Law (London School of Economics and Political Science)

THOMAS D. MUSGRAVE
Senior Lecturer (University of Wollongong)

ALEXANDER ORAKHELASHVILI
Lecturer in Law (University of Birmingham)

LLUÍS PARADELL TRIUS
Counsel (Freshfields Bruckhaus Deringer LLP)

KATE PARLETT
Senior Associate (Freshfields Bruckhaus Deringer LLP)

YAËL RONEN
Professor of International Law (Sha'arei Mishpat Academic Center)

DONALD R. ROTHWELL
Professor of International Law (Australian National University)

PHILIPPE SANDS, QC
Professor of Law (University College London), Barrister (Matrix Chambers)

IVAN SHEARER
Emeritus Professor of Law (University of Sydney), Adjunct Professor of Law (University of Adelaide), Adjunct Professor of Law (University of South Australia)

OLE SPIERMANN
Partner (Bruun & Hjejle) and previously Professor of International Law (University of Copenhagen)

CHRISTIAN J. TAMS
Professor of International Law (University of Glasgow)

ISABELLE VAN DAMME
Référendaire (Court of Justice of the European Union), Visiting Lecturer (Université Catholique de Louvain)

RALPH WILDE
Reader in Law (University College London)

MARGARET A. YOUNG
Associate Professor of Law (Melbourne University)

INETA ZIEMELE
Judge, Section President (European Court of Human Rights), Professor of International Law and Human Rights (Riga Graduate School of Law)

EDITORS' PREFACE

James Crawford has been a towering figure in international law and practice over the past decades, in universities (primarily in his native Australia and the United Kingdom), in international, regional and national courts and tribunals and in governmental (national and international) bodies. He has performed multiple roles in each of these sites: scholar, teacher, supervisor, dean, college fellow and director of a research centre; advocate, expert witness and arbitrator; and law reform commissioner in Australia and on the International Law Commission. His energy and work rate are legendary. He has given his time and expertise to non-governmental organisations, for instance as Director of Studies of the International Law Association. He has also received multiple honours including honorary doctorates, being elected a Fellow of the British Academy and, most recently, Companion in the General Division of the Order of Australia.

James's publications make clear that his academic research and writing interests are both prolific and range widely, especially across public international law, private international law and constitutional law. James is not associated with any 'school' of international law; rather, his commitment is to international law as an 'open system', a practical tool for the resolution of often apparently intractable international problems. But he is also 'open' to diverse theories and methodologies of international law, traditional positivist approaches as well as historical, interdisciplinary and critical work – as is evident from even a brief look at the contents of the co-edited (with Martti Koskenniemi) *Cambridge Companion to International Law*. In an era of international legal specialisation, James is a 'generalist' who has illuminated foundational concepts of international law: sovereignty, States, statehood, territory, self-determination, State responsibility. But he is also a specialist, for as is said by one of the contributors to this volume, no one can be a specialist without first being a generalist. Unsurprisingly, the range of topics chosen by contributors for their doctoral work under James's supervision is great. The constraints of commercial publication did not allow us to give a free hand to contributors, reflecting their past and current academic interests. Instead we sought to bring together a volume that reflects upon three concepts that have pervaded James's work over the past four decades and where he has made an outstanding intellectual contribution: sovereignty (the unique, intangible and yet essential characteristic of States), statehood (what it means to be(come) a State; the process of acquiring, or losing, statehood) and State responsibility (the legal component of what being a State entails). The unifying theme between these topics – apart from James's seminal work on each of them – is that they have always been, and will in the future continue to form, part of the foundation of public international law.

This volume is a tribute and token of gratitude to James Crawford on his retirement from academia in one of his many roles, that of doctoral supervisor and thus as scholar and mentor, rather than practitioner. All the contributors to the volume were former doctoral candidates under James's supervision at the law faculties at the University of Sydney and the University of Cambridge and are now themselves active in legal academia, in international legal practice, or both – hence its appellation as a *Liber Doctorandorum.*

We thank the authors for their contributions to the volume. We also give a special thank you to Elina Zlatanska and Sophie Starrenburg for their invaluable research and editing work which assisted us in finalising the volume. We also thank Cambridge University Press, and especially Finola O'Sullivan for her support and enthusiasm for this project.

Christine Chinkin, LSE

Freya Baetens, Leiden University

JAMES CRAWFORD: THE EARLY YEARS*

James Richard Crawford was born in Adelaide, South Australia on 14 November 1948. He is the oldest of the seven children of James Allen Crawford and Josephine Margaret Crawford (née Bond). He was educated first at Brighton High School, Adelaide, whose motto is *fac omnia bene* ('do everything well'), an admonition that James has evidently ever since taken to heart. The school also has a special focus on music, which remains an important part of James's life.

James's school record was one of outstanding achievement. He ended his time at school as co-head prefect. Along the way he was president of the Public Speaking and Debating Club, co-edited the school magazine and the school newspaper, played in the soccer A team and the cricket B team, was on the committee of the Senior French Club and acted in the Revue. His valedictory editorial in the 1965 issue of the school magazine demonstrates an early maturity of vision. Taking issue with a narrow definition of what education is about, the seventeen-year-old James wrote:

> [Then] what is education? Something like this: a leading out, through discipline and balance, of latent abilities in youth, and thus a preparation for life . . . For the purposes of the school, balance must mean intelligent participation in a wide range of activities; participation that is both giving and receiving. This year the school has had a wider range than ever before, with increased prefect and house activities, more clubs and sports teams. Intelligent participation in all facets of school life, or, if you like, the correct balance between 'work' and 'play' on a creative level; this is the way to a good education. And a good education is the way to a good life; the fulfilment of the aims of the individual, the society and therefore the school.

* I wish to acknowledge with thanks the assistance I have received from members of James's family, the Principal of Brighton High School (now named Brighton Secondary School), Ms Olivia O'Neill and the Dean of the Faculty of Law of the University of Adelaide, Professor John Williams.

James left school to enter the University of Adelaide in 1966, with the support of a government scholarship waiving fees, as a student in the faculties of arts and law. He collected a number of prizes and awards in both faculties, including the Angas Parsons Prize in Law in his final year, which was at that time the nearest equivalent to a university medal. In the faculty of arts he was awarded the Sir Archibald Strong Memorial Prize for Literature and the Bundey Prize for English verse (poetry remains important to him). The degrees of Bachelor of Arts and Bachelor of Laws (Honours) were conferred in 1972.

The University of Adelaide is one of Australia's oldest universities, established in 1874. Its first vice-chancellor, Dr Augustus Short, came to South Australia in 1847, eleven years after the foundation of the colony, as the first Anglican Bishop of Adelaide, after a notable career as a Fellow of Christ Church, Oxford. Among Dr Short's famous pupils at Oxford was the later prime minister W. E. Gladstone. Short's vision for the University of Adelaide was not tied to the model of the ancient universities of Great Britain. He foresaw the need for the developing colony to allow for an exploration of fields of scholarship beyond the classical mode of his own university. Before the end of the nineteenth century, faculties were established, as well as in arts, in science (in 1882, the first Australian university to establish such a faculty), law, medicine and music. Mathematics, philosophy, languages and mining engineering were also taught. The law faculty at Adelaide ranks as the second oldest in Australia (1883).

The University of Adelaide remains an institution with liberal traditions and a spirit of free inquiry. The vice-chancellor just before James's time was A. P. Rowe, whose habit of personally dropping in on rooms whose lights were burning late at night to find out what interesting developments were being hatched, in whatever field, led to his being humorously dubbed 'the Abominable Rowe Man'. His successor, Sir Henry Basten, had similarly wide interests and peripatetic habits, which led on one occasion to his arrest as a suspected intruder. An anguished late-night telephone call to the university's registrar was needed to confirm his identity.

The law school in James's time included some notable scholars, although some subjects were still being taught by local barristers and solicitors. The days of major expansion in all Australian law schools were still to come. His teachers included Arthur Rogerson and John Keeler (recent arrivals from Oxford), Alex Castles, Horst Luecke, David Kelly and Michael Detmold. Some notable visiting teachers during James's time were David Williams of Cambridge and Rupert Cross of Oxford. Among the part-time teachers were John Bray QC, a leading advocate and a classics scholar, who later became Chief Justice of South Australia, and Roma Mitchell QC, successively Australia's first female Queen's Counsel, first female Supreme Court judge and first female state governor.

James's teacher of international law was D. P. O'Connell, who in the year of James's graduation (1972) was elected to the Chichele Chair of International Law at Oxford. The teaching of international law at Adelaide had had an interrupted history. It was taught, both as public and private international law, from the early twentieth century by Sir John Salmond, better known for his treatise on torts, and later a judge of the Supreme Court of New Zealand, then by Professor Jethro Brown and, in the early 1920s, by Professor Coleman Phillipson, author of a magisterial work on international law in ancient Greece and Rome. A break of some thirty years in the teaching of public international law followed, although not of private international law. The subject was not revived until some years after the arrival of O'Connell in 1951.

O'Connell was a New Zealander who won a postgraduate scholarship to Cambridge where he read for a doctorate under Professor Sir Hersch Lauterpacht. His subject was State succession, and his thesis first appeared in print in 1956. It was later expanded into a two-volume work. He later became known for his work on the law of the sea, and for his general treatise on international law (second edition, 1970). O'Connell's teaching was clearly influential in James's intellectual development even while James was somewhat reserved as to its theoretical underpinnings in natural law. O'Connell's mastery of detail and the telling anecdote, based on his wide practice as counsel (he appeared for Australia before the International Court in the Nuclear Tests case), could not have failed to impress and inspire a young student.

James won a postgraduate Shell Scholarship to pursue his interest in international law at Oxford, where he became a member of University College. Although he and O'Connell arrived in Oxford at much the same time, James chose to be supervised by Professor Ian Brownlie (later to be O'Connell's successor in the Chichele Chair, after O'Connell's untimely death in 1979). Brownlie provided a contrast in style and substance to O'Connell; his influence is evident in James's work in a similar economy of style and rigorous method of doctrinal inquiry. However, it cannot be said that James was an avid disciple of either of his teachers: he soon developed a distinctive approach and voice of his own.

James's thesis at Oxford was on the subject of statehood. His choice was an early indication of his willingness, indeed eagerness, to tackle large topics. He graduated as doctor of philosophy (DPhil) in 1977. An adaptation of his thesis was published in 1979 by Oxford University Press under the title *The Creation of States in International Law.* The work was greeted with wide acclaim and was awarded the Certificate of Merit by the American Society of International Law in 1981. A revised second edition was published in 2006.

James returned to Adelaide immediately after Oxford and taught international law and constitutional law. His rise through the academic ranks was rapid: he was awarded a personal chair in 1983. His students were understandably in awe of him; they dubbed him 'JC'. But like that other renowned teacher he combined authoritative and stimulating teaching with a kind nature.

Marriage followed, and the birth of two daughters, both of whom have followed him in outstanding scholarly careers.

James's second major publication appeared in 1982. *Australian Courts of Law* purported to be a student textbook but in reality it served a far wider audience. It was a comprehensive survey of the entire court system of Australia with all its many problems of federal, state and territory jurisdictions. Far from being a student text it came to be an essential library acquisition for judges and the practising legal profession. Its success can be measured by the fact that it is now its fourth edition (co-authored by Brian Opeskin, Oxford University Press, 2004).

In early 1982 James took leave from the University to accept a three-year appointment as a full-time commissioner of the Australian Law Reform Commission. This body had been established in 1974 by the Whitlam government to examine all matters referred to it that were appropriate to the exercise of Commonwealth (federal) powers and to make recommendations for reform. It conducted wide community consultation through the production of discussion papers and was supported by highly qualified research teams. The chairman during James's first appointment was Michael Kirby, later to become a Justice of the High Court of Australia. James was assigned as Commissioner-in-Charge of three major references: Foreign State Immunity, Civil Admiralty Jurisdiction, and the Recognition of Aboriginal Customary Laws.

Foreign State Immunity was clearly a subject for an international lawyer. At the time of the reference there was doubt in Australia whether the traditional common law approach of absolute immunity should give way to developing judicial trends elsewhere towards restrictive or qualified immunity. There was as yet no decision of the higher Australian courts on the question; the decision of the Judicial Committee of the Privy Council in *The Philippine Admiral* case (1977) was considered persuasive but not binding since it did not come on appeal from Australia. James had the benefit of the experience of many other common law jurisdictions which had pronounced on the matter, some legislatively, in preparing his report and draft legislation. In recommending that Australia adopt the approach of absolute immunity subject to exceptions (especially with respect to commercial transactions) the report considered that such an approach would accord with practice elsewhere, including the likely approach of the International Law Commission. In unaltered form it was passed into law as the Foreign States Immunities Act 1985.

The second of the two references dealt with a relic of Australia's colonial history. Admiralty jurisdiction, both civil and criminal, was tied to English law and was unsuited to the needs of an independent nation. Already before James was appointed to the commission, admiralty criminal jurisdiction had been supplanted in Australia by the passage of the Crimes at Sea Act 1979 (now replaced by the Crimes at Sea Act 2000). That Act cured the anomaly of having to lay charges of crimes committed at sea under English law and not the criminal law of the adjacent Australian state. The civil admiralty jurisdiction, exercisable by state courts, was stuck in the mould of the Colonial Courts of Admiralty Act 1890 (Imp). It was necessary, on a national basis, to resolve uncertainties about, and unjustified limitations on, the scope of that jurisdiction. The Report, under James's direction, succeeded in forming the basis of the Admiralty Act 1988.

The third reference took James into relatively uncharted and potentially controversial areas, far removed from international law. At a time when it was increasingly being questioned whether Australia should be regarded as having been unoccupied, and thus as *terra nullius*, upon British settlement in 1788, or whether the Aboriginal population should be regarded as having retained root title to their lands (matters that were to be decided by the High Court of Australia later in the *Mabo* case in 1992), there were many other matters of a more immediately pressing nature to be examined. These included whether Aboriginal customary law could be invoked before Australian courts, or should be considered in administrative decisions, regarding such matters as the criminal law and sentencing, traditional marriage and family status, child custody, traditional hunting and fishing and many others. Consultations provided a rich source of experience as the Commission took soundings all around the country, including in aboriginal areas. The final report did not recommend comprehensive legislation (although, piecemeal at various levels, some state and federal laws resulted) but rather proposed a set of recommendations to be implemented or considered at appropriate levels of government.

James returned to Adelaide at the conclusion of his full-time term on the commission at the end of 1984, but continued to be a part-time member until 1990. In 1985 he was elected an Associate Member of the Institut de Droit International, the youngest member to have been appointed in recent times. He was promoted into full membership in 1991. After the death of Julius Stone he was the only Australian member of the Institut until the recent election of Hilary Charlesworth.

It soon became clear that James would have greater opportunities on the eastern seaboard of Australia. Adelaide is hardly a backwater, but Australian public life tends to be dominated by the 'Sydney–Melbourne–Canberra triangle'. In 1986 he was appointed Challis Professor of International Law at the University of Sydney. That endowed chair has had an uninterrupted history from its first incumbent, Pitt Cobbett, in 1890. James succeeded D. H. N. Johnson, formerly of London (LSE), who in turn had succeeded Julius Stone. Johnson's appointment had seen the separation of the once unitary Chair of International Law and Jurisprudence into two separate Challis Chairs.

The departure of James, Marisa and their two daughters from Adelaide to settle permanently in Sydney was marked by an unfortunate event. All their possessions went into storage during the Christmas and New Year break. The storage facility caught fire and everything within it was destroyed. Their possessions included irreplaceable personal records, papers and photographs. The effects of that experience were highly unsettling to them all.

James was appointed dean of the faculty of law at the University of Sydney in 1990. During the three years that followed he instituted international law as a compulsory subject in the LLB curriculum, in place of the elective status enjoyed by that subject previously. An innovation was to view international law widely, embracing both public and private international law. As an introductory course it thus ensured that all students would have at least a nodding acquaintance with the basic sources and principles considered by James to be essential to the education of lawyers in a globalised world. Students inspired by this immersion were able to follow as separate elective subjects advanced courses in both branches of international law. Sydney's example has since been followed by many other Australian law schools, including Adelaide.

James always saw it as desirable that academic lawyers in Australia should have strong links with the practising legal profession. He was thus called to the Bar of New South Wales in 1987. He was later appointed Senior Counsel (a rank that replaced, but is of equal status to, Queen's Counsel) in 1997. This distinction, unlike in Canada, is rarely conferred on Australian academic lawyers.

With James's election to the Whewell Chair of International Law at Cambridge in 1992, and his election in the same year to the International Law Commission of the United Nations, this account of the earlier years comes to an end.

Ivan Shearer

AN AUSTRALIAN IN ENGLAND

James Crawford arrived in Cambridge in the autumn of 1992, with the internet and globalisation, to take up the position of Whewell Chair of International Law and a Fellowship at Jesus College. I had come to know him five years earlier, at the 1987 meeting of the Institut de Droit International in Cairo, when he engaged actively with the secretariat on which I served. He was a razor-sharp and open Australian, direct, engaged and humorous.

For twenty-one years James's academic work has centred on the law faculty in Cambridge. This second life has included three years as Chair and two stints as Director of the Lauterpacht Research Centre for International Law (characterised by long hours spent in an office that is now on the first floor, regular visits to the kitchen and library on the ground floor and a work ethic so 'punishing' that the word does not begin to do justice to his personal style).

The Cambridge years have spanned both undergraduate and LLM teaching, across a range of international law subjects, and also embracing a remarkable *fifty-seven* doctoral students (not a typographical error). The engagement with the classroom reflects an undying commitment to the power of nurture and encouragement, irrespective of creed or culture or politics. The body of protégés crosses all these barriers, although it must be said that young Australians interested in international law are attracted to him like bees to honey (does any country today have more international lawyers per capita, or a greater proportion of its GNP devoted to international legal scholarship and other services?). Many of James's pupils have entered academic life across the UK and Australia and beyond, allowing the Crawford effect – international law as an 'open system', as he likes to put it, that is real and modern – to spread well beyond the Fens. His impact at Cambridge is hard to overstate: international law was already a central part of the life of the law faculty, but somehow it has expanded even further, a thriving part of the life of the faculty. The classroom credo is not revolutionary transformation, but incremental change over time and subject area. The teaching style – understated and humorous, with a touch of irreverence and a recognition of the limits of the subject in the real world of power and politics – has been widely attractive. I am yet to meet a single person anywhere in the world who has complained about James as a teacher.

Over these two decades James has also managed to complete the odd book or ten, along with innumerable articles and publications the citation of which would exhaust my permitted word limit. The standouts surely include the second edition of *The Creation of States in International Law* (which appeared in 2006), and the eighth edition of *Brownlie's Principles of International Law* (in 2012), a minor miracle produced with a small orchestra of willing and able assistants, to whom credit is offered in full. The book offers longevity to the work's originator (and James's teacher), whilst maintaining its characteristic ethos.

Elsewhere, the Crawford world of international law has expanded to encompass water, people, rights, courts, investments and responsibility (a recurring theme), amongst many other subjects. It has also touched, on occasion, the realm of theory, although James will be the first to recognise that the world of practice and process offers particular attractions. This is reflected in the general course on international law offered at The Hague Academy in the summer of 2013, *The Course of International Law*. It was a characteristic feature of his industry that he was able to hand over the entire manuscript at the end of his final lecture, notwithstanding his concurrent role as senior counsel for Australia, arguing against Japan's 'scientific whaling' in the Antarctic.

James's arrival in Cambridge coincided with his election to the International Law Commission, and summers in Geneva. This was no sinecure. The Commission had spent five decades working on two subjects of keen importance and growing interest – the idea of a statute for an international criminal court, and a set of articles on State responsibility – and there was little prospect of an end in sight when James arrived. He brought his special forensic and diplomatic skills to bear on what might have seemed a fruitless task, and a unique ability to create a sense of collegiality and common purpose. He served as Rapporteur on these efforts, bringing both to completion to a standard and quality that ensured the product would find traction in the practical world. The draft articles on an international criminal court paved the way for the creation of the International Criminal Court, just four years later; the draft articles on State responsibility are probably amongst the most cited texts in modern international law (assisted by a commentary of crisp and concise prose that is characteristic of James's style).

Such contributions as those already touched upon might be thought to be sufficient for most living souls, but not for James. The Cambridge years have somehow allowed time to engage in the odd case, prepare an occasional advice or opinion, and sit as arbitrator and judge. In 2000 he was a founder member of Matrix Chambers, and has contributed to the life of the international and English bar as international law increasingly permeates domestic and European law.

There have been cases in Hamburg, Washington, Paris and Istanbul, not to mention the second home that is The Hague. There have been more than two score cases at the International Court of Justice alone (James is not a 'numbers' person and would object strongly to the totting up), and dozens in other places. It might be said that James has been midwife for the transformation of the international justice system. His unique ability to get to the nub of the central legal issue in any case, and to roll up his sleeves and immerse himself in the muck of facts, makes him the principal public international lawyer of our age. To international litigation he has brought a distinct style of advocacy – referred to by some as 'the Australian way' – that is direct, subtle and fearsome. In one hand a surgeon's knife, in the other a sledgehammer. The arguments are relevant, efficient and humorous.

This was encapsulated for many in an early effort, made on behalf of a group of four Pacific island countries, when he sought to persuade a somewhat sceptical bench that the use of nuclear weapons was unlawful in all circumstances. There's a difference between deterrence and the actual threat to use weapons to achieve one's ends, he told the Court, adopting an approach that surprised some. 'Mr President', he said boldly, looking straight in the eye at the diminutive, older gentleman who sat before him, 'I may be big enough and strong enough to hurt you, if you punch me in the nose . . . but I am not threatening you, not in the event that you do not punch me on the nose – it is simply a fact.' The look on the judge's face – was it awe, or incomprehension? – remains embedded in the memory of many who were present.

He has served as arbitrator and judge, displaying fearsome independence and collegiality in the struggle for consensus. Occasionally this might generate a sense of frustration on the part of the party that appointed him, yet it will be overcome by the knowledge that his presence on the tribunal invariably leads to a judgment or award that ticks the quality boxes. It might be said that he is generous in the extreme as to the assumptions about the uses (and abuses) to which a decision might be put (yes, dear James, many *still* find it hard to swallow aspects of the decision of the annulment committee in *CMS Gas Transmission Company* v. *Argentine Republic*!).

James likes litigation, and litigation likes him. He's a natural and highly effective, even after a twenty-four-hour flight (who else would take in trips to Europe, South America and Australia in *a single week*, and then be willing and able to appear in an international court?). To be gently savaged by him in the course of a hearing is a badge of honour, a pleasurable rite of passage. As many have learnt, to seek to savage in return, and to do it well (or even not), invariably catalyses a generous and warm word of appreciation after the hearing, a pat on the shoulder and perhaps an invitation for a beer.

James's arrival in Britain coincided with a transformation in the international law scene in his adoptive country. International law came into the mainstream of legal life in the United Kingdom (a country the future make-up of which he may have contributed to by the opinion he prepared on Scottish independence, following on from his work in relation to Quebec and Canada), and to a significant extent its political life too. Cause or effect? It will always be difficult to know, and James would never seek to overstate (or even state) his influence. But many others have recognised his impact. That he put his name and weight to a March 2003 letter to the then British prime minister, warning him of the illegality of using force in Iraq without an explicit Security Council Resolution, undoubtedly added to its authority and effect. It reflected a characteristic willingness to do the right thing, to jump out of the ivory tower and get his hands dirty with the great issues of the day. As so often, his leadership made it easier for others to join. The same may be said of his efforts in challenging the Bush administration on its legal policies in the aftermath of 9/11. 'The American Society of International What?', he asked, sitting on a panel in Washington, with a great grin on his face, when it was put to him that the Society should avoid becoming embroiled in such delicate matters. Less than a decade later the society honoured him with the prestigious Manley Hudson Medal, one of the growing number of prizes and honours that reflect the reach of his ideas and imprint.

What are the qualities that have informed this global recognition? They have rightly catalysed the respect of legal rags, for which he would have little regard, which refer (no doubt to his considerable embarrassment) to his 'profound influence on the development of international law' and to the observable facts that public international law 'forms part of his

DNA' and that he is 'the most brilliant performer of his generation'. The intellectual qualities are widely noted, but there is something else. It's a personal style and human qualities that are brought to bear across the range of his activities, both academic and professional. There is, for a start, a generosity of spirit and humility that stands out in a world often marked by self-importance. There is the openness to ideas, even if they are not ones to which he is himself attached, and irrespective of their individual provenance. It is the substance that matters, not the messenger. These are disarming qualities that allow the force of the intellectual arguments to extend their reach, cutting through political and cultural opposition. There is, too, a driving belief in the rule of law and its reach, a commitment to the system of international law *for all*, individuals, associations, corporations and States.

'Why does he take on so much?' is a frequent question. Because he loves it and because he cares, is the only possible answer. The personal characteristics inspire a sense of affection and collegiality that allows things to get done, results to be achieved, sacred cows to be destroyed. It is true too that beyond the love of international law – and the encyclopaedic store of information – there is an understanding that there is more to life (a point more often appreciated perhaps in the lives of others), that the law has its limits and that one should be sanguine about the prospects and possibilities of one's own actions or impact.

There is too a particular sense of humour, invariably attached to words and language. The emails are short and to the point, and often generate a laugh. A personal favourite amongst the numerous 4.00 a.m. emails relates to proceedings that Bangladesh brought against India and Myanmar, on the delimitation of the Bay of Bengal. Bangladesh opted for two separate cases: one, against Myanmar, went to the International Tribunal for the Law of the Sea (and on which sat the Indian judge P. C. Rao) and the other, against India, went to an Annex VII arbitration tribunal. The day after India appointed as arbitrator its former legal adviser P. S. Rao, James sent a short email, the subject header of which said: *Two Raos, One Dispute.*

Nothing really goes to the head. A tad more stretched, he is as generous and open as the day he arrived in Cambridge, as committed to making things right, as kindly irreverent and unwilling as ever to defer to sacred cows. There is, finally and forever, that commitment to his Australian roots (and passport). This has not been without its cost, namely hundreds of additional hours forced to stand in line waiting to get through the non-EU immigration lines at European airports. This price he has willingly paid to open the door to (an even fuller) life in The Hague (Tom Bingham once told me that he saw no reason why an Australian – well, this Australian – might not succeed the former British judge at the court). It is fitting that he reaches the likely end of this stage of his career – a second grown-up life – in the year that Australia retained the cricket Ashes with a crushing – nay, humiliating – victory against England, and in which he was made Companion of the Order of Australia in the Australian Queen's Birthday Honours List.

James's arrival in England made life different for a great many people, myself included. He was, I believe, the first non-UK national to take up the Whewell Chair, a sign of changing times, encouraging new areas to explore and a new style to apply. In the first case on which we worked together, two decades ago, as team leader he encouraged all in the room to express their views, on facts and law, even to challenge his views, dispensing with any vestige of formal hierarchy in the team. Of course, he told us, at the end of the day it would be for him to decide what advice to give the government client, but to be able to do so he wanted to hear from all what their ideas were. It was not a style I was used to, as a junior academic, or at the English bar. James has brought to us the qualities of openness and listening. Deference to the existing order, to following patterns of behaviour simply because that is how things have always been done, was to be cast aside unless justifiable on their merits. For that, for the humour, for the generosity and for the sheer power of the intellect we have reason to be very grateful that this Australian came to England.

Philippe Sands, QC

CASES

International Tribunals

Arbitration Awards

General international arbitration

Air Services Agreement of 27 March 1946 (United States *v.* France), Reports of International Arbitral Awards, vol. XVIII, 416 (1979) 357

Arbitration between Barbados and the Republic of Trinidad and Tobago, Relating to the Delimitation of the Exclusive Economic Zone and the Continental Shelf between them, Decision of 11 April 2006, Reports of International Arbitral Awards, vol XXVII, 147 (2008) 264

Case concerning a dispute between Argentina and Chile concerning the Beagle Channel, Award, 18 February 1977, Reports of International Arbitral Awards, vol. XXI, 53 (1977) 259

Case concerning the audit of accounts between the Netherlands and France in application of the Protocol of 25 September 1991 Additional to the Convention for the Protection of the Rhine from Pollution by Chlorides of 3 December 1976 (Netherlands *v.* France) Award, 12 March 2004, Reports of International Arbitral Awards, vol. XXV, 267 (2004) 440

Case concerning the delimitation of maritime boundary between Guinea-Bissau and Senegal, Decision of 31 July 1989, Reports of International Arbitral Awards, vol. XX, 119 (2006) 249, 257

Cyne (Responsibility of Germany for acts committed subsequent to 31 July 1914 and before Portugal entered the war) (Portugal *v.* Germany) Reports of International Arbitral Awards, vol. II, 1035 (1930) 396

Island of Palmas case (or Miangas) (United States *v.* Netherlands), Reports of International Arbitral Awards, vol. II, 829 (1928) 112, 141

Lighthouses Arbitration (France *v.* Greece), (18 April 1956), Reports of International Arbitral Awards, vol. XII, 155 (1956) 298

Rainbow Warrior Arbitration (New Zealand *v.* France), (30 April 1990), Reports of International Arbitration Awards, vol. XX, 215 (1990) 299

Responsabilité de L'Allemagne a Raison des Dommages Causés dans les Colonies Portugaises du Sud de L'Afrique, (Portugal *v.* Germany), (Naulilaa case), Reports of International Arbitral Awards, vol. II, 1027 (1928) 356

The Channel Tunnel Group Limited and France-Manche S.A. *v.* The Secretary of State for Transport of the Government of the United Kingdom of Great Britain and Northern Ireland and Le Ministre de l'Équipement des Transports, de l'Aménagement du Territoire, du Tourisme et de la Mer du Gouvernement de la République Française, ILR, vol. 132, 1 (2007) 422
The Netherlands *v.* United States of America (4 April 1928), Reports of International Arbitral Awards, vol. II, 829 (1928) 112

Investment arbitration

Archer Daniels Midland Company and Tate & Lyle Ingredients Americas, Inc. *v.* United Mexican States, ICSID Case No. ARB(AF)/04/05, Award, 21 November 2007 398
Asian Agricultural Products Ltd *v.* Sri Lanka, ICSID Case No. ARB 87/3, Award, 27 June 1990 316
Camuzzi International SA *v.* Argentine Republic, ICSID Case No. ARB/03/2, Decision on Objections to Jurisdiction, 11 May 2005 392
Cargill, Inc. *v.* United Mexican States, ICSID Case No. ARB(AF)05/2, Award, 18 September 2009 398, 401
Corn Products International, Inc. *v.* United Mexican States ICSID Case No. ARB(AF)/04/01, Decision on Responsibility, 15 January 2008 397, 399
Iberdrola Energía S.A. *v.* Republic of Guatemala ICSID Case No. ARB/09/5, Award, 17 August 2012 109
Jan de Nul NV and Dredging International NV *v.* Arab Republic of Egypt, ICSID Case No. ARB/04/13, Decision on Jurisdiction, 16 June 2006 387
Noble Ventures, Inc. *v.* Romania, ICSID Case No. ARB/01/11, Award, 12 October 2005 387
Robert Azinian, Kenneth Davitian, & Ellen Baca *v.* The United Mexican States, ICSID Case No. ARB (AF)/97/2, Award, 1 November 1999 109
Saar Papier Vertriebs GmbH *v.* Republic of Poland (UNCITRAL), Final Award, 16 October 1995 106
Técnicas Medioambientales Tecmed, S.A. *v.* The United Mexican States ICSID Case No. ARB (AF)/00/2, Award, 29 May 2003 107
Total S.A. *v.* The Argentine Republic, ICSID Case No. ARB/04/01, Decision on Liability, 27 December 2010 107
Toto Costruzioni Generali S.p.A. *v.* The Republic of Lebanon, ICSID Case No. ARB/07/12, Award, 7 June 2012 108
United Postal Service of America, Inc. *v.* Government of Canada, ICSID Arbitration, Award on the Merits, 24 May 2007 181

Central American Court of Justice

El Salvador *v.* Nicaragua, Central American Court of Justice, Judgment, 9 March 1917, 11 American Journal of International Law 674 (1917) 258

Court of Justice of the European Union (CJEU)

Joined cases C-176/97 and C-177/97, Commission *v.* Belgium and Luxembourg [1998] ECR I-3557 415
Case 22/70, Commission *v.* Council – AETR [1971] ECR 263 407
Case C-45/07, Commission *v.* Greece [2009] ECR I-00701 409, 414
Case C-459/03, Commission *v.* Ireland [2006] ECR I-4635 408
Case C-266/03, Commission *v.* Luxembourg [2005] ECR I-4805 408, 414
Case C-55/00, Elide Gottardo *v.* Istituto nazionale della previdenza sociale (INPS) [2002] ECR I-413 414
C-379/87, Groener *v.* Minister for Education and the City of Dublin [1989] ECR I-3967 104
Case C-308/06, The Queen, on the application of International Association of Independent Tanker Owner (Intertanko) and others *v.* Secretary of State for Transport [2008] ECR I-4057 410
Case C-432/92, R *v.* Minister of Agriculture, Fisheries and Food, ex parte S. P. Anastasiou (Pissouri) Ltd and others (Anastasiou I) [1994] ECR I-3116 178
Case C-159/90, Society for the Protection of the Unborn Children Ireland *v.* Grogan, [1991] ECR I-4685 104

European Court of Human Rights (ECtHR)

Al-Adsani *v.* the United Kingdom, Application No. 35763/97, ECtHR, Judgment, 21 November 2001, 34 EHRR 11 (2002) 187
Al-Jedda *v.* United Kingdom, Application No. 27021/08, ECtHR (GC), Judgment (Merits and Just Satisfaction), 7 July 2011 421
Bankovic and others *v.* Belgium and others, Application No. 52207/99, ECtHR (GC), Judgment, 12 December 2001 66
Behrami and Behrami *v.* France, Application No. 71412/01, ECtHR (GC), 2 May 2007 421
Cyprus *v.* Turkey, Application No. 25781/94, ECtHR (GC), 10 May 2001 199
Demopoulos and others *v.* Turkey, Application No. 46113/99, ECtHR, Admissibility Decision, 1 March 2010 178
Fogarty *v.* the United Kingdom, Application No. 37112/97, ECtHR, 21 November 2001 185
Ilascu and others *v.* Moldova and Russia, Application No. 48787/99, ECtHR (GC), 8 July 2004 323
Loizidou *v.* Turkey, Application No. 40/1993/435/514, ECtHR, 23 February 1995 323
Öcalan *v.* Turkey, Application No. 46221/99, ECtHR (GC), 12 May 2005 56
Saramati *v.* France, Germany and Norway, Application No. 78166/01, ECtHR (GC), 2 May 2007 421

Kosovo Human Rights Advisory Panel

S.C. *v.* UNMIK, Case No. 02/09, 6 December 2012 162

Human Rights Committee

Lilian Celiberti de Casariego *v.* Uruguay, Communication No. 56/1979, UN Doc. CCPR/C/13/D/56/1979 (29 July 1981) 56, 61

Sergio Euben Lopez Burgos *v.* Uruguay, Communication No. R.12/52, UN Doc. Supp. No. 40 (A/36/40) (6 June 1979) 56, 61

International Court of Justice (ICJ)

Accordance with International Law of the Unilateral Declaration of Independence in Respect of Kosovo, Advisory Opinion, 22 July 2010, ICJ Reports 403 (2010) 163, 193, 199, 207, 236, 275

Antarctica cases (UK *v.* Argentina; UK *v.* Chile), ICJ Pleadings (1956) 110

Application of the Convention on the Prevention and Punishment of the Crime of Genocide (Bosnia and Herzegovina *v.* Serbia and Montenegro), Order of 13 September 1993, ICJ Reports 325 (1993) 33

Application of the Convention on the Prevention and Punishment of the Crime of Genocide (Bosnia Herzegovina *v.* Serbia and Montenegro), Judgment, 26 February 2007, ICJ Reports 43 (2007) 300, 323, 326, 377, 380

Armed Activities on the Territory of the Congo (Congo *v.* Uganda), Judgment, 19 December 2005, ICJ Reports 168 (2005) 52, 324

Barcelona Traction, Light and Power Company Limited (Belgium *v.* Spain), Judgment, 5 February 1970, ICJ Reports 3 (1970) 298, 304, 341

Case concerning Ahmadou Sadio Diallo (Republic of Guinea *v.* Democratic Republic of the Congo) (Preliminary Objections), 24 May 2007, ICJ Reports 582 (2007) 392

Case concerning Armed Activities on the Territory of the Congo (New Application: 2002) (Democratic Republic of the Congo *v.* Rwanda), Jurisdiction of the Court and Admissibility of the Application, Judgment, 3 February 2006, ICJ Reports 6 (2006) 205

Certain Phosphate Lands in Nauru (Nauru *v.* Australia), Judgment on Preliminary Objections, 26 June 1992, ICJ Reports 240 (1992) 438

Corfu Channel case (UK *v.* Albania) (Merits), Judgment, 9 April 1949, ICJ Reports 4 (1949) 47, 302, 315

Difference Relating to Immunity from Legal Process of a Special Rapporteur of the Commission on Human Rights, Advisory Opinion, 29 April 1999, ICJ Reports 62 (1999) 380

East Timor case (Portugal *v.* Australia), Judgment, 30 June 1995, ICJ Reports 90 (1995) 227

Frontier Dispute (Burkina Faso/Republic of Mali), Judgment, 22 December 1986, ICJ Reports 554 (1986) 199, 256

Jurisdictional Immunities of the State (Germany *v.* Italy: Greece intervening), Judgment, 3 February 2012, ICJ Reports 99 (2012) 187

LaGrand case (Germany *v.* United States of America), Judgment, 27 June 2001, ICJ Reports 466 (2001) 152

Land and Maritime Boundary between Cameroon and Nigeria (Cameroon *v.* Nigeria: Equatorial Guinea intervening), Judgment, 10 October 2002, ICJ Reports 303 (2002) 262

Land, Island and Maritime Frontier Dispute (El Salvador/Honduras: Nicaragua intervening), Judgment, 11 September 1992, ICJ Reports 3 (1992) 260, 269, 270

Legal Consequences of the Construction of a Wall in the Occupied Palestinian Territory, Advisory Opinion, 9 July 2004, ICJ Reports 136 (2004) 51, 56, 63, 69, 108, 348, 385

Legal Consequences of the Continued Presence of South Africa in Namibia (South-West Africa) notwithstanding Security Council Resolution 276, Advisory Opinion, 21 June 1971, ICJ Reports 16 (1971) 58, 177, 195

Legality of the Threat or Use of Nuclear Weapons, Advisory Opinion, 8 July 1996, ICJ Reports 226 (1996) 82, 148

Maritime Delimitation in the Black Sea (Romania *v.* Ukraine), Judgment, 3 February 2009, ICJ Reports 61 (2009) 270

Military and Paramilitary Activities in and against Nicaragua (Nicaragua *v.* USA), Judgment, 27 June 1986, ICJ Reports 14 (1986) 40, 301, 323

Nuclear Test cases (Australia *v.* France; New Zealand *v.* France), Judgment, 20 December 1974, ICJ Reports 253, 457 (1974) 199

Oil Platforms (Islamic Republic of Iran *v.* United States of America), Judgment, 6 November 2003, ICJ Reports 161 (2003) 173

Pulp Mills on the River Uruguay (Argentina *v.* Uruguay), Judgment, 20 April 2010, ICJ Reports 14 (2010) 316, 321

Reparation for Injuries Suffered in the Service of the United Nations, Advisory Opinion, 11 April 1949, ICJ Reports 174 (1949) 82, 297

South West Africa cases (Ethiopia *v.* South Africa; Liberia *v.* South Africa) (Preliminary Objections), 21 December 1962, ICJ Reports 624 (1962) 295

Territorial and Maritime Dispute (Nicaragua *v.* Colombia), Merits, Judgment, 19 November 2012, ICJ Reports 624 (2012) 267

Territorial and Maritime Dispute (Nicaragua *v.* Colombia), Preliminary Objections, Judgment, 13 December 2007, ICJ Reports 832 (2007) 267

Territorial and Maritime Dispute between Nicaragua and Honduras in the Caribbean Sea (Nicaragua *v.* Honduras), Judgment, 8 October 2007, ICJ Reports 659 (2007) 265

United States Diplomatic and Consular Staff in Tehran (United States of America *v.* Iran), Judgment, 24 May 1980, ICJ Reports 3 (1980) 298

Western Sahara, Advisory Opinion, 16 October 1975, ICJ Reports 12 (1975) 139, 157

International Criminal Tribunal for the former Yugoslavia (ICTY)

Prosecutor *v.* Tihomir Blaskic, Case No. IT-95–14-T, Trial Chamber, 3 March 2000 334
Prosecutor *v.* Delalic et al., Case No. IT-96–21-T, ICTY Trial Chamber, 16 November 1998 326
Prosecutor *v.* Galic, Case No. IT-98–29-T, Trial Chamber, Judgment, 5 December 2003 325
Prosecutor *v.* Dario Kordic and Mario Cerkez, Case No. IT-95–14/2-T, ICTY Trials Chamber, Judgment 26 February 2001 334
Prosecutor *v.* Dario Kordic and Mario Cerkez, Case No. IT-95–14/2-A, ICTY Appeals Chamber, 17 December 2004 334
Prosecutor *v.* Krstic, Case No. IT-98–33-A, Appeals Chamber, 19 April 2004 326
Prosecutor *v.* Dusko Tadic (Decision on the Defence Motion for Interlocutory Appeal on Jurisdiction), Case No. IT-94–1, ICTY, Appeals Chamber, 2 October 1995 33
Prosecutor *v.* Dusko Tadic, Case No. IT-94–1-A, ICTY Appeals Chamber, Judgment, 15 July 1999 301

International Tribunal for the Law of the Sea (ITLOS)

ARA Libertad case (Argentina *v.* Ghana), ITLOS Case No. 20 390
M/V 'Saiga' (No. 2) (Saint Vincent and the Grenadines *v.* Guinea), ITLOS Case No. 2, 1 July 1999, ITLOS Reports 1999, 65 308
Responsibilities and Obligations of States Sponsoring Persons and Entities with respect to Activities in the Area (Advisory Opinion), ITLOS Case No. 17, 1 February 2011 386

Iran–United States Claims Tribunal

Rankin *v.* Islamic Republic of Iran, Award No. 326–10913–2, 3 November 1987, 17 IRAN-U.S. C.T.R. 135, 141 386

Nuremberg and Tokyo Trials

The Hostage Trial (Trial of Wilhelm List and others), Law Reports of Trials of War Criminals, 8 (1949) 333
Trial of Alfred Felix Alwyn Krupp and Eleven Others (The Krupp Trial), Law Reports of Trials of War Criminals, 10 (1949) 333

Permanent Court of International Justice (PCIJ)

Factory at Chorzów (Germany *v.* Poland) (Merits), Judgment, 13 September 1928, PCIJ Series A, No. 17 (1928) 295

Free Zones of Upper Savoy and the District of Gex, Judgment, 7 June 1932, PCIJ, Series A/B, No. 4 (1932) 294

Greco-Bulgarian 'Communities', Advisory Opinion, 31 August 1930, PCIJ, Series B, No. 17 (1930) 294

Jurisdiction of Courts of Danzig, Advisory Opinion, 3 March 1928, PCIJ Series B, No. 15 (1928) 151

Legal Status of Eastern Greenland (Norway *v.* Denmark), Judgment, 5 September 1933, PCIJ Series A/B, No. 53 (1933) 111

Mavrommatis Palestine Concessions (Greece *v.* Britain), Judgment, 30 August 1924, PCIJ Series A, No. 2 (1924) 295

Nationality Decrees Issued in Tunis and Morocco (French Zone), Advisory Opinion, 7 February 1923, PCIJ Series B, No. 4 (1923) 147

Phosphates in Morocco (Italy *v.* France), Judgment, 14 June 1938, PCIJ Series A/B, No. 74 (1938) 294

SS Lotus (France *v.* Turkey), Judgment, 7 September 1927, PCIJ Series A, No. 10 (1927) 148, 293, 303, 311

SS Wimbledon (United Kingdom *v.* Germany), Judgment, 17 August 1923, PCIJ Series A, No. 1 (1923) 149, 294, 302

Status of Eastern Carelia, Advisory Opinion, 23 July 1923, PCIJ Series B, No. 5 (1923) 147

Treatment of Polish Nationals and Other Persons of Polish Origin or Speech in the Danzig Territory, Advisory Opinion, 4 February 1932, PCIJ, Series A/B, No. 44 293

Special Tribunal for Lebanon

Interlocutory Decision on the Applicable Law: Terrorism, Conspiracy, Homicide, Perpetration, Cumulative Charging, STL-11–01/I, 16 February 2011 162

United Nations Committee on the Rights of the Child

Concluding Observations of the Committee on the Rights of the Child: Israel, UN Doc. CRC/C/15/Add.195, 4 October 2002 57

World Trade Organization

Panel and appellate dispute settlement reports

Australia – Measures Affecting Importation of Salmon – Recourse to Article 21.5 of the DSU by Canada ('Australia – Salmon (Article 21.5 – Canada)'), WT/DS18/RW, adopted 20 March 2000 373

Canada – Certain Measures Affecting the Automotive Industry ('Canada – Autos'), WT/DS139/R, WT/DS142/R, adopted 19 June 2000, as modified by Appellate Body Report WT/DS139/AB/R, WT/DS142/AB/R 378

Canada – Measures Affecting the Importation of Milk and the Exportation of Dairy Products ('Canada – Dairy'), WT/DS103/R, WT/DS113/R, adopted 27 October 1999, as modified by Appellate Body Report WT/DS103/AB/R, WT/DS113/AB/R 373, 386

Decision by the Arbitrators, Brazil – Export Financing Programme for Aircraft – Recourse to Arbitration by Brazil under Article 22.6 of the DSU and Article 4.11 of the SCM Agreement ('Brazil – Aircraft (Article 22.6 – Brazil)'), WT/DS46/ARB, 28 August 2000 374

Decision by the Arbitrator, United States – Subsidies on Upland Cotton – Recourse to Arbitration by the United States under Article 22.6 of the DSU and Article 4.11 of the SCM Agreement ('US – Upland Cotton (Article 22.6 – US I)'), WT/DS267/ARB/1, 31 August 2009 374

EC – Measures Affecting the Approval and Marketing of Biotech Products WT/DS291/R, WT/ DS292/R, WT/DS293/R 79

European Communities – Customs Classification of Frozen Boneless Chicken Cuts ('EC – Chicken Cuts'), WT/DS269/AB/R, WT/DS286/AB/R, adopted 27 September 2005, and Corr.1 384

European Communities and Certain Member States – Measures Affecting Trade in Large Civil Aircraft ('EC and Certain Member States – Large Civil Aircraft'), WT/DS316/AB/R, adopted 1 June 2011 374, 384

Japan – Measures Affecting Consumer Photographic Film and Paper ('Japan – Film'), WT/DS44/R, adopted 22 April 1998 378

Korea – Measures Affecting Government Procurement ('Korea – Government Procurement'), WT/DS163/R, adopted 19 June 2000 374

Mexico – Tax Measures on Soft Drinks and Other Beverages (Mexico – Taxes on Soft Drinks), WTO Doc. WT/DS308/AB/R, adopted 6 March 2006 397

United States – Continued Existence and Application of Zeroing Methodology ('US – Continued Zeroing'), WT/DS350/AB/R, adopted 19 February 2009 373, 384

United States – Continued Suspension of Obligations in the EC – Hormones Dispute ('US – Continued Suspension'), WT/DS320/AB/R, adopted 14 November 2008 373

United States – Countervailing Duty Investigation on Dynamic Random Access Memory Semiconductors (DRAMS) from Korea ('US – Countervailing Duty Investigation on DRAMS'), WT/DS296/AB/R, adopted 20 July 2005 376

United States – Definitive Safeguard Measures on Imports of Circular Welded Carbon Quality Line Pipe from Korea ('US – Line Pipe'), WT/DS202/AB/R, adopted 8 March 2002 373

United States – Import Prohibition of Certain Shrimp and Shrimp Products WT/DS58/AB/R, WTO Appellate Body, adopted 12 October 1998 81

United States – Measures Affecting the Cross-Border Supply of Gambling and Betting Services ('US – Gambling'), WT/DS285/R, WTO Panel Report, adopted 20 April 2005, as modified by Appellate Body Report WT/DS285/AB/R 373
United States – Measures Relating to Zeroing and Sunset Reviews – Recourse to Article 21.5 of the DSU by Japan ('US – Zeroing (Japan) (Article 21.5 – Japan)'), WT/DS322/AB/RW, adopted 31 August 2009 373
United States – Sunset Review of Anti-dumping Duties on Corrosion-Resistant Carbon Steel Flat Products from Japan ('US – Corrosion-Resistant Steel Sunset Review'), WT/DS244/AB/R, adopted 9 January 2004 378
United States – Transitional Safeguard Measure on Combed Cotton Yarn from Pakistan ('US – Cotton Yarn'), WT/DS192/AB/R, WTO Appellate Body, adopted 5 November 2001 373

National Courts

Australia

Horta *v.* Commonwealth, High Court of Australia, 14 August 1994 (1994) 123 ALR 1 195
Humane Society International, Inc. *v.* Kyodo Senpaku Kaisha Ltd [2004] FCA 1510 116
Humane Society International, Inc. *v.* Kyodo Senpaku Kaisha Ltd [2008] FCA 3 116
Wright *v.* Cantrell (Supreme Court of New South Wales, 1943) [1943] ALR 427 312

Bolivia

Sentencia del Tribunal Constitucional de Bolivia sobre constitucionalidad de leyes ratificadoras de Convenios y Tratados, No. 0031/2006, 10 May 2006 90

Brazil

In re Gilbert (Brazil, Supreme Federal Court, 1944) 13 ILR 86 312

Canada

Reference Re Secession of Quebec, Supreme Court of Canada, 29 August 1998 (1998) 161 DLR (4th) 385 199
The Council of Canadians et al. *v.* Her Majesty in Right of Canada (Ontario Supreme Court of Justice), 8 July 2005 91
The Council of Canadians et al. *v.* Her Majesty in Right of Canada (Ontario Court of Appeal), 30 November 2006 91

Columbia

Sentencia de la Corte Constitucional de Colombia C-294/02, 23 April 2002 90

France

Clerget *v.* Banque Commerciale pour Europe du Nord & Banque du Commerce Extérieur du Vietnam (Court of Appeal, Paris, 7 June 1969) 202

Germany

Internationale Handelsgesellschaft von Einfuhr- und Vorratsstelle für Getreide und Futtermittel (Solange I), decision of 29 May 1974, BVerfGE 37, 271 [1974] CMLR 540 102
F.a. Steinike & Weinlig *v.* Bundesamt für Ernährung & Forstwirtschaft (Vielleicht), BVerfG 25 July 1979 103
Wünsche Handelsgesellschaft (Solange II), BVerfG 22 October 1986 103

Guatemala

Belize case, Case No. 290 and 292/91 (Constitutional Court of Guatemala, 1992) 100 ILR 304 195

India

German Democratic Republic *v.* Dynamic Industrial Undertaking Ltd (High Court of Bombay, 14–16 October 1970) 195
Republic of Italy & Ors *v.* Union of India & Ors, Writ Petition (Civil) No.135 of 2012 (Supreme Court of India, 18 January 2013) 313

Italy

Frontini et altri *v.* Ministro delle finanze et altri (C. cost., 27 December 1973) 102
Spa Granital *v.* Amministrazione delle finanze dello Stato (C. cost., 5 June 1984) 102
Fragd *v.* Amministrazione delle Finanze dello Stato (C. cost., 21 April 1989) 102

Japan

Japan *v.* Girard (Maebashi District Court, 1957) 26 ILR 203 312

The Netherlands

In re Rauter, Special Court of Cassation, 12 January 1949, 16 Annual Digest and Reports of Public International Law Cases 526 (1949) 333
The Netherlands *v.* Hasan Nuhanovic (12/03324 LZ/TT), Supreme Court of the Netherlands, Judgment (First Chamber), 6 September 2013 421

Singapore

Civil Aeronautics Administration *v.* Singapore Airlines, 14 January 2004 [2004] SGCA 3 (Singapore Court of Appeals) 199

United Kingdom

Air Corporation *v.* Iraqi Airways Company and others [1995] 1 WLR 1147 234
Alcom *v.* Republic of Colombia [1984] AC 580 185
Caglar *v.* Billingham (Inspector of Taxes), 7 March 1996 (England, Special Commissioners) 202
Carl-Zeiss-Stiftung *v.* Rayner and Keeler, Ltd and others (No. 2) [1966] 2 All ER 536 195
Czarnikow Ltd *v.* Rolimpex [1979] AC 351 176, 186
Gur Corporation *v.* Trust Bank of Africa Ltd [1987] 1 QB 599 195
Hesperides Hotels *v.* Aegean Holidays [1978] QB 205 177
I Congreso del Partido [1983] 1 AC 244 183
Jones *v.* Saudi Arabia [2006] UKHL 16 187
Khurts Bat *v.* The Investigating Judge of the German Federal Court [2011] EWHC 2029 (Admin) 312
Kibris Turk Hava Yollari *v.* Secretary of State for Transport [2010] EWCA Civ 1093 178
R (Abassi) *v.* Secretary of State for Foreign and Commonwealth Affairs [2002] EWCA Civ 1598 18
R (on the application of Al-Skeini and others) *v.* Secretary of State for Defence (The Redress Trust intervening) [2007] UKHL 26; [2007] 3 WLR 33 57
R (on the application of Al-Skeini and others) *v.* Secretary of State for Defence [2005] EWCA Civ 1609 (21 December 2005) 57
R (on the application of Al-Skeini and others) *v.* Secretary of State for Defence [2004] EWHC 2911 (Admin), 14 December 2004 57
R *v.* Immigration Officer at Prague Airport and another (Respondents), ex p. European Roma Rights Centre and others (Appellants) [2004] UKHL 55, 9 December 2004 64
Regina *v.* Bow Street Metropolitan Stipendiary Magistrate and others, ex p. Pinochet Ugarte (No. 3) [2000] 1 AC 147 187
The Charkieh (1872–75) 4 LR 59 183
Trendtex Trading Corporation *v.* Central Bank of Nigeria [1977] 1 QB 529 186
Westland Helicopters Ltd *v.* Arab Organisation for Industrialisation [1995] 2 All ER 387 203

United States

Bertrand *v.* Sava, 684 F2d 204, 218–19 (2d Cir, 1982) 98
Camacho *v.* Rogers, 199 FSupp 155 (SDNY 1961) 98

Frolova *v.* USSR, 761 F2d 370, 374 (7th Cir, 1985) 98
In re Alien Children Educ. Litig., 501 FSupp 544, 590 (SD Tex 1980) 98
International Association of Machinists and Aerospace Workers *v.* Organization of Petroleum Exporting Countries (OPEC), 649 F2d 1354 (9th Cir, 1981) 184
Namba *v.* McCourt, 204 P2d 569 (1949) 96
Oyama *v.* California, 332 US 633 (1948) 95
Pan American World Airways, Inc. *v.* Aetna Casualty and Surety Co., 505 F2d 989 (2nd Cir, 1974) 203
Pauling *v.* McElroy, 164 FSupp 390 (1958) 98
Pemex Corporación Mexicana de Mantenimiento Integral, S. De R.L de C.V. *v.* Pemex-Exploración y Producción, No. 10 Civ. 206 (AKH), 2013 WL 4517225 (SDNY Aug 27, 2013) 184
People of Saipan *v.* United States Dep't of Interior, 502 F2d 90 (9th Cir, 1974) Plyler *v.* Doe, 457 US 202 (1982) 98
Plyler *v.* Doe, 457 US 202 (1982) 98
Schooner Exchange *v.* McFaddon, 11 US (7 Cranch) 116 (1813) 312
Sei Fujii *v.* State of California, 217 P2d 481 (Cal D Ct App 1950) 96
Sei Fujii *v.* State of California, 242 P2d 617 (1952) 97
Shelley *v.* Kraemer, 334 US 1 (1948) 95
Spiess *v.* C. Itoh & Co. (America), Inc., 643 F2d 353 (5th Cir, 1981) 98
Stanford *v.* Kentucky, 492 US 361 (1989) 99
The Maret, 145 F.2d 431, 442 (3rd Cir, 1944) 194
Thompson *v.* Oklahoma, 487 US 815 (1988) 99
Ungar *v.* Palestine Liberation Organization, 402 F3d 274 (1st Cir, 2005) 194
United States *v.* Palestine Liberation Organization, 695 F Supp 1456 (SDNY, 1988) 194
United States *v.* Postal, 589 F2d 862 (5th Cir, 1979) 98
Vlissidis *v.* Anadell, 262 F2d 398 (7th Cir, 1959) 98

DOMESTIC LEGISLATION

Australia

Australian Antarctic Territory Acceptance Act 1933 115
Foreign States Immunities Act 1985 314
Environment Protection and Biodiversity Conservation Act 1999 115
Seas and Submerged Lands (Limits of Continental Shelf) Proclamation 2012 115

Belgium

Constitution of Belgium (1970 amendment) 100

Canada

State Immunity Act 1982 (Canada), 1980–83 314
Amendments of the State Immunity Act (R.S.C. 1985, c. S-18), 13 March 2012 185

Denmark

Constitution of Denmark (1953) 100

France

French Constitution (1946) 100
French Constitution (1958) 100
Constitutional Law 92–554, 25 June 1992 101

Germany

German Constitution (1949) 100

Greece

Constitution of Greece (1975) 100

India

Suppression of Unlawful Acts against Safety of Maritime Navigation and Fixed Platforms on Continental Shelf Act 2002 (Act No. 69 of 2002) 311

Ireland

Constitution of Ireland (1937, consolidated 2012) 100

Italy

Constitution of Italy (1948) 100

Luxembourg

Constitution of Luxembourg (1956 amendment) 100

Portugal

Constitution of Portugal (1976) 100

Spain

Constitution of Spain (1978) 100

The Netherlands

Constitution of the Netherlands (as amended in 1953) 100

United Kingdom

Firearms Act 1968 319
Immigration Act 1971 426
European Communities Act 1972 100
State Immunity Act 1978 185
The Channel Tunnel (International Arrangements) Order 1993 426
Immigration and Asylum Act 1999 425
The Export Control Order 2008 319

Instruments of the European Union

Regulation No. 847/2004 on the Negotiation and Implementation of Air Service Agreements between Member States and Third Countries, 2004 411

Council Regulation (EC) No. 389/2006, 27 February 2006 206

Directive 97/67/EC of 15 December 1997 on common rules for the development of the internal market of Community postal services and the improvement of quality of service, OJ L 15, as amended by Directive 2002/39/EC of 10 June 2002; and Directive 2008/6/EC of 20 February 2008 416

Regulation No. 662/2009 of 13 July 2009 establishing a procedure for the negotiation and conclusion of agreements between Member States and third countries on particular matters concerning the law applicable to contractual and non-contractual obligations (2009) 411

Treaty on the Functioning of the European Union (2010) 407

European Parliament Resolution of 22 November 2012 on the forthcoming World Conference on International Telecommunications (WCIT-12) of the International Telecommunication Union, and the possible expansion of the scope of international telecommunication regulations 418

TREATIES

Bilateral Treaties

Treaty of Tordesillas (1494) 258
Treaty of Madrid of 1750 (annulled in 1761) 258
Treaty of San Ildefonso (1777) 258
Treaty of Peace, Friendship and Alliance between Ecuador and Peru (1860) 253
Treaty between Colombia and Venezuela for submitting to Arbitration the Question of the Boundary between the two Republics (1881) 253
Treaty of Peace, Friendship, Commerce and Navigation between Argentina and Chile (1855) 259
Treaty concerning Territorial Questions at Issue between Colombia and Nicaragua (1928) 267
Treaty concerning the Construction and Operation by Private Concessionaires of a Channel Fixed Link, Canterbury (1986), 1497 UNTS 334 423
Treaty of Peace between the State of Israel and the Hashemite Kingdom of Jordan (1994), 2042 UNTS 351 197
Interim Accord between Greece and the Former Yugoslav Republic of Macedonia (1995), 1891 UNTS 3 197

Multilateral Treaties

Convention Respecting the Limitation of Employment of Force for the Recovery of Contract Debts (1907), 205 CTS 250 342
Convention respecting the Laws and Customs of War on Land and its Annex: Regulations concerning the Laws and Customs of War on Land (1907), 205 CTS 277 35, 335
London Declaration concerning the Laws of Naval War (1909), 208 CTS 338 336
Convention on the Rights and Duties of States (1933), 165 LNTS 21 198
Charter of the United Nations (1945), 1 UNTS XVI 24, 95, 156, 210, 235, 256
Statute of the International Court of Justice (1945), 33 UNTS 933 108, 235, 303, 387
Convention for the Amelioration of the Condition of the Wounded and Sick in Armed Forces in the Field (1949), 75 UNTS 31 335

Convention relative to the Protection of Civilian Persons in Time of War (1949), 75 UNTS 287 336
European Convention for the Protection of Human Rights and Fundamental Freedoms (1950), 213 UNTS 221 54, 67, 68
International Convention for the Unification of Certain Rules Relating to Penal Jurisdiction in Matters of Collisions and Other Incidents of Navigation (1952), 233 UNTS 439 311
Convention for the Protection of Cultural Property in the Event of Armed Conflict (1954), 249 UNTS 240 336
Convention on the High Seas (1958), 450 UNTS 11 309
Antarctic Treaty (1959), 402 UNTS 71 110, 114
International Convention on the Elimination of All Forms of Racial Discrimination (1965), 660 UNTS 195 55
International Covenant on Economic, Social and Cultural Rights (1966), 993 UNTS 3 55
International Covenant on Civil and Political Rights (1966), 999 UNTS 171 55
Vienna Convention on the Law of Treaties (1969), 1155 UNTS 331 24, 79, 205, 235, 244, 364, 374
European Convention on State Immunity (1972), 1495 UNTS 182 314
Convention on International Trade in Endangered Species of Wild Fauna and Flora (1973), 983 UNTS 243 80
Convention on the Prohibition of Military or any Hostile Use of Environmental Modification Technique (1976), 1108 UNTS 151 330
Agreement for the Protection of the Rhine against Chemical Pollution (1976), 1124 UNTS 406 440
Protocol Additional to the Geneva Conventions of 12 August 1949, and Relating to the Protection of Victims of International Armed Conflicts, (1977) (Protocol I) 325
Convention on the Elimination of All Forms of Discrimination Against Women (1979), 1249 UNTS 13 53, 55
United Nations Convention on the Law of the Sea (1982), 1833 UNTS 397 117, 123, 309, 390
Agreement for the Implementation of Provisions of the United Nations Convention on the Law of the Sea of 10 December 1982 Relating to the Conservation and Management of Straddling Fish Stocks and Highly Migratory Fish Stocks (1995), 2167 UNTS 3 309
Convention Against Torture and Other Cruel, Inhuman or Degrading Treatment or Punishment (1984), 1465 UNTS 85 55, 180
Convention for the Suppression of Unlawful Acts against the Safety of Maritime Navigation (1988), 1678 UNTS 221 311
Convention on the Rights of the Child (1989), 1577 UNTS 3 55
United Nations Framework Convention on Climate Change (1992), 31 ILM 849 73

North American Free Trade Agreement, Canada–Mexico–United States (1992), 32 ILM 289 181
General Framework Agreement for Peace in Bosnia and Herzegovina (Bosnia and Herzegovina-Croatia-Federal Republic of Yugoslavia) (1995) UN Doc. A/50/79C, S/1995/999, 30 November 1995 197
Protocol on Prohibitions or Restrictions on the Use of Mines, Booby-Traps and Other Devices annexed to the Convention on Prohibitions or Restrictions on the Use of Certain Conventional Weapons Which May be Deemed to be Excessively Injurious or to Have Indiscriminate Effects (1996) 325
Rome Statute of the International Criminal Court (1998), 2187 UNTS 90 244, 326
Optional Protocol to the Convention on the Rights of the Child on the Involvement of Children in Armed Conflict (2000), 2173 UNTS 222 53
Agreement concerning Cooperation in Suppressing Illicit Maritime and Air Trafficking in Narcotic Drugs and Psychotropic Substances in the Caribbean Area (2003) 309
United Nations Convention on Jurisdictional Immunities of States and Their Property (2004) 173, 314
Protocol of 2005 to the Convention for the Suppression of Unlawful Acts against the Safety of Maritime Navigation (2005) 309
Arms Trade Treaty (2013) 45

International Bank for Reconstruction and Development

Charter Establishing the Forest Carbon Partnership Facility (2010) 81

Organization of African Unity (OAU) and African Union (AU)

Charter of the Organization of African Unity (1963), 479 UNTS 39 255
African Charter on Human and Peoples' Rights (1981) 53
Constitutive Act of the African Union (2002) 29

Organization of American States (OAS)

American Declaration of the Rights and Duties of Man, 1948, OAS Res. XXX (1948) 53
American Convention on Human Rights (1969), 1144 UNTS 123 55

World Trade Organization (WTO)

Agreement Establishing the World Trade Organization (1994) 368

RESOLUTIONS

(in chronological order)

United Nations General Assembly Resolutions

Resolution 195 (III) (1948) 232
Resolution 296 (IV) (1949) 232
Resolution 377 (V) (1950), Uniting for Peace 28
Resolution 620 (VII) (1952) 232
Resolution 1017 (X) (1957) 232
Resolution 1514 (XV) (1960), Declaration on the Granting of Independence to Colonial Countries and Peoples 144, 155, 211, 222, 256
Resolution 1541 (XV) (1960), Principles which should Guide Members in Determining whether or not an Obligation Exists to Transmit the Information Called for under Article 73e of the Charter of the United Nations 155, 211, 224
Resolution 2625 (XXV) (1970), Declaration on Principles of International Law concerning Friendly Relations and Cooperation among States in Accordance with the Charter of the United Nations 41
Resolution 3151 (XXVIII) (1973) 238
Resolution 3314 (1974) 173
Resolution 36/172 (1981) 41
Resolution 43/177 (1988) 229, 238, 243
Resolution 52/520 (1998) 243
Resolution 56/83 (2001) 194
Resolution 58/314 (2004) 239
Resolution 59/38 (2004) 315
Resolution 61/295 (2007), Declaration on the Rights of Indigenous Peoples 87
Resolution 67/19 (2012), Status of Palestine in the United Nations 229

United Nations Security Council Resolutions

Resolution 138 (1960) 47
Resolution 221 (1966) 25
Resolution 379 (1975) 157
Resolution 380 (1975) 157
Resolution 621 (1988) 157

Resolution 658 (1990) 157
Resolution 690 (1991) 157
Resolution 733 (1992) 25
Resolution 743 (1992) 25
Resolution 755 (1992) 25
Resolution 788 (1992) 48
Resolution 794 (1992) 25
Resolution 819 (1993) 25
Resolution 836 (1993) 26
Resolution 866 (1993) 48
Resolution 867 (1993) 167
Resolution 873 (1993) 167
Resolution 940 (1994) 167
Resolution 1181 (1998) 48
Resolution 1203 (1998) 162
Resolution 1244 (1999) 162
Resolution 1373 (2001) 164
Resolution 1429 (2002) 158
Resolution 1483 (2002) 170
Resolution 1495 (2003) 158
Resolution 1528 (2004) 169
Resolution 1529 (2004) 168
Resolution 1542 (2004) 168
Resolution 1590 (2005) 159
Resolution 1674 (2006) 33
Resolution 1706 (2006) 34
Resolution 1933 (2010) 170
Resolution 1962 (2010) 169
Resolution 1970 (2011) 43
Resolution 1973 (2011) 34, 43
Resolution 1975 (2011) 170
Resolution 1996 (2011) 36
Resolution 2014 (2011) 36
Resolution 2099 (2013) 159
Resolution 2118 (2013) 349

OTHER INTERNATIONAL INSTRUMENTS AND REPORTS

Badinter Commission

Arbitration Commission of the Peace Conference on Yugoslavia, Opinion No. 3 (Borders) 3 EJIL (1992) 184 248

Arbitration Commission of the Peace Conference on Yugoslavia, Opinion No. 10 (Federal Republic of Yugoslavia – Serbia and Montenegro) 4 July 1992, 4 EJIL 1 (1993) 74 193

United Nations Reports

'Preventing War and Disaster: A Growing Global Challenge', Kofi Annan (UN Annual report on the work of the Organization, 1999) 28

Report of the Secretary-General concerning the Situation in Western Sahara, UN Doc. S/2001/613 annex 1, 20 June 2001 157

Report of the Secretary-General concerning the Situation in Western Sahara, UN Doc. S/2003/565, 23 May 2003 158

'A More Secure World: Our Shared Responsibility', Report of the High-level Panel on Threats, Challenges and Change, UN Doc. A/59/565, 2 December 2004 31

'In Larger Freedom: Towards Development, Security and Human Rights for All', Report of the Secretary-General, UN Doc. A/59/2005, 21 March 2005 32

Report of the Secretary-General on the Situation concerning Western Sahara, UN Doc. S/2006/249, 19 April 2006 159

Report of the Special Envoy of the Secretary-General on Kosovo's future status, UN Doc. S/2007/168, 26 March 2007 164

Report of the Secretary-General on the United Nations Interim Administration Mission in Kosovo, UN Doc. S/2008/692, 24 November 2008 165

Twenty-sixth progress report of the Secretary-General on the United Nations Operation in Côte d'Ivoire, UN Doc. S/2010/600, 23 November 2010 169

Twenty-seventh progress report of the Secretary-General on the United Nations Operation in Côte d'Ivoire, UN Doc. S/2011/211, 30 March 2011 169

Report of the Secretary-General on the Situation concerning Western Sahara, UN Doc. S/2013/220, 8 April 2013 59

Report of the Secretary-General on the United Nations Interim Administration Mission in Kosovo, UN Doc. S/2013/254, 30 April 2013 165

United Nations International Law Commission

Commentaries to the ILC Articles concerning the Law of the Sea (1956) 309
Draft Articles on the Responsibility of States for Internationally Wrongful Acts (1996) 194, 421
Articles on Responsibility of States for Internationally Wrongful Acts and Commentary (2001) 173, 179, 289, 310, 322, 334, 364, 391, 421
Guiding Principles Applicable to Unilateral Declarations of States Capable of Creating Legal Obligations, UN Doc. A/61/10 (2006) 201, 235

ILC Reports

ILC Report (2000), UN Doc. A/55/10 340
ILC Report (2001), UN Doc. A/56/10 343
'Report of the International Law Commission on the Work of its Thirty-second Session', ILC Yearbook (1980) 336

ILC Study Group

Fragmentation of International Law: Difficulties Arising from the Diversification and Expansion of International Law – Finalized by Martti Koskenniemi; and Draft Conclusions of the Work of the Study Group, Doc. A/CN.4/L.682 and Add.1 and Corr.1, 2 May 2006 71, 374
'Fragmentation of International Law: Difficulties Arising from the Diversification and Expansion of International Law, Conclusions of the Work of the Study Group' (A/CN.4/L.702) (18 July 2006) 71

Special Rapporteurs

Roberto Ago, 'First Report on State Responsibility', ILC Yearbook (1969) 292
Roberto Ago, 'Eighth Report on State Responsibility', ILC Yearbook (1979) 352
Willem Riphagen, 'Preliminary Report on State Responsibility', ILC Yearbook (1980) 351
Willem Riphagen, 'Fourth Report on State Responsibility', ILC Yearbook (1983) 358
Willem Riphagen, 'Fifth Report on State Responsibility', ILC Yearbook (1984) 353
Willem Riphagen, 'Sixth Report on State Responsibility', ILC Yearbook (1985) 353
Mohamed Bennouna, 'Preliminary Report on Diplomatic Protection', ILC Yearbook (1998) 341

Gaetano Arangio-Ruiz, 'Seventh Report on State Responsibility', ILC Yearbook (1995) 353
John Dugard, 'First Report on Diplomatic Protection', ILC Yearbook (2000) 341
James Crawford, 'Third Report on State Responsibility', ILC Yearbook (2000) 342
James Crawford, 'Fourth Report on State Responsibility', ILC Yearbook (2001) 340

Other UN Documents

UN Human Rights Committee, Consideration of Country Report – United Nations Interim Administration Mission in Kosovo (initial report), UN Doc. CCPR/C/UNK/CO/1, 14 August 2006 163
UN General Assembly, Responsibility of States for Internationally Wrongful Acts – Compilation of Decisions of International Courts, Tribunals and Other Bodies – Report of the Secretary-General, UN Doc. A/62/62, 1 February 2007 387
UN General Assembly, Responsibility of States for Internationally Wrongful Acts – Compilation of Decisions of International Courts, Tribunals and Other Bodies – Report of the Secretary-General, UN Doc. A/65/76, 30 April 2010 387

World Health Organisation

Report of the Committee of Experts on Tobacco Industry Documents, 'Tobacco Company Strategies to Undermine Tobacco Control Activities at the World Health Organization', (July 2000) 85

PART I

Sovereignty

1

The war against cliché: dispatches from the international legal front

KAREN KNOP AND SUSAN MARKS*

'To idealize', writes Martin Amis, 'all writing is a campaign against cliché. Not just clichés of the pen, but clichés of the mind and clichés of the heart.' He goes on: 'When I dispraise, I am usually quoting clichés. When I praise, I am usually quoting the opposed qualities of freshness, energy, and reverberation of voice.'[1] Amis is a justly respected leader in the war against cliché. But if we, the authors of this chapter, hope to consider ourselves partisans of that campaign, in our case the spur to enlist came from another source.

It was at the time when we were both doctoral students working under the supervision of James Crawford. One of us was busy finding the devil in the detail. The other was wondering whether at the end of the day everything really was so cut and dried. Well, suffice it to say (for clichés are surely hard to avoid altogether), we changed our tune (ditto) when there began to appear in the margins of our drafts that shaming rebuke, that call to arms: 'cliché'.

We wish to use the present occasion to explore a little further what happened then. What exactly was it that James was signalling to us as aspiring scholars of international law when he cautioned us against cliché? Are the clichés of international legal field clichés of the pen, or also clichés of the mind and even clichés of the heart? Why are they to be deprecated? And if, once deprecated, they still remain (as we have already suggested) hard to avoid, why is that so? Does cliché always stand opposed to freshness, energy and reverberation of voice, or might it be that, behind the over-familiarity, there is potential for vitality and insight yet?

* We thank Simon Stern for his valuable suggestions on the subject of cliché and the Global Law Students Association, Melbourne Law School for the opportunity to discuss a draft of this chapter.

[1] Martin Amis, *The War against Cliché* (London: Vintage, 2002), xv.

It is a cliché of writing about cliché that, while we think we know a cliché when we're confronted with one, that is not always the case. Perhaps because of this, much work on the subject takes the form of inventories or 'dictionaries' of clichés.[2] We do not offer here a list of international legal clichés (assuming such could exist). The issue for us is, rather, cliché – the phenomenon of cliché – as a problem of international law. What does it mean, we ask, and what does it not mean, to wage the war against cliché on the international legal front?

I

We begin with the concept of cliché itself. In the introduction to a dictionary of clichés that is now in its fifth edition, Eric Partridge writes that a cliché is 'an outworn commonplace; a phrase or short sentence that has become so hackneyed that careful speakers and scrupulous writers shrink from it because they feel that its use is an insult to the intelligence of their audience or public'.[3] This definition highlights a number of features. In the first place, there is the *hackneyed* character of the cliché. Clichés are banal, trite, ho-hum. Secondly, the concept of cliché brings with it the idea of loss or degeneration.[4] A cliché is an *outworn* commonplace, in the sense that it originally had a point but repetition has now blunted that point and effaced the meaning and intensity which the cliché once had. And thirdly, cliché is a pejorative term. To apply the label is to condemn that to which it is applied as boring, predictable, inane, jejune and/or specious – an *insult* to the collective intelligence.

Partridge's concern is the verbal cliché – the phrase or short sentence – but, at any rate today, the concept of cliché plainly extends much further than that. Thus, for instance, we speak of musical clichés, architectural clichés, theatrical clichés and culinary clichés. We take cliché to apply not only to language, but also to the aural, visual and other sensory domains, as well as to the realm of gestures and actions. Underlying all this is an idea of cliché as a particular mode of thought – a markedly unreflective mode of thought, indeed a mode of non-thought, a kind of automatism. For Walter Redfern, the central characteristic of cliché is 'dependence'

[2] See e.g. Eric Partridge, *A Dictionary of Clichés*, 5th edn (London: Routledge, 1978); James Rogers, *The Dictionary of Clichés* (New York: Ballantine, 1991); and Lucy Fisher, *Clichés: A Dictionary of Received Ideas* (Kindle, 2012).

[3] Partridge, *A Dictionary of Clichés*, 2.

[4] On this, see Elizabeth Barry, *Beckett and Authority: The Uses of Cliché* (Basingstoke: Palgrave Macmillan, 2006), 3.

in this sense.[5] When you use a cliché, you short-circuit cognition. You renounce your independent-mindedness and obviate the inconvenience and effort of thinking for yourself. There is felt to be a laziness about the use of cliché. There is also felt to be an undertone of self-legitimation, inasmuch as clichés tie us to normality, to respectability, to authority. In her study of the trial of Adolf Eichmann, Hannah Arendt remarks on Eichmann's tendency to repeat 'word for word the same stock phrases and self-invented clichés', observing that 'when he did succeed in constructing a sentence of his own, he repeated it until it became a cliché'.[6]

At the same time, Gillian Beer poses a fair question when she asks: '[H]ow would we live or communicate without clichés?'[7] Clichés frequently belong to the category of phatic communication, meeting the need for general sociability, rather than putting across any specific proposition. As Beer explains, 'cliché assures us that we all belong together . . . It wards off extreme intimacy of encounter', while signalling comfortable 'communality'.[8] Redfern recalls that the French word 'répétition' has the double sense of reiteration and rehearsal.[9] The repetition of familiar tropes facilitates the performance of social interaction. The darker side of that is, of course, that cliché is also exclusionary. Outworn, it is by no means washed-up; there is a potency in its very banality. Thus, clichés function as *shibboleths* that distinguish those in the know from those who fail to understand the clichéd expression or to appreciate its character as a cliché. At the same time, clichés serve as carriers of *ideology* that uphold the status quo by making the received version of right-thinking common sense too banal to question. Arendt's attention to Eichmann's patterns of speech has been read in this light: 'To identify the cliché is to try to open up the possibility of dissent in the domain of the obvious.'[10] Finally, clichés give expression to *stereotypes* that reinforce prejudices and perpetuate the marginalisation of low-status groups.

The concept of the stereotype takes us directly to the origin of the word 'cliché'. Borrowed from French, the term comes from the world of printing. It refers to a moulded metal plate – a stereotype – cast for printing

[5] Walter Redfern, *Clichés and Coinages* (Oxford: Basil Blackwell, 1989), 16.

[6] Hannah Arendt, *Eichmann in Jerusalem* (London: Penguin, 1994 [1963]), 49. See further Jakob Norberg, 'The Political Theory of Cliché: Hannah Arendt Reading Adolf Eichmann', *Cultural Critique*, 76 (2010), 74.

[7] Gillian Beer, 'The Making of a Cliché: "No Man is an Island"', *European Journal of English Studies*, 1 (1997), 33.

[8] *Ibid.* [9] Redfern, *Clichés and Coinages*, 8.

[10] Norberg, 'The Political Theory of Cliché', 81.

blocks of text. Whereas at first individual letters had always to be set one by one, in the early nineteenth century a process developed whereby phrases that were likely to appear frequently could be prefabricated as single units – 'clichés'. The word is believed to be onomatopoeic: *clicher* is a variant of the more common *cliquer* (to click), and is understood to evoke the 'click-clack' sound made by the moulding matrix when it struck the surface of the molten metal to produce the plate. By extension, cliché came also to refer to plates for the printing of images, and later to other printing technologies, including photographic negatives. The figurative usage of cliché as a 'prefabricated' or stereotyped mode of expression had apparently gained currency in France by the 1860s. That figurative usage (though not, it seems, the literal usage) was then imported into English.[11] The *Oxford English Dictionary* dates the first occurrence in English to 1892.

The cliché, then, is a phenomenon of the nineteenth century that is bound up with processes of mechanisation, industrialisation and rationalisation, and with the emergence of a print culture enabling the mass circulation of texts. In tracing its history, Elizabeth Barry highlights the shift from the positively or neutrally coded 'commonplace' to the negatively coded 'cliché'.[12] In classical antiquity commonplaces formed part of the study of rhetoric, and referred to particular starting points or thematics to be used in formal argument (*topoi*). Early modern European thought likewise embraced the idea of the commonplace, though not so much as an aspect of rhetoric, which fell widely out of favour insofar as it came to be associated with manipulative and insincere speech. Instead, the activity of 'commonplacing' and the 'commonplace book' became private pursuits, the collection of material in personal scrapbooks. According to Barry, what set the scene for the concept of cliché was the emergence of a mass market for the consumption of texts. Anxiety about vulgarisation, banalisation and inauthenticity arose as a concomitant of the increasingly wide and fast dissemination of words and ideas that was made possible by the new technologies of mechanical reproduction. Barry reports that an analogy became prevalent in Romantic literary aesthetics between 'a mechanical use of language and the technical equipment of printing'.[13]

The first work thematising the concept of the cliché is often said to be Gustave Flaubert's satirical novel *Bouvard and Pécuchet*, written in 1880,

[11] The *Oxford English Dictionary* refers to cliché in its literal sense as the French name for what in English is simply called a cast or, in a more technical idiom, a 'dab'.

[12] Barry, *Beckett and Authority*, 11 *et seq.*

[13] *Ibid.*, 16.

in which two copy-clerks embark on a search for knowledge that brings only errors, failures and disasters.[14] The clerks' putative commonplace book – published separately under the title of *Dictionary of Received Ideas* – catalogues clichés in such entries as 'Rhyme: Never in accord with reason'; 'Thicket: Always "dark and impenetrable"'; and 'Unleash: Applied to dogs and evil passions'.[15] By the middle of the next century, the denunciation of cliché had become considerably less subtle – a trend perhaps nowhere better exemplified than in George Orwell's famously intemperate essay on politics and the English language.[16]

For Orwell, 'the English language is in a bad way', and a key aspect of the pathology is the prevalence of clichés.[17] All too often, and especially in the discourse of politics and government, recourse is had to 'ready-made phrases' and 'worn-out metaphors which have lost all evocative power and are merely used because they save people the trouble of inventing phrases for themselves'.[18] Echoing the association mentioned above of 'mechanical' language with printing technology, Orwell writes that a 'speaker who uses that kind of phraseology has gone some distance towards turning himself into a machine. The appropriate noises are coming out of his larynx, but his brain is not involved as it would be if he were choosing his words for himself.'[19] The essay culminates in a series of rules for overcoming this state of affairs, of which rule 1 is 'Never use a metaphor, simile or other figure of speech which you are used to seeing in print.'[20]

II

Let us now begin to connect this discussion to international law.[21] In doing so, we should note one further feature of cliché on which we have not yet touched. This is that cliché is, as Ruth Amossy and Elisheva Rosen observe, an inescapably relative phenomenon.[22] There is no such thing as a 'cliché in itself'.[23] Rather, clichés are specific to particular times.

14 Gustave Flaubert, *Bouvard and Pécuchet, with Dictionary of Received Ideas*, tr. A. Krailsheimer (London: Penguin, 1976).

15 *Ibid.*, 324, 328.

16 George Orwell, 'Politics and the English Language', reprinted in *Why I Write* (London: Penguin, 2004), 102.

17 *Ibid.* 18 *Ibid.*, 112, 106. 19 *Ibid.*, 114. 20 *Ibid.*, 119.

21 We join here a wider literature on law as rhetoric and the roles of imagery in law, including international law. What distinguishes clichés is that they involve failed metaphors, whereas the legal literature tends to focus on successful imagery.

22 Ruth Amossy and Elisheva Rosen, *Le Discours du cliché* (Paris: Société d'édition d'enseignement supérieur, 1982), 9.

23 *Ibid.*

We mentioned earlier Partridge's dictionary of clichés. It runs to some 250 pages, and puts asterisks next to clichés that are 'particularly hackneyed or objectionable'.[24] Yet who today speaks of 'heaping coals of fire on a person's head', or of 'Lares and Penates', 'the clerk of the weather', 'in one's palmy days' or 'hewers of wood and drawers of water' – all of them asterisked as especially egregious clichés in Partridge's most recent edition of 1978?

Clichés are also specific to particular places. To stay with verbal clichés, 'Monday morning quarterback', 'fall off the turnip truck', 'blow this pop stand' and 'talk turkey' might be – or once have been – used and understood by some people in the United Kingdom, but if so, these phrases would not be likely to be – or have been – heard as particularly clichéd. That said, the global circulation of language, or at any rate English, and perhaps especially American English, is a widely remarked phenomenon of our time, and it may be accelerating. As Hephzibah Anderson remarks, 'Twitter, digital memes and the 24-hour news cycle can coin a cliché overnight, it seems.'[25]

Finally, clichés are specific to particular contexts and communities. Hence Redfern's remark near the beginning of his book on cliché that there is 'no way of knowing whether my clichés are yours'.[26] Amossy and Rosen explain that clichés depend on conditions of reception that permit them to be recognised as such.[27] Along with the other aspects of relativity, this is, of course, a feature shared by the related phenomenon of idiom. But whereas idioms are unmarked lexical items, we have seen that it belongs with the distinctiveness of the cliché that it gives off an aura of loss or degeneration.[28] In order for that to occur, there must exist a situation in which, and an audience by whom, it is apprehended as exhausted, stale and devitalised, something that once fired the imagination, but does so no longer.

Learning to sort a field's clichés from its idioms is an important competence that may serve as a badge of proficiency for those who have it and a handicap and barrier to entry for those who don't. It is a competence that is often acquired through relationships of training or apprenticeship. We have already mentioned the training which we both received from James Crawford. Of course, that training was not limited to specialised international legal language. The clichés of international law are the clichés of

24 Partridge, *A Dictionary of Clichés*, 9.
25 Hephzibah Anderson, 'In Praise of the Cliché', *Prospect*, 14 November 2012.
26 Redfern, *Clichés and Coinages*, 3. 27 Amossy and Rosen, *Le Discours du cliché*, 9.
28 On the distinction between cliché and idiom, see further Barry, *Beckett and Authority*, 4.

everyday communication – and they are the clichés of policy debate, legal practice, institutional organisation and academic life as well. On the other hand, those wider terrains are not all-encompassing. As with Orwell's domain of politics, there also exist clichés that are rooted in the distinctive history, literature, institutions and traditions of international law itself.

Thinking about cliché as a problem of international law, we might start by recalling the usage in international legal communication of banal and specious phases in general currency. 'The reality on the ground', 'all the stakeholders', 'going forward' and 'drill down' are a few contemporary examples. We can then notice the emergence of clichés peculiar to international law. These mostly arise from the overuse of language borrowed from academic literature or from the pronouncements of courts and tribunals. 'The invisible college',[29] 'compliance pull',[30] 'a legal black hole'[31] and 'the dark sides'[32] are some phrases that may be thought to exemplify this turn of events whereby resonant expressions become, in some sense, victims of their own success. To these figurative noun-phrases, one might add sentence-length propositions. It is now trite to say – as the cliché of legal discourse would have it – that 'almost all nations observe almost all principles of international law and almost all of their obligations almost all of the time'.[33] So too, repetition has dimmed the rhetorical power of Judge Dillard's chiasmus: 'It is for the people to determine the destiny of the territory and not the territory the destiny of the people.'[34]

But the clichés of international law are not, of course, only verbal. Perhaps the most notorious international legal clichés lie, in fact, in the visual domain – the domain of book covers, website homepages, institute logos and the like. Robert Musil once wrote that '[t]here is nothing in this world as invisible as a monument',[35] and certainly the iconography of international law is replete with 'monuments' that have become more

[29] Oscar Schachter, 'The Invisible College of International Lawyers', *Northwestern University Law Review*, 72 (1977–8), 217.

[30] Thomas Franck, *The Power of Legitimacy among Nations* (New York: Oxford University Press, 1990), 16.

[31] *R (Abassi)* v. *Secretary of State for Foreign and Commonwealth Affairs* [2002] EWCA Civ 1598, para. 64; Johan Steyn, 'Guantanamo Bay: The Legal Black Hole', *International and Comparative Law Quarterly*, 53 (2004), 1.

[32] David Kennedy, *The Dark Sides of Virtue: Reassessing International Humanitarianism* (Princeton University Press, 2004).

[33] Louis Henkin, *How Nations Behave: Law and Foreign Policy*, 2nd edn (New York: Council on Foreign Relations, 1979), 47 (emphasis omitted).

[34] *Western Sahara*, Advisory Opinion, 16 October 1975, ICJ Reports (1975), 12, 116.

[35] Robert Musil, 'Monuments' in *Posthumous Papers of a Living Author*, tr. Peter Wortsman (London: Penguin, 1993), 61.

or less invisible. Maps are one example. Their overuse on the dust jackets of international legal books has largely drained them of the capacity to engage us imaginatively. We register them, of course, as images of the global scale of international law or of its preoccupation with boundaries, spaces and territories, but they do not detain us for long. They do not hold our attention or invite our scrutiny. Their evocative spark has gone faint. Yellowing antique maps, favoured in recent times to emphasise international law's Eurocentric viewpoint (whether to place it comfortingly in the past or disturbingly in the present), scarcely escape this fate.

Images of justice – the blindfolded goddess Justitia or the set of scales she holds – together with the Earth as a globe are another example. A staple of logos of programmes, journals and professional associations in the international legal field, these once-inspiring representations now project reassuring normality, safe respectability and a rather bland, humdrum authority. As a final example, we might take the scenes of important people doing momentous things in settings of international law-making and adjudication that adorn international legal publications and promotional materials for international legal activities – statesmen shaking hands, diplomats negotiating around a table, Heads of State signing documents, representatives voting at the United Nations, international judges on the bench and other similar images. Are we to focus on who is present at these occasions or on who is absent from them? The images are so familiar that it becomes hard to remember even to ask such questions.

Alongside verbal and visual clichés, any discussion of cliché as a problem of international law must reckon with a further category of clichés that come rather less neatly packaged for inspection. We shall call this the category of 'conceptual clichés'. Inasmuch as they are expressed through language, conceptual clichés might, of course, be assimilated to verbal clichés. But the focus here is less on the manner of speaking than on the manner of conceptualising things. Conceptual clichés are outworn ways of framing, analysing, thematising or otherwise thinking about the issues under investigation. In expressing conceptual clichés, we can usefully take our cue from Flaubert's copy-clerks. Thus, some international legal examples might be 'State sovereignty: Either eroding or persisting'; 'The individual: Always emerging as a subject of international law'; 'International legal system: Young, embryonic, primitive'; and 'Balancing: Applied to freedom and security, state sovereignty and human rights, military necessity and humanitarian protection, etc.' Stamped machine-like on the texts of international law, these *topoi* operate as stereotypes, shibboleths and performances of comfortable 'communality'.

III

On the basis of what we have said so far, it seems that international law is as problematic when it comes to cliché as Orwell took politics to be. Rule 1 may well be more honoured in the breach than the observance. And, of course, there we go breaching it yet again. Orwell concedes that he breaches it too. 'The debased language I have been discussing is in some ways very convenient', he writes. 'Look back through this essay, and for certain you will find that I have again and again committed the very faults I am protesting against.'[36] Does that make Orwell a hypocrite? For Christopher Ricks, the 'only way to speak of a cliché is with a cliché', with the result that 'even the best writers against clichés are awkwardly placed'.[37] The problem, as he sees it, is that some of them do not always 'winc[e] enough'.[38] But Ricks also shows that the issue is not only about wincing enough. Orwell is surely one of the best writers against clichés, and Ricks has something very interesting to say about the passage with which Orwell's essay 'Politics and the English Language' ends.

The passage goes like this:

> One cannot change this all in a moment, but one can at least change one's own habits, and from time to time one can even, if one jeers loudly enough, send some worn-out and useless phrase – some *jackboot, Achilles' heel, hotbed, melting pot, acid test, veritable inferno* or other lump of verbal refuse – into the dustbin where it belongs.[39]

Ricks comments that 'Orwell's darkest urgings' have, in these words, a 'weirdly bright undertow'.[40] How so? Because 'what is most alive in that sentence is not the sequence where Orwell consciously put his polemical energy' – the 'argumentative train of serviceable clichés' that takes him from 'worn-out and useless', through 'lump of verbal refuse', to 'into the dustbin where it belongs' – but rather the sequence that lists the spurned clichés themselves:

> The *jackboot* has, hard on its heels, *Achilles' heel*; then the *hotbed* at once melts in the heat, into *melting pot*, and then again (a different melting) into *acid test* – with perhaps some memory of Achilles, held by the heel when he was dipped into the Styx; and then finally the *veritable inferno*, which

36 Orwell, 'Politics and the English Language', 116.

37 Christopher Ricks, 'Clichés' in Leonard Michaels and Christopher Ricks (eds.), *The State of the Language* (Berkeley: University of California Press, 1980), 54.

38 *Ibid.*, 55. 39 Orwell, 'Politics and the English Language', 120.

40 Ricks, 'Clichés', 55.

> not only consumes *hotbed* and *melting pot* but also, because of *veritable*, confronts the truth-testing *acid test.*[41]

Ricks concludes that 'Orwell may have set his face against those clichés, but his mind . . . was another matter.'[42] For even as Orwell disdains and dismisses this language as a useless heap of verbal rubbish, even as he sets schoolmasterish rules designed to ban it, he uses it to 'create a bizarre vitality of poetry'.[43] The key word in that last sentence is actually 'uses'. Ricks explains: '[u]sing is the nub'; the point is to use clichés, not be 'used by them'.[44] Orwell proposes that clichés 'anaesthetize a portion of one's brain',[45] but on the evidence of Orwell's own writing, Ricks demonstrates that the great essayist is wrong. 'Clichés invite you not to think', Ricks writes, 'but you may always decline the invitation'.[46] In a similar vein, Redfern remarks that 'clichés are first thoughts', but 'we have the capacity for second thoughts'.[47]

Ricks and Redfern belong to a critical tradition that urges contemplation of the imaginative possibilities of clichés. Rather than simply banning clichés, for these critics the more productive approach is often to *do something with them*. In any case, experience teaches us that a ban will not work. It will only serve to make everyone feel bad. As Redfern rightly avers, 'we are all vulgarians'.[48] We can't and won't avoid using metaphors, similes and other figures of speech which we are used to seeing in print, even if it were a good idea for us to try. That means we also need to be careful as critics. For if clichés can serve as shibboleths – door-openers that also shut out those not in the know – so too the criticism of cliché can risk spilling over into self-delusion and snobbery. Besides, if clichés were really so worthless, why would they have such tenacity?

We have mentioned more than once that it is a characteristic feature of clichés that they are taken to be outworn and degraded, the trace of something once potent that has been dissipated through overuse. In the case of verbal clichés, what has been dissipated often seems to be their figurative charge. When we speak of an 'acid test', the acid is no longer vivid in our mind's eye (or ear or nose). Because of this, clichés are sometimes thought of as 'dead metaphors' – that is to say, metaphors that we no longer recognise as figurative, metaphors in respect of which the comparison made in the metaphor is no longer imaginatively registered.

[41] *Ibid.*, 55–6. [42] *Ibid.*, 56. [43] *Ibid.*, 55. [44] *Ibid.*, 57.
[45] Orwell, 'Politics and the English Language', 117. [46] Ricks, 'Clichés', 58.
[47] Redfern, *Clichés and Coinages*, 7. [48] *Ibid.*, 5.

The classic examples are expressions like 'the foot of a mountain, 'the leg of a table', 'to run in the family'. Some analysts of language dispute this concept, arguing that even in expressions of that kind there is some 'bare spark of life'.[49] But certainly, when it comes to clichés, those who highlight the possibility of their creative deployment insist that 'dead metaphor' is not, in fact, the right way to think of them. Of course, no one disputes that it is a defining feature of cliché that it has lost vigour, but rather than taking clichés for dead, these scholars encourage us to see them as merely 'sleeping'.[50]

The implications of seeing metaphors as sleeping are explored by Chaim Perelman and Lucie Olbrechts-Tyteca in their celebrated treatise on the 'new rhetoric'.[51] (The term actually used in the English edition of their book is 'dormant'.) To characterise a metaphor as dormant, they propose, is to intimate that it is inactive, but that 'this state of inactivity may only be transitory', so that 'the metaphor can be awakened and become active again'.[52] We can be led again to see, hear and smell the fizz of the unverified substance as it hits the acid, and through that, we can be led to reflect on the imagery of the 'acid test' and on how it directs, channels and frames our thinking about the nature of truth and of truth-testing. Perelman and Olbrechts-Tyteca describe a number of ways in which dormant metaphors may be awakened. They may be awakened by being placed in a context that is different from their usual one (recontextualisation).[53] They may be awakened by being set alongside another cliché or other clichés (juxtaposition). They may be awakened by being developed or extended in a new way (development or extension). And they may be awakened by being taken literally (literalisation).

The awakening of dormant metaphors is the stuff of much everyday playfulness and humour.[54] It can make us laugh, but in doing so, it can also make us think. In a book about cliché published in 1970, Marshall McLuhan reports a funny story that illustrates the first of Perelman and

[49] George Lakoff and Mark Johnson, *Metaphors We Live By* (University of Chicago Press, 1980), 55.

[50] See esp. Barry, *Beckett and Authority*, 3. On the idea that metaphors may be 'not dead but sleeping', see William Empson, *Seven Types of Ambiguity* (London: Hogarth Press, 1991), 25.

[51] Chaim Perelman and Lucie Olbrechts-Tyteca, *The New Rhetoric: A Treatise on Argumentation*, tr. John Wilkinson and Purcell Weaver (London: Notre Dame Press, 1969), 405 *et seq.*

[52] *Ibid.*, 405.

[53] The bracketed terms are our own.

[54] As Ricks, among others, observes. See Ricks, 'Clichés', 58.

Olbrechts-Tyteca's methods of metaphor-awakening – recontextualisation:

> A teacher asked her class to use a familiar word in a new way. One boy read: 'The boy returned home with a cliché on his face.' Asked to explain his phrase, he said, 'the dictionary defines *cliché* as a "worn-out expression"'.[55]

The boy in this story has placed the cliché of clichés as 'worn-out expressions' in a context that is different from its usual one, and in so doing, he has jolted it awake. To be sure, the awakening took a bit of explanation. But once it happened, the imagery of exhaustion and expression would have become, for his teacher and classmates, at once strikingly vivid and newly, comically strange.

Many of the authors to whom we have referred in this section, McLuhan included, highlight the prominence of metaphor-awakening in the work of modernist writers like James Joyce, T. S. Eliot, Eugene Ionesco and Samuel Beckett. Here is one example from Beckett's *Happy Days*:

> *Winnie:* Oh well what does it matter, that is what I always say, it will come back, that is what I find so wonderful, all comes back... Floats up, one fine day, out of the blue... The comb is here. The brush is here. Perhaps I put them back after use. But normally I do not put things back after use, no, I leave them lying about and put them back all together, at the end of the day. To speak in the old style. The sweet old style... That is what I find so wonderful, that not a day goes by – to speak in the old style – without some blessing in disguise.[56]

Beckett uses here the second of Perelman and Olbrechts-Tyteca's methods – juxtaposition. The clichés tumble out, one on top of the other, in a way that draws attention to their clichéness: the 'old style' of speaking. What is that old style? Is it really 'old' – or also new? Sweet – or also bitter? A style – or also a regime of knowledge and power? H. Porter Abbott observes that, in passages such as this, Beckett exposes 'a still-active power in clichés, a power that works on us in our slumber'. For, Abbott suggests, 'it is not really the metaphors that sleep but we who use them'.[57]

[55] Marshall McLuhan with Wilfred Watson, *From Cliché to Archetype* (New York: Viking Press, 1970), 54 (quoted by Ricks, 'Clichés', 59).

[56] Samuel Beckett, *The Complete Dramatic Works* (London: Faber and Faber, 1986), 135, 144, 146–7.

[57] H. Porter Abbott, 'The Art of Making it New, Revisited: Beckett and Cliché', *Poetics Today*, 29 (2008), 596.

IV

To recognise international law as a domain of cliché is also to grasp international law as a domain in which *things can be – and have been – done with cliché.* In this final section, we want to illustrate the potential for rousing (or, as the case may be, not rousing, even further enervating) international legal clichés by returning to some of the verbal, visual and conceptual clichés to which we referred earlier. In particular, we want to return to 'the invisible college', the erosion or persistence of sovereignty, 'a legal black hole' and images of maps and important people. Beginning, then, with the first of these, it is part of the cliché of the invisible college to recall that this phrase was coined by Oscar Schachter in an article published in 1977.[58] Schachter wrote that 'the professional community of international lawyers . . . , though dispersed throughout the world and engaged in diverse occupations, constitutes a kind of invisible college dedicated to a common intellectual enterprise'.[59] He referred to this community's role in giving 'meaning and effect' to the conception of '*la conscience juridique*',[60] but said that, in order to fulfil that role, it had to become more visible to State officials. There was also a need for wider 'participation embracing persons from various parts of the world and from diverse political and cultural groupings'.[61]

In 2001 the American Society of International Law chose as the theme of its annual meeting 'The Visible College of International Law'. The organisers explained that they found:

> Professor Oscar Schachter's famous observation, made nearly a quarter century ago in 1977 . . . to be an intriguing characterization, one that demanded a kind of reflection particularly suitable for observance of the (true) millennium and the extraordinary changes that had occurred in the nature of international law – and its practice – over the past quarter century.[62]

They said that their theme was designed to focus attention on the 'historical evolution, our current status, and our future prospects as a college, we submit, an increasingly visible college, of international legal scholars, practitioners, policy makers, and social scientists'.[63] To speak of the

[58] Schachter, 'The Invisible College of International Lawyers', 217.

[59] *Ibid.* [60] *Ibid.*, 226. [61] *Ibid.*, 222.

[62] David Bederman and Lucy Reed, 'The Visible College of International Law: An Introduction', *American Society of International Law Proceedings*, 95 (2001), ix.

[63] *Ibid.*

'visible' college of international law is to *develop* the cliché by replacing 'invisible' with 'visible'. In Beckett's *Waiting for Godot* Estragon similarly replaces the usual terms of a cliché with different ones when he says: 'On the other hand it might be better to strike the iron before it freezes.'[64]

What makes Beckett's formulation arresting is that he plays against the cliché about striking while the iron is hot (and also perhaps adds into the mix another cliché about hell freezing over). Suddenly we see again the blacksmith sweating over his forge – the image that had become displaced by the idea of acting while conditions are right. In contrast, the American Society of International Law plays *into* the clichéd call for transparency and diversity in the discipline of international law, leaving that call largely undisturbed. The same may be said of a blog that *recontextualises* the cliché of the invisible college by taking it as its name. The 'Invisible College' blog is linked to the Netherlands School of Human Rights Research.[65] Again evoking 'Schachter's famous article of 1977', its stated aim is to provide interesting commentary on international law and also to serve as a community resource for the contemporary invisible college, publicising courses, job opportunities, web materials etc.

More promising, perhaps, is the title given by Hilary Charlesworth to an article on 'feminist futures for the United Nations': 'Transforming the United Men's Club'.[66] In substituting the openly exclusive concept of the club, and combining it with both 'United Nations' and '(gentle)men's club', Charlesworth *literalises* the invisible college of international lawyers. That is to say, she makes it not simply a metaphor for relative opacity and homogeneity, but an actual body or institution, like the College of Cardinals or the Garrick Club. Schachter has said that he chose the metaphor of a college because the 'group that formed the international law community in the past... used to be a fairly small community made up almost entirely of upper-class, European, French-speaking, male lawyers who knew or were related to one another'.[67] Charlesworth restores the whiff of cigars, bringing it into the present and implicitly reminding us

64 Samuel Beckett, *Waiting for Godot*, 2nd edn (London: Faber and Faber, 1965), 18. See Barry, *Beckett and Authority*, 206. For an account of this passage as an illustration of the strategy of *literalisation*, see Abbott, 'The Art of Making it New, Revisited', 596–7.

65 http://invisiblecollege.weblog.leidenuniv.nl.

66 Hilary Charlesworth, 'Transforming the United Men's Club: Feminist Futures for the United Nations', *Transnational Law and Contemporary Problems*, 4 (1994), 421.

67 Mieke Clincy, 'An Interview with Oscar Schachter', *American Society of International Law Proceedings*, 95 (2001), 18.

that colleges, like clubs, permit only so much democratisation. In her hands, the 'college' becomes less a project to be advanced than a reality to be transformed.

Passing now to sovereignty, Louis Henkin once declared his belief that this word should be dropped from the vocabulary of international law.[68] '[I]t is time', he wrote, 'to bring "sovereignty" down to earth, cut it down to size, discard its overblown rhetoric . . . ; to repackage it, even rename it, and slowly ease the term out of polite language in international relations, surely in law.'[69] Henkin's approach to the clichés that cluster around the concept of sovereignty highlights a point on which we have not yet had occasion to touch, though it may have been implicit in our discussion so far. This is that if, as we have seen, clichés are apprehended as exhausted, stale and devitalised, they are indeed apprehended as *so* exhausted, stale and devitalised that they are not only unworthy of use; they are unworthy even of critical interrogation. They are simply to be avoided, banished, abjured. This explains why, to a much greater extent than other kinds of self-evident truth or taken-for-granted representation, clichés fly under the critical radar, escaping all forms of consideration other than censure.

In contrast, David Kennedy has the cliché firmly in his sights when he characterises sovereignty as 'a rhetorical toolkit, a glimmering and shifting style of presentation and address, at once fashionable and passé, fighting words and cliché'.[70] He goes on: 'We could call it [sovereignty] a shrewd balance, a recurring contradiction, an enduring problem at the core of the discipline, updated in each era.'[71] And again: 'A thousand calls for [sovereignty's] elimination over the last hundred years, its death announced a thousand times in speeches and articles about the "new" interdependence, still it continues to structure our legal positions, our political alliances, our discipline's imagination.'[72] Finally: '[H]owever much we love to hate sovereignty, it reappears in our dreams as desire.'[73] As in *Happy Days*, the clichés come tumbling out here, producing – as Ricks discerns also in Orwell's writing – a bizarre vitality of poetry. The 'shrewd balance' corrects the 'recurring contradiction', which results

68 Louis Henkin, 'The Mythology of Sovereignty', *Canadian Council on International Law Proceedings*, 21 (1992), 16. See also Louis Henkin, 'That "S" Word: Sovereignty, and Globalization, and Human Rights, Et Cetera', *Fordham Law Review*, 68 (1999), 1.

69 *Ibid.*, 16.

70 David Kennedy, 'Some Reflections on "The Role of Sovereignty in the New International Order"', *Canadian Council on International Law Proceedings*, 21 (1992), 245.

71 *Ibid.*, 244. 72 *Ibid.*, 238. 73 *Ibid.*, 239.

from the 'enduring problem at the core'. 'Reports of my death are greatly exaggerated' by the 'thousand calls'. The 'face that launched a thousand ships' is someone we 'love to hate', but would marry 'in our dreams'. Far from censuring the clichéd 'issues' of State sovereignty, Kennedy embeds them in a series of *juxtapositions* that invite attention to, and interest in, the sovereignty tropes *as clichés*.

Our next cliché – that of Guantánamo Bay as a legal black hole – exemplifies the speed with which clichés may arise. First coined in the context of a judgment rendered by the English Court of Appeal in 2002,[74] and used again a year later by the English judge Johan Steyn as part of the title of a lecture on the detentions at Guantánamo Bay,[75] the image of the legal black hole became timeworn very quickly. Along the way, it attracted more than the usual amount of critical attention. In one of the most insightful critiques, Fleur Johns argued that the metaphor was flawed and misleading, insofar as it implied that Guantánamo Bay was a lawless zone or a place empty of law.[76] In fact, as she reminded us, the United States's island prison was not at all lawless or legally empty; it was 'filled to the brim'[77] with law, whether as a result of the processes of international, constitutional, administrative, military, regulatory, immigration or some other kind of law. It followed that the problems of arbitrary detention, unfair trials and abusive treatment could not simply be solved by the application of law.

Although it was not part of Johns's purpose to propose that people should stop using the phrase 'legal black hole' to describe Guantánamo Bay and similar spaces, her analysis pointed in that direction. But what if the metaphor had layers of meaning that were not specious in this context? And what if, with regard to those layers, it was simply dormant, and could be awakened? The US National Aeronautics and Space Administration (NASA) explains black holes in the following terms:

> Don't let the name fool you: a black hole is anything but empty space. Rather, it is a great amount of matter packed into a very small area – think of a star ten times more massive than the Sun squeezed into a sphere

[74] *R (Abassi)* v. *Secretary of State for Foreign and Commonwealth Affairs*, para. 64.

[75] Steyn, 'Guantanamo Bay', 1.

[76] Fleur Johns, 'Guantánamo Bay and the Annihilation of the Exception', *European Journal of International Law*, 16 (2005), 613. See also Fleur Johns, *Non-Legality in International Law* (Cambridge University Press, 2012), ch. 3.

[77] *Ibid.*, 618.

> approximately the diameter of New York City. The result is a gravitational field so strong that nothing, not even light, can escape.[78]

NASA also explains that:

> [s]cientists can't directly observe black holes with telescopes that detect x-rays, light, or other forms of electromagnetic radiation. We can, however, infer the presence of black holes and study them by detecting their effect on other matter nearby.[79]

In a recent book on the Black Hole of Calcutta, Partha Chatterjee shows that, in that very different context, the phrase 'black hole' has somewhat analogous connotations.[80] On the one hand, the Black Hole of Calcutta was a cell in which 123 British soldiers taken prisoner by the Nawab of Bengal allegedly died by suffocation in 1756. (By extension, 'the black hole of Calcutta' later became synonymous with any confined and suffocating space.) On the other hand, very little is directly known about the Black Hole of Calcutta. Inasmuch as there are conflicting accounts of where exactly it was located, and what happened inside it, it remains obscure.

All this points to the possibility that the 'legal black hole' might be made actually to align with Johns's critique. Instead of jettisoning the metaphor, we might *extend* it so as to recover and reawaken a twofold sense of being stuffed full and not easily comprehended.[81] As in Johns's analysis, Guantánamo Bay could then seem a highly legalised space, not one empty of law. And as in her analysis too, the challenge it throws up could be less to secure the application of law than to understand the law's complicities and limitations. But, of course, the 'legal black hole' does not only express the condition of the law. It also expresses the condition of the people held. In a never-ending war on terror, these detainees cannot be released, any more than light can escape from a black hole. Moreover, like the prisoners of the Nawab in the story of the Black Hole of Calcutta, they have been cruelly treated. Is the scandal of the 'legal black hole' that the administration of the United States is being likened to an 'uncivilised' eighteenth-century Bengali ruler? Or does the parallel

78 http://science1.nasa.gov/astrophysics/focus-areas/black-holes/. 79 *Ibid.*

80 Partha Chatterjee, *The Black Hole of Empire* (Princeton University Press, 2012), xi, 1.

81 For a play on the clichéd meaning, see David Dyzenhaus, '*Schmitt* v. *Dicey*: Are States of Emergency Inside or Outside the Legal Order', *Cardozo Law Review*, 27 (2006), 2018 ('grey holes').

work the other way, chiming with criticism that the most high-profile detainees at Guantánamo Bay have been citizens of Western countries whose governments have intervened on their behalf or whose cases have been aired in the Western media?

To complete this brief illustrative review, let us turn finally to visual clichés. We referred earlier to the overuse in connection with international legal publications of maps and of scenes of important people in international law-related settings. Consider the following cover image. A man is sitting at his desk in a high-backed leather chair. He is white, in late middle age, and is wearing a three-piece mid-grey suit with wide 1950s-style lapels. His arms are folded, and his face is expressionless. His gaze is directed off to one side. He leans back in his chair. On the wall behind the man is a map. It takes up the entirety of the space behind him. The North Atlantic Ocean is to his right, the Indian Ocean to his left. The scale of the picture is such that his head is about the same size as West-Central Africa. Indeed, his head largely blocks those regions from view, along with the rest of the sub-Saharan continent. In front of the man, on the desk, is a large blurry shape that appears to be an open hard-sided attaché case. We see an extended diagonal hinge, again out of focus, ending at about Washington DC. This is the image on the cover of Sundhya Pahuja's *Decolonising International Law*. It's a black and white photograph, and a note on the back of the book informs us that the man is Eugene R. Black, president of the World Bank from 1949 to 1963.[82]

Pahuja's cover reawakens the visual clichés of international legal publishing by *literalising* them and inviting attention to the material realities behind them. One of the characteristics of cliché, as we have seen, is evanescence; clichés fade into the background, unable to hold our attention or induce us to examine their detail. In the photograph on the cover of Pahuja's book, the map is *literally* in the background. Furthermore, the map itself is not a representation of a map; it is a *literal* map hanging on the wall of Black's office. As Black sits with his back to it, he *literally* claims a place in the order of international development before, or in front of, Africa. The fact that he obscures most of the continent also makes *literal* the old cliché of the 'dark continent'. The hinge of the attaché case connects Black's chair with the approximate location on the map of Washington DC, similarly *literalising* the seat of the World Bank. We get

[82] Sundhya Pahuja, *Decolonising International Law* (Cambridge University Press, 2011).

a good view of Black's face, but the rest of his body is partly obscured by the attaché case and desk. He is *literally* a Head. What then of the organisation of which he is head – is the World Bank *literally* a world bank? The picture's blurry foreground suggests that, on certain questions raised by an enquiry into the decolonisation of international law, we currently have no clear answers.

Conclusion

Faced with the phenomenon of cliché, we have contrasted two approaches which we have found in the literature on this subject. One approach is to say '*Away with cliché!*'. This is epitomised by George Orwell in his essay 'Politics and the English Language', with its injunction never to use phrases which you are accustomed to seeing in print. The other approach is to say '*Do something with cliché!*'. Samuel Beckett was a master of this, but Christopher Ricks encapsulates the point of it when he speaks of using clichés, rather than allowing oneself to be used by them. The first of these two approaches is – to us, at least – the more familiar; the second, the more challenging. Together, they express what Elizabeth Barry has termed 'the impasse of attraction and resistance to cliché'.[83]

International law designates a field of cliché. That field overlaps with, or is partly encompassed by, other fields of cliché, both specialised and everyday. But it is also partly distinct. Clichés specific to international law often originate as quotations from academic literature, from the pronouncements of courts and tribunals, or from the language of international institutions. Quotation – repetition – is key to the emergence of clichés. Of course, repetition also has a wider significance in law, including international law. The click-clack of cliché is integral to all jurisgenerative processes. As a problem of international law, however, cliché is fundamentally about international legal thought – its independence, vitality and creativity.

A 'war against cliché' has been declared, and is going on around us. What is, or should be, the situation on the international legal front? As we approach now the end of our discussion, we confine ourselves to one further observation. This is that it is among the *clichés* of clichés that they need to be 'attacked' and defeated militarily.[84] That is to say, the 'war against cliché' is itself a cliché. To engage in it is to be undermined in one's

[83] Barry, *Beckett and Authority*, 5. [84] See Ricks, 'Clichés', 58.

efforts to pursue it by that very gesture. And if, somehow, the war could be won, what would victory look like? Would it not serve only, as Ricks puts it, to replace 'tyranny-by-clichés' with 'tyranny-over-clichés'?[85] Here is Redfern's friendly advice: 'Clichés will not go away, nor should we even desire them to. Use them. Know them. Use them knowingly.'[86]

85 *Ibid.* 86 Redfern, *Clichés and Coinages*, 256.

2

International law and the responsibility to protect

MICHAEL BYERS

Introduction

'[W]e surely have a responsibility to act when a nation's people are subjected to a regime such as Saddam's.'[1] During its short life, the 'responsibility to protect' (R2P) has experienced gains and setbacks, with the greatest setback coming in March 2004 when Tony Blair invoked the concept in an attempt to justify the previous year's invasion of Iraq.

R2P is of interest to international lawyers and international relations scholars alike. It is a result of 'norm entrepreneurship'.[2] It achieved prominence quickly, with only four years separating its birth in 2001 from its inclusion in the United Nations World Summit Outcome Document in 2005. But with success came controversy and compromise. On the key issue of the use of military force, R2P has – by widespread agreement – been confined to the context of UN Security Council decision-making, where it remains non-binding.

This chapter examines the interaction between R2P, the prohibition on the use of force set out in the UN Charter, and the discretionary power of the Security Council to determine the existence of a 'threat to the peace' and authorise military action.[3] It asks: to what degree, if any, has R2P

1 Tony Blair, 'The Global Threat of Terrorism', speech, Sedgefield, 5 March 2004, BBC News, full text available at http://news.bbc.co.uk/2/hi/3536131.stm.

2 On norm entrepreneurs, see Martha Finnemore and Kathryn Sikkink, 'International Norm Dynamics and Political Change', *International Organization*, 52 (1998), 887; Margaret Keck and Kathryn Sikkink, *Activists Beyond Borders: Advocacy Networks in International Politics* (Ithaca: Cornell University Press, 1998); Ian Johnstone, 'The Secretary-General as Norm Entrepreneur' in Simon Chesterman (ed.), *Secretary or General?: The UN Secretary-General in World Politics* (Cambridge University Press, 2007), 123.

3 The broader aspects of R2P are well-documented elsewhere. See e.g. Gareth Evans, *The Responsibility to Protect: Ending Mass Atrocity Crimes Once and For All* (Washington, DC: Brookings Institution, 2008); Ramesh Thakur, *The Responsibility to Protect: Norms, Laws, and the Use of Force in International Politics* (London: Routledge, 2011).

become part of contemporary international law concerning the use of force? And what does the history of R2P tell us, more generally, about 'norm entrepreneurship' and processes of legal change?

The chapter concludes that R2P has neither acquired legal status as a new exception to the prohibition on the use of force, nor exerted much influence on the rest of the international legal system. At the same time, the concept may – on an *ad hoc* basis – be influencing how States respond when another State violates the law while seeking to prevent atrocities. If so, the principal legal effect of R2P might concern mitigation of the consequences of rule-breaking, rather than any changes to the rules themselves.

Development of R2P

The central obligation of the UN Charter is set out in Article 2(4):

> All Members shall refrain in their international relations from the threat or use of force against the territorial integrity or political independence of any state, or in any other manner inconsistent with the Purposes of the United Nations.[4]

According to the international rules on treaty interpretation, a treaty 'shall be interpreted in good faith in accordance with the ordinary meaning to be given to the terms of the treaty in their context and in the light of its object and purpose'.[5] The ordinary meaning of Article 2(4) is clear: the use of force across borders is prohibited. This meaning is supported by the context of the terms and the object and purpose of the treaty, with the Charter's preamble affirming the determination of its members 'to ensure by the acceptance of principles and the institution of methods, that armed force shall not be used, save in the common interest'.[6] The Charter allows only two exceptions to the prohibition: Security Council authorisation and the right of self-defence. Only the first of these exceptions is of much relevance to R2P.

Under Chapter VII of the UN Charter, the Security Council has wide powers to 'determine the existence of any threat to the peace, breach of the

[4] Art. 2(4), UN Charter (San Francisco, adopted 26 June 1945, entered into force 24 October 1945), 1 UNTS XVI.

[5] Art. 31, Vienna Convention on the Law of Treaties (Vienna, adopted 22 May 1969, entered into force 27 January 1980), 1155 UNTS 331. The Vienna Convention codified the customary international law of treaty interpretation, as to which see Lord McNair, *The Law of Treaties* (Oxford University Press, 1961), 366–82.

[6] UN Charter.

peace, or act of aggression' and authorise military action. These powers went unexercised during the Cold War, apart from a possible authorisation in Korea in 1950 and a clear but tightly constrained authorisation concerning Southern Rhodesia in 1966. In the latter situation, the Security Council took a significant step in determining that human rights violations – in this case the racist policies of a white minority government – constituted a threat to the peace. It imposed a wide-reaching embargo and, in Resolution 221, called upon the United Kingdom 'to prevent, by the use of force if necessary, the arrival of vessels reasonably believed to be carrying oil destined for Southern Rhodesia'.[7]

Somalia (1992–3)

After the Cold War, the Security Council used Chapter VII in a number of human rights or humanitarian crises. In January 1992, the Council determined that civil strife and famine in Somalia constituted a threat to the peace and imposed an arms embargo.[8] Later that year, the Council authorised a UN-led peacekeeping force[9] as well as a second, US-led, force with a broad mandate to 'use all necessary means to establish as soon as possible a secure environment for humanitarian relief operations'.[10]

One year later, the killing of eighteen US Army Rangers in Mogadishu prompted a public outcry in the United States that led to the collapse of both the US- and UN-led operations. But Somalia nevertheless represented an important step for the Security Council, which for the first time in the post-Cold War era had authorised the use of force for humanitarian ends.

Bosnia (1992–5)

The post-Cold War break-up of Yugoslavia resulted in bloody cleavages between ethnic groups. In 1992, the Security Council used Chapter VII to establish the United Nations Protection Force (UNPROFOR) to provide basic peacekeeping.[11] The next year, it extended UNPROFOR's mandate to include the creation and protection of so-called 'safe havens' for Bosnian civilians.[12] Later in 1993, Security Council Resolution 836 authorised NATO aircraft to bomb Serbian weapons and supply lines, but only

[7] SC Res. 221, 9 April 1966.
[8] SC Res. 733, 23 January 1992.
[9] SC Res. 755, 28 August 1992.
[10] SC Res. 794, 3 December 1992.
[11] SC Res. 743, 21 February 1992.
[12] SC Res. 819, 16 April 1993.

after specific targeting decisions were co-ordinated and approved by both NATO and the UN Secretary-General.[13] As with the Somalia resolutions, Resolution 836 was significant in authorising force for humanitarian ends. But the complex mandate proved ineffective and, in 1995, more than 7,000 men and boys were slaughtered in Srebrenica as UN peacekeepers stood by, their pleas for NATO air support unanswered.

Rwanda (1994)

As the Rwandan genocide began in April 1994, the commander of a small UN peacekeeping operation desperately requested more troops. The Security Council responded by reducing his force from 2,500 to 270 peacekeepers. The withdrawal cannot be attributed to any lack of knowledge on the part of Security Council members. On 23 April, a classified document prepared for senior US officials spoke matter-of-factly about 'the genocide, which relief workers say is spreading south'.[14] Six days later, during a Security Council meeting, the British ambassador reportedly cautioned against designating the massacre as 'genocide' because doing so might compel a response.[15] As in Bosnia, where inadequate and complex mandates hindered action, the problem was a lack of political will. And yet the failure to act in Rwanda might subsequently have shamed some countries into action in Kosovo.

Kosovo (1999)

In 1999, NATO countries launched an air campaign to protect the Albanian population of Kosovo from Serbian forces. The intervention took place without Security Council authorisation and over the strong objections of Russia, China and numerous developing countries. Although the United Kingdom claimed a right of 'unilateral' (i.e. not Security Council-authorised) humanitarian intervention,[16] the United States was more circumspect, referring repeatedly to 'humanitarian concerns' but

13 SC Res. 836, 4 June 1993.

14 Central Intelligence Agency, 'National Intelligence Daily', 23 April 2004, available at www.gwu.edu/~nsarchiv/NSAEBB/NSAEBB117/Rw34.pdf.

15 Linda Melvern, *A People Betrayed: The Role of the West in Rwanda's Genocide* (London: Zed Books, 2000), 180.

16 See Sir Jeremy Greenstock, UK Permanent Representative to the UN, statement to the Security Council on 24 March 1999, UN Doc. S/PV.3988, 11–12, reproduced in *British Yearbook of International Law*, 70 (1999), 580–1. See also 'Fourth Report of the House of Commons Foreign Affairs Committee', (2000) HC-28-I, which points out that the

never explicitly claiming a third exception to the prohibition on the use of force.[17] Germany supported the NATO action but insisted it 'must not be allowed to become a precedent'.[18]

The Kosovo War put proponents of human rights and humanitarian assistance in a difficult position. UN Secretary-General Kofi Annan's initial reaction was to say: 'Emerging slowly, but I believe surely, is an international norm against the violent repression of minorities that will and must take precedent over concerns of State sovereignty.'[19] Following the war, the United Kingdom proposed a framework for a limited right of unilateral humanitarian intervention. According to the British criteria, armed force should only be used as a last resort, in the face of 'an overwhelming humanitarian catastrophe, which the government has shown it is unwilling or unable to prevent or is actively promoting'. The force 'should be proportionate to achieving the humanitarian purpose', carried out 'in accordance with international law', and 'collective'.[20] But the Kosovo War did nothing to alleviate concerns about powerful states abusing any new right to intervene. In 1999 and 2000, the 133 developing states of the Group of 77 twice adopted declarations that unequivocally affirmed the illegality of humanitarian interventions not specifically authorised by the Security Council.[21]

UK government justified humanitarian intervention only 'as an exceptional measure in support of purposes laid down by the UN Security Council . . . where that is the only means to avert an immediate and overwhelming humanitarian catastrophe'.

17 See e.g. 'In the President's Words: "We Act to Prevent a Wider War"', *New York Times*, 25 March 1999, A15. After the war, Secretary of State Madeleine Albright stressed that Kosovo was 'a unique situation *sui generis* in the region of the Balkans' and that it was important 'not to overdraw the various lessons that come out of it'. Press conference with Russian Foreign Minister Igor Ivanov, Singapore, 26 July 1999, cited in vol. II of the ICISS report, 'The Responsibility to Protect' (Ottawa: International Development Research Centre, 2002), 128.

18 Foreign Minister Klaus Kinkel said: 'With their decision, NATO states did not intend to create any new legal instrument that could ground a general power of authority of NATO for intervention. The NATO decision must not be allowed to become a precedent. We must not enter onto a slippery slope with respect to the Security Council's monopoly on the use of force.' Deutscher Bundestag, Plenarprotokoll 13/248, 16 October 1998, 23129 (author's translation). German original available at http://dip21.bundestag.de/dip21/btp/13/13248.asc.

19 Kofi Annan, 'No Government Has the Right to Hide Behind National Sovereignty in Order to Violate Human Rights', *The Guardian*, 7 April 1999, available at www.guardian.co.uk/world/1999/apr/07/balkans.unitednations.

20 Foreign Secretary Robin Cook, 'Speech to the American Bar Association, 19 July 2000', *British Yearbook of International Law*, 71 (2000), 646.

21 See Ministerial Declaration, 23rd Annual Meeting of the Ministers for Foreign Affairs of the Group of 77, 24 September 1999, para. 69, available at www.g77.org/doc/Decl1999.

This negative reaction was likely what caused Annan, later in 1999, to acknowledge that any norm of unilateral humanitarian intervention had not yet achieved legal status and could have undesirable consequences for the international order: 'What is clear is that enforcement action without Security Council authorisation threatens the very core of the international security system founded on the Charter of the UN. Only the Charter provides a universally accepted legal basis for the use of force.'[22]

International Commission on Intervention and State Sovereignty (2001)

After the Kosovo War, the Canadian government established the International Commission on Intervention and State Sovereignty (ICISS) and charged it with finding 'some new common ground'.[23] However, a careful reading of the ICISS report, released in December 2001 and entitled 'The Responsibility to Protect', shows the commissioners failing to agree on the central issue of the use of force. Some passages seem to favour a right of humanitarian intervention in the absence of Security Council authorisation:

> Based on our reading of state practice, Security Council precedent, established norms, emerging guiding principles, and evolving customary international law, the Commission believes that the Charter's strong bias against military intervention is not to be regarded as absolute when decisive action is required on human protection grounds.[24]

Other passages lean the other way, albeit with a nod to the 'Uniting for Peace' Resolution adopted by the General Assembly in 1950:

> As a matter of political reality, it would be impossible to find consensus . . . around any set of proposals for military intervention which acknowledge the validity of any intervention not authorized by the Security Council or General Assembly.[25]

html; Declaration of the Group of 77 South Summit, Havana, Cuba, 10–14 April 2000, para. 54, available at www.g77.org/doc/docs/summitfinaldocs_english.pdf.

22 Kofi Annan, 'Preventing War and Disaster' (United Nations: Annual report on the work of the Organization, 1999), 8, para. 66, UN Doc. A/54/1.

23 ICISS, 'The Responsibility to Protect', I, vii.

24 *Ibid.*, 16, para. 2.27.

25 *Ibid.*, 54–5, para. 6.36. On 'Uniting for Peace' see UNGA Res. A-RES-377(V) (3 November 1950); and Dominik Zaum, 'The Security Council, the General Assembly and War: The Uniting for Peace Resolution' in Vaughan Lowe *et al.* (eds.), *The United Nations Security*

In addition to coining the term 'responsibility to protect', the ICISS usefully expanded the focus of attention to include preventive and post-crisis measures. But it did little to resolve the controversy over unilateral humanitarian intervention, leaving that for states to decide.

Constitutive Act of the African Union (2002)

In 2002, the Organisation of African Unity renamed and reconstituted itself through the Constitutive Act of the African Union.[26] Part of the reconstitution was a provision described by Dan Kuwali as 'by and large, on all fours with the notion of R2P'.[27] Article 4(h) asserts the 'right of the Union to intervene in a Member State pursuant to a decision of the Assembly [of Heads of State and Government] in respect of grave circumstances, namely: war crimes, genocide and crimes against humanity'.[28] Article 4(h) also implies that African Union member states do not consider themselves bound to obtain UN Security Council authorisation when using force collectively in response to such atrocities.[29]

Despite having faced some major human rights and humanitarian crises, the African Union has yet to invoke Article 4(h). Paul Williams has identified three possible reasons for this: 'first, the strength of the host state; second, the residual power of the principles of non-interference and anti-imperialism within the African society of states; and third, the AU's lack of practical military capacity for humanitarian intervention'.[30] A fourth and equally important reason may be that, whenever the African

Council and War: The Evolution of Thought and Practice since 1945 (Oxford University Press, 2008), 154.

26 Constitutive Act of the African Union, 11 July 2002, OAU Doc. CAB/LEG/23.15.

27 Dan Kuwali, 'The End of Humanitarian Intervention: Evaluation of the African Union's Right of Intervention', *African Journal on Conflict Resolution*, 9 (2009), 48.

28 In 2003, the adoption of a 'Protocol Relating to the Establishment of the Peace and Security Council of the African Union' provided an implementing mechanism for decisions to intervene taken by the Assembly. Available at: www.africa-union.org/root/au/organs/psc/Protocol_peace%20and%20security.pdf.

29 Art. 17(1) of the Protocol (*ibid.*) reads: 'In the fulfillment of its mandate in the promotion and maintenance of peace, security and stability in Africa, the Peace and Security Council shall cooperate and work closely with the United Nations Security Council, which has the primary responsibility for the maintenance of international peace and security.' Nothing in the words 'cooperate and work closely with' or 'primary responsibility' implies a relationship of legal dependence.

30 Paul D. Williams, 'The African Union's Conflict Management Capabilities', Council on Foreign Relations, October 2011, 5, available at www.cfr.org/content/publications/attachments/IIGG_WorkingPaper7.pdf.

Union has wished to intervene in a human rights or humanitarian crisis, the UN Security Council has provided a Chapter VII resolution.

There may well be a causal connection between the 2001 ICISS report and the Constitutive Act of the African Union, since the former preceded the latter by just six months. At the same time, the right asserted in Article 4(h) is entirely consistent with established international law because the member states of the African Union, when ratifying the Constitutive Act, consented to the new power.[31] Article 4(h) is analogous to Chapter VII, where the powers of the Security Council are derived from the consent expressed by member states when ratifying the UN Charter. For this reason, Article 4(h) is not a precedent for unilateral humanitarian intervention, even if it does create a new, strictly regional, treaty-based exception to the prohibition on the use of force.

Iraq War (2003)

Again, Tony Blair has provided a worrisome example of how R2P could be abused. One year after the Iraq War, the British prime minister implied that a right of unilateral humanitarian intervention already existed in situations of 'humanitarian catastrophe':

> It may well be that under international law as presently constituted, a regime can systematically brutalise and oppress its people and there is nothing anyone can do, when dialogue, diplomacy and even sanctions fail, *unless* it comes within the definition of a humanitarian catastrophe . . . [32]

He then invoked R2P in support of a right to intervene in less severe circumstances:

> The essence of a community is common rights and responsibilities. We have obligations in relation to each other . . . [W]e do not accept in a community that others have a right to oppress and brutalise their people. We value the freedom and dignity of the human race and each individual in it. Emphatically I am not saying that every situation leads to military action. But . . . we surely have a responsibility to act when a nation's people are subjected to a regime such as Saddam's.[33]

Thus, a war that Blair had previously sought to justify with contested readings of Security Council resolutions was suddenly being rationalised with a concept that, as a possible legal basis for force, had already been

[31] See similarly Kuwali, 'The End of Humanitarian Intervention', 45–6.
[32] Blair, 'The Global Threat of Terrorism' (emphasis added). [33] *Ibid.*

widely rejected by most governments.[34] This development was of pivotal importance for the future direction of R2P.

High-level Panel on Threats, Challenges and Change (2004)

After Blair's invocation of R2P, many proponents of the concept refocused their efforts on addressing the problem of political will within the context of existing legal constraints. This adjustment was visible in a speech given to the UN General Assembly by Canadian Prime Minister Paul Martin in September 2004.[35] Martin stressed that the 'responsibility to protect is not a licence for intervention; it is an international guarantor of political accountability'. Although 'customary international law is evolving to provide a solid basis in the building of a normative framework for collective humanitarian intervention', this basis was not yet complete. Martin called for the Security Council to 'establish new thresholds for when the international community judges that civilian populations face extreme threats'.

In December 2004, the UN Secretary-General's High-level Panel on Threats, Challenges and Change reported that 'the Council and the wider international community have come to accept that, under Chapter VII . . . it can always authorize military action to redress catastrophic internal wrongs if it is prepared to declare that the situation is a "threat to international peace and security", not especially difficult when breaches of international law are involved'.[36] With respect to R2P specifically, the Panel wrote:

> There is a growing recognition that the issue is not the 'right to intervene' of any State, but the 'responsibility to protect' of *every* State when it comes to people suffering from avoidable catastrophe – mass murder and rape, ethnic cleansing by forcible expulsion and terror, and deliberate starvation and exposure to disease.[37]

[34] Russian Foreign Minister Sergey Lavrov likewise invoked the term 'responsibility to protect' to justify the invasion of Georgia in 2008, but it is clear that he was referring to a principle in Russian *domestic* law concerning the duty of the Russian government to protect its citizens. See 'Interview by Minister of Foreign Affairs of the Russian Federation Sergey Lavrov to BBC', Moscow, 9 August 2008, available at www.un.int/russia/new/MainRoot/docs/off_news/090808/newen2.htm.

[35] 'Address by Prime Minister Paul Martin at the United Nations', 21 September 2004, available at http://news.gc.ca/web/article.

[36] 'A More Secure World: Our Shared Responsibility', Report of the High-level Panel on Threats, Challenges and Change, 2 December 2004, UN Doc. A/59/565, 57, para. 202.

[37] *Ibid.*, 56–7, para. 201.

The Panel stressed that this 'emerging norm' was – in terms of military intervention – only 'exercisable by the Security Council'.[38] It proposed 'criteria of legitimacy' for when force should be used: seriousness of intent, proper purpose, last resort, proportional means and balance of consequences.[39] It recommended that these criteria be embodied in declaratory resolutions of the Security Council and General Assembly.[40]

Secretary-General's Report and World Summit Outcome Document (2005)

In March 2005, Kofi Annan issued a report entitled 'In Larger Freedom' in which he endorsed R2P while affirming the Security Council's monopoly on the use of force:

> [I]f national authorities are unable or unwilling to protect their citizens, then the responsibility shifts to the international community to use diplomatic, humanitarian and other methods to help protect the human rights and well-being of civilian populations. When such methods appear insufficient, the Security Council may out of necessity decide to take action under the Charter of the United Nations, including enforcement action, if so required.[41]

Six months later, at the conclusion of the UN World Summit, the member states not only endorsed R2P; they declared themselves 'prepared to take collective action . . . in a timely and decisive manner'.[42] However, they also specified that any such action would take place 'through the Security Council, in accordance with the Charter, including Chapter VII', that it would only be 'on a case-by-case basis' and only 'should peaceful means be inadequate and national authorities are manifestly failing to protect their populations from genocide, war crimes, ethnic cleansing and crimes against humanity'.

The inclusion of R2P in the World Summit Outcome Document was a significant development. At the same time, the role of the concept was deliberately limited by: (1) the reaffirmation of the exclusivity of

[38] *Ibid.*, 57, para. 203. [39] *Ibid.*, 57–8, para. 207. [40] *Ibid.*, 58, para. 208.

[41] 'In Larger Freedom: Towards Development, Security and Human Rights for All', Report of the Secretary-General, 21 March 2005, UN Doc. A/59/2005, paras. 132 and 135.

[42] 'World Summit Outcome Document', 15 September 2005, paras. 138 and 139, available at www.un.org/summit2005/documents.html.

Security Council decision-making;[43] (2) the use of non-committal language such as 'prepared' and 'on a case-by-case basis'; and (3) the raising of the ICISS threshold of 'population suffering serious harm' to 'genocide, war crimes, ethnic cleansing, and crimes against humanity'. Moreover, the World Summit Outcome Document did not create any new rights, obligations or limitations for the Security Council, since the Council already had the discretionary power to authorise the use of force for the full range of human rights and humanitarian concerns. At most, the World Summit Outcome Document created a new point of *political* leverage, since proponents of action can now point to this collective statement of intent.

Security Council Resolution 1674 (2006)

In April 2006, the Security Council followed the recommendation of the High-level Panel by adopting a declaratory resolution. Resolution 1674 addresses numerous aspects of the 'protection of civilians in armed conflict', including R2P. Paragraph 4 '*[r]eaffirms* the provisions of paragraphs 138 and 139 of the World Summit Outcome Document regarding the responsibility to protect populations from genocide, war crimes, ethnic cleansing and crimes against humanity'.[44] It thus confirms the Council's post-Cold War practice of including human rights and humanitarian crises within the scope of possible determinations of 'threats to the peace'. However, it does not signal or contribute to any change in international law, because the scope of the Council's discretionary power is so very wide that, from a legal perspective, it might only be limited by *jus cogens* rules.[45]

[43] That said, Carsten Stahn has argued that 'states did not categorically reject the option of (individual or collective) unilateral action in the Outcome Document. This discrepancy leaves some leeway to argue that the concept of responsibility to protect is not meant to rule out such action in the future.' Carsten Stahn, 'Responsibility to Protect: Political Rhetoric or Emerging Legal Norm?', *American Journal of International Law*, 101 (2007), 120. However, as a general principle of interpretation, a text's silence on any particular issue does not imply a gap.

[44] SC Res. 1674, 28 April 2006.

[45] See *Application of the Convention on the Prevention and Punishment of the Crime of Genocide (Bosnia and Herzegovina* v. *Serbia and Montenegro)*, Order of 13 September 1993, 440, para. 100 (Separate Opinion of Judge ad hoc Elihu Lauterpacht). In the *Tadić* case, the International Criminal Tribunal for the Former Yugoslavia wrote: 'the determination that there exists such a threat [to the peace] is not a totally unfettered discretion, as it has to remain, at the very least, within the limits of the Purposes and Principles of the Charter'. However, the tribunal went on to note that 'the practice of the Security Council is rich

The adoption of Resolution 1674 might increase the likelihood of the Security Council acting in situations of 'genocide, war crimes, ethnic cleansing and crimes against humanity', but only because its references to R2P and the World Summit Outcome Document give proponents of military action an additional point of political leverage. It is important to note that the Resolution does not include any criteria such as those recommended by the High-level Panel.[46] Nor did the Council follow the lead of the General Assembly and declare it was 'prepared to take collective action . . . in a timely and decisive manner'.[47]

The greatest challenge with respect to humanitarian and human rights crises remains generating the political will to act, which in the context of the Security Council means both adopting *and* implementing a resolution. That political will is required over both stages was demonstrated with respect to Darfur. In August 2006, after more than two years of atrocities, the Security Council finally used its Chapter VII powers to authorise the deployment of a UN peacekeeping force with a robust mandate to protect civilians.[48] Resolution 1706 made an indirect reference to R2P by noting that Resolution 1674 'reaffirms inter alia the provisions of paragraphs 138 and 139 of the 2005 United Nations World Summit outcome document'.[49] But most governments, instead of rushing to participate in this new and legally robust mission, either ignored the authorisation or cited commitments elsewhere.[50]

Security Council Resolution 1973 (Libya, 2011)

In March 2011, Libyan dictator Muammar Gaddafi used deadly force against peaceful protesters and threatened to show no mercy to the

with cases of civil war or internal strife which it classified as a "threat to the peace" and dealt with under Chapter VII, with the encouragement or even at the behest of the General Assembly'. *Prosecutor* v. *Duško Tadić* (Decision on the Defence Motion for Interlocutory Appeal on Jurisdiction), Case No. IT-94–1, ICTY Appeals Chamber, Judgment, 2 October 1995.

46 See discussion, n. 39.

47 'World Summit Outcome Document'.

48 In para. 12 of Resolution 1706, adopted on 31 August 2006, the Security Council, 'Acting under Chapter VII of the Charter of the United Nations: (a) *Decides* that UNMIS is authorized to use all necessary means, in the areas of deployment of its forces and as it deems within its capabilities . . . to protect civilians under threat of physical violence . . . '

49 *Ibid.*

50 See e.g. 'UN Force for Darfur Takes Shape', *New York Times*, 1 August 2007, available at www.nytimes.com/2007/08/01/world/africa/01iht-darfur.4.6942617.html?_r=0.

residents of rebel-held cities.[51] The Security Council responded by adopting Resolution 1973 which provided two parallel authorisations to use force, the first of which was much broader than the second.[52]

In paragraph 4, the Council: '*Authorizes* Member States . . . to take all necessary measures . . . to protect civilians and civilian populated areas under threat of attack in the Libyan Arab Jamahiriya, including Benghazi, while excluding a foreign occupation force of any form on any part of Libyan territory'.

This first authorisation would cover a great deal of military activity, because 'all necessary measures' is the language normally used by the Council to grant full powers to intervening countries.[53] Even the exclusion of a 'foreign occupation force' does not preclude the use of some ground forces, since 'occupation' is a technical term of international humanitarian law defined in the 1907 Hague Regulations: 'Territory is considered occupied when it is actually placed under the authority of the hostile army. The occupation extends only to the territory where such authority has been established and can be exercised.'[54]

The second authorisation that deals with airspace is arguably redundant, because it concerns a measure that could also fall within the scope of 'all necessary measures . . . to protect civilians and civilian populated areas'. It appears in paragraph 6 where the Council '*Decides* to establish a ban on all flights in the airspace of the Libyan Arab Jamahiriya in order to help protect civilians', and in paragraph 8 where the Council '*Authorizes* Member States . . . to take all necessary measures to enforce compliance with the ban on flights imposed by paragraph 6 above, as necessary'.

Resolution 1973 does not endorse an expansive conception of R2P, with just one paragraph in the preamble making reference to it: '*Reiterating* the responsibility of the Libyan authorities to protect the Libyan population

[51] In one TV broadcast, Gaddafi told the residents of Benghazi to lay down their arms; otherwise, he warned, his troops would come that night and 'find you in your closets; we will have no mercy and no pity'. Dan Bilefsky and Mark Landler, 'As U.N. Backs Military Action in Libya, U.S. Role Is Unclear', *New York Times*, 17 March 2011, available at www.nytimes.com/2011/03/18/world/africa/18nations.html.

[52] SC Res. 1973, 17 March 2011.

[53] Of course, all military actions remain subject to the rules of international humanitarian law, including those set out in the 1949 Geneva Conventions and 1977 Additional Protocols.

[54] Art. 42, Hague Regulations concerning the Laws and Customs of War on Land, as annexed to the 1907 Convention (IV) respecting the Laws and Customs of War on Land (The Hague, adopted 18 October 1907, entered into force 26 January 2010), 205 CTS 277.

and *reaffirming* that parties to armed conflicts bear the primary responsibility to take all feasible steps to ensure the protection of civilians'.[55] Apart from the word 'primary', there is nothing in the paragraph that suggests a responsibility to protect on the part of outside countries.

Nor does Resolution 1973 declare that any of the crimes identified by the World Summit Outcome Document as falling within the ambit of R2P are occurring. Although the resolution condemns 'the gross and systematic violation of human rights, including arbitrary detentions, enforced disappearances, torture and summary executions', it adopts a decidedly cautious stance as to these actually being crimes against humanity, '*considering* that the widespread and systematic attacks currently taking place in the Libyan Arab Jamahiriya against the civilian population may amount to crimes against humanity'.

Resolution 1973 is consistent with R2P insofar as it authorises the use of force for human rights purposes.[56] But in terms of the development of R2P, Resolution 1973 proves only that the concept has become part of the context of Security Council deliberations. Of course, in some situations that role as context may still be significant.

Post-Libya consequences for R2P

There are those who believe that the evolution of R2P was set back by the controversy over NATO's campaign in Libya, and that this reversal is evident in the lack of a meaningful response by the Security Council to the Syrian civil war.[57] As Vitaly Churkin, Russia's ambassador to the United Nations, has said:

[55] Similar references appear in the preambles of SC Res. 1975, 30 March 2011 (Côte d'Ivoire), SC Res. 1996, 8 July 2011 (South Sudan) and SC Res. 2014, 21 October 2011 (Yemen).

[56] That human rights were the principal motivating factor behind Resolution 1973 is supported by the fact that, at the time of the intervention, the Libyan regime posed no threat to other countries. Gaddafi forswore his nuclear and chemical weapons programmes in 2003 and was removed from the US list of state sponsors of terror in 2006.

[57] See e.g. Gareth Evans, Ramesh Thakur and Robert A. Pape, 'Humanitarian Intervention and the Responsibility to Protect (R2P)', *International Security*, 37 (2013), 206 ('[T]he R2P consensus underpinning Resolution 1973 fell apart over the course of 2011, damaged by gaps in expectation, communication, and accountability between those who mandated the operation and those who executed it.'); Spencer Zifcak, 'The Responsibility to Protect after Libya and Syria', *Melbourne Journal of International Law*, 13 (2012), 1; Noele Crossley, 'The Responsibility to Protect in 2012: R2P Fails in Syria, Brazil's "RWP" Emerges', Global Policy Journal blog, 28 December 2012, available at www.globalpolicyjournal.com/blog/28/12/2012/.

> The situation in Syria cannot be considered in the Council separately from the Libyan experience. The international community is alarmed by statements that compliance with Security Council resolutions on Libya in the NATO interpretation is a model for the future actions of NATO in implementing the responsibility to protect . . . [58]

However, the authorisations in Resolution 1973 gave space for different public positions concerning the permissible extent of force.[59] This would not be the first time the Security Council has crafted a resolution with a view to providing room for divergent interpretations.[60] The result is an intermediate zone on the legal–illegal spectrum of military action: between the legal and the illegal, there is now the deliberately arguable. One benefit of this grey zone is that it provides space for states to disagree in public while 'agreeing to disagree' in private. Another benefit may be that it creates a form of temporary, conditional permission that can harden into legality or illegality, depending on how contested facts are subsequently clarified – for instance, by the presence or absence of weapons of mass destruction, or the actual existence and scale of atrocities.

It is also significant that Resolution 1973 had the support of the Arab League. Indeed, the resolution refers explicitly to 'the decision of the Council of the League of Arab States of 12 March 2011 to call for the imposition of a no-fly zone on Libyan military aviation, and to establish safe areas in places exposed to shelling as a precautionary measure that allows the protection of the Libyan people and foreign nationals residing in the Libyan Arab Jamahiriya'. The involvement of the Arab League made it politically difficult for China and Russia to cast their vetoes, and thus increased the incentive to agree on language that enabled the resolution to be interpreted in different ways.

The Arab League has also been active with respect to the Syrian crisis: suspending Syria's membership of the League, imposing economic sanctions, pushing for a Security Council resolution that would have called on President Bashar al-Assad to step aside and proposing a UN-authorised

58 UN SCOR, 66th Session, 6627th Meeting, UN Doc. S/PV.6627 (4 October 2011), 4.

59 As Hugh Roberts writes, 'Those who subsequently said that they did not know that regime change had been authorised either did not understand the logic of events or were pretending to misunderstand in order to excuse their failure to oppose it.' Hugh Roberts, 'Who Said Gaddafi Had to Go?', 33, *London Review of Books*, 17 November 2011.

60 Michael Byers, 'Agreeing to Disagree: Security Council Resolution 1441 and Intentional Ambiguity', *Global Governance*, 10 (2004), 165.

peacekeeping mission.[61] However, there are many factors associated with Security Council decision-making. In the case of Syria, complicating factors include its geographic location, the presence of Russian electronic intelligence-gathering and naval facilities and advanced air defences which would likely cause the loss of aircraft and pilots if any attempt was made to impose a no-fly zone.[62]

After a chemical-weapons attack in Damascus in August 2013, the United Kingdom, United States and France prepared for air strikes against the Syrian regime. Significantly, the term 'responsibility to protect' was largely absent from official statements concerning the legal basis for military action. The British government released a document setting out its legal position that stated, in part:

> If action in the Security Council is blocked, the UK would still be permitted under international law to take exceptional measures in order to alleviate the scale of the overwhelming humanitarian catastrophe in Syria by deterring and disrupting the further use of chemical weapons by the Syrian regime. Such a legal basis is available, under the doctrine of humanitarian intervention, provided three conditions are met:
>
> (i) there is convincing evidence, generally accepted by the international community as a whole, of extreme humanitarian distress on a large scale, requiring immediate and urgent relief;
>
> (ii) it must be objectively clear that there is no practicable alternative to the use of force if lives are to be saved; and
>
> (iii) the proposed use of force must be necessary and proportionate to the aim of relief of humanitarian need and must be strictly limited in time and scope to this aim (i.e. the minimum necessary to achieve that end and for no other purpose).[63]

The British government's position was similar to the framework it had proposed after the Kosovo War, without the requirements that the intervention be carried out 'in accordance with international law' and

[61] 'The League and Syria' in 'Times Topics: Arab League', *New York Times* website, available at http://topics.nytimes.com/topics/reference/timestopics/organizations/a/arab_league/index.html.

[62] Julian Borger, 'Russian Military Presence in Syria Poses Challenge to US-led Intervention', *The Guardian*, 23 December 2012, available at www.guardian.co.uk/world/2012/dec/23/syria-crisis-russian-military-presence.

[63] 'Chemical Weapon Use by Syrian Regime – UK Government Legal Position', 29 August 2013, available at www.gov.uk/government/uploads/system/uploads/attachment_data/file/235098/.

'collective'.[64] For the purposes of this chapter, its relevance lies in the lack of any reference to R2P despite the emergence of that concept over the previous decade. It is also significant that the House of Commons rejected Prime Minister David Cameron's call for military action, thus preventing any State practice from accompanying the *opinio juris* of the legal position.[65]

The US government also avoided any reference to R2P, focusing instead on the use of chemical weapons, which killed at most several thousand people, as compared to the 100,000 or more deaths caused in Syria by conventional arms. Secretary of State John Kerry stated that any military action would be 'a limited and tailored response to ensure that a despot's brutal and flagrant use of chemical weapons is held accountable'.[66]

Only French President François Hollande referred explicitly to R2P, saying that '[International law] is the best way of ensuring borders are respected, disputes are settled and collective security prevails. But international law must evolve with the times. It cannot be a pretext for allowing large-scale massacres to be perpetrated. This is why I recognise the principle of "the responsibility to protect" civilians, which the United Nations General Assembly voted for in 2005.'[67] However, earlier in the same speech, Hollande made clear that the catalyst for any French military action was the use of chemical weapons, rather than the broader humanitarian crisis: 'The international community cannot fail to react to the use of chemical weapons. France stands ready to punish those who took the appalling decision to gas innocent people.'[68]

These controversies over the implementation of Resolution 1973 in Libya and the legal bases for using force in Syria will eventually subside, for there is more pragmatism in international relations than the public statements of governments might indicate. The concept of R2P will

64 Foreign Secretary Robin Cook, 'Speech to the American Bar Association, 19 July 2000'.

65 Andrew Grice, 'David Cameron's Plans for Military Action in Syria Shot Down in Dramatic Commons Vote', *The Independent*, 30 August 2013, available at www.independent.co.uk/news/uk/politics/david-camerons-plans-for-military-action-in-syria-shot-down-in-dramatic-commons-vote-8788612.html.

66 Secretary of State John Kerry, 'Statement on Syria', 30 August 2013, available at www.state.gov/secretary/remarks/2013/08/213668.htm.

67 '21st Ambassadors' Conference – Speech by François Hollande', 27 August 2013, available at www.diplomatie.gouv.fr/en/the-ministry-158/events-5815/article/21st-ambassadors-conference-speech.

68 *Ibid.*

survive, and have influence politically, even if it never changes the core legal prohibition on the use of force.

Legal status of R2P

Prior to Blair's 2004 speech, much of the literature on R2P either continued the debate that had previously been framed as 'unilateral humanitarian intervention', or discussed the concept in the post-9/11 context of self-defence and preventive military action.[69] But even before Blair's demonstration of the potential for the abuse of R2P by powerful states, it was already apparent that the threshold for changing the prohibition on the use of force was unachievable. Both the widespread opposition of developing States and the *jus cogens* character of the prohibition rendered the idea of an R2P exception a non-starter in a legal system where rules are changed through the actions and opinions of nearly 200 states, and where a small number of rules are more deeply entrenched than the others.[70] Gareth Evans, one of the 'norm entrepreneurs' behind R2P, has summarised the new consensus: 'The 2005 General Assembly position was very clear that, when any country seeks to apply forceful means to address an R2P situation, it must do so through the Security Council . . . Vigilante justice is always dangerous.'[71]

This chapter could end here: with the conclusion that R2P, insofar as it concerns the use of force, is now limited to being part of the content of Security Council decision-making. However, it may prove useful to extend the analysis one step further, by examining whether R2P is having any influence on the margins of the prohibition on the use of force, and specifically on the rules proscribing the provision of aid, assistance, training, equipment and arms to rebels.[72]

[69] See, perhaps most problematically, Lee Feinstein and Anne-Marie Slaughter, 'A Duty to Prevent', *Foreign Affairs*, 83 (2004), 136.

[70] See Michael Byers and Simon Chesterman, 'Changing the Rules about Rules? Unilateral Humanitarian Intervention and the Future of International Law' in J. L. Holzgrefe and Robert O. Keohane (eds.), *Humanitarian Intervention: Ethical, Legal and Political Dilemmas* (Cambridge University Press, 2003), 183–4.

[71] Gareth Evans, 'Russia and the 'Responsibility to Protect', *Los Angeles Times*, 31 August 2008, available at http://www.latimes.com/la-oe-evans31-2008aug31-story.html.

[72] As the International Court of Justice explained in the *Nicaragua* case, it is sometimes necessary 'to distinguish the most grave forms of the use of force (those constituting an armed attack) from other less grave forms'. *Military and Paramilitary Activities in and against Nicaragua (Nicaragua* v. *US)*, Judgment, 27 June 1986, ICJ Reports (1986), 101, para. 191.

Support for rebels

The prohibition on the use of force has long been understood to encompass the provision of aid, assistance, training, equipment and arms to rebels.[73] In 1970, the UN General Assembly adopted the 'Friendly Relations Resolution' that encapsulated the rule in two paragraphs:

> Every State has the duty to refrain from organizing, instigating, assisting or participating in acts of civil strife or terrorist acts in another State or acquiescing in organized activities within its territory directed towards the commission of such acts, when the acts referred to in the present paragraph involve a threat or use of force . . .
>
> Also, no State shall organize, assist, foment, finance, incite or tolerate subversive, terrorist or armed activities directed towards the violent overthrow of the régime of another State, or interfere in civil strife in another State.[74]

Although the rule was often violated during the Cold War, as the two superpowers engaged in 'proxy wars', it was not altered by that contrary practice. One explanation for the lack of change is that support for rebels was usually provided covertly, and only overt actions can contribute to changing international law.[75]

The rule was affirmed in the 1986 *Nicaragua* case where the International Court of Justice found that the United States had illegally trained and equipped rebels.[76] The Court addressed the possibility that the law might be different when rebels have a 'particularly worthy' cause:

> [The Court] has to consider whether there might be indications of a practice illustrative of belief in a kind of general right for States to intervene, directly or indirectly, with or without armed force, in support of an internal

[73] See Ian Brownlie, *International Law and the Use of Force by States* (Oxford University Press, 1963), 70–1. The only possible and controversial exception to this ban has concerned the provision of support to groups engaged in wars of 'national liberation'. For example, in 1981 the UN General Assembly appealed 'to all States to provide all necessary humanitarian, educational, financial and other necessary assistance to the oppressed people of South Africa and their national liberation movement in their legitimate struggle'. GA Res. 36/172 (1981), para. 16.

[74] Declaration on Principles of International Law concerning Friendly Relations and Co-operation Among States in Accordance with the Charter of the United Nations, GA Res. 2625 (XXV) (1970).

[75] See Anthony D'Amato, *The Concept of Custom in International Law* (Ithaca: Cornell University Press, 1971), 469, where the author writes, with respect to the widespread use of torture by states, that the 'objective evidence shows hiding, cover-up, minimization, and non-justification – all the things that betoken a violation of the law'.

[76] *Nicaragua* case.

> opposition in another State, whose cause appeared particularly worthy by reason of the political and moral values with which it was identified. For such a general right to come into existence would involve a fundamental modification of the customary law principle of non-intervention.[77]

The Court went on to emphasise that, 'for a new customary rule to be formed, not only must the acts concerned "amount to a settled practice", but they must be accompanied by the *opinio juris sive necessitatis*'. In short, '[r]eliance by a State on a novel right or an unprecedented exception to the principle might, if shared in principle by other States, tend towards a modification of customary international law', but only if States 'justified their conduct by reference to a new right of intervention or a new exception to the principle of its prohibition'.[78] The Court in the *Nicaragua* case found neither a settled practice nor evidence of *opinio juris*.

The end of the Cold War brought three developments that might have affected the rule. First, there was an increase in the practice of selling weapons to rebel groups, as arms producers, squeezed by a reduction in military spending by NATO and former Warsaw Pact countries, became less scrupulous about their buyers.[79] Secondly, and as explained above, the Security Council expanded its conception of 'threat to the peace' to include human rights and humanitarian crises. Thirdly, a difficult debate about unilateral humanitarian intervention took place, which ultimately led to the ICISS reframing the issue as 'responsibility to protect'.

The debate about unilateral humanitarian intervention has also spilled over into an academic debate over the permissibility of supplying weapons to rebels who are fighting to prevent atrocities.[80] There are authors who support arms transfers based on an inherent right to self-defence against genocide,[81] and those who accept the 'normative legitimacy' of such transfers but insist on the continued requirement of 'some form of approval within the UN system'.[82] But there has been little movement with respect to State practice and *opinio juris*, as an examination of some recent developments demonstrates.

[77] *Ibid.*, 108, para. 206. [78] *Ibid.*, 108–9, para. 206.

[79] See Joanna Spear, 'Arms Limitations, Confidence-building Measures, and Internal Conflict' in Michael Edward Brown (ed.), *The International Dimensions of Internal Conflict* (Cambridge, MA: Center for Science and International Affairs, 1996), 383.

[80] See Frederic Mégret, 'Beyond the "Salvation" Paradigm: Responsibility to Protect (Others) vs the Power of Protecting Oneself', *Security Dialogue*, 40 (2009), 575.

[81] Daniel D. Polsby and Don B. Kates, 'Of Holocausts and Gun Control', *Washington University Law Quarterly*, 75 (1997), 1237.

[82] Kenneth D. Heath, 'Could We Have Armed the Kosovo Liberation Army: The New Norms Governing Intervention in Civil War', *UCLA Journal of International Law and Foreign Affairs*, 4 (1999–2000), 259.

Bosnia-Herzegovina

Bosnia-Herzegovina was recognised as an independent State before Iran began shipping weapons in 1994, in an effort to help the Bosnian government counter well-armed Serbian paramilitaries who were committing atrocities against civilians. As a result, the legal controversy that ensued was not over any possible infraction of the rule prohibiting arms shipments to rebels, but rather of the apparent violation of a UN arms embargo that had been imposed on both sides.

Nevertheless, the situation cast some light on whether – and how – the justness of a cause might matter to the legality of weapons shipments. When the *Los Angeles Times* reported that the United States had known about the Iranian shipments and failed to discourage them,[83] the White House responded that it had 'upheld the letter of the law and the requirements of the UN Security Council resolution' imposing the embargo.[84] But another newspaper reported an anonymous US official as saying: 'Were we in a position to stop them? Not really. And was there sympathy for Bosnia here? The answer is, yes.'[85]

Libya

In February 2011, the Security Council imposed an arms embargo on Libya by way of paragraph 9 of Resolution 1970.[86] One month later it adopted Resolution 1973, which authorised 'all necessary measures, *notwithstanding paragraph 9 of resolution 1970 (2011)*, to protect civilians and civilian populated areas'.[87] This language can easily be interpreted as authorising the supply of weapons to the rebels, and arguably reflects something of a change in the international community's attitude to providing such support. However, the 'notwithstanding paragraph 9' language in no way contributed to a change in the general rule because the authorisation was provided by the Security Council. The question, as to

[83] James Risen and Doyle McManus, 'U.S. OKd Iranian Arms for Bosnia, Officials Say', *Los Angeles Times*, 5 April 1996, available at http://articles.latimes.com/1996-04-05/news/mn-55275_1_iranian-arms-shipments.

[84] James Risen, 'Administration Defends its OK of Bosnia Arms', *Los Angeles Times*, 6 April 1996, available at http://articles.latimes.com/1996-04-06/news/mn-55492_1_arms-embargo.

[85] Rupert Cornwell, 'US "Secretly Agreed Iran Arms for Bosnia"', *The Independent*, 6 April 1996, available at www.independent.co.uk/news/world/us-secretly-agreed-iran-arms-for-bosnia-1303474.html.

[86] SC Res. 1970, 26 February 2011.

[87] SC Res. 1973, para. 4 (emphasis added).

whether there has been any change in the rule *outside* of Chapter VII, remained unanswered.

Syria

In 2011–13, Syria was not subject to a UN arms embargo because Russia and China were opposed to such a measure. Syria thus provides an opportunity to examine whether the prohibition on providing aid, assistance, training, equipment and arms to rebels has been relaxed in parallel with (and perhaps as a consequence of) the development of international human rights and R2P. As we will see, a number of governments have been willing to openly provide aid, assistance and 'non-lethal' equipment to the Syrian rebels. But some of those governments have stopped short of providing arms, while others have only done so covertly.

In July 2012, Switzerland suspended arms exports to the United Arab Emirates after a Swiss-made hand grenade originally shipped to that country was found in Syria.[88] The next month, *Reuters* reported that US President Barack Obama had 'signed a secret order authorizing U.S. support for rebels seeking to depose Syrian President Bashar al-Assad and his government' but that the United States was 'stopping short of giving the rebels lethal weapons'.[89] France also indicated that it would provide 'non-lethal elements' to the rebels, including 'means of communication and protection'.[90] And when British Foreign Secretary William Hague announced that his government would provide £5 million in non-lethal equipment to the Syrian opposition, he emphasised that the funding would go to 'unarmed opposition groups, human rights activists and civilians'.[91] In January 2013, when Hague announced that the United Kingdom was seeking modifications to EU sanctions on Syria 'so that the

[88] 'Switzerland Halts Arms Exports to UAE, as Report says Swiss Arms Used by Syria Rebels', *Haaretz and Reuters*, 5 July 2012, available at www.haaretz.com/news/middle-east/switzerland-halts-arms-exports-to-u-a-e-as-report-says-swiss-arms-used-by-syria-rebels-1.449022.

[89] Mark Hosenball, 'Exclusive: Obama Authorizes Secret U.S. Support for Syrian Rebels', *Reuters*, 1 August 2012, available at www.reuters.com/article/2012/08/01/us-usa-syria-obama-order-idUSBRE8701OK20120801.

[90] 'France Gives Non-lethal Military Aid to Syrian Opposition: PM', *Al Arabiya News*, 22 August 2012, available at: http://english.alarabiya.net/articles/2012/08/22/233570.html.

[91] 'Syria Conflict: UK to Give Extra £5m to Opposition Groups', *BBC News*, 10 August 2012, available at www.bbc.co.uk/news/uk-19205204.

possibility of additional assistance [to the rebels] is not closed off',[92] he indicated any military equipment provided would still be of a non-lethal character, such as body armour.[93]

This differentiation between the provision of aid, assistance, training and non-lethal equipment on the one hand, and weapons on the other, was consistent with another recent development in international politics. For it has become widely accepted that curtailing arms transfers to non-State groups is one of the most effective means of reducing long-term risks to civilians. This new acceptance has led to an Arms Trade Treaty that was adopted by the United Nations in April 2013.[94] The treaty makes no exception for the provision of arms to rebels, not even those fighting to prevent atrocities, and ratifications of the treaty are now contributing important State practice to the prohibition against such transfers.[95]

Of course, weapons still find their way into rebel hands. In June 2012, the *New York Times* reported that CIA operatives in southern Turkey were helping to direct arms – paid for by Turkey, Saudi Arabia and Qatar – to Syrian opposition fighters.[96] In January 2013, *The Guardian* reported that: 'Along with Qatar, Turkey and the UAE, the Saudis are believed to be the rebels' principal suppliers and financiers.'[97] However, the latter report also observed that 'public discussion of the issue is extremely rare and the demarcation between government and private initiatives is blurred'.

In other words, although there is State practice in support of providing arms to rebels, it is not accompanied by the *opinio juris* necessary to change a rule of customary international law, and certainly not one of *jus cogens* status that is set out in a foundational treaty such as the UN Charter.

[92] 'Hague: "Options Open" on Military Support for Syrian Rebels', *BBC News*, 10 January 2013, available at www.bbc.co.uk/news/uk-politics-20969386.

[93] *Ibid.* [94] Arms Trade Treaty (New York, adopted 2 April 2013, not yet in force).

[95] On the role of treaties as state practice, see Richard Baxter, 'Treaties and Custom', *Recueil des Cours*, 129 (1970-I), 25; D'Amato, *The Concept of Custom in International Law*, 89–90 and 160; Mark Villiger, *Customary International Law and Treaties* (Dordrecht: Martinus Nijhoff, 1985).

[96] Eric Schmitt, 'C.I.A. Said to Aid in Steering Arms to Syrian Opposition', *New York Times*, 21 June 2012, available at www.nytimes.com/2012/06/21/world/middleeast/cia-said-to-aid-in-steering-arms-to-syrian-rebels.html.

[97] Ian Black, 'Arm Syrian Rebels to Contain Jihadis, says Saudi Royal', *The Guardian*, 25 January 2013, available at www.guardian.co.uk/world/2013/jan/25/arm-syrian-rebels-jihadis-saudi.

Even the United States' June 2013 decision to supply some of the Syria rebels with weapons is clouded with regards to its legal relevance. The decision was announced by a spokesman and not by the president or a cabinet member. Weapons were not specifically mentioned; instead, the spokesman simply said that the military aid would be 'different in scope and scale to what we have provided before'. Moreover, the decision was explicitly linked to the Syria government's use of chemical weapons, rather than the human suffering caused.[98] As a result, the United States did not contribute substantially to the State practice and *opinio juris* in favour of relaxing the more general rule against providing arms to rebels. And of course the United States cannot change international law on its own; what matters, more than its actions, is how other countries respond.

For the moment, the situation has not changed from that described by former US State Department Legal Adviser John B. Bellinger III in January 2013:

> The U.N. Charter prohibits member states from using force against or intervening in the internal affairs of other states unless authorized by the U.N. Security Council or justified by self-defense. These rules make it unlawful for any country to use direct military force against the Assad regime, including establishing 'no-fly zones' or providing arms to the Syrian opposition without Security Council approval.[99]

However, states are increasingly behaving as if the same general prohibition on the use of force no longer precludes the provision of aid, assistance, training and 'non-lethal' equipment to rebels – at least in cases where the rebels are fighting to prevent atrocities. States could also, in future, behave as if the general prohibition on the use of force no longer precludes the supply of arms to rebels who are fighting against a regime that uses chemical weapons. And to the degree these changes occur, they do so in parallel with, and perhaps partly as a result of, developments concerning international human rights that include the Security Council taking a broader approach to 'threat to the peace', as well as the emergence of R2P.

[98] Mark Mazzetti, Michael R. Gordon and Mark Landler, 'U.S. Is Said to Plan to Send Weapons to Syrian Rebels', *New York Times*, 13 June 2013, available at www.nytimes.com/2013/06/14/world/middleeast/syria-chemical-weapons.html.

[99] John B. Bellinger III, 'U.N. Rules and Syrian Intervention', *Washington Post*, 17 January 2013, available at http://articles.washingtonpost.com/2013–01–17/opinions/36410395_1_syrian-opposition-assad-regime-intervention.

Role of R2P in contributing to mitigation

When a State feels compelled by humanitarian concerns to violate the prohibition on the use of force, the circumstances might be taken into account in mitigation. Mitigation is a concept familiar to international law. In the 1949 *Corfu Channel* case, when Albania took the United Kingdom to the International Court of Justice in circumstances where both countries had acted illegally, the Court held that a declaration of illegality was a sufficient remedy for the British violation.[100] In 1960, after Israel abducted Adolf Eichmann from Argentina to face criminal charges, Argentina lodged a complaint with the Security Council, which passed a resolution stating that the sovereignty of Argentina had been infringed and requesting Israel to make 'appropriate reparation'.[101] However the Council, 'mindful' of 'the concern of people in all countries that Eichmann be brought to justice', made no indication that Eichmann should be returned to Argentina.[102]

Shortly after the Kosovo War, Simon Chesterman and I wrote:

> In accordance with such an approach, the human rights violations that prompted a unilateral humanitarian intervention would have to be considered, and to some degree weighed against the actions of the intervening state, in any determination as to whether compensation for violating the rules concerning the use of force is required. Given the fundamental character of the rights violated when mass atrocities occur . . . the intervening state might fare quite well in any such after-the-fact balancing of relative violations.[103]

Since then, the development of R2P has introduced criteria that might guide the Security Council and individual states on the appropriateness and degree of mitigation. Resolution 1674 identified that 'genocide, war crimes, ethnic cleansing and crimes against humanity' are of particular concern to the Council, and therefore most likely to trigger an authorised intervention.[104] The paragraphs on R2P in the World Summit Outcome Document, which were 'reaffirmed' in Resolution 1674, specified that an intervention may only be contemplated 'should peaceful means be inadequate and national authorities are manifestly failing to protect their

[100] *Corfu Channel (United Kingdom* v. *Albania)*, Judgment, 9 April 1949, ICJ Reports (1949), 4, 36.
[101] SC Res. 138, 23 June 1960. [102] *Ibid.*
[103] Byers and Chesterman, 'Changing the Rules about Rules?', 200–1.
[104] See discussion, nn. 44–5.

populations'.[105] And while the report of the High-level Panel on Threats, Challenges and Change was not explicitly endorsed by the Security Council or General Assembly, its 'criteria of legitimacy' – seriousness of intent, proper purpose, last resort, proportional means and balance of consequences – might be considered by the Council and individual states as they decide how to respond to another State's violation of the prohibition on force.[106]

Mitigation itself could come in the form of *ex post facto* authorisation from the Security Council, and it is instructive that such authorisation was granted with respect to the ECOWAS interventions in Liberia and Sierra Leone but not the US-led interventions in Kosovo or Iraq.[107] It could also come in the form of a waiver or reduction of reparations owed, a possibility foreseen in Article 39 of the International Law Commission's Articles on State Responsibility: 'In the determination of reparation, account shall be taken of the contribution to the injury by wilful or negligent action or omission of the injured State or any person or entity in relation to whom reparation is sought.'[108]

Mitigation may already be happening with respect to transfers of weapons to rebels. As was explained above, such transfers are generally covert, and covert actions cannot make or change international law.[109] However, to the degree such transfers are known to be happening, as in Syria, they now attract little reprobation from other states – if and when they are directed at rebels who are fighting to prevent atrocities. One can therefore speculate that, instead of changing the rule to accommodate the exception, the international community is simply choosing to ignore or at least downplay particular violations.

Implications for the international legal system

The on-going development of R2P offers a number of insights into the international legal system. First, 'norm entrepreneurs' who act strategically and persistently can have a significant influence on the framing of debates concerning specific issues of international law.

[105] See discussion, nn. 42–3. [106] See discussion, nn. 36–9.

[107] See SC Res. 788 and 866, 19 November 1992 and 22 September 1993 (Liberia) and 1181, 13 July 1998 (Sierra Leone).

[108] James Crawford, *The International Law Commission's Articles on State Responsibility: Introduction, Text and Commentaries* (Cambridge University Press, 2002).

[109] See discussion, nn. 75–8.

Secondly, such efforts can be interrupted by unanticipated events, including attempts to distort or hijack the norm by other actors.

Thirdly, unanticipated events can necessitate compromise and redirection, which in the case of R2P has involved the limitation of the concept, insofar as it concerns the use of force, to being part of the context of Security Council decision-making.

Fourthly, compromise and redirection may also result when 'norm entrepreneurs' realise that some aspects of the international legal system, such as the prohibition on the use of force, are deeply imbedded and therefore highly resistant to change. This is not to say that ICISS members were naïve about the existence of *jus cogens* rules or the necessity for widespread support from the developing world for any change. Strategically, it is sometimes useful to set one's public goals higher than the results one realistically hopes to achieve. For this reason, acceptance of R2P as relevant context for Security Council decision-making has to be considered a victory, even if some proponents of the concept remain dissatisfied.[110]

Fifthly, the failure of 'norm entrepreneurs' to change a rule does not necessarily mean that they have failed to influence associated or derivative aspects of the legal system. In the case of R2P and the prohibition on the use of force, the failure to change the rule concerning military interventions has not precluded a possible change to the same rule as it applies to the provision of aid, assistance, training and non-lethal equipment to rebels fighting to prevent atrocities, and perhaps even of weapons. Practitioners and scholars of international law would be wise to pay attention, not just to the central aspect of any rule, but also to its often-more-mutable margins.

Finally, the effects of 'norm entrepreneurship' can include changes that are additional or alternative to changes to rules. In the case of R2P, both as it concerns unilateral humanitarian intervention and the provision of arms to rebels, it is important to consider whether the development of the concept will lead to increased mitigation of the consequences – for States

[110] See e.g. the International Coalition for the Responsibility to Protect, a coalition of forty-nine NGOs which includes the following 'essential element' in its 'common understanding' of R2P: 'when a state "manifestly fails" in its protection responsibilities, and peaceful means are inadequate, the international community *must* take stronger measures including Chapter VII measures under the UN Charter, including but *not limited to the collective use of force authorized by the Security Council*'. Available at www.responsibilitytoprotect.org/index.php/about-coalition/our-understanding-of-rtop (emphasis added).

whose moral compulsion to violate international law is both genuinely felt and well-founded.

In the future, R2P may lead to more changes in the international legal system. But instead of beginning at the core of the prohibition on the use of force, the changes will most likely commence at the margins. International law is often like that, moving forward sideways.

3

Human rights beyond borders at the World Court

RALPH WILDE*

Introduction

It was an immense privilege, pleasure and honour to work as a research assistant for, and then be supervised as a doctoral student by, James Crawford. Whereas the opportunity to contribute to a volume in tribute to him by some of his former doctoral students follows from that, it has its own special significance. The passage of time since those days has deepened the sense of great fortune one feels at having had the opportunity of sustained and deep contact, at a particularly formative period in one's life, with someone capable of having such a tremendously positive personal impact. One is reminded by the inevitable ups and downs of life that things could easily have been very different, and so how precious, in the light of that, the experience then was. James was frank, honest, unsparing in criticism, unwaveringly supportive, fair and sensible. He always gave one the impression of considerable faith in and commitment to one's ability and merit and, when I felt that this was unwarranted, it made me raise my game.

More personally, for me as a British person from a family where no one had previously stayed at school beyond the age of sixteen, James's lack of pretention and absence of grandness, and his exclusive focus on aspirations to merit and excellence, were of immense significance. To have a Cambridge experience that enabled me to move further away from, not

* The work on this piece was funded by the Leverhulme Trust and the European Research Council. It reproduces, with permission, some parts of a longer article, 'Human Rights beyond Borders at the World Court: The Significance of the International Court of Justice's Jurisprudence on the Extraterritorial Application of International Human Rights Law Treaties', *Chinese Journal of International Law*, 12(4) (2013), 639–77, open access at http://chinesejil.oxfordjournals.org/cgi/content/full/jmt039?ijkey=4g2d5iTs7GmwWHX&keytype=ref.

closer to, the horrors of the British class system is a mark of the positive significance of James's personal character and the especially beneficial impact of that on the university in general and his students and colleagues in particular. The atmosphere at the Lauterpacht Centre for International Law under his tenure was, I now see, a model of collegiality, with people working in very different roles in an atmosphere marked by a remarkably unhierarchical, friendly and mutually supportive tone. My memories of that time combine stimulating work challenges and inspiring lectures and discussions with the warmth, fun and friendship of the regular morning coffee meetings, lunches, dinners, barbecues and parties.

In paying tribute to James, I offer a critical evaluation of the significance of the International Court of Justice's (ICJ) express pronouncements on the extraterritorial application of human rights treaties in the context of determinations on this area of law by other courts and tribunals. These pronouncements were made in three decisions: the *Wall* Advisory Opinion of 2004; the 2005 Judgment in the *DRC* v. *Uganda* case; and the 2008 Provisional Measures Order in the *Georgia* v. *Russia* case.[1] As will be discussed, the significance of these pronouncements to the law on the extraterritorial application of human rights law built on a statement in the Court's *Namibia* Advisory Opinion from decades earlier, 1971.[2] Although not about this area of law as such, that statement can nonetheless be regarded as foundational to how the law is now understood. This piece forms part of a body of scholarship on the broader issue of the ICJ and international human rights law.[3]

[1] *Legal Consequences of the Construction of a Wall in the Occupied Palestinian Territories*, Advisory Opinion, 9 July 2004, ICJ Reports (2004), 136 (*Wall* Advisory Opinion); *Case concerning Armed Activities on the Territory of the Congo (Democratic Republic of the Congo v. Uganda)*, Judgment, 19 December 2005, ICJ Reports (2005) (*DRC* v. *Uganda*); *Application of the International Convention on the Elimination of All Forms of Racial Discrimination (Georgia v. Russian Federation)*, Order Indicating Provisional Measures, 15 October 2008 (*Georgia* v. *Russia* Provisional Measures).

[2] *Legal Consequences for States of the Continued Presence of South Africa in Namibia (South West Africa) Notwithstanding Security Council Resolution 276 (1970)*, Advisory Opinion, ICJ Reports (1971), 16 (*Namibia* Advisory Opinion).

[3] See the following, and the sources cited therein: Gentian Zyberi, *The Humanitarian Face of the International Court of Justice: Its Contribution in Interpreting and Developing International Human Rights and Humanitarian Law and Rules* (Antwerp: Intersentia, 2008); Sandesh Sivakumaran, 'The International Court of Justice and Human Rights' in Sarah Joseph and Adam McBeth (eds.), *Research Handbook on International Human Rights Law* (Cheltenham: Edward Elgar, 2010), 299–325; Bruno Simma, 'Mainstream Human Rights: The Contribution of the International Court of Justice', *Journal of International Dispute Settlement*, 3 (2012), 7–29. For the human rights instruments whose provisions will be

There are certain direct connections between some of these cases and James Crawford. He was counsel for Palestine in the *Wall* advisory proceedings and for Georgia in *Georgia* v. *Russia.* The position of these two States on the topic at issue in the present chapter – whether or not certain human rights treaties apply extraterritorially – prevailed and was endorsed by the Court in the decisions under evaluation. The *Namibia* Advisory Opinion dates of course from a different era, but even here there are significant links. The year it was issued, 1971, was the same one that James was awarded his joint honours LLB-BA degrees from Adelaide University. The *Namibia* Opinion constitutes a landmark not only, as will be argued, on the present topic of the extraterritorial application of human rights law, but also more generally on the law of self-determination (not unconnected), a subject on which that graduate of the same year went on to become one of the leading, if not *the* leading, academic authorities.

More broadly, the topic of this chapter, and James's intellectual career, challenge the banal generalist/specialist distinction that has arisen in the context of the massive increase in the range and depth of international law that, indeed, one might also say has occurred since 1971 – a further trend that links the topic to the person. Just as James, the quintessential 'generalist', has made seminal contributions in every 'specialist' area of law he has engaged with (of course one cannot hope to appreciate the specific without a complete, authoritative understanding of the general)

addressed in the present piece, see American Declaration of the Rights and Duties of Man, 1948, OAS Res. XXX (1948) (American Declaration) [not a treaty]; European Convention for the Protection of Human Rights and Fundamental Freedoms (Rome, adopted 4 November 1950, entered into force 3 September 1953), 213 UNTS 221 (ECHR); International Covenant on Economic, Social and Cultural Rights (New York, adopted 16 December 1966, entered into force 23 March 1976), 993 UNTS 3 (ICESCR); International Covenant on Civil and Political Rights (New York, adopted 16 December 1966, entered into force 23 March 1976), 999 UNTS 171 (ICCPR); American Convention on Human Rights, 1969, 1144 UNTS 123 (ACHR); International Convention on the Elimination of All Forms of Racial Discrimination (New York, adopted 7 March 1966, entered into force 4 January 1969), 660 UNTS 195 (ICERD or CERD); International Convention on the Elimination of All Forms of Discrimination Against Women (New York, adopted 18 December 1979, entered into force 3 September 1981), 1249 UNTS 13 (CEDAW); African Charter on Human and Peoples' Rights (OAU Doc. CAB/LEG/67/3 rev. 5, Nairobi, adopted 27 June 1981, entered into force 21 October 1986) (ACHPR); Convention on the Rights of the Child (New York, adopted 20 November 1989, 2 September 1990), 1577 UNTS 3 (CRC); Optional Protocol to the Convention on the Rights of the Child on the Involvement of Children in Armed Conflict of 2000 (CRC Optional Protocol) (New York, adopted 25 May 2000, entered into force 12 February 2002), 2173 UNTS 222; Convention Against Torture and Other Cruel, Inhuman or Degrading Treatment or Punishment (New York, adopted 10 December 1984, entered into force 26 June 1987), 1465 UNTS 85 (CAT).

it will be suggested that the ICJ's pronouncements on this area of law are just as, and in some cases more, significant than what has been said by specialist human rights bodies. There is a further, more basic but still significant, stylistic link in the importance of brief, pithy remarks that convey a depth of authority, significance and, ultimately, merit.

The contested issue and treaty law framework on extraterritoriality

The Court's determinations on the question of the extraterritorial application of human rights treaty law obligations were made at the time when this question was highly contested.[4] The entry-level matter of the very applicability of the obligations themselves – as distinct from consequential questions, such as what they would mean were they to apply, or how this meaning would be mediated by the interplay with other applicable law – was disputed.[5] Such a situation was possible in part because the relevant provisions of the treaties contain terminology on applicability that lack a clear indication of spatial scope.

Some of the main treaties addressing civil and political rights, the International Covenant on Civil and Political Rights (ICCPR), the American Convention on Human Rights (ACHR) and the European Convention on Human Rights (ECHR) and their Protocols, the Convention Against Torture (CAT), as well as the Convention on the Rights of the Child (CRC), which also covers economic, social and cultural rights, conceive obligations as operating in the State's 'jurisdiction'. Under the ECHR (and

[4] See the following, and the sources cited therein: Fons Coomans and Menno Kamminga (eds.), *Extraterritorial Application of Human Rights Treaties* (Antwerp and Oxford: Intersentia, 2004); Michael J. Dennis, 'Application of Human Rights Treaties Extraterritorially in Times of Armed Conflict and Military Occupation', *American Journal of International Law*, 99 (2005), 119; Ralph Wilde, 'Legal "Black Hole"?: Extraterritorial State Action and International Treaty Law on Civil and Political Rights', *Melbourne Journal of International Law*, 26 (2005), 739; Michał Gondek, *The Reach of Human Rights in a Globalising World: Extraterritorial Application of Human Rights Treaties* (Antwerp: Intersentia, 2009); Ralph Wilde, 'Compliance with Human Rights Norms Extraterritorially: "Human Rights Imperialism"?' in Laurence Boisson de Chazournes and Marcelo Kohen (eds.), *International Law and the Quest for its Implementation: Liber Amicorum Vera Gowlland-Debbas* (The Netherlands: Brill/Martinus Nijhoff, 2010); Marko Milanovic, *Extraterritorial Application of Human Rights Treaties: Law, Principles, and Policy* (Oxford University Press, 2011); Karen da Costa, *The Extraterritorial Application of Selected Human Rights Treaties* (The Netherlands: Brill, 2012). Sandesh Sivakumaran highlights this significance in the Court's intervention on the topic. See Sivakumaran, 'The International Court of Justice and Human Rights', 307.

[5] See the sources cited *ibid.*

some of its Protocols) and the ACHR, the State is obliged to 'secure' the rights contained in the treaty within its 'jurisdiction'.[6] Under the CAT, the State is obliged to take measures to prevent acts of torture 'in any territory under its jurisdiction'.[7] Under the CRC, States parties are obliged to 'respect and ensure' the rights in the treaty to 'each child within their jurisdiction'.[8] The ICCPR formulation is slightly different from the others in that applicability operates in relation to those 'within [the State's] territory and subject to its jurisdiction'.[9]

Thus a nexus to the State – termed 'jurisdiction' – has to be established before the State's obligations are in play (the significance of the separate reference to 'territory' in the ICCPR will be addressed below).

Certain other international human rights instruments do not contain a general provision, whether using the term 'jurisdiction' or some other equivalent expression, stipulating the scope of applicability of the obligations they contain: the 1948 (Inter-)American Declaration of the Rights and Duties of Man (not a treaty), the 1981 African Charter on Human and Peoples' Rights, the 1965 International Convention on the Elimination of All Forms of Racial Discrimination (CERD), the 1979 International Convention on the Elimination of All Forms of Discrimination Against Women (CEDAW) and the Optional Protocol to the Convention on the Rights of the Child on the Involvement of Children in Armed Conflict of 2000.[10] That said, as far as the Inter-American Declaration is concerned, the Inter-American Commission on Human Rights has treated the instrument as if it does contain the 'jurisdiction' trigger, without any explanation for this assumption.[11]

The obligation to secure the economic, social and cultural rights contained in the International Covenant on Economic, Social and Cultural Rights (ICESCR) does not include a dedicated stipulation concerning spatial applicability. The relevant provision simply obliges parties 'to take steps, individually and through international assistance and co-operation . . . with a view to achieving progressively the full realization of the rights recognized in the present Covenant'.[12]

The vagueness of the provisions in the instruments reviewed enables the scope of their spatial applicability to be easily disputed. 'Jurisdiction'

[6] See ECHR, Art. 1; ACHR, Art. 1. [7] CAT, Art. 2.
[8] CRC, Art. 2.1. [9] ICCPR, Art. 2.
[10] American Declaration; ACHPR; CEDAW; CERD; CRC Optional Protocol.
[11] *Coard* v. *U.S.*, Case 10.951, Report No. 109/99, OEA/Ser.L./V/II.85, doc. 9 rev. (1999) (*Coard*), para. 37.
[12] ICESCR, above n. 3, Art. 2.

could be regarded as a synonym for presence in sovereign territory only, thereby ruling out extraterritorial applicability. Alternatively, it could be defined in some way that includes, but is not limited to, a State's presence in its sovereign territory, but is defined in a manner that only covers a subset of extraterritorial activities (for instance, requiring a certain level of control), thereby creating the possibility for disagreements over which activities are covered. 'Free-standing' obligations could be regarded as operating in any spatial zone in which the State is present, or, alternatively, a claim could be made that a limitation to sovereign territory should be read into them.

Decisions by other bodies and the Court

By the time the ICJ came to pronounce upon the extraterritorial applicability of certain of the aforementioned human rights treaties, there were already other decisions (judicial, quasi-judicial, advisory) on the topic, and the process of overlapping deliberations continued during the period in which the Court became seized of the topic. Prominent were decisions of the United Nations Human Rights Committee (expressed through its Views and General Comments),[13] the Inter-American Commission of Human Rights,[14] the European Commission and Court of Human Rights,[15] the United Nations Committee Against Torture,[16] the

[13] General Comment No. 31, UN Doc. CCPR/C/21/Rev.1/Add. 13 (26 May 2004) (HRC General Comment No. 31); para. 10; HRC, *Lilian Celiberti de Casariego* v. *Uruguay*, Communication No. 56/1979, UN Doc. CCPR/C/13/D/56/1979 (29 July 1981) (*Celiberti de Casariego*), para. 10.3; HRC, *Sergio Euben Lopez Burgos* v. *Uruguay*, Communication No. R.12/52, UN Doc. Supp. No. 40 (A/36/40) (6 June 1979) (*Lopez Burgos*).

[14] *Coard*, paras. 37, 39, 41.

[15] *WM* v. *Denmark*, Application No. 17392/90, 73 Eur Comm'n HR Dec. and Rep. 193 (1992), 196, Section 'The Law', para. 1 (*WM*); *Loizidou* v. *Turkey*, Application No. 40/1993/435/514, Judgment, 23 February 1995, 1996-VI ECtHR, Ser. A, 2216 (GC) (Merits), paras. 52–6; *Cyprus* v. *Turkey*, Application No. 25781/94, Judgment, 10 May 2001, 2001-IV, ECtHR, 1 (GC), para. 77; *Banković and others* v. *Belgium and others*, Application No. 52207/99, Judgment, 12 December 2001, 2001–XII ECtHR (GC), 333, paras. 70–1; *Öcalan* v. *Turkey*, Application No. 46221/99, ECtHR (GC), 12 May 2005 (*Öcalan*), para. 91; *Isaak v Turkey*, Application No. 44587/98, ECtHR, Judgment, 28 September 2006 (Admissibility) (*Isaak*), p. 21; *Issa and others* v. *Turkey*, ECtHR, Admissibility Decision, 30 May 2000 (*Issa* (Admissibility)) and 41 ECtHR 27 (2004) (Merits) (*Issa* (Merits)), para. 71; *Al-Saadoon and Mufdhi* v. *United Kingdom*, Application No. 61498/08, ECtHR, Chamber decision, 2 March 2010 (*Al-Saadoon*); *Al Skeini and others* v. *United Kingdom*, Application No. 55721/07, ECtHR, Judgment, 7 July 2011.

[16] Consideration of Reports Submitted by States Parties under Article 19 of the Convention, Conclusions and Recommendations: United States of America, UN Doc.

United Nations Committee on the Rights of the Child[17] and judgments of domestic courts such as in the United Kingdom.[18]

The question of the extraterritorial applicability of human rights law treaties raised in the ICJ cases concerned the applicability of the treaties to Israel in the Palestinian Territories in the context of the occupation in general and the construction of the separation barrier in particular, to Uganda in the DRC in the context of the military action by the latter in the territory of the former and to Russia in Georgia in the context of Russia's support for the breakaway Republics of Abkhazia and South Ossetia, including through military action in 2008. The treaties at issue were the ICCPR (*Wall* and *DRC* v. *Uganda*), the CRC (*DRC* v. *Uganda*), the CRC Optional Protocol (*DRC* v. *Uganda*), the African Charter (*DRC* v. *Uganda*), the ICESCR (*Wall* Advisory Opinion) and the CERD (*Georgia* v. *Russia*).

Just as in general many of the States who act extraterritorially – and whose legal position is, therefore, directly at stake – refute applicability in this context, so the three States whose obligations were being determined in these cases – Israel, Uganda and Russia – advanced the view that the treaties at issue did not apply to them in the territories under consideration.

The way the Court rejected these positions, and affirmed extraterritorial applicability, involved a series of assertions with a more general significance for the debates on applicability. Moreover, as will be explained, the Court's contribution to understandings of what obligations should mean in the extraterritorial context builds upon what it had said decades previously in the *Namibia* Advisory Opinion concerning South Africa's obligations to the people of that territory. The Court's contribution in this field can be divided up into five distinct elements; these are set out in the following sections.

CAT/C/USA/CO/2 (25 July 2006), para. 15; General Comment No. 2: Implementation of Article 2 by States Parties, 23 November 2007, UN Doc. CAT/C/GC/2 (24 January 2008), para. 16.

17 Concluding Observations of the Committee on the Rights of the Child: Israel, UN Doc. CRC/C/15/Add.195, 4 October 2002, paras. 2, 5, 57–8.

18 *R* v. *Immigration Officer at Prague Airport and another (Respondents), ex p. European Roma Rights Centre and others (Appellants)* [2004] UKHL 55, 9 December 2004; *R (on the application of Al-Skeini and others)* v. *Secretary of State for Defence (The Redress Trust intervening)* [2007] UKHL 26, [2007] 3 WLR 33; *R (on the application of Al-Skeini and others)* v. *Secretary of State for Defence* [2005] EWCA Civ 1609, 21 December 2005; *R (on the application of Al-Skeini and others)* v. *Secretary of State for Defence* [2004] EWHC 2911 (Admin), 14 December 2004.

In the first place, in the *Namibia* Advisory Opinion, the Court established the principle that territorial control, rather than the enjoyment of territorial sovereignty (that is, title) should be the basis for the operation of State obligations in general. Although not a determination specifically about international human rights treaty obligations, this broad proposition paved the way for later decisions about human rights law by both human rights bodies and, subsequently, the Court itself.

In the second place, for treaties containing the 'jurisdiction' trigger for applicability, the Court both supported prior affirmations by other bodies that this trigger has an extraterritorial dimension and offered original affirmations of its own.

In the third place, for treaties that have a 'free-standing' model of applicability, the Court has for some instruments treated them as if they did contain a 'jurisdiction' clause, which operates extraterritorially, and for other instruments affirmed extraterritorial application in a simpler fashion.

In the fourth place, the Court's pronouncement upon the 'exceptional' nature of extraterritorial activities is potentially significant for the regulation of these activities by human rights law when compared to similar pronouncements by certain other bodies.

Similarly, in the fifth place, the Court's approach to the application of human rights treaty obligations to a State acting in territory not forming part of the territory of another State that is a party to the same treaty is highly significant given what has been suggested by certain other decisions on this matter.

The Court's contribution (1): *Namibia* – control not sovereignty; effective control a trigger

In the *Namibia* Advisory Opinion the ICJ stated that South Africa, which at the time was unlawfully occupying Namibia, was:

> accountable for any violations . . . of the rights of the people of Namibia. The fact that South Africa no longer has any title to administer the Territory does not release it from its obligations and responsibilities under international law towards other States in respect of the exercise of its powers in relation to this Territory. Physical control of a territory, and not sovereignty or legitimacy of title, is the basis of State liability for acts affecting other States.[19]

[19] *Namibia* case, 54, para. 118.

This opinion was issued before the main decisions by human rights bodies on the extraterritorial application of human rights treaties. It is not, of course, a decision about human rights-specific treaty law as such, although it concerns the 'rights of the people of Namibia'. The reference to 'obligations and responsibilities under international law towards other States' and 'liability for acts affecting other States' assumes an inter-State focus, although such a focus can include human rights given that obligations of this type are contained in treaties between States, and that certain such obligations (including those at issue here, the prohibition of racial discrimination and the right of self-determination) are regarded as operating *erga omnes*, implicating a generalised community interest on the part of all States.

Whatever the intended meaning in the case of South Africa and the people of Namibia, and the significance for rules concerning applicable law in general and human rights law in particular, as a general proposition the echo of this statement can be traced through later decisions on the applicability of human rights treaty law in two related but distinct respects. First, the fundamental point that State responsibility should not be limited to situations where a State enjoys title is the basic underpinning of extraterritorial applicability. Secondly, the particular concept of 'physical control over territory' as a basis for determining where obligations should subsist has been adopted in later human rights decisions, notably those made in interpreting the meaning of 'jurisdiction' in the European Convention on Human Rights, as one of the two main triggers for extraterritorial applicability, the second being a concept of control exercised over individuals.[20] The extraterritorial applicability of human rights treaties based on the exercise of control over territory – the 'spatial' or 'territorial' trigger – finds its origin in this more general concept from the ICJ.[21]

It would be no exaggeration to say, then, that the ideas first judicially affirmed by the ICJ are both the underpinning of the notion of the extraterritorial application of human rights law itself, and also one of the two main ways in which the trigger for such application has been defined. They foreground subsequent approaches taken on these issues by human rights bodies and the Court itself.[22] In retrospect, it can be said that the

20 The two triggers are discussed below, nn. 29 and 30 and accompanying text.

21 *Ibid.*

22 Sandesh Sivakumaran observes that the Court's later decisions on the extraterritorial application of the ICCPR, ICESCR and CRC (addressed below) are 'timely and important'

ground-breaking decision on the extraterritorial application of human rights law came from the ICJ, not from a human rights tribunal, and well before the canonical decisions were issued on the topic by such tribunals.

Just as the Court paved the way for later approaches taken on extraterritorial applicability that were directly concerned with human rights treaty law, so too the Court later became involved in offering approaches of its own to the topic. Its contribution here can be split into different elements, beginning with the question of the extraterritorial meaning of the term 'jurisdiction' as used in human rights treaties.

The Court's contribution (2): affirming the extraterritorial meaning of 'jurisdiction'

The general refutation of the extraterritorial application of human rights law made by many of the States which would be subject to the obligations were they to apply – including Israel, Uganda and Russia with respect to the three ICJ decisions in this field – has been primarily concerned with the term 'jurisdiction' in some of the main human rights treaties. This term, it is argued, means the State's presence in its sovereign territory only, and so in circumstances where it serves as the trigger for applicability, the relevant obligations do not apply extraterritorially.[23] In the particular case of the ICCPR provision on applicability, which as mentioned earlier addresses those 'within [the State's] territory and subject to its jurisdiction', the argument is made that the inclusion of the word 'territory' in addition to 'jurisdiction' should be read to suggest that jurisdiction is limited to territory, thereby ruling out extraterritorial applicability.[24] Arguments have also been made against the extraterritorial application of the ICESCR, for example by Israel in the context of the situation in the Palestinian territories.[25]

Even before the *Wall* Advisory Opinion and the *DRC* v. *Uganda* and *Russia* v. *Georgia* decisions were issued by the ICJ, the consistent

but also 'no more than the specific application to human rights treaties of' this earlier idea. Sivakumaran, 'The International Court of Justice and Human Rights', 309.

23 See e.g. the discussion in Wilde 'Legal "Black Hole"?', 776–8, and sources cited therein.

24 See the discussions in the literature cited above, n. 4; for one example of a commentator who advocates this position, see Dennis, 'Application of Human Rights Treaties Extraterritorially in Times of Armed Conflict and Military Occupation'. For Israel's position with respect to the ICCPR, see e.g. *Wall* Advisory Opinion, para. 110, and sources cited therein.

25 See the *Wall* Advisory Opinion, para. 112.

position adopted in relation to international human rights instruments by international review bodies was the opposite of the rejectionist position. The term 'jurisdiction' in the ECHR, ACHR, CAT and CRC has been interpreted to operate extraterritorially in certain circumstances.[26] The aforementioned treatment of the applicability of the (Inter-)American Declaration by the Inter-American Commission on Human Rights in terms of the exercise of 'jurisdiction' was in the context of extraterritorial activity, which it regarded as capable of constituting the exercise of jurisdiction and thereby falling under the scope of the obligations in the Declaration.[27] Similarly, the ICCPR was interpreted as applying extraterritorially by the UN Human Rights Committee in Views issued in 1981 and a General Comment of 2004.[28] In general, the term 'jurisdiction' has been defined extraterritorially as the exercise of control over either territory – the concept, indicated earlier, which has its origins in the *Namibia* Advisory Opinion, sometimes referred to as the 'spatial' or 'territorial' definition[29] – or individuals, sometimes referred to as the 'individual', 'personal' or, because of the identity of the foreign State actor involved, 'State agent authority' definition.[30]

The significance of the ICJ's determinations on this issue was to bolster some of the affirmations of extraterritorial applicability that had already been made by expert bodies in relation to the ICCPR and the CRC.

In the *Wall* Advisory Opinion and the *DRC* v. *Uganda* Judgment the Court affirmed that the ICCPR is capable of extraterritorial application.[31] This bolsters the credibility of the Human Rights Committee's position on this question, and, by the same token, the credibility of the rejectionist view is weakened. It is also significant more broadly within the Court's jurisprudence because the Human Rights Committee's position is expressly cited by the Court in its reasoning on the issue in the *Wall* Advisory Opinion, both as a general matter and as far as the position of Israel in the Palestinian territories in particular is concerned (the reasoning in *DRC* v. *Uganda* merely invokes the Court's earlier reasoning in

[26] See decisions cited above nn. 14–17. [27] *Coard*, above n. 11, para. 37.

[28] General Comment No. 31, *Celiberti de Casariego, Lopez Burgos*, above n. 13.

[29] See e.g. *Cyprus* v. *Turkey*; *Loizidou* v. *Turkey* (Preliminary Objections), Merits; *Banković*; *Al-Skeini* (DC), (CA), (HL), (ECtHR); *Issa*.

[30] *Celiberti de Casariego*, para. 10.3; *Lopez Burgos*, para. 12.3; *Öcalan*; *Isaak*, p. 21; *Coard*, paras. 1–4, 37, 39, 41; *Al-Skeini* (DC), (CA), (HL), (ECtHR), passim; *Al-Saadoon*, passim; *WM*, p. 196, section 'The Law', para. 1.

[31] *Wall* Advisory Opinion, para. 113.

the *Wall* Advisory Opinion in summary form).[32] Just as its decisions on extraterritorial applicability constitute some of the main decisions by the Court on human rights law generally, so here a decision in this category is a landmark in the broader theme of the Court's express use of the decisions of other courts and tribunals.

In a similar fashion, in the same two decisions, the Court provided authority for the extraterritorial application of the CRC, as with the Human Rights Committee and the ICCPR earlier, bolstering the position of the Committee on the Rights of the Child on this issue (although, by contrast, without referring to the latter Committee's position on the issue).[33]

Before the ICJ made its pronouncements on the topic, the position on the extraterritorial applicability of the term 'jurisdiction' when used in human rights treaties was limited to affirmation by the UN Human Rights Committee and the Committee on the Rights of the Child – whose decisions, although important and influential, are formally non-judicial and non-binding – and the European Commission and Court of Human Rights – whose decisions are necessarily specific to the ECHR and its Protocols even if often containing logic that is clearly transferable to equivalent provisions in other treaties. The extraterritorial applicability of the ICCPR and the CRC could be rejected by dissenting States on the grounds that it had not been affirmed by a body other than the Committees associated with the two instruments, that the position of those Committees were non-binding and that decisions made with respect to the European Convention on Human Rights were irrelevant.[34]

After these ICJ cases, the positions of the Human Rights Committee and the Committee on the Rights of the Child with respect to the ICCPR and the CRC were no longer isolated and, moreover, had been endorsed by a body with formal judicial status, and in a multifaceted fashion that both affirmed the position as general proposition and applied it to the facts of two separate situations, Israel in Palestine and the DRC in Uganda (in the latter case in a binding judgment).

32 *Ibid.*, para. 109 (on the Committee's general position on extraterritorial applicability) and para. 110 (on the Committee's position on Israel in the Palestinian territories in particular); *DRC* v. *Uganda*, para. 216.

33 *Wall* Advisory Opinion, para. 113; *DRC* v. *Uganda* Judgment, paras. 216–7. On the decision of the Committee on the Rights of the Child, see above, n. 17.

34 See the discussions in the literature cited above n. 4; for one example of a commentator who advocates this position, see Dennis, 'Application of Human Rights Treaties Extraterritorially in Times of Armed Conflict and Military Occupation'. For Israel's position with respect to the ICCPR, see e.g. *Wall* Advisory Opinion, para. 110, and sources cited therein.

More broadly, the quantum of authoritative interpretation on the question of the extraterritorial applicability of the term 'jurisdiction' across international human rights treaties generally had become significantly greater, in that jurisprudence from specialist human rights bodies was joined by the pre-eminent, generalist Court.

The Court's contribution (3): affirming the extraterritorial applicability of other treaties with free-standing obligations

As mentioned above, some treaties operate in a free-standing sense, in that they do not contain express provisions stipulating their general spatial field of application. Debates about this spatial field are concerned not with the meaning of an ambiguous term (as in the earlier contest over the meaning of 'jurisdiction') but, rather, on whether the lack of an express provision renders the treaties always applicable to States parties anywhere in the world, or whether some sort of spatial test for applicability should be read into them and, if so, what constitutes the limits of that test.

The Court has made an important contribution to these debates, through adopting two distinct approaches to extraterritorial applicability. First, the Court in effect read into treaties a concept of jurisdiction, which it then determined to apply extraterritorially. Secondly, the Court offered a more simple affirmation of extraterritorial applicability, without explaining the basis for this.

As indicated above, the Inter-American Commission on Human Rights had read a concept of 'jurisdiction' into the American Declaration on Human Rights (not a treaty), which did not contain an express reference to this word, as a way of affirming its extraterritorial applicability. This approach was taken up (without acknowledgement of its origins, as an idea, in the Commission's decision about the Declaration) and applied by the ICJ in relation to the ICESCR in the *Wall* Advisory Opinion, the African Charter and the CRC Optional Protocol in *DRC* v. *Uganda*. All of these instruments were treated as if they contained the 'jurisdiction' trigger, as a way of affirming that they were capable of extraterritorial application on the basis of the performance of activity by the State which fell within the scope of this concept.[35] In the *Wall* Advisory Opinion, the Court mentions the positions of Israel and the Committee on Economic, Social and Cultural Rights on the question of the applicability of the

[35] On the ICESCR, see *Wall* Advisory Opinion, paras. 111–12; on the ACHPR and the CRC Optional Protocol, see *DRC* v. *Uganda* Judgment, paras. 216–7.

ICESCR to Israel in the Palestinian territories.[36] Whereas it rejects Israel's advocacy of inapplicability, in contrast to its discussion of the position of the Human Rights Committee in relation to the ICCPR, it does not expressly associate the position of the Committee on Economic, Social and Cultural Rights advocating applicability (either generally or in relation to Israel in the Palestinian territories in particular) with its own affirmation of this view.[37]

Here it is a matter not, as earlier, of interpreting a treaty provision termed 'jurisdiction' as having an extraterritorial meaning, but, rather, of affirming the extraterritorial applicability of the obligations in the instrument by reading into it a concept for applicability called 'jurisdiction', which has an extraterritorial component. This takes (without acknowledgement) an approach adopted in one decision by a regional body in relation to one instrument, not at issue in the case before it, and treats it as relevant more generally to certain other human rights treaties that do not have an explicit concept of 'jurisdiction' triggering applicability.

A second approach to the extraterritorial scope of treaties with a free-standing conception of applicability provisions is simpler. It was adopted by the UK House of Lords (as it was called then) in the *Roma Rights* case of 2004 concerning the posting of UK immigration officials at Prague airport.[38] Lady Hale and Lord Steyn both assumed that the prohibition of discrimination on grounds of race in CERD applied extraterritorially, without recourse to a particular factual doctrine such as the exercise of 'jurisdiction', which had to be met in order for the obligations to be in play.[39]

The effect of the ICJ's 1998 Order for provisional measures in the *Georgia* v. *Russia* case is to offer further support to this 'free-standing' approach to applicability. The Court stated that it:

> observes that there is no restriction of a general nature in CERD relating to its territorial application; whereas it further notes that, in particular, neither Article 2 nor Article 5 of CERD, alleged violations of which [by Russia in Georgia] are invoked by Georgia, contain a specific territorial limitation . . . the Court consequently finds that these provisions of CERD generally appear to apply, like other provisions of instruments of that nature, to the actions of a State party when it acts beyond its territory;[40]

[36] *Wall* Advisory Opinion, para. 112. [37] *Ibid.*

[38] See Opinion of Lord Bingham, *Roma Rights* case, para. 4.

[39] See Opinion of Lady Hale, *Roma Rights* case, paras. 97–102 and Opinion of Lord Steyn, paras. 44 and 46.

[40] *Georgia* v. *Russia* (Provisional Measures), para. 109.

The Court's order called upon '[b]oth Parties, within South Ossetia and Abkhazia and adjacent areas in Georgia' to take certain acts to comply with the Convention, a determination that assumed the extraterritorial application of CERD to Russian forces in Georgia.[41]

This decision offers a particular approach to understanding the extraterritorial application of those treaties such as the CERD with free-standing models of applicability not expressly qualified by jurisdiction: the absence of a restriction on applicability, whether of a general character, or specific to the particular obligations in the treaty at issue, should be taken to suggest that the provisions *should* apply. In other words, as far as the significance of treaty provisions is concerned, the enquiry on extraterritorial applicability depends on not establishing this in a positive sense, but, rather, establishing whether it has been ruled out negatively through restrictive provisions. Such an approach to treaties with free-standing provisions can be seen as offering a potential explanation for the approach adopted by the UK House of Lords in *Roma Rights*, and a general doctrine to be followed in relation to such treaties as an alternative to the approach of reading a concept of 'jurisdiction' into them.

The Court's contribution (4): on the 'exceptional' nature of extraterritorial activity and its regulation by human rights law

However controversial and important extraterritorial State actions are, and however fundamental they may be in certain cases to the interests of the relevant States and those in the territories affected, taken as a whole they are exceptional when compared with the presence and activities of State authorities within their sovereign territories. Thus in the *Wall* Advisory Opinion the ICJ stated in relation to the ICCPR that 'while the exercise of jurisdiction is primarily territorial, it may sometimes be exercised outside the State territory'.[42] The Court went on to say that:

> Considering the object and purpose of the . . . Covenant . . . it would seem natural that, even when such is the case, States parties to the Covenant should be bound by its provisions.[43]

Similarly, in relation to the ICESCR, the Court stated that:

> this Covenant guarantees rights which are essentially territorial. However, it is not to be excluded that it applies *both* to territories over which a State

[41] *Ibid.*, para. 149.
[42] *Wall* Advisory Opinion, para. 109. [43] *Ibid.*

> party has sovereignty *and* to those over which that State exercises territorial jurisdiction.[44]

Here, then, the Court is being descriptive about the exercise of jurisdiction in the sense of a State presence (the particular activity performed by Israel at issue before it) reflecting the fact that States parties to the Covenant (taken as a whole) do not normally engage in this activity *as a matter of fact* outside their territory. These observations are significant because of how they echo an earlier statement made by the European Court of Human Rights, and how they have potentially a significantly different import, in terms of the implications for the scope of extraterritorial applicability, from an earlier statement by the Strasbourg Court.

In the *Banković* decision concerning the NATO bombing of Serbia in 1999, the European Court of Human Rights stated that jurisdiction is 'essentially' territorial, with extraterritorial jurisdiction subsisting only in 'exceptional' circumstances.[45] However, in this observation the Court seemed to suggest that somehow the 'exceptional' character of extraterritorial jurisdiction should be understood not only in a factual sense; it should also have purchase in attenuating the scope of the meaning of 'jurisdiction' in international human rights law, and should perform this function in an autonomous manner from the factual exceptionalism. The autonomous nature of this exceptionalism creates the possibility that even if a State *is* acting 'exceptionally' as a *matter of fact* outside its territory, such a situation might not fall within its 'jurisdiction' for the purposes of human rights law. In other words, only a subset of extraterritorial activity will be regulated by human rights law.

The dictum from *Banković* was affirmed at certain stages in the English courts of the *Al-Skeini* case concerning the UK's military presence in Iraq, although by way of simple recitation only.[46] In the Strasbourg judgment in that case, the European Court of Human Rights stated:

> A State's jurisdictional competence under Article 1 is primarily territorial... Jurisdiction is presumed to be exercised normally throughout the State's territory... Conversely, acts of the Contracting States performed, or producing effects, outside their territories can constitute an exercise of jurisdiction within the meaning of Article 1 only in exceptional cases...
>
> To date, the Court in its case-law has recognised a number of exceptional circumstances capable of giving rise to the exercise of jurisdiction by a

[44] *Ibid.*, para. 112. [45] *Banković*, para. 67.
[46] See *Al-Skeini* (HC), paras. 245 and 269; *Al-Skeini* (CA), paras. 75–6.

> Contracting State outside its own territorial boundaries. In each case, the question whether exceptional circumstances exist which require and justify a finding by the Court that the State was exercising jurisdiction extra-territorially must be determined with reference to the particular facts.[47]

This statement seems to suggest that, necessarily, human rights law does not apply to all the extraterritorial actions of States – even if States perform 'acts . . . outside their territories', such acts can only 'constitute an exercise of jurisdiction within the meaning of Article 1', that is to be regulated by the obligations in the treaty, 'in exceptional cases'.

This doctrine of the 'exceptional' extraterritorial application of human rights obligations has only ever been affirmed in the context of the ECHR. Moreover, even in relation to that instrument it was absent from the case law before the *Banković* decision of 2001. Nonetheless, it appears to suggest a significantly different approach to 'exceptionalism' from that articulated by the ICJ in the *Wall* Advisory Opinion, which was issued after *Banković*. For the ICJ, exceptionalism was only an issue in terms of the frequency of extraterritorial State action; it was not also a doctrine to limit the circumstances when this action would be regulated by human rights law when it occurred.

The absence of an affirmation of the latter doctrine places the *Wall* Advisory Opinion alongside the decisions of other bodies such as the Inter-American Commission of Human Rights and the Human Rights Committee, supporting the absence of such a doctrine from human rights law generally and further marginalising the apparent affirmation of the doctrine in the context of the ECHR.

The Court's contribution (5): whether human rights treaty obligations should apply to a State acting in territory not falling within the sovereign territory of another contracting party to the treaty

An idea has become associated with the ECHR, based on an interpretation of a dictum from the European Court of Human Rights in the aforementioned *Banković* decision, about the 'legal space' or '*espace juridique*' of the Convention, which has fundamental consequences for the question of extraterritorial applicability. Although advanced and affirmed only with respect to the European Convention, as an idea it is transferrable to other human rights treaties.

[47] *Al Skeini* (ECtHR), paras. 131–2.

This idea is as follows: a particular action taken by one State in the territory of another State would not be governed by the Convention obligations of the first State if the second State is not also a party to the Convention, even if in other respects the act in question meets the test for extraterritorial jurisdiction under the Convention (for instance the State exercises effective territorial control). Under this view, although the concept of 'jurisdiction' under the ECHR is not limited to a State's own territory, the applicability of the treaty as a whole is limited to the overall territory of contracting States. In consequence, States acting outside the 'territorial space' of the ECHR are not bound by their obligations in that instrument, even if they are exercising effective control over territory and/or individuals. This is a severe limitation as far as the ECHR is concerned, since most of the world's States, including some of the key sites of extraterritorial action by certain European States, fall outside the 'legal space' of the ECHR.

This concept, although articulated in relation to the ECHR, is of significance more broadly to situations where States act in territory in respect of which they lack title, and which does not form part of another State that is also bound by the same human rights obligations as they are. This would cover territory of a State that is not a party to the same human rights treaty and non-State territory that, necessarily, does not fall within the territory of any State bound by any human rights treaties at all. It would also cover territory of a State that is party to the same treaty but subject to different obligations under it, whether through reservations, declarations or a divergent position as far as additional instruments such as optional protocols to the treaty are concerned. This is not, then, a rejection of the extraterritorial application of human rights law *in toto*; it is a rejection of human rights norms that have not yet been universally accepted or accepted at least by a State with sovereignty (as title) over the territory concerned, even if they have been accepted by the foreign State acting in that territory.

The significance of this idea is illustrated by the following two examples of exclusions that would be effected by this limitation. First, no European State acting in Afghanistan, or taking action in the territorial waters of States and/or the high seas off the Horn of Africa with respect to so-called 'piracy', or taking migration-related action in the territorial waters of North African States and/or the high seas in the Mediterranean, would be bound by the ECHR. Secondly, no action by any State on the high seas, or off the coast of the Western Sahara (a non-State territory), whether piracy- or migration-related, is covered by any human rights treaty obligations whatsoever.

This sets up a two-tier system of human rights protection: States may act abroad in a manner that impacts on human rights, but such action is only regulated by human rights obligations if these had already been in operation in the territories in question. Such a system echoes legal distinctions operating in the colonial era in levels of civilisation and as between the metropolis and the colony as far as the level of rights protection is concerned. Indeed, with the ECHR the distinction in rights protection necessarily operates according to a European/non-European axis – Turkey in northern Cyprus: yes; that State and other European States in Iraq: no.

Whether or not such an exclusion actually operates with respect to the ECHR and its Protocols has been addressed in both case law and academic commentary.[48] Such discussion has included coverage of broader normative issues concerning whether the absence of such a limitation, and the consequent application of human rights standards that were not previously applicable in the territory, would constitute 'human rights imperialism' and also potentially risk, where it is co-applicable, adherence to certain norms of occupation law.

In *DRC* v. *Uganda*, the Court held that the nature of the extraterritorial action by the State at issue, Uganda, met the test for triggering the law of occupation. Applying Uganda's human rights obligations was not capable of raising a 'legal space' problem as set out above, however, because the DRC was also a party to the treaties at issue. Similarly, in *Georgia* v. *Russia*, the Court was concerned with the extraterritorial application of a human rights treaty that was binding on both the State acting extraterritorially, and the State in whose territory the former State was acting. These two cases were equivalent, then, to the Strasbourg cases about Turkey in northern Cyprus: one State being bound by its obligations when acting in the territory of another State also a party to the treaty or treaties containing the obligations at issue. Everything was happening within the 'legal space' of the treaty or treaties.

In the *Wall* Advisory Opinion, however, the Court was considering the applicability of human rights treaties that were not already in operation in the particular sense that the territory – Palestine – did not itself constitute a State party to human rights treaties (a position that has since changed), nor was it regarded as forming part of the territory of another State party to such treaties. The situation was therefore, in this sense, outside the 'legal space' of these instruments. It might have been said, then, that to apply the

48 See *Banković*; *Al-Skeini* (DC), (CA), (HL), (ECtHR), 63; Wilde, 'Compliance with Human Rights Norms Extraterritorially'.

treaty obligations to Israel in the Occupied Palestinian Territories would fall foul of a limitation on applicability to the 'legal space' of the treaties at issue. However, such a view was not expressed by the Court and the treaties were regarded as applicable to Israel, thereby necessarily rejecting the 'legal space' limitation idea in its entirety.

Conclusion

When the ICJ issued the *Namibia* Advisory Opinion in 1971, the development of international human rights treaty law, and its expert-body interpretation, was at a very early stage – the two global human rights Covenants, for example, had been adopted (in 1966) but were not yet in force (that happened in 1976).[49] The question of the extraterritorial application of this law had not been subject to any general expert determination. When that happened later, the ideas expressed by the Court can be clearly identified. Although, then, the Court did not itself pronounce upon international human rights treaty law for some time after *Namibia*, that opinion nonetheless deserves a central place in the canon of international human rights law jurisprudence, not only for the commonly acknowledged significance it has for UN law and the law of self-determination, but also because of this link with later expert-body determinations on the extraterritorial application of human rights law. Moreover, when the Court offered its own contribution on the latter subject to sit alongside the expert-body determinations, this had an important role in consolidating and supplementing a critical mass of authoritative interpretation on what was and remains the highly contested and fundamentally important question of whether human rights treaty obligations apply extraterritorially. In a few brief statements in three decisions, the Court bolstered the case for an affirmative answer to this question. It has done this in a manner that has widened the scope of the judicial and quasi-judicial conversation from an isolated, treaty-specific treatment by dedicated interpretation bodies on what is a common matter across the human rights treaty framework.

[49] See ICCPR and ICESCR.

4

Fragmentation, regime interaction and sovereignty

MARGARET A. YOUNG

Introduction

The fragmentation of international law is a long-observed phenomenon that demonstrates uneven normative and institutional development and evolution in inter-State relations, with little or no hierarchical order or overall coherence. Separate legal regimes such as the international trade regime and the international regime to mitigate climate change have developed largely independently from one another, often instigated by non-identical groupings of States. Conflicts of norms between these regimes give rise to 'post modern anxieties' about disorder and uncertainty,[1] and in response, the United Nations International Law Commission (ILC), in a seminal study led by Martti Koskenniemi, advocates a toolbox of professional techniques for international lawyers.[2] These techniques seek first and foremost to ascertain the common intention of States parties to the relevant regimes in resolving normative conflicts. In doing so, the techniques promote adherence to sovereign concerns.

Yet even aside from the potential for large-scale conflicts between rules or rule-systems, the fragmented and diversified legal landscape and the plethora of legal regimes give rise to challenges of a more mundane character. Given that issues of global concern such as climate change, fisheries depletion and human rights do not fall neatly into one regime, there is a constant need to mediate and understand the interaction between

[1] Martti Koskenniemi and Päivi Leino, 'Fragmentation of International Law? Postmodern Anxieties', *Leiden Journal of International Law*, 15 (2002), 553.

[2] ILC Study Group, 'Fragmentation of International Law: Difficulties Arising from the Diversification and Expansion of International Law, Conclusions of the Work of the Study Group', A/CN.4/L.702 (18 July 2006); see also Report of the ILC Study Group, 'Fragmentation of International Law: Difficulties Arising from the Diversification and Expansion of International Law', finalised by Martti Koskenniemi, A/CN.4/L.682 and Corr.1 (13 April 2006).

regimes.[3] Joint work programmes, the common advancement of 'multi-sourced equivalent norms'[4] and shared institutional practices are a routine feature of the implementation of international law. This interaction between regimes sometimes occurs with the full awareness and consent of States parties, but oftentimes it does not. For example, States sometimes allow secretariats of international organisations to enter into memoranda of understanding with other secretariats; at times, institutional co-operation exists without such arrangements. If regime interaction occurs without the apparent consent of States, what is the risk to sovereignty?

The situation is further complicated when one considers the growth of non-traditional legal regimes and 'transnational law' beyond the confines of the State. An example from forestry regulation illustrates this phenomenon. Forested areas are simultaneously governed by States for a range of uses including timber extraction and agricultural plantation; they also form part of complex and localised normative arrangements of indigenous and other communities. Such pluralism is destined to become even more complex. Imminent global attempts to reduce carbon emissions from deforestation and forest degradation (known as 'REDD' programmes) promise to provide public and private entities with opportunities to establish carbon markets, adding a layer of governance that is grounded on State participation and yet dependent on global and 'de-nationalised' authorities. The interaction between these areas of law provides additional challenges to notions of sovereignty. Can States retain control? Should they?

This chapter addresses the dilemma posed for sovereignty by regime interaction. The first part identifies the multiple meanings of 'regime'. The term is useful in drawing attention to specialised areas of practice and institutional development, notwithstanding the risks that accompany such analysis.[5] This part considers the influence of international inter-governmental organisations and non-governmental organisations (NGOs) in these arrangements. Such influence may even exceed the

[3] See generally, Margaret A. Young (ed.), *Regime Interaction in International Law: Facing Fragmentation* (Cambridge University Press, 2012).

[4] Tomer Broude and Yuval Shany, 'The International Law and Policy of Multi-sourced Equivalent Norms' in Tomer Broude and Yuval Shany (eds.), *Multi-sourced Equivalent Norms in International Law* (Oxford: Hart, 2011), 1.

[5] For the risks in defining regimes and theorising their interactions (especially with respect to reductive thinking and essentialising tendencies), see Margaret A. Young, 'Introduction: The Productive Friction between Regimes' in Margaret A. Young (ed.), *Regime Interaction in International Law: Facing Fragmentation* (Cambridge University Press, 2012), 10–11.

influence of States, especially for some privately developed 'transnational regimes'.

The second part focuses on sovereignty and its demands. Traditional conceptions of sovereignty emphasise the full and independent authority of States to govern their citizens and their territory. When States ratify treaties and become members of legal regimes, the delegation of power is seen by some to be a diminution of sovereignty. Perhaps even more keenly felt is the impact on sovereignty of interacting regimes and this part examines examples of international organisations within one regime finding facts and drawing upon law from another regime. Examples from regimes relating to liberalised trade, climate change mitigation and fisheries protection are provided to demonstrate the current practice surrounding intersecting regimes. If such activities go beyond the implied powers of international organisations, sovereignty's demand for State consent in situations of authority and control may go unmet.

The third part provides a normative argument for regime interaction that attenuates the concept of sovereignty to allow for the participation of international organisations and NGOs in regime interaction. It explores ways in which regime interaction satisfies the demands of sovereignty by ensuring legitimacy. Issues such as accountability, transparency and cross-regime scrutiny become important at both a practical and theoretical level. An account of sovereignty that allows international law to confront issues of global concern, even as those issues traverse multiple regimes with disparate (and sometimes non-existing) State membership and differing organisational structures, is a necessary part of an open system of international law.

A 'Regimes' of international laws and institutions

'Regimes' is a term that delineates professional specialisations, treaty and institutional arrangements and subject disciplines bounded by functional, teleological, organisational and geographical domains. The international trade regime, headed by the World Trade Organization (WTO);[6] the climate change regime, led by the Conferences of Parties to the United Nations Framework Convention on Climate Change (UNFCCC);[7] and

[6] Agreement Establishing the World Trade Organization (Marrakesh, 15 April 1994, 1 January 1995), 33 ILM 1143.

[7] United Nations Framework Convention on Climate Change (New York, adopted 9 May 1992, entered into force 21 March 1994), 31 ILM 849.

the law of the sea regime, dominated by the United Nations Convention on the Law of the Sea,[8] exemplify common descriptions of separate but connected areas of international law.

Such arrangements conform to the idea of regimes as 'sets of norms, decision-making procedures and organisations coalescing around functional issue-areas and dominated by particular modes of behaviour, assumptions and biases'.[9] This definition is a hybrid of terms deployed and developed within international law and international relations (IR) scholarship.[10] In the latter context, 'regime theory' concentrates on normative developments by States (and more specifically, governments) within regimes. Similarly, a growing body of work on 'regime complexes'[11] identifies how narrowly framed regimes devised by States are linked together to address set issues.

A similar preoccupation with the interests of States pervades the understanding of 'regimes' in international law. Early usage of the term 'regimes' by the International Court of Justice combined it with the adjective 'self-contained', to emphasise a system of legal prescriptions (relating to diplomatic law) that contained its own rules on the consequences of breach.[12]

[8] United Nations Convention on the Law of the Sea (Montegobay, adopted 10 December 1982, entered into force 16 November 1994), 1833 UNTS 397.

[9] Young, 'Introduction: The Productive Friction between Regimes', 11, building on Stephen Krasner's seminal definition in his 'Structural Causes and Regime Consequences: Regimes as Intervening Variables' in Stephen Krasner (ed.), *International Regimes* (Ithaca: Cornell University Press, 1983), 3 (regimes are 'sets of implicit or explicit principles, norms, rules, and decision-making procedures around which actors' expectations converge in a given area of international relations'); see also Oran Young, *International Cooperation: Building Regimes for Natural Resources and the Environment* (Ithaca: Cornell University Press, 1989), 1. Note the different use of the term 'regime' to refer to government authority within a state, see e.g. James Crawford, 'Sovereignty as a Legal Value' in James Crawford and Martti Koskenniemi (eds.), *The Cambridge Companion to International Law* (Cambridge University Press, 2012), 127; also exemplified by the genteelism 'regime change' when governmental authority is challenged by intervention in domestic affairs by an external state.

[10] The following overview is a brief summary of the more detailed analysis in Young, 'Introduction: The Productive Friction between Regimes', 4–11.

[11] See e.g. Kal Raustiala and David Victor, 'The Regime Complex for Plant Genetic Resources', *International Organization*, 58 (2004), 277; Robert Keohane and David Victor, 'The Regime Complex for Climate Change', *Perspectives on Politics*, 9 (2011), 7.

[12] *Consular Staff in Tehran (USA* v. *Iran)*, ICJ Reports (1979), para. 86. See further Bruno Simma, 'Self-Contained Regimes', *Netherlands Yearbook of International Law*, 16 (1985), 115 and 117. For criticism of the Court's use of the term, see James Crawford and Penelope Nevill, 'Relations between International Courts and Tribunals: The "Regime Problem"' in Margaret A. Young (ed.), *Regime Interaction in International Law: Facing Fragmentation* (Cambridge University Press, 2012), 235, 259.

The ILC now prefers the term 'special regimes' in its conceptualisation of the operation of *lex specialis* in the context of resolving conflicts of norms arising from the fragmentation and diversification of international law.[13]

Whilst the ILC's use of the term 'special regimes' generally reiterates the centrality of States in regime formation and operation, the third of its three offered definitions hints at a broader conception.[14] If 'regimes' are defined to include bodies of 'functional specialization or teleological orientation', such as environmental law or trade law,[15] arguably a wide number of actors besides States are included in the definition. Specialisation connotes an expertise, and possibly a 'professional mindset',[16] most commonly belonging to technical experts operating within secretariats but also within tribunals, NGOs and other bodies. Understanding the contribution made by these actors to regimes underpins IR scholarship on 'epistemic communities'.[17] It is also part of the broader realisation that the conflict between regimes in international law reflects wider societal conflicts.[18]

Two consequences relevant to the current chapter flow from this broad understanding of regimes. First, the enhanced recognition of the role of non-State actors – especially international inter-governmental organisations and NGOs – in the formation and operation of regimes[19] displaces sovereign States as the sole drivers of regime interaction. Secondly,

[13] See ILC Study Group Analytical Study, 81–2 (para. 152), 248 (para. 492). For definitions, see ILC Study Group Conclusions, 11–12, para. 12.

[14] This usage applies when 'all the rules and principles that regulate a certain problem area are collected together so as to express a "special regime". Expressions such as "law of the sea", "humanitarian law", "human rights law", "environmental law" and "trade law", etc. give expression to some such regimes. For interpretative purposes, such regimes may often be considered in their entirety.' Conclusions, *ibid.*

[15] ILC Analytical Study, 72, para. 136.

[16] On the influence of experts on international law, see Martti Koskenniemi, 'The Fate of Public International Law: Between Technique and Politics', *Modern Law Review*, 70 (2000), 1; David Kennedy, 'The Mystery of Global Governance', *Ohio Northern University Law Review*, 34 (2008), 827. See also Andrew T. F. Lang, 'Legal Regimes and Professional Knowledges: The Internal Politics of Regime Definition' in Margaret A. Young (ed.), *Regime Interaction in International Law: Facing Fragmentation* (Cambridge University Press, 2012), 113.

[17] See e.g. Peter Haas, 'Introduction: Epistemic Communities and International Policy Coordination', *International Organization*, 46 (1992), 1.

[18] Andreas Fischer-Lescano and Gunther Teubner, 'Regime-collisions: The Vain Search for Legal Unity in the Fragmentation of Global Law', *Michigan Journal of International Law*, 25 (2004), 999.

[19] See Oran Young, 'The Politics of International Regime Formation: Managing Natural Resources and the Environment', *International Organization*, 43 (1989), 353–4.

accounting more clearly for institutions allows for a greater understanding of the changing nature of sovereignty, not only when such institutions facilitate compliance with international law,[20] but also when they facilitate regime interaction.

Institutions are central in efforts to promote interaction within and between regimes. A surprising array of examples document *intra*-regime co-operation. In the human rights field, for example, NGOs have moved far beyond the original expectations which encapsulated their formal consultative status in order to forge normative development and links between UN human rights bodies.[21] In the environmental field, institutional interplay accompanies a great deal of the growth in norms[22] (otherwise termed 'treaty congestion').[23] The trade regime,[24] private property rights and regulation,[25] indigenous peoples' rights[26] and the protection of cultural expression[27] have all undergone further specialisation and internal fragmentation.

Aside from *intra*-regime interaction, a plethora of examples document the growing normative overlap and institutional co-operation *between* regimes. These are too numerous to list in the current chapter,[28] but notable analyses are available on the links between, for instance,

[20] Abram Chayes and Antonia Handler Chayes, *The New Sovereignty: Compliance with International Regulatory Agreements* (Cambridge, MA: Harvard University Press, 1995).

[21] Dianne Otto, 'Institutional Partnership or Critical Seepages? The Role of Human Rights NGOs in the United Nations' in Mashood A. Baderin and Manisuli Ssenyonjo (eds.), *International Human Rights Law: Six Decades After the UDHR and Beyond* (Aldershot: Ashgate, 2010), 317.

[22] Thomas Gehring and Sebastian Oberthür, 'Institutional Interaction: Ten Years of Scholarly Development' in Sebastian Oberthür and Olav Schram Stokke (eds.), *Managing Institutional Complexity: Regime Interplay and Global Environmental Change* (Cambridge, MA: MIT Press, 2011), 25.

[23] Rüdiger Wolfrum and Nele Matz, *Conflicts in International Environmental Law* (Berlin: Springer-Verlag, 2003), 3 and references cited therein.

[24] Jagdish Bhagwati, *Termites in the Trading System: How Preferential Agreements Undermine Free Trade* (Oxford University Press, 2008), 63.

[25] Steven R. Ratner, 'Regulatory Takings in Institutional Context: Beyond the Fear of Fragmented International Law', *American Journal of International Law*, 102 (2008), 475.

[26] Claire Charters, 'Multi-sourced Equivalent Norms and the Legitimacy of Indigenous Peoples' Rights under International Law' in Tomer Broude and Yuval Shany (eds.), *Multi-sourced Equivalent Norms in International Law* (Oxford: Hart, 2011), 289.

[27] Toshiyuki Kono and Steven van Uytsel (eds.), *The UNESCO Convention on the Diversity of Cultural Expressions: A Tale of Fragmentation in International Law* (Cambridge: Intersentia, 2012).

[28] Especially as one considers how the rhetoric of fragmentation has been used strategically throughout history: Anne-Charlotte Martineau, 'The Rhetoric of Fragmentation: Fear and Faith in International Law', *Leiden Journal of International Law*, 22 (2009), 1.

human rights and humanitarian intervention,[29] climate change and human rights,[30] fisheries agreements and trade law,[31] and biodiversity and forests.[32] These regimes are supported by different (and differently empowered)[33] international organisations, have different (or, at the very least, non-identical) members and came into being with laws that were developed at different times and with different functions. Whilst the most obvious clashes between regimes occur during the settlement of disputes,[34] it is clear that the relations between these regimes extend far beyond the headline act of a tribunal forced to identify priority in conflicting norms.[35] Their on-going interactions are often productive for international law and its beneficiaries,[36] yet also present challenges for sovereignty.

The growth of regimes that are detached from sovereign States (but which still conform to the definition of regimes offered at the start of this part[37]) must also be noted. Certain regimes, such as the indigenous legal arrangements relating to the forest, or 'transnational regimes' motivated by sectoral differentiation such as the law of the internet, are not dependent on States and may even be antagonistic to their interests.[38] Clearly, the interaction of regimes in these contexts gives rise to particular

[29] See e.g. Alexander Orakhelashvili, 'The Interaction between Human Rights and Humanitarian Law: Fragmentation, Conflict, Parallelism, or Convergence?', *European Journal of International Law*, 19 (2008), 161.

[30] Stephen Humphreys, 'Introduction: Human Rights and Climate Change' in Stephen Humphreys (ed.), *Human Rights and Climate Change* (Cambridge University Press, 2009), 1.

[31] Margaret A. Young, *Trading Fish, Saving Fish: The Interaction between Regimes in International Law* (Cambridge University Press, 2011).

[32] Harro van Asselt, 'Managing the Fragmentation of International Environmental Law: Forests at the Intersection of the Climate and Biodiversity Regimes', *New York University Journal of International Law and Politics*, 44 (2012), 1205.

[33] Powers relate not only to enforcement (with the WTO regime notably the strongest), but also to the ability of organisations to establish their own administrative arrangements.

[34] For examples, see Crawford and Nevill, 'Relations between International Courts and Tribunals', 235–60.

[35] See also Jeffrey L. Dunoff, 'A New Approach to Regime Interaction' in Margaret A. Young (ed.), *Regime Interaction in International Law: Facing Fragmentation* (Cambridge University Press, 2012), 136.

[36] Young, 'Introduction: The Productive Friction between Regimes'.

[37] See above n. 9 and associated text.

[38] See Gunther Teubner and Peter Korth, 'Two Kinds of Legal Pluralism: Collision of Transnational Regimes in the Double Fragmentation of World Society' in Margaret A. Young (ed.), *Regime Interaction in International Law: Facing Fragmentation* (Cambridge University Press, 2012), 23.

challenges for sovereignty, especially when private legal regimes seek a global, unifying reach that mirrors aspects of constitutionalism.[39]

The ILC Study Group noted the growth in 'quasi-autonomous normative sources' arising at the international level,[40] and the complexity associated with non-governmental participants and other actors.[41] While its recommendations were addressed to States and accorded with a traditional conception of sovereignty (whereby situations of conflict or interpretation were to be resolved by seeking to ascertain the intentions of States parties), it also concluded its pioneering study by calling for further work to be done on 'the notion and operation of "regimes"'.[42] This wider task animates the present chapter, and the next part considers in greater depth the impact on sovereignty wrought by regime interaction.

B Sovereignty and its demands

The concept of sovereignty, though contested,[43] contains a 'presumption of full governmental authority over a polity and territory'.[44] Sovereignty has historically evolved to attach only to States. Regimes are made up of more than just States: as set out above, they include institutions and those actors possessing relevant functional expertise. Though these non-State actors are central to regime interaction, they do not possess sovereignty. Even less relevant to them is sovereign equality, especially considering the wildly divergent concentrations of power and interests they represent.

Modern sovereignty is currently said to be in crisis, with national authority struggling to retain control over challenges presented by an increased trans-boundary movement of people, capital, information and goods.[45] The establishment of regimes, in part to address the challenges of globalisation, is argued to be a specific threat to sovereignty, given the delegation of power from States to collective agreements.[46] The

[39] See, generally, Christian Joerges, Inger-Johanne Sand and Gunther Teubner (eds.), *Transnational Governance and Constitutionalism* (Oxford: Hart, 2004).

[40] ILC Analytical Study, 249. [41] *Ibid.*, 252. [42] *Ibid.*, 249.

[43] Hent Kalmo and Quentin Skinner, 'Introduction: A Concept in Fragments' in Hent Kalmo and Quentin Skinner (eds.), *Sovereignty in Fragments: The Past, Present and Future of a Contested Concept* (Cambridge University Press, 2011), 1.

[44] Crawford, 'Sovereignty as a Legal Value', 132.

[45] See Richard Joyce, *Competing Sovereignties* (Abingdon: Routledge, 2013), 1–2, and sources therein; see also Stephen Krasner, *Sovereignty: Organized Hypocrisy* (Princeton University Press, 1999), 3.

[46] Thomas M. Franck, 'Can the United States Delegate Aspects of Sovereignty to International Regimes?' in Thomas M. Franck (ed.), *Delegating State Powers: The Effect of Treaty*

counter-argument is that States may (and do) withdraw from regimes, and thus retain their sovereignty in the face of new and emerging international law. In addition, sovereignty may be reinforced by the establishment of regimes that enable States to achieve long-term aims that would otherwise be elusive.[47]

When regimes interact, sovereignty is challenged in a related but slightly different way. At its heart, the challenges posed to sovereignty by regime interaction go to a loss of authority and control by States. If States have ratified the agreements that underpin the interacting regimes, or have otherwise consented to the interaction, sovereignty is not unduly affected. But if the States have not, even *impliedly*, permitted international secretariats to share information, work together, assist in the drafting of new rules, interpret norms or otherwise be influenced by other international regimes, threats to sovereignty may be said to arise. Similar pressures arise when international tribunals within particular regimes take into account laws and material from other regimes in their decisions.

The following examples of regime interaction illustrate the variability of its impacts on sovereignty. Regime interaction apparently most reverential to sovereignty arises if States are members of the relevant regimes before they interact. This situation is promoted by some interpretations of Article 31(3)(c) of the Vienna Convention on Law of Treaties (VCLT),[48] which provides that a treaty may be interpreted with reference to:

> (c) any relevant rules of international law applicable in the relations between the parties.

Though not a mainstream view, a notorious WTO Panel has ruled that Article 31(3)(c) requires overlapping membership between the treaty being interpreted and the treaty (or 'relevant rules') that is said to form the context.[49] According to that Panel, the WTO legal agreements may only be interpreted with reference to other rules of international law, if all

Regimes on Democracy and Sovereignty (New York: Transnational Publishers, 2000), 1. See also Oona Hathaway, 'International Delegation and State Sovereignty', *Law and Contemporary Problems*, 71 (2008), 115.

47 Hathaway, 'International Delegation and State Sovereignty', 141–5.

48 Vienna Convention on the Law of Treaties (Vienna, adopted 22 May 1969, entered into force 27 January 1980), 1155 UNTS 331.

49 Panel Report, *EC – Measures Affecting the Approval and Marketing of Biotech Products* WT/DS291/R, WT/ DS292/R, WT/DS293/R (circulated 29 September 2006), para. 7.68. See further Margaret A. Young, 'The WTO's Use of Relevant Rules of International Law: An Analysis of the *Biotech* Case', *International and Comparative Law Quarterly*, 56 (2007), 907.

WTO members have signed up to those rules. If there is explicit consent by all parties to both sets of regimes, interaction does not unduly affect States parties' rights and duties, and the traditional notion of sovereignty appears to prevail.[50] Yet, like many arguments surrounding sovereignty, the real question is 'whose sovereignty?'[51] On one view, sovereignty is threatened rather than preserved by a rigid prescription of parallel membership. At least notionally, the requirement that regimes have common membership before they share norms grants those States which are *not* members of the relevant regimes a power of veto over the evolution of international law.[52]

A second example also demonstrates apparent fidelity to sovereignty in regime interaction. States often agree that regimes will influence one another, even if they are not parties to all relevant regimes. Rules that allow observer status to international organisations – in negotiations or on-going committee work – are a common feature in bodies such as the WTO, the Food and Agriculture Organisation (FAO) and the Conference of the Parties to the Convention on the International Trade in Endangered Species (CITES).[53] Common membership by States is not a prerequisite to regime interaction, but State consent is.

[50] The domestic analogue to this is a presumption of full policy co-ordination within state agencies, with the state then presenting a united and coherent front to all international regimes. For examples demonstrating the fiction behind such ideals, see Young, *Trading Fish, Saving Fish*, 249–53.

[51] The following statement by the Permanent Court of Justice is often pointed to as a founding argument for sovereignty: 'International law governs relations between independent States. The rules of law binding upon States therefore emanate from their own free will as expressed in conventions or by usages generally accepted as expressing principles of law . . . Restrictions upon the independence of States cannot therefore be presumed.' See *SS Lotus Case (France* v. *Turkey)*, Judgment, 7 September 1927, PCIJ Series A, No. 10 (1927), 18. Yet, as James Crawford points out, the presumption is lessened in external affairs, since the equal rights of other States must be taken into account: James Crawford, 'The Criteria for Statehood in International Law', *British Yearbook of International Law*, 48 (1976), 108. In the *Lotus* case, the Permanent Court was concerned with the freedoms of Turkey (in prosecuting a French officer of the watch after a collision between a French and a Turkish steamship). At Cambridge, we students of James Crawford were prompted to consider how the jurisdictional issue would have been resolved had France's freedoms been at issue.

[52] Margaret A. Young, 'Regime Interaction in Creating, Implementing and Enforcing International Law' in Margaret A. Young (ed.), *Regime Interaction in International Law: Facing Fragmentation* (Cambridge University Press, 2012), 85, 95–6.

[53] Convention on International Trade in Endangered Species of Wild Fauna and Flora (Washington, DC adopted 3 March 1973, entered into force 1 July 1975), 983 UNTS 243. See further *ibid.*, 96–7.

A third set of examples of regime interaction has a less certain link with State consent, and therefore with sovereignty. In one example, the WTO Appellate Body referred to the law of international environmental regimes when interpreting WTO norms in the *US–Shrimp* dispute, notwithstanding a lack of parallel membership.[54] Its secretariat also issued a directive for the submission of *amicus* briefs during highly controversial asbestos litigation between Canada and the European Union – an act that foreshadowed the receipt of information from a range of sources, including NGOs from public health regimes.[55] In determining threats to marine species, the CITES secretariat has collaborated with the FAO on scientific and research data, and ultimately entered into a memorandum of understanding on how CITES may protect such species. Finally, the World Bank's Forest Carbon Partnership Facility has forged links with a range of States and non-State entities to develop capacity in forestry governance, despite the absence of a multilateral forestry convention. These activities are part of attempts to establish programmes to reduce emissions from deforestation and forest degradation (the 'REDD' programmes identified above) through incentives paid by States and funding bodies to particular governments.[56] The World Bank's efforts can be viewed as part of an 'assemblage' that includes local forest dwelling and indigenous communities, merchant banks, agricultural companies, environmental NGOs, satellite remote-sensing experts and State regulators.[57]

These examples may satisfy the direct demands of sovereignty if the relevant international organisations are acting within their powers. According to international law, as developed from the early *Reparations* case,

[54] Appellate Body Report, *United States – Import Prohibition of Certain Shrimp and Shrimp Products* WT/DS58/AB/R (circulated 12 October 1998); the Appellate Body was following norms of interpretation in the VCLT, especially Art. 31(1); see further Young, *Trading Fish, Saving Fish*, 189–240.

[55] Duncan Hollis, 'Private Actors in Public International Law: Amicus Curiae and the Case for the Retention of State Sovereignty', *Boston College International and Comparative Law Review*, 25 (2002), 235.

[56] See International Bank for Reconstruction and Development, *Charter Establishing the Forest Carbon Partnership Facility* (March 2010), Recital B ('[T]he Forest Carbon Partnership Facility [aims] to build partnerships among developed and developing countries, public and private sector entities, international organizations, non-governmental organizations, forest-dependent indigenous peoples and forest dwellers to prepare for possible future systems of positive incentives for REDD, including innovative approaches to sustainable use of forest resources and biodiversity conservation').

[57] William Boyd, 'Climate Change, Fragmentation, and the Challenges of Global Environmental Law: Elements of a Post-Copenhagen Assemblage', *University of Pennsylvania Journal of International Law*, 32 (2010), 457.

international organisations have international legal personality and certain powers may be implied.[58] It may be argued that in situations of legal fragmentation, international inter-governmental organisations impliedly possess relevant powers to interact with other regimes in certain circumstances where such interaction is functionally necessary (just as the United Nations was implied to possess the power to bring an international claim for reparations on behalf of itself and its slain agent). As such, international organisations acting independently of their members in particular circumstances of legal fragmentation do not threaten the sovereignty of their members.

Such a construction, however, does not conform to the current majority view within international institutional law. The International Court of Justice has held that, in construing the implied powers of international organisations, regard will be had to what is functionally necessary given that international organisations have specific specialisations: according to this construction, the World Health Organisation was held *not* to have implied powers to request an advisory opinion on the legality of nuclear weapons, given that this remained the realm of the Security Council.[59] On this view, international competences are parcelled up appropriately as between international organisations, and it will not be necessary for them to interact even as new global issues traversing multiple regimes arise (or at least, if such issues do arise, States parties need to directly consent to inter-regime competences in addressing them).

Apart from the uncertainties surrounding the legal capacity of institutions acting independently from States in situations of regime interaction, threats to sovereignty arise from the enhanced role of experts. These experts are a necessary part of regime interaction (when, for example, data on the decline of fish stocks is sought by the FAO from the CITES secretariat; or when satellite technology and climate modelling is needed by the World Bank to determine REDD recipients). Yet managerial procedures and the resultant decision-making by the privileged and isolated few who are proficient in modes of exchanges between regimes may be part of a wider phenomenon of what has been called a 'technicalisation' of

[58] *Reparation for Injuries Suffered in the Service of the United Nations*, Advisory Opinion, 11 April 1949, ICJ Reports (1949), 174. See further James Crawford, 'International Law as an Open System' in James Crawford, *International Law as an Open System: Selected Essays* (London: Cameron May, 2002), 19–22.

[59] *Legality of the Use by a State of Nuclear Weapons in Armed Conflict*, Advisory Opinion, 8 July 1996, ICJ Reports (1996), 79.

international affairs.[60] Significant risks may arise from allowing experts within regimes greater latitude in regime interplay. The resultant regime interaction may suggest a rational and coherent resolution of global problems, but in fact may be reinforcing a dominant set of preferences that simply further the agenda of particular regimes.[61] While the interests of some powerful States may well be satisfied by this interaction, the interests – and sovereignty – of others are clearly strained.[62] This seems to replay the historical engagement between power and technology that established early forms of sovereignty and territory through mapping and other techniques.[63]

Yet amongst all these pressures on established notions of sovereignty, it must be recognised that the expertise and interests held by non-State actors are often necessary to confront global issues that cross over many regimes. As James Crawford notes, whilst States maintain some monopolies, such as the collective capacity to determine peremptory norms, 'we now reject other claims to State monopoly formerly associated with the doctrine of sovereignty, in particular the monopoly of rights and the monopoly of representation'.[64] Moreover, even if the interests pursued by non-State actors are *not* considered representative of a citizen majority, they may provide useful perspectives for deliberation and debate.[65] Affected stakeholders are often in the best position to review information.[66] Open participation leads to better implementation

60 Koskenniemi, 'The Fate of Public International Law'; see also Martti Koskenniemi, 'International Law: Constitutionalism, Managerialism and the Ethos of Legal Education', *European Journal of Legal Studies*, 1 (2007) (online reference: see www.ejls.eu/1/4UK.pdf); Stephen Toope, 'Emerging Patterns of Governance and International Law' in Michael Byers (ed.), *The Role of Law in International Politics* (Oxford University Press, 2000), 106.

61 Martti Koskenniemi, 'Hegemonic Regimes' in Margaret A. Young (ed.), *Regime Interaction in International Law: Facing Fragmentation* (Cambridge University Press, 2012), 305.

62 For an analysis of how powerful states maintain their dominance in conditions of fragmentation, see Eyal Benvenisti and George W. Downs, 'The Empire's New Clothes: Political Economy and the Fragmentation of International Law', *Stanford Law Review*, 60 (2007), 595.

63 Michael Biggs, 'Putting the State on the Map: Cartography, Territory, and European State Formation', *Comparative Studies in Society and History*, 41 (1999), 399.

64 Crawford, 'International Law as an Open System', 38.

65 See e.g. the call for NGO participation in WTO decision-making to ensure the inclusion of ideas that are 'overlooked or undervalued by governments': Steve Charnovitz, 'WTO Cosmopolitics', *NYU Journal of International Law and Politics*, 34 (2002), 343.

66 Michael Dorf and Charles Sabel, 'A Constitution of Democratic Experimentalism', *Columbia Law Review*, 98 (1998), 267.

of rules,[67] and promotes learning, information-exchange, peer review and cross-forum experimentation across a range of international organisations.[68] The challenge is therefore to identify how the demands of sovereignty can be met through the participation of a multitude of actors besides States in regime interaction.

C How regime interaction can satisfy the demands of sovereignty

This chapter has pointed to the involvement of a range of actors in global issues that traverse the boundaries of multiple international regimes. These include non-State actors advancing divergent interests and expertise in subject areas such as public health (in the case of the *amicus* briefs at the WTO), marine species preservation (in the case of the CITES secretariat), forest subsistence (in the case of indigenous communities) and even wealth maximisation (in the case of merchant banks involved in REDD projects). Their involvement demonstrates that international law is not simply an inter-State system but instead can be viewed as a multiplicity of State and non-State actors participating in a range of globalising processes.[69]

In some examples, States explicitly or impliedly consent to regime interaction, thus satisfying a pure, positivist conception of sovereignty. But in others, non-State actors appear to be participating independently of the wishes of sovereign States. When these actors shape the production of knowledge, determine facts and draw upon law, they join States parties in controlling the intersections between regimes and their outcomes. Can the demands of sovereignty be satisfied in these situations? This part argues in the affirmative, by setting out the necessary legal conditions for international law to address issues of real complexity that cover multiple fields of functional and professional specialisation whilst retaining legitimacy.

[67] See e.g. David Victor, Kal Raustiala and Eugene Skolnikoff, 'Introduction and Overview' in David Victor, Kal Raustiala and Eugene Skolnikoff (eds.), *The Implementation and Effectiveness of International Environmental Commitments: Theory and Practice* (Cambridge, MA: MIT Press, 1998), 21–4.

[68] See e.g. the need for a wide range of inter-governmental organisations, besides the ones with traditional mandates for fisheries, to co-operate on sustainability: Young, *Trading Fish, Saving Fish*, 275.

[69] On multiplicity of actors, see further Saskia Sassen, *Territory, Authority, Rights: From Medieval to Global Assemblages* (Princeton University Press, 2006), 340.

Without direct consent, sovereignty can be satisfied by determining the representative or deliberative credentials of non-State actors according to known public law traditions for assessing accountability.[70] The assessment differs as between international inter-governmental organisations and NGOs. The substance and mode of development of the relevant intersecting norms will also determine the legitimacy of regime interaction. There will be times when legitimacy is not satisfied and it will not be appropriate for international organisations and NGOs to control the interaction between regimes, as set out below.

For international organisations mediating the boundaries between regimes, there is a constant and continuous need for inter-regime scrutiny, not just of the relevant norms but also of the actors conveying those norms. For example, when the CITES secretariat collaborates with the FAO about the status of fish stocks, its recommendations to list species will be subject to a vote by CITES parties.[71] When a WTO Panel draws upon norms developed by international standard-setting bodies, it must determine that the relevant body was open to all WTO members.[72] There are examples when international organisations will determine that the requisite standards for regime interaction are not met. Consider, for example, the World Health Organisation's decision to restrict the involvement of tobacco lobbies in the development of the Framework Convention on Tobacco Control: whilst those lobbies represent 'affected stakeholders', their lack of open, transparent and ethical practices were grounds to deny them participation.[73]

This legal framework for regime interaction posits a kind of gatekeeper role for relevant international organisations to use norms that are exogenous to their own regime. International organisations are empowered to have regard to whether there is a high degree of international consensus

[70] The following is developed from what I have argued to be a 'legal framework for regime interaction' in the context of fisheries governance: see Young, 'Regime Interaction in Creating, Implementing and Enforcing International Law', 98–109. See further, Young, *Trading Fish, Saving Fish*, 241–306.

[71] Young, *Trading Fish, Saving Fish*, 278.

[72] Relatedly, standard setting bodies are also encouraged to operate with open, impartial and transparent procedures: see WTO Doc. G/TBT/1/Rev.8 (Decision of the TBT Committee on Principles for the Development of International Standards, Guides and Recommendations), discussed in Young, *Trading Fish, Saving Fish*, 279.

[73] World Health Organisation, Report of the Committee of Experts on Tobacco Industry Documents, 'Tobacco Company Strategies to Undermine Tobacco Control Activities at the World Health Organization' (July 2000), 244, cited in Young, *Trading Fish, Saving Fish*, 283–4.

to those norms. This may include inquiries into whether the norm has been agreed by a range of developing countries as well as developed countries. The substance of the norm will also dictate its relevance: for example, where norms developed by transnational regimes exhibit a 'tunnel vision' that disregards broader questions of public interest more commonly absorbed in the norms of national legal systems, this may lessen its relevance.[74] Moreover, whether the norm was *itself* developed in an open and accessible way is relevant in a decision to accord it influence.[75]

The gatekeeper role of international organisations also requires them to assess the deliberative credentials of NGOs wishing to influence regime interaction. Such assessment will have regard to an NGO's relevant functions, constituencies and intended beneficiaries and also ask whether it operates in an open, accessible, transparent and participatory way.[76] Disclosure of funding, as required by some but not all international organisations, would seem necessary in this process.[77] Private bodies that seek to accredit NGOs[78] can provide evidence of good practice, in a tantalising example of sovereignty being strengthened by non-State processes.

This suggestion of a mediating role for international organisations accords with sociological theories of Gunter Teubner and others who support polycentric constitutionalism, where State-based norm-generative processes are supplemented and sometimes supplanted by processes within particular regimes.[79] As has been observed within those theories, the State continues to play an important role in such processes.[80] Sovereignty remains important even if it is somewhat hidden under layers

[74] Teubner and Korth, 'Two Kinds of Legal Pluralism'.

[75] *Cf.* the OECD, which is a closed group representing only thirty developed countries; see further Young, *Trading Fish, Saving Fish*, 282.

[76] See Sasha Courville, 'Understanding NGO-based Social and Environmental Regulatory Systems: Why We Need New Models of Accountability' in Michael W. Dowdle (ed.), *Public Accountability: Designs, Dilemmas and Experiences* (Cambridge University Press, 2006), 271.

[77] The United Nations, for example, requires NGOs to provide details about funding, but the World Intellectual Property Organisation does not. See further Young, *Trading Fish, Saving Fish*, 282–3. The guidelines issued by the WTO Appellate Body in the *EC-Asbestos* appeal (see above n. 55 and surrounding text) required *amicus* briefs to state the nature of their interest.

[78] See e.g. the International Social and Environmental Accreditation Alliance (ISEAL Alliance), available at www.isealalliance.org.

[79] See Gunther Teubner, 'Constitutionalizing Polycontexturality', *Social and Legal Studies*, 20 (2011), 210.

[80] Gert Verschraegen, 'Hybrid Constitutionalism, Fundamental Rights and the State: A Response to Gunther Teubner', *Netherlands Journal of Legal Philosophy*, 40 (2011), 216.

of other legal – or even constitutionalising – activities. However, sovereignty may be said to rise to the surface in some particular situations of normative conflict. For example, when intersecting regimes involve indigenous norms, the resulting clashes between the social embeddedness of legal systems of indigenous societies and the formal law of modern international regimes are not resolvable through general conflict rules.[81] Instead, institutionalised and proceduralised protection of the basic rights of those groups that are otherwise marginalised is more appropriate. In mediating regime interaction in REDD policies, for example, the inclusion of the interests of indigenous and forest-dwelling communities must, at the very least, require prior informed consent and benefit-sharing. While such guarantees are beginning to be located in international regimes,[82] the fulfilment of such rights for indigenous peoples often depends once again on laws and processes within sovereign States.

These arguments for a legal framework of regime interaction seek to safeguard an attenuated form of sovereignty. The framework prioritises administrative law-type procedures of openness, transparency and reason-giving,[83] although these procedures operate at the level of regimes rather than within internal regulatory agencies.[84] The emphasis on inclusivity in situations of polycontextuality also follows existing literature on transnational governance, which rests an ideal of democratic legitimacy on the involvement of a broad sphere of actors.[85] An extension of these ideas could even found a renewed set of sovereign responsibilities, which require States to be *other-regarding* in their dealings with intersecting

[81] Teubner and Korth, 'Two Kinds of Legal Pluralism'.

[82] See Nagoya Protocol on Access to Genetic Resources and the Fair and Equitable Sharing of Benefits Arising from their Utilisation to the Convention on Biological Diversity, foreshadowed in Teubner and Konth, 'Two Kinds of Legal Pluralism', 52; see also the United Nations Declaration on the Rights of Indigenous Peoples, A/RES/61/295, 2 October 2007 and UNFCCC Cancun Agreement, Decision 1/CP. 16, FCCC/CP/2010/7/Add. 1 (2010), Appendix I.

[83] For related attempts to locate accountability structures in non-traditional sites of globalised law-making, see Benedict Kingsbury, Nico Krisch and Richard Stewart, 'The Emergence of Global Administrative Law', *Law and Contemporary Problem*, 68 (2005), 15.

[84] On the classification of norms from global administrative law, see Teubner, 'Constitutionalizing Polycontexturality', 219.

[85] Patrizia Nanz, 'Democratic Legitimacy and Constitutionalisation of Transnational Trade Governance: A View from Political Theory' in Christian Joerges and Ernst-Ulrich Petersmann (eds.), *Constitutionalism, Multilevel Trade Governance and Social Regulation* (Oxford: Hart, 2006), 80; see also Inger-Johanne Sand, 'Polycontextuality as an Alternative to Constitutionalism' in Christian Joerges, Inger-Johanne Sand and Gunther Teubner (eds.), *Transnational Governance and Constitutionalism* (Oxford: Hart, 2004), 41.

regimes.[86] The promotion of structures of accountability for States and non-State actors is necessary within an enriched theory of sovereignty that allows international law to better address global complexity.

Conclusion

While noting the stability and continuity of sovereignty as a key notion of international law, James Crawford also recognises that in times of vast political change, international law will change. He notes, '[t]he difficulty is to envision appropriate forms of change, and at the same time to hold to those aspects of international law which embody the stable outcomes of the interaction between peoples, societies and their governments over many years'.[87] This chapter demonstrates that the modern phenomenon of fragmentation, which has seen international law develop into myriad regimes of different specialisations, norms, memberships and scope, leads to challenges for sovereignty. Global problems do not fall neatly into existing regimes, and international organisations and other actors must often work together, or at least concurrently, on global issues. If sovereignty demands that the consent of States underlies the flow of norms and the shaping of knowledge between regimes, such activities cannot be accounted for. Nor can a purely positivist conception of sovereignty account for situations of normative pluralism when the relevant intersecting regimes include private transnational arrangements, or indigenous systems, some of which have developed separately from, or specifically without, national support.

This chapter has argued that these challenges to sovereignty can be met by structures of accountability that ensure the accessibility and participation of a range of State and non-State actors. Such a system builds on already established roles of international organisations, and provides them with guidance in mediating the norms and practices of exogenous regimes. It also acknowledges situations where participation is legitimately denied, if international organisations and NGOs fail to demonstrate requisite credentials and credibility. Furthermore, for special situations of indigenous systems, substantive protections may also be necessary. In current and

[86] For one examination of whether sovereigns must incorporate in their decision-making the concerns of those they affect, see Eyal Benvenisti, 'Sovereigns as Trustees of Humanity: On the Accountability of States to Foreign Stakeholders', *American Journal of International Law*, 107 (2013), 295.

[87] James Crawford, 'Democracy and International Law', *British Yearbook of International Law*, 63 (1993), 113, 133.

emerging situations of regime interplay, including between forestry governance and carbon markets, health and trade and fisheries management and conservation, State sovereignty may co-exist, and even be strengthened, by such arrangements. The interaction of regimes in situations of legal fragmentation, if based on an open, but rigorous, conception of membership and participation, can ensure the viability and application of international law to the issues of our day.

5

The legitimacy of investment treaties

Between Exit, Voice and James Crawford's quest for a more democratic international law

LLUÍS PARADELL TRIUS

Introduction

In the last decade, controversy has arisen regarding the compatibility of investment protection treaties and the ICSID Convention with national constitutions and State sovereignty. The focus of concerns has been the alleged lack of equality, transparency, predictability and accountability of investor–State arbitration under those treaties.[1] Horacio Rosatti, former attorney general of Argentina, was among the first to complain in 2003, when starting to defend Argentina from the avalanche of investment treaty claims brought by investors aggrieved by Argentina's 2002 measures to fight its economic crisis.[2]

Many more similar comments of unease followed suit in Argentina, including a book by the judge of the Supreme Court, Carlos Fayt.[3] Draft laws were prepared by Argentine MPs to declare bilateral investment treaties (BITs) unconstitutional.[4] Further, while Colombian and Bolivian courts heard and rejected constitutional challenges against investment treaties,[5] in Ecuador some BITs were declared unconstitutional and

[1] e.g. Public Statement on the International Investment Regime, 31 August 2010, available at www.osgoode.yorku.ca/public_statement.

[2] Horacio D. Rosatti, 'Los tratados bilaterales de inversión: el arbitraje internacional obligatorio y el sistema constitucional argentino', *La Ley*, 58 (2003), 1.

[3] Carlos S. Fayt, *La Constitución Nacional y los tribunales internacionales de arbitraje* (Buenos Aires: La Ley, 2007).

[4] e.g. Draft Law 4504-S-04, presented by Senator Capitanich in February 2005 and 532-S-05 presented by Senator Müller in March 2005.

[5] Sentencia de la Corte Constitucional de Colombia C-294/02, 23 April 2002, available at http://corte-constitucional.vlex.com.co/vid/-43618351. Sentencia del Tribunal Constitucional de Bolivia sobre constitucionalidad de leyes ratificadoras de Convenios y

others are still under review in Ecuador.[6] In Canada, NAFTA Chapter 11 investment protections were also attacked as unconstitutional.[7] Australia announced in 2011 that it would no longer include investor–State arbitration in its trade agreements, given its impact on State sovereignty.[8] Recently, a columnist of the UK newspaper *The Guardian* mounted a furious attack on the investment protection chapter of the EU–US Transatlantic Trade and Investment Partnership, which is being negotiated, because it 'would let rapacious companies subvert our laws, rights and national sovereignty' and 'kill regulations protecting people and the living planet'.[9] Professor Martti Koskenniemi has also argued that this agreement is 'a transfer of power from public authorities to an arbitration body, where a handful of people would be able to rule whether a country can enact a law or not and how the law must be interpreted'.[10]

The complaints have often been tainted by ideological opinions and political interests. Disapproval of investment treaties by States has frequently been a reaction to being sued under such treaties. The opposition to open market policies may also have influenced the doctrinal charge against the investment treaty regime. Thus, the critics have in turn been attacked for echoing prejudice and preconception, or at least an overstated and one-sided focus on the shortcomings of investment treaty arbitration, under the banner of the system's 'legitimacy crisis', rather than engaging in more fine-grained analysis.[11] Empirical research, in turn, has shown

Tratados, No. 0031/2006, 10 May 2006, available at http://italaw.com/sites/default/files/treaty-interpretations/ita0940.pdf.

6 'Ecuadorian Constitutional Court rulings on the constitutionality of UK, German, Chinese and Finish bilateral investment treaties', Investment Arbitration Reporter, 28 August 2010, available at http://iareporter.com/articles/20100830_2; 'Ecuador to Set Up Commission to Audit Bilateral Investment Treaties', *Practical Law Arbitration*, 16 October 2013.

7 Ontario Supreme Court of Justice, *The Council of Canadians et al.* v. *Her Majesty in Right of Canada*, Decision of 8 July 2005 and Ontario Court of Appeal Decision of 30 November 2006, available at http://italaw.com/sites/default/files/treaty-interpretations/ita0941.pdf.

8 Gillard Government Trade Policy Statement, 'Trading Our Way to More Jobs and Prosperity' (Department of Foreign affairs and Trade, April 2011), available at http://blogs.usyd.edu.au/japaneselaw/2011_Gillard%20Govt%20Trade%20Policy%20Statement.pdf.

9 George Monbiot, 'This Transatlantic Trade Deal is a Full-frontal Assault on Democracy', *The Guardian*, 4 November 2013.

10 'Professor Martti Koskenniemi: Finland's Legislative Power May Be in Jeopardy', *Helsinki Times*, 16 December 2013, available at http://www.helsinkitimes.fi/finland/finland-news/domestic/8717-professor-finland-s-legislative-power-may-be-in-jeopardy.html.

11 Devashish Krishan, 'Thinking about BITs and BIT Arbitration: The Legitimacy Crisis that Never Was' in Todd Weiler and Freya Baetens (eds.), *New Directions in International*

(arguably) that States often prevail in investment treaty cases, so that the concern that investment treaties unduly constrain sovereignty and regulatory action may be somewhat exaggerated.[12]

There is no intention here to join either side of the debate, but to suggest that its mere existence should give pause for thought. Similar legitimacy issues have arisen in relation to other areas of international law and other international norm-generation institutions, like the WTO, the free trade provisions of the NAFTA and the international criminal courts.[13] Monroe Leigh's contention that due-process concerns generated by some of the decisions of the existing war crimes tribunals indicated the need 'to commence a campaign to add a Bill of Rights to the UN Charter'[14] is reminiscent of the familiar debate on the need to incorporate human rights protections in European Community law. Hence, 'critical transnational constitutional crises'[15] are not unheard of.

Two precedents of legitimacy crises will be reviewed here: the debate in US law in the 1950s and '60s on the constitutionality of human rights' treaties in the context of the civil rights movement; and the constitutionality problems linked to the supremacy of European Community (EC) law

Economic Law: In Memoriam Thomas Wälde (Leiden: Martinus Nijhoff, 2011), 107, providing a long list of references at n. 32.

[12] For empirical research see Susan Franck, 'Empirically Evaluating Claims about Investment Treaty Arbitration', *North Carolina Law Review*, 86 (2007), 1; Susan Franck, 'Empiricism and International Law: Insights for Investment Treaty Dispute Resolution', *Virginia Journal of International Law*, 48 (2008), 767; Susan Franck, 'Development and Outcomes of Investment Treaty Arbitration', *Harvard International Law Journal*, 50 (2009), 435; Kassi Tallent, 'State Responsibility by the Numbers: Towards an Understanding of the Prevalence of the Latin America Countries in Investment Arbitration', *Transnational Dispute Management*, 1 (2010).

[13] Paul D. Marquardt, 'Law without Borders: The Constitutionality of an International Criminal Court', *Columbia Journal of Transnational Law*, 33 (1995), 73; Gordon A. Christenson and Kimberly Gambrel, 'Constitutionality of Binational Panel Review in Canada–U.S. Free Trade Agreement', *International Lawyer*, 23 (1989), 401; Bruce Ackerman and David Golove, 'Is NAFTA Constitutional?', *Harvard Law Review*, 108 (1995), 4; John Jackson, 'The Great 1994 Sovereignty Debate: United States Acceptance and Implementation of the Uruguay Round Results', *Columbia Journal of Transnational Law*, 36 (1997), 157; Steven Croley and John Jackson, 'WTO Dispute Procedures, Standard of Review, and Deference to National Governments', *American Journal of International Law*, 90 (1996), 193; Robert Kushen and Kenneth Harris, 'Surrender of Fugitives by the United States to the War Crimes Tribunals for Yugoslavia and Rwanda', *American Journal of International Law*, 90 (1996), 510.

[14] Monroe Leigh, 'The Yugoslav Tribunal: Use of Unnamed Witnesses against Accused', *American Journal of International Law*, 90 (1996), 238.

[15] W. Michael Reisman, 'Introductory Remarks', Symposium: Constitutionalism in the Post-Cold War World, *Yale Journal of International Law*, 19 (1994), 192.

in EC Member States. The US controversy resulted in the non-ratification by the US of human rights' treaties, and still today international law has a somewhat precarious status in the US legal system. Conversely, the EC debate resulted in the reinforcement of the EC system through dialogue and cross-fertilisation between national courts and the European Court of Justice (ECJ).

The suggestion in this chapter is that the investment treaty regime may learn some lessons from these crises. Before delving further into them, however, a brief explanation of the framework for the analysis is needed.

The Exit and Voice dichotomy, and James Crawford's quest for a more democratic international law

The disparity of approaches to an international regime's legitimacy crisis may be explained by the dichotomy between 'Exit' and 'Voice', used by Joseph Weiler to explain some of the dynamics in the EC legal order: 'Exit is the mechanism of organizational abandonment in the face of unsatisfactory performance. Voice is the mechanism of intraorganizational correction and recuperation.'[16] Thus, the legitimacy and constitutionality problems of international regimes may lead to opposite forces: withdrawal from the system (Exit) or demand for more participation (Voice). The greater the opportunities for Voice, the less the tendency for Exit.

In investment arbitration Exit has already appeared in the form of denunciation of the ICSID Convention[17] and termination of some BITs.[18] Voice too has been felt in the amendment of model investment treaties,[19] the issuance of biding interpretations of their provisions[20] and the participation of States as non-disputing parties in some cases. But the question here is whether the dynamics of Voice may also be heard on a day-to-day basis in the case law of investment treaty tribunals, in the way they

16 Joseph H. H. Weiler, 'The Transformation of Europe', *Yale Law Journal*, 100 (1991), 2411.

17 Denunciations by Bolivia (16 May 2007), Ecuador (5 December 2007) and Venezuela (26 January 2012). See https://icsid.worldbank.org/ICSID/ICSID/ViewNewsReleases.jsp.

18 'Ecuadorian President Reportedly Asks Congress to Terminate 13 Bits; Move Comes on Heels of Earlier Termination of Multiple BITs', *Investment Arbitration Reporter*, 30 October 2009, available at www.iaireporter.com/articles/20091124_8.

19 See e.g. the modification of the US Model BIT in 2012, available at www.ustr.gov/about-us/press-office/press-releases/2012/april/united-states-concludes-review-model-bilateral-inves.

20 e.g. North American Free Trade Agreement, Notes of Interpretation of Certain Chapter 11 Provisions, NAFTA Free Trade Commission, 31 July 2001, available at www.sice.oas.org/tpd/nafta/Commission/CH11understanding_e.asp.

integrate national legal concepts and interact with domestic courts. If so, the tendency for Exit may be mitigated.

Inspiration is drawn, as ever, from James Crawford, my esteemed professor and mentor, an exceptional man and friend who has made international law and to whom this modest contribution is dedicated. Now that he is retiring from his chair as Whewell Professor of International Law at the University of Cambridge, I want to recall his inaugural lecture back in 1993, entitled 'Democracy in International Law', which I had the pleasure to attend and which influenced my PhD thesis on the interaction between international law and national constitutions, supervised by him.[21] In that lecture he addressed a number of facets of the relationship between international law and democratic principles. One of his arguments was to question the continuing acceptability of the rule of international law which provides that, except for treaties entered into in manifest violation of a rule of constitutional law of fundamental importance, national constitutional standards do not affect the international validity of international commitments and obligations.[22] In his lecture James referred to this rule as one of the 'deeply undemocratic features of classical international law'.[23]

No doubt the traditional rule of irrelevance of domestic law is required at a practical level, for international law to be able to function as a legal system binding its subjects, the States. However, at a more conceptual level this paradigm may not be fit for the increasing overlap between international and national constitutional law. Hence in 1997 James wrote as follows:

> [T]he relation between the international and constitutional levels can be reciprocal, and if there is to be a 'constitutionalisation' of international law and treaty making – which their effects on the individual increasingly seems to call for – it may occur by way of the co-opting of national constitutional limitations in the interests of international regularity.[24]

[21] Lluís Paradell Trius, 'International Law in National Legal Systems: Constitutional Obstacles and Opportunities', *TDM* 5 (2005).

[22] Arts. 27 and 46 of the 1969 Vienna Convention of the Law of Treaties (Vienna, adopted 22 May 1969, entered into force 27 January 1980), 1155 UNTS 331.

[23] James Crawford, *Democracy in International Law* (Cambridge University Press, 1994), 8 (reprinted in *British Yearbook of International Law*, 64 (1993), 113).

[24] James Crawford, 'International Law and Australian Federalism: Past, Present and Future' in Brian Opeskin and Donald R. Rothwell (eds.), *International Law and Australian Federalism* (Carlton: Melbourne University Press, 1997), 325.

The demands of national constitutions cannot be ignored if developments in international law, notably its growing concern with the relationship between the State and the individual, are to be accepted. Some fundamental principles of national constitutions may be externalised and thus condition the development of international law. As public power is exercised and reviewed internationally, and international law is in many domains reconceived as a system of public law, constitutional principles may operate as constraints on international or supranational action, thereby reinforcing its legitimacy. If these dynamics appear, then Voice prevails over Exit. Conversely, exaggerated criticism leads to Exit, which represents the defeat of the fruitful interaction between international law and national law.

The risks of Exit: international law in US civil rights litigation

Writing in 1948, Paul Sayre criticised the Supreme Court landmark decision in *Shelley* v. *Kraemer* (1948)[25] because it had neglected to refer to the US obligations under the UN Charter as a basis for refusing to judicially enforce a racially restrictive covenant relating to private property. He added that the UN Charter 'is now not only part of our constitution, but by our constitutional act we are part of the United Nations . . . we are morally and legally bound to give them [the Charter's provisions] all full effect all the time'.[26] These were the early days of the American civil rights movement, in which civil liberties groups filed suits in both state and federal courts citing the Universal Declaration of Human Rights and Articles 55 and 56 of the UN Charter to challenge racial discrimination.[27] According to these human rights clauses of the Charter, each member pledges itself to promote, and to take action for the achievement of, 'universal respect for, and observance of, human rights and fundamental freedoms for all without distinction as to race, sex, language, or religion'.

Sayre's contention seemed to find immediate support in two judicial decisions. In *Oyama* v. *California* (1948), the Supreme Court found that the California Alien Land Law, as applied to the case, deprived the applicant of the equal protection by discriminating against citizens of Japanese

[25] *Shelley* v. *Kraemer*, 334 US 1 (1948).
[26] Paul Sayre, '*Shelley* v. *Kraemer* and United Nations Law', *Iowa Law Review*, 34 (1948), 1.
[27] See generally Bert B. Lockwood, 'The United Nations Charter and United States Civil Rights Litigation: 1946–1955', *Iowa Law Review*, 69 (1984), 901.

origin.[28] The opinion did not reach the question of constitutionality of the Law, nor did it cite the UN Charter. However, two separate concurring opinions, in which four of the justices joined, not only mentioned the Charter but would have struck down the Law partially as infringing the international obligations there assumed.[29] These arguments were extensively relied on by the Oregon Supreme Court in *Namba* v. *McCourt* (1949).[30] In this decision, the Oregon Alien Land Law was held unconstitutional as racially discriminatory in violation of the equal protection clause of the Fourteenth Amendment, interpreted in the light of the UN Charter human rights provisions.[31]

This initial trend was to be halted by the landmark 1952 decision of the California Supreme Court in *Sei Fujii* v. *State* (1952).[32] The case concerned a challenge by a Japanese resident in California against the validity of the California Alien Land Law, which discriminated against Japanese landowners. It was alleged that the Law was racially discriminatory and that it violated Articles 1, 55 and 56 of the United Nations Charter, as well as the equal protection clause of the Fourteenth Amendment. The California District Court of Appeal held that the constitutional arguments would fail on the grounds of the authority of Supreme Court case law upholding the constitutionality of alien land laws, and went on to strike down the Law as infringing the human rights provisions of the UN Charter.[33]

This decision was followed by vivid controversy and widespread criticism, generated in particular by those that sought to prevent bringing an end to racial segregation by international agreement.[34] Together with

[28] *Oyama* v. *California*, 332 US 633 (1948).

[29] *Ibid.*, 649–50 (Black, J., concurring), 673 (Murphy, J., concurring).

[30] *Namba* v. *McCourt*, 204 P2d 569 (1949).

[31] *Ibid.*, 579.

[32] *Sei Fujii* v. *State*, 217 P2d 481 (Cal D Ct App 1950), rehearing denied 218 P2d 595 (1950), affirmed on other grounds 242 P2d 617 (1952).

[33] *Ibid.*, 217 P2d 481, 484–8 (Cal D Ct App 1950).

[34] See on the controversy e.g. George Finch, 'The Need to Restrain the Treaty-making Power of the United States within Constitutional Limits', *American Journal of International Law*, 48 (1954), 57; Quincy Wright, 'National Courts and Human Rights: The Fujii Case', *American Journal of International Law*, 45 (1951), 62; Oscar Schachter, 'The Charter and the Constitution: The Human Rights Provisions in American Law', *Vanderbilt Law Review*, 4 (1951), 643. See also Lockwood, 'The United Nations Charter and United States Civil Rights Litigation: 1946–1955', 924 *et seq.* The main criticism of the decision came from the American Bar Association as reflected in the pages of its journal. See e.g. Frank E. Holman, 'Treaty Law-making: A Blank Check for Writing a New Constitution', *American Bar Association Journal*, 36 (1950), 707; and Frank Ober, 'The Treaty-making and Amendment Powers: Do They Protect Our Fundamental Rights?', *American Bar Association Journal*, 36 (1950), 715.

the US signature of the Convention on the Prevention and Punishment of Genocide in 1948,[35] concern arose that international commitments might undermine State sovereignty, national autonomy and the US form of government. This set off a campaign to limit the treaty power, culminating in the proposed Bricker Amendment, which would have made all treaties non-self-executing.[36]

In response to all this debate, the California Supreme Court affirmed the lower court's decision solely on constitutional grounds, and held the human rights clauses of the UN Charter to be non-self-executing.[37] The Court found the Charter provisions to be vague and lacking the intent necessary to make them self-executing. The examination of the position taken by the US negotiators, and by the political branches in ratifying the Charter, led also to the conclusion that the US had not undertaken an immediate obligation to supersede conflicting national legislation. Thus, the Court held that the provisions Charter's invoked were not intended to become rules of law for the judiciary to apply.[38]

The debate around the self-executing doctrine generated by the *Fujii* case and the Bricker Amendment exerted very considerable influence thereafter. The US did not ratify any major human rights treaty until 1986. Since then it has ratified the Genocide Convention in 1986, the Convention Against Torture and Other Cruel, Inhuman or Degrading Treatment or Punishment in 1990, the International Covenant on Civil and Political Rights in 1992 and the Convention of the Elimination of All Forms of Racial Discrimination in 1994. However, ratification has been subjected to comprehensive reservations which raise questions about the seriousness of the US's commitment, and to declarations establishing that the treaties are non-self-executing.

The constitutionality of these declarations is doubtful because they prevent judges from applying treaty law, for which they are empowered by the Constitution, and which contradicts the purpose of the Supremacy Clause.[39] In any case, this episode evidences the risks linked to Exit. As a result of the *Fujii* case and the ensuing controversy, courts revitalised and expanded the self-executing treaty doctrine to hold a series of human

[35] But not ratified (Senate advice and consent) until 1986.

[36] See Ch. 1, nn. 29 *et seq.*, and accompanying text.

[37] *Sei Fujii* v. *State*, 242 P2d 617 (1952). [38] *Ibid.*, 619–22.

[39] See Thomas Buergenthal, 'Modern Constitutions and Human Rights Treaties', *Columbia Journal of Transnational Law*, 36 (1997), 211; and Louis Henkin, 'U.S. Ratification of Human Rights Conventions: The Ghost of Senator Bricker', *American Journal of International Law*, 89 (1995), 341.

rights treaties to be non-self-executing.[40] International law was ousted from the civil rights litigation, and as a consequence it probably took longer for US racial segregation to end, even if the UN Charter may have had an indirect effect on the civil rights jurisprudence.[41] More generally, courts discovered the use of the doctrine of non-self-executing treaties to circumvent the consequences that the enforcement of treaty obligations may have upon internal law.

This is why multilateral treaties, with much greater impact in internal law than bilateral treaties, are almost always regarded as non-self-executing in US law.[42] Whenever the position of the US government is opposed to the enforcement of a treaty provision, or the latter may bring the court in conflict with, or embarrass, the political branches, courts may find a way out by determining the provisions of a treaty non-self-executing. In these situations courts avoid deciding substantive international law issues that cases may raise, so that the non-self-executing doctrine serves the same purpose as the 'political question' doctrine. The controlling rationale for both is the courts' understanding of the demands of the constitutional separation of powers: the need to preserve the authority of the political organs in matters which have been considered particularly within their competence.[43]

[40] *Vlissidis* v. *Anadell*, 262 F2d 398 (7th Cir, 1959) (Arts. 55 and 56 of the UN Charter non-self-executing); *Pauling* v. *McElroy*, 164 FSupp 390 (1958), affirmed 278 F2d 252 (DC Cir, 1960), certiorari denied 364 US 835 (1960) (same); *Camacho* v. *Rogers*, 199 FSupp 155, 158 (SDNY 1961) (same); *Frolova* v. *USSR*, 761 F2d 370, 374 (7th Cir, 1985) (same); *In re Alien Children Educ. Litig.*, 501 FSupp 544, 590 (SD Tex 1980), affirmed mem. (5th Cir, 1981), affirmed sub nom. *Plyler* v. *Doe*, 457 US 202 (1982) (OAS Charter non-self-executing); *Bertrand* v. *Sava*, 684 F2d 204, 218–19 (2nd Cir, 1982) (Refugees Protocol non-self-executing); *Spiess* v. *C. Itoh & Co. (America), Inc.*, 643 F2d 353 (5th Cir, 1981) (UN Charter non-self-executing).

[41] Lockwood, 'The United Nations Charter and United States Civil Rights Litigation: 1946–1955', 901.

[42] See e.g. *United States* v. *Postal*, 589 F2d 862 (5th Cir, 1979), certiorari denied 444 US 832 (1979); and *People of Saipan* v. *United States Dept of Interior*, 502 F2d 90 (9th Cir, 1974), certiorari denied 420 US 1003 (1975). See also Stefan Riesenfeld, 'The Doctrine of Self-Executing Treaties and *U.S.* v. *Postal*: Win at Any Price?', *American Journal of International Law*, 74 (1980), 892; and Richard Lillich and Hurst Hannum, 'Linkages between International Human Rights and U.S. Constitutional Law', *American Journal of International Law*, 79 (1985), 161.

[43] Thomas Buergenthal, 'Self-executing and Non-self-executing Treaties in National and International Law', *Collected Courses of the Hague Academy of International Law*, 235 (1992), 303; Charles Stotter, 'Self-executing Treaties and the Human Rights Provisions of the United Nations Charter: A Separation of Powers Problem', *Buffalo Law Review*, 25 (1976), 773; Wright, 'National Courts and Human Rights: The Fujii Case', 62; Carlos

The potential and fruitful interaction between international law and national law, including constitutional law, came out unfulfilled. One example is that while an increasing number of States favour the normativity of international law, notably human rights law, by resorting to it in interpreting 'open – textured' provisions of the national constitution, this trend is much less perceptible in the United States. In particular, the Supreme Court has shown considerable disinclination towards using international instruments as a guiding principle for constitutional interpretation.

In *Stanford* v. *Kentucky* (1989), for instance, the question of the relevance of international and comparative law for constitutional interpretation was raised before the Court in a case concerning the imposition of capital punishment upon juveniles aged sixteen and seventeen. The Supreme Court examined whether the punishment was contrary to 'evolving standards of decency that mark the progress of a maturing society', the criterion for the determination of the infringement of the Eighth Amendment's prohibition against cruel and usual punishment. The majority's opinion, written by Justice Scalia, held that in examining the 'evolving standard of decency' only US conceptions of decency were relevant, and refused to take into consideration comparative and international law practice in connection with the death penalty.[44]

The virtues of Voice: constitutional dialogues in the EC legal order

It is well known that EC law has evolved 'into a vertically-integrated legal regime conferring judicially enforceable rights and obligations on all legal persons and entities, public and private, within EC territory'.[45] This evolution was not explicitly envisaged by the founding treaties, but

Manuel Vázquez, 'The Four Doctrines of Self-Executing Treaties', *American Journal of International Law*, 89 (1995), 696, 722–3 (argues that the doctrine has an 'allocation of powers function', and is thus a matter of the proper institutional role of national courts).

44 *Stanford* v. *Kentucky*, 492 US 361, 369 n. 1 (1989). This decision contrasts with the earlier one in *Thompson* v. *Oklahoma*, 487 US 815, 821 (1988), another case concerning the execution of juveniles, in which a different Supreme Court majority had favoured the use of international and comparative law in eighth amendment analysis. The new majority in the Supreme Court abandoned any attempt to reconcile international and internal law regarding the death penalty, and tended to exacerbate the differences between the two legal orders. See generally Joan Fitzpatrick, 'The Relevance of Customary International Norms to the Death Penalty in the United States', *Georgia Journal of International and Comparative Law*, 25 (1995–6).

45 Alec Stone Sweet, 'Constitutional Dialogues in the European Community' in Anne-Marie Slaughter, Alec Stone Sweet and Joseph H. H. Weiler (eds.), *European Court and the*

resulted, first and foremost, from a series of landmark decisions of the ECJ starting in the 1960s which established the doctrines of direct effect and supremacy of EC law in national legal systems, pre-emption, interpretation of national law in conformity with EC law, and the doctrine of governmental liability for failure to properly implement EC law.[46]

The deepening legal integration involved the need for national legal orders to come to terms with the vast constitutional implications of European Community integration. Recognition of the Community order meant the introduction of EC law among the sources of national law, with primacy over them; the transfer of law-making powers, policy determination authority and executive competences to Community institutions in ever-expanding fields; as well as, in many cases, the reinforcement of the judicial branch by introducing the principle of judicial review of the consistency of national legislation with EC law.

The alteration of the national constitutional structures and their adaptation to the EC legal order was achieved primarily by constitutional interpretation, effectuated by the supreme and constitutional courts of the Member States.[47] In some cases, constitutions contained provisions permitting limitations of sovereignty and transfers of sovereign powers to international organisations.[48] In other cases, such general clauses on membership of international organisations were adopted with the prospect of the country's participation or accession to the EC.[49] These rules were interpreted extensively so as to legitimise the constitutional

National Courts – Doctrine and Jurisprudence: Legal Change in its Social Context (Oxford: Hart, 1998), 306.

46 On these developments see, among many others, *ibid.*; Weiler, 'The Transformation of Europe', 2403; Jean-Victor Louis, *L'Ordre juridique communautaire*, 5th edn (Luxembourg: Office des publications officielles des Communautés européennes, 1990).

47 For an excellent and comprehensive description of the reception of the EC 'constitutional' doctrines in the various legal orders of the Member States see Henry Schermers and Denis Waelbroeck, *Judicial Protection in the European Communities* (Deventer: Kluwer, 1992). See also Thibaut de Berranger, *Constitutions nationales et construction communautaire* (Paris: LGDJ, 1995); and Santiago Muñoz Machado, *La Unión europea y las mutaciones del Estado* (Madrid: Alianza Universidad, 1993).

48 Art. 11, Italian Constitution (1948); Art. 24(1), German Constitution (1949); Para. 15, Preamble to the French Constitution (1946), in force as part of the preamble of the 1958 Constitution.

49 Art. 67 Netherlands Constitution (as amended in 1953, now renumbered Art. 92); Art. 49(bis) Luxembourg Constitution (1956 amendment); Art. 25(bis) Belgian Constitution (1970 amendment); Art. 20(1) Danish Constitution (1953); Art. 28(2) and (3) Greek Constitution (1975); Art. 93 Spanish Constitution (1978); Art. 7(5) Portuguese Constitution (1976). In the UK a legislative act, the European Communities Act (1972), was adopted at the time of accession.

adjustments required by the EC legal order. In addition, some countries inserted stipulations in their constitutions giving specific constitutional basis to European integration, notably in France and Germany in view of the ratification of the Maastricht Treaty (1992).[50]

However, the acceptance of the doctrines of EC legal integration and their consequences within national legal orders was not unconditional, nor did it necessarily comprise the endorsement of the ECJ's rationale for the constitutionalisation of the EC legal order. In particular, the highest courts in the Member States did not seem to subscribe to the legal basis for EC supremacy offered by the ECJ – namely, the EC as a new and autonomous legal system prevailing over national law of its own force. Instead they insisted on a national constitutional basis[51] or, exceptionally, an international law basis,[52] for EC supremacy. Further, some supreme or constitutional courts specified that the constitutional provisions which mediate in the relationship between EC law and national law are subordinated to other constitutional provisions. In so doing, they established constitutional limits on European integration as well as reserved for them the ultimate authority to control the legality of EC law.

Thus, for instance, accepting supremacy of EC law without a guarantee that this supreme law would not violate the essential constitutional principles and fundamental rights enshrined in the constitution of a Member State would have been practically impossible. This was made particularly clear in Italy and Germany, given that in these countries human rights enjoy constitutional protection, post-war national identity is to a large extent founded on and shaped by the Constitution, and the constitutional legality is safeguarded by specialised constitutional courts.

In Italy, for example, the EC legal order was subject to the so-called 'counter-limits' (*controlimiti*) – that is, EC law's respect for the fundamental principles of the constitutional system and the inalienable rights of individuals. The correlation in the jurisprudence of the Italian

50 Title XIV of the French Constitution (as amended by Constitutional Law 92–554, 25 June 1992); Art. 23 German Constitution (as amended on 21 December 1992). In Ireland, a specific reference to the EC has existed since 1972, in Art. 29(4)(3)–(6) of the Constitution, amended to permit the ratification of the Single European Act (1986) and the Maastricht Treaty (1992).

51 See Andrew Oppenheimer (ed.), *The Relationship between European Community Law and National Law: The Cases* (Cambridge University Press, 1994), 4–5, and the cases there cited and compiled. In the UK, supremacy was accepted on the basis of s. 2(1) of the 1972 European Communities Act.

52 In Belgium and Luxembourg. See Oppenheimer, *The Relationship between European Community Law and National Law.*

Constitutional Court between constitutional openness to European integration and its constitutional limitations arose for example in the *Frontini* case (1973).[53] Here the Italian Constitutional Court affirmed that the Constitution authorised restrictions of the legislative power by effect of EC law, but if ever EC law led to 'unacceptable power to violate the fundamental principles' of the constitutional order 'or the inalienable rights of man' 'the guarantee would always be assured that this Court would control the continuing compatibility of the Treaty with the above-mentioned fundamental principles'.[54]

Likewise, in its *Granital* decision (1984), the Constitutional Court recognised the immediate applicability and superiority of Community law over conflicting Italian legislation but also affirmed that 'the law implementing the Treaty could be subject to review by this Court with regard to the basic principles of the municipal legal order and the inalienable rights of man'.[55]

In the *Fragd* decision (1989) the Constitutional Court declared itself competent 'to verify whether or not a treaty norm, as interpreted and applied by the institutions and organs of the EEC, is in conflict with the fundamental principles of the Italian Constitution or violates the inalienable rights of man . . . Such a conflict, whilst being highly unlikely, could still happen.'[56]

In Germany, in the famous *Solange I* decision (1974)[57] the Constitutional Court held that the German constitutional openness to the EC had to 'be understood in the overall context of the Constitution', and did not consent to 'amending the basic structure of the Constitution, which forms the basis of its identity'. The Constitutional Court admitted that basic rights could be guaranteed on multiple levels but that, 'as long as' (*Solange*) 'the integration process has not progressed so far that Community law also receives a catalogue of fundamental rights decided on by a parliament and of settled validity, which is adequate in comparison with the catalogue of fundamental rights contained in the Constitution', the Constitutional Court would still control the constitutional legitimacy of EC law.[58]

[53] *Frontini et altri* v. *Ministro delle finanze et altri* (C. cost., 27 December 1973 no. 183), *Rivista di diritto internazionale*, 57 (1974), 130; 93 ILR 514 (English translation).

[54] *Ibid.*, 93 ILR, 525.

[55] *Spa Granital* v. *Amministrazione delle finanze dello Stato* (C. cost., 5 June 1984 no. 170), *Rivista di diritto internazionale*, 67 (1984), 360; 93 ILR 527, 536 (English translation).

[56] *Fragd* v. *Amministrazione delle Finanze dello Stato* (C. cost., 21 April 1989 no. 232), *Rivista di diritto internazionale*, 72 (1989), 104; 93 ILR 538, 542–3 (English translation).

[57] *Solange I* - Internationale Handelsgesellschaft von Einfuhr- und Vorratsstelle für Getreide und Futtermittel, decision of 29 May 1974, BVerfGE 37, 271 [1974] CMLR 540.

[58] *Ibid.*, 395.

After this decision, the Constitutional Court gradually showed more and more willingness to relinquish its control, on the very basis of the *Solange I* doctrine, as the Community system developed certain structural characteristics which ensured that the exercise of the competences transferred would not be contrary to the Constitution. The doctrine thus identified in the jurisprudence of the Constitutional Court a principle of structural congruence (*strukturelle Kongruenz*) – that is, the need for a substantial equivalence between the structure of the German constitutional order and the international organisation to which competences are transferred.[59] Thus, in its *Vielleicht* ('Maybe') decision of 1979, the Constitutional Court declared in *obiter dictum* that it left open 'whether and, if so, to what extent – maybe in view of political and legal developments in the European sphere occurring in the meantime – the principles contained in its decision of 29 May 1974 can continue to claim validity without limitation'.[60]

A turning point in the case law of the German Constitutional Court was its *Solange II* decision (1986).[61] The Court held that, at the EC level, 'there should be a guarantee of the application of fundamental rights which in substance and effectiveness is essentially similar to the protection of fundamental rights required unconditionally by the Constitution',[62] and that 'so long as' (*Solange*) an effective protection was thus ensured, the Court would not exercise its jurisdiction 'to decide on the applicability of secondary Community legislation cited as the legal basis for any acts of German courts or authorities . . . and it will no longer review such legislation by the standard of the fundamental rights contained in the Constitution'.[63] Thus, the Constitutional Court stressed the 'functional interlocking of the jurisdiction of the European Communities with those of the Member-States'.[64] This strengthened the position of the ECJ, now considered the effective 'ordinary' guardian of fundamental rights, but also implied the Constitutional Court's final say in conflicts with the ECJ.

[59] Filippo Donati, *Diritto comunitario e sindacato di costituzionalità* (Milano: Giuffrè, 1995), 263; Enzo Cannizzaro, *Trattati internazionali e giudizio di costituzionalità* (Milano: Giuffrè, 1991), 340, and doctrinal references there cited.

[60] *F.a. Steinike & Weinlig* v. *Bundesamt für Ernährung & Forstwirtschaft (Vielleicht)*, BVerfG 25 July 1979, 52 BVerfGE 187; [1980] CMLR 531, 537 (English translation) (emphasis added). In the CMLR the word *vielleicht* is translated as 'for instance', although 'maybe' is a more common translation and also gives name to the decision.

[61] *Wünsche Handelsgesellschaft (Solange II)*, BVerfG 22 October 1986, 73 BVerfGE 339; 93 ILR 403 (English translation).

[62] *Ibid.*, 93 ILR, 427–8. [63] *Ibid.*, 436. [64] *Ibid.*, 420.

That all this concern for fundamental constitutional values may not have been unfounded may be illustrated with some practical examples. In *Groener* (1989), for instance, the ECJ balanced the protection of the Gaelic language in Ireland with the EC principle of free movement of labour, in holding that the Irish laws requiring teachers to pass a Gaelic-language exam to obtain a job was a reasonable and non-discriminatory restriction to EC law.[65] In *Grogan* (1991), the freedom to supply services was balanced against the Irish prohibition of the distribution of information concerning abortion services in another Member State. The ECJ held that while abortion could be considered a service under EC law, the Irish prohibition in cause did not violate EC law because in this case the link between the providers of information and the providers of abortion in another Member State was too indirect.[66]

In general, the ECJ has been cautious in giving a decision that may directly clash with national constitutional values. Further, it has incorporated human rights into the EC legal order, adopting for its criteria the constitutional traditions common to the Member States and the international human rights conventions to which they have subscribed.[67] Thus, the interaction between the ECJ and national constitutional courts has led to 'stable accommodations on rights and to the obligation of ordinary courts to enforce EC law'.[68] However, the problem remains who is the ultimate authority to determine the constitutionality of EC acts. This was recast in the *Maastricht* judgment of the German Constitutional Court in the form of the *Kompetenz-Kompetenz* problem, 'the question as to which jurisdiction, Community or national, has the ultimate authority to declare the unconstitutionality of Community measures on the

[65] Case C-379/87, *Groener* v. *Minister for Education and the City of Dublin* [1989] ECR I-3967.

[66] Case C-159/90, *Society for the Protection of the Unborn Children Ireland* v. *Grogan* [1991] ECR I-4685. See also Diarmuid Rossa Phelan, 'Right to Life of the Unborn v. Promotion of Trade in Services', *Modern Law Review*, 55 (1992), 670; Jason Coppel and Aidan O'Neill, 'The European Court of Justice: Taking Rights Seriously?', *Common Market Law Review*, 29 (1992), 669.

[67] On this jurisprudence see e.g. Joseph H. H. Weiler, 'Eurocracy and Distrust: Some Questions Concerning the Role of the European Court of Justice in the Protection of Fundamental Rights within the Legal Order of the European Communities', *Washington Law Review*, 61 (1986), 1103. The status of human rights as an integral part of EC law is now clearly stated in Art. F of the European Union Treaty (1992), amended by the Amsterdam Treaty (1997). See generally on this evolution F. Sudre, 'La Communauté européenne et les droits fondamentaux après le Traité d'Amsterdam: vers un nouveau système européen de protection des droits de l'homme?', *Juris classeur periodique*, part I, 100 (1998).

[68] Sweet, 'Constitutional Dialogues in the European Community', 319.

grounds of ultra vires and effectively to become the arbiter of the jurisdictional limits of the Community legal order'.[69] The German Constitutional Court's assertion of its competence reflects democracy concerns within national legal systems arising from the ever-expanding competences of the Community.

Thus, the legal integration with national legal systems attained by EC law was achieved in close partnership with national constitutional systems, which sanctioned, and therefore conditioned, the profound transformations of the EC legal order. It is precisely such legal integration that seemed 'to be more solicitous to an involvement of national jurisdictions in the determination of jurisdictional limits of the Community legal order'.[70]

While international law would not justify, except in the narrowest circumstances, a State's use of national law including constitutional law for non-performance of an international obligation, paradoxically this seems more acceptable in a vertically integrated system. As stated by Joseph Weiler and Ulrich Haltern, the approach of national constitutional courts 'is an insistence on a more polycentred view of constitutional adjudication and will eventually force a more even conversation between the European Court and its national constitutional counterparts'.[71]

This conferred on European integration a new dimension, as it demanded the reconciliation of EC law with fundamental constitutional values.[72] Constitutional limitations acted not as external constraints to the EC legal order but as demands that this had to satisfy within its own structure. While national constitutions were adapted to European integration, EC law 'draws on and integrates the national constitutional orders'.[73]

Voice in investment treaty case law: the comparative law perspective

The investment treaty regime does not have an institutional structure anywhere similar to the EU. It is still largely an inter-governmental framework which allows for traditional forms of Voice, such as direct amendment

[69] Joseph H. H. Weiler and Ulrich Haltern, 'Constitutional or International? The Foundations of the Community Legal Order and the Question of Judicial Kompetence-Kompetence' in Anne-Marie Slaughter, Alec Stone Sweet and Joseph H. H. Weiler (eds.), *European Court and the National Courts – Doctrine and Jurisprudence: Legal Change in its Social Context* (Oxford: Hart, 1998), 331.

[70] *Ibid.*, 336. [71] *Ibid.*, 363.

[72] Marta Cartabia, *Principi inviolabili e integrazione europea* (Milano: Giuffrè, 1995), 136–7.

[73] Weiler and Haltern, 'Constitutional or International?', 363.

by States of existing investment treaties or the issuance of binding interpretations of its terms. However, the investment treaty regime also has supranational features. Investment arbitration tribunals settle disputes in a binding form, allegedly constrain State action, and act as lawmakers in international investment law.[74] The question is whether, within these supranational dynamics, a more system-internal type of Voice may be developing, along the lines of the stable accommodation and dialogue between legal orders characteristic of the EU system.

One such phenomenon may be the comparative public law approach in the interpretation of investment treaty protections, that draws on domestic administrative and constitutional law in construing the scope of such standards. The genuinely public law nature of international investment law would justify it, and the approach could be a way to legitimise the investment treaty regime by making it more acceptable to national legal orders.[75]

The comparative law methodology is not a new development in the field. It was already present in the second award ever issued in investment treaty arbitration made public only recently, the *Saar Papier* v. *Poland* award.[76] The tribunal in this case made explicit use of domestic administrative law to interpret the provisions on indirect expropriation in the Germany–Poland BIT.[77] The tribunal pointed out that '[t]o interpret the Treaty administrative law practice in Germany and Poland would be helpful' and, after complaining that '[d]espite repeated requests, the arbitral tribunal received little help from the parties on German and Polish administrative law', relied on 'general administrative law and the principle of good faith to interpret the Treaty',[78] particularly the law of the States of nationality of the two arbitrators that formed the majority opinion, Germany and Switzerland.

[74] Stephan Schill, 'System-building in Investment Treaty Arbitration and Lawmaking', *German Law Journal*, 12 (2011), 1083.

[75] See e.g. Stephan Schill, 'International Investment Law and Comparative Public Law: An Introduction' in Stephan Schill (ed.), *International Investment Law and Comparative Public Law* (Oxford University Press, 2010), 3; Anthea Roberts, 'Clash of Paradigms: Actors and Analogies Shaping the Investment Treaty System', *American Journal of International Law*, 107 (2013), 45.

[76] *Saar Papier Vertriebs GmbH* v. *Republic of Poland* (UNCITRAL), Final Award, 16 October 1995.

[77] Jarrod Hepburn, '*Saar Papier* v. *Poland*: Comparative Public Law and the Second-ever Investment Treaty Award', *EJIL: Talk!*, 3 February 2014, available at www.ejiltalk.org/saar-papier-v-poland-comparative-public-law-and-the-second-ever-investment-treaty-award/.

[78] *Saar Papier Vertriebs GmbH* v. *Republic of Poland*, para. 79.

The tribunal found that '[i]n administrative law practice two approaches converge to deal with this type of problem', meaning the definition of indirect expropriation. First, the tribunal referred to an effects and proportionality test:

> [I]f the right of property is limited in a way that in its economic effect must be equated to expropriation, compensation must be paid. This is called '*materielle Enleignung*' ... A 'materielle Enteignung' is present in particular if a measure has a general impact but nevertheless burdens a particular right of ownership far more than all others.[79]

Secondly, the tribunal alluded to a legitimate expectations approach:

> The second approach was developed mostly after World War II and starts from the general proposition that there is an *obligation of good faith in public law* which applies to all branches of government. Under certain circumstances a law is not applied to certain private persons or, if it is applied, they must be fully compensated even though the application of the law is lawful. *This* principle applies where the state has given *misleading information* about the law or where the law or administrative or court practice have changed.[80]

As noted by a commentator, the arbitrators in this case seemed to be 'unaware of relevant international jurisprudence' and 'simply reached for the closest analogy that they could find'.[81] This may be right, and indeed it is curious that, for example, no case of the Iran–US Claims Tribunal is cited as international law authority for the effects test. In any case, the fact remains that this is the first example of the comparative public law approach in investment treaty case law, providing comparative administrative law support for international law doctrines that have been subject to much criticism in today's commentary.

Reasoning similar to the *Saar Papier* tribunal only resurfaced in investment treaty case law many years later, for example in the *Tecmed* v. *Mexico* award as far as the good faith principle and proportionality test is concerned.[82] For its part, the comparative public law approach reappeared even later. In fact, this approach was not fully and explicitly used until the liability decision in *Total* v. *Argentina*, dated 27 December 2010. In this case the tribunal found that the comparative law analysis was justified in interpreting the fair and equitable treatment standard:

[79] *Ibid.*, paras. 81, 83. [80] *Ibid.*, para. 92.

[81] Hepburn, '*Saar Papier* v. *Poland*: Comparative Public Law and the Second-ever Investment Treaty Award'.

[82] *Técnicas Medioambientales Tecmed, S.A.* v. *The United Mexican States* (ICSID Case No. ARB (AF)/00/2), Award, 29 May 2003.

> In determining the scope of a right or obligation, Tribunals have often looked as a benchmark to international or comparative standards. Indeed, as is often the case for general standards applicable in any legal system (such as 'due process'), a comparative analysis of what is considered generally fair or unfair conduct by domestic public authorities in respect of private firms and investors in domestic law may also be relevant to identify the legal standards under BITs. Such an approach is justified because, factually, the situations and conduct to be evaluated under a BIT occur within the legal system and social, economic and business environment of the host State.[83]

The tribunal elaborated on the comparative law perspective, in particular in relation to the legitimate expectations doctrine:

> Since the concept of legitimate expectations is based on the requirement of good faith, one of the general principles referred to in Article 38(1)(c) of the Statute of the International Court of Justice as a source of international law, the Tribunal believes that a comparative analysis of the protection of legitimate expectations in domestic jurisdictions is justified at this point.[84]

In this same line, the tribunal in *Toto* v. *Lebanon* stated that '[t]he fair and equitable treatment standard of international law does not depend on the perception of the frustrated investor, but should use public international law and comparative domestic public law as a benchmark'.[85]

The comparative law perspective is not without problems, for example that of the criteria for the selection of the comparative legal orders, and the inherent abstraction involved in assessing the recognition of a specific legal principle across different legal systems. Further, investment arbitration tribunals interpret treaty provisions and as such must apply international law. In this context, whether a certain principle of comparative law may be regarded as either a rule of customary international law or a general principle of law under Article 38(1) of the ICJ Statute may be arguable in many cases. No doubt this problem will need to be addressed in the jurisprudence if the comparative law perspective, with (and perhaps because of) its system-building capabilities, is to be applied in future cases.

[83] *Total S.A.* v. *The Argentine Republic* (ICSID Case No. ARB/04/01), Decision on Liability, para. 111.

[84] *Ibid.*, para. 128.

[85] *Toto Costruzioni Generali S.p.A.* v. *The Republic of Lebanon* (ICSID Case No. ARB/07/12), Award, 7 June 2012, para. 166; see also para. 193.

Conclusion

The *ad hoc* nature of investment treaty tribunals makes it more likely, and perhaps even desirable,[86] that tribunals focus on the application of the law to a given dispute rather than on systemic elucidations. This, however, does not exclude the emergence in the case law of some system-building paradigms regarding the interaction between the investment treaty regime and domestic legal principles and courts. One such phenomenon may be the comparative law perspective, which is reminiscent of the dynamics of Voice, in the form of a dialogue between legal orders, in the EC framework. Other forms of Voice, existing or to be developed in further case law, may concern a more clear division of competence between national courts and investment tribunals depending on the nature and substantiation of disputes,[87] and the possibility of contract or domestic law counterclaims in investment cases.

Voice is a mechanism for the enhanced participation of domestic legal systems in the realm of international law. It has the virtue of contributing to the shaping of the international regime, gradually enriching it, and reinforcing its legitimacy. In contrast, Exit is the abandonment of the international regime altogether with the associated defeat of its fruitful interaction with national legal systems. In the investment treaty framework, both dynamics are at play. While exaggerated criticism pushes for Exit, Voice may be allowed to be heard in the more day-to-day workings of its supranational features – that is, investment treaty arbitration. As James Crawford suggested in 1997, 'the relation between the international and constitutional levels can be reciprocal' and this helps international law by 'the co-opting of national constitutional limitations in the interests of international regularity'.[88]

[86] W. Michael Reisman, '"Case Specific Mandates" versus "Systemic Implications": How Should Investment Tribunals Decide? – The Freshfields Arbitration Lecture', *Arbitration International*, 29 (2013), 131.

[87] See e.g. the application for the 'prima facie' test of jurisdiction *ratione materiae* in *Iberdrola Energía S.A.* v. *Republic of Guatemala* (ICSID Case No. ARB/09/5), Award, 17 August 2012. See also similarly, *Robert Azinian, Kenneth Davitian, & Ellen Baca* v. *The United Mexican States* (ICSID Case No. ARB (AF)/97/2), Award, 1 November 1999.

[88] Crawford, 'International Law and Australian Federalism: Past, Present and Future', 325.

6

Polar territorial and maritime sovereignty in the twenty-first century

DONALD R. ROTHWELL*

Introduction

Polar sovereignty was a relatively dormant issue in the second half of the twentieth century. The disputes that had emerged in Antarctica over territorial claims, which at one point had made their way to the International Court of Justice,[1] had been effectively resolved with the adoption in 1959 of the Antarctic Treaty.[2] Article IV of the Treaty proved capable of suppressing sovereignty tensions between the seven Antarctic territorial claimants,[3] and also keeping in abeyance the interests of potential territorial claimants including the United States and the Soviet Union/Russian Federation.[4] In the Arctic, territorial claims had also been settled by the time of World War II and, while the Cold War introduced military and security tensions into the Arctic, none of these directly related to contested territorial sovereignty.[5]

Nevertheless, there remain on-going sovereignty tensions, which if not properly managed have the potential to erupt into significant international disputes with implications reaching well beyond Antarctica and the Arctic. While Article IV of the Antarctic Treaty set aside sovereignty

* With acknowledgement to James Crawford, who along with Ivan Shearer, supervised my University of Sydney PhD entitled 'The Polar Regions and the Development of International Law' (1995).

1 *Antarctica* cases *(UK* v. *Argentina*; *UK* v. *Chile)*, ICJ Pleadings (1956).

2 Antarctic Treaty (Washington, adopted 1 December 1959, entered in force 23 June 1961), 402 UNTS 71.

3 The seven claimant States are: Argentina, Australia, Chile, France, New Zealand, Norway and the United Kingdom.

4 David Day, *Antarctica: A Biography* (North Sydney: Random House/Knopf Australia, 2012), 434–91.

5 Shelagh D. Grant, *Polar Imperative: A History of Arctic Sovereignty in North America* (Toronto: Douglas & McIntyre, 2010), 193–246.

issues for the duration of the Treaty, tensions have been raised over recent submissions to the Commission on the Limits of the Continental Shelf (CLCS) over Southern Ocean outer continental shelf claims and by Japan's refusal to acknowledge Australia's proclaimed Whale Sanctuary offshore Antarctica and the on-going conduct of its Southern Ocean 'scientific' whaling programme. Arctic outer continental shelf claims are also a source of tension, placing a spotlight upon the CLCS as it reviews claims and how Arctic States resolve overlapping maritime claims. The status of certain waters also remains in dispute, including the Northwest Passage where the United States questions Canadian sovereignty over those waters. Melting ice means that the Arctic Ocean is also becoming more accessible to shipping, raising issues with respect to the freedom of navigation being exercised by non-Arctic States such as China.[6] This chapter will review these issues and make observations as to how polar sovereignty may be understood in coming decades and, in doing so, will build upon some of James Crawford's analysis of these issues.[7]

Polar sovereignty

Polar sovereignty and the effective assertion of territorial title to polar lands have held a fascination for international lawyers for over a century. This has no doubt been driven by the relative contemporary exploration of polar lands, which resulted in both the North and South Pole being first reached early in the twentieth century, and also because of the challenges in effectively asserting sovereignty over polar lands. As a result, notwithstanding discovery of polar lands and the assertions of title that were often associated with those discoveries, claims over Antarctica or the Arctic represented classic examples of inchoate titles in need of perfection. That the *Eastern Greenland* case acknowledged the challenges associated with the effective assertion of title over polar lands[8] provided an additional legal basis for appreciating the distinctiveness of these issues.

6 See e.g. Olya Gayazova, 'China's Rights in the Marine Arctic', *International Journal of Marine and Coastal Law*, 28 (2013), 61–95.

7 Crawford's contributions to matters associated with polar sovereignty can be found in James Crawford and Donald Rothwell, 'Legal Issues Confronting Australia's Antarctica', *Australian Yearbook of International Law*, 13 (1992), 53–88; James Crawford, *Brownlie's Principles of Public International Law*, 8th edn (Oxford University Press, 2012), 241–2.

8 *Legal Status of Eastern Greenland (Norway* v. *Denmark)*, Judgment, 5 September 1933, PCIJ Series A/B, No. 53.

There are five recognised methods of acquiring sovereignty over territory: occupation, annexation, accretion, prescription and cession.[9] During early expeditions to the Arctic and Antarctic, various territorial claims were made, predominantly based upon acts of discovery, the raising of the flag and an act of proclamation.[10] However, as was held in the *Island of Palmas Arbitration*,[11] states whose basis of claim is discovery only have an inchoate title which must be perfected by later acts demonstrating an actual intent to exercise sovereignty over the discovered lands. This raised questions as to how traditional principles of territorial sovereignty could be applied in areas remote from the metropolitan power and where there was no immediate prospect of colonising those lands.

Throughout the twentieth century the effective exercise of sovereignty over polar lands was problematic given their relative inaccessibility and distance from metropolitan lands. Judge Huber in *Island of Palmas* recognised that differential standards may apply 'according to conditions of time and place', and also whether territory was inhabited or uninhabited.[12] However, it was in *Eastern Greenland* that the Permanent Court made express reference to the particular challenges associated with fulfilling the requirements of effective occupation in the polar regions, noting that:

> It is impossible to read the records of the decisions in cases as to territorial sovereignty without observing that in many cases the tribunal has been satisfied with very little in the way of the actual exercise of sovereign rights, provided that the other State could not make out a superior claim. This is particularly true in the case of claims to sovereignty over areas in thinly populated or unsettled countries.[13]

While publicists have agreed that the strict standards applied to more temperate lands do not apply to the polar regions,[14] they have maintained that some of the traditional incidents of effective occupation must still

9 See e.g. Ivan Anthony Shearer (ed.), *Starke's International Law*, 11th edn (London: Butterworths, 1994), 145; Robert Jennings and Arthur Watts (eds.), *Oppenheim's International Law*, 9th edn, 2 vols. (London: Longman, 1992), I, Parts II–IV, 679 (who substitute subjugation for annexation).

10 In the case of Antarctica, see the discussion in Day, *Antarctica: A Biography*, 227–52.

11 *The Netherlands* v. *United States of America* (4 April 1928), Reports of International Arbitral Awards, II, 829.

12 *Ibid.*, 840.

13 *Legal Status of Eastern Greenland (Norway* v. *Denmark)*, 46.

14 See e.g. F. M. Auburn, *Antarctic Law and Politics* (Canberra: Croom Helm, 1982), 13; Gillian D. Triggs, *International Law and Australian Sovereignty in Antarctica* (Sydney: Legal Books, 1986), 82; Philip C. Jessup and Howard J. Taubenfeld, *Controls for Outer Space and the Antarctic Analogy* (New York: Columbia University Press, 1959), 141.

be made out.[15] This opens for consideration whether different standards should be applied to the determination of polar territorial claims in the twenty-first century than was previously the case. Two factors immediately would appear relevant. The first is that the polar regions are now more accessible than was the case at the time they were first discovered and when the early cases were decided. While they cannot necessarily be equated with 'temperate lands', they can be reached with an ease that would have been unimaginable a century ago and as such are no longer as 'distant' as previously imagined. The second is that modern technology has rendered the polar regions capable of settlement in much the same fashion as other parts of the globe. In the Arctic, the Russian city of Murmansk is the biggest city north of the Arctic Circle with a population of over 330,000.[16] In Antarctica, the American base at McMurdo Sound has an austral winter population of up to 200 and a summer population of up to 1,100, while at the South Pole the American Amundsen/Scott base is also capable of accommodating 245 persons in summer.[17]

An unresolved aspect of polar sovereignty is the status of claims based upon the so-called 'sector theory' which is that States can assert a territorial claim along lines of latitude that run directly to the Pole, thereby effectively dividing up the region. A significant feature of Antarctic claims is that, with the exception of Norway, they are all based on a sector as all the claims commence at points along the Antarctic coast and converge along degrees of longitude at the geographic South Pole. The sector theory has also been influential in debates over Arctic territorial claims, where it was thought to have been based upon principles such as contiguity, 'hinterland' or the 'spheres of influence' doctrine.[18] In the Arctic, sector claims are based on the geographic proximity of the claimant State, and have from time to time been asserted as a basis of claim to Arctic lands by Canada and Russia. In Antarctica, only Argentina and Chile are sufficiently geographically proximate to be able to rely upon a form of sector

15 See e.g. A. C. Castles, 'The International Status of the Australian Antarctic Territory' in Daniel Patrick O'Connell (ed.), *International Law in Australia* (Sydney: Law Book Company, 1966), 355.

16 Charles Emmerson, *The Future History of the Arctic* (London: Vintage, 2010), 68.

17 United States Antarctic Program, *United States Antarctic Program Participant Guide*, 2010–12 edn (US Antarctic Program, 2010), 72.

18 Jennings and Watts, *Oppenheim's International Law*, I, Parts II–IV, 693; Daniel Patrick O'Connell, *International Law*, 2nd edn, 2 vols. (London: Stevens and Son, 1970), I, 449; Gustav Smedal, *Acquisition of Sovereignty over Polar Areas* (Oslo: I Kommisjon Hos Jacob Dybwad, 1931), 54–76; Oscar Svarlien, 'The Sector Principle in Law and Practice', *Polar Record*, 10 (1960), 248–63.

claim linked to contiguity or related bases of claim. Ultimately, sector theory has never been the subject of final determination by an international court or tribunal, has never been officially relied upon by claimant states to polar lands, and has been subject to widespread critique from commentators. Crawford has recently assessed the principle as one that 'remains a rough method of delimitation, and has not become a separate rule of law',[19] while Shaw characterises it as a 'political proposition'.[20] Crawford's further reservations extend to the observation that the sector principle inherits some of the defects of contiguity, that 'its application is a little absurd insofar as there is a claim to a narrow sliver of sovereignty stretching to the Pole' and that it cannot apply to areas of the high seas.[21] It can therefore be observed that while the standard international law principles associated with the assertion of sovereignty and the perfection of territorial title apply to polar lands, there has also been some recognition of the distinctive aspects of polar sovereignty. Whether those points of distinction, including particular theories that have been applied in the past to polar lands such as the sector theory, have much contemporary application is a matter for determination.

Antarctic sovereignty

In 1959, when the Antarctic Treaty was negotiated, sovereignty over the continent was unresolved. To that end, Article IV of the Antarctic Treaty is a remarkable provision which has proven itself capable of multiple interpretations and some evolution over the more than fifty years the Treaty has been in force.[22] Initially, the goal was to reach a settlement amongst the seven territorial claimants and the United States and Soviet Union so as to allow for the orderly management of Antarctic affairs and neutralise sovereignty from Antarctic discourse. This proved to be a major strength when the Antarctic Treaty became the focus of sustained criticism in the United Nations General Assembly during the 1980s. By being able to demonstrate that traditional notions of State sovereignty were not exercised in Antarctica, the Antarctic Treaty parties were able to successfully mount a diplomatic response, deflecting criticism of the Treaty and the

19 Crawford, *Brownlie's Principles of Public International Law*, 241; see also Auburn, *Antarctic Law and Politics*, 31.

20 Malcolm N. Shaw, *International Law*, 6th edn (Cambridge University Press, 2008), 535.

21 Crawford, *Brownlie's Principles of Public International Law*, 241.

22 See the discussion in Crawford and Rothwell, 'Legal Issues Confronting Australia's Antarctica', 79–82.

Antarctic Treaty System (ATS).[23] More recently, as some claimant States have sought to secure their positions with respect to maritime claims in the Southern Ocean, Article IV and its interpretation has once again become a live issue within the ATS.[24]

The issues concerning Antarctic sovereignty are highlighted by considering Australia's position. Australia has been a long-standing player in polar affairs, formally commencing with Sir Douglas Mawson's 1911–14 expedition which eventually paved the way for Australian interests in Antarctica to be formalised by way of the declaration of the Australian Antarctic Territory (AAT) in 1936.[25] Australia's polar interests have been predominantly realised through territorial claims to the AAT, and through its sub-Antarctic islands: Macquarie Island, Heard Island and McDonald Island. Those claims remain of considerable significance to Australia as was highlighted in 2012 when Australia proclaimed outer continental shelves offshore Heard Island and Macquarie Island, which extend deep into the Southern Ocean.[26] Nevertheless, Australian sovereignty over Antarctica is not positively recognised by many States and, with the exception of the reciprocal recognition accorded Antarctic claims between Australia, France, New Zealand and the United Kingdom, lingering doubts remain over whether Australia's claim to the AAT has been perfected.[27]

In the past decade, Australian sovereignty in Antarctica has been confronted with the challenges of Japanese whaling and outer continental shelf claims. Since the 1970s Australia has progressively adopted a pro-conservation position towards whales, and these developments have been reflected in Australian law. The Environment Protection and Biodiversity Conservation Act 1999 (EPBC Act) creates an Australian Whale Sanctuary, which applies offshore the Australian continent, offshore territories and the AAT. Whaling within the Australian Whale Sanctuary is prohibited and the Act applies to all persons and vessels,[28] giving no consideration to possible Antarctic Treaty constraints on the application of

23 See discussion in Richard Woolcott, *The Hot Seat: Reflections on Diplomacy from Stalin's Death to the Bali Bombings* (New South Wales: Harper Collins, 2003), 209–18.

24 Donald R. Rothwell, 'Sovereignty and the Antarctic Treaty', *Polar Record*, 46 (2010), 17–20.

25 Australian Antarctic Territory Acceptance Act 1933 (Australia).

26 Seas and Submerged Lands (Limits of Continental Shelf) Proclamation 2012 (Australia), Federal Register of Legislative Instruments F2012L01081 (24 May 2012).

27 The most thorough contemporary analysis can be found in Triggs, *International Law and Australian Sovereignty in Antarctica*; see also Crawford and Rothwell, 'Legal Issues Confronting Australia's Antarctica', 59–61.

28 Environment Protection and Biodiversity Conservation Act 1999 (Australia), s. 229.

Australian law to foreign nationals.[29] Notwithstanding Japan's conduct of whaling operations within the Australian Whale Sanctuary, no Australian government agency has to date sought to enforce the prohibition on whaling. In 2004 a non-governmental organisation, Humane Society International (HSI), contested this view and commenced proceedings in the Australian courts, arguing that Japanese whaling activity was contrary to the EPBC Act. In a series of proceedings before the Federal Court from 2004–8,[30] declaratory and injunctive relief was sought concerning whaling alleged to have been carried out by Kyodo Senpaku Kaisha, a corporation holding a licence from the Japanese government to conduct 'special permit' whaling in the Southern Ocean. Following a series of legal proceedings in 2008,[31] the Federal Court of Australia delivered its final judgment in the matter.[32] Satisfied that a 'significant number of whales were taken inside the Australian Whale Sanctuary',[33] the Court concluded that Kyodo had contravened a number of relevant provisions of the EPBC Act in relation to both minke whales and fin whales, and issued orders that Kyodo be restrained from engaging in any such further acts.[34] HSI arranged for the Federal Court's judgment to be served upon Kyodo in Japan in late January 2008.[35] These orders have not deterred Kyodo from continuing with its whaling programme and there have been continual infringements of the Australian Whale Sanctuary since 2008.[36]

What may be perceived as Australian reticence over the active enforcement of Australian law in the case of whaling can be contrasted with the more active assertion of Australian sovereignty over its Southern Ocean continental shelf. In 2004 Australia made its CLCS submission of data with respect to an outer continental shelf in the Southern Ocean, and

[29] As to the issues arising regarding the enforcement of Australian law offshore the AAT see Crawford and Rothwell, 'Legal Issues Confronting Australia's Antarctica', 78–85.

[30] Commencing with *Humane Society International, Inc.* v. *Kyodo Senpaku Kaisha Ltd* [2004] FCA 1510.

[31] See discussion in Tim Stephens and Donald Rothwell, 'Japanese Whaling in Antarctica: *Humane Society International, Inc.* v. *Kyodo Senpaku Kaisha Ltd*', *Review of European Community and International Environmental Law*, 16 (2007), 243–6.

[32] *Humane Society International, Inc.* v. *Kyodo Senpaku Kaisha Ltd* [2008] FCA 3.

[33] *Ibid.*, para. 39. [34] *Ibid.*, para. 55.

[35] Peter Alford, 'Aussie Judgment Served on Whalers', *The Australian* (Sydney), 24 January 2008, 7.

[36] In 2012 vessels from the Japanese whaling fleet entered the Australian Whale Sanctuary offshore Macquarie Island which brought about a response from the Australian government; see Nicola Roxon MP, 'Japanese Whaling Vessels Nearing Macquarie Island', Attorney-General for Australia Media Release, 25 February 2012, available at www.attorneygeneral.gov.au/Media-releases/.

more generally offshore the Australian continent and territories.[37] This process, made consistently with mechanisms provided for under Article 76 of the 1982 United Nations Convention on the Law of the Sea (LOSC),[38] asserted a potential Australian Southern Ocean outer continental shelf claim offshore the AAT, Heard and McDonald Islands, and Macquarie Island. However, mindful of the fact that the Commission does not consider continental shelf claims with respect to disputed territory, Australia requested the CLCS 'not to take any action for the time being' with respect to the continental shelf appurtenant to Antarctica.[39] Nevertheless, Australia's submission generated responses from eight states, of which six made direct observations regarding a claimed outer continental shelf off the AAT coast.[40] Japan, for example, indicated in its communication to the United Nations Secretary-General that it 'does not recognize any State's right of or claims to territorial sovereignty in Antarctica'.[41] Because Australia was the first State to go before the CLCS with data associated with continental shelf claims offshore Antarctica, some reaction could have been anticipated,[42] and to that end Australia paved the way for other Antarctic claimants in their CLCS dealings. Likewise, Australia was also the first State to assert an outer continental shelf in the Southern Ocean. In May 2012 Australia formally proclaimed adjusted outer limits of the Australian continental shelf, which in the case of both the Heard and McDonald Islands, and Macquarie Island, at their southern limit terminate within the Antarctic Treaty area.[43]

[37] For analysis see Andrew Serdy, 'Towards Certainty of Seabed Jurisdiction beyond 200 Nautical Miles from the Territorial Sea Baseline: Australia's Submission to the Commission on the Limits of the Continental Shelf', *Ocean Development and International Law*, 36 (2005), 201–17.

[38] United Nations Convention on the Law of the Sea (Montego Bay, adopted 10 December 1982, entered into force 10 November 1994), 1833 UNTS 397.

[39] 'Note from the Permanent Mission of Australia to the Secretary-General of the United Nations Accompanying the Lodgement of Australia's Submission', Note 89/2004 (November 2004) available at www.un.org/Depts/los/clcs_new/submissions_files/submission_aus.htm.

[40] The States that directly commented on this matter were Germany, India, Japan, the Netherlands, Russian Federation and USA.

[41] The Permanent Mission of Japan to the United Nations (SC/05/039) (19 January 2005) available at www.un.org/depts/los/clcs_new/submissions_files/aus04/clcs_03_2004_los_jap.pdf.

[42] See discussion in Alan D. Hemmings and Tim Stephens, 'The Extended Continental Shelves of Sub-Antarctic Islands: Implications for Antarctic Governance', *Polar Record*, 46 (2010), 312–27.

[43] See above n. 26.

Arctic sovereignty

Arctic territorial sovereignty has been less contentious than in Antarctica, superficially because there has been less disputed territory. Following the period of intense discovery of Arctic lands in the late nineteenth and early twentieth century, which included the 'race for the Pole', Arctic territorial disputes were settled in a relatively orderly fashion, including by reference to the Permanent Court of International Justice (PCIJ). At present, the only territorial dispute is that between Canada and Denmark over Hans Island, which is a very small island that straddles Nares Strait between Greenland and Ellesmere Island.[44] There have, nevertheless, been sovereignty tensions in the Arctic, especially as discussed below between Canada and the United States over the characterisation of the Northwest Passage as either internal waters or an international strait.

The dawn of the twenty-first century has seen a significant shift in the debate over Arctic sovereignty and this has been due to a number of factors. The first is the effects of the melting of the sea ice of the Arctic Ocean. In recent years the effect of the melt has been dramatic, with significant tracts of open water appearing in parts of the Arctic Ocean and a shifting ice pattern becoming discernible.[45] The permanent disappearance of Arctic sea ice throughout much of the region during the summer months has resource access implications. Previously inaccessible areas of the Arctic Ocean will potentially become accessible for various forms of resource exploitation, ranging from the non-living resources of the sea-bed, to fish stocks and other living resources of the water column. With increased resource exploitation, there is the potential for demands for greater foreign access by States which may not traditionally have had an interest in the region. This may especially be the case with respect to Arctic fisheries and that area of Arctic high seas beyond the limits of coastal State jurisdiction. It follows that this will in turn raise issues of increased navigational interest in Arctic waters, not only with respect to navigation

[44] Christopher Stevenson, 'Hans Off! The Struggle for Hans Island and the Potential Ramifications for International Border Dispute Resolution', *Boston College International and Comparative Law Review*, 30 (2007), 263–75.

[45] The first time that consistent reports emerged of the Northwest Passage being ice-free was 2007, which coincided with a then record minimum sea ice extent being recorded for Arctic sea ice. See John Roach, 'Arctic Melt Opens Northwest Passage', *National Geographic News*, 17 September 2007, available at http://news.nationalgeographoc.com/news/pf/38614724.html.

within the Arctic but by members of the international community eager to gain access to new shipping routes between the North Pacific and North Atlantic. A second factor is the rising tension associated with outer continental shelf claims, which will potentially converge in the central Arctic Ocean, resulting in the need for resolution of additional maritime boundaries to settle overlapping claims.[46]

The combination of climate change and the potential for at least a partially ice-free Arctic Ocean, combined with an acknowledgement of continental shelf rights in an area that is becoming more accessible to a range of maritime activities, has generated considerable political interest, with accompanying legal and policy implications.[47] One particular dimension of this renewed interest in the Arctic has been the attention given to Arctic shipping in general, and navigational issues in particular.[48] Two Arctic shipping routes have traditionally attracted attention. The first – the so-called Northern Sea Route[49] – runs along Russia's northern coast primarily within coastal waters. As there has been little dispute over Russia's capacity to control navigation within these waters consistent with the law of the sea, the Northern Sea Route has rarely been the subject of controversy. This has not been the case with respect to the Northwest Passage. A variety of interconnected sea routes which pass between the islands that make up the Canadian Arctic Archipelago, the status of the Northwest Passage has been the subject of on-going dispute between Canada and the US ever since the voyage of the SS *Manhattan* in 1969. In response to the *Manhattan* voyage, which attempted to demonstrate the capacity of a supertanker to shuttle between the Alaskan oil fields and the United States's eastern seaboard, Canada adopted the Arctic Waters Pollution Prevention Act, placing significant constraints on the passage of vessels through its Arctic waters on environmental grounds. Canada took further steps in the 1980s to bolster its control of its Arctic waters through the declaration of straight baselines around the outer

46 See e.g. Timo Koivurova, 'The Actions of Arctic States Respecting the Continental Shelf: A Reflective Essay', *Ocean Development and International Law*, 42 (2011), 211–26.

47 See e.g. James Kraska (ed.), *Arctic Security in an Age of Climate Change* (Cambridge University Press, 2011); Scott G. Borgerson, 'Arctic Meltdown: The Economic and Security Implications of Global Warming', *Foreign Affairs*, 87 (2008), 63–77.

48 See e.g. Aldo Chircop, 'The Growth of International Shipping in the Arctic: Is a Regulatory Review Timely?', *International Journal of Marine and Coastal Law*, 24 (2009), 355–80; E. J. Molenaar, 'Arctic Marine Shipping: Overview of the International Legal Framework, Gaps, and Options', *Journal of Transnational Law and Policy*, 18 (2009), 289–325.

49 Also referred to as the Northeast Passage.

limits of its Arctic islands with the effect that all vessels passing through the Northwest Passage would be within Canadian internal waters. The significance of Canada's initiatives has been to convert waters that may at one time have been a part of the territorial sea or exclusive economic zone, within which certain navigational rights existed for foreign ships, into waters over which Canada has complete sovereignty and the capacity to regulate all shipping – including the right to deny entry to foreign vessels.[50] Canada's position with respect to navigation through the Northwest Passage has been tolerated, though subject to protest by the United States. It has not been tested, however, before any international court or tribunal, and while Canada's position finds some support in Article 234 of the LOSC granting to coastal States a capacity to adopt additional environmental measures for ice-covered waters,[51] this does not provide a foundation for Canada's baselines interpretation or the constraints which have been placed on navigation. This remains a dormant legal issue which has the potential to erupt directly as a result of climate change and the new opportunities for safe and efficient navigation through the Northwest Passage.

A significant increase in Arctic shipping has the potential to stoke new sovereignty tensions. The 2009 Arctic Maritime Shipping Assessment (AMSA) Report[52] highlighted the potential for an increase in not only destinational Arctic shipping, but also trans-Arctic shipping via shipping routes that cross the Arctic Ocean from a point of entry to a point of exit. Such shipping routes may operate via the Northern Sea Route or Northwest Passage, or through the Central Arctic Ocean, with the effect that the Bering Strait (where the Russian Federation and United States are the littoral states) would become a pivotal route for access or egress to the Arctic.[53] A trans-Arctic shipping route through the Bering Strait, across the Arctic Ocean and then via the Fram and Greenland Straits to Iceland, is almost 5,000 miles shorter than using the Panama Canal between Hamburg and Yokohama. Polar class vessels, capable of operating

[50] See Donat Pharad, *Canada's Arctic Waters in International Law* (Cambridge University Press, 1988).

[51] Ted L. McDorman, *Salt Water Neighbors: International Ocean Law Relations between the United States and Canada* (Oxford University Press, 2009), 93–5.

[52] Arctic Council, *Arctic Marine Shipping Assessment 2009 Report* (Arctic Council, 2009) (AMSA Report).

[53] Donald R. Rothwell, 'International Straits and Trans-Arctic Navigation', *Ocean Development and International Law*, 43 (2012), 267–82.

in a substantially ice-reduced Arctic, are on order and are being built in order to take advantage of these opportunities.[54]

In the case of the Arctic, much of the Arctic Ocean remains beyond the limits of existing 200-nautical-mile continental shelf claims, including the seabed at the North Pole. A great deal of the Arctic Ocean is potentially susceptible to an outer continental shelf claim by the Arctic Ocean littoral states, which include Canada, Denmark (Greenland), Norway, the Russian Federation and the United States. The potential of these claims to raise sovereignty hackles was famously highlighted in August 2007 by the planting of a Russian flag by a mini-submarine on the Arctic Ocean seabed at the North Pole.[55] More substantively, the growing number of claims before the CLCS by Arctic States, including Canada's anticipated claim, plus the uncertainty as to the position of the United States and its claims offshore Alaska, has contributed to not only a growing media fascination with Arctic sovereignty but parallel consideration of Arctic legal issues and governance that was absent for much of the twentieth century.[56] Russia was the first Arctic State to make its CLCS submission in 2001, which has since been followed by Norway, and Denmark. A Canadian claim is anticipated in 2013 while the position of the United States is uncertain as it has yet to become a party to the LOSC.

Contemporary challenges

The contemporary issues confronting the polar regions ultimately reflect the phenomenon of globalisation. A century ago Antarctica and the Arctic were literally the last places on earth subject to exploration, and even

[54] Chircop, 'The Growth of International Shipping in the Arctic', 356–7.

[55] C. J. Chivers, 'Russia Plants Underwater Flag at North Pole', *New York Times*, 2 August 2007, available at www.nytimes.com/2007/08/02/world/europe/02cnd-artic.html?module=Search&mabReward=relbias%3; T. Parfitt, 'Russian plants flag on North Pole seabed', *The Guardian*, 2 August 2007, available at www.guardian.co.uk/world/2007/aug/02/russia.arctic.

[56] See e.g. 'Special Report: The Arctic', *The Economist*, 16–22 June 2012. Some of the recent literature relevant includes Tessa Mendez, 'Thin Ice, Shifting Geopolitics: The Legal Implications of Arctic Ice Melt', *Denver Journal of International Law and Policy*, 38 (2010), 527–47; Tavis Potts and Clive Schofield, 'An Arctic Scramble? Opportunities and Threats in the (Formerly) Frozen North', *International Journal of Marine and Coastal Law*, 23 (2008), 151–76; Louise A. de La Fayette, 'Oceans Governance in the Arctic', *International Journal of Marine and Coastal Law*, 23 (2008), 531–66.

after the Poles were conquered it was not really until the advent of reliable polar air transportation that comprehensive mapping of polar lands was completed in the 1950s. In the twenty-first century another type of exploration is taking place as the polar seabed is mapped to support CLCS submissions. The consequence has been that as a result of the dual effects of climate change and the contemporary law of the sea polar sovereignty has again come into the public and political spotlight.

International law does provide a framework for the resolution of these issues, a fact the five Arctic littoral States recognised in May 2008 when they issued the Ilulissat Declaration. The Declaration affirms the capacity of the law of the sea to provide 'important rights and obligations concerning the delineation of the outer limits of the continental shelf, the protection of the marine environment, including ice-covered areas, freedom of navigation, marine scientific research, and other uses of the sea'.[57] In a direct reference to resolution of Arctic maritime boundaries, the Declaration also stated that 'We remain committed to this legal framework and to the orderly settlement of any possible overlapping claims.'[58] The law of the sea is therefore central to how polar maritime sovereignty is to be determined and ultimately exercised, within which the CLCS will play a pivotal part.

The CLCS operates under a mandate based upon Article 76 and Annex II of the LOSC, and its Rules of Procedure make clear that it will not become engaged in political or legal disputes. To date, the CLCS has sought to strictly maintain its role as a scientific and technical body, and as such the Commission has sought to neatly side-step claims which have been asserted offshore disputed territories, or which may result in overlapping claims between two or more states. In the Southern Ocean, both Australia and New Zealand indicated their desire for the CLCS to set aside for the time being potential outer continental shelf claims that could be asserted offshore their Antarctic territories. An alternative approach was taken by Argentina whose 2009 CLCS submission claimed an outer continental shelf offshore its Antarctic territories and adjacent islands.[59] While Argentina has notified the CLCS as to the

[57] See the Ilulissat Declaration, available at www.arcticgovernance.org/the-ilulissat-declaration.4872424.html.

[58] *Ibid.*

[59] Outer Limits of the Continental Shelf: Argentine Submission (Executive Summary) (21 April 2009), available at www.un.org/depts/los/clcs_new/submissions_files/arg25_09/arg2009e_summary_eng.pdf.

existence of disputes with the United Kingdom with respect to the Falkland Islands, South Georgia and the South Sandwich Islands, no such indication was made in the case of its claim over continental Antarctica, or whether there existed constraints upon Argentina's capacity to assert such a claim under the Antarctic Treaty.[60] Argentina's CLCS submission, which remains queued for the time being with no immediate prospect of consideration by the Commission in the near future, has been the subject of diplomatic communications made via the United Nations Secretary-General to the Commission from six Antarctic Treaty parties.[61]

The position in the Arctic is also complex, not because of issues regarding territorial sovereignty but because the configuration of the Arctic Ocean is such that the continental shelf claims will predominantly converge in the Central Arctic Ocean, necessitating the resolution of maritime boundaries between the littoral states whose claims overlap. On current projections, this would potentially involve the resolution of boundaries between Denmark (Greenland) and Canada, Canada and the United States, the United States and Russia, Russia and Norway, and Norway and Denmark (Greenland).[62] The CLCS is therefore set to become an important forum for resolving some of the controversies over Arctic seabed claims, and this may prove to be a catalyst for forcing the US to reassess its position towards the LOSC. Because there is to date so little State practice with respect to outer continental shelf claims under the LOSC, it cannot be said – unlike the general position with respect to 200-nautical-mile continental shelf claims – to be reflective of customary international law. There could be no basis for the United States asserting a unilateral claim to an outer continental shelf without having first acceded to the Convention and having made a submission before the CLCS. This is not to suggest that the United States would have to sit on the sidelines indefinitely whilst other Arctic states assert claims to the Arctic Ocean. One option may be

60 *Ibid.*, 8–9; Argentina refers to these islands as Islas Malvinas, Georgias del Sur and Sandwich del Sur.

61 See e.g. Permanent Mission of Japan to the United Nations (SC/09/390) (19 November 2009) available at www.un.org/Depts/los/clcs_new/submissions_files/arg25_09/jpn_re_arg_2009. Other States to have lodged communications on this matter were the United Kingdom, United States, the Russian Federation, India and the Netherlands.

62 Alex G. Oude Elferink, 'The Outer Continental Shelf in the Arctic: The Application of Article 76 of the LOS Convention in a Regional Context' in Alex G. Oude Elferink and Donald R. Rothwell (eds.), *The Law of the Sea and Polar Maritime Delimitation and Jurisdiction* (The Hague, New York: Martinus Nijhoff, 2001), 149.

for the United States to collaborate in submitting a joint CLCS Arctic claim. There is certainly precedent for the CLCS considering such claims, but in each instance the relevant claimant States have been parties to the LOSC and this may prove to be a hurdle for the United States adopting such a strategy. For this reason the United States may be forced in the very near future to accede to the LOSC.

Concluding remarks

Polar territorial and maritime sovereignty is significantly advanced in the twenty-first century compared to when it was first contemplated one hundred years ago. However, notwithstanding the developments in international law including the specific recognition of particular issues associated with polar sovereignty in the *Eastern Greenland* case and the Antarctic Treaty, and the manner in which maritime sovereignty can be claimed and exercised under the LOSC, there remain tensions over polar sovereignty which show no sign of abating. The stewardship of polar lands has been a dominant theme in political discourse and has been responsible for some remarkable diplomatic about-turns with respect to mining in the Arctic and Antarctica.[63] However, as climate change continues its onward march and the polar regions become more accessible, polar stewardship will be further challenged and in its place polar sovereignty will inevitably assume even greater significance. In the Arctic this will raise particular issues for indigenous peoples whose culture and livelihoods will be threatened by climate change and by new visitors challenging indigenous notions of sovereignty.[64] The polar regions are therefore rapidly approaching a crossroads where decisions will need to be made as to whether to continue the status quo which has served regional legal governance relatively well in recent decades, whether more traditional notions of State sovereignty are (re)applied or in the Arctic there is a significant rethinking of what is meant by sovereignty so as to encompass the views of indigenous peoples who have been the

[63] See e.g. Andrew Jackson and Peter Boyce, 'Mining and "World Park Antarctica", 1982–1991' in Marcus Haward and Tom Griffiths (eds.), *Australia and the Antarctic Treaty System: 50 Years of Influence* (Sydney: University of New South Wales Press, 2011), 300–19.

[64] See, generally, James Crawford, 'The Rights of Peoples: Some Conclusions' in James Crawford (ed.), *The Rights of Peoples* (Oxford: Clarendon, 1988), 159–75.

custodians of the region for centuries. Whatever the outcomes, international law will be tested by these developments and innovative solutions may be needed to ensure Antarctica and the Arctic remain areas of relative international peace and harmony where protection of the environment is a fundamental principle.

7

An enquiry into the palimpsestic nature of territorial sovereignty in East Asia – with particular reference to the Senkaku/Diaoyudao question*

KEUN-GWAN LEE

I Introduction

China is rising (or it has already risen). According to press reports, in 2010 China replaced Japan as the second biggest economy of the world.[1] The inexorable rise of China has led some international relations scholars to predict the inevitable conflict between China and the incumbent hegemon – that is, the United States.[2] China, which would like to avoid confrontation with the other superpower while it pursues the policy of economic modernisation, calls into question the conventional wisdom of the realist bent, in particular its thesis of the inevitability of conflict in the case of big change in power relations. China in 2012 promoted its own revisionist theory entitled 'a new type of great power relationship' (*Xinxing Daguo Guanxi*).[3]

Against this background, an important question for international law scholars is whether and how the rise of China will translate into (hopefully

* Part of this chapter is based on the presentation the author made at the 2011 ILA Asia-Pacific Regional Conference (Taipei, 29 May–1 June 2011) under the title 'Territorial Questions in the East China Sea from a Trans-temporal Perspective'.

1 Mure Dickie, 'China Economy Overtakes Japan', *Financial Times*, 14 February 2011.

2 e.g. John J. Mearsheimer, *The Tragedy of Great Power Politics* (New York: W. W. Norton, 2001); *ibid.*,'China's Unpeaceful Rise', *Current History* (April 2006), 160–2. For detailed discussions of the question, see Steve Chan, *China, the U.S. and the Power-Transition Theory: A Critique* (London and New York: Routledge, 2008); Barry Buzan, 'China in International Society: Is "Peaceful Rise" Possible?', *The Chinese Journal of International Politics*, 3 (2010), 5–36.

3 Cui Tiankai and Pang Hanzhao, 'China–US Relations in China's Overall Diplomacy in the New Era: On China and US Working Together to Build a New-Type Relationship Between Major Countries' (20 July 2012), available at www.fmprc.gov.cn/ce/cggb/eng/gyzg/xwdt/t953682.htm.

peaceful) change in the normative configurations of international society. To adduce an example, the rise of China brings with it a renewed and even (to some ears) 'retro-sounding' emphasis on the principle of (State) sovereignty. Recently, there have been premature rumours of the death of sovereignty, and the concept of sovereignty is often criticised for being a stumbling block in the increasingly globalising world. In contrast, the newly rising (or, to use Kissinger's perceptive expression, 'returning'[4]) China unabashedly claims itself to be 'a most enthusiastic champion' for the principle.[5]

The impact of China's rise on current international law is strongly felt, among others, in the field of territorial sovereignty that delineates the space within which State sovereignty (*imperium*, *jurisdictio*) is exercised.[6] The recent flare-up between China and Japan over the Senkaku/Diaoyudao Islands is a case in point. In 2013, China began to call into doubt even the territorial status quo of Okinawa.[7] It is well known that China has fervently emphasised the principle of territorial integrity[8] and is faced with some thorny territorial issues (actual or potential) of its own. An immediate question is why and on what ground China raises such claims vis-à-vis Japan that carry the risk of boomeranging back to itself.

If one looks at the question from a broader historical perspective, one can ask whether the historical fact that the traditional East Asian

[4] Henry Kissinger, *On China* (New York: Penguin, 2012), 546.

[5] Wang Tieya, 'International Law in China: Historical and Contemporary Perspectives', *Recueil des Cours*, 221 (1990), 288; Li Zhaojie, 'Legacy of Modern Chinese History: Its Relevance to the Chinese Perspective of the Contemporary International Legal Order', *Singapore Journal of International and Comparative Law*, 5 (2001), 318. For a detailed discussion of the principle of sovereignty from Chinese perspective, see Xue Hanqin, *Chinese Contemporary Perspectives on International Law: History, Culture and International Law* (Martinus Nijhoff Publishers, 2012), 68–96; Yang Zewei, *Zhuquanlun: Guojifa shangde Zhuquan Wenti ji qi Fazhan Qushi Yanjiu* [On Sovereignty: Sovereignty and Its Development Tendency in International Law] (Peking University Press, 2005).

[6] For a detailed discussion of the relationship between *souveraineté territoriale* (*territoriale Souveränität*) and *suprématie territoriale* (*Gebietshoheit*), see Julio A. Barberis, 'Les Liens juridiques entre l'état et son territoire: perpspectives théoriques et évolution du droit international', *Annuaire Français de Droit International*, 45 (1999), 132–46; Alfred Verdross, Bruno Simma and Rudolf Geiger, *Territoriale Souveränität und Gebietshoheit: Zur völkerrechtlichen Lage der Oder-Neiße-Gebiete* (Bonn: Kulturstiftung der Deutschen Vertriebenen, 1980).

[7] Reiji Yoshida, 'Japan Protests China's Okinawa Commentary', *Japan Times*, 10 May 2013.

[8] The principle of mutual respect for sovereignty and territorial integrity is the first among the Five Principles of Peaceful Co-existence that were promulgated by China and India in 1954. Xue, *Chinese Contemporary Perspectives on International Law*, 36.

world order (which enjoyed an exceptional longevity spanning a couple of millennia[9]) was abruptly and violently replaced by a new normative order called the 'public law of Europe' bears on the issue of territorial sovereignty over the islands.

It is in this connection that the metaphors of *tabula rasa* and *palimpsest* come in handy. Is international law in East Asia a *tabula rasa* onto which only the European set of norms are indelibly etched? Or is it a *palimpsest*– that is, a parchment which, though overwritten, still retains traces from the past practices of East Asia? As will be shown below, China seems to subscribe to the latter conceptualisation in dealing with its territorial differences with Japan. Then the question arises of whether and how these traces, if any, will impact on the articulation and functioning of international law in East Asia and, in particular, on the equitable resolution of territorial issues in the region.

I will begin by presenting a brief historical overview of the question (II). I will go on to describe the respective claims of Japan and China over the Senkaku/Diaoyu Islands (III) and then offer some critical remarks on the respective positions (IV). This will be followed by an attempt to elucidate what I called the palimpsestic nature of territorial sovereignty in East Asia (V). I will also provide brief concluding remarks (VI).

II Historical overview of the question of the Senkaku/Diaoyu Islands

It is beyond argument that many Chinese books and maps (dating from the Ming (1386–1644) and Qing periods (1644–1911)) recorded the group of uninhabited islands and rocks called Senkaku by the Japanese and Diayudao by the Chinese.[10] They were used as navigational markers by various investiture missions sent to Ryukyu (present-day Okinawa) by

9 For a classical discussion of this subject, see John King Fairbank (ed.), *The Chinese World Order: Traditional China's Foreign Relations* (Harvard University Press, 1968).

10 Due to space constraints, I will not provide a detailed description of the Senkaku/Diayudao question, which one can find elsewhere. For instance, Tao Cheng, 'The Sino-Japanese Dispute over the Tiao-yu-tai (Senkaku) Islands and the Law of Territorial Acquisition', *Virginia Journal of International Law*, 14 (1974), 221–65; Yoshiro Matsui, 'International Law of Territorial Acquisition and the Dispute over the Senkaku (Diaoyu) Islands', *Japanese Annual of International Law*, 40 (1997), 3–31; Han-yi Shaw, *The Diaoyutai/Senkaku Islands Dispute: Its History and an Analysis of the Ownership Claims of the P.R.C., R.O.C., and Japan* (Occasional Papers/Reprints Series in Contemporary Asian Studies No. 3–1999 (152)); Unryu Suganuma, *Sovereign Rights and Territorial Space in Sino-Japanese Relations: Irredentism and the Diaoyu/Senkaku Islands* (Hawaii University Press, 2000); Seokwoo Lee, 'Territorial Disputes among Japan, China and Taiwan Concerning the Senkaku Islands', *Boundary and Territory Briefings*, 3 (2002), 1–37; Junwu Pan, *Toward a New Framework for Peaceful Settlement of China's Territorial and Boundary Disputes* (Leiden: Martinus Nijhoff

China. More importantly, the islands were incorporated into the coastal defence system of the Ming Dynasty in 1561.[11]

A change to this state of affairs took place with the annexation of the Ryukyu Kingdom into Japan in 1879. According to Japan, five years later a Japanese explorer 'discovered' these islands. In January 1895, when Japan's victory over China in the Sino-Japanese War was virtually sealed, Japan formally annexed these islands as *terra nullius*.

During World War II, the Allies adopted the Cairo Declaration on 1 December 1943 and declared their 'purpose... that all the territories Japan has stolen from the Chinese, such as Manchuria, Formosa and the Pescadores, shall be restored to the Republic of China'.[12] The implementation of this Declaration was confirmed by Paragraph 8 of the Potsdam Proclamation of 26 July 1945, which Japan undertook to carry out in the Instrument of Surrender of 2 September 1945.[13] China claims that in accordance with these documents 'Diaoyu Dao, as affiliated islands of Taiwan, should be returned, together with Taiwan, to China.'[14]

After the end of World War II, these islands were put under the trusteeship of the United States in accordance with the 1951 San Francisco Peace Treaty with Japan. The United States exercised effective administration over these islands, using them as firing ranges. However, there was no protest from the Chinese side from 1945 until late 1971.

It was only in the late 1960s that the Chinese interest in the islands resurfaced upon the publication of a report by the UN Economic Commission for Asia and the Far East indicating potential oil and gas reserves in the vicinity of the islands.[15] On 30 December 1971 the government of the People's Republic of China (PRC) raised its territorial claim over the islands (the Republic of China government did so on 12 June 1971).[16]

Publishers, 2009); Masahiko Asada, 'Diaoyu/Senkaku Islands', *Max Planck Encyclopedia of Public International Law*, 10 vols. (Oxford University Press, 2011), III, 90–3.

[11] Information Office of the State Council, The Peoples' Republic of China, 'Diaoyu Dao, an Inherent Territory of China' (Foreign Language Press, 2012), available at www.fmprc.gov.cn/eng/topics/diaodao/t973774.htm.

[12] *Supplement to the American Journal of International Law*, 38 (1944), 8.

[13] James Crawford, *The Creation of States in International Law*, 2nd edn (Oxford University Press, 2006), 198.

[14] Information Office of the State Council, PRC, 'Diaoyu Dao, an Inherent Territory of China', 12.

[15] Committee for Co-ordination of Joint Prospecting for Mineral Resources in Asian Offshore Areas, United Nations Economic Commission for Asia and the Far East, 'Geological Structure and Some Water Characteristics of the East China Sea and Yellow Sea', *Technical Bulletin* 2 (1969), 39–40.

[16] According to the PRC, 'On December 30, 1971, the Chinese Ministry of Foreign Affairs issued a solemn statement, pointing out that "it is completely illegal for the government

China argues that both sides recognised the existence of a territorial dispute over the Senkaku/Diaoyudao Islands in 1972 and 1978 and agreed to defer its settlement to a later date. Japan denies the existence of such an agreement.[17]

China and Japan remained in a 'stagnant confrontation'[18] until recently. The problem of delimiting the Exclusive Economic Zone (EEZ)/continental shelf in the East China Sea was compounded by the territorial question over the islands.[19] The stagnant confrontation flared up into an open diplomatic and even military confrontation after September 2010 when a Chinese fishing boat collided with the patrol boats of the Japan Coast Guard. Upon the 'nationalisation' of three islands (including the biggest one, Uotsurishima/Diaoyudao) by the Japanese government in September 2012, the Chinese government upped the ante by establishing straight baselines around the islands.[20] China has also tried to erode the *status quo ante* by sending naval ships to patrol the waters near the Senkaku/Diaoyudao Islands.[21]

Based on this summary, let me now proceed to a brief description and analysis of the respective claims of China and Japan.

III The respective positions of China and Japan on the Senkaku/Diaoyu Islands

I will present brief descriptions of the respective positions of China and Japan concerning title to the Senkaku/Diaoyu Islands, limiting myself to

of the United States and Japan to include China's Diaoyu Dao Islands into the territories to be returned to Japan in the Okinawa Reversion Agreement and that it can by no means change the People's Republic of China's territorial sovereignty over the Diaoyu Dao Islands". The Taiwan authorities also expressed firm opposition to the backroom deal between the United States and Japan.' Above n. 11, at 13.

17 For the Japanese position on whether the question was shelved in 1972 and 1978, see Ministry of Foreign Affairs of Japan, 'Q&A on the Senkaku Islands' (in particular, Question No. 14), available at www.mofa.go.jp/region/asia-paci/senkaku/qa_1010.html#qa14.

18 Steven Wei Su, 'The Territorial Dispute over the Tiaoyu/Senkaku Islands: An Update', *Ocean Development and International Law*, 36 (2005), 45.

19 For a detailed discussion of this question, see Gao Jianjun, 'Joint Development in the East China Sea: Not an Easier Challenge than Delimitation', *The International Journal of Marine and Coastal Law*, 23 (2008), 39–75.

20 'Statement of the Government of the People's Republic of China on the Baselines of the Territorial Sea of Diaoyu Dao and Its Affiliated Islands' (September 10, 2012), available at www.un.org/depts/los/LEGISLATIONANDTREATIES/PDFFILES/DEPOSIT/chn_mzn89_2012_e.pdf.

21 Martin Fackler, 'Japan Says China Aimed Radar at Ship', *New York Times*, 5 February 2013.

the facts that are closely related to the main argument of this chapter, the palimpsestic structure or nature of territorial sovereignty in East Asia.

1 *Overview of the Chinese position*

Until recently, it was not necessarily easy to ascertain the official position of China in sufficient detail. Because of the lack of official statements, interested parties had to rely mainly on scholarly writings. This situation has changed in the past couple of years with the publication of *Zhongguo Guojifa Shijianyu Anli* (International Law in China: Cases and Practice)[22] in March 2011 and the official pamphlet titled *Diaoyu Dao She Zhonggude Lingtu* (Diaoyu Dao, an Inherent Territory of China)[23] compiled by the Information Office of the State Council, a Peoples' Republic of China in September 2012. The former was compiled by the Department of Treaty and Law, the PRC Ministry of Foreign Affairs.[24] China's position on the Diaoyu Islands appears in pages 134–8. The latter publication was published in the pivotal month of September 2012 when Japan 'nationalised' the three islands of the Senkaku/Diaoyu group. The pamphlet is very helpful in that it contains the most detailed official view of the Chinese government, in particular, the legal grounds China invokes to found its territorial sovereignty for the islands. Another pamphlet that is largely similar in its main points was published by the PRC National Marine Data and Information Service under (rather confusingly) the same English title.

The central pillar of the Chinese claim is that the group of islands is part of 'China's inherent territory'. The expression 'inherent territory', which is widely used in East Asia (for instance, Takeshima – known as Dokdo in Korea – is claimed to be 'an inherent part of the territory of Japan',[25] and 'the Senkaku Islands are clearly an inherent part of the territory of Japan'[26]), appears to signify historic title.[27] Indeed, China's

[22] Duan Jielong (ed.), *Zhongguo Guojifa Shijianyu Anli* (International Law in China: Cases and Practice) (Beijing: Law Press China, 2011).

[23] Above n. 11.

[24] The publication is available from the following website: www.soa.gov.cn/soa/news/specialtopic/diaoyudao/gylt/webinfo/2012/09/1347338540445425.htm.

[25] Ministry of Foreign Affairs of Japan, 'Japan's Inalterable Position on the Sovereignty of Takeshima', available at www.mofa.go.jp/region/asia-paci/takeshima/index.html.

[26] *Ibid.*, and 'The Basic View on the Sovereignty over the Senkaku Islands' (May 2013), available at www.mofa.go.jp/region/asia-paci/senkaku/basic_view.html.

[27] For a concise discussion of historic title, see Andrea Gioia, 'Historic Titles', *Max Planck Encyclopedia of Public International Law*, 10 vols. (Oxford University Press, 2011), IV, 814–23.

position as indicated in the 2012 pamphlet, in the 2011 book compiled by the PRC Foreign Ministry, and in scholarly and media materials, gives central focus to this title. In so doing, China adamantly refutes Japan's contention that the Senkaku/Diaoyu Islands were *terra nullius* in January 1895.[28]

To corroborate its argument founded on historic title, China adduces a substantial amount of historical records dating back to as early as 1403. These records document a long series of Chinese practices or actions relating to the islands such as their usage as navigational aids for various investiture missions, at the latest, since 1534. China also invokes many cases of the islands' entry in the local gazetteers and, more importantly, the practices of incorporating the islands within the Chinese coastal defence system.[29] Cartographic evidence is also proffered, such as the inclusion of the islands as Chinese territory in an official Chinese map entitled Imperial Map of Native and Foreign Lands (*Huangchao Zhongwai Yitong Yutu*, 1863).[30]

In discussing whether the islands were *terra nullius* in January 1895, Chinese commentators hint at the existence of not a single normative system, but of a double-layered normative order in East Asia at the end of the nineteenth century. In other words, as far as China is concerned, the question of the Senkaku/Diaoyu Islands being *terra nullius* or not in January 1895 should not be assessed solely according to 'modern international law' (that had been recently 'introduced' into the region). The traditional concept of territorial sovereignty as practiced in East Asia should be taken into account (at least, along with modern international law) in the evaluation of the question.

In this vein, a Chinese commentator mentions the need to '[consider] as special the Chinese ancient values on territorial sovereignty, instead of disqualifying the legal effect of [China's "obviously ineffective display of sovereignty" in the pre-1895 period]'.[31] He admits that '[traditionally]

[28] For a detailed discussion of various modes of territorial acquisition, see James Crawford, *Brownlie's Principles of Public International Law*, 8th edn (Oxford University Press, 2012), ch. 9.

[29] Information Office of the State Council, PRC, 'Diaoyu Dao, an Inherent Territory of China', 5; Shaw, *The Diaoyutai/Senkaku Islands Dispute*, 55–7; Cheng, 'The Sino-Japanese Dispute over the Tiao-yu-tai (Senkaku) Islands and the Law of Territorial Acquisition', 256–7.

[30] Information Office of the State Council, PRC, 'Diaoyu Dao, an Inherent Territory of China', 6; Shaw, *The Diaoyutai/Senkaku Islands Dispute*, 55.

[31] Su, 'The Territorial Dispute over the Tiaoyu/Senkaku Islands: An Update', 52.

China's approaches to displaying its sovereignty are all alien to Western international law doctrines'.[32] These arguments are offered, in part, to counter Japan's attempt to discredit the relevance of the pre-1895 Chinese records and practices.[33] From the standpoint of China, it would be highly inappropriate to apply the yardstick of modern international law in appreciating the facts that took place under a substantially different normative order.

2 Overview of the Japanese position

While China presented its official position in an elaborate manner only recently, the Japanese government had already published a document titled 'The Basic View on the Sovereignty over the Senkaku Islands' (hereinafter, 'Basic View') in March 1972. The following discussion is based on this document, together with the supplementary information such as 'Q&A on the Senkaku Islands', which is available on the homepage of the Japanese Ministry of Foreign Affairs.[34] The 'Basic View' has evolved since its first appearance in 1972 and it is worthwhile to compare the 1972 version and the currently available one.[35]

The first paragraph of the currently available 'Basic View' summarises the Japanese position. According to the provisional translation offered at the homepage of the Japanese Ministry of Foreign Affairs, the central part of the paragraph reads: '[t]here is no doubt that the Senkaku Islands are clearly an inherent part of the territory of Japan, in light of historical facts and based upon international law'.[36]

The current version of the 'Basic View' contains four more paragraphs that serve to elaborate the main argument as put forth in the first paragraph. The main grounds Japan invokes to support its claim of territorial sovereignty over the islands can be summarised as follows:

(a) historic title as reconfirmed by the act of annexation as *terra nullius* in 1895

32 *Ibid.*

33 e.g. Toshio Okuhara, 'Senkaku Retto no Ryoyuken Kizoku Mondai' (The Problem of To Whom the Territorial Sovereignty over the Senkaku Islands Belongs), *Asahi Asia Review*, 3 (1972).

34 Above n. 7.

35 The most recent version is effective as of May 2013. The following discussion is based on this version.

36 The 'Basic View on the Sovereignty over the Senkaku Islands'.

(b) confirmation of Japan's sovereignty in the 1951 San Francisco Peace Treaty
(c) China's acquiescence in (or even recognition of) Japan's territorial sovereignty until 1971.

According to Japan, 'the Senkaku Islands have continuously been an integral part of the Nansei Shoto Islands [present-day Okinawa Islands], which are the territory of Japan'.[37] Normally, such a statement would be followed by the enumeration of records and practices proving the claimant State's historic title over the islands in question. However, in the case of the Senkaku Islands, very curiously, Japan states that after confirming that 'the Senkaku Islands had been not only uninhabited but also showed no trace of having been under the control of the Qing Dynasty of China',[38] it annexed the islands as *terra nullius* on 14 January 1895. An acute logical problem implicit in this argument will be discussed in more detail later.

Japan also invokes the resounding and prolonged silence of China regarding the islands from 1895 until 1971. It goes further by adducing some evidence which, Japan argues, proves China's recognition of Japan's territorial sovereignty over the islands. One prominent example is an article of the *People's Daily*, the official newspaper of the Communist Party of China, which appeared on 8 January 1953. The article, titled 'Battle of People in the Ryukyu Islands against the U.S. Occupation', stated that 'the Ryukyu Islands . . . consist of 7 groups of islands; the Senkaku Islands, the Sakishima Islands'.[39] Based on these practices, Japan argues that China acquiesced in and even recognised Japanese territorial sovereignty over the islands. This would constitute an 'Achilles' heel' for China in a judicial setting.

IV Some critical remarks on the respective positions of China and Japan

This section will offer some critical remarks on the respective positions of China and Japan over the question of the Senkaku/Diaoyu Islands. It will focus on the questions that have an immediate relevance to the main question under consideration – that is, whether modern international

[37] *Ibid.* [38] *Ibid.*

[39] Ministry of Foreign Affairs of Japan, 'Q&A on the Senkaku Islands' (in particular, Question No. 4).

law alone should be taken into account when tackling the problem of determining territorial sovereignty over the Senkaku/Diaoyu Islands.

1 Critique of the Chinese position

The Chinese position is mainly anchored on historic title – a claim about which the Japanese side raises serious doubt, calling into question the relevance of the historical documents and maps that China relies upon. According to Japan, these documents and maps fall short of the legal standards set by modern international law and, as such, do not deserve to be taken into account in resolving the question.

For this reason some Chinese commentators put forth the need to evaluate these documents not from the standpoint of modern European international law, but from the viewpoint of a different normative order contemporaneous with the alleged annexation of the islands by Japan – that is, the traditional East Asian world order.[40] China holds a deep sense of mistrust and victimisation in regard to modern international law given that it perceives itself to have been on the receiving end of the instrumental (ab)use of such law by the Western and Japanese powers throughout the 'century of humiliation'.[41]

To this extent, China's reliance on the double-layered nature of international law in the region is understandable. However, China's approach is riddled with serious problems. First, it is a highly daunting task to come up with an articulate description of the traditional normative order in East Asia as a sophisticated and coherent system. Secondly, supposing one could reconstruct this order in an elaborate and coherent way, it should be recalibrated to ensure its compatibility with the fundamental principles of modern international law. For instance, the basic tenet of the traditional order is the (axiomatic) positional superiority of China and the resultant verticality of its relationship with the other members of the order. It is obvious that this verticality is diametrically opposed to the founding principle of modern international law – that is, the principle of sovereign equality of states. Thirdly, the no less difficult task of securing an interface between this order and modern international law remains.

[40] e.g. Shaw discusses the relevance of the 'East Asian World Order' throughout his book *The Diaoyutai/Senkaku Islands Dispute*.

[41] Xue observes that 'China's persistent stand on the primacy of State sovereignty has its deep roots embedded in the miserable experience in its modern history', *Chinese Contemporary Perspectives on International Law*, 71.

At the present stage, it appears that Chinese commentators are resorting to and invoking the traditional regional order without articulating the architecture and concrete contents of the order. From this, it follows that they do not know how to articulate the relationship between this order and modern international law.

2 Critique of the Japanese position

In contrast to the Chinese position, Japan appears to operate under a single normative system – that is, modern international law originating from Europe. The seemingly straightforward position of the Japanese government gives the impression that both points in time – namely, the year 1895 (when the islands were annexed as *terra nullius*) and the present – are placed within a single and seamlessly continuing normative space, obviating the need to discuss the double-layered nature of international law in East Asia.

The main Japanese position is built on historic title as reconfirmed by the act of annexation as *terra nullius* in 1895. When one compares the 1972 'Basic View' with its current version, there is a subtle yet important difference concerning the title of occupation of *terra nullius.* In the older version, this title is accorded the central role in establishing Japan's territorial sovereignty over the islands. The original claim was that '[s]ince [January 1895] the Senkaku Islands have been consistently a part of Japan's territory of Nansei Shoto'.[42] In stark contrast, the current 'Basic View' states that '[h]istorically, the Senkaku Islands have continuously been an integral part of the Nansei Shoto Islands, which are the territory of Japan'. Thus, there has been a substantial shift in the Japanese position with respect to when the islands have been regarded as the 'inherent territory' of Japan. In sum, according to the 1972 'Basic View', the islands have been a part of Japan's territory of Nansei Shoto since January 1895, while the current 'Basic View' regards them as having been an integral part of the Nansei Shoto Islands *historically*, seemingly indicating that they have been so 'from time immemorial'.

This difference is not merely temporal. It compels one to reconstruct the logical relationship between the titles. According to the 1972 'Basic

[42] The English version of the 1972 'Basic View' of Japan is available from the following source: Jerome Alan Cohen and Hungdah Chiu, *People's China and International Law: A Documentary Study*, 2 vols. (Princeton University Press, 1974), I, 351–2.

View', this relationship is straightforward. The islands were annexed as *terra nullius* in 1895 and have since then remained a part of Japan's territory. Under the current 'Basic View', Japan annexed the islands not as *terra nullius*, but in order to reconfirm its historic title over them. It is clear that an acute logical problem ('annexing as *terra nullius* the islands that have been a historically inherent part of your territory') lurks in the new formulation.

An important question is why Japan is taking the risk of committing such a logical fallacy. If nothing had happened to the once unassailable superiority of modern international law, such retreat into a logical quagmire by Japan would not have been necessary. The compulsion, as it were, to take such a substantial risk suggests that a significant change has taken place to, generally, the international legal order of East Asia, and, more specifically, to the normative parameters of territorial questions in the region. The unquestionable superiority of modern international law (in particular, the positivity and legitimacy of annexation of *terra nullius* as a title of territorial acquisition), obviating the need to look at any other normative system, gave way to the necessity to reformulate Japan's argument concerning its territorial title, even at the risk of logical inconsistency.

3 Preliminary conclusion

The critical survey conducted above suggests that the rise or return of China as a world power has dented the unquestionable authority of modern international law as the ultimate normative benchmark for the region. This probably has led China to invoke the 'pre-modern' documents and practices with more ease and conviction. Japan seems to be compelled to take into account this change, even at the risk of logical self-contradiction.

Does this imply that the contemporary legal order in East Asia is of a palimpsestic nature? Supposing that that order is (at least partially) palimpsestic, how can one secure an 'interface' between modern international law and the traditional regional order in an articulate and coherent manner? Is this mode of viewing contemporary international law applicable to the other non-European regions? Does this approach not carry the risk of further aggravating the 'fragmentation of international law' about which much concern has been expressed from various angles? One can come up with a very long list of questions concerning the palimpsestic nature or structure of international law, some of which are discussed in the next section.

V The palimpsestic nature of territorial sovereignty in East Asia

This chapter does not aim to evaluate the merits of the respective claims of China and Japan over the Senkaku/Diaoyu Islands, but to examine the fundamental question underlying China's argument: the existence and relevance of the traditional concept of territorial sovereignty and its implications for the resolution of the Senkaku/Diaoyu dispute. I will first describe the dilemma faced by the Chinese side and then suggest a strategy for a palimpsestic reconstruction of its claims over the Senkaku/Diaoyu Islands.

1 Dilemma faced by the Chinese scholars

A fundamental difference between the approaches of China and Japan concerning the Senkaku/Diaoyu Islands lies in the choice of normative system(s) to be applied to the question at hand. In this connection, the Chinese side places a substantial reliance on the traditional concept of territorial sovereignty.

Concerning the Chinese argument based on the double-layered structure of international law in East Asia, let me first point out that a substantial degree of uncertainty surrounds such resort to the traditional order. Chinese commentators do not elaborate what the substantive contours or contents of this order are in reference to territorial acquisition. They stop at suggesting the existence and relevance of this order. While unable to articulate the architecture and contents of this order, they still believe that this normative dimension exists and could (or should) impact, in one way or another, the resolution of the question. There exists a perception that there is 'something important', but it remains on the furthest edges of their epistemological horizon, defying a comprehensible and detailed exposition.

Without a clear idea of what this traditional order is, it is very difficult to expect scholars to proceed to the 'Herculean' task of securing and clarifying the relationship or interaction between the traditional order and modern international law. Until and unless this relationship or interface is constructed in an intelligible and coherent manner, the traditional order is in danger of remaining just that, a hodge-podge of 'pre-modern' practices not susceptible of scientific or systemic treatment or categorisation by modern international law. That this is not an idle worry is amply demonstrated by a series of decisions of the International Court of Justice and international arbitral tribunals.[43]

2 Strategy for a palimpsestic reconstruction

Let me now address the question of how to ascertain the substantive contours or contents of the traditional East Asian order, often known as the Sino-centric order. The late Professor Wang Tieya observed in his 1990 Hague Lectures that 'for thousands of years in the context of Chinese traditional order, no international law of any kind could possibly exist'.[44] The veracity of this sweeping statement can be questioned in many ways. However, the question of the correctness of the 'Wang thesis' should not detain us here. What is important for our purposes is that the supposed or professed cultural or moral character of the order (or, seen from a different angle, the alleged absence of an 'inter-State' relationship) resulted in a dearth of reflections or scientific treatments of the subject now called international law. For example, books were written dealing with diplomatic rituals. However, little literature on the 'legal' nature of the tributary relations (often assimilated to 'suzerainty', a highly misleading term having a European origin) was produced.[45] To use the Hegelian terms, the Sino-centric order existed and functioned as a 'being-in-itself' (*an-sich-sein*), lacking in self-awareness and remaining 'self-identical'. In other words, the order did not reach the stage of 'being-for-itself' (*für-sich-sein*), 'the fully deployed, exteriorized, which therefore lies, as it were "before itself"'.[46]

As a result, it is not surprising that Chinese scholars could not present a systematic exposition of the substantive contents of the order in spite of their repeated invocations of it. There lies the difficult task for the scholars

[43] Cases involving territorial sovereignty in which arguments based on 'pre-modern' legal concepts or practices were rejected by international judicial organs include, among others, *Western Sahara (Advisory Opinion)* (1975), *Case concerning the Territorial Dispute (Libya/Chad)* (1994) and *Eritrea-Yemen Arbitration, Phase I Award* (1998).

[44] Wang, 'International Law in China', 219. See also Fairbank, *The Chinese World Order*, 5 ('the traditional Chinese world order can hardly be called international').

[45] For discussions on the history of international law in East Asia, see Keishiro Iriye, 'The Principles of International Law in the Light of Confucian Doctrine', *Recueil des Cours*, 120 (1967), 1–57; Onuma Yasuaki, 'When Was the Law of International Society Born? – An Inquiry of the History of International Law from an Intercivilizational Perspective', *Journal of the History of International Law*, 2 (2000), 27–32, 51–4.

[46] Charles Taylor, *Hegel* (Cambridge University Press, 1975), 112.

who are interested in the palimpsestic nature of international law in East Asia and other non-European regions. They have first to articulate the traditional orders in their regions in a systematic and coherent manner. Given the absence or dearth of academic or reflective heritage in this regard and the resultant need to work from scratch, the enormity of the task can be readily understood.

It is beyond my ability to provide an articulate description of the order in this chapter. All I can do is merely to suggest a research strategy for the future. The first task is to collate cases or practices relating to territorial questions from historical materials. In analysing these cases, one needs to find recurrent patterns and determine whether they have normative implications. In doing so, the risk of uncritically subsuming these practices under the ready-made categories and concepts of modern international law should be avoided. One should not overlook or ignore a certain overlap or commonality between the two normative orders. At the same time, every effort should be made to remain aware of and alert to the characteristics peculiar to the traditional East Asian order.

Let me adduce an example. China accords substantial weight to the fact that the Chinese first discovered and named the Diaoyu Islands. In this connection, let me discuss an official Chinese map entitled Imperial Map of Native and Foreign Lands (*Huangchao Zhongwai Yitong Yutu*, 1863). In the explanatory part to the compilation of maps, a co-compiler of the maps, Yan Shusen, stated the principle of 'the name follows its owner' (*mingcongzhuren*). He strengthened the authority of the principle by tracing it to one of the canonical texts of Confucianism, 'The Commentary of Gongyang to the Springs and Autumns Annals'. If a certain locality on the map belonged to non-Sinic frontier lands (*siyi*), both the Chinese and vernacular names were used. He subsequently provided a select list of vernacular expressions for, among others, river, mountain, castle, lake and their Chinese counterparts.[47]

In connection with the Senkaku/Daioyu question, this principle could assume a certain importance. On the 1863 map, the three islands belonging to the Senkaku/Diaoyu Islands are indicated in Chinese names only, while those islands belonging to the present-day Okinawa are indicated in both Chinese and the vernacular – that is, Ryukyuan – names. According

[47] e.g. Toshio Okuhara, 'Senkaku Retto no Ryoyuken Kizoku Mondai' (The Problem of to Whom the Territorial Sovereignty over the Senkaku Islands Belongs), *Asahi Asia Review*, 3 (1972).

to the Chinese side, this fact is interpreted to reflect Qing China's clear conception of territorial ownership of the Diaoyu Islands.[48]

There is much need for further research into the significance of the principle as expressed in the 1863 map. The Chinese interpretation would be further strengthened if one could prove that this supposed principle, rather than being a one-off in 1863, was in fact widely used in traditional East Asia. Then the Chinese side could be justified in claiming that the islands in question fell under the Chinese *dominium* under the traditional East Asian order, thereby refuting Japan's argument based on the annexation of the islands as *terra nullius*.[49]

To address this thorny question, interdisciplinary and international co-operation among scholars is required. Even if one were able to articulate the substantive contours or contents of the traditional order, the no less daunting challenge of securing an interface between this order and modern international law remains. In carrying out this difficult task, one should not conceptualise the relationship between the two orders as two separate circles that never overlap. This would be as grave an error as supposing that both an island dispute in mid-nineteenth-century East Asia and one in early twenty-first-century Europe occupy the same normative space. There should be a certain level of overlap or commonality between the orders in respect of the conception of territory (and the concomitant rules such as its inviolability in time of peace), the catalogue of valid territorial titles, the probative value of maps and so on. In so doing, one should construct the interface in such a way as to ensure compatibility between the traditional order and modern international law.

VI Concluding remarks

In this short chapter, I have conducted a preliminary investigation into China's 'rise' or 'return' and its implications for the resolution of a territorial question between China and Japan, concerning the Senkaku/Diaoyu Islands. In so doing, I have attempted to demonstrate that while Japan

[48] Shaw, *The Diaoyutai/Senkaku Islands Dispute*, 55.

[49] China could argue that under the standard of modern international law the inclusion of these uninhabited and remote islands in an official map can amount to not only 'symbolical' but 'effective' occupation. On the other hand, Japan could invoke the case law as elaborated in the *Island of Palmas* arbitration and regard the 1863 act of China, at most, as creating an 'inchoate' title. For a detailed discussion of discovery creating only an inchoate title, see *Island of Palmas or (Miangas), United States* v. *Netherlands*, Arbitration (1928), Reports of International Arbitral Awards, vol. 2, 843–6.

operates under the European version of territorial law that has enjoyed a monopolistic authority in the region since the latter half of the nineteenth century, China places a substantial reliance on, in addition to contemporary international law, the normative discourse that reigned supreme in traditional East Asia. I have used the metaphor of palimpsest to delve into the (at least partially) double-layered structure or nature of international law in today's East Asia. The metaphor can be utilised in other non-European regions of the world.

One may ask about the differences between China's rise and its challenge for contemporary public international law, on the one hand, and the other challenges coming from outside Western Europe in the past, on the other. As regards the latter, three examples come to mind. First, Japan's rise in the post-1945 period was partial in the sense that it was limited to the economic and financial field. More importantly, Japan seems to lack an *animus* to change the international legal order. Secondly, the rise of the Soviet Union led to a fierce rivalry between the capitalist and the socialist camps and posed a great challenge to the unity and continuity of international law. The theory of peaceful co-existence, firmly premised on the fundamental incompatibility between the two camps,[50] is an apt example. However, 'peaceful co-existence' meant co-survival in a state of 'cold peace' without meaningful interchange. This constitutes a significant contrast to the relationship between China and the rest of the world that can be characterised as one of profound entanglement. Thirdly, there was a serious attempt by the G-77 states to reformulate the international legal order during the period of de-colonisation, as is exemplified by the effort to establish a new international economic order or a new international information order. However, the rise of this group of states at the discursive level was not matched by a rise at the material level. In other words, their rise, if ever, had only *animus*, lacking in *corpus*. Thus looked at, the challenge China's rise poses for current international law is unprecedented and, therefore, requires a focused and, at the same time, flexible response.

To use the metaphor of giant, China can be described as a giant that does not yet know how to articulate its normative past. The rise of China will surely impact on the configurations of the international normative system in one way or another, thus ensuring that the current international law is recalibrated to reflect the normative experiences and expectations of

[50] For a detailed discussion of the subject, see Grigory I. Tunkin, 'Coexistence and International Law, *Recueil des Cours*, 95 (1958), 1–81.

China. In the region, discomfort with the current system of international law is not limited to China. The late Professor Han-key Lee, who is regarded as one of the pioneers of modern international law research in Korea, proposed the establishment of a Regional International Court of Justice of Asia for the pacific settlement of disputes, especially disputes arising from State boundary or territory problems. This court was to 'solve regional problems on the basis of regional philosophy of law and practices'.[51]

The re-conceptualisation of international law in East Asia from a palimpsestic perspective and the resultant recalibration of current international law carry the risk of furthering the centrifugal tendency of international law. This exercise cannot be a nostalgic and unreflective attempt to return to an ostensibly idyllic past, which is unfeasible given that international law has been transformed (probably irrevocably) by the 'public law of Europe'. East Asians cannot return to the days when the positional superiority of China was the founding principle of the regional order. In particular, one should beware the danger of the palimpsestic approach to territorial questions in East Asia falling prey to the siren call of irredentism, which runs diametrically counter to the fundamental principle of the stability of boundaries. It should aim at a more modest and pragmatic goal of achieving a peaceful change or polyphonic reconstruction of international law without radically undermining the stability and security of the current international order.

[51] Han-Key Lee and MyongWhai Kim, 'Background Paper on Hongkong Conference in International Law', *Korean Journal of International Law*, 12 (1967), 181–2.

8

General legal characteristics of States

A view from the past of the Permanent Court of International Justice

OLE SPIERMANN

Contributors to this book share the privilege of having been supervised by Professor Crawford in an atmosphere combining theoretical curiosity and vast practical experience that is unique to James: a truly open system. These were supervisions at their most effective, open-minded and thought-provoking; they were also supervisions by a master not to be imitated by his students, as this chapter will confirm. With James Crawford in the Whewell chair, international law at Cambridge acknowledged a close relationship between law and history long before it became flavour of the month. This chapter will take the general characteristics of States listed in *The Creation of States in International Law* and discuss these, albeit not quite in the Crawfordian style, with a view to the past of the Permanent Court of International Justice.

The Permanent Court stands as a monument to the possible impact to be exercised on and from the bench of the World Court by eminent scholars. In their generation, Max Huber and Dionisio Anzilotti were second to none. The Permanent Court was the first significant court of justice at the international level. Obscure cases decided by the Permanent Court are household names, familiar to present generations of international lawyers, because they were, by chance, the first place for authoritative expression of various principles of general international law. Such statements of principle have found wide use far beyond their original context. Many are also to the point today. As Crawford has noted, '[o]ur system is one which international lawyers of four generations ago would have had no particular difficulty in recognizing or working with, once they had got over its bulk'.[1] To the question 'what are the constitutional underpinnings

[1] James Crawford, *International Law as an Open System* (London: Cameron May, 2002), 17.

of the processes that are producing such developments as these?', Crawford's answer has been: 'the same old concepts of consent, treaty-making and state authority'. To the question 'what are the legal techniques at play in determining the results of these processes?', he has answered: '[t]he same old techniques'.[2]

General legal characteristics of States

In *The Creation of States in International Law*, Crawford lists five general legal characteristics of States, including the following:

(1) In principle, States have plenary competence to perform acts, make treaties and so on in the international sphere: this is one meaning of the term 'sovereign' as applied to States.

(2) In principle, States are exclusively competent with respect to their internal affairs, a principle reflected by Article 2(7) of the United Nations Charter. This does not of course mean that international law imposes no constraints: it does mean that their jurisdiction over internal matters is prima facie both plenary and not subject to the control of other States.

...

(4) In international law States are regarded as 'equal', a principle recognized by the Charter (Article 2(1)). This is in part a restatement of the foregoing principles, but it has other corollaries. It is a formal, not a moral principle. It does not mean, for example, that all States are entitled to an equal vote in international organizations: States may consent to unequal voting rights by becoming members of organizations with weighted voting... Still less does it mean that they are entitled to equal voice or influence. But it does mean that at a basic level, States have equal status and standing...[3]

Essentially, these three general characteristics of States combine three notions that are fundamental to international law and international lawyers.

First, sovereignty: States have 'plenary competence', both 'in the international sphere' (1) and 'with respect to their internal affairs' (2).

[2] *Ibid.*, 37.

[3] James Crawford, *The Creation of States in International Law*, 2nd edn (Oxford University Press, 2006), 40–1.

Secondly, independence: States are 'prima facie . . . not subject to the control of other States', in international matters (4) as well as in 'internal matters' (2).

Thirdly, international/national divide: sometimes States act 'in the international sphere' (1 and 4), sometimes in 'their internal affairs' (2).

It takes a plurality of States, and the acknowledgement thereof, to move from sovereignty to independence and the international/national divide. This move cannot be explained or questioned within international law. It is axiomatic to international law. International lawyers have an understanding of what constitutes 'the international sphere' before they become, or see themselves as, international lawyers. This minimum of internationalism is beyond sovereign will. Sovereignty is competence while independence is restriction upon competence, something to be accepted in order to secure the sovereignty of other states through international law.

Yet another general legal characteristic of States, as formulated by Crawford, is the following:

(3) In principle States are not subject to compulsory international process, jurisdiction, or settlement without their consent, given either generally or in the specific case.[4]

Independence translates into a variety of principles, which are substantive in kind, the necessary minimum of international law and, in terms of scope, an international sphere, as distinct from internal affairs. The substantive principles into which independence translates have been categorised by tradition as customary international law, sometimes supplemented by general principles of civilised nations. Some have tried to introduce avant-gardist terms such as 'international law of co-existence'. Crawford prefers the more appropriate term 'general international law'.

It is a choice to include the absence of compulsory jurisdiction in general international law as a general, and legal, characteristic of States. It means that jurisdiction takes consent and treaty form. It is an aspect of substantive international law. Instead of this negative aspect of general international law, one could just as well refer to some of the positive aspects as general legal characteristics of States, such as the principle of peaceful settlement of disputes.

The last general legal characteristic of States listed by Crawford is the following:

[4] *Ibid.*, 41.

(5) Derogations from these principles will not be presumed: in case of doubt an international court or tribunal will tend to decide in favour of the freedom of action of States, whether with respect to external or internal affairs, or as not having consented to a specific exercise of international jurisdiction, or to a particular derogation from equality. This presumption – rebuttable in any case – has declined in importance, but it is still invoked from time to time and is still part of the hidden grammar of international legal language. It will be referred to as the Lotus presumption – its classic formulation being the judgment of the Permanent Court in *The Lotus*.[5]

This last general characteristic of States is accompanied by a footnote occupying almost a full page, and it is controversial, not least from the point of view of the Permanent Court.

Independence and the Permanent Court

The flow of grand statements from the Permanent Court that are still quoted today are almost exclusively the fruits of the work of the Permanent Court in its first composition in the 1920s. This period saw a tendency to employ the most general principles in deciding the most specific issues, and an interest in 'developing' international law.

The first thing to note about this period is that the focus of the Permanent Court was on independence, as distinct from sovereignty, as illustrated by the following cases.

In the *Eastern Carelia* Opinion, independence was characterised as 'a fundamental principle of international law [*la base même du droit international*]'. The Permanent Court added: 'It is well established in international law that no State can, without its consent, be compelled to submit its disputes with other States either to mediation or to arbitration, or to any other kind of pacific settlement.'[6]

Just before the *Eastern Carelia* Opinion, in the *Nationality Decrees* Opinion, the Permanent Court took independence (in the form of a principle of non-intervention) as a blueprint when interpreting Article 15(8) of the Covenant of the League of Nations. According to Article 15(8), the Council of the League of Nations should make no recommendations in

[5] *Ibid.*, 41–2.

[6] *Status of Eastern Carelia (USSR* v. *Finland)*, Advisory Opinion, 23 July 1923, PCIJ Series B, No. 5 (1923), 27.

matters 'within the domestic jurisdiction'. In the view of the Permanent Court, 'at a given point' the League's interest in being able to make recommendations gave 'way to the equally essential interest of the individual State to maintain intact its independence in matters which international law recognises to be solely within its jurisdiction'.[7] 'Without this reservation', the Permanent Court explained, 'the internal affairs of a country might, directly they appeared to affect the interests of another country, be brought before the Council and form the subject of recommendations by the League of Nations'. However, a caveat was entered. According to the same paragraph of the *motifs*, '[t]he question whether a certain matter is or is not solely within the jurisdiction of a State is an essentially relative question; it depends upon the development of international relations'.[8] Article 15(8) was 'limited by rules of international law' so that if a State had undertaken treaty obligations, Article 15(8) 'then ceases to apply as regards those States which are entitled to invoke such rules', the dispute taking on 'an international character'. In short, independence was not synonymous with sovereignty nor a principle of *in dubio pro libertate*, a presumption against international law.

In *The Lotus* then, the Permanent Court was again dealing with independence, as distinct from sovereignty:

> International law governs relations between independent States. The rules of law binding upon States therefore emanate from their own free will as expressed in conventions or by usages generally accepted as expressing principles of law and established in order to regulate the relations between these co-existing independent communities [*la co-existence de ces communautés indépendantes*] or with a view to the achievement of common aims. Restrictions upon the independence of States cannot therefore be presumed.[9]

The last sentence, '[r]estrictions upon the independence of States cannot therefore be presumed', has been taken by many academics to imply that the Permanent Court saw no need for international law, that each State was sovereign and self-contained, and that it supported a presumption against international law.

In the *Nuclear Weapons* Opinion, the International Court of Justice for the first and only time confronted that particular sentence, just in

[7] *Nationality Decrees Issued in Tunis and Morocco (French Zone)*, Advisory Opinion, 7 February 1923, PCIJ Series B, No. 4 (1923), 25.

[8] *Ibid.*, 24.

[9] *SS Lotus (France* v. *Turkey)*, Judgment, 7 September 1927, PCIJ Series A, No. 10 (1927), 18.

order to side-step it. According to the International Court, none of the States appearing before the Court had disputed that 'their independence to act was indeed restricted by the principles and rules of international law'.[10] Therefore, the International Court assumed that the Permanent Court had been using the word 'independence' as synonymous with 'sovereignty', while the approach of the Permanent Court was, in fact, the exact opposite. In 1931, Max Huber had made it known that the majority opinion in *The Lotus* 'a été quelquefois mal interprété par les critiques du dit arrêt'.[11] Åke Hammerskjöld, the ingenious Registrar of the Permanent Court, was equally critical of the readers, writing under pseudonym.[12]

What the Permanent Court dealt with in that critical passage of the judgment in *The Lotus* was the making of international law outside general international law, namely treaty law. Clearly the Permanent Court assumed that only states can make international law and, because 'independent', no State could lay down international law with binding effect on another State: 'The rules of law binding upon States therefore emanate from their own free will.' This was the only way to make international law. At least, '[r]estrictions upon the independence of States cannot therefore be presumed'. Accordingly, this statement referred back to the *Eastern Carelia* Opinion, according to which 'the principle of independence of States' is 'a fundamental principle of international law'.

Sovereignty and the Permanent Court

It was in decisions other than *The Lotus* that the Permanent Court explored notions of sovereignty, not always entirely successfully, beginning with *The Wimbledon.* Pleadings on the part of the German government were taken to imply that the matter concerned 'a personal and imprescriptible right, which forms an essential part of her sovereignty and which she neither could nor intended to renounce by anticipation'. The Permanent Court responded eagerly:

[10] *Legality of the Threat of Using Nuclear Weapons*, Advisory Opinion, 8 July 1996, ICJ Reports (1996), 226, para. 21.

[11] Max Weber, 'Observations de M. Huber', *Annuaire de l'institut de droit international*, 36-I (1931), 79.

[12] Michel de la Grotte, 'Les Affaires traitées par la Cour Permanente de Justice Internationale pendant la période 1926–1928', *Revue de droit international et de législation comparée*, 10 (1929), 387.

> The Court declines to see in the conclusion of any Treaty by which a State undertakes to perform or refrain from performing a particular act an abandonment of its sovereignty. No doubt any convention creating an obligation of this kind places a restriction upon the exercise of the sovereign rights of the State, in the sense that it requires them to be exercised in a certain way. But the right of entering into international engagements is an attribute of State sovereignty.[13]

The Permanent Court agreed to proceed on the basis of sovereignty, upon which, it said, 'an obligation of this kind places a restriction'. But, invoking the international/national divide, the counter-argument simply transferred sovereignty from the national to the international sphere: 'the right of entering into international engagements is an attribute of State sovereignty'. This playing with words has amused scholars ever since, and it has attracted much less criticism than *The Lotus*, albeit it would have been much more straightforward had the Permanent Court simply stated that treaty obligations are binding as a matter of international law.

In *The Wimbledon*, as in a number of other decisions, the Permanent Court alluded to a principle of restrictive interpretation. According to the majority:

> the fact remains that Germany has to submit to an important limitation of the exercise of the sovereign rights which no one disputes that she possesses over the Kiel Canal. This fact constitutes a sufficient reason for the restrictive interpretation, in case of doubt, of the clause which produces such a limitation. But the Court feels obliged to stop at the point where the so-called restrictive interpretation would be contrary to the plain terms of the article and would destroy what has been clearly granted.[14]

In the context of the motifs, this was an empty gesture, as the Permanent Court had already held that the text of the treaty provision in question was 'clear'. Yet it was again a less than ideal way in which to overcome sovereignty. As Crawford has noted:

> These days that concession would not be made: the language of treaties is not subject to any particular presumption but will be read so as to give effect to the object and purpose of the treaty in its context.[15]

[13] *SS Wimbledon (United Kingdom* v. *Germany)*, Judgment, 17 August 1923, PCIJ Series A, No. 1 (1923), 25.

[14] *Ibid.*, 24–5.

[15] James Crawford, 'Sovereignty as a Legal Value' in James Crawford and Martti Koskenniemi (eds.), *The Cambridge Companion to International Law* (Cambridge University Press, 2012), 117, para. 123.

The international/national divide and the Permanent Court

The international/national divide played into decisions of the Permanent Court other than *The Wimbledon* in various ways, but none is more thought-provoking than the treatment given to non-State actors. The *Jurisdiction of Courts of Danzig* Opinion went down in history. The Polish government contended that an international agreement (between two states or State-like entities) could not create rights and obligations for individuals. The Permanent Court's response was memorable, at least to a degree:

> It may be readily admitted that, according to a well established principle of international law, the *Beamtenabkommen*, being an international agreement, cannot, as such, create direct rights and obligations for private individuals. But it cannot be disputed that the very object of an international agreement, according to the intention of the contracting Parties, may be the adoption by the Parties of some definite rules creating individual rights and obligations and enforceable by the national courts.[16]

According to Dionisio Anzilotti, the Permanent Court's opinion:

> ne dit pas qu'un traité, comme tel, peut créer des droits et des obligations pour des individus, sans besoin que les règles y afférentes soient incorporées dans le droit interne: il dit seulement que l'intention des Parties contractantes peut être celle d'adopter des règles déterminées créant des droits et des obligations pour des individus et susceptibles d'être appliquées par les tribunaux nationaux.[17]

That being said, Anzilotti pointed to an argument that had been put at the end of the *motifs*:

> Poland would contend that the Danzig Courts could not apply the provisions of the *Beamtenabkommen* because they were not duly inserted in the Polish national law, the Court would have to observe that, at any rate, Poland could not avail herself of an objection which, according to the construction placed upon the *Beamtenabkommen* by the Court, would amount to relying upon the non-fulfilment of an obligation imposed upon her by an international engagement.[18]

16 *Jurisdiction of Courts of Danzig*, Advisory Opinion, 3 March 1928, PCIJ Series B, No. 15 (1928), 17–18.

17 Dionisio Anzilotti, *Cours de droit international* (1929), 407–8. [Translation: 'The Court's opinion does not say that a treaty can, in itself, create rights and obligations for individuals, obviating the need to incorporate the rules pertaining to it into internal law: it only says that the contracting parties might resolve to adopt specific rules which create rights and obligations for individual and can be applied by national tribunals.']

18 *Jurisdiction of Courts of Danzig*, 26–7.

Here then, the Permanent Court found comfort in treaty obligations simply being binding as a matter of international law, rather than sovereignty.

Many years later, in the judgment from 2001 in the *LaGrand* case, the International Court confirmed rather unobtrusively that a treaty may create individual rights.[19] International law is no longer a law of exclusion. Nevertheless, relatively few international lawyers have been willing unhesitatingly to characterise individuals as international legal subjects or persons.

In *The Creation of States in International Law*, having emphasised the position of individuals as holders of international rights and obligations, Crawford adds: 'But it remains true that these forums are created and ultimately controlled by States or by intergovernmental organizations, and it is these entities that remain the gatekeepers and legislators of the international system.'[20] In a footnote, Crawford states explicitly that individuals are not 'in any meaningful sense "international legal persons"', the reason being that '[a]s holders of rights and even obligations they do not cease to be subject to the State of their nationality, residence or incorporation, as the case may be'.[21] This may be mainly a question of terminology, as suggested by Crawford's characterisation of international law as an open system. In his words, '[i]t may be that the system is so open in this respect that the former threshold concept [of legal personality] has ceased to have much significance'.[22]

[19] *LaGrand case (Germany* v. *United States of America)*, Judgment, 27 June 2001, ICJ Reports (2001), 466, para. 77.

[20] Crawford, *The Creation of States in International Law*, 29.

[21] *Ibid.*, 30, note 132.

[22] Crawford, *International Law as an Open System*, 21.

PART II

Statehood

9

The Security Council and statehood

CHRISTINE CHINKIN

1 Introduction

The increased use and expanded scope of United Nations Security Council (SC) power following the end of the Cold War have been widely acknowledged. This chapter focuses on two separate, but perhaps linked, examples of the exercise of SC power: the impact of the Council's authority on the creation (or otherwise) of States and its interventions into dysfunctional or 'failed'[1] States in the name of democracy, State- and capacity-building, governance and the rule of law. As is evident from the choice of these topics, they recall and honour two aspects of James Crawford's inestimable contribution to international law and practice: his work on the creation of States in international law[2] and on democracy and international law.[3]

The United Nations General Assembly (GA), rather than the SC, has historically been the major organ of the UN with respect to territorial disposition, in particular its responsibility for issues relating to decolonisation and achievement of the right of self-determination in accordance with Resolutions 1514[4] and 1541[5] through its Decolonisation Committee.[6] The

[1] James Crawford, *Brownlie's Principles of Public International Law*, 8th edn (Oxford University Press, 2012), 133.

[2] James Crawford, *The Creation of States in International Law*, 2nd edn (Oxford University Press, 2006).

[3] James Crawford, 'Democracy and International Law', *British Yearbook of International Law*, 64 (1993), 113–33.

[4] GA Res. 1514 (XV), Declaration on the Granting of Independence to Colonial Countries and Peoples, 14 December 1960.

[5] GA Res. 1541 (XV), Principles which should guide Members in determining whether or not an obligation exists to transmit the information called for under article 73e of the Charter of the United Nations, 15 December 1960.

[6] Special Committee on the Situation with regard to the Implementation of the Declaration on the Granting of Independence to Colonial Countries and Peoples.

exception has been where the Security Council's primary responsibility for the maintenance of international peace and security has been called into play,[7] as for example in the termination of the Trusteeship Agreement with respect to the so-called 'strategic' trust territories and the creation of the Federated States of Micronesia, the Republic of the Marshall Islands and Palau.[8] The changed geopolitical situation following the termination of the Cold War has furthered the practice of negotiated peace agreements entailing territorial disposition being endorsed by the SC, as well as the use of the Council's 'international dispositive powers'[9] leading to Crawford's conclusion that where necessary 'to maintain or restore international peace and security',[10] transfer or otherwise disposing of territory by the SC would not be contrary to the 'structure' of the Charter.[11]

2 The Security Council and territorial disposition

This section considers SC action in two well-trodden disputes over the status of territory, primarily picking up from where the second edition of *The Creation of States* finished, that is 2005. In one case (Western Sahara) the SC has found no way to end an illegal status quo and statehood remains in abeyance, while in the other (Kosovo) it has effectively facilitated *de facto* status and regime change. The creation (and denial) of statehood 'is a matter in principle governed by international law'.[12] However, despite receiving often detailed factual reports from the Secretary-General on situations on its agenda, SC decisions rarely involve judicial or even quasi-judicial considerations of fact and law, but are political and inevitably subject to the interests of major powers, including those dictated by 'the brave new world of the "war against terror"'.[13] While its response to disparate incidents may be discounted as anomalies, without any precedential effect, the outcomes also have a destabilising potential that may have unexpected repercussions elsewhere.

[7] Charter of the United Nations (San Francisco, adopted 26 June 1945, entered into force 24 October 1945), 1 UNTS XVI, Art. 24(1). The wording is deliberately chosen to recall James's liking for cricket.

[8] Crawford, *The Creation of States*, 581–4. [9] *Ibid.*, ch. 12.

[10] Art. 39, Charter of the United Nations.

[11] Crawford, *The Creation of States*, 552. For the view that creation of states by the SC is contrary to international law see Alexander-Georg Rackow, 'The Law of Nationbuilding: Does the UN Security Council have Authority to Create New States?', available at www.kentlaw.edu/perritt/courses/seminar/alex-rackow-finalversion.htm#_ftn45.

[12] Crawford, *The Creation of States*, preface, v. [13] *Ibid.*, vi.

2.1 The case of the Western Sahara

The first is the unresolved position of the Western Sahara. The Western Sahara story encompasses a leftover from colonisation (it is one of the sixteen territories remaining on the list of non-self-governing territories), a Cold War impasse, optimism for a peace settlement fostered by the weakening and subsequent end of the Cold War, and the still further undermining of the hopes of the Saharawi people in the climate of counter-terrorist priorities. Although the principles and policies applicable to the exercise of self-determination are those agreed by the GA and the situation was before that body, as advised by the International Court of Justice,[14] the Security Council became seised of the matter in 1975. It urged the parties to avoid any unilateral action that might escalate tension and 'deplored' the so-called 'Green March' into the territory by Morocco.[15] However there was no further SC Resolution on the issue for thirteen years until 1988 when the Council authorised the Secretary-General (S-G) to appoint a special representative to pursue with the Organisation of African Unity the possibility of a referendum on self-determination.[16] This process – undertaken precisely at the moment of the thawing of the Cold War[17] – bore fruit and in 1990 the SC adopted the Settlement Plan,[18] which proposed a referendum for independence or integration with Morocco. It was accepted by both sides but implementation was stalled by Morocco over disputes as to voter registration. The identification process had ground to a halt by 1995 and in May 1996 the SC recognised the collapse and suspended the process. An attempt to reactivate the process was made by the UN Special Envoy, James Baker, who was appointed in 1997. After failing to reactivate the 1988 Settlement Plan he pursued a new approach that shifted some distance away from the 'zero-sum game' of the Settlement Plan (independence or integration) and was presented in the 2001 Baker Plan (Framework Agreement).[19] The Baker Plan envisaged autonomy

[14] *Western Sahara*, Advisory Opinion, 16 October 1975, ICJ Reports (1975), 12.

[15] SC Res. 379, 2 November 1975; SC Res. 380, 6 November 1975.

[16] SC Res. 621, 20 September 1988.

[17] Unlike in other crisis areas of that time (e.g. Namibia, Cambodia and Kuwait), Western Sahara did not benefit from the apparent determination to ensure the international rule of law.

[18] SC Res. 658, 22 June 1990 (containing the full plan); SC Res. 690, 29 April 1991; SC Res. 690, 29 April 1991 mandated MINURSO (the United Nations Mission for a Referendum in Western Sahara) to implement the Settlement Plan and to supervise the proposed referendum.

[19] Report of the Secretary-General concerning the Situation in Western Sahara, UN Doc. S/2001/613 annex 1, 20 June 2001.

for Western Sahara under the Moroccan Constitution for a transitional period. Morocco would have exclusive control over some attributes of statehood – foreign relations, national security and external defence. The eligible voters of Western Sahara would elect an executive body to run the territory's internal affairs, but Morocco would appoint the judges and be responsible for law and order during the transition. After four years of transition a referendum would decide the future status of Western Sahara, but with changed voter qualifications from 'peoples' (with the associated commitment to the legal right of self-determination) to 'population'.[20] Unlike the Settlement Plan, where voter identification rested upon the 1974 Spanish census, the Framework Agreement made Moroccan settlers who had remained in Western Sahara for more than a year eligible to vote in the referendum. Following further deadlock, the then UN Secretary-General, Kofi Annan, suggested a further change of direction by outlining a number of options to the SC that no longer required the parties' concurrence – that is, a non-consensual solution.[21] The SC did not accept any of these more coercive options and urged the S-G and his Special Representative to continue their efforts to find a political solution.[22] This led in 2003 to a modified version of the Framework Agreement, the Peace Plan for Self-determination of Western Sahara.[23] The Peace Plan seeks a compromise solution by attempting to bring together elements of the Settlement Plan into the Framework Agreement. It proposes that Western Sahara become a semi-autonomous region of Morocco for a transition period of up to five years, followed by a referendum in which voter identification is limited to those who have been resident in the territory since 1999. The Plan was supported (although not 'endorsed'[24]) by the SC 'as an optimum political solution on the basis of agreement between the two parties'.[25] The Resolution reaffirmed the Council's 'commitment to . . . a just, lasting and mutually acceptable political solution, which will provide for the self-determination of the people of Western Sahara', but it also

[20] Toby Shelley, *Endgame in the Western Sahara: What Future for Africa's Last Colony?* (London: Zed Books, 2004), 148.

[21] Report of the Secretary-General concerning the Situation in Western Sahara, UN Doc. S/2003/565, 23 May 2003, paras. 44–7. One option was division of the Territory, favoured by Algeria and the *Frente Polisario*, para. 43.

[22] SC Res. 1429, 30 July 2002.

[23] Report of the Secretary-General concerning the Situation in Western Sahara, UN Doc. S/2002/565 and Corr.1, 23 May 2003.

[24] As had been proposed by the US but opposed by France in support of Morocco, which now rejected the plan; Shelley, *Endgame*, 162.

[25] SC Res. 1495, 31 July 2003.

considered that a political solution was 'critically needed'. While Algeria and the *Frente Polisario* indicated their acceptance, the Peace Plan was not accepted by Morocco, because the possibility of independence remained as one of the options in the proposed referendum.[26] Baker resigned in 2004.

In his April 2006 Report the S-G considered the possibility of a 'step back'[27] for the UN through direct negotiations between the parties. He suggested that what is unacceptable by imposition – a plan without the possibility of independence at least some time in the future – might not be unacceptable by political negotiation, and posited that such direct negotiations be held without any preconditions. Any compromise agreement reached would be based on 'relevant principles of international law and current political realities'.[28] In April 2007 both the *Frente Polisario* and Morocco submitted proposals and further rounds of negotiation have since taken place, but without result. The SC considers 'consolidation of the status quo' not to be acceptable and that 'realism and a spirit of compromise by the parties are essential to achieve progress in negotiations'.[29] Meanwhile the Saharawi people continue to live in refugee camps, or under occupation in Morocco. Protests are responded to by Moroccan security forces and human rights violations persist.[30] Morocco rejected a recommendation made through the universal periodic review process of the UN Human Rights Council for the establishment of a permanent human rights component in MINURSO,[31] labelling calls for

26 The creation of the newest state, South Sudan, was through such a process. The Comprehensive Peace Agreement between the Government of the Republic of Sudan and the Sudan People's Liberation Movement/Sudan People's Liberation Army (CPA) 2005, Chapter I (Machakos Protocol), Art. 1.3 recognised the right to self-determination of the people of South Sudan 'through a referendum to determine their future status'. The SC welcomed the CPA and mandated UNMIS to support its implementation; SC Res. 1590, 24 March 2005. The referendum took place in January 2011 and the Republic of South Sudan gained its independence on 9 July 2011 and was admitted to the UN on 14 July 2011. On innovative responses to self-determination claims see Marc Weller, 'Settling Self-determination Conflicts: Recent Developments', *European Journal of International Law*, 20 (2009), 111.

27 Report of the Secretary-General on the Situation concerning Western Sahara, UN Doc. S/2006/249, 19 April 2006, para. 35.

28 *Ibid.*, para. 38.

29 SC Res. 2099, 25 April 2013.

30 *Ibid.*: 'Stressing the importance of improving the human rights situation in Western Sahara and the Tindouf camps'. Unlike UN human rights bodies, the resolution does not attribute violations to Morocco; Report of the Secretary-General on the Situation concerning Western Sahara, UN Doc. S/2013/220, 8 April 2013, paras. 80–97.

31 *Ibid.*, para. 93.

independent human rights monitoring in the territory 'an attack on its sovereignty'.[32]

SC action has not led to the creation of a Saharawi State. Although it has not endorsed the annexation of the territory into Morocco, it has avoided a coercive approach and urged compromise. Morocco's actions in violation of the right to self-determination have never been condemned.[33] The 1991 Settlement Plan was not adopted under UN Charter Chapter VII; the situation has never been designated as a threat to international peace and security and continues to be governed by UN Charter Chapter VI;[34] no coercive measures for non-compliance have been adopted; and the SC has not imposed an obligation of collective non-recognition.[35] It did take the 'very unusual step'[36] of seeking an opinion from the Under-Secretary for Legal Affairs and Legal Counsel of the UN on the 'legality in the context of international law . . . of actions allegedly taken by the Moroccan authorities consisting in the offering and signing of contracts with foreign countries for the exploration of mineral resources in Western Sahara'.[37] The Legal Counsel's conclusion was that while the contracts were not of themselves illegal 'if further exploration and exploitation activities were to proceed in disregard of the interests and wishes of the people of Western Sahara, they would be in violation of the principles of international law'. This constituted a 'very clear message with respect to the legality of the activities in question: Morocco would have to engage in proper consultations with persons authorised to represent the people of Western Sahara before such activities would be allowed'.[38] The Security Council has not responded to this legal opinion. In contrast, reference to the good offices of the S-G implies mediation and compromise, and emphasis on a 'political solution' indicates conciliation rather than enforcement. The SC has allowed Morocco to use delaying tactics to frustrate the voter identification process since the 1990s.

32 'US to redeploy Morocco in Western Sahara spat', BBC, 17 April 2013, available at www.bbc.co.uk/news/world-africa-22189197.

33 Thomas Franck, 'The Stealing of the Sahara', *American Journal of International Law*, 70 (1976), 694.

34 Report of the Secretary-General on the Situation concerning Western Sahara, UN Doc. S/2013/220, 8 April 2013, para. 20.

35 Crawford, *The Creation of States*, 158–73.

36 Hans Correll, 'The Legality of Exploring and Exploiting Natural Resources in Western Sahara' in Neville Botha, Michèle Olivier and Delarey van Tonder (eds.), *Multilateralism and International Law with Western Sahara as a Case Study* (Pretoria: VerLoren van Themaat Centre, University of South Africa Press, 2010), 234. The opinion was delivered to the SC on 29 January 2002; UN Doc. S/2002/161.

37 *Ibid.*, 232. 38 *Ibid.*, 240.

As noted by Crawford, the '"failed State" problem has been vastly complicated by its relation to questions of international security and the use of force'.[39] Western Sahara is not, of course, a 'failed' State since it has never attained statehood, but its uncertain status and the long-standing refugee camps in Algeria have been described as a 'ticking time bomb'.[40] Security concerns have escalated since 2012 with the fighting in Mali involving 'armed elements linked to Al-Qaida' and fears that the violence could spill over and contribute to radicalising the refugee camps.[41] Condemning another generation of Saharawi – a predominantly Muslim – people to dispossession and displacement in those camps could serve as an inducement to recruitment; nor is it conducive to either their own or regional security. Kidnapping concerns are high. The vastness and isolation of the territory – geographically and politically – make border control difficult and infiltrations likely.[42] MINURSO, UN agencies and *Frente Polisario* have worked to co-ordinate security; Morocco however has argued that it is justified in undertaking military actions in violation of the Military Agreement because of the security challenges in the region.[43] That the long-standing support that Morocco has received, from permanent members of the SC, especially France but also the US, is unlikely to be changed in the current security environment is indicated by its success in persuading the US to withdraw its demand that the 2013 renewal of MINURSO include a human rights monitoring component.[44]

2.2 The case of Kosovo

The case of Kosovo brings forcible intervention into the picture through NATO's military response to oppression and human rights abuses by the Federal Republic of Yugoslavia (FRY). Perceptions of the different

39 Crawford, *The Creation of States*, 721.

40 Report of the Secretary-General on the Situation concerning Western Sahara, UN Doc. S/2013/220, 8 April 2013, para. 34.

41 *Ibid.*

42 A growing number of illegal migrants found in the territory that MINURSO lacks capacity to deal with has previously been described as adding to the tension; e.g. Report of the Secretary-General on the Situation concerning Western Sahara, UN Doc. S/2006/249, 19 April 2006, paras. 21–3. The April 2013 Report of the Secretary-General states that 'no irregular migrants were recorded' in the latest reporting period, UN Doc. S/2013/220, 8 April 2013, para. 79.

43 Report of the Secretary-General on the Situation concerning Western Sahara, UN Doc. S/2006/249, 19 April 2006, para. 40.

44 Morocco had called off military exercises with the US, but these were resumed. 'Morocco Forces Change to UN Text on W. Sahara', 23 April 2013, available at http://reliefweb.int/report/western-sahara/morocco-forces-change-un-text-w-sahara.

actors are interesting. In 1998 the Security Council had condemned 'all acts of violence by any party, as well as terrorism in pursuit of political goals by any group or individual' and supply of arms or training for terrorist activities in Kosovo.[45] The SC did not identify the perpetrators of terrorism, but did insist that the Kosovo Albanian leadership 'condemn all terrorist actions'.[46] But by 1999, the FRY was increasingly perceived in the West as a pariah State[47] and NATO intervened in effect on behalf of the Kosovo Albanians. While the NATO action led swiftly to regime change and acceptance of the inevitability of status change, it was also followed by widespread attacks – systematic killings, abductions, arbitrary detentions, sexual and gender-based violence, beatings and harassment – by Kosovo Albanian armed groups against non-Albanian Kosovars.[48]

Although the intervention had not received SC authorisation, the Council accepted the 'general principles on a political solution' that were agreed prior to the SC's adoption of Resolution 1244 and are annexed thereto.[49] The general principles presaged the establishment of an effective, international, transitional civil and military presence in Kosovo. Resolution 1244 simultaneously reasserted the territorial integrity and political independence of the FRY while denying the State the right to exercise related powers in Kosovo. The fiction of consent to such intervention is maintained through the SC's welcoming of the agreement of the FRY to its stripping of authority in Kosovo.

[45] SC Res. 1203, 24 October 1998.

[46] There is no widely accepted definition of international terrorism. The Special Tribunal for Lebanon has determined that under customary international law terrorism is: '(i) the perpetration of a criminal act . . . or threatening such an act; (ii) the intent to spread fear among the population (which would generally entail the creation of public danger) or directly or indirectly coerce a national or international authority to take some action, or to refrain from taking it; (iii) when the act involves a transnational element'. *Interlocutory Decision on the Applicable Law: Terrorism, Conspiracy, Homicide, Perpetration, Cumulative Charging*, STL-11–01/I, 16 February, 2011, para. 85.

[47] Although its president, Slobodan Milošević, had been a principal participant at the 1995 Dayton peace talks, representing the Bosnian Serbs, in US terms 'Towards the end of the decade, the Serbian Government of Slobodan Milosevic brought ethnic cleansing to Kosovo.' UN Doc. S/PV.5839, 18 February 2008. The International Tribunal for former Yugoslavia indicted Milošević for genocide, war crimes and crimes against humanity in May 1999, shortly before the end of the Kosovo conflict.

[48] Kosovo Human Rights Advisory Panel, *S.C.* v. *UNMIK*, Case No. 02/09, 6 December 2012.

[49] SC Res. 1244, 10 June 1999, Annex I, Statement by the Chairman on the conclusion of the meeting of the G-8 Foreign Ministers held at the Petersberg Centre on 6 May 1999, and Annex II. The general principles were to be implemented 'taking full account of the Rambouillet accords'.

The Secretary-General was authorised to establish an international civil presence in Kosovo to act as an interim international territorial administration. Accordingly, by its first Regulation all legislative and executive authority, including the administration of the judiciary, was vested in the Special Representative of the Secretary-General (SRS-G). Under the authority of the SC, the UN Interim Administration in Kosovo (UNMIK) exercised its powers through the adoption of multiple regulations and directives ranging through privatisation of socially owned enterprises, determining disputed property claims, private law, policing and taxation. In effect UNMIK had vested itself with the same powers as a State government but without regard to the democratic principle of the separation of governmental powers and the appropriate checks and balances.[50] This was somewhat ironic since Resolution 1244 mandated UNMIK to organise and oversee 'the development of provisional institutions for democratic and autonomous self-government', but as Crawford has noted, 'certain features of international law are themselves non-democratic'.[51] Similarly, concerns were expressed about UNMIK's compliance with human rights in the exercise of its powers.[52] This led it to establish the Human Rights Advisory Panel with jurisdiction to consider individual complaints of alleged violations of human rights treaties by UNMIK.[53] In this way the international administration assumed some further accoutrements of a State, accountability and responsibility for internationally wrongful acts.[54]

The SC had temporarily suspended 'Serbia's exercise of its authority flowing from its continuing sovereignty',[55] by transferring the exercise of that authority to an international organisation under its supervision, but subsequently leaving the existence of Kosovo in a legal limbo. The authority of the Security Council to take such a decision is not clear-cut.

50 Ombudsperson Institution in Kosovo, 2nd Annual Report 2001–2002, 10 July 2002.

51 Crawford, *The Creation of States*, 153.

52 UN Human Rights Committee, Consideration of country report – United Nations Interim Administration Mission in Kosovo (initial report) UN Doc. CCPR/C/UNK/CO/1, 14 August 2006; Venice Commission, *Human Rights in Kosovo: Possible Establishment of Review Mechanisms*, Opinion no. 280/2004, 8–9 October 2004.

53 UNMIK Regulation 2006/12, On the Establishment of the Human Rights Advisory Panel, 23 March 2006, as amended by Regulation 2007/3, 12 January 2007.

54 For the Panel's concern about UNMIK's lack of public reaction to its recommendations see Kosovo Human Rights Advisory Panel, Annual Report 2012, para. 88, available at www.unmikonline.org/hrap/Eng/Pages/Annual-Report.aspx.

55 *Accordance with International Law of the Unilateral Declaration of Independence in Respect of Kosovo*, Advisory Opinion, 22 July 2010, ICJ Reports (2010), 403, para. 98.

Under Article 41 of the UN Charter the Council may decide upon measures not involving the use of force to give effect to its decisions. This competence has been determined to be sufficiently broad to support, *inter alia*, the creation of the *ad hoc* international criminal tribunals,[56] far-reaching intrusions into national legal systems for the prevention and suppression of terrorist acts[57] and the overriding of treaty provisions regulating military occupation. Nevertheless it remains questionable 'for the United Nations to administer . . . territory in a situation where (whatever may be said about territorial integrity) the issue of secession following ethnic cleansing is very much on the agenda'.[58]

Alongside its extensive regulatory programme, UNMIK acted quickly to establish the Provisional Institutions of Self-government in Kosovo. In 2005 efforts intensified to find a permanent solution to the issue of final status. After sustained attempts at achieving a negotiated solution, the UN Special Envoy, Martti Ahtissari, put forward a plan for independence under international supervision.[59] His reasoning provides an instrumentalist view of statehood in contemporary international law: the *sui generis* status of Kosovo is described as a 'major obstacle to Kosovo's democratic development, accountability, economic recovery and inter-ethnic reconciliation'. Uncertainty leads to 'further stagnation, polarizing [Kosovo] communities and resulting in social and political unrest. Pretending otherwise and denying or delaying resolution of Kosovo's status risks challenging not only its own stability but the peace and stability of the region as a whole.' Nevertheless the SC was split and thus unable to accept the plan. Russia, in continued support of Serbia, condemned 'the illegal acts of the Kosovo Albanian leadership and of those who support them' as a 'dangerous precedent' and noted that the deployment of EULEX did not come within the power conferred by Resolution 1244. China too was 'gravely concerned'. EU Member States (Belgium, Italy, the United Kingdom and France) and the US recognised Kosovo's independence to be an 'irreversible fact'.[60] The response – the unilateral declaration of independence made by the 'democratically elected leaders' of Kosovo on 8 February 2008 – accepts fully 'the obligations for Kosovo contained in the Ahtisaari Plan' – that is, a form of supervised

[56] *Prosecutor* v. *Tadić* (Decision on the Defence Motion for Interlocutory Appeal on Jurisdiction), Case No. IT-94–1AR72, ICTY Appeals Chamber, Judgment, 2 October 1995.

[57] SC Res. 1373, 28 September 2001. [58] Crawford, *The Creation of States*, 560.

[59] Report of the Special Envoy of the Secretary-General on Kosovo's future status, UN Doc. S/2007/168, 26 March 2007.

[60] UN Doc. S/PV.5839, 18 February 2008.

independence.[61] Weller comments that the declaration was an attempt to replace the binding nature of Resolution 1244, adopted under UN Charter Chapter VII with a 'self-imposed limitation of sovereignty'. But qualified sovereignty does not necessarily deny statehood.[62]

As of June 2013, the International Court of Justice (ICJ) has advised that the assertion of independence is not in violation of either general international law or SC Resolution 1244[63] and Kosovo has been recognised by over one hundred States. UNMIK clearly no longer has either the legitimacy or the capacity to exercise executive authority and is not taken into account by the Kosovo Constitution. UNMIK has accordingly reconfigured its position and transferred much responsibility (notably in the context of the rule of law) to EULEX.[64] However, legally Kosovo remains subject to SC Resolution 1244. The SRS-G continues to report to the SC in accordance with the Resolution,[65] which can only be repealed by the SC itself ('unless the SC deems otherwise') and thus remains technically still applicable.

Some contrasts between Western Sahara and Kosovo are striking, while there are also similarities. In the former case, the SC has not adopted a normative, regulatory or administrative role by placing the territory under UN administration[66] as it did with Kosovo 'pending a final settlement, of substantial autonomy and self-government'.[67] Unlike UNMIK (and UNTAET in East Timor),[68] MINURSO constituted a minimalist SC response: it is a small force (213 personnel as of March 2013)[69] with

[61] Kosovo Declaration of Independence, 17 February 2008, paras. 1 and 3, available at www.assembly-kosova.org/?cid=2,128,1635.

[62] Crawford, *Brownlie's Principles of Public International Law*, 135.

[63] *Accordance with International Law of the Unilateral Declaration of Independence in Respect of Kosovo*, 403.

[64] Report of the Secretary-General on the United Nations Interim Administration Mission in Kosovo, UN Doc. S/2008/692, 24 November 2008; UN Doc. S/PRST/2008/44, 26 November 2008.

[65] Report of the Secretary-General on the United Nations Interim Administration Mission in Kosovo, UN Doc. S/2013/254, 30 April 2013.

[66] After the 2001 Framework Plan Algeria proposed that the UN should assume sovereignty over the Western Sahara in order to implement provisions that appeared identical to the 1988 Settlement Plan. The S-G and S-GSR considered this option to have no more likelihood of working than the Settlement Plan; Report of the Secretary-General concerning the Situation in Western Sahara, UN Doc. S/2003/565, 23 May 2003, para. 40.

[67] SC Res. 1244.

[68] UNTAET was established pending 'self-government' in East Timor; SC Res. 1272, 25 October 1999.

[69] Report of the Secretary-General on the Situation concerning Western Sahara, UN Doc. S/2013/220, 8 April 2013, para. 37.

a limited mandate and no administrative or regulatory powers. Despite the difference between a 'light' and a 'heavy' institutional touch, in neither case has SC action led unequivocally to the creation of a new State. In the case of the Western Sahara, attempts within the UN to reach a peace settlement acceptable to all parties have failed, leaving the SC with limited options with respect to the status of the territory. In Kosovo principles for settlement of the conflict were endorsed by the SC, despite the unauthorised military intervention preceding it, and encompassing its own territorial administration. However, with the rejection of the Ahtisaari plan, there too the SC ran out of options, leaving the democratically elected leaders to take matters into their own hands. Indeed, if the SC were to repeal Resolution 1244 and UNMIK finally to withdraw, there might be debate as to whether the creation of the State of Kosovo was through secession from Serbia, or from the intervening interim administration. The options and plans put forward at different times in both cases illustrate the tension between a solution grounded in traditional principles of international law based upon self-determination and non-intervention, and one grounded in political expediency and the abdication of legal principle to the situation on the ground.

SC participation bestows a 'top-down' emphasis on determination of status. In both instances popular, armed movements resisted control by Morocco and Serbia respectively. As States, Morocco and Serbia can put their positions directly before the SC, but the opinions of the leaders of the disputed territories become mediated through those of UN Special Envoys and Representatives. While vocal in the world outside, civil society voices are not heard within the SC. In Western Sahara the right of the Saharawi people has been subordinated to the will of Morocco, while in Kosovo the objectives of the Kosovo Albanians have prevailed, albeit by way of an unwanted UN administration.

3 The SC and regime change

The traditional stance of the SC towards the form or ideology of internal governance was one of indifference; the rare call for collective non-recognition of an entity rested upon its creation through international illegality or 'fundamentally unlawful policies'.[70] However, the end of the

[70] Crawford, *The Creation of States*, 338.

Cold War has seen expressed SC policies in furtherance of democratically elected government, the rule of law and human rights, especially in post-conflict contexts. The SC has associated effective statehood (meaning government commitment to these values) to the maintenance of international peace and security, authorising expansive but inconsistent intrusion into the domestic jurisdiction of fragile States. Especially in the light of controversy over the NATO intervention in Kosovo and the aftermath of the terrorist attacks of 11 September 2001, issues of security, protection of human rights, capacity and development have become linked bases for intervention. This is not an issue of State creation,[71] but has become one of regime change. For instance, the emergent concept of the responsibility to protect[72] includes the responsibility to rebuild, which may be presaged on regime change: as Kosovo itself demonstrates, this may in fact entail changed status and statehood, especially where State fragility is based upon, or is exposed by, ethnic and other difference. The impact of such interventions on the creation of States remains unclear, but may in the long term require another chapter to *The Creation of States.*

The first intervention by the SC explicitly in the name of democracy was 'Operation Uphold Democracy' in Haiti. In response to the escalation of 'politically motivated violence' following a military coup against the elected government, the SC authorised the establishment of a UN Mission in Haiti (UNMIH) in September 1993,[73] which owing to events elsewhere was unable immediately to deploy.[74] In July 1994, the Security Council authorised the use of 'all necessary means' to restore democracy in Haiti and the prompt return of the legitimately elected president, Jean-Bertrand Aristide.[75] This brought a new dimension to post-Cold War military intervention: the overthrow of a democratically elected government was deemed to constitute a threat to international peace and security and measures were authorised to reverse it. Ten years later, in 2004, the SC again intervened for the purpose of State-building, this time against Aristide, who had been re-elected in 2000, but had 'unacceptable aspirations to shift

[71] While 'there is room for the insistence on general standards of human rights and of democratic institutions as an aspect of the stability and legitimacy of a new State . . . this has not matured into a peremptory norm disqualifying an entity from statehood', *ibid.*, 155.

[72] Report of the International Commission on Intervention and State Sovereignty, 'The Responsibility to Protect' (December, 2001).

[73] SC Res. 867, 23 September 1993. [74] SC Res. 873, 13 October 1993.

[75] SC Res. 940, 31 July 1994.

power in Haiti somewhat towards the poor and grassroots'.[76] He was now overthrown and expelled from Haiti. Citing the 'rapid deterioration of the humanitarian situation . . . and its destabilizing effect on the region', the Council drew upon traditional bases for intervention; it noted Aristide's 'resignation' and the 'appeal' of the newly installed president to the UN for assistance, and authorised the deployment of a Multinational Interim Force 'to contribute to a secure and stable environment . . . in order to support Haitian President Alexandre's request for international assistance to support the constitutional political process under way in Haiti'.[77]

But there is another story obscured by the oblique language of the SC. Critiques of coercive democratic promotion have demonstrated its association with neo-liberal capitalism and ensuing inequality.[78] In a petition to the Inter-American Commission on Human Rights, Haitian human rights groups alleged a 'long-term, systematic plan' that undermined the 'democratically elected Haitian government through a development-assistance embargo' and supported armed opposition groups in overthrowing the democratically elected Haitian government and replacing it with a government with no constitutional or electoral legitimacy'.[79] The petition is brought against the United States and Dominican Republic.

US government officials are alleged to have forced President Aristide to sign a letter of resignation and to have taken him out of Haiti against his will. The US is also accused of sending guns to the Dominican Republic, 'many of which made it into the hands of the Haiti rebels'. These events can thus be construed in two different ways: the official narrative of SC-authorised assistance in restoring constitutional order to Haiti, providing humanitarian support and promoting human rights; and the alternative narrative of the forced removal of an elected government that challenged Washington's imperial interests and of terror in Haiti unleashed and supported by MINUSTAH.[80] What is unarguable is the SC authority to bestow legality upon such action, the lack of any process for review, and academic silence.[81]

[76] China Miéville, 'Multilateralism as Terror: International Law, Haiti and Imperialism', *Finnish Yearbook of International Law*, 19 (2008), 77.

[77] SC Res. 1529, 29 February 2004. This was replaced by the United Nations Stabilization Mission in Haiti (MINUSTAH) established by SC Res. 1542, 30 April 2004.

[78] Susan Marks, 'What Has Become of the Emerging Right to Democratic Governance?', *European Journal of International Law*, 22 (2011), 507.

[79] Complaint Regarding Violations of the Right to Participate in Representative Government, 2 February 2006, available at www.teledyol.net/IJDH/IACHRPet_v.pdf.

[80] Miéville, 'Multilateralism as Terror', 63.

[81] *Ibid.*, 76.

The concept of the responsibility to protect was explicitly engaged in the case of Côte d'Ivoire. Against a complex background of social division and armed conflict between the south of the country controlled by the government and the north, held by the rebel Forces Nouvelles, in 2004 the SC mandated the United Nations Operation in Côte d'Ivoire (UNOCI) with an extensive civilian and peacekeeping mandate.[82] UNOCI incorporated an earlier SC-mandated political mission, an ECOWAS peacekeeping mission and French forces authorised 'to use all necessary means' to support UNOCI, in particular to contribute to general security in the area of operation of the international forces. A peace agreement was signed in Ouagadougou in 2007, although aspects of it remained unimplemented at the time of presidential elections in 2010 (delayed since 2000). The elections were held in a peaceful manner and international observers 'expressed overall satisfaction with the conduct of the election'.[83] As neither the incumbent president, President Gbagbo, nor the principal contender, Mr Ouattara, received an overall majority, a run-off election was arranged. Some violence followed this election. The Constitutional Court of Côte d'Ivoire determined that there had been massive electoral fraud, discounted several thousand votes for the contender, Ouattara, and thereby secured victory for the incumbent, President Gbagbo. This was contrary to the position of the Independent Electoral Commission, whose findings were endorsed by the SRS-G.[84] Further violence ensued and following the position of ECOWAS and the African Union (but not that of the Constitutional Court), the Security Council urged recognition of Ouattara as properly elected.[85] This decision legitimised the imposition of economic measures against Gbagbo and his supporters and, as no longer the legitimate government, made his consent to the deployment of UN and French peacekeepers legally irrelevant.[86] Multiple attempts were made, primarily through ECOWAS and the African Union, at finding a negotiated solution amidst concerns about civilian security and the potential for the commission of mass atrocities. The situation on the ground worsened and in March 2011, expressing concern about the possibility

[82] SC Res. 1528, 27 February 2004.

[83] 26th Progress Report of the Secretary-General on the United Nations Operation in Côte d'Ivoire, UN Doc. S/2010/600, 23 November 2010, para. 18.

[84] 27th Progress Report of the Secretary-General on the United Nations Operation in Côte d'Ivoire, UN Doc. S/2011/211, 30 March 2011, para. 16.

[85] SC Res. 1962, 20 December 2010.

[86] Alex Bellamy and Paul Williams, 'The New Politics of Protection? Côte d'Ivoire, Libya and the Responsibility to Protect', *International Affairs*, 87 (2011), 833.

of civil war between the sides (and with intercommunal and inter-ethnic dimensions) the Security Council stressed UNOCI's mandate to protect civilians. The SC reaffirmed the primary responsibility of the State to protect its citizens and authorised UNOCI 'to use all necessary means . . . to protect civilians under imminent threat of physical violence, within its capabilities and its areas of deployment'.[87] Military action by UNOCI and French troops enabled Ouattara to be installed as president.

The Côte d'Ivoire situation raises questions about the extent to which authorisation of intervention for civilian protection legitimates regime change and SC intervention into domestic elections. Elections in divided countries may be a flashpoint for violence and SC support for one side may trigger State fragmentation. In this instance, reunification of the country remained fragile and with the potential for a further outbreak of civil war. In such circumstances, creation of a further State remained conceivable, but has been avoided and territorial integrity upheld. There was disagreement, even among those States that had voted for it, about whether SC Resolution 1975 extended UNOCI's protective mandate or simply reiterated the mandate as set out in earlier Resolutions.[88] India stressed that peacekeepers 'cannot be made instruments of regime change' and the Russian foreign minister stated that '[w]e are looking into the legality of this situation [taking the side of Ouattara against Gbagbo] because the peacekeepers were authorised to remain neutral, nothing more'.[89]

4 Conclusion

SC decision-making with respect to territorial disposition and State governance enhances the legitimacy of the entity and simultaneously augments the Council's relevance in global politics and power. This partly explains why there has been a return to the SC after an unauthorised military action,[90] or following a peace agreement conducted outside its auspices. But it has also become compromised by the use of multilateral decision-making to pursue what is essentially the US political agenda behind the smokescreen of democracy, good governance and human rights. While

87 SC Res. 1975, 30 March 2011.

88 SC Res. 1933, 30 June 2010; SC Res. 1962, 20 December 2010.

89 Cited in Bellamy and Williams, 'The New Politics of Protection?', 835.

90 As with Kosovo; see also SC Res. 1483, 22 May 2003 which provided a needed façade of legality after the divisiveness within the Council caused by the invasion of Iraq.

decisions around statehood and State authority have always been subject to the interests of the great powers,[91] the security priorities created by fears of terrorism have added a further dimension that discounts or co-opts local choices. The SC is a variously, even simultaneously, active player, a latecomer to a prearranged outcome and a frustrated bystander to the formation and constitution of States.

91 Gerry Simpson, *Great Powers and Outlaw States Unequal Sovereigns in the International Legal Order* (Cambridge University Press, 2004).

10

The dynamics of statehood in the practice of international and English courts

ALEXANDER ORAKHELASHVILI

1 Introduction

To honour James Crawford on this special occasion, it is proposed to examine statehood in its dynamic aspect, drawing on legal aspects of recognition, State responsibility and State immunity that most prominently feature among the multiple areas of law that he has mastered as a distinguished scholar and practitioner.

From Althusius and Grotius onwards, the study of statehood has focused upon the original derivation of sovereignty and the options to share or alienate it.[1] The doctrinal consolidation along with the positivist approach was led by the nineteenth-century German classical school, notably Paul Laband and Georg Jellinek, to identify the initial criteria of what makes a State.[2] These criteria – territory, population and government (or public authority) – have eventually developed into the commonly accepted standard for State creation. These have been thoroughly examined,[3] so there is no pressing need to revisit them.

The focus will instead be upon the continuous exercise of sovereign authority once the above static criteria of statehood are both established and undisputed in relation to the relevant entity. The dynamic aspect of statehood relates to manifesting the State's sovereign character through regular acts of public authority that draw on the patterns of daily operation of the international legal system, and their opposability on the international plane.

[1] *Cf.* Hugo Krabbe, *The Modern Idea of the State* (New York and London: D. Appleton and Company, 1922), 17–28.

[2] Paul Laband, *Staatsrecht des deutschen Reiches*, 1st edn (Freiburg and Leipzig: Mohr, 1895), 164 *et seq.*; Georg Jellinek, *Allgemeine Staatslehre* (Berlin: O. Häring, 1914), 394 *et seq.*

[3] James Crawford, *Creation of States in International Law*, 2nd edn (Oxford University Press, 2006), chs. 2–3.

2 Introducing the dynamic aspect of statehood

The key conceptual issue is the unity and divisibility of statehood. The commentary to the International Law Commission's (ILC) Article 4 on State responsibility specifies that 'The principle of the unity of the State entails that the acts or omissions of all its organs should be regarded as acts or omissions of the State for the purposes of international responsibility.'[4] However, in an early but extremely important contribution on State immunity, Crawford has articulated the non-absolute nature of State immunity as following from the divisibility of sovereign authority that every State possesses.[5]

The divisibility or unity of States can be seen either in factual terms of the structural arrangement of States, or in terms of the substantive scope of their sovereign powers. Whether statehood is structurally indivisible, in relation to which question the national law of the State will, according to the principle stated in the ILC's Article 4(2), be an initial starting point, is not a question identical to whether the substantive scope of the sovereign authority encompasses the totality of State activities. For, through any of its structural components, the State can enter into the multitude of dealings and transactions that do not require the exercise of sovereign authority. If, along these lines, sovereignty is divisible, then international law cannot invariably attach identical consequences to all acts performed by the State in both sovereign and non-sovereign areas.

As Krabbe has explained, this dilemma, either the State is a power arrangement (*Machterscheinung*) that creates law and thus is not subject to private law or, if it is indeed subjected to private law just like any other private entity, then its essence cannot be explained by reference to sovereign authority alone. The State exercises public authority differently from the way it administers postal services or a railway network. Krabbe proposed relying on the concept of legal sovereignty instead of that of State sovereignty, which would then mean that the legal standing of the State in relation to citizens, including its 'added value' (*Mehrwertigkeit*) in the area

4 Report of the International Law Commission on the Work of its 53rd Session, *ILC Yearbook*, 2 (2001), 40. Other possible examples of defining the State structure include Art. 2(1)(b) United Nations Convention on Jurisdictional Immunities of States and their Property (New York, adopted 2 December 2004, not yet in force); *Oil Platforms* (*Islamic Republic of Iran* v. *United States of America)*, Judgment, 6 November 2003, ICJ Reports (2003), 191, and Art. 3(e) in UNGA Resolution 3314 (1974) defining aggression, respectively associating with the State structure ships and armed forces lawfully stationed abroad.

5 James Crawford, 'International Law and Foreign Sovereigns: Distinguishing Immune Transactions', *British Yearbook of International Law*, 54 (1983), 75.

of public authority proper, would materialise only through the framework of law.[6] If Krabbe's equation could be exported to the international legal realm when particular acts and transactions of States fall to be assessed for their public and sovereign character, then the sovereign authority of the State would validly exist to the extent that international law recognises it as such.

In any case, the scope and essence of the public, sovereign or governmental authority of the State must be seen in prescriptive, not factual, terms, for authority as such is a prescriptive construct, not a fact; it is created and maintained through prescriptive ordering. Whether seen through Sir Henry Maine's articulation of legal fictions,[7] or through Hans Kelsen's imputation theory,[8] governmental authority is not what the organ in question is doing factually, but the scope of functions that the legal system bestows upon that organ in its particular capacity as an organ of the State.

Some clues as to the substance of the prescriptive standard are provided in the ILC's commentary to Article 5 on State responsibility. This suggests that the 'governmental authority' of the State does not cover situations where domestic law confers powers upon, or authorises conduct by, citizens or residents generally, or as part of the general regulation of the affairs of the community, but only where it specifically authorises the conduct as involving the exercise of public authority. 'Governmental authority' does not attach to private activities. As for the specific content of this standard, the ILC has observed that '*Beyond a certain limit*, what is regarded as "governmental" depends on the particular society, its history and traditions.'[9]

The ILC's is a nuanced statement, which effectively suggests that there may be a complementary international standard with respect to the valid and internationally opposable exercise of governmental authority. A shared international understanding of public, sovereign and governmental authority would, in the first place at least, be premised on the inherent nature of States that all States share and aspire to maintain. As Hans Kelsen has observed, the State is similar to the individual in its aspiration

[6] Hugo Krabbe, *Die Lehre der Rechtssouveränität – Beitrag zur Staatslehre* (Groningen: J. B. Wolters, 1906), 29–31, 38.

[7] Henry Sumner Maine, *Ancient Law* (London: J. Murray, 1920), 31.

[8] Hans Kelsen, *General Theory of Law and State*, tr. Anders Wedberg (New York: The Lawbook Exchange, 1945), 196 *et seq.*

[9] Report of the International Law Commission on the Work of its 53rd Session, 43 (emphasis added).

to achieve its aims, to develop and prosper.[10] Philip Jessup has similarly observed that States, too, have 'feelings'.[11]

But these factors are not among the immediate concerns of international law. Whether we take a dualist position that States are at the roots of the international legal system, or subscribe to Kelsen's monist approach that statehood is the characterisation imputed by international law to the entities that qualify, it obtains in either case that international law does not initially create States as socio-political realities. It merely attaches certain consequences to the fact of their existence. The State initially gets organised on a basis unrelated to international law; the latter has hardly any say as to the reasons and factors – historical, socio-economic, trade-related, cultural and so on – that motivate the organisation of an entity as a State,[12] still less does it pronounce on the ultimate justification of statehood. The formation, transformation and related development of States constitute a complex socio-political process displayed through the specificity of individual situations that do not lend themselves to a crude generalisation. International law can, then, only take cognisance of the essence of statehood as is inherent to it across the board; it cannot construct the substantive rationale of statehood afresh.

In a way that applies to all States, Ludwig Gumplowicz has described the State as the organisation of power and domination through the legal order.[13] Similarly, if we follow Max Weber's approach, statehood relates to the organised use of coercion, legitimating and monopolising the use of force within the relevant territorial boundaries, and the corresponding obedience from men and women. The justification of domination – and depending also on its extent – can be explained through religious considerations, habitual traditional obedience, charisma and grace, or alternatively through legality that consists in the validity of the legal rules that the State enacts by virtue of its functionally delimited authority. In

[10] Hans Kelsen, *Hauptprobleme der Staatsrechtslehre Entwickelt aus der Lehre vom Rechtssatze*, 2nd edn (Tübingen: Mohr, 1923), 496.

[11] Philip C. Jessup, *A Modern Law of Nations* (New York: The Macmillan Company, 1948), 28.

[12] The reasons are diverse, and often contested or obscured. For instance, in a somewhat unlikely manner, one reason that led to the unification of North American colonies into the United States of America was the need to raise the Navy adequate to deal with the Barbary piracy threat from North Africa: Michael B. Oren, *Power, Faith and Fantasy: America in the Middle East, 1776 to the Present* (New York: W. W. Norton & Company, 2007). See more generally, Francis Fukuyama, *The Origins of Political Order: From Prehuman Times to the French Revolution* (London: Profile Books, 2011).

[13] Ludwig Gumplowicz, *Allgemeines Staatsrecht* (Innsbruck: Wagner, 1907), 24.

all those cases obedience could in practice be determined by what Weber denotes as 'highly robust motives of fear and hope – fear of the vengeance of magical powers or of the power-holder'.[14]

What Weber thus focuses upon is how the power-holder sells the justification and how that justification comes across to people. The two may not always overlap in practice, and the visions of legitimation may thus diverge at the opposing ends of the equation. Nor does that actual process of legitimation always have to be concomitant with the 'terms and conditions' officially stated in the relevant State's constitution, but could also embrace more informal but widely perceived grounds.

Out of the approximately 200 States to which international law applies, not all operate in the same way. Some States are premised on a more or less straightforward constitutional pattern of representation and accountability, the use of coercion being limited to carefully demarcated instances of violating legal prescriptions, beyond which individuals retain complete freedom of choice as to their activities in various areas of social life without fearing coercion, oppression or reprisal. Other States, however, are dominated by more unspoken premises that often divide rather than unite communities and, in order to survive, carry on and command submission, either in terms of domestic governance or of occupation and colonisation of foreign territories. The political systems in question need to rely on fear and violence. For instance, the concept of public and sovereign authority underlying Denmark or the Netherlands shows no viable similarity with that on which the current political regime in Zimbabwe or the Turkish domination of Northern Cyprus (created through massive eviction of inhabitants and importing settlers) are premised. The latter will, quite simply, not survive without oppression and continuing efforts to consolidate the fruits of those oppressive efforts factually, and validate them both domestically and internationally.

If, as observed above, international law does not specify the nature of States and their political regimes in any *a priori* or comprehensive manner, it should not be the task of courts to draw themselves into those complex processes. It was in this spirit that Lord Wilberforce warned against 'involv[ing] English courts in difficult and delicate questions as to the motivation of a foreign State, and as to the concept of public good, which would be unlikely to correspond with ours'.[15] Nor has a top-down attempt at excluding, totally or partially, States from the international legal

[14] H. H. Gerth and G. Wright Mills (eds.), *From Max Weber: Essays in Sociology* (London: Routledge, 1948), 78–9.

[15] *Czarnikow Ltd* v. *Rolimpex* [1979] AC 351, 364.

system proposed, for instance, by liberal theory,[16] succeeded in its aims any more than radical monism succeeded in ensuring the supremacy of international law. The task of international law and of the courts that apply it seems to be more modest, namely to evaluate the nature of particular State activities when it comes to the application of international law to facts.

3 Applying the dynamic aspect of statehood

(a) The law of recognition – addressing the Namibia exception

In its Advisory Opinion on *Namibia* the International Court of Justice had to examine the legal consequences of the illegal presence of South Africa in Namibia. The Court pronounced the duty of third States not to accord recognition to official acts of South Africa in Namibia, so that its sovereign powers there would not be given effect. That, however, did not extend to acts such as 'the registration of births, deaths and marriages, the effects of which can be ignored only to the detriment of the inhabitants of the Territory'.[17] The Court thus effectively proposed a two-pronged guideline for applying this test: whether the recognition of the relevant act serves the interests of the inhabitants; and whether such recognition permits the illegal occupier to assert such public authority as the occupation purports to generate.

The litigation before English courts in the case of *Hesperides*[18] dealing with property deprivation by the illegal authorities of the Turkish Republic of Northern Cyprus (TRNC) addressed the whole matter through the prism of private international law and applied, in relation to title to property, the law of the place where the property was situated. The Court of Appeal did not address the public international law issue of the legality of the TRNC's status, which was antecedent to those private law questions. The *Namibia* two-pronged guidance was not addressed either. Instead, Lord Denning was content to observe that the Northern Turkish administration was factually effective and that was enough for its laws – the inherently public acts validating the initial invasion and separation – to be recognised internationally.

16 See Anne-Marie Slaughter, 'International Law in a World of Liberal States', *European Journal of International Law*, 6 (1995), 504.

17 *Legal Consequences of the Continued Presence of South Africa in Namibia (South-West Africa) notwithstanding Security Council Resolution 276*, Advisory Opinion, 21 June 1971, ICJ Reports (1971), 16, 56, para. 125.

18 *Hesperides Hotels* v. *Aegean Holidays* [1978] QB 205, 221 (*per* Lord Denning).

The European Court of Justice took a more properly strict position in *Anastasiou*, by denying the TRNC the power to issue export certificates for exporting goods to the EU market, which was essentially a public power available, in relation to the territory of the whole of Cyprus, only to the government based in Nicosia.[19] Strasbourg jurisprudence has also addressed the matter, but what was at stake there was not the legality of the TRNC's public law authority that it had effectively stolen from the Republic of Cyprus, but merely the remedies available to individuals within the TRNC before they could take their cases to the European Court of Human Rights. *Cyprus* v. *Turkey* addressed this one single aspect head-on.[20] This narrow focus of adjudication, coupled with the Court's stated policy to admit the *Namibia* exception only to the extent necessary not to strip inhabitants of their basic rights,[21] is a possible countervailing factor that could constrain this exception within its proper limits. That much is also obvious from the subsequent case of *Demopoulos*.[22]

The difference between public authority and private law is what is at stake in this area, for it is essentially a legislative exercise beyond the gift of international tribunals, to expand the *Namibia* exception from private law to public law relationships, and correspondingly to trim down the scope of the duty of non-recognition that is reflected in Article 41 of the Articles on State Responsibility (ASR), or actually render that duty nugatory.

That the *Namibia* exception does not extend to public acts was also confirmed by the Court of Appeal in *Kibris Turk Hava Yollari* v. *Secretary of State for Transport*. As Richards LJ most pertinently observed:

> It is almost certainly true that the opening up of international flights to northern Cyprus would be of great practical significance for persons resident in the territory... But that does not bring the case within the [*Namibia*] exception. The mere fact that the impugned public law decision has a knock-on effect on private lives cannot be sufficient for the purpose.[23]

The standard upheld by the European Court of Human Rights is thus different from that under *Hesperides* and that which was advanced, but

[19] *R* v. *Minister of Agriculture, Fisheries and Food, ex p. S. P. Anastasiou*, Case C-432/92, 100 ILR 258, 296.

[20] *Cyprus* v. *Turkey*, Application No. 25871/94, ECtHR, Judgment, 10 May 2001.

[21] *Ibid.*, para. 96.

[22] *Demopoulos and others* v. *Turkey*, Application No. 46113/99, ECtHR, Admissibility Decision, 1 March 2010, para. 96.

[23] *Kibris Turk Hava Yollari* v. *Secretary of State for Transport* [2010] EWCA Civ 1093, 12 October 2010, para. 80.

rejected, in *Anastasiou* and subsequently by the Court of Appeal of England and Wales in *Kibris*. This latter position, most prominently represented by *Hespreides*, tries to modify the initial legal position by reference to, and effectively in support of, the factual realities on the ground, most profoundly including the illegal occupation. As every State displays in time and space, recognising sovereign prerogatives in illegal entities essentially amounts to stealing the same prerogatives from the rightful owner – the State, or prospectively the non-State entity seeking to become a State – that has the rightful title to the relevant territory. The very purpose of the valid version of the *Namibia* exception is to safeguard the scope of sovereign authority that the rightful owner legally retains.

(b) The law of State responsibility

As it happens, the approach of the law of State responsibility to State activities is, in the first place at least, highly factual, referring to the factual connection between the act of the State and breach of an international obligation, without at that stage introducing any further requirement as to the sovereign or other nature underlying the relevant act. Attribution requirements under Article 4 ASR follow from the already established premise that the organ in question acts as a State organ. However, in relation to non-State entities, whose status as an organ of the State is not obvious, the nature of the activity assumes predominant importance in ascertaining whether their conduct entails the responsibility of the State for which they act.

Whether we are dealing with contexts involving States with different socio-economic systems, or the increasing pattern of privatisation and outsourcing of multiple State activities, whether through the prisons system or the use of private military companies, the issue as to the extent to which the State can alienate its sovereign functions and therefore evade responsibility becomes pressing. For outsourcing of public functions to non-State entities whose identity is separate from that of the State, importantly raises the question as to the precise (non-)sovereign nature of the relevant activities, ultimately to answer the question whether the relevant State should still be held responsible for what has, strictly speaking, been done by someone else. A positive answer to this question is possible only if the non-State entity in question has been given the powers to act in lieu of the State – that is, to do whatever would not be doable but for being a State.

Commentary to the ILC's Article 5 suggests that to attract responsibility, 'the conduct of an entity must accordingly concern governmental activity';

and the person or entity [must be] acting in that capacity in the particular instance'.[24] The criterion seems to be whether the relevant entity has been doing that for which the State would have to use its sovereign capacity were it to perform the same act itself. An inevitable conclusion, however contextual, is that even if the law of State responsibility does not associate the responsibility of the State as such (under Article 4) with the governmental, public or sovereign nature of its activities, it still provides for the test to identify the scope of such activities.

Other, more specialised, areas of responsibility follow suit. The requirement of 'official capacity' under Article 1 of the 1984 UN Convention Against Torture (CAT),[25] to regulate the responsibility of non-State entities for torture[26] is quite similar in essence to 'governmental authority' the way Article 5 ASR addresses it. In this particular case, it is about non-State entities (rebels, insurgents and other *de facto* arrangements) that, although not being a State nor having been delegated official functions from any State, have come to exercise the relevant public functions that would, were other things equal, be exercised in that dimension of time and space by one or another State.

The involvement of private military companies (PMC) in various conflicts has given rise to a debate as to how attribution and 'governmental authority' works in relation to them.[27] The factual context, including at its most extreme a PMC being drawn into combat situations, may not, as such, be crucial. It depends upon the purpose for which force is being used and the nature of that force. The example of food supply or premises security is invoked,[28] arguably to emphasise that PMCs should enjoy security in performing their tasks. It is not the PMCs' but rather the State's public authority, of which a PMC is merely a dedicated servant, that holds the key in determining responsibility. Even the use of force in self-defence, provided that its proper limits under the relevant domestic law are observed, may not be that different from a similar action undertaken by a private individual on the streets of an average town in

[24] Report of the International Law Commission on the Work of its 53rd Session, 43.

[25] Art. 2 of the Convention Against Torture and Other Cruel, Inhuman or Degrading Treatment or Punishment (New York, adopted 10 December 1984, entered into force 26 June 1987), 1465 UNTS 85.

[26] Manfred Nowak and Elizabeth McArthur, *The United Nations Convention Against Torture: A Commentary* (Oxford University Press, 2008), 78–9.

[27] Chia Lenhardt, 'Private Military Companies and State Responsibility' in Simon Chesterman and Chia Lenhardt (eds.), *From Mercenaries to Market: The Rise and Regulation of Private Military Companies* (Oxford University Press, 2007), 139.

[28] *Ibid.*, 148.

Texas. What matters is whether the State has tasked the company to perform the activities that only States can perform as part of their public authority, either as ordinary State functions in peacetime, or those related to war and foreseen under humanitarian law treaties, such as the interrogation of prisoners or maintaining law and order in occupied territories; and then also whether the PMC's particular conduct is performed at the service of that public authority.

The Arbitral Award in *United Postal Service of America Inc. (UPS)* v. *Canada* provides a rare example of judicial articulation of the 'governmental authority' test.[29] Canada Post – operating as part of the Canadian State machinery – prevented the United Postal Services from having access to the Canadian postal market the way it had enabled other operators, arguably breaching Canada's obligations under sections 1102 and 1105 of the North American Free Trade Agreement (NAFTA).[30] The tribunal had to assess whether the acts of Canada Post were attributable to Canada directly and, if not, whether Canada could be held responsible pursuant to Articles 1502(3)(a) and 1503(2) NAFTA, which require parties to ensure that government-owned or -designated monopolies, or State enterprises exercising certain delegated authority, comply with Chapter 11 of the same Agreement.[31] The relevant NAFTA provisions, 'read as a whole [led] the Tribunal to the conclusion that the general residual law reflected in Article 4 of the ILC text' was replaced by 'the special rules of law stated in chapters 11 and 15'.

The particular provisions of chapter 15 themselves distinguish in their operation between the Party on the one side and the monopoly or enterprise on the other. It is the Party which is to ensure that the monopolies or enterprises meet the Party's obligations stated in the prescribed circumstances. The obligations remain those of the State Party; they are not placed on the monopoly or enterprise.

Thus, the Canadian State and Canada Post each possessed separate identities; the latter's acts would not per se become the former's for the purposes of NAFTA, even if they could be attributable to Canada under the general law of responsibility.[32] The principle of the 'unity of the State' was effectively derogated from.

[29] *United Postal Service of America, Inc.* v. *Canada*, ICSID Arbitration, Award on the Merits (24 May 2007).

[30] North American Free Trade Agreement, Canada–Mexico–United States (adopted 17 December 1992, entered into force 1 January 1994), 32 ILM (1992), 605.

[31] *United Postal Service of America, Inc.* v. *Canada*, paras. 45–6.

[32] *Ibid.*, paras. 55, 59, 62.

All then turned on whether Canada Post exercised 'governmental authority'. Sections 1502 and 1503 were contingent on 'establish[ing] that the monopoly or State enterprise in question is exercising a "regulatory, administrative or other governmental authority that the Party has delegated to it"', so that 'a State Party does not avoid its own obligations under the Agreement as a whole . . . by delegating governmental authority to a monopoly (private or public) or to a State enterprise'. Thus, not all acts inconsistent with NAFTA were caught; the two 'provisions operate[d] only where the monopoly or enterprise exercises the defined authority and not where it exercises other rights or powers. They have a restricted operation'. The tribunal observed that '[t]o be contrasted with the exercise of that [governmental] authority is the use by a monopoly or State enterprise of those rights and powers which it shares with other businesses competing in the relevant market and undertaking commercial activities'. Therefore, in relation to access to market and use of infrastructure, Canada Post was not acting on terms foreseen under the ILC's Article 5.[33] Liability would materialise if Canada Post would act not just in contradiction to Canada's NAFTA obligations, but *additionally* do so in the exercise of governmental powers that the Canadian government would have delegated to it.

The tribunal's observation as to the general scope of public authority is also instructive:

> In terms of the instances listed in [sections 1502 and 1503] the body exercising this authority *expropriates* the property, *grants* the license, *approves* the commercial transaction (such as a merger), or *imposes* the quota, fee or charge – in all cases by the unilateral exercise of the governmental authority delegated to it. While that list of authorities is not exhaustive, it helps to identify a genus which involves binding decision-making. So too does the word 'authority' when read with its three adjectives – 'regulatory, administrative or governmental'.

The tribunal's open-ended approach is further instructive in the sense that responsibility does not depend on whether outsourced activities involve the exercise of coercive powers.[34]

(c) The Law of State Immunity

Addressing the area of sovereign immunity requires focusing on the restrictive immunity doctrine, which centres on distinguishing sovereign

[33] *Ibid.*, paras. 68, 70, 72–4, 78. [34] *Ibid.*, para. 79 (emphasis original).

from non-sovereign acts. What matters is the nature of State acts rather than their perpetration by organs of a sovereign State.

As an instance illustrating underlying distinctions, socialist States ordinarily used to claim absolute immunity, for the restrictive doctrine did not admit immunity 'in those cases in which a state performs acts that are also open to private persons'. Socialist States entered 'into a whole series of such contracts on the ground of its state monopoly of foreign trade', and it was thus 'impossible to split up the socialist State into two subjects: a sovereign power and an entity subject to private law rules'.[35] Even after the demise of the Socialist camp, this problem retains its relevance, for both directions of interaction between the State and private activity – the State entering the private marketplace and the State outsourcing its public functions – remain part of modern socio-economic life.

Although the restrictive doctrine is deemed to have been introduced into international law since the mid-twentieth century, its roots can be found in the pronouncements by Sir Robert Phillimore in *The Charkieh*, to the effect that:

> No principle of international law, and no decided case, and no dictum of jurists of which I am aware, has gone so far as to authorize a sovereign to assume the character of a trader, when it is for his benefit; and when he incurs an obligation to a private subject to throw off, if I may so speak, his disguise, and appear as a sovereign, claiming for his own benefit, and to the injury of a private person, for the first time, all the attributes of his character.[36]

This reasoning addresses how and in what manner the sovereign enters the marketplace, or more generally into private relations, that are available to any private actor. In whichever quality or capacity they enter it, so they are supposed to carry on. If the State as a public entity ventures into private dealings the way that everyone else can act, that demonstrates that it can be subjected to the ordinary law applicable to individuals. This approach was further crystallised in the *Congreso* case where Lord Wilberforce clearly emphasised that if an act can be performed by private persons it is no longer a sovereign act.[37] The purpose of immunities under the restrictive doctrine is to protect privileges inherently deriving from statehood, not the totality of State activities.

35 M. M. Boguslavsky, 'Foreign State Immunity: Soviet Doctrine and Practice', *Netherlands Yearbook of International Law*, 10 (1979), 169–70.

36 *The Charkieh* (1872–5) 4 LR 59, 99–100.

37 *I Congreso del Partido* [1983] 1 AC 244, 268.

It is on this narrower version that immunity shields acts contradicting international law. When the act in question is a valid exercise of sovereign authority in the first place, the immunity for it will not fall away merely for the reason that the same act violates international law; not that the unlawful could attract immunity without its sovereign nature being demonstrated in an antecedent manner.

The ways of identifying the connection between the relevant act and the scope of sovereign powers have been articulated in jurisprudence. In the practice of American courts, this has been done in relation to the ownership and control by the State of its natural resources. It was observed in the *Pemex* case that:

> The Court must regard carefully a sovereign's conduct with respect to its natural wealth. A very basic attribute of sovereignty is the control over its mineral resources and short of actually selling these resources on the world market, decisions and conduct concerning them are uniquely governmental in nature.[38]

In the case of *International Association of Machinists and Aerospace Workers* v. *OPEC*, another US court has similarly observed that:

> The control over a nation's natural resources stems from the nature of sovereignty. By necessity and by traditional recognition, each nation is its own master in respect to its physical attributes. The defendants' control over their oil resources is an especially sovereign function because oil, as their primary, if not sole, revenue-producing resource, is crucial to the welfare of their nations' peoples.[39]

The sovereign nature thus accrued only to that narrow area of sovereign activity and decision-making process. This narrow area of control – initial and ultimate decision-making if not the day-to-day administration – is a cardinally important aspect of sovereignty; not least because it essentially follows from the permanent sovereignty over natural resources in line with Resolution 1803(1962) adopted by the UN General Assembly. There can be no serious doubt about this falling within sovereign authority before many other activities will be so labelled.

[38] *Pemex Corporación Mexicana de Mantenimiento Integral, S. De R.L de C.V v. Pemex-Exploración y Producción*, No. 10 Civ. 206 (AKH), 2013 WL 4517225 (SDNY Aug 27, 2013).

[39] For the overview of both cases and other relevant jurisprudence see G. R. Delaume, 'Economic Development and Sovereign Immunity', *American Journal of International Law*, 79 (1985), 325, 327.

The same principle was upheld by the European Court of Human Rights in a different context, distinguishing between the organisational policy underlying the arrangement of a foreign embassy that falls within the area of sovereignty and may attract sovereign immunity, and the more specific issue of the embassy's compliance with an employee's contractual rights, which may not.[40]

The restrictive immunity doctrine does not always overlap with the way national immunity legislation, for instance the 1978 UK State Immunity Act (SIA), regulates the relevant matters. As Lord Diplock emphasised in the *Alcom* case, the SIA does not codify the restrictive doctrine that requires examining the precise (non-)sovereign nature of the relevant act, but grants foreign States absolute immunity unless the matter falls within the specific exceptions set out under the same Act.[41] However, States are not bound by these statutory standards internationally. Court decisions based on the letter of domestic statutes are premised on the exclusion of international law from judicial consideration. They are thus not constitutive of State practice that could possibly build customary law on immunities.[42] States can amend their legislation the way that the United States and Canada have done in relation to terrorist activities,[43] effectively manifesting their position that there is no such indivisible concept of sovereignty which requires that States should be able to claim their sovereign privileges in relation to terrorist activities.

One area where restrictive doctrine and the ensuing sovereign authority test can be used even within domestic statutory frameworks relates to 'separate entities' under section 14(2) of the SIA, which prescribes that the entity affiliated with the governmental apparatus of the foreign State is immune only if 'the proceedings relate to anything done by it in the exercise of sovereign authority'. This was confirmed in *Kuwait Air Co.*, where Lord Goff emphasised that 'it is not enough that the entity should have acted on the directions of the State, because such an act need not

[40] *Fogarty* v. *UK*, Application No. 37112/97, ECtHR, Judgment, 21 November 2001, paras. 22, 30, 38.

[41] *Alcom* v. *Republic of Colombia* [1984] AC 580, 600.

[42] F. A. Mann, 'The State Immunity Act 1978', *British Yearbook of International Law*, 51 (1980), 43; James Crawford, 'A Foreign State Immunities Act for Australia?', *Australian Yearbook of International Law*, 8 (1983), 105–6.

[43] See, for an overview, Ronald Bettauer, 'Germany Sues Italy at the International Court of Justice on Foreign Sovereign Immunity: Legal Underpinnings and Implications for US Law', *ASIL Insight*, 19 November 2009; and the amendments to the Canadian State Immunity Act (RSC 1985, c. S-18), 13 March 2012.

possess the character of a governmental act. To attract immunity under section 14(2), therefore, what is done by the separate entity must be something which possesses that character.'[44] Thus, section 14(2) requires the Court first to identify the character of the organ and then to apply the restrictive doctrine to its action.

The issue was addressed before the SIA came into force, in the *Trendtex* case where Shaw LJ and Stephenson LJ refused to consider the Central Bank of Nigeria as an organ of the Nigerian State, for the relevant legislative amendments that drew on the Bank's status fell short of revealing legislative intention to that effect.[45] A similar philosophy underlies the pronouncements in *Rolimpex* that the entity in question was not part of the Polish State since, even if it 'bought and sold for the State', it retained a considerable freedom in relation to day-to-day commercial activities.[46] To some extent, then, the very status of a 'separate legal entity' as *Trendtex* had it, will depend on the nature of its tasks and the degree of its affiliation with the sovereign functions of the State. In *Rolimpex* the entity in question was confirmed in that status, enabling it to claim a substantive defence against non-compliance with contractual obligations due to government intervention beyond its control – an issue unrelated to immunities. But the underlying test of State public authority remained the same in both areas of law; in both cases the core issue was, and was answered in the negative, whether the entity in question was acting as part of the State and exercising its sovereign functions. Capitalising on previous jurisprudence, Lord Goff concluded in *Kuwait Air Co.* that 'in the absence of such [governmental] character, the mere fact that the purpose or motive of the act was to serve the purposes of the state will not be sufficient to enable the separate entity to claim immunity under section 14(2) of the Act'.[47]

As for the governing law on this issue, it was emphasised in *Trendtex* that:

> the constitution and powers of a Nigerian corporation must be viewed in the light of the domestic law of Nigeria. But its status in the international scene falls to be decided by the law of the country in which an issue as to its status is raised. In civilised states that law will derive from those principles of international law which have been generally accepted among such states.[48]

44 *Kuwait Air Corporation* v. *Iraqi Airways Company and others* [1995] 1 WLR 1147, 1160 (*per* Lord Goff).

45 *Trendtex Trading Corporation* v. *Central Bank of Nigeria* [1977] 1 QB 529, 565, 573.

46 *Czarnikow Ltd* v. *Rolimpex*, 364 (*per* Lord Wilberforce), 367 (*per* Viscount Dilhorne).

47 *Kuwait Air Corporation* v. *Iraqi Airways Company and others*, 1160.

48 *Trendtex Trading Corporation* v. *Central Bank of Nigeria*, 575 (*per* Shaw LJ).

It is therefore affirmed that the domestic forum must, whenever possible, select international law as the law determining the (non-)sovereign status of the entity. As Shaw LJ observed, even if the Bank was a sub-serving agent for government departments, that was not sufficient to make it part of the government.[49] Domestic law provided the initial point of reference, while international law assessed the nature of the relevant domestic legal arrangements, and ultimately determined where sovereign authority lies.

Similar choice-of-law issues are confronted in cases where States themselves, or their officials, claim immunity. The use of the restrictive doctrine under international law in the criminal case of *Pinochet* crucially determined the scope of sovereign functions and that they do not include international crimes.[50] It may be tempting to conclude that, after the thread of jurisprudence culminating with the International Court's judgment in *Germany* v. *Italy*, civil cases are different.[51] Care should be taken, however, not to take this jurisprudence in a casuistic manner, for the nature of judicial reasoning must always be put above judicial statistics. If we use this approach, it will be easily discovered that all pertinent cases confirming immunity in civil proceedings fail to focus on the requirements under the restrictive doctrine. The Strasbourg decision in *Al-Adsani* did not utter a single word regarding the (non-)sovereign nature of torture, the way the restrictive doctrine as detailed above would require it to do.[52] The House of Lords in *Jones* did not focus on the restrictive doctrine either, instead asserting that once the relevant acts were attributable to Saudi Arabia under the law of State responsibility these acts attracted immunity as well.[53] In other words the House of Lords concluded that attributing an act to the State will invariably lead to according it immunity. The *Germany* v. *Italy* judgment did not examine the restrictive doctrine in any detail, and instead relied on the Italian concession that German war crimes were sovereign acts. When focusing on the acts of armed forces,

[49] *Ibid.*, 575.

[50] *Regina* v. *Bow Street Metropolitan Stipendiary Magistrate and others, ex p. Pinochet Ugarte (No. 3)* [2000] 1 AC 147.

[51] *Cf. Jurisdictional Immunities of the State (Germany* v. *Italy: Greece intervening)*, Judgment, 3 February 2012, General List No. 143, para. 87.

[52] *Al-Adsani* v. *UK*, Application No. 35763/97, ECtHR, Judgment, 21 November 2001, 34 EHRR 11 (2002). Twelve years later, in *Jones* v. *UK*, the Fourth Chamber of the European Court has not provided any more substantiated explanation of the rationale and basis of State immunity than its derivation from the sovereignty of States either (*Jones and others* v. *UK*, Applications Nos. 34356/06 and 40528/06, ECtHR, Judgment, 14 January 2014, not reported yet).

[53] *Jones* v. *Saudi Arabia* [2006] UKHL 16, 14 June 2006, paras. 11–12 (*per* Lord Bingham), 76 (*per* Lord Hoffmann).

the International Court focused on the identity of the perpetrator, not the nature of acts, and essentially accorded immunity to Germany on the basis of the – now outdated – absolute immunity doctrine.[54]

Thus, all the three above cases – *Al-Adsani*, *Jones* and *Germany* v. *Italy* – fall short of being good law, for they allowed the relevant States to claim immunity for what are not acts of their sovereignty. It is furthermore odd, to say the least, to contend that the relevant crime could be a sovereign act for civil but not for criminal proceedings. It is a misconception that the denial of immunity for serious violations of human rights and humanitarian law contradicts the State-centric nature of international law. Protecting the internationally recognised valid scope of statehood and public authority is just as much – and as little – as the State-centric nature of international law actually requires.

4 The three areas evaluated

The dynamic aspect of statehood addresses the extent to which a State can validly use its sovereign authority or rely on it to evade responsibility. Obviously the test of governmental or sovereign authority is bound to be the same for all pertinent areas of international law, focusing on the authority available only to States, not acts or rights that can also be performed by private or other non-State entities. A State cannot be more or less sovereign in different areas or contexts. To operate viably and predictably, the three above areas of international law rely on that single overarching concept of public authority for their own purposes and focus upon the aspects of it to be applied to each of those areas, thereby reinforcing the unity of that test and mutual interconnectedness of its various elements.

The law of recognition and State responsibility law are concerned only with situations when the entity other than the State acts in a legitimate or purported exercise of State authority. The law of immunities aims not just to prove facts of State involvement but to classify them for the further additional purpose, and to delimit the extent to which the ordinary course of justice can be evaded. In the end, the historical process of elaboration upon all these standards has served the common and overriding goal to secure efficient accountability.

[54] *Jurisdictional Immunities of the State (Germany* v. *Italy: Greece intervening)*, paras. 60 *et seq.*

Furthermore, the notion of 'separate entity' operates to enable the State to get away from foreign proceedings when the relevant act is *jure imperii*. Thus, in the law of immunities, 'governmental authority' assumes the same dimension as in the law of State responsibility as per *UPS*, the way that it includes – and in this case immunises – actions performed within the valid scope of sovereign authority as recognised under international law, and excludes other actions.[55] The application of section 14 SIA in *Kuwait Air Co.* broadly fits within this approach.

Thus, if a State delegates public authority to a 'separate entity' for whatever purpose, that State is responsible for everything factually done in the exercise of that delegated or outsourced authority; even though, depending on its substance, the actual specific act performed within the area covered by Article 5 ASR, that is under the guise of 'governmental authority', may or may not be a genuine exercise of that authority. The ILC commentary does not require that it should be. Nor does it have to be, for the use of the 'governmental authority' test in Article 5 is merely to channel the factually occurred incidents back to the State so that the latter's liability materialises. Again, Article 5 is not about the governmental or official nature of specific acts, it is about the *a priori* generalised conferral, by the State to a non-State entity, of the authority to perform activities in that particular area.

If the 'governmental authority' test is used in terms of defining the nature of a particular wrongful act, it could be used homogenously for the purposes of both State responsibility and State immunity. For Article 5 purposes, the delegating State does not, at the point of delegation or conferral, determine unilaterally what 'governmental authority' covers; it merely ends up transferring to the non-State entity the powers that, under international law and independently of State will expressed at the point of delegation, already possess such governmental character. The underlying formula is not 'I determine if X is governmental and then delegate it', but 'I delegate what already is governmental.'

The outcome specifically for the purposes of immunities is that the State can claim immunity for acts of a 'separate entity' only if those acts were validly performed as part of that delegated 'governmental authority', with the effect that the outsourcing State itself would, as a matter

[55] After all, the articulation of this test in *United Postal Service of America, Inc.* v. *Canada*, para. 79 is fairly similar to the criteria of *jure imperii* acts in *Contemporary Problems Concerning the Immunity of States*, Institute of International Law, Basel Session, 1991, Art. 2(3) (Special Rapporteur Ian Brownlie).

of international law, be validly entitled to claim immunity for those acts under the restrictive doctrine of immunity. For, the restrictive doctrine addresses not just general systemic and constitutional patterns of delegation and outsourcing, but also crucially focuses on the governmental or private nature of that very specific act in relation to which immunity is being claimed.

The relevant activities can initially be described as governmental or private: compare an arrest with the sale of tickets. What also matters, however, is whether individual acts are undertaken within the area that broadly involves governmental authority, whether by the State or delegated to a non-State entity. We can thus contrast a general context of policing or maintenance of discipline in prisons to the supply of food to or torture of inmates, which are specific acts undertaken within the broader task of governmental authority to run prisons. If the government outsources to a private entity the broader governmental authority to run the prison, particular acts performed within this framework will be channelled back to the State through the principle stated in Article 5 ASR. For the private entity would not commit these acts if governmental authority had not been delegated to it from the State. Once attribution to the State is determined, however, its responsibility will attach to individual acts, not to that overall framework of governmental authority. Correspondingly, for the purposes of the law of immunities, it is these specific acts that fall to be assessed for their sovereign or private character. Thus, for instance, acts perpetrated by a PMC and channelled to the State through Article 5 ASR would not, under the restrictive doctrine, attract immunity.

A PMC interrogating prisoners and torturing them enters the field through the use of conferred public authority, but the act in question does not become sovereign for the purposes of State immunity. For immunities focus on specific acts, not general authority; the latter does not cover, nor would be intended at the point of conferral to authorise, those specific acts. Similarly, the State torturing in peacetime enters the field through the private activity in the first place and is thus not immune. The State would not thus be immune for the PMC's torture either.

5 Conclusion

The advantage of focusing on the dynamic aspects of statehood, as developed in judicial practice and the ILC's work, is to promote effective accountability of States in various contexts, on inclusive terms and through the application of the existing law. The areas examined above demonstrate that in the twenty-first century there could hardly be room for the absolute and indivisible version of statehood. The reasoning that preaches pragmatism, and alludes to imaginary needs of stability that could be threatened by human rights litigation, in effect tries to superimpose a preconceived ideology over the merit of legal evidence, and is essentially a reasoning developed from the position of intellectual and evidentiary weakness.

The comparative advantage, and thus power, of judicial reasoning is that it holds the grip on the continuous process of the application of established rules and principles of international law. Instead of projecting some liberal transnational compact and on that basis discriminating between States, the focus on the role of courts is premised on the inclusive approach that applies to all States, great or small, liberal or 'rogue', integrating them all within the same process of lawmaking and law enforcement. It is not completely free of inconsistencies, but the difference it has already made is undeniable. Following this route is far more feasible than unrealistically waiting for some great systemic changes leading to a constitutional revolution – especially if it is a revolution that most of us do not want to happen.

11

How to recognise a State (and not)

Some practical considerations

TOM GRANT

The mechanisms and procedures of recognition: a practical problem

A wide variety of situations arise in international relations upon which States may judge it necessary to express a view. Claims by States to territory or maritime jurisdiction, attempts to transfer the assets of an international organisation, challenges to the status and immunities of government officers, alterations in the public law of an occupied territory and constitutional crises which cast doubt on the representative capacity of a government as agent of a State are among the recurring examples. Perhaps the most notable is that where a new State is claimed to have emerged. Where an existing State resists relinquishing responsibility over the territory of the putative new State, the situation is particularly delicate.

There were tentative suggestions at the start of the United Nations era that the international response to the putative emergence of new States should be resolved centrally – not by the individual State exercising a unilateral discretion, but by a collective organ of the international community acting in the name of all its members and, perhaps, even applying international law rules. Norway, at the Dumbarton Oaks Conference, proposed that the Member States vest in the United Nations an exclusive authority to recognise new States; the idea attracted little support.[1] Perhaps it was thought that recognition, in the relevant sense, was a decision for States alone and not one to be taken by an organisation; but, if that were the case, then certainly it would have been for States, if they chose, to confer the power over that decision to an organisation of their own making. The Secretary-General, not long after, evidently saw no obstacle in principle

[1] See United Nations Conference on International Organization, Amendments and Observations on the Dumbarton Oaks Proposals (Norway), 4 May 1945, UNCIO Doc. 2, G/7 (n 1), 2–3.

to the organisation recognising new States: he proposed that, by Charter amendment or by treaty, the Member States might assign the organisation a power in this respect – in the Secretary-General's words, '[t]o establish the rule of collective recognition'.[2] That and similar proposals such as Hersch Lauterpacht's[3] notwithstanding, the traditional position – recognition as a unilateral and discretionary act – was left undisturbed.

And so has it been largely since. Thus Serbia could reassert the unilateral and discretionary character of recognition in the advisory proceedings in respect of Kosovo;[4] and Western European States, like France and the United Kingdom, while disagreeing with Serbia as to most aspects of the situation, agreed on that threshold point.[5] The European Union (EU), in respect of Eritrea, seems to have confirmed that recognition of a new State is not an action restricted by any general rule to States – the EU established a European position on recognition of Eritrea[6] – but, in respect of Kosovo, where a consensus of all its Member States (as at 2008) did not exist, the EU refrained from asserting a position. According to the Council of the EU, 'Member States will decide, in accordance with national practice and international law, on their relations with Kosovo.'[7] The evidence is, then, that the law has changed little since the early 1990s, when the Badinter Commission had been able to reach much the same conclusion.[8] The law indeed has changed little on the point since the United States' Permanent Representative famously referred to recognition as that 'high political act' which '[n]o country on earth can question',[9] even if States and their

[2] See Memorandum on the Legal Aspects of the Problem of Representation in the United Nations, S/1466, 9 March 1950.

[3] See Hersch Lauterpacht, *Recognition in International Law* (Cambridge University Press, 1947 [repr., with a foreword by James Crawford, 2012]), 68–73. *Cf.* Josef L. Kunz, 'Critical Remarks on Lauterpacht's "Recognition in International Law"', *American Journal of International Law*, 44 (1950), 713.

[4] Written Comments of Serbia, 15 July 2009, *Accordance with International Law of the Unilateral Declaration of Independence in Respect of Kosovo (Request for Advisory Opinion)*, 199, para. 501 ('*Kosovo* case').

[5] Written Statement by France, 17 April 2009, *Kosovo* case, 15–16, 45, paras. 1.16, 2.70; Written Statement of the United Kingdom, 17 April 2009, *Kosovo* case, 99, para. 5.51.

[6] EC Bull. No 36, 314, 8 May 1993.

[7] Council Conclusions on Kosovo, 18 February 2008, 2851st External Relations Council Meeting.

[8] See *Opinion No 10, Commission of Arbitration of the Conference on Yugoslavia* (Badinter, Chairman; Corasaniti, Herzog, Petry and Tomas Valiente, Members), 4 July 1992, 92 International Law Reports, 206, 208, para. 4.

[9] Warren Austin, 18 May 1948 quoted P. M. Brown, 'The Recognition of Israel', *American Journal of International Law*, 42 (1948), 621.

representatives in recent times would be unlikely to express the matter as stridently as that; and even given the general rule of non-recognition in respect of situations created by a serious breach of a peremptory norm.[10]

When States deal with a question of recognition 'in accordance with national practice and international law', international law, depending on the situation, thus may entail some substantive constraints, but it is the national practice which will be of primary importance when it comes to the mechanisms and procedures of recognition. It comes as little surprise, where a matter has remained de-centralised to this extent, that little if any systematic treatment has been given to the mechanisms or procedures.

Yet the mechanisms and procedures may be important when disputes arise over statehood. Disputes over statehood arise from time to time at the international level, for example in respect of the treatment an international organisation is to accord an entity.[11] It would seem that disputes over statehood are at least as frequent, perhaps more so, at the municipal level, such as in respect of how a national court is to treat the entity,[12] its acts,[13] agents[14] or property.[15] It hardly can be expected in national systems which respect the rule of law that courts in all circumstances will automatically defer to the executive determinations of the government; but when it comes to recognition of States, executive certification is important in many jurisdictions.[16] Few courts, if any, ignore entirely

[10] International Law Commission (ILC), Draft Articles on Responsibility of States for Internationally Wrongful Acts, *ILC Yearbook*, 2(2) (2001), 29; GA Res. 56/83, 12 December 2001, annex, corrig. A/56/49 (vol. I)/Corr.4, Art. 41, para. 2.

[11] E.g. treatment of the Sahrawi Arab Democratic Republic in the OAU: Gino J. Naldi, 'The Organization of African Unity and the Saharan Arab Democratic Republic', *Journal of African Law*, 26 (1982), 152–62. See also Gino J. Naldi, 'Peace-keeping Attempts by the Organisation of African Unity', *International and Comparative Law Quarterly*, 34 (1985), 595–601.

[12] *Ungar* v. *Palestine Liberation Organization*, 402 F3d 274, 287–92 (1st Cir, Selya CJ) (31 March 2005) (sovereign immunity).

[13] Case C-432/92, *The Queen* v. *Minister of Agriculture, Fisheries and Food, ex p. S. P. Anastasiou (Pissouri) Ltd and others*, Judgment, ECJ, 5 July 1994 (*Anastasiou I*), [1994] ECR I-3116 (on reference by High Court of Justice (Queen's Bench Division)) (movement and phytosanitary certificates issued by authorities of the 'Turkish Republic of Northern Cyprus').

[14] *United States* v. *Palestine Liberation Organization*, 695 F Supp 1456, 1459 (SDNY, Palmieri DJ) (29 June 1988) (representation of 'Palestine' or the 'Palestinian people' at UN headquarters by PLO).

[15] *The Maret*, 145 F2d 431, 442 (3rd Cir, Biggs CJ) (17 October 1944) (putative title of a Soviet State agency to an Estonian ship).

[16] See e.g. the position in India, with reference to United Kingdom and United States practice, *German Democratic Republic v. Dynamic Industrial Undertaking Ltd* (High Court of

whether or not the executive offices of the State have recognised (or declined to recognise) the entity in question.[17] Only in unusual circumstances would a court be likely to adjudicate a challenge against the act of recognition itself.[18]

In any circumstance, it might be supposed that whether or not recognition has taken place is easy to determine. After all, the executive organs of the State, when called on to do so, usually have been perfectly clear whether or not the State has recognised a given situation. This is why it is possible to 'presuppose . . . that the judiciary can understand what the executive has said'.[19] In some cases, however, the executive has not been so clear. Consequently, the question may itself be one of contention between parties to a dispute. This is one way in which the mechanisms and procedures of recognition may assume a practical significance – that is to say, in the forensic process.

There is also the case where the State is obliged not to recognise a given situation but seeks to preserve some scope for normal transactions. The International Court of Justice (ICJ) addressed this as a matter of protecting the interests of the inhabitants of a territory subject to a rule of non-recognition.[20] In practice, it well may be that persons or institutions elsewhere wish to invest in the territory or to engage in commerce with its inhabitants and thus are concerned that the rule of non-recognition

Bombay, 14–16 October 1970) (Mody and Vaidya JJ), paras. 35–48, repr. 64 International Law Reports, 504, 514–19.

17 Even where courts have been relatively liberal in how they apply executive statements in light of the circumstances of the case, the inquiry starts with the question of the certification – recall *Carl-Zeiss-Stiftung* v. *Rayner and Keeler, Ltd and others (No. 2)* [1966] 2 All ER 536.

18 See *Horta* v. *Commonwealth*, High Court of Australia, 14 August 1994, (1994) 123 ALR 1, 7, repr. 104 International Law Reports, 450, 456:

> nothing in this judgment should be understood as lending any support at all for the proposition that, in the absence of some real question of sham or circuitous device to attract legislative power, the propriety of the recognition by the Commonwealth Executive of the sovereignty of a foreign nation over foreign territory can be raised in the courts of this country.

Supporting the position that it requires a question of constitutional propriety to give rise to a justiciable challenge, see *Belize* case, Case No. 290 and 292/91 (Constitutional Court of Guatemala, 3 November 1992): repr. 100 International Law Reports, 304.

19 *Gur Corporation* v. *Trust Bank of Africa Ltd*, 22 July 1986 (Nourse LJ) [1987] 1 QB 599, 626, repr. 75 International Law Reports, 675, 698.

20 *Legal Consequences for States of the Continued Presence of South Africa in Namibia (South West Africa) notwithstanding Security Council Resolution 276 (1970)*, Advisory Opinion, 21 June 1971, ICJ Reports (1971), 56, para. 125.

not get in the way of *their* interests.[21] There, too, what mechanisms and procedures are understood as conferring recognition is an important question, for it is those mechanisms and procedures from which the State must refrain if it is to remain in accord with the obligation not to recognise.

The difficulty, as suggested above, is that the mechanisms and procedures have been subject to little systematic consideration. It is well enough established that, in considering close questions of statehood, recognition is a probative factor; whether a given act is to be understood as conferring recognition is the question which now may be considered.

Recognition expressly indicated

The case where a State has adopted a clear statement that it recognises the situation in question may be dealt with briefly. For example, Japan, through a statement by its foreign minister, said as follows: 'Japan recognized the Republic of South Sudan as a new state as of today.'[22] The United States, in a statement through its president, said, 'the United States formally recognizes the Republic of South Sudan as a sovereign and independent state upon this day'.[23] India recognised South Sudan through a letter from its prime minister to the president of the new State.[24] The Member States of the European Union did so jointly through a declaration.[25] The United States recognised Bosnia and Herzegovina, Croatia and Slovenia by a presidential statement in the following terms: 'The United States recognizes Bosnia-Hercegovina, Croatia, and Slovenia as sovereign and independent states.'[26]

There are also occasions when a State has incorporated a statement recognising another in a treaty. Greece did this in the Interim Accord

[21] E.g. the building company and bank involved in the dispute arising out of a bank guarantee and contracts for the construction of schools and a hospital in Ciskei, South Africa: *Gur Corporation* v. *Trust Bank of Africa Ltd.*

[22] Statement of the Foreign Minister of Japan on the Independence of the Republic of South Sudan (provisional trans.), para. 2, 9 July 2011, available at www.mofa.go.jp/announce/announce/2011/7/0709_01.html.

[23] White House, Office of the Press Secretary, Statement of the President: Recognition of the Republic of South Sudan, 9 July 2011.

[24] Letter of 9 July 2011 from Prime Minister Manmohan Singh to President General Salva Kiir Mayardit, reported at www.thehindu.com/news/national/article2215972.ece.

[25] Declaration by the EU and its Member States on the Republic of South Sudan's Independence, 9 July 2011, 12679/11 – PRESSE 232.

[26] President George H. W. Bush, Statement of 7 April 1992, repr. 1992 (i) *Public Papers of the Presidents of the United States*, 553.

of 13 September 1995, under Article 1, paragraph 1, of which Greece recognised the Former Yugoslav Republic of Macedonia:

> Upon entry into force of this Interim Accord, the Party of the First Part recognizes the Party of the Second Part as an independent sovereign state ...[27]

Then there are reciprocal exchanges of recognition, such as that between the Federal Republic of Yugoslavia and the Republic of Bosnia and Herzegovina:

> The Federal Republic of Yugoslavia and the Republic of Bosnia and Herzegovina recognize each other as sovereign independent States within their international borders.[28]

Israel and Jordan took a similar approach:

> The Parties will apply between them the provisions of the Charter of the United Nations and the principles of international law governing relations among states in time of peace. In particular:
> 1. They recognise and will respect each other's sovereignty, territorial integrity and political independence;
> 2. They recognise and will respect each other's right to live in peace within secure and recognised boundaries ...[29]

These are statements announcing recognition in terms; they do not leave recognition to inference.

The matter becomes more complicated, where the State has given no explicit indication that it recognises the situation but its practice, in other respects, presents the possibility that it has. There, inquiry will turn to the intention of the State to recognise (or not to recognise). This raises a question: by what evidence can the intention be established? As will be seen, there has been a tendency to answer the question categorically by reference to particular types of conduct – for example, by saying that by entering into an agreement the State necessarily evinces the intention to recognise the other party as a State. Whether the State's conduct, in

[27] Interim Accord between Greece and the Former Yugoslav Republic of Macedonia (New York, adopted 13 September 1995, entered into force 13 October 1995), 1891 UNTS 3, 5.

[28] General Framework Agreement for Peace in Bosnia and Herzegovina (Bosnia and Herzegovina–Croatia–Federal Republic of Yugoslavia), 14 December 1995, Art. X, repr. 35 *International Law Materials*, 75, 90.

[29] Art. 2, Treaty of Peace between the State of Israel and the Hashemite Kingdom of Jordan (adopted 26 October 1994, entered into force 10 November 1994), 2042 UNTS 351, 393–4.

itself, will necessarily settle the question is far from clear, however. Before turning to the question of how conduct may be identified as entailing the intention to recognise, it is worth considering how intention relates to recognition.

Recognition as an intentional act

Intention has been ascribed importance in the field of recognition for some time. The Institut de Droit International addressed the matter in 1936 as follows:

> La reconnaissance *de jure* résulte, soit d'une déclaration expresse, soit d'un fait positif, marquant clairement l'intention d'accorder cette reconnaissance, tel l'établissement de relations diplomatiques; en l'absence de déclaration ou de fait semblable, la reconnaissance ne saurait être considérée comme acquise.[30]

This made clear that the act of recognition is not necessarily an explicit statement like the examples given above. The act of recognition need not be '*une déclaration expresse*'. If the act is one '*marquant clairement l'intention d'accorder cette reconnaissance* . . . ' then the State adopting the act has recognised the situation in question.

The formula is obviously of limited utility. To determine that a given act is an act of recognition, the formula has us ask whether the act is intended to be an act of recognition. Without more, this is circular. The one multilateral instrument to address the matter around the time of the Institut's Resolution is no more helpful. According to Article 7 of the Montevideo Convention:

> [T]he recognition of a state may be express or tacit. The latter results from any act which implies the intention of recognizing the new state.[31]

So, again, the emphasis is removed from form: the act need not be express; it may be 'tacit'. This hardly narrows the category of potential acts; it widens it. Recognition may result from 'any act', so long as it 'implies the intention of recognizing'. The problem is that these statements say nothing

[30] 11th Commission, Resolution, Art. 4: (1936) 9(ii) *Annuaire de l'institut de droit international*, 300, 301. '*De jure* recognition results either from an express declaration or from a positive fact, clearly indicating the intention to grant such recognition, such as the establishment of diplomatic relations; in the absence of a similar statement or fact, recognition cannot be considered to have been granted.'

[31] Art. 7, Convention on the Rights and Duties of States adopted by the 7th International Conference of American States (Montevideo, adopted 26 December 1933, entered into force 26 December 1934), 165 LNTS 21, 25.

as to the content of the intention to which they refer. And attempts to pinpoint the intention behind recognition, in terms of legal effects, run up against the oft-noted uncertainty as to the legal character of recognition. To complete the picture, it seems there may be no better way forward than further analysis of the practice.

Courts considering recognition have done so in connection with particular disputes and so have not aimed to systematise the matter. The Singapore Court of Appeal, for example, was asked to consider the extensive relations that the Singapore government maintained with Taiwan as possible evidence of recognition. The Court of Appeal concluded that it could not infer that Singapore had recognised Taiwan as a State because '[f]or there to be implied recognition, the acts must leave no doubt as to the intention to grant it'.[32] The European Court of Human Rights also seems to have understood recognition to require intention: to acknowledge that a functioning court system exists in a territory, absent an intention to extend recognition, is not to imply recognition.[33]

In the *Kosovo* Advisory Opinion, it was not necessary for the ICJ to say what acts amount to recognition. The Court restricted its observations about recognition to saying that it had not been asked 'about the validity or legal effects of the recognition of Kosovo by those States which have recognized it as an independent State'.[34] In other cases, the Court has referred to the intentional element in connection with unilateral declarations. In the *Nuclear Tests* cases, the Court said, 'When it is the intention of the State making the declaration that it should become bound according to its terms, that intention confers on the declaration the character of a legal undertaking.'[35] It referred to this passage in *Burkina Faso/Mali* and added (it would seem for emphasis) that 'it all depends on the intention of the State in question'.[36] The Court was considering certain acts in these

[32] *Civil Aeronautics Administration* v. *Singapore Airlines*, 14 January 2004 [2004] SGCA 3 (Singapore Court of Appeals) (Chao Hick Tin JA), para. 36, repr. 133 International Law Reports, 371, 383–4.

[33] See *Cyprus* v. *Turkey*, Application No. 25781/94, ECtHR, 10 May 2011, para. 238, repr. 120 International Law Reports, 10, 76.

[34] *Accordance with International Law of the Unilateral Declaration of Independence in Respect of Kosovo*, Advisory Opinion, 22 July 2010 ('*Kosovo* Advisory Opinion'), ICJ Reports (2010), 403, 423, para. 51. *Cf. Reference Re Secession of Quebec*, Supreme Court of Canada, 29 August 1998, (1998) 161 DLR (4th) 385, 443, para. 142, repr. 115 International Law Reports, 536, 589.

[35] *Nuclear Test cases (New Zealand* v. *France; Australia* v. *France)*, Judgment, 20 December 1974, ICJ Reports (1974), 472, para. 46; ICJ Reports (1974), 267, para. 43.

[36] *Frontier Dispute (Burkina Faso/Republic of Mali)*, Judgment, 22 December 1986, ICJ Reports (1986), 573, para. 39.

cases because it was possible that they gave rise to specific legal obligations for the declarant States.[37] Because what specific legal obligations arise from an act of recognition remains a matter of uncertainty – as noted, the Court would not say what the 'legal effects of... recognition' might be – the Court's earlier observations about intention and obligation do not necessarily apply strictly to recognition. Yet, while recognition is not exactly the type of unilateral act which the Court was considering in *Nuclear Tests* or *Burkina Faso/Mali*, recognition in its classic sense has been a unilateral act. To identify intention as a necessary element of unilateral acts seems, at least in a general way, to say something about recognition.

The modern law codification projects, like their forebears, have identified intention as an element in recognition. In the 1965 Restatement, the American Law Institute (ALI) said, 'Implied recognition may take place in a variety of ways by which a state manifests its intention to treat an entity as a state.'[38] The 1987 Restatement described recognition as an act 'confirming that the entity is a state, and expressing the intent to treat it as a state'.[39]

The International Law Commission (ILC) Special Rapporteur for unilateral acts acknowledged that '[i]t is not easy to define the act of recognition, specifically the recognition of a State' and then rallied to the intention requirement:

> The act of recognition could... be defined as follows:
>
> A unilateral expression of will formulated by one or more States, individually or collectively, acknowledging the existence of a de facto or de jure situation or the legality of a legal claim, with the intention of producing specific legal effects, and in particular accepting its opposability as from that time or from the time indicated in the declaration itself.[40]

Agreement, in the end, was not reached to associate recognition with the topic. As the Special Rapporteur admitted, it had not been included with

[37] See Memorial of Burkina Faso, 3 October 1985, 117 and 119, paras. 13 and 18. The statements of the French government (to the effect that atmospheric atomic tests would cease) deprived the litigation of any further object: ICJ Reports (1974), 477–8, paras. 61–65; ICJ Reports (1974), 271–2, paras. 58–62.

[38] Restatement (Second) Foreign Relations Law (1965), § 104. Manifestation of Intention to Recognize, Comment b.

[39] Restatement (Third) Foreign Relations Law (1987), § 202. Recognition or Acceptance of States, Reporters' Note 1.

[40] Rodríguez Cedeño, 6th Report, ILC 55th Session, 30 May 2003, A/CN.4/534, 17, para. 67.

the Commission's mandate as such.[41] The *Guiding Principles* which the ILC eventually adopted in respect of unilateral acts were restricted 'to unilateral acts *stricto sensu*, i.e., those taking the form of formal declarations formulated by a State with the intent to produce obligations under international law'.[42] So this text is relevant to the act of recognition, only when the act takes 'the form of a formal declaration', and only if the act is performed with the intent to produce obligations – which it is not always clear it is, given the uncertainties surrounding the legal effects of recognition. Nor under other topics has the ILC yet adopted a text to address recognition of States.[43] Thus the conclusions which can be drawn about recognition from the ILC's work are limited, but the possible connections to recognition were certainly being considered under the topic of unilateral acts. And there the Commission as a whole placed stress on intentionality: the concern there is with '[d]eclarations publicly made and manifesting the will to be bound'.[44]

Modern writers who address recognition in its strict sense largely agree that the element of intent is central. According to Pellet, '*l'essentiel est que la volonté de reconnaître soit établie de façon certaine* . . . '[45] Shaw, too, places the stress on intention: 'recognition is founded upon the will and intent of the state that is extending the recognition'.[46] *Brownlie's Principles of Public International Law*, though with a slightly different emphasis, draws attention to intent as well:

> Above all, recognition is a political act and is to be treated as such. Correspondingly, the term 'recognition' does not absolve the lawyer from inquiring into the intent of the recognizing government, placing this in the context of the relevant facts and law.[47]

[41] Rodríguez Cedeño (Special Rapporteur), 65th Session, 2818th Meeting, para. 41, *ILC Yearbook*, 1 (2004), 185.

[42] Guiding Principles Applicable to Unilateral Declarations of States Capable of Creating Legal Obligations, preambular para. five: *ILC Yearbook*, 2(2) (2006), 369, para. 177.

[43] Recognition of States and governments was one of the topics originally proposed for the Commission, see *ILC Yearbook* (1949), 37–8, paras. 1–13. The topic as yet has not been taken up, about which see Outline of the Working Group on the Long-term Programme of Work, A/51/10, *ILC Yearbook*, 2(2) (1996), Annex II, repr. James Crawford, *Creation of States in International Law*, 2nd edn (Oxford University Press, 2006), 757.

[44] Guiding Principles Applicable to Unilateral Declarations of States Capable of Creating Legal Obligations, Principle (1), 370.

[45] Patrick Daillier *et al.*, *Droit international public*, 8th edn (Paris: LGDJ, 2009), 631, §370 ('what is essential is that the will to recognise be established with certainty').

[46] Malcolm N. Shaw, *International Law*, 6th edn (Oxford University Press, 2008), 462. *Cf. ibid.*, 453.

[47] James Crawford, *Brownlie's Principles of Public International Law*, 8th edn (Oxford University Press, 2012), 147. See also *ibid.*, 149.

Verhoeven[48] and Jennings and Watts[49] also referred to intent as a requirement.

Recognition is not like strict liability; an act does not constitute recognition unless it evinces the intention to recognise. That much is clear from judicial practice, the work of codifiers and academic commentary. The question, however, remains: how is it to be determined whether a given act evinces the requisite intention?

Categories of acts and the intention to recognise

States at one time believed that a wide variety of acts were tantamount to recognition – to the extent that it may be asked whether intention was necessary to the act at all. For example, the legal advisors to the Privy Council said that private commerce by British subjects would not be consistent with non-recognition of the independence of St Domingo.[50] Sending a consul to Warsaw could 'be considered . . . as amounting in fact to a recognition of [Poland's] independence'.[51]

Sending a consular officer today would still likely suggest an intention to recognise,[52] but even extensive and continuous contacts do not in themselves necessarily amount to recognition.[53] The fact that France negotiated the Geneva Agreements of 20 July 1954 did not mean it had recognised the Democratic Republic of Viet Nam.[54] The Croat, Muslim and Serb communities in Bosnia and Herzegovina participated in negotiations but this did not deprive Bosnia and Herzegovina of its territorial integrity.[55] Certainly, negotiating with aeroplane hijackers does not

48 Joe Verhoeven, *Droit international public* (Brussels: Larcier, 2000), 64.

49 Robert Jennings and Arthur Watts (eds.), *Oppenheim's International Law*, 9th edn (Harlow: Longman, 1992) 169, § 50.

50 Nicholl, Piggott and Romilly to Privy Council, 22 March 1806, repr. Arnold McNair, *International Law Opinions*, 3 vols. (Cambridge University Press, 1956), I, 132.

51 Jenner to Palmerston, 30 June 1831, repr. McNair, *International Law Opinions*, I, 134.

52 See 'United Kingdom Materials in International Law', *British Yearbook of International Law*, 67 (1996), 717.

53 *Civil Aeronautics Administration* v. *Singapore Airlines*, paras. 32–6, repr. 133 International Law Reports, 371, 382–3 (commercial, trade and cultural representations); *Caglar* v. *Billingham (Inspector of Taxes)*, 7 March 1996 (England, Special Commissioners) (Oliver and Brice, Commissioners), para. 45, repr. 108 International Law Reports, 510, 519 (tax and law enforcement liaisons).

54 *Clerget* v. *Banque Commerciale pour Europe du Nord & Banque du Commerce Extérieur du Vietnam* (Court of Appeal, Paris, 7 June 1969), repr. 52 International Law Reports, 310, 312.

55 See Written Observations of the Federal Republic of Yugoslavia, *Application of the Convention on the Prevention and Punishment of the Crime of Genocide (Bosnia and Herzegovina* v.

say anything about their representative capacity or about the legal identity of the movement they purport to represent.[56] In conferences[57] and in standing organisations[58] States undertake a range of contacts without implying recognition.

The substantial flexibility evident in practice notwithstanding, this is a field where the limits are still sometimes characterised in categorical terms. The act of concluding an agreement at the international level in particular has been said necessarily to imply recognition. For example, under the heading 'Manifestation of Intention to Recognize', the American Law Institute (ALI) says as follows:

> (2) The coming into effect of a bilateral international agreement between a state and an entity implies recognition of that entity as a state and recognition, as its government, of the regime that makes the agreement for it.[59]

The ILC Special Rapporteur for unilateral acts also identified the conclusion of an agreement as an implicit act of recognition:

> When a State . . . concludes an agreement with an entity that it has not recognized as such, it will be recognizing it from that point in time onwards . . .[60]

These are categorical positions, in that they attribute the intention to a category of acts; there is no reservation here for examples of agreements which do not imply recognition.

The difficulty is that the adoption of an international agreement does not necessarily in itself imply the statehood of either party. By entering into an agreement with a multilateral organisation, a State does not intend to recognise the organisation as a State.[61] The view from the early stages of the drafting of the International Centre for Settlement of Investment Disputes (ICSID) Convention had been that an investor and a State may

Serbia and Montenegro) (*Genocide case*), 9 August 1993, 8, para. 8; and Judgment, 11 July 1996 (Preliminary Objections), ICJ Reports (1996), 595, 611, 613, paras. 19, 26.

56 *Pan American World Airways, Inc.* v. *Aetna Casualty & Surety Co.*, 505 F2d 989, 1012 (2nd Cir, Hays CJ) (15 October 1974).

57 E.g. London Somalia Conference, in which participated Somaliland and Puntland: FCO Communique, Lancaster House, 23 February 2012, paras. 6 and 16, available at www.gov.uk/government/news/london-conference-on-somalia-communique--2.

58 See 'United Kingdom Materials in International Law', *British Yearbook of International Law*, 60 (1989), 590.

59 Restatement (Second) Foreign Relations Law, § 104.

60 Rodríguez Cedeño, 6th Report, 8, para. 28.

61 See *Westland Helicopters Ltd* v. *Arab Organisation for Industrialisation* [1995] 2 All ER 387.

enter into an agreement to arbitrate,[62] and this could well be an international agreement.[63] Nobody would say that the host State thinks it is the respondent in an inter-State proceeding when the investor institutes arbitration!

So it is not satisfactory to say that all such acts necessarily evince the intention to confer recognition. Other factors must be considered.

Factors identifying the act of recognition

As noted above, the factor which makes it easiest to identify an act of recognition is the content of the statement which a State adopts; express acts of recognition largely remove the doubt. Some suggestions may briefly be made as to factors which are relevant in the closer cases.

The organ or agent which acts toward the entity

Where an act does not expressly confer recognition, one factor which may be considered is the functional purpose of the organ or agent which acts toward the entity in question.

As observed already, absent a centralised mechanism, it is unsurprising that international law does not specify a particular procedure or apparatus that a State must use to confer recognition. The suggestion nevertheless once was made that allocation of this competence might be under a general international law principle. The Institut de Droit International said that recognition:

> émane de l'autorité compétente, suivant le droit public de l'État, pour le représenter dans les relations extérieures.[64]

This suggests a degree of symmetry with the international law rules concerning formation of legal obligation. Article 7, paragraph 2 of the Vienna

[62] International Bank for Reconstruction and Development, 'Report of the Executive Directors on the Convention on the Settlement of Investment Disputes between States and Nationals of Other States (18 March 1965)' repr. *History of the ICSID Convention: Documents Concerning the Origin and the Formulation of the Convention*, 4 vols. (ICSID, Washington 1968), II(2), 1077 [24] ('ICSID Hist.'); *ibid.*, II(1), 275 (Consultative Meeting of Legal Experts, Summary Record of Proceedings (30 April 1964) 5th Session, 18 December 1963).

[63] Memorandum of the Meeting of the Committee of the Whole, 27 December 1962, SID/62–2 (7 January 1963) ICSID Hist., vol. II(1), 68 [48]; Paper prepared by the General Counsel and transmitted to the members of the Committee of the Whole, SID/63–3 (18 February 1963) ICSID Hist. (n 115), vol. II(1), 74, 79–80 [8], [18].

[64] Institut de Droit International, 11th Commission, Resolution, Art. 2, (1936) 9(ii) *Annuaire de l'institut de droit international* 300, 301.

Convention on the Law of Treaties identifies the organs which presumptively bind the State as those which perform the general foreign policy functions.[65] Other organs might bind the State as well, but this is constrained by the particular functions they are assigned. The ICJ in *Armed Activities on the Territory of the Congo* alluded to the constraint as follows:

> with increasing frequency in modern international relations other persons representing a State in specific fields may be authorized by that State to bind it by their statements in respect of matters falling within their purview. This may be true, for example, of holders of technical ministerial portfolios exercising powers in their field of competence in the area of foreign relations, and even of certain officials.[66]

Other organs may act, but their field of action is 'in respect of matters falling within their purview'. The ILC Special Rapporteur may have gone too far when he said that '[t]here is a limitative criterion in the case of recognition of a State, which is probably different from other unilateral acts such as promise, in which case a broader criterion can be established'.[67] States remain free to organise their internal functions as they please; no international rule or principle prevents a State from giving the director of the forestry department the mandate to confer recognition. The point is nevertheless valid that such an officer's statements are not generally to be presumed to indicate the intent of the State in that branch of international relations.

Disclaimer

In an area of practice where intent is of central importance, disclaimer, where adopted, inevitably has a corresponding role. The ALI said that 'certain relations or associations between the state and the entity or regime' will imply recognition – 'unless such an implication is prevented by disclaimer of intention to recognize'.[68] This would suggest a mirror effect of express statements: an express affirmation of recognition establishes the State's position with clarity; an express statement the other way does so as well, at least where the act to which the disclaimer is attached leaves some margin of doubt as to the intention behind it.

65 Art. 7, para. 2, Vienna Convention on the Law of Treaties (Vienna, adopted 22 May 1969, entered into force 27 January 1980), 1155 UNTS 332, 334.

66 *Case concerning Armed Activities on the Territory of the Congo (New Application: 2002) (Democratic Republic of the Congo* v. *Rwanda)*, Jurisdiction of the Court and Admissibility of the Application, Judgment, 3 February 2006, ICJ Reports (2006), 27, para. 47.

67 Rodríguez Cedeño, 6th Report, 18, para. 72.

68 Restatement (Second) Foreign Relations Law, § 104.

The European Union, in adopting an agreement with Macedonia, included a disclaimer that the fact of adoption 'cannot be interpreted as acceptance or recognition by the European Communities and their Member States in whatever form or content of a denomination other than the "former Yugoslav Republic of Macedonia"'.[69]

But disclaimers have not been adopted in all situations in which a question might arise. The EU adopted no disclaimer when it established a financial support mechanism for northern Cyprus.[70] Nor did it adopt a disclaimer in respect of Taiwan when it adopted a further procedural understanding in respect of the World Trade Organization (WTO) Dispute Settlement Understanding with Chinese Taipei (Taiwan).[71] It could be that the general policy of non-recognition spoke for itself in both situations. It also could be that the language of the respective instruments entailed an implicit disclaimer. In addressing northern Cyprus, the Council referred to the 'reunification of Cyprus' and recalled the suspension of the *acquis communautaire* pending a 'solution to the Cyprus problem'; in the agreement with Taiwan, the EU referred to that entity as the 'Separate Customs Territory of Taiwan, Penghu, Kinmen and Matsu'. Recognition tends to assume that the situation being recognised has achieved a degree of permanence; the language referring to the provisional character of arrangements in Cyprus acknowledged that the situation there is not permanent. And it would be peculiar to recognise a territory using a title which was adopted to avoid the inference of statehood; the title used in dealings with Taiwan was adopted precisely to avoid that inference.[72]

Third-party statements

Serbia, in the *Kosovo* advisory proceedings, recalled that the UN Secretary-General had indicated that the UN maintained a position of 'strict status neutrality', that is to say, the UN did not recognise Kosovo as an

[69] Letter from the European Communities and their Member States to Prime Minister of the Government of the former Yugoslav Republic of Macedonia, 9 April 2001, OJ L 084, 20/03/2004, 0003–0012.

[70] Council Regulation (EC) No. 389/2006, 27 February 2006, L 65/5, §§ (2), (3).

[71] Understanding between the European Union and Chinese Taipei Regarding Procedures under Articles 21 and 22 of the Dispute Settlement Understanding, 11 July 2011, WT/DS277/15.

[72] I.e. the accommodation by which Taiwan acceded to the WTO: Accession of the Separate Customs Territory of Taiwan, Penghu, Kinmen and Matsu, Decision of 11 November 2001, WT/L/433.

independent State.[73] According to Serbia, it 'would clearly run counter to this position to now interpret the behaviour of either the Secretary-General or his Special Representative as a tacit acceptance of the UDI'.[74] It certainly would not be credible for Serbia later to say that that behaviour *did* amount to tacit acceptance.

Other circumstances surrounding the conduct

Finally, before imputing (or denying) the intention to recognise, it may be necessary to consider other circumstances surrounding the statement or conduct in question. It would be strange to impute the intention to recognise where the object of putative recognition is nothing like a State, nor shows any sign of becoming one. The concern instead is with a territorial entity exercising real governmental competences and at least a degree of international capacity and, moreover, which claims to be a State. Entities like Kosovo, the 'Turkish Republic of Northern Cyprus' or the 'Republic of China' in Taiwan, when these have entered into international transactions, have presented the more serious questions.

Conclusion

The purpose here has been to consider a particular dimension of a well-known problem in international law. States, by making their positions explicit one way or the other, typically have avoided the question whether they intend to recognise a given situation. The conduct of States, however, is not always clear.

In summary, four factors may help identify whether a particular act amounts to recognition:

(i) the content of the relation or statement
(ii) the usual functions performed by the organ or agent which operationalises the relation or adopts the statement
(iii) disclaimers accompanying the establishment or adoption of the relation or statement
(iv) the positions expressed by third parties

[73] Letter dated 12 June 2008 from the Secretary-General to Boris Tadić: S/2008/354, quoted Written Comments of Serbia, 15 July 2009, *Accordance with International Law of the Unilateral Declaration of Independence in Respect of Kosovo (Request for Advisory Opinion)*, 193, para. 488.

[74] *Ibid.*

(v) any other circumstances, including especially the conduct and characteristics of the entity with which the relation is entered or toward which the statement is adopted.

In a situation where non-recognition is obligatory, States may wish to enter into relations which would imply at least certain capacities in the other party. Whether the act of entering into a given relation or adopting a particular statement would amount to recognition there will have practical significance as the State seeks to maintain accordance between its conduct and its obligations.

12

An analysis of the 1969 Act of Free Choice in West Papua

THOMAS D. MUSGRAVE*

1 Introduction

This chapter will examine the so-called 'Act of Free Choice', which took place in West Papua in 1969, and which resulted in the incorporation of West Papua into Indonesia. 'West Papua' is the name by which the Papuans themselves refer to their homeland. The territory was originally known in colonial times as West New Guinea, and the territory is referred to as 'West Irian' in Indonesia. In this chapter the term 'West Papua' will be used to refer to the territory, except in those instances when it has been officially referred to either as West New Guinea or West Irian. The population of West Papua will be referred to as 'Papuans'.

Leaders of the West Papuan independence movement assert that the population of West Papua was not accorded any real opportunity to exercise its right of self-determination upon the decolonisation of the territory in 1969. They argue that the so-called 'Act of Free Choice' administered by Indonesia was manipulated so as to ensure that West Papua was absorbed into Indonesia, without the true will of the population having been taken into account. As a result, the events surrounding the Act of Free Choice remain a source of deep and abiding grievance amongst Papuans. Indonesia, on the other hand, has always denied that there was anything untoward about the Act of Free Choice, and that West Papua was legally incorporated into Indonesia and now forms an integral part of the country. Recently no less a personage than Indonesian President Yudhoyono, referring to West Papua, declared that there 'exist no manipulations

* I wish to acknowledge my research assistant, Ms Anne Thomas, and to express my heartfelt thanks to her for her very helpful contributions to this chapter.

of history that must be revised'.[1] This chapter will examine the events leading up to and involving the 1969 Act of Free Choice, in the context of the legal requirements of the right of self-determination as it existed at that time, in order to ascertain whether the West Papuans were indeed denied a real opportunity to exercise their right to self-determination, and, if so, to analyse the consequences which flow from such a denial.

2 The development of self-determination in international law

In examining the legality of the 1969 act of self-determination in West Papua, it is first necessary to consider the status of self-determination in international law at that time. Up until World War II, self-determination had for the most part been solely a political process. Since then, it has increasingly become an established legal right in international law. This began with its inclusion in the Charter of the United Nations (UN), in Articles 1(2) and 55. Self-determination was not defined in the Charter, but in the 1950s it came to mean the process of decolonisation, for a majority of the members of the General Assembly. Colonies, or 'dependent territories', were addressed in Chapters XI, XII and XIII of the Charter. Although the term 'self-determination' was not utilised in these chapters, the fact that the term was increasingly associated with decolonisation meant that the provisions of these chapters were understood to constitute a primary application of the principle.

The UN Charter categorised these territories into two types: trust territories, which were addressed in Chapters XII and XIII of the Charter, and non-self-governing territories, which were addressed in Chapter XI. West Papua had been declared to be a non-self-governing territory by the General Assembly in 1960,[2] and therefore the provisions of Chapter XI applied to it. Chapter XI comprised two articles, Articles 73 and 74. Article 73 obliged Member States administering non-self-governing territories to develop self-government in those territories. However, the Charter had not defined when a territory would be considered to be non-self-governing, nor when it would cease to be non-self-governing.[3]

[1] Jennifer Robinson, 'Self-determination and the Limits of Justice: West Papua and East Timor' in Helen Sykes (ed.), *Future Justice* (Albert Park, Victoria: Future Leaders, 2010), 177.

[2] John Saltford, *The United Nations and the Indonesian Takeover of West Papua, 1962–1969* (London, New York: Routledge, 2003), 180.

[3] Thomas D. Musgrave, *Self-determination and National Minorities* (Oxford University Press, 1997), 69, 70.

Consequently the General Assembly sought to define and elaborate these issues in a number of Resolutions adopted in the 1950s, and to exert pressure on administering states to end the non-self-governing status of such territories as quickly as possible. Amongst the many Resolutions adopted by the General Assembly in this regard, the two most important ones were Resolution 1514(XV) of 14 December 1960 and Resolution 1541(XV) of 15 December 1960.

Resolution 1514(XV) was entitled 'The Declaration on the Granting of Independence to Colonial Countries and Peoples'. This Resolution equated self-determination with decolonisation. This can be seen in the juxtaposition of paragraphs 1 and 2. Paragraph 1 condemned the 'subjection of peoples to alien subjection and exploitation' and declared that this was 'contrary to the Charter of the United Nations and is an impediment to promotion of world peace and co-operation'. The Resolution then linked the reference to 'peoples' in Article 1 to their right to self-determination in Article 2:

> All peoples have the right to self-determination; by virtue of that right they freely determine their political status and freely pursue their economic, social and cultural development.[4]

The preamble declared 'the necessity of bringing to a speedy and unconditional end colonialism in all its forms and manifestations'. Paragraphs 3 and 5 provided further elaboration in this regard. Paragraph 5 called for the immediate transfer of 'all powers to the peoples of those territories, without any conditions or reservations, in accordance with their freely expressed will and desire, without any distinction as to race, creed or colour in order to enable them to enjoy complete independence and freedom'. This grant of independence to non-self-governing territories was not to be delayed, according to paragraph 3, by any inadequacy of political, economic, social or educational preparedness.

Paragraph 6 emphasised that the process of decolonisation was not to affect or alter the territorial boundaries of the newly independent State from the boundaries which had defined it as a colony:

[4] Para. 2 simply reiterated the identical wording of Art. 1(1) of the International Covenant on Civil and Political Rights and the International Covenant on Economic, Social and Cultural Rights. Although these two covenants did not open for signature and ratification until 19 December 1966, and did not come into force until 1976, common Art. 1(1) had been drafted in its final form and approved by the General Assembly in 1955.

> Any attempt aimed at the partial or total disruption of the national unity and the territorial integrity of a country is incompatible with the purposes and principles of the Charter of the United Nations.

Resolution 1514(XV) was adopted by the General Assembly by a vote of eighty-nine in favour, none against, and nine abstentions. Both Indonesia and the Netherlands voted for the Resolution.[5]

The day following the adoption of Resolution 1514(XV) the General Assembly adopted Resolution 1541(XV). This Resolution was also directed at dismantling colonialism. It laid down twelve principles with regard to Article 73 of the Charter and non-self-governing territories. Principle I specified that Chapter XI applied to territories which were 'known to be of the colonial type'. Principle VI set out the three ways in which a non-self-governing territory could obtain a full measure of self-government: independence, free association with an independent State or integration with an independent State. General Assembly Resolutions up to this point had stressed that independence was 'the normal and expected way in which a full measure of self-government would be achieved'.[6] It was therefore assumed in Resolution 1541(XV) that independence would be the usual outcome of an act of self-determination, and as a result Resolution 1541(XV) did not enumerate conditions for the attainment of independence by a non-self-governing territory. For the other two types of self-government, which were seen to be derogations from the normal and expected outcome of independence, the Resolution did lay down conditions. The conditions laid down for integration were particularly stringent, because integration was considered to be irreversible. Principle VIII declared that integration must occur 'on the basis of complete equality'. Principle IX declared that integration 'should come about' as follows:

(a) The integrating territory should have attained an advanced stage of self-government with free political institution, so that its peoples would have the capacity to make a responsible choice through informed and democratic processes.
(b) The integration should be the result of the freely expressed wishes of the territory's peoples acting with full knowledge of the change to

[5] Dusan J. Djonovich (ed.), *United Nations Resolutions Series I: Resolutions Adopted by the General Assembly, VIII: 1960–1962* (Dobbs Ferry, New York: Oceana Publications, 1974), 21, 38.

[6] Musgrave, *Self-determination and National Minorities*, 72.

> their status, their wishes having been expressed through informed and democratic processes, impartially conducted and based on universal adult suffrage. The United Nations could, when it deems it necessary, supervise these processes.[7]

Integration was thus discouraged in all but the most politically advanced of territories, that is those which would be the least likely to adopt this alternative.[8] Resolution 1541(XV) was adopted by the General Assembly by a vote of sixty-nine in favour, two against, and twenty-one abstentions. Indonesia voted for the Resolution; the Netherlands abstained.[9]

3 The uncertain status of West New Guinea

On 17 August 1945 the Indonesian nationalist leader Sukarno proclaimed the independence of the Republic of Indonesia, becoming its first president.[10] The new State of Indonesia emerged from the colony of the Dutch East Indies, and the Dutch attempted unsuccessfully to reassert control over their colonial possession. In 1949 the United Nations Commission on Indonesia was established. The Commission set up the 'Round Table Conference' at The Hague in order to resolve the Indonesian question. On 27 November 1949 the Netherlands and Indonesia signed the Hague Agreement, by which the Netherlands transferred sovereignty over the Dutch East Indies to Indonesia.[11]

During the Round Table negotiations the two sides could not agree on whether West Papua,[12] which had been a constituent part of the Dutch East Indies, should be transferred to Indonesia, or whether it should remain under Dutch sovereignty. There were on-going but fruitless negotiations on the status of West Papua throughout the 1950s. The Dutch argued that West Papua should develop as a separate colony under Dutch administration and should eventually become an independent State in

[7] United Nations General Assembly, Resolution 1541 (XV) Principles which should guide Members in determining whether or not an obligation exists to transmit the information called for under Article 73e of the Charter, Fifteenth session, 948th plenary meeting, 15 December 1960, Resolutions adopted on the reports of the Fourth Committee, 29–30.

[8] Musgrave, *Self-determination and National Minorities*, 73.

[9] Djonovich, *United Nations Resolutions Series I*: VIII, 22, 40.

[10] Philip C. Jessup, *The Birth of Nations* (New York, London: Columbia University Press, 1974), 44; Saltford, *The United Nations and the Indonesian Takeover of West Papua, 1962–1969*, xvi.

[11] Saltford, *The United Nations and the Indonesian Takeover of West Papua, 1962–1969*, 5.

[12] Then officially known as 'West New Guinea'.

its own right, because the population of West Papua had nothing in common with the population of Indonesia. The Melanesian population of West Papua was not only racially different from the Malay Indonesians, but also differed completely from them in terms of languages spoken, culture and religion.[13] The population of West Papua was also at a much lower level of social and political development than the population of Indonesia, and the Dutch seriously doubted whether the Indonesians would be capable of administering a population which was so different and so undeveloped in comparison with other parts of Indonesia.

Indonesia argued that the territory of West Papua rightly belonged to it, and that the exercise of continued Dutch sovereignty over the territory amounted to a violation of its territorial integrity. Indonesia noted that West Papua had been administered by the Dutch as an integral part of the colony of the Dutch East Indies.[14] Whatever differences might exist between the Malay Indonesians and the Melanesian West Papuans were not relevant, according to the Indonesians, because the essential factor which united all of the diverse groups within the former Dutch East Indies was that they had all equally suffered under Dutch colonialism.[15] Moreover, because Indonesian nationalists had been imprisoned by the Dutch in West Papua during the struggle for independence, Indonesia argued that West Papua had become 'a sacred site in the national imagining'.[16]

In 1950 the Netherlands proposed that the question of West Papua be dealt with either by the United Nations Commission on Indonesia or by the International Court of Justice. Indonesia, however, rejected this proposal out of hand.[17] Indonesia sought instead to mobilise the General Assembly into supporting Indonesia's claim on West Papua. Between 1954 and 1957 Indonesia put forward four draft Resolutions to the General Assembly, but in each case the Resolution was not adopted by the Assembly.[18] Indonesia thereupon decided that it had to embark on a different course of action in order to obtain West Papua. Throughout Indonesia

[13] Anthony L. Smith and Angie Ng, 'Papua: Moving Beyond Internal Colonialism?', *New Zealand Journal of Asian Studies*, 4 (2002), 97.

[14] The Dutch countered this argument by asserting that the territory of West Papua had been administered from Batavia (Jakarta) by the same governor and colonial administration simply because it had not been practical to create a separate administrative apparatus when there had been such a small Dutch presence in West Papua.

[15] Clinton Fernandes, *Reluctant Indonesians* (Melbourne: Scribe Publications, 2006), 54.

[16] *Ibid.*

[17] Pieter Drooglever, *An Act of Free Choice* (Oxford: Oneworld Publications, 2009), 326.

[18] Saltford, *The United Nations and the Indonesian Takeover of West Papua, 1962–1969*, 6.

the securing of West Papua had become the primary focus of nationalist expression, extending 'across the entire political spectrum'.[19] Amongst Indonesians the dispute over West Papua was understood as simply the most recent episode in their on-going struggle against the Dutch imperialists. This struggle, as Smith and Ng point out, was 'at the heart of Indonesian nationalism' and was one of its most fundamental aspects.[20] In December 1957 the 50,000 Dutch nationals living in Indonesia were expelled from the country and their businesses were nationalised. Indonesia now began a campaign which involved threats of military force, as well as the infiltration of armed Indonesians into West Papua, in order to attain its end.[21]

4 The growth of West Papuan nationalism

Throughout the 1950s the Dutch began to prepare the population of West Papua for eventual independence. Schools were set up in the territory, in order to train Papuans as teachers, bureaucrats, paramedics, police and tradesmen. The Dutch made sure that this small but educated class of Papuans found employment within the colonial administration as well as in the wider community,[22] and they cultivated the notion of greater autonomy amongst this local elite.[23] The rapid expansion of opportunities intensified pro-independence sentiments within the territory and several political parties were formed, all of which supported the eventual independence of West Papua, apart from one party which was exclusively Indonesian in composition.[24] However, the growth of this pro-independence sentiment amongst the educated class of West Papuans must be seen in light of the fact that approximately half of the population of West Papua at this time still lived in areas which were not even under Dutch administration.[25] Most West Papuans in these areas lived in very primitive conditions, and had no understanding whatsoever of such concepts as self-determination, autonomy and independence.[26]

[19] *Ibid.* [20] Smith and Ng, 'Papua: Moving Beyond Internal Colonialism?', 96.

[21] Peter King, *West Papua and Indonesia since Suharto* (Sydney: University of New South Wales Press, 2004), 21; Saltford, *The United Nations and the Indonesian Takeover of West Papua, 1962–1969*, xvii, 6.

[22] Fernandes, *Reluctant Indonesians*, 53; Smith and Ng, 'Papua: Moving Beyond Internal Colonialism?', 97.

[23] Fernandes, *Reluctant Indonesians*, 21.

[24] Saltford, *The United Nations and the Indonesian Takeover of West Papua, 1962–1969*, 9, 10.

[25] *Ibid.*, 10. The population of West Papua has been estimated at approximately 700,000 to 800,000 persons at this time.

[26] Saltford, *The United Nations and the Indonesian Takeover of West Papua, 1962–1969*, 9, 10.

Nevertheless, the Dutch pushed ahead with plans to implement self-government in West Papua, preparatory to the eventual grant of independence to the territory. In 1959 the Dutch set up both a central representative body, known as the West New Guinea Council, as well as regional councils throughout the territory. The first election for the West New Guinea Council was held in February 1961. Sixteen councillors were elected in the developed areas from amongst ninety candidates, and an additional twelve councillors were appointed by the Dutch to represent those areas thought not to be politically ready for the electoral process.[27]

In September 1961 the Netherlands submitted a Resolution to the General Assembly, in which it proposed to relinquish sovereignty over West Papua, which would then be administered by a United Nations Commission. The Commission would organise a plebiscite amongst the population in order to determine West Papua's ultimate political status.[28] The proposed Resolution received a majority of votes in the General Assembly, but failed to achieve the two-thirds majority required for its adoption.[29] The West New Guinea Council, however, endorsed the proposed Resolution on 1 December 1961, and issued a statement calling on all states to respect the right of the West Papuans to self-determination.[30] The Council renamed the territory West Papua, and adopted a national anthem and a national flag, known as the 'Morning Star'.[31]

Indonesia reacted forcefully to these moves by the Netherlands and the West New Guinea Council. On 19 December 1961 President Sukarno delivered a speech in which he declared that Indonesia would never permit the Dutch to set up a 'puppet State' in West Irian, and that it was the Indonesian flag which must inevitably fly over this territory. Sukarno called for a general mobilisation of the Indonesian people in order to 'liberate' West Irian, and proceeded to set up a military task force to integrate West Papua into Indonesia by force.[32]

[27] *Ibid.*, 10. Of the sixteen elected councillors, three were Dutch, two were Eurasians, and eleven were Papuans.

[28] Fernandes, *Reluctant Indonesians*, 54; Saltford, *The United Nations and the Indonesian Takeover of West Papua, 1962–1969*, 10, 11.

[29] There were 53 votes in favour, and 41 votes against: Saltford, *The United Nations and the Indonesian Takeover of West Papua, 1962–1969*, xviii.

[30] Fernandes, *Reluctant Indonesians*, 54.

[31] Smith and Ng, 'Papua: Moving Beyond Internal Colonialism?', 98; Fernandes, *Reluctant Indonesians*, 54; Saltford, *The United Nations and the Indonesian Takeover of West Papua, 1962–1969*, 11.

[32] Fernandes, *Reluctant Indonesians*, 21; Saltford, *The United Nations and the Indonesian Takeover of West Papua, 1962–1969*, 11.

5 The New York Agreement

Since 1957 the Soviet Union had been supplying arms to Indonesia and giving it diplomatic support with regard to the 'liberation' of West Papua.[33] During this same period the Indonesian Communist Party had become the largest political party in the country. It garnered significant support among Indonesians by promoting a nationalist campaign for the integration of West Papua into Indonesia.[34]

These developments caused considerable alarm in the United States. In the broad context of the Cold War the primary concern of the United States was to ensure that Indonesia did not become aligned to the Communist bloc. From the United States' perspective, Indonesia's claim on West Papua seemed to be a very minor issue and certainly not one which should jeopardise the Cold War balance of power.[35] The Americans therefore began to bring considerable pressure upon the Dutch to come to some sort of agreement with Indonesia concerning West Papua. Negotiations between the two sides began in March 1962, with the American diplomat, Ellsworth Bunker, appointed by the United Nations as mediator.

The negotiations between the Netherlands and Indonesia proved to be very difficult, and talks were broken off several times. The Dutch sought to ensure that the West Papuans were accorded an act of self-determination, whereas the Indonesians were only 'prepared to give the Papuans the opportunity to confirm that they wanted to continue on as part of Indonesia'.[36] The United States proposed a plan whereby administration of the territory would be granted for an initial period to the United Nations, and then administration would pass to the Indonesians, with an act of self-determination for the Papuans taking place some years later. This proposal eventually became the basis for the New York Agreement, which was signed by the Netherlands and Indonesia on 15 August 1962. At no point in the proceedings did any Papuans take part.[37]

By virtue of Article II of the Agreement the Netherlands was to transfer administration of West Papua to a United Nations Temporary Executive Authority (UNTEA). UNTEA would then administer the territory for a

[33] King, *West Papua and Indonesia since Suharto*, 21. [34] *Ibid.*

[35] One advisor to the Kennedy administration went so far as to declare that self-determination for the 'stone-age' Papuans would be meaningless: Memo from Rostow, Deputy Special Assistant for National Security Affairs to President J. F. Kennedy, 13 October 1961. *US Foreign Relations 1961–62*, 440. Quoted in Saltford, *The United Nations and the Indonesian Takeover of West Papua, 1962–1969*, 11.

[36] Drooglever, *An Act of Free Choice*, 429.

[37] John Saltford, 'United Nations Involvement with the Act of Self-Determination in West Irian (Indonesian West New Guinea) 1968 to 1969', *Indonesia*, 69 (2000), 72.

minimum period of seven months. At the end of the minimum period the head of UNTEA would then determine, pursuant to Article XII, when to transfer administration to Indonesia, and the territory would then be administered by Indonesia. Article XIV stated that once administration of West Papua had been transferred to Indonesia, Indonesian national laws and regulations would be applicable in the territory. However, Article XXII(1) specified that both UNTEA and Indonesia would 'guarantee fully the rights, including the rights of free speech, freedom of movement and of assembly, of the inhabitants of the area'. The Article went on to state that these rights would 'include the existing rights of the inhabitants of the territory at the time of the transfer of administration to the UNTEA'.

Article XX specified that the 'act of self-determination' was to be 'completed before the end of 1969'.[38] Of particular note were Articles XVII and XVIII. Article XVII specified that the arrangements for 'the Act of Free Choice', as it was referred to, were the 'responsibility of Indonesia', but that the 'Representative of the Secretary-General' would 'advise, assist and participate in the arrangements' together with Indonesia. The Representative, by virtue of Article XVI, would be supported by a 'number of United Nations experts', who would 'participate at the appropriate time in the arrangements for self-determination', but whose functions would 'be limited to advising on, and assisting in, preparations for carrying out the provisions for self-determination'. Indonesia was thus to have effective control in the organising and implementation of the 'act of free choice', and the role of the United Nations was to be limited to 'advising ' and 'assisting'.

Article XVIII set out the parameters for the Act of Free Choice, as follows:

> Indonesia will make arrangements, with the assistance and participation of the United Nations Representative and his staff, to give the people of the territory the opportunity to exercise freedom of choice. Such arrangements will include:
>
> (a) Consultations (*Musyawarah*) with the representative councils on procedures and appropriate methods to be followed for ascertaining the freely expressed will of the population;
>
> (b) The determination of the actual date of the exercise of free choice within the period established by the present Agreement;
>
> (c) Formulation of the questions in such a way as to permit the inhabitants to decide (a) whether they wish to remain with Indonesia; or (b) whether they wish to sever their ties with Indonesia;

[38] Arts. X and XVII also used the term 'self-determination' in their wording.

(d) The eligibility of all adults, male and female, not foreign nationals, to participate in the act of self-determination to be carried out in accordance with international practice, who are resident at the time of the signing of the present Agreement and at the time of the act of self-determination, including those residents who departed after 1945 and who return to the territory to resume residence after the termination of Netherlands administration.

Thus, although Indonesia had control over the way in which the Act of Free Choice would be conducted, the parameters of such arrangements were circumscribed by the provisions set out in Article XVIII.

6 The Act of Free Choice

Although no maximum period had been set for the administration by UNTEA, the UN Authority transferred the administration of West Papua to Indonesia within the precise minimum period of time set out in the Agreement, on 1 May 1963.[39] The territory was thereafter administered by Indonesia. On 4 May 1963, the newly installed Indonesian administration banned all existing Papuan political parties, and prohibited unauthorised political activity. Protests by West Papuans against Indonesian rule were brutally suppressed, and the Indonesian military undertook a 'sustained campaign of violence, conditioning and intimidation' against the West Papuans.[40] This led to a number of mutinies amongst Papuan policemen, and an on-going series of armed rebellions in the various parts of the territory. In 1965 the Papuan resistance movement known as the OPM (*Organisasi Papua Merdaka*, or 'Free Papua Movement') was formed to fight the Indonesians.[41] The Indonesian military responded with counter-insurgency operations, in which many thousands of West Papuans were killed.

When the UN team arrived in 1968 to assist in the arrangements for the act of self-determination they discovered that the Indonesians had already decided on the method to be used. There would not be a 'one person, one vote' process. Instead, the Indonesian practice of *musyawarah* would be used. Smith and Ng define *musyawarah* as a 'process of consultation towards consensus to secure the people's approval'.[42] In the context

39 Saltford, 'United Nations Involvement with the Act of Self-Determination in West Irian', 72.

40 Robinson, 'Self-determination and the Limits of Justice', 172.

41 Saltford, *The United Nations and the Indonesian Takeover of West Papua, 1962–1969*, xxi–xxiv.

42 Smith and Ng, 'Papua: Moving Beyond Internal Colonialism?', 100.

of the self-determination of West Papua the Indonesians decided that *musyawarah* would involve a consultation process with the representatives of an enlarged version of the eight regional councils of West Papua. The existing members of the regional councils had been appointed by Indonesia and, as it turned out, the additional members were also handpicked by Indonesian officials. The membership of the eight enlarged councils amounted to 1,022 representatives. Only these representatives would be involved in the process of *musyawarah*, which, according to Indonesia, would then constitute the appropriate act of self-determination for West Papua. Indonesia justified the use of *musyawarah* on the basis that West Papua was 'one of the most primitive and undeveloped communities in the world' and that Western democratic procedures would therefore be totally inappropriate.[43] The eight regional councils voted successively in the Act of Free Choice throughout July 1969, and into the first week of August 1969. From early July the representatives of the councils had been isolated by Indonesian authorities, and there is very credible evidence that most, if not all, of them were either bribed, threatened or otherwise intimidated by the Indonesian military or other Indonesian officials.[44] When the votes of the representatives were tallied, not unsurprisingly all 1,022 had voted that West Papua be integrated into Indonesia.

The Act of Free Choice was clearly nothing of the kind, and certainly did not represent the view of the vast majority of Papuans, who had shown their resistance to becoming a part of Indonesia through repeated demonstrations and armed rebellions throughout the entire period of Indonesian administration. Numerous observers remarked on the fact that the Papuans manifestly did not want to be integrated into Indonesia. The UN team of experts, sent to 'assist and advise' the Indonesians, privately expressed the view that some 95 per cent of Papuans did not want to become a part of Indonesia, and instead wanted to become independent.[45] A confidential briefing paper written by a member of the British Foreign Office was even more blunt, noting that 'the people of West Irian have no desire to be ruled by the Indonesians who are of an

43 Saltford, *The United Nations and the Indonesian Takeover of West Papua, 1962–1969*, 165.

44 Drooglever, *An Act of Free Choice*, 721; Saltford, *The United Nations and the Indonesian Takeover of West Papua, 1962–1969*, 158; Robinson, 'Self-determination and the Limits of Justice', 172; Smith and Ng, 'Papua: Moving Beyond Internal Colonialism?', 100; King, *West Papua and Indonesia since Suharto*, 22.

45 Smith and Ng, 'Papua: Moving Beyond Internal Colonialism?', 100.

alien (Javanese) race, and that the process of consultation did not allow a genuinely free choice to be made'.[46]

The matter was then brought to the General Assembly. Although there was some debate about the legitimacy of the Act of Free Choice, particularly from African states, the General Assembly adopted Resolution 2504(XXIV) on 19 November 1969.[47] The wording of this Resolution was cloyingly vague and anodyne, but the thrust of it was that the General Assembly granted its imprimatur to the Act of Free Choice.[48] Thus, with the blessing of the General Assembly, West Papua was incorporated into Indonesia.

7 Analysis

During the Paris Peace Conference of 1919, the principle of self-determination had been applied by its progenitor, President Woodrow Wilson, largely on an ethnic basis. This meant that the reconfiguration of European boundaries, in conformity with this understanding of the principle, occurred largely on the basis that the new states of Europe would reflect as much as possible the geographic distribution of particular ethnic groups. Ideally, each new State would comprise a single ethnic group.

However, as has been seen above, a new understanding of self-determination arose subsequent to World War II, one which equated self-determination with decolonisation.[49] This new understanding of self-determination did not sit well with the older understanding. Many colonies had been arbitrarily established with no consideration of the various ethnic groups within a particular colony. In such situations the question for the General Assembly was how appropriately to effect the decolonisation of a non-self-governing territory in a way which would accommodate the political needs and desires of that colony's diverse and often mutually hostile ethnic groups. In the 1950s the practice of the General Assembly was occasionally to permit the division of a non-self-governing territory into a number of states when it was apparent that the ethnic groups comprising that non-self-governing territory would not be

46 PRO: FCO 24/449. (FWD1/4). FCO briefing on West Irian prepared for the British delegation to the UNGA (10 September 1969). Quoted in Saltford, *The United Nations and the Indonesian Takeover of West Papua, 1962–1969*, 171.

47 Dusan J. Djonovich (ed.), *United Nations Resolutions Series I, XII: 1968–69* (Dobbs Ferry, New York: Oceana Publications, 1975), 213.

48 The vote was eighty-four in favour, none against, and thirty abstentions: *ibid.*, 75.

49 See pp. 210–13 above.

able to co-exist in a single independent State.[50] This was precisely the situation pertaining in the Dutch East Indies, where the population of West Papua could not have been more different from the Malay population of the rest of the colony, and where the vast majority of Papuans repeatedly made it clear that they did not want to be a part of an independent Indonesia. That such a radically different group as the West Papuans should be entitled to determine their own political destiny was recognised not only as a legitimate but as a 'paramount' right by no less than the legal counsel of the United Nations, Constantin Stavropoulos, who in 1962 wrote as follows:

> Our study has revealed that the subject of self-determination is a complex one, presenting many facets. However, at least since President Wilson enunciated the principle of self-determination in 1918, there appears to emerge a strong presumption in favour of self-determination in situations such as that of Western New Guinea on the basis of the wishes of the peoples of the territory concerned, irrespective of the legal stands or interests of other parties to the question. While other factors may also be taken into account, there seems to be a growing practice of recognising that the wishes of the local population should be paramount, and should thus be ascertained before a final disposition is made of any particular territory.[51]

Indonesia, however, countered the argument that the West Papuans were entitled to a separate right of self-determination by pointing to paragraph 6 of Resolution 1514(XV), which required that a non-self-governing territory retain its territorial integrity upon decolonisation.[52] The necessary concomitant of paragraph 6 was that the population of West New Guinea could not be entitled to self-determination, because the 'people' who are so entitled under Resolution 1514(XV) must comprise the entire population of the non-self-governing territory.

This argument, however, cannot apply in the context of the relationship of Indonesia to West New Guinea. This is so for two reasons. First, when the General Assembly in 1960 listed West Papua specifically as a separate non-self-governing territory, this necessarily meant that it was then the population of West Papua who constituted the 'people' who were entitled

[50] This occurred, for example, in the partitions of the Palestine mandate into Jewish and Arab states in 1947, British India into the two states of India and Pakistan in 1947, the British Cameroons in 1958 and the trust territory of Ruanda-Urundi in 1962. See Musgrave, *Self-determination and National Minorities*, 157, 158.

[51] UN Series 100, Box 2, File 7. Stavropoulos to U Thant, 29 June 1962. Quoted in Saltford, *The United Nations and the Indonesian Takeover of West Papua, 1962–1969*, 169, 170.

[52] See p. 212 above, where para. 6 is set out *verbatim*.

to the right of self-determination by virtue of paragraphs 2 and 5 of Resolution 1514(XV), and whose territory, the territory of West Papua, was protected from dismemberment by virtue of paragraph 6.[53] Secondly, once West Papua had been recognised by the General Assembly as a separate non-self-governing territory, Indonesia could not then rely on Paragraph 6 as the basis for its claim to West Papua, because the provisions of the Resolution were now applicable to West Papua rather than to Indonesia.

By signing the New York Agreement, Indonesia itself explicitly acknowledged, particularly in Articles X and XVIII(d),[54] that the population of West Papua was entitled to an act of self-determination. This meant that the population of West Papua did indeed constitute a 'people', since only 'peoples' are entitled to self-determination at international law.[55] It also meant that Indonesia was barred from relying on paragraph 6 to claim the territory of West Papua.

Resolution 1514(XV) addresses those cases of decolonisation in which the act of self-determination results in the independence of the non-self-governing territory. However, with West Papua it was questionable whether this was actually the issue to be decided. The wording of Article XVIII(c) of the New York Agreement frames the issue in terms of the Papuans having to decide whether or not to separate themselves from Indonesia and become an independent State in their own right.[56] In this scenario, the provisions of Resolution 1514(XV) only would apply. But the wording of Article XVIII(c) does not reflect the true nature of the dispute between the Netherlands and Indonesia or the context in which that dispute was to be resolved, in several respects. Whereas Article XVIII(c) referred to the 'inhabitants' of West Papua, the population of West Papua was actually a 'people', as indicated above. Moreover, as the General Assembly had listed West Papua as a separate non-self-governing territory in 1960, the wording of Article XVIII(c), in framing the issue in terms of whether the Papuans desired 'to remain with Indonesia', was at variance with reality, because at this point West Papua was not a part of Indonesia. The real issue to be decided by the people of West Papua was not whether they wished to 'remain' with Indonesia, but rather whether they wished to become integrated into Indonesia.

[53] See p. 212 above, with regard to paras. 2 and 5.

[54] See p. 218, n. 38, and p. 219 above.

[55] Musgrave, *Self-determination and National Minorities*, 148, 167.

[56] See p. 218 above.

The provisions of Resolution 1514(XV) govern those cases of self-determination in which the independence of the non-self-governing territory is the end result. But in those exceptional cases in which integration of a non-self-governing territory into another State is in issue, it is the provisions of Resolution 1541(XV) which apply. The integration of West Papua into Indonesia should therefore have conformed to the conditions set out in Resolution 1541(XV) in order to constitute a legitimate act of self-determination. The reference to 'international practice' in Article XVIII(d) of the New York Agreement underscores this requirement. But the conditions set out in Resolution 1541(XV) were egregiously violated by Indonesia.[57]

Under the conditions set out in Principles VIII and IX of Resolution 1541(XV) an act of self-determination involving the integration of West Papua into Indonesia should not have taken place, as it was premature, given the level of political and social development of the people of West Papua. Principle VIII required integration to occur only 'on the basis of complete equality', and Principle IX(a) required that the integrating territory have 'attained an advanced stage of self-government with free political institutions', so that its people 'have the capacity to make informed and democratic processes'.[58] When the Act of Free Choice took place in 1969 the people of West Papua clearly had not yet attained the level of political and social development envisaged in Resolution 1541(XV). Indonesia itself acknowledged as much when it argued that *musyawarah* was the appropriate voting procedure for the 'primitive Papuans'.[59]

Although paragraph 3 of Resolution 1514(XV) declares that the 'inadequacy of political, economic, social, or educational preparedness' cannot be invoked to delay the process of decolonisation, Indonesia cannot rely on this provision, because paragraph 3 declares that the enumerated forms of unpreparedness 'should never serve as a pretext for delaying independence'. In other words, paragraph 3 applies only in the context of an act of self-determination resulting in independence. But when the act of self-determination involves the integration of a non-self-governing territory into another State, as was the case with West Papua, it is Resolution 1541(XV) which applies: *inclusio unius, exclusio alterius.* When

[57] It should be recalled that Indonesia voted in favour of Resolution 1541(XV).

[58] See pp. 212–13 above for the full text of Principle IX.

[59] Indonesian Foreign Minister Adam Malik justified the use of *musyawarah* by declaring that the 'primitive Papuans' should not be entitled to a voting procedure which the 'so much further advanced people of Java and Sumatra' did not yet have: Drooglever, *An Act of Free Choice*, 680.

integration is in issue, the provisions of Resolution 1541(XV) derogate from paragraph 3 of Resolution 1514(XV), and very stringent conditions with regard to the preparedness of the people must be complied with.

However, even if the people of West Papua could be said to have reached a stage of preparedness which would have enabled them to engage in an act of self-determination involving the question of integration, Indonesia itself, during the period of its administration of West Papua, fundamentally violated the requirements set out in Resolution 1541(XV), in ways which ensured that the act of self-determination could not comply with those requirements. Principle IX(a) required that an act of self-determination involving integration occur only after the integrating territory had attained 'an advanced stage of self-government with free political institutions'. Principle IX(b) required the act of self-determination to occur 'through informed and democratic processes' and to be 'based on universal suffrage'. Upon assuming control of West Papua, the Indonesian administration banned all political parties, appointed the members of the regional councils, and suppressed free speech and demonstrations. For its part the Indonesian military brutally oppressed the local population and resorted to violence whenever it encountered Papuan opposition to Indonesian domination. These acts were all flagrant breaches of Article XXII of the New York Agreement.[60] There was thus nothing remotely resembling real self-government in West Papua during this time, nor were there in place 'free political institutions' and 'informed and democratic processes'. The process of *musyawarah* was a blatant violation of the requirement set out in Principle IX for 'universal adult suffrage'.

The use of *musyawarah* was, however, not simply a violation of the requirement of universal adult suffrage set out in Principle IX, but was also a violation of the terms of the New York Agreement itself. Indonesia argued that neither the word 'referendum' nor that of 'plebiscite' had been used in the New York Agreement, whereas the word *musyawarah* had been explicitly used in Article XVIII(a). Indonesia also stressed that Article XVIII(a) granted it, in consultation with the representative councils, the right 'to determine the procedures and appropriate methods to be followed for ascertaining the freely expressed will of the population'. In the light of these provisions and given the political and social level of the West Papuans, *musyawarah*, in Indonesia's opinion, was the most appropriate method of determining the will of the population.

[60] See p. 218 above.

Although the term *musyawarah* was used in Article XVIII(a), the Article as a whole makes it clear that the *musyawarah* form of proceeding was to be limited to the initial consultation process between the Indonesian authorities and the regional councils in determining the appropriate method of proceeding.[61] Moreover, although Indonesia was granted the right to determine the appropriate method of proceeding, the method chosen had to be one which enabled the entire population of West Papua to participate. The wording of Article XVIII allows for no other interpretation. The introductory clause of Article XVIII specifies that Indonesia was to make arrangements 'to give the people of the territory the opportunity to exercise freedom of choice'. Subsection XVIII(a) contains the phrase 'for ascertaining the freely expressed will of the population'. Subsection XVIII(d) refers to the 'eligibility of all adults, male and female, not foreign nationals, to participate in the act of self-determination to be carried out in accordance with international practice'. These phrases indicate unequivocally that, whatever the form of proceeding Indonesia might adopt to determine the will of the people of West Papua, it had to be one which allowed for universal suffrage by the population of West Papua. The reference to 'international practice' in Article XVIII(d) is particularly significant. International practice with regard to the integration of a non-self-governing territory, as has already been seen, specifically requires universal suffrage. Moreover, should the issue fall solely within the parameters of Resolution 1514(XV) rather than those of 1541(XV), 'international practice', as Robinson points out, also connotes universal suffrage.[62] Therefore not only did Indonesia not comply with the requirements set out in Resolutions 1514(XV) and 1541(XV), but in addition it failed to fulfil the clear and unambiguous requirements of the New York Agreement.

Indonesia failed even to conduct a valid act of *musyawarah*, because the Papuan representatives chosen to participate in the act were isolated, coerced and bribed by the Indonesian authorities to ensure that they voted for integration. It is self-evident that in such circumstances the Papuan representatives were unable to give a valid consent to the integration of West Papua. It is an elementary principle of law that there cannot be a valid consent when that consent has been obtained through coercion or corruption.[63]

[61] Drooglever, *An Act of Free Choice*, 758.

[62] Robinson, 'Self-determination and the Limits of Justice', 173.

[63] This principle is reflected, for example, in Arts. 50 and 51 of the Vienna Convention on the Law of Treaties (Vienna, adopted 22 May 1969, entered into force 27 January 1980),

In his report to the General Assembly, the head of the UN Mission to West Papua failed to make mention of the coercion and corruption by which Indonesia manipulated the votes of the *musyawarah* representatives. The report did acknowledge, albeit in vague language, that Indonesia had complied with neither the requirements of Resolution 1541(XV), nor with the terms of the New York Agreement, by noting that the Indonesian administration had 'exercised at all times a tight political control over the population' and that 'an act of free choice' had taken place in West Irian 'in accordance with Indonesian practice' by the 'representatives of the population'.[64] Yet in adopting Resolution 2504(XXIX) the General Assembly 'chose to do nothing about the terrible abuses of the consultation process'.[65]

8 Conclusion

There is no doubt whatsoever that the process of self-determination in West Papua was nothing more than a sham and amounted to a gross travesty. From whatever angle the situation is considered, be it the requirements of Resolutions 1514(XV) and 1541(XV), or the terms of the New York Agreement, or basic principles of general international law, Indonesia not only failed to fulfil its international obligations but in fact consistently acted in a manner which traduced those obligations. As a result, the people of West Papua were never given any real opportunity to exercise their right of self-determination and West Papua was incorporated into Indonesia without the true consent of its people.

In November 1969, after the General Assembly had confirmed the Act of Free Choice, and West Papua was incorporated into Indonesia, President Suharto declared that Indonesia had no further territorial ambitions. A mere six years later, however, Indonesia invaded the Portuguese colony of East Timor and incorporated this non-self-governing territory into the country. This also occurred without the people of East Timor having any opportunity to exercise their right of self-determination. But in 1995, the International Court of Justice addressed the issue of self-determination for the people of East Timor, in the *East Timor case (Portugal* v. *Australia)*.[66]

1155 UNTS 331. Art. 50 addresses the corruption of a representative of a State, and Art. 51 the coercion of a representative of a State.

64 UNGA Official Record, Agenda item 98, Doc. A/7723 (6 November), Annex I, paras. 251 and 253. Quoted in Saltford, *The United Nations and the Indonesian Takeover of West Papua, 1962–1969*, 166.

65 King, *West Papua and Indonesia since Suharto*, 22.

66 *East Timor case (Portugal* v. *Australia)*, Judgment, 30 June 1995, ICJ Reports (1995), 90.

Although the Court decided that it did not have jurisdiction to hear the case, the Court nevertheless noted that the right of self-determination was a right *erga omnes*, and that the people of East Timor continued to possess this right.[67] In other words, they possessed it against Indonesia. On 27 January 1999 Indonesia announced that it would permit a referendum to be held in East Timor and on 30 August 1999 the people of East Timor voted in favour of independence, by a margin of 78.5 per cent.[68]

Like the people of East Timor until 1999, the people of West Papua have not been able to exercise a genuine act of self-determination, and like the people of East Timor, their territory was incorporated into Indonesia without their consent. And therefore like the people of East Timor, the people of West Papua are still entitled to exercise a right of self-determination, which right is exercisable *erga omnes*. In other words, the people of West Papua possess a right to self-determination which neither Indonesia nor the General Assembly can gainsay.

East Timor seemed irrevocably integrated into Indonesia in 1975. But twenty-four years later, the East Timorese exercised their right of self-determination, and when they did so, it was to separate themselves from Indonesia and to create their own independent State. The West Papuans have now been waiting to exercise a genuine right of self-determination for forty-six years. When they finally get the opportunity to do so, they may very well take the example of East Timor to heart in determining their chosen future.

[67] *Ibid.*, 102. [68] Musgrave, *Self-determination and National Minorities*, xii.

13

Recognition of the State of Palestine

Still too much too soon?

YAËL RONEN*

1 Introduction

In 1990 James Crawford wrote 'The Creation of the State of Palestine: Too Much Too Soon?', rejecting the claim that in Resolution 43/177 the UN General Assembly (UNGA) recognised the existence of a State of Palestine.[1] Surprisingly, perhaps, in 2012 a similar question arose, whether UNGA Resolution 67/19, in the operative part of which the General Assembly decided 'to accord to Palestine non-member observer State status in the United Nations',[2] recognised the existence of the State of Palestine. And no less than in 1990, '[i]t seems difficult for international lawyers to write in an impartial and balanced way about the Palestine issue'.[3] Scholars who support the Palestinian cause at times converge the 'ought' with the 'is', citing the resolution as confirmation of their position that a State of Palestine already exists, without delving into the resolution's content;[4] while those less convinced that such a State already

* I am grateful to James Crawford as well as to Dapo Akande, Yehuda Blum, Shai Dothan, Guy Harpaz, Nimrod Karin, David Kretzmer, Ido Rosenzweig, Yuval Shany and Jure Vidmar for comments on earlier versions, and to Yael Naggan for excellent research assistance.

[1] James Crawford, 'The Creation of the State of Palestine: Too Much Too Soon?', *European Journal of International Law*, 1 (1990), 307.

[2] UN General Assembly, Status of Palestine in the United Nations, Resolution 67/19, UN Doc. A/RES/19/67, 29 November 2012.

[3] Crawford, 'The Creation of the State of Palestine', 307. A telling admission of this is John Quigley's statement that his position, that a state of Palestine has been in existence at least since 1924 is disputed 'among scholars, even scholars who generally are taking positions supportive of the Palestinian cause'. Russell Tribunal on Palestine, John Quigley, October 2012, available at www.russelltribunalonpalestine.com/en/sessions/future-sessions/new-york-session-video-presentations/john-quigley.

[4] Jean Salmon, 'La Qualité d'état de la Palestine', *Revue belge de droit international*, 2012/1 (2013), 13; Richard Falk, 'Forward' in Mutaz Qafishe (ed.), *Palestine Membership in the*

existed prior to the resolution, are correspondingly more reserved about the legal consequences of the resolution.[5] The differences of view concern practically every element involved, including an assessment of the effectiveness criteria, of the effect of recognition and of whether Resolution 67/19 constituted an act of recognition. Partisanship is not unavoidable; it is nonetheless useful to articulate one's point of departure in order to establish a common ground with the reader. Those who contest it, while unlikely to convert, might nonetheless find interest in the intellectual journey proffered in the following lines.

This chapter adopts the view that the declaratory approach is preferable to the constitutive one. While the comparison between the two, and the drawbacks of the latter, have been discussed primarily with regard to situations where recognition has been denied (at least in part) despite effective functioning, this chapter concerns the converse situation, where recognition is extended in the absence of effectiveness. Acknowledgement of statehood in this situation, too, is problematic, since it accords rights and obligations to an entity which is not fully able to act upon them. With respect to Palestine, this chapter shares in the view that irrespective of the desirability of the establishment of a Palestinian State, such a State probably did not exist prior to the adoption of UNGA Resolution 67/19 because it lacked sufficient independence and consequently effectiveness, and that treating a Palestinian entity as a State for the purposes of international law, be it represented by the PA or the PLO, required engaging in legal fiction, which is undesirable as a matter of legal policy, and not necessarily conducive to rendering statehood a political reality. Nonetheless, whatever the drawbacks of the constitutive approach on the doctrinal, prescriptive level, practice suggests that a critical amount of recognitions combined with some objective features of effectiveness may render statehood close to objective. In other words, that collective

United Nations (Cambridge Scholars, 2013), xviii; John Dugard, 'Palestine and the International Criminal Court: Institutional Failure or Bias?', *Journal of International Criminal Justice*, 11 (2013), 563–70.

[5] Joseph H. H. Weiler, 'Differentiated Statehood? "PreStates"? Palestine @ the UN', *European Journal of International Law*, 24 (2013), 1; John Cerone, 'Legal Implications of the UN General Assembly Vote to Accord Palestine the Status of Observer State', *ASIL Insight*, 16 (2012); Dapo Akande, 'Palestine as a UN Observer State: Does this Make Palestine a State?', *EJIL: Talk!*, 3 December 2012; Jure Vidmar, 'Palestine and the Conceptual Problem of Implicit Statehood', *Chinese Journal of International Law*, 12 (2013), 21; Martin Wählisch, 'Beyond a Seat in the United Nations: Palestine's UN Membership and International Law', *Harvard International Law Journal*, 53 (2012), 236 (writing in anticipation of the resolution).

recognition is actually constitutive may be the more accurate description of a political reality.[6]

The history of Palestinian participation in the work of the UN leading to UNGA Resolution 67/19 has been canvassed elsewhere, including the request for admission of Palestine as a member to the UN, which is formally still pending before the Security Council, and Palestine's admission as member of UNESCO.[7] This chapter focuses on UNGA Resolution 67/19 itself. First, it examines whether the General Assembly can generate an objective statehood through collective recognition. It then examines whether UNGA Resolution 67/19 actually recognises the existence of – or creates – a State of Palestine. If the answer is negative, this does not mean that the Resolution has no consequences; those are considered in the final section. The article does not purport to settle the question of whether the entity under Palestinian Authority governance presently fulfils the effectiveness criteria, since the situation on the ground has not changed as a result of the adoption of the resolution.

2 Can a General Assembly resolution on recognition create objective statehood?

The drafters of the Charter did not intend for the General Assembly resolutions to have, in themselves,[8] binding authority other than in its relations with other organs of the UN.[9] However, while General Assembly resolutions do not directly create obligations for States, in practice they may have legal effect and operative consequences.[10] It is in this category that a General Assembly resolution on recognition may fall, in that it

[6] Dan Joyner, 'The UNGA Recognizes the State of Palestine', *Arms Control Law* (3 December 2012), available at http://armscontrollaw.com/2012/12/03/the-unga-recognizes-the-state-of-palestine/. Kevin Jon Heller, 'Palestinian Statehood and Retroactive Jurisdiction', *Opinio Juris* (2 December 2012), available at http://opiniojuris.org/2012/12/01/palestinian-statehood-and-retroactive-jurisdiction/.

[7] An excellent account is that by Paul Eden, 'Palestinian Statehood: Trapped between Rhetoric and *Realpolitik*', *International and Comparative Law Quarterly*, 62 (2013), 225.

[8] As opposed to their constituting *opinio juris*, representing State practice or codifying customary international law.

[9] M. J. Peterson, 'General Assembly' in Thomas G. Weiss and Sam Daws (eds.), *The Oxford Handbook on the United Nations* (Oxford University Press, 2007), 103.

[10] *Legal Consequences for States of the Continued Presence of South Africa in Namibia (South West Africa) Notwithstanding Resolution 276 (1970)*, Advisory Opinion, 21 June 1971, ICJ Reports (1971), 16, para. 105. On the changing role of resolutions of international organisations see Rosalyn Higgins, *Problems and Process: International Law and How We Use It* (Oxford: Clarendon Press, 1994), 22–8.

purports to establish a new state of legal relations, or at least declare a fact that carries legal consequences.

A General Assembly resolution on admission is generally perceived as confirming 'objective' statehood of the new member, triggering the applicability not only of the UN Charter but also of customary international law between the new member and all other States, regardless of the stance they had taken towards the admission and of their bilateral relations with that State. While the jurisprudential basis for this law is neither agreed upon nor beyond controversy, it is reflected in practice.[11]

A separate question is whether a UN General Assembly resolution recognising the statehood of an entity but stopping short of admitting the latter as a member of the Organisation can also create an objective status. Dugard suggests that the answer is positive, since admission is, ultimately, a matter of procedure[12] that is unrelated to the merits of the case, and therefore non-admission does not necessarily indicate failure to fulfil the criteria for statehood. As an example he cites the 1948 General Assembly resolution declaring that 'there has been established a lawful government (the Government of the Republic of Korea) having effective control and jurisdiction over that part of Korea . . . in which the great majority of the people of all Korea reside',[13] which was regarded as recognition of the fulfilment of the criteria of statehood with respect to Korea for all purposes.[14] However, it is submitted that the various possible

[11] John Dugard, *Recognition and the United Nations* (Cambridge: Grotius Publications, 1987), 43. Dugard's thesis was based mainly on decolonisation practice; however, its practice review remains exhaustive since there has been no subsequent practice of admission to the UN of entities while their statehood was controversial (although controversies over status persist, e.g. whether the Federal Republic of Yugoslavia was the successor of the Social Federal Republic of Yugoslavia or not).

[12] *Ibid.*, 50.

[13] UN General Assembly, UNGA Resolution 195(III), UN Doc. A/RES/195(III), 12 December 1948, operative para. 2.

[14] Herbert W. Briggs, 'Community Interest in the Emergence of New States: The Problem of Recognition', *Proceedings of the American Society of International Law at Its Annual Meeting (1921–1969)*, 44 (1950), 171, 175. Dugard, *Recognition and the United Nations*, 59–60. This resolution differs from numerous resolutions declaring that certain aspiring members are peace-loving States (e.g. UN General Assembly Resolution 296 (IV), 22 November 1949, concerning Austria, Ceylon, Finland, Ireland, Italy, Jordan, Portugal and Nepal; UN General Assembly Resolution 620(VII), UN Doc. A/RES/620(VII), 21 December 1952, concerning Japan (Part B), Vietnam (Part C), Cambodia (Part D), Laos (Part E), Libya (Part F), Jordan (Part G); UN General Assembly Resolution 1017(X), UN Doc. A/RES/1017, 28 February 1957, concerning Korea (Part A) and Viet-Nam (Part B)) in that it establishes not eligibility for membership but statehood. It differs from other resolutions which have been adopted in the face of Security Council vetoes, in that it

jurisprudential grounds for regarding a resolution on admission to the UN as evidence of, or confirming, objective statehood, do not apply in the same manner to a resolution on recognition that does not encompass UN membership.

For example, if admission resolutions are universally binding because under UN Charter Article 4(1) States have delegated their competence to recognise new States to the organisation, as advocated by Kelsen,[15] then resolutions outside Article 4(1) do not necessarily have the same universal effect. States may have subjected themselves to majority vote in order to facilitate effective functioning of the organisation, which would be hampered if member status was non-uniformly applicable; but they cannot be deemed to have made the same concession to majority vote with respect to all other matters. Similarly, if the universally binding character of the resolution derives from co-membership in the organisation, as proposed by Briggs,[16] then a resolution that does not lead to co-membership does not have the same binding effect.

A different strand of views is that admission to the UN provides compelling[17] or *prima facie*[18] evidence of a determination by States individually, or by the international community as a whole,[19] that an entity fulfils the criteria for statehood. These views differ from the previous ones in that they perceive UN admission resolutions as establishing only a *factual presumption* of objective statehood, rather than normative status. In other words, while recognition according to the previous views is constitutive, the present strand perceives recognition as declaratory. Whether the presumption of objective statehood is equally compelling when the resolution concerns recognition short of admission to the UN can be debated. Since a vote on recognition does not trigger the applicability of the UN Charter, it is reasonable to argue that the weight of a vote in favour of recognition as indicating an assessment on the fulfilment

anticipated admission to the UN, rather than aimed to balance the failure of the attempt at admission.

15 Dugard, *Recognition and the United Nations*, 46. See also Weiler, 'Differentiated Statehood?', 4–5, doubting that States which have accepted the voting rules of other international organisations have also accepted that this entailed replacing their discretion in according recognition of statehood by that of the organisation.

16 Briggs, 'Community Interest in the Emergence of New States', 178.

17 James Crawford, *The Creation of States in International Law*, 2nd edn (Oxford University Press, 2006), 545.

18 James Crawford, *Brownlie's Principles of Public International Law*, 8th edn (Oxford University Press, 2012), 150.

19 Wright, cited by Dugard, *Recognition and the United Nations*, 49.

of the effectiveness criteria is not the same as that of a vote in favour of admission.

Finally, the weight of practice in developing the law differs with regard to recognition through admission and to direct resolutions on recognition. The conclusiveness of recognition through admission is largely a matter of practice,[20] based on numerous instances where admission to the UN preceded bilateral recognition, including some in which entities were admitted despite strong controversy as to their compliance with the effectiveness requisites.[21] In contrast, collective recognition short of admission occurred in the single resolution regarding the Republic of Korea. Practice can therefore hardly be said to have led to the crystallisation of new law on collective recognition that is unaccompanied by admission to the UN.[22]

In conclusion, no immediate extrapolation can be made from the law regarding collective recognition through admission to the UN, to collective recognition that is not linked to admission. There is (at least as yet) no rule that majority recognition outside the framework of admission to the UN is binding on third States.[23] To the extent that Resolution 67/19 constitutes recognition of statehood, it might of course add to the development of such law. This leads, naturally, to the question of whether the resolution purports to recognise or establish a Palestinian State.

3 Does General Assembly Resolution 67/19 constitute collective recognition of a State of Palestine?

While admission to the UN is generally perceived as implying recognition of statehood since only States may become members of the organisation,[24] the grant of observer status (to a State or any other actor) is not regulated

[20] Dugard, *Recognition and the United Nations*, 43; Crawford, *The Creation of States in International Law*, 150.

[21] E.g. Israel, Guinea-Bissau, Angola; Dugard, *Recognition and the United Nations*, 60–3, 73–5.

[22] Briggs argued the opposite. However, the practice he cited concerned Israel, which had been admitted to the UN, as well as the resolutions on Korea, Jordan, Nepal and Ceylon, following the failure of their admission bids on political grounds. Briggs, 'Community Interest in the Emergence of New States', 174–5.

[23] Crawford, *The Creation of States in International Law*, 438.

[24] For a contrary view see Vidmar, 'Palestine and the Conceptual Problem of Implicit Statehood', paras. 72–3, who maintains that statehood cannot be held hostage to procedure and deteremined by reverse effect.

by the Charter, and since it does not entail any pre-set organisational substantive rights or obligations, it cannot be regarded as an implicit confirmation of legal status.[25] However, this does not preclude the possibility that the content of the resolution constitutes recognition of statehood, whether express or implicit – irrespective of the organisational status that it confers.

That Resolution 67/19 does not expressly recognise the existence of a State is obvious. This is no bar since recognition may be implicit; but it must be unequivocal.[26] It is therefore necessary to ascertain whether the references in the resolution to the 'State of Palestine' are an acknowledgement of existing statehood (in which case the resolution may generate legal consequences if it is regarded as universally binding) or merely an exhortation for future development. There are no established rules on interpretation of General Assembly resolutions. Nor is there much practice or scholarship on the matter. The lack of interest in interpreting General Assembly resolutions is not surprising since they are not, in themselves, binding sources under international law. Guidance on interpretation of international instruments other than treaties is generally sparse, and, with the exception of the ILC's Guiding Principles applicable to unilateral declarations of States capable of creating legal obligations,[27] is almost entirely limited to interpretation of Security Council resolutions adopted under Chapter VII.

It has repeatedly been proposed that the point of departure for interpretation of international instruments other than treaties should be by analogy from the Vienna Convention on the Law of Treaties (VCLT),[28] namely an exercise to give effect to the drafters' intention as expressed by the use of the words in light of surrounding circumstances,[29] taking into account the particular character of the instrument in question.[30] For

[25] *Ibid.*, 5, 23–4, para. 16. The UN Charter does however mention non-member States, Arts. 2(6), 11(2), 32, 35(2), 50.

[26] Yaël Ronen, 'Entities that Can Be States but Do Not Claim to Be' in Duncan French (ed.), *Statehood and Self-Determination: Reconciling Tradition and Modernity in International Law* (Cambridge University Press, 2013), 47–8.

[27] International Law Commission, Guiding Principles Applicable to Unilateral Declarations of States Capable of Creating Legal Obligations, UN Doc. A/61/10 (2006).

[28] Vienna Convention on the Law of Treaties (Vienna, adopted 22 May 1969, entered into force 27 January 1980), 1155 UNTS 331.

[29] *Ibid.*, Art. 31(1).

[30] *Fisheries Jurisdiction (Spain* v. *Canada)*, Merits, Judgment, 4 December 1998, ICJ Reports (1998), 453, para. 46. Regarding interpretation of declarations under ICJ Statute Art. 36(2), endorsed by ILC, Guiding Principles Applicable to Unilateral Declarations

example, the *a priori* non-binding nature of General Assembly resolutions might require that endowing them with a binding quality be subject to the rigorous demand relating to a unilateral declaration, which 'entails obligations for the formulating State only if it is stated in clear and specific terms'.[31] In addition, interpretation of General Assembly resolutions might resemble that of Security Council resolutions, given the essentially political character of both types of resolutions. Nonetheless, there are pertinent differences: the interpretation of Security Council resolutions, for example, involves limited reliance on preambular language for interpreting operative parts, since preambles tend to be used as dumping grounds for proposals that are not acceptable in the operative paragraphs.[32] In contrast, with respect to General Assembly resolutions which are prima facie non-binding, the absence of normative gap between preambular and operative paragraphs invites a greater interpretative role for preambular paragraphs.

The present analysis proceeds on the basis of these guidelines. It begins with an interpretation of the ordinary meaning to be given to the terms of the treaty in their context and in the light of its object and purpose, taking into account surrounding circumstances. Where the outcome is inconclusive, the circumstances of adoption and preparatory work may be of particular significance,[33] namely statements in anticipation of and following the vote.

(a) Textual interpretation

Some mentions in the operative paragraphs of UNGA Resolution 67/19 can be interpreted as referring to an existing State: Operative paragraph 1 reaffirms 'the right of the Palestinian people to self-determination

of States Capable of Creating Legal Obligations, Guiding Principle 7, commentary para. (3); *Accordance with International Law of the Unilateral Declaration of Independence in Respect of Kosovo*, Advisory Opinion, ICJ Reports (2010), 403, para. 94; Michael Wood, 'The Interpretation of Security Council Resolutions' (United Nations 2008), Audiovisual Library of International Law.

31 ILC, Guiding Principles Applicable to Unilateral Declarations of States Capable of Creating Legal Obligations, Guiding Principle 7.

32 Michael Wood, 'The Interpretation of Security Council Resolutions', *Max Planck Yearbook of United Nations Law*, 2 (1998), 86–7.

33 *Ibid.*; Michael Wood, 'The Interpretation of Security Council Resolutions'; Bart Smit Duijzentkunst, 'Interpretation of Legislative Security Council Resolutions', *Utrecht Law Review*, 4 (2008), 205–8.

and to independence in their State of Palestine'. The use of 'State of Palestine'[34] instead of the 'independent State of Palestine' and the use of 'independence' as a goal may imply that an occupied, non-independent State is deemed to already exist.[35] The State of Palestine is also mentioned in the call on the Security Council to consider favourably the application for UN membership,[36] which is reserved to States, thereby implying the existence of a State capable of being admitted. Operative paragraph 6 urges States and UN-related organisations 'to continue to support and assist the Palestinian people in the early realisation of their right to self-determination, independence and freedom'.[37] The absence of mention of 'sovereignty' might imply that such is deemed to already inhere in the Palestinian entity.

Importantly, however, operative paragraph 2, which accords Palestine the new status, does not refer to it as the 'State of Palestine'. In addition, operative paragraph 5 speaks of the 'a permanent two-State solution' as a goal yet to be achieved, and refers to 'the Palestinian and Israeli sides', suggesting that treating them on an equal footing requires that the term 'State' be avoided. Unlike the resolution on Korea, Resolution 67/19 is also vague on the fulfilment of the effectiveness criteria. It welcomes assessments that the Palestinian Authority fulfils the threshold requisites of effective government,[38] but stops short of making a clear or independent statement on the matter. In the preamble, the phrase 'State of Palestine' appears as a normative claim (the right of the Palestinian people to their independent State of Palestine),[39] or as the goal of a political commitment of the General Assembly ('to the two-state solution of an independent, sovereign, democratic, viable and contiguous State of Palestine living side by side with Israel').[40] Insofar as the preamble is indicative, it therefore also weakens the claim that Resolution 67/19 holds a State to exist.

The reference to the PLO within the resolution may provide some context for interpretation. Operative paragraph 2 stipulates that the General Assembly accords Palestine non-member observer State status in the United Nations, 'without prejudice to the acquired rights, privileges

34 Preambular para. 2.

35 Similarly see John Quigley, 'Palestinian Statehood: A Rejoinder to Professor Robert Weston Ash', *Rutgers Law Record*, 36 (2010), 257–8.

36 Operative para. 3.

37 Operative paras. 3 and 6.

38 Preambular para. 21.

39 Preambular para. 2.

40 Preambular para. 18, operative para. 4.

and role of the Palestine Liberation Organization in the United Nations as the representative of the Palestinian people'. The use, within the same paragraph, of the terms 'Palestine' and 'Palestine Liberation Organisation' (PLO), and the regulation of the relations between Palestine and the PLO, suggest that 'Palestine' now means something other than a designation of the PLO[41] – presumably a State. This also implies that within the UN system there are now two entities representing the Palestinian people: a State, and a national liberation movement. This apparent duplication has been interpreted as preserving the right of the PLO to represent diaspora Palestinians.[42] However, there is no precedent for a national liberation movement continuing to operate in the UN alongside the government.[43] In practice there is only one entity operating in the UN, designated by the UN secretariat as the 'non-member State' of Palestine, effectively identical to the former PLO-designating Palestine.[44] The 'no prejudice' clause might alternatively be interpreted as providing procedural continuity between Palestine as designating the PLO and Palestine as a State observer, thereby avoiding the need to stipulate the accruing benefits, an exercise which would have been time-consuming and possibly controversial.

It has been suggested that the grant of 'non-member observer state *status*' (emphasis added) indicates that the resolution is solely concerned with a procedural status. This emerges from comparison of the resolution with past conferrals of observer status in the UN, which did not contain

41 UN General Assembly, 'Question of Palestine, Resolution A/RES/43/177', 15 December 1988.

42 Nadia Hijab, 'The Fine Print of Palestinian Statehood', *Aljazeera* (4 December 2012); Al Haq, 'Al-Haq's Questions and Answers: Palestine's UN Initiatives and the Representation of the Palestinian People's Rights' (2011) 23, available at www.alhaq.org/publications/publications-index/item/al-haq-s-questions-and-answers-palestine-s-un-initiatives. On the significance of maintaining PLO representation irrespective of the status within the UN of a State of Palestine, see Sir Guy S. Goodwin-Gill, 'Opinion re the Palestine Liberation Organization, the Future State of Palestine, and the Question of Popular Representation' (10 August 2011), available at http://s3.documentcloud.org/documents/238962/final-pdf-plo-statehood-opinionr-arb.pdf.

43 Except in the case of the ANC and South Africa, since the ANC was seeking popular liberation from that very government. Policies of *apartheid* of the Government of South Africa, UN General Assembly Resolution 3151(XXVIII)(B) operative para. 4(d), 14 December 1973. In contrast, the PLO is not recognised as a national liberation movement as against the PA. On the other hand, even in the South African case there was only one entity operating within the formal UN system – the State. In the Palestinian case, neither entity is operating within the formal UN system.

44 Available at www.un.org/en/members/nonmembers.shtml, http://www.un.int/wcm/content/site/palestine/.

the word 'status'.[45] This view is supported by statements such as that of Georgia (voting in favour), that 'the resolution confers on Palestine privileges and rights that are equivalent to those of non-member States and only within the General Assembly. Georgia does not consider that the decision endows Palestine with the automatic right to join international institutions and treaties as a State.'[46] However, a perusal of the explanations of vote reveals that states did not attach particular significance to the 'status' terminology. For example, the Turkish delegate speaks of 'the Palestinian bid to become a non-member observer State' but also of '[g]ranting Palestine the status of a non-member observer State'.[47]

Despite the absence of explicit or even unambiguous recognition in any of the resolution's provisions, the cumulative effect of the repeated references to the right to statehood and to political steps towards consolidation of international status could be tantamount to recognition. Such a contextual interpretation would support the political goal of the resolution, which is beyond dispute an attempt to secure the Palestinian entity the widest measure of recognition as a State despite the obstacle to its admission as a member of the UN. However, that this was the drafters' original motive for pursuing the adoption of the resolution does not mean that it was ultimately achieved. Given the ambiguity of the resolution, it is helpful to turn to States' statements explaining their votes in order to ascertain what they believed the effect of the resolution to be.

(b) *The circumstances of adoption: explanations of votes*

Fifty-four States took the floor to explain their votes. Only a dozen of those seemed to consider the resolution as recognising or establishing the existence of a Palestinian State for all purposes. For the most part, these states voted in support of the resolution.[48] Some states referred to the legal obligations and rights associated under international law

[45] Oded Eran and Robbie Sabel, 'The Status of "Palestine" at the United Nations', *INSS Insight*, 387 (2012), 3, *inter alia* comparing the terminology of the resolution with UN Doc. A/RES/58/314 of 16 July 2004, in which UN General Assembly granted observer status to the Holy See, stating that it 'acknowledges that the Holy See, in its capacity *as an Observer State*, shall be accorded the rights and privileges' (operative para. 1), without 'status'.

[46] UN Doc. A/67/PV.45, 4. [47] UN Doc. A/67/PV.44, 10.

[48] In addition to the survey below, see the statements in UN Doc. A/67/PV.44 (29 November 2012) 17 (Honduras); UN Doc. A/67/PV.45 (29 November 2012) 1 (Honduras), 13 (Kuwait), 16-17 (UAE), 24 (Morocco) and 3 (Guatemala – abstaining).

with statehood, that accrue to Palestine following the adoption of the resolution, thereby implying that they regarded the Resolution as bringing about a new legal status. Switzerland said that '[t]he elevation of Palestine to the status of a United Nations observer State endows Palestine not only with rights but also with obligations, in particular that of refraining from the threat or use of force as enshrined in the Charter of the United Nations'.[49] According to Japan, 'following the adoption of that historic Resolution, Palestine will assume greater responsibility as a member of the international community'.[50] Other statements refer directly to statehood: South Africa found it 'satisfying that the Organization has now cemented in the books of history the fact that Palestine is indeed a State'.[51] Turkey addressed the objections to the resolution as 'misguided efforts aimed at stopping the Palestinians from winning statehood at the United Nations', adding '[w]hen will it be the right time for the Palestinians to achieve their right to statehood, if not today?'[52] Costa Rica stated that 'our decision is consistent with the recognition that we granted to the State of Palestine in 2008 and with our support for its admission into UNESCO'.[53] Canada explained its opposition to the resolution on the ground that it constituted a unilateral measure contrary to the 1995 Interim Agreement between Israel and the PLO[54] which (implicitly) prohibited the Palestinians from pursuing statehood. This implies that it regarded the Resolution as intended to bring about recognition of statehood.

In contrast, some States clarified that the resolution (and consequently their own in support) votes did not constitute recognition of Palestinian statehood. New Zealand (in favour) was most explicit, that the resolution 'is a political symbol of the commitment of the United Nations to a two-State solution. New Zealand has cast its vote accordingly based on the assumption that our vote is without prejudice to New Zealand's position on its recognition of Palestine.'[55] Belgium (in favour) also noted 'a significant step towards the creation of a State of Palestine, which we all look forward to . . . For Belgium, the Resolution adopted today by the General Assembly does not yet constitute a recognition of a State in the full sense.'[56] Finland (in favour) stressed that

[49] Switzerland's statement is particularly interesting given that it also stated: 'This decision does not involve a bilateral recognition of a Palestinian State, which will depend on future peace negotiations.' UN General Assembly, UN Doc. A/67/PV.44, 29 November 2012, 16.

[50] UN Doc. A/67/PV.45, 3. [51] *Ibid.*, 15. [52] UN Doc. A/67/PV.44, 11.

[53] *Ibid.*, 3. [54] *Ibid.*, 8. [55] *Ibid.*, 20.

[56] *Ibid.*, 16. See also the statements by Georgia, UN Doc. A/67/PV.45, 4, and Romania, *ibid.*, 6.

'the Assembly's vote did not entail a formal recognition of a Palestinian State'.[57]

Other states, such as the US (against), UK and Singapore (abstaining), opined that the resolution could not create a State because the factual criteria had not been fulfilled and nothing has changed on the ground.[58] These statements indicate that these states regarded the Resolution as a purported act of recognition – but a premature one.

Perhaps the most telling, and in fact setting the terms for the debate, are the statements by Sudan, which introduced the resolution, and by Mahmoud Abbas, speaking on behalf of the Palestine Liberation Organization. The Sudanese careful paraphrasing of the draft resolution[59] indicates that the sponsors took care not to digress from a delicately crafted text so that nothing could be read into it beyond what was already in the text. Abbas, too, spoke repeatedly of acquiring 'non-member observer status for Palestine' and nothing more concrete. After mentioning UNGA Resolution 181(III) of 1947, which recommended the partition of mandatory Palestine into two States, as 'the birth certificate for Israel',[60] Abbas asked the General Assembly 'to issue a birth certificate of the reality of the State of Palestine'.[61] The comparison to Resolution 181 indicates that Resolution 67/19 is merely a call for the establishment of a State. On the other hand, the reference to 'the reality of the state' implies that a State is already in existence.

In general, however, beyond a generally shared focus on the necessity to progress towards peace and a two-State solution to the conflict, most statements were confused and impenetrable. France (in favour), for example, held that '[t]he international recognition that the Assembly has today given the proposed Palestinian State can become fact only through an agreement based on negotiations',[62] introducing the unprecedented notion of 'recognition of proposal', or of recognition of statehood not sufficing for the latter to become 'fact' until a political agreement is achieved. Jamaica (in favour) said that its support for the resolution was 'based on the understanding that the granting of non-member observer State status to Palestine within the United Nations is on the same basis as that given to the Holy See',[63] leaving it unclear whether the 'same basis' was statehood or merely procedural benefits. Bulgaria abstained on the ground that

[57] UN Doc. A/67/PV.44, 20; See also Norway, UN Doc. A/67/PV.44, 21.

[58] UN Doc. A/67/PV.44, 13 (US), 15 (UK), 14 (Singapore).

[59] *Ibid.*, 1. [60] *Ibid.*, 5. [61] *Ibid.*

[62] *Ibid.*, 14. [63] UN Doc. A/67/PV.45, 5.

'unilateral actions by either side are counterproductive', implying that the resolution constituted recognition of statehood, but also noted that direct negotiations are 'the only sustainable way to achieve the establishment of a sovereign . . . Palestinian State',[64] suggesting that sovereignty was still lacking (although, as it stated, it had already recognised Palestine bilaterally). Germany (abstaining) noted that 'a Palestinian State can be achieved only through direct negotiations between Israelis and Palestinians',[65] leaving it unclear whether it considered recognition of statehood through the resolution to be objectionable or simply ineffective.

(c) Conclusion

The immediate object and purpose of UNGA Resolution 67/19, clearly articulated, was to accord Palestine non-member observer status. Beyond that – that is, insofar as concerns recognition of statehood or other non-procedural status – the ambiguity of the resolution is intentional. It was drafted in terms which leave matters sufficiently vague as to garner the widest support possible, including from States which, while supporting the Palestinian cause, did not feel that they could subscribe to a Resolution that expressly recognised Palestinian statehood.

Little can be gleaned from the explanations of vote. While a few reflect clear – and conflicting – understandings of the resolution, the majority are drafted in an elusive manner, whether due to failure to comprehend the complexities of the matter or in an attempt to appease all sides without undertaking any commitment.

However, the onus of proof is on whoever claims that a General Assembly resolution carries legal consequences, as well as on whoever asserts that there has been an act of recognition. The ambiguity of UNGA Resolution 67/19 precludes it from being held as an act of collective recognition of a State of Palestine.

4 The consequences of Resolution 67/19

The conclusion that General Assembly Resolution 67/19 does not establish Palestinian statehood does not mean that it is entirely without consequence. First and foremost it has a procedural consequence within the UN. The effect of the vote was well captured by Cuba (in favour), which laconically congratulated 'the Palestinian people and authorities on their

[64] UN Doc. A/67/PV.44, 16. [65] *Ibid.*, 15.

victory in this Hall today on obtaining the new status of a non-member observer State'.[66]

If the only outcome of the resolution is the upgrade in status, the victory is a hollow one. There are various differences between observer States and other observers, but Palestine (the PLO) already enjoyed most of the preferential benefits of observer States, such as participation in Security Council debates, placement on the list of speakers, and the right to have documents circulated.[67] A benefit that has now been added is the right of an observer to change its designation upon informing the Secretariat and without requiring prior approval by the General Assembly,[68] but clearly it was not for this that the Palestinian campaign had been launched. Moreover, the reactions to the adoption of General Assembly Resolution 67/19 indicate that both its proponents and its opponents assume that its impact goes beyond cosmetic changes within UN procedures, even if the Resolution does not put the existence of a State of Palestine beyond dispute.

Arguably, the minutiae of the resolution's wording and States' linguistic and diplomatic acrobatics are all of limited significance, if – correctly or otherwise – States perceive the resolution as having recognised or established a State of Palestine. In this vein, Akande suggests that if the resolution 'is capable of effecting the legal changes hoped for (by proponents) or feared (by those who oppose the decision), this will provide strong support to the view that collective recognition is capable of creating Statehood'.[69] Prima facie, this proposition turns the matter on its head: consequences should follow from the resolution rather than the resolution being interpreted on the basis of subsequent events. Thus, if the resolution does not (in itself) effect any legal change, it can only give political support for subsequent measures. Accordingly, any decision by States or international organisations such as to recognise Palestine on a bilateral level, to admit it into an organisation reserved to states, or to hold it responsible under customary international law applicable only to states, can rely on UNGA Resolution 67/19 no more than it can rely, for example, on UNGA Resolution 43/177.[70] Whether the accumulated effect of such legal changes would eventually amount to the emergence of a State

66 *Ibid.*, 18.
67 General Assembly Resolution 52/520, 13 July 1998.
68 S-G letter to Palestine 17 December 2012, available at http://unterm.un.org/dgaacs/.
69 Akande, 'Palestine as a UN Observer State'.
70 This analysis assumes, of course, that Resolution 43/177 also did not, in itself, constitute recognition of Palestine.

if such was not previously recognised is a separate question, which will not be discussed here. However, doctrine does recognise the proposition that subsequent practice in the application of the treaty establishes the agreement of the parties regarding its interpretation.[71] It may well apply also to General Assembly resolutions.

The distinction between the resolution's political and (absence of) legal effect cannot be completed without making reference to a particular type of reliance on General Assembly resolutions, the UN Secretary-General's practice as depositary of multilateral treaties. This is particularly pertinent in the present instance, since the 2012 campaign for UN recognition was carried out very much in the shadow of the debate on the capacity of the Palestinians to consent to ICC jurisdiction,[72] either by accession to the ICC Statute or by consenting to jurisdiction under Article 12(3).

The Statute of the International Criminal Court (ICC) allows accession by 'all states'.[73] Whether the Palestine is a 'state' is a matter to be decided, in the first instance, by the despositary, namely the UN Secretary-General. It is the UN Secretary-General's practice as the depositary of multilateral treaties which refer to accession by 'all states' to follow General Assembly practice in determining whether an entity wishing to deposit an instrument of accession should be regarded as a State.[74] This is intended to relieve the Secretary-General of having 'to determine, on his own initiative, the highly political and controversial question of whether or not the areas whose status was unclear were States'.[75] To date, the Secretary-General has relied, in accepting instruments of accession in cases of doubt, on unequivocal indications from the Assembly that it considered particular entities to be States,[76] as well as on resolutions which noted 'the accession to independence' of various countries.[77] As demonstrated above, Resolution 67/19 is neither an unequivocal statement that Palestine is a State, nor even an implicit one. As for independence, the resolution

[71] VCLT, Art. 31(3)(b).

[72] UN Doc. A/67/PV.44, 15 (UK); also Italy: 'Italy decided to vote in favour of resolution 67/19 . . . in the light of the information . . . from President Abbas . . . to refrain from seeking membership in other specialized agencies in the current circumstances, or pursuing the possibility of the jurisdiction of the International Criminal Court . . . ' UN Doc. A/67/PV.44, 18–19. See also the statement by Egypt, UN Doc. A/67/PV.45, 8.

[73] ICC Statute, Art. 125(3). Note that this is not the 'Vienna formula' which allows also accession of members of the UN specialised agencies.

[74] UN Secretariat, Office of the Legal Advisor, Summary of Practice of the Secretary-General as Depositary of Multilateral Treaties, UN Doc. ST/LEG/7/Rev.1, 1999, para. 81. However, it is UNGA Resolution 67/19 which seems to have prompted the debate on the matter.

[75] UN Doc. ST/LEG/7/Rev.1, para. 81. [76] *Ibid.*, para. 82. [77] *Ibid.*, para. 84.

indicates that this is a goal yet to be achieved.[78] Thus, notwithstanding numerous claims that following the adoption of UNGA Resolution 67/19 Palestine can now accede to the ICC Statute,[79] it is doubtful whether the Resolution delivers the goods so vehemently sought. Moreover, the resolution may actually block other routes previously adopted by the Secretary-General. For example, in the past the Secretary-General has relied on a decision on statehood by the World Health Assembly. The reliance on a special agencies' resolutions was justified by the Secretary-General where their 'membership was fully representative of the international community'. However, such reliance is appropriate only if '[t]he guidance the Secretary-General might have obtained from the General Assembly, had he requested it, would evidently have been substantially identical' to the decision of the special agency.[80] In the case of Palestine, there is a resolution admitting Palestine into membership in UNESCO.[81] If the Palestinians had attempted to accede to the ICC Statute prior to the adoption of UNGA Resolution 67/19, the Secretary-General might have been able to rely on the UNESCO resolution. But once UNGA Resolution 67/19 has been adopted, it is clear that the General Assembly's guidance (or lack thereof) is substantially different form that of UNESCO. The Secretary-General's ability to rely on the latter now is at least questionable.[82]

Taking the matter a step further, it should be noted that admission to international legal institutions such as treaty relations, even when those are reserved only to States, does not necessarily imply a general recognition of statehood. In addition to the doctrinal difficulties in deducing statehood from procedural processes[83] based on diverse political agendas,[84]

78 Operative paras. 4, 6.

79 Andreas Zimmerman, 'Palestine and the International Criminal Court Quo Vadis? Reach and Limits of Declarations under Article 12(3)', *Journal of International Criminal Justice*, 11 (2013), 303; Dugard, 'Palestine and the International Criminal Court', 568. Kevin Jon Heller, 'Placard? I Don't See No Stinking Placard!', *Opinio Juris* (24 January 2013), available at http://opiniojuris.org/2013/01/23/.

80 UN Doc. ST/LEG/7/Rev.1, para. 86.

81 UNESCO General Conference, Admission of Palestine as a Member of UNESCO, 36C/Resolution 76, 31 October 2011.

82 After completion of this text, in August 2014 the prosecutor of the International Criminal Court stated that following the adoption of Resolution 67/19, 'Palestine could now join the Rome Statute.' Fatou Bensouda, 'Fatou Bensouda: The Truth about the ICC and Gaza', *The Guardian*, 29 August 2014, http://www.theguardian.com/commentsfree/2014/aug/29/icc-gaza-hague-court-investigate-war-crimes-palestine.

83 Vidmar, 'Palestine and the Conceptual Problem of Implicit Statehood'.

84 Weiler, 'Differentiated Statehood?', 5.

international practice evinces a distinction between treaty membership and statehood. For example, when in the 1980s the UN Council for Namibia joined several international treaties on behalf of Namibia, Namibia continued to be regarded as not yet being a State. One might hazard to suggest that even within UNESCO, Palestinian statehood is not beyond debate; this is hinted in the Executive Committee's Resolution in the lead-up to admission which noted that 'the status of Palestine is the subject of ongoing deliberations at the United Nations'; and by the fact that membership was accorded to 'Palestine' rather than to the 'State of Palestine'.[85]

A separate but equally political issue would arise if the ICC Prosecutor decides to revisit the question of accepting a declaration by Palestine under Article 12(3) on the basis of General Assembly Resolution 67/19. This provision engages the ICC Prosecutor's authority to determine whether Palestine is a State or not. It is not clear that the test for jurisdiction is the same as that applied by the Secretary-General with respect to accession to treaties. The ICC Prosecutor's decision of April 2012 suggested that a General Assembly resolution might seal the matter also for the purpose of jurisdiction under ICC Article 12(3). In explaining why he could not regard Palestine as a State, the Prosecutor noted, *inter alia*, that despite wide bilateral recognition, 'the current status granted to Palestine by the United Nations General Assembly is that of "observer", not as a "Non-member State"'.[86] By implication, the new status is a game-changer. The position of the new ICC Prosecutor, however, may be different. Reportedly, she regards Resolution 67/19 as paving the way for Palestinian accession to the ICC Statute,[87] but not necessarily for acceptance of its declaration under Article 12(3).[88] Treaty accession is, ultimately, an institutional procedure. Jurisdiction of the ICC requires a direct determination of statehood as an objective legal status.

[85] UNESCO Executive Board, UNESCO 187 EX/Decision 40, 2011; Admission of Palestine as a Member of UNESCO.

[86] ICC, Office of the Prosecutor, 'The Situation in Palestine' (3 April 2012), para. 7, available at www.icc-cpi.int/NR/rdonlyres/C6162BBF-FEB9–4FAF-AFA9–836106D2694A/284387/SituationinPalestine030412ENG.pdf.

[87] John V. Whitbeck, 'Palestine and the ICC', *The Palestine Chronicle*, 6 April 2013.

[88] This is evident in her statement that the ball is in the Palestinian court. In the context of determining the ICC's jurisdiction, Whitbeck, Palestine and the ICC'.

5 Conclusion

The legal significance of Resolution 67/19 might not be as great as would appear at first sight. For those who regarded Palestine as a State prior to the adoption of the resolution, the latter merely removes procedural obstacles.[89] For those who considered that Palestine lacked certain requisites for statehood, Resolution 67/19 does not necessarily fill the gap. It might give political courage to leading international players, such as the UN Secretary-General. But notwithstanding its political significance, it is submitted that the Resolution should not be viewed as effecting any legal change.

Supporters of the Palestinian cause strove for an all-round recognition of statehood. Realising that they could not achieve that directly, they settled for a formulation which would be acceptable to all. However, the ambiguity which allowed the adoption of the resolution is critical, since being all things to all men (and women), it does not feature the definitive statement that is necessary for statehood to be confirmed. As noted by Crawford, '[f]or a Palestinian State to be properly described as "*nasciturus*", what is needed is statesmanship on all sides, and respect for the rights of the peoples and states of the region. The manipulation of legal categories is unlikely to advance matters.'[90] More than twenty years down the road, these words have lost none of their poignancy.

[89] As candidly suggested by John Quigley, even before the adoption of the resolution, above n. 3.

[90] Crawford, 'The Creation of the State of Palestine', 313.

14

The role of the *uti possidetis* principle in the resolution of maritime boundary disputes

SUZANNE LALONDE

In the fall of 1993, I arrived at Cambridge University where I had the incredible good fortune to have Professor James Crawford as my thesis supervisor. It was Professor Crawford who first alerted me to the importance the principle of *uti possidetis* was increasingly having on the determination of boundaries and who convinced me of the need for further research into its legal status.

A rather obscure Latin American colonial principle, *uti possidetis* had been catapulted into the limelight the previous year by the Yugoslavia Arbitration Commission. In its third Advisory Opinion delivered in January 1992,[1] the Commission had recommended that the explosive issue of Yugoslavia's boundaries be resolved according to the *uti possidetis juris* principle: the internal boundaries dividing the former constituent republics should automatically become the international boundaries of the new States.[2] Elated by what seemed a clear and workable solution to an impossible problem, the international community proceeded to impose the 'binding' principle of *uti possidetis* on all the parties involved. A few short months later in the spring of 1992, five renowned international law experts,[3] relying heavily on the Badinter interpretation of *uti possidetis*, had assured the Quebec government that in the event of separation from Canada, Quebec could assume legal entitlement to its existing provincial boundaries.[4]

1 Arbitration Commission of the Peace Conference on Yugoslavia, Opinion No. 3 (Borders), International Law Reports, 92 (1993), 170.

2 *Ibid.*, 172.

3 The final opinion was drafted by Alain Pellet in close collaboration with the other four signatories: Thomas M. Franck, Rosalyn Higgins, Malcolm N. Shaw and Christian Tomuschat.

4 Thomas M. Franck *et al.*, 'L'Intégrité territoriale du Québec dans l'hypothèse de l'accession à la souveraineté' in *Commission d'étude des questions afférentes à l'accession du Québec à la souveraineté: Projet de Rapport* (Québec, 1992).

The question in Professor Crawford's mind as we discussed those new developments and which became the focus of my own PhD thesis, was whether these recent interpretations of the *uti possidetis* principle might not have exaggerated its legal status under international law. I therefore spent the next three and a half years examining the Roman origins of the *uti possidetis* principle, its manifestation in the law of war and peace, its colonial roots as well as State practice in the nineteenth and twentieth centuries, to try and clarify its true nature and evaluate its potential as a guarantor of international peace and stability. In devising my thesis plan after a few months of preliminary research, I made the deliberate choice of excluding from the scope of my enquiry the issue of *uti possidetis* and maritime boundaries.

My decision was largely founded on Judge Bedjaoui's arguments in his dissenting opinion in the *Guinea Bissau/Senegal* case militating against the extension of *uti possidetis* to maritime delimitations.[5] Such an opinion, coming from one the most qualified and tenacious supporters of *uti possidetis* as a legal norm for the determination of land boundaries in the colonial context, warranted in my opinion, the greatest deference. The Algerian jurist had been, after all, president of the Chamber of the International Court of Justice (ICJ) which had declared in the course of its decision in the 1986 *Burkina Faso/Mali* affair that *uti possidetis* was:

> not a special rule which pertains solely to one specific system of international law. It is a general principle, which is logically connected with the phenomenon of the obtaining of independence, wherever it occurs.[6]

This dictum was later cited by the Badinter Commission in its Opinion No. 3 as authority for the proposition that *uti possidetis* had become a general principle of international law.[7]

Conscious of the strict word limit imposed by the Law Faculty, I reduced Judge Bedjaoui's careful and detailed arguments to a few short lines and presented them as a justification for my decision in the final paragraphs of the introduction to my thesis and the eventual book which was published in 2002 by McGill-Queen's Press:

> The issue of *uti possidetis* and maritime boundaries is not included in our enquiry, as the latter have their own distinctive character. Maritime

[5] *Case concerning the Delimitation of Maritime Boundary between Guinea-Bissau and Senegal*, Decision of 31 July 1989, Reports of International Arbitral Awards, 20 (2006), 154.

[6] *Frontier Dispute (Burkina Faso/Republic of Mali)*, Judgment, 22 December 1986, ICJ Reports (1986), 565.

[7] Arbitration Commission of the Peace Conference on Yugoslavia, Opinion No. 3, 172.

> territory is not subject to human occupation as such, nor do historical considerations generally have a strong impact in this area. Furthermore, the relationship between maritime boundaries and the principle of self-determination is of a different nature.[8]

In his dissenting opinion, Judge Bedjaoui had strongly emphasised the differences between the two domains (land and maritime), considering them 'to be manifest and irreducible', adding that the concept of sovereignty and its consequences such as territorial integrity did not have or *did not yet have* any relevance for maritime spaces.[9] Judge Bedjaoui, writing in 1986, could therefore not be entirely certain that his conclusion might not be called into question by future developments.

Over the course of the last few decades, the significance of maritime boundaries in international relations has been steadily growing as a result of the increasing territorialisation of marine spaces[10] and the development of new deep-sea technologies – processes, it must be readily acknowledged, well underway by 2002 when my thesis was published. As the International Law Discussion Group which met at Chatham House in February 2006 pointed out:

> An acre of sea may be worth more than an acre of barren land, especially if there is oil or gas on the subsoil or on the seabed. Therefore boundary-making is now a major task for coastal States and relatively few of them have a full set of maritime boundaries.[11]

Current overlapping claims and maritime disputes in various parts of the world involve such fundamental and sensitive issues as State sovereignty, sovereign rights and jurisdiction, title to valuable natural resources and economic sustainability and even questions of national pride and honour. For these reasons, they may also pose a real threat to international stability.

Thus, and mindful of Cicero's admonition that 'any man [or woman] can make mistakes, but only an idiot persists in his error', I feel compelled to take up the challenge which I set aside two decades ago and attempt to discover, whether, as Judge Bedjaoui speculated, *uti possidetis* has today become relevant for the determination of maritime spaces.

8 Suzanne Lalonde, *Determining Boundaries in a Conflicted World: The Role of Uti Possidetis* (Montreal: McGill-Queen's University Press, 2002), 9.

9 *Case concerning the Delimitation of Maritime Boundary between Guinea-Bissau and Senegal*, 167, para. 34.

10 Georges Labrecque, *Les Frontières maritimes internationales* (Montréal: Hamattan, Inc., 1998), 34.

11 'Methods of Resolving Maritime Boundary Disputes', Summary Document of a Meeting of the International Law Discussion Group at Chatham House (UK) on 14 February 2006, available at www.chathamhouse.org/publications/papers/view/108176.

Of course, the potential application of the *uti possidetis* principle to the maritime domain has been the subject of some scholarship[12] and it has been endorsed by international tribunals in a handful of cases. Yet some confusion remains as to the actual scope of application of *uti possidetis* in the maritime context. For instance, there has been some academic debate as to its role for the allocation of insular features and islands between claimant States.[13] Nesi[14] and Kohen,[15] for example, see no reason to distinguish insular from continental *terra firma* and do not consider that this type of situation concerns the possible extension of *uti possidetis* to maritime delimitations.[16]

Without a doubt, the critical *uti possidetis* question is what impact the principle can have in regard to pre-existing lines in the sea. However, as a consequence of the credo that 'land dominates the sea', States have attached vital importance to the ownership of land features out at sea because of the generous maritime claims they can generate, a strategy that has given rise to a number of acrimonious disputes around the world. As my aim is to continue the study which I began under the careful guidance of Professor Crawford – the assessment of what real or practical impact the principle of *uti possidetis* has played in the actual determination of boundaries – my investigation will include cases of disputed sovereignty over insular features and the possible effect *uti possidetis* may thus indirectly have on maritime delimitations.

Nearly all writers emphasise that the modern principle of *uti possidetis* was founded amidst the disintegration of the Iberian empires in South America. Sorel and Medhi, for example, declare 'it is in Latin America that *uti possidetis* was first officially baptized',[17] while De Pinho

[12] Giuseppe Nesi, '*Uti possidetis juris* e delimitazioni maritime', *Rivista di Diritto Internazionale*, 74 (1991), 534; Sánchez Rodríguez, '*Uti possidetis*: la reactualización jurisprudencial de un viejo principio', *Revista española de derecho internacional*, (1988), 121; Sánchez Rodriguez, 'L'uti possidetis: application à la délimitation maritime' in INDEMER, *Le Processus de délimitation maritime: étude d'un cas fictif* (Paris: Pedone, 2004), 303; Daniel Bardonnet, 'Frontières terrestres et frontières maritimes', *Annuaire français de droit international*, 35 (1989), 59–64; Marcelo G. Kohen, *Possession contestée et souveraineté territoriale* (Paris: Presses universitaires de France, 1997), 461–4; Constantine Antonopoulos, 'The Principle of *Uti Possidetis Iuris* in Contemporary International Law', *Revue hellénique de droit international* (1996), 45–8.

[13] Rodríguez, '*Uti possidetis*: la reactualización jurisprudencial de un viejo principio', 135–7.

[14] Nesi, '*Uti possidetis juris* e delimitazioni maritime', 539.

[15] M. Kohen, 'Le Principe de l'*uti possidetis* juris', Corso di stampa, par. II.2, quoted in Nesi, '*Uti possidetis juris* e delimitazioni maritime', 539.

[16] *Ibid.*

[17] Jean-Marc Sorel and Rostane Medhi, 'L'*Uti possidetis* entre la consécration juridique et la pratique', *Annuaire français de droit international*, 40 (1994), 13.

Campinos asserts that 'the principle of *uti possidetis* was born in Latin America'.[18] African State practice during the period of decolonisation is then inevitably considered by the majority of commentators, as the most significant application of the 'Latin American principle of *uti possidetis*'.[19] For this reason, the role of *uti possidetis* in the decolonisation of Latin America and Africa was at the heart of my thesis and will also be the focus of this chapter.

The starting point to this enquiry must be a clear and accurate understanding of the *uti possidetis* principle itself. In the first part of the chapter, I will therefore revisit my principal conclusions with regard to the practical contribution of *uti possidetis* to the determination of boundaries between the newly independent Latin American and African States and its status under international law.

The second part of the chapter will provide a brief summary of key international decisions in which the *uti possidetis* principle has been invoked as a relevant rule for the determination of maritime boundaries. As the entire edifice of *uti possidetis* as a general principle of international law rests on Latin American and African State practice in the decolonisation period, only cases involving States from those continents will be considered. Furthermore, only cases presenting the classic *uti possidetis* scenario have been selected: instances of maritime delimitation between two former colonies belonging to the same metropolitan power.

On the basis of this brief overview of relevant cases, I will consider whether my original conclusions with regard to the *uti possidetis* principle and land boundaries must be revised or whether my rather harsh assessment of the principle's track record is still defendable in the maritime context.

A The colonial *uti possidetis* principle

Calls to extend and apply the *uti possidetis* principle in maritime situations are based upon its purported success in the past in resolving conflicts over

[18] Jorge de Pinho Campinos, 'L'Actualité de l'*uti possidetis*' in Société française pour le droit international, *La Frontière* (Paris: Pedone, 1979), 95.

[19] See e.g. D. Bourjorl-Flécher, 'Heurs et malheurs de l'*uti possidetis*: l'intangibilité des frontières africaines', *Revue juridique et politique indépendance coopération*, 35 (1981), 812; Ian Brownlie (ed.), *Basic Documents on African Affairs* (Oxford: Clarendon Press, 1971), 360; A. O. Cukwurah, 'The Organization of African Unity and African Territorial and Boundary Problems: 1963–1973', *Indian Journal of International Law*, 13 (1973), 181; Boutros Boutros-Ghali, 'The Addis Ababa Charter', *International Conciliation*, 546 (1964), 29, among many others.

land boundaries, especially in colonial Latin America and Africa. Before joining the debate on the merits of a maritime *uti possidetis*, I feel it is essential to summarise my previous findings with regard to the actual impact of the principle in the colonial context.

As a result of my in-depth study of nineteenth-century Latin American State practice and breaking with the general doctrinal trend, I argued in my thesis that the *uti possidetis* principle had played neither a significant nor a particularly successful role in settling boundary issues between the new Iberian republics. References to colonial territorial units in early instruments represented the application of established rules on State succession and did not address the question of the precise location of the new international boundaries. Only once their independence had been consolidated, and international recognition had been extended, did the new States turn to the question of the precise delimitation of their mutual frontiers. And even in this limited role, *uti possidetis* had precious little impact because of theoretical and practical problems.

One of the most problematic aspects of the Latin American *uti possidetis* principle was the conflicting meanings it came to possess, particularly the Brazilian *uti possidetis de facto* formula and the Spanish American version, *uti possidetis juris*. According to Brazil's interpretation, the *uti possidetis* principle referred to actual and effective possession. Territorial limits were to be determined on the basis of what each State actually possessed at the time of independence. However, as interpreted by the Spanish American republics, *uti possidetis* constituted a rule of constructive possession. The territorial extent of each State was to be founded on royal titles and official Spanish colonial instruments granting a right of jurisdiction, a type of fictitious possession at the theoretical date of independence. In addition to these two dominant interpretations of the principle, State practice during the period of decolonisation also revealed a number of other alternative interpretations of the principle: for example, *uti possidetis* before independence;[20] *uti possidetis* of 1826;[21] *uti possidetis* of 1874;[22] *uti possidetis juris* of 1880.[23]

[20] Treaty of Peace, Friendship and Alliance between Ecuador and Peru, 25 January 1860, 50 *British and Foreign State Papers*, 1086.

[21] Political Constitution of the Republic of Costa Rica, 22 November 1848, 37 *British and Foreign State Papers*, 777.

[22] République Dominicaine, Haiti, 3 July 1895, 23 *Nouveau recueil général de traités et autres actes relatifs aux rapports de droit international* (2d), 79.

[23] Treaty between Colombia and Venezuela for submitting to Arbitration the Question of the Boundary between the two Republics, 14 September 1881, 73, *British and Foreign State Papers*, 1107.

It must be emphasised that the commitment to respect the colonial heritage found in all of the different Latin American versions of the *uti possidetis* principle concerned lines dividing units that the struggle for independence had already placed under the control of the new international actors. Indeed, the *uti possidetis* principle was never allowed to displace boundary lines established as a result of revolutionary activity, force of arms or unequal bargaining power.

In addition to competing interpretations of the principle, inconsistent State practice also prevented *uti possidetis* from having much of an impact in Latin America. Though the Spanish American Republics professed adherence to the *uti possidetis juris* principle, there is clear evidence that the Latin American Republics were inconsistent in their reliance on any given interpretation of the principle, choosing the particular version which, in a given dispute, most favoured their claim.[24]

A number of practical difficulties also severely curtailed the effectiveness of the *uti possidetis* principle in the colonial Latin American context. Many regions in Spanish America were unexplored and other parts were only vaguely known. Consequently, jurisdictional limits between the administrative units were often imprecise and, in certain areas, had not been fixed at all. Furthermore, in some of the more remote regions, the territory had in fact never been allocated to any particular unit. Thus, even in those fairly rare cases where the parties were able to agree on a precise and common definition of the principle and then to submit their dispute to international adjudication, decision-making bodies were in most instances unable to apply the principle because of insufficient information; the decisions were ultimately based on post-independence

[24] Peru, Venezuela and Bolivia each concluded a treaty with Brazil on the basis of the *uti possidetis de facto* – that is to say, on the basis of actual possession – yet on 25 January 1860, Peru concluded the Treaty of Peace, Friendship and Alliance with Ecuador on the basis of the *uti possidetis juris* formula. Similarly, the preamble of the 1881 treaty concluded between Venezuela and Colombia refers to the *uti possidetis juris* of 1880, while Art. 8 of the General Arbitration Treaty between Bolivia and Peru instructed the arbitrator to resolve the dispute in strict obedience with the principle of *uti possidetis* of 1810. See Lalonde, *Determining Boundaries in a Conflicted World*, 34–5. Kohen also notes: '[T]he notion of *uti possidetis de facto* . . . was invoked by Paraguay in its dispute with Bolivia over the *Chaco boreal*, by Guatemala in its frontier dispute with Honduras . . . and to a certain extent, by Salvador in the *Case concerning the Land, Island and Maritime Frontier Dispute*. All these theses have in common the fact of favouring the situation on the ground rather than juridical titles, in other words possession in relation to the right to possess.' Kohen, *Possession contestée et souveraineté territoriale*, 449–50.

effectivités or equitable considerations or by reference to natural geographical features.[25]

Therefore, despite many cavalier references to the 'Latin American' principle of *uti possidetis*, I argued that it was difficult to maintain that the nineteenth-century Latin American Republics had bequeathed to international law a clearly defined and consistently applied principle that could then serve as a precedent in other boundary disputes or that could elevate *uti possidetis* to the status of a general principle of international law.

In the period of independence, African leaders debated the principles of regional organisation, and in 1963 the Organisation of African Unity (OAU) was created. The outcome of the debate was the adoption of a general programme of African unity, but in practical terms this was to be based upon a unity of action between independent States. Article 3(3) of the OAU Charter affirmed every member's adherence to 'respect for the sovereignty and territorial integrity of each State and for its inalienable right to independent existence'.[26] As an important aspect of the policy-making of this period, the members of the OAU, meeting in Cairo the following year, adopted a Resolution in which the Assembly of Heads of State and Government reaffirmed 'the strict respect by all member States of the organisation for the principles laid down in Article III, paragraph 3 of the Charter' and declared 'that all member States pledge themselves to respect the frontiers existing on their achievement of national independence'.[27]

As noted, many commentators have argued that this respect for boundaries inherited from the colonial past is simply the application in the African context of the Latin American principle of *uti possidetis*. Indeed, the Charter and the Resolution of the OAU are considered strong evidence that the *uti possidetis* had a major impact in the decolonisation of the African continent. One such commentator is Quéneudec: 'It was therefore possible to consider, from that time, that the Heads of State and of Government meeting in Addis Ababa in 1963 had defended "the principle of an African *uti possidetis*".'[28]

[25] See e.g. the discussion of the 1891 Colombia–Venezuela award rendered by Queen Regent Marie-Christine and the 1909 Bolivia–Peru arbitral award as well as other cases in Lalonde, *Determining Boundaries in a Conflicted World*, 41–51.

[26] OAU Charter (Addis Ababa, adopted 25 May 1963, entered into force 13 September 1963), 479 UNTS 39.

[27] Brownlie, *Basic Documents on African Affairs*, 361.

[28] Jean Pierre Quéneudec, 'Remarques sur le règlement des conflits frontaliers en Afrique', *Revue générale de droit international public*, 74 (1970), 70–1.

The Chamber of the International Court of Justice tasked with determining a sector of the Burkina Faso–Mali land frontier also shared this vision, declaring in its 1986 judgment that elements of *uti possidetis* were latent in many declarations made by African leaders 'in the dawn of independence'.[29] The Chamber emphasised at the outset that the *uti possidetis* principle was not a special rule pertaining solely to one specific system of international law:

> The fact that the new African States have respected the administrative boundaries and frontiers established by the colonial powers must be seen not as a mere practice contributing to the gradual emergence of a principle of customary international law, limited in its impact to the African continent as it had previously been to Spanish America, but as the application in Africa of a rule of general scope.[30]

However, unlike the process in nineteenth-century Latin America, independence in Africa was a goal promoted by the UN Charter under Chapter XI and a right conferred by Chapter XII upon those territories within the international trusteeship system. This obligation to promote and support the self-government of the African colonies was subsequently confirmed by the Colonial Declaration.[31] An international legal framework was therefore in place to oversee the accession to independence of the African colonies. The right of self-determination, which was territorially defined and was thus granted to each colonial people as a whole, together with the principle of territorial integrity, which then protected the new State from internal and external claims, largely accounted for the maintenance of colonial boundary lines into the period of independence. In addition, as independence was conferred through acts of devolution, the *nemo dat* principle – that a sovereign entity can only relinquish as much territory as it actually possesses – would also have contributed to maintaining the policy of the territorial status quo in Africa.

In fact, no actual reference to the *uti possidetis* principle can be found in any of the official African instruments or pronouncements of the decolonisation period. Early calls to revise the arbitrary colonial lines[32] cast considerable doubt on the existence of a binding rule of international

[29] *Frontier Dispute (Burkina Faso/Republic of Mali)*, 565–6.

[30] *Ibid.*, 566. [31] GA Res.1514, 15 UN GAOR, Supp. (No. 16) 66, UN Doc. A/4684 (1960).

[32] The revisionist movement culminated in the resolution proclaimed by the All-African Peoples Conference held in Accra in December 1958, which called for the abolition or readjustment of colonial frontiers at an early date. A. C. McEwen, *International Boundaries of East Africa* (Oxford: Clarendon Press, 1971), 73.

law mandating the automatic transformation of administrative lines into international boundaries. And even once African leaders had agreed that the risks inherent in redrawing the map of Africa were too great, the solution adopted, which international law already provided, was to accept the boundary lines existing at the date of independence. However, this pledge to respect existing borders concerned the *de facto* colonial lines on the ground and did not entail referring back to legal instruments of the former colonial power to determine the legitimacy of those lines. Therefore, if African State practice was evidence of a commitment to the *uti possidetis* principle, it did not support the dominant *uti possidetis juris* version favoured by the Spanish American Republics. Howsoever described, the African status quo policy was never intended to create new legal obligations and simply reflected the rights and duties of States as defined according to well-established rules of international law.

A final disturbing aspect concerned claims that *uti possidetis* guaranteed the sanctity of African borders established by treaty between two distinct metropolitan powers.[33] This interpretation appeared to signal a misplaced belief that *uti possidetis* had become the incarnation of every principle and rule of international law bearing on the question of territory, for such boundaries were already protected by long-established and undisputed rules concerning State succession to treaties and fundamental change of circumstances. In the final analysis, and despite later interpretations, it did not appear as if African State practice in the period of independence had consecrated *uti possidetis juris* as a rule of customary international law 'connected with the phenomenon of the obtaining of independence wherever it occurred'.[34]

While African State practice and judgments of the International Court of Justice, particularly in cases such as *Burkina Faso/Mali*, might have conferred a normative status on the colonial *uti possidetis* principle, I argued that its status had been inflated. Though undoubtedly an influential rule for the determination of the international land boundaries of States that had emerged from the colonial rule of a single metropolitan power, *uti possidetis* was no more than a presumption as to the location of the boundaries of an entity which had achieved independence. It was

[33] See *Case concerning the Delimitation of Maritime Boundary between Guinea-Bissau and Senegal*, 35, wherein the tribunal declared that in Africa, *uti possidetis* had a broader meaning 'because it concerns both the boundaries of countries born of the same colonial empire and boundaries which during the colonial era had already an international character because they separated colonies belonging to different colonial empires'.

[34] *Frontier Dispute (Burkina Faso/Republic of Mali)*, 565.

not a binding solution which could be imposed in advance of formal independence under the mantle of a customary rule of international law.

B A brief overview of some international decisions in favour of the application of the *uti possidetis* principle to maritime delimitations

Latin American State practice in the nineteenth century does not provide much of a context for an analysis of the role of *uti possidetis* in maritime delimitations. International norms regarding the maritime domain were embryonic and rights over maritime zones were considered very limited. This fact explains why Spain and Portugal did not include any references to their respective maritime zones in the principal treaties which divided the Latin American continent between them.[35]

Yet by virtue of a Royal Decree dated 17 December 1760, Spain did claim that its territorial waters off the coasts of Latin America extended for 6 nautical miles. There is also formal evidence that certain areas of the sea, like bays and estuaries, were historically considered by the Spanish Crown as being subject to a special regime. This was notably the case of the Gulf of Fonseca on the western coast of Central America. In the first round of the dispute between El Salvador and Nicaragua in 1917, the Central American Court of Justice declared that the Gulf constituted a historic bay:

> The historic origin of the right of exclusive ownership that has been exercised over the waters of the Gulf during the course of nearly four hundred years is incontrovertible, first, under the Spanish dominion – from 1522, when it was discovered and incorporated into the royal patrimony of the Crown of Castile, down to the year of 1821 – then under the Federal Republic of the Center of America . . . and, subsequently, on the dissolution of the Federation . . . the States of El Salvador, Honduras and Nicaragua . . . incorporated into their respective territories . . . both the Gulf and its archipelago.[36]

The case, however, does not shed any light on the issue of pre-existing colonial maritime lines and their treatment by successor States or international judicial tribunals. Both parties in the course of their pleadings had

[35] The Treaty of Tordesillas of 1494, the Treaty of Madrid of 1750 (annulled in 1761) and the Treaty of San Ildefonso of 1777.

[36] *El Salvador* v. *Nicaragua*, Central American Court of Justice, Judgment, 9 March 1917, *American Journal of International Law*, 11 (1917), 700.

in fact recognised that no demarcation lines existed between them prior to their constitution as independent entities. Indeed, the Court concluded that, with the exception of a short line of division agreed to by Honduras and Nicaragua in 1900, the great majority of the waters of the Gulf had remained undivided.[37] Thus according to the majority, 'since it is true in principle that the absence of demarcation always results in community',[38] the three riparian States (El Salvador, Honduras and Nicaragua) were co-owners of the waters of the Gulf.[39]

In the *Beagle Channel arbitration* (1977) between Argentina and Chile, the Court of Arbitration was asked to determine sovereignty over Picton, Nueva and Lennox islands and to fix the maritime boundary in the area of the Beagle Channel. The award does consider the *uti possidetis* principle but only in its traditional role as a mechanism for the determination of ownership of certain tracts of land – in this case, islands, islets and rocks near the extreme end of the South American continent.

While both Argentina and Chile had formally recognised in their 1855 Treaty of Peace, Friendship, Commerce and Navigation 'as the boundaries of their respective territories those existing at the time when they broke away from Spanish dominion in the year 1810',[40] no attempt had been made to define what those boundaries were, including in the Beagle Channel. Rather, the two neighbours had agreed 'to defer the questions that have arisen or may arise regarding this matter in order to discuss them later'. Thus, for decades following their independence, the limits between the two former Spanish colonial divisions had remained uncertain. In fact, both Argentina and Chile had at various times relied on *uti possidetis* to claim most of the continent south of the Rio Negro and east of the Andes down to the far south.

The Court concluded that it was 'no part of its task to pronounce on what would have been the rights of the Parties on the basis of the *uti possidetis juris* of 1810' because those rights, whatever they might have been, had been overtaken and transcended by the regime deriving from the 1881 Treaty.[41] Indeed, with the exception of the limits of the two countries' respective claims in Antarctica, the boundaries between Argentina and

[37] *Ibid.*, 711. [38] *Ibid.*

[39] The Court excluded from the regime of co-ownership a marine league of exclusive ownership adjacent to the coasts of the parties' mainlands and islands. *Ibid.*, 716.

[40] Art. 39, Treaty of Peace, Friendship, Commerce and Navigation between Argentina and Chile of 1855, 49, *British and Foreign State Papers*, 1200.

[41] *Case concerning a Dispute between Argentina and Chile Concerning the Beagle Channel*, Award, 18 February 1977, Reports of International Arbitral Awards, 21 (1997), 82.

Chile had been fixed by the 1881 Treaty, Article III of which provided for the allocation of islands in Tierra del Fuego and in the vicinity of the Beagle Channel. Applying the literal method of interpretation and also taking into consideration the context and overall effectiveness of the Treaty,[42] sovereignty over the disputed islands was awarded to Chile. The Court then proceeded to draw a median line through the Beagle Channel, with some minor adjustments for reasons of coastal configuration, convenience and navigability.[43] Thus like a number of other boundary disputes in Latin America,[44] the Beagle Channel dispute was resolved on the basis of an existing treaty which reflected the will of the parties, and not as a result of the operation of the *uti possidetis* principle.

The 1992 decision of a Chamber of the ICJ in the *Land, Island and Maritime Frontier Dispute*[45] considers at some length the *uti possidetis juris* principle and has in fact come to exert the same kind of influence in the maritime context as has the *Burkina Faso/Mali* judgment in cases involving *uti possidetis* and former colonial land frontiers. For the purposes of this chapter, only the Court's reasoning with respect to the maritime issues submitted to it by the parties (El Salvador, Honduras with Nicaragua intervening) will be examined.

The Special Agreement concluded at Esquipulas (Guatemala) on 24 May 1986 between the Republic of El Salvador and the Republic of Honduras requested a determination of the legal status of the islands in dispute between the parties within the Gulf of Fonseca, which the Court identified as El Tigre, Meanguera and Meanguerita islands. It was El Salvador's claim that, on the basis of the *uti possidetis juris* principle, it should be recognised as the successor of the Spanish Crown in respect of all the islands in the Gulf.[46] It was also Honduras's contention that the only law applicable to the dispute was the *uti possidetis juris* of 1821. And the Chamber of the Court agreed with both parties as to the relevance of the *uti possidetis juris* principle:

42 Division for Ocean Affairs and the Law of the Sea, Office of Legal Affairs, *Digest of International Cases on the Law of the Sea* (New York: United Nations, 2007), 14.

43 *Ibid.*, 146 and 216.

44 See e.g. the influence of the Additional Arbitration Convention concluded between Peru and Ecuador on 15 December 1895 in Paul de Lapradelle, *La Frontière: étude de droit international* (Paris: Les éditions internationales, 1928), 85. See also Lalonde, *Determining Boundaries in a Conflicted World*, 58.

45 *Land, Island and Maritime Frontier Dispute (El Salvador/Honduras: Nicaragua intervening)*, Judgment, 11 September 1992, ICJ Reports (1992), 351.

46 El Salvador also relied upon the existence or display of sovereignty over the islands.

> The Chamber has no doubt that the starting-point for the determination of sovereignty over the islands must be the *uti possidetis juris* of 1821. The islands were discovered in 1522 by Spain and remained under the sovereignty of the Spanish Crown for three centuries. When the Central American States became independent in 1821, none of the islands were *terra nullius*; sovereignty over the islands could not therefore be acquired by occupation of territory. The matter was one of the succession of the newly-independent States to all former Spanish islands in the Gulf. The Chamber will therefore consider whether it is possible to establish the appurtenance in 1821 of each disputed island to one or the other of the various administrative units of the Spanish colonial structure in Central America.[47]

Recognising that in the case of the islands there were no land titles of the kind which it had taken into account to reconstruct the limits of the *uti possidetis juris* on the mainland, the Chamber declared that it could have regard not only to administrative and legislative texts of the colonial period, but also to 'colonial *effectivités*'.[48] However, after a brief consideration of the essential contentions of the parties on the historical basis of their respective claims, the Chamber was forced to conclude that the evidence was confused and conflicting and of no practical value:

> The Chamber considers it unnecessary to analyse in any further detail the arguments of each Party directed to showing that that Party acquired sovereignty over some or all of the islands in the Gulf by the application of the *uti possidetis juris* principle. It has reached the conclusion, after careful consideration of those arguments, that the material available to the Chamber, whether presented as evidence of title (as in the case of the *Reales Cédulas*) or of pre-independence *effectivités*, is too fragmentary and ambiguous to be sufficient for any firm conclusion to be based upon it.[49]

The Chamber felt it therefore had to proceed on the basis of the conduct of the parties in the period following independence as indicative of what must have been the 1821 position. It also decided that such evidence could be supplemented by considerations wholly unconnected with the *uti possidetis juris* principle, in particular, the possible significance of the same conduct, or the conduct of the parties in more recent years, as possibly constituting acquiescence.[50] Thus, and despite the Chamber's strong endorsement of the principle, *uti possidetis juris* as a rule of constructive

[47] *Land, Island and Maritime Frontier Dispute (El Salvador/Honduras: Nicaragua intervening)*, 558, para. 333.

[48] *Ibid.* [49] *Ibid.*, 563, para. 341. [50] *Ibid.*

possession ultimately had no impact whatsoever on the Chamber's final award of sovereignty over the three islands.

As for the legal situation of the waters of the Gulf of Fonseca, the Chamber indicated that it was 'necessary to enquire into the legal situation of the waters of the Gulf in 1821 at the time of succession from Spain; for the principle of *uti possidetis juris* should apply to the waters of the Gulf as well as to the land'.[51] However, in the very next sentence of its judgment, the Chamber acknowledged that no evidence had been presented suggesting that there was for these waters prior to, or at 1821, 'anything analogous to those boundaries of provincial sway, which have been so much discussed in respect of the land'.[52] In light of the absence of any maritime administrative boundaries at the time of inheritance, the Chamber confirmed the *ratio decidendi* of the 1917 judgment of the Central American Court of Justice.

The Chamber therefore declared that the Gulf was a historic bay and that its waters, except for a 3-mile belt, were historic waters subject to the joint sovereignty of El Salvador, Honduras and Nicaragua.[53] The Court also determined that the closing line should be the one referred to in the 1917 judgment (from Punta Ampala to Punta Cosigüina) and recognised by the three coastal States in practice.[54] Finally, the Chamber adjudged that given the tri-partite presence at the closing line, all three of the joint sovereign States had legal entitlements to ocean waters outside the bay.

On 10 October 2002, the International Court of Justice rendered its decision in the *Case concerning the Land and Maritime Boundary between Cameroon and Nigeria, Equatorial Guinea intervening*.[55] The application filed by the government of the Republic of Cameroon in March 1994 referred to a dispute with the Federal Republic of Nigeria 'relating essentially to the question of sovereignty over the Bakassi Peninsula'. However, Cameroon further stated in its application that the delimitation of the maritime boundary between the two States had remained a partial one and that despite many attempts to complete it, the two parties had been unable to do so. In a bid to avoid further incidents between the two countries, Cameroon therefore requested the Court to 'determine the course of the maritime boundary between the two States beyond the line fixed in 1975'.

[51] *Ibid.*, 589, para. 385. [52] *Ibid.*, 589, para. 386.
[53] Division for Ocean Affairs, *Digest*, 24. [54] *Ibid.*
[55] *Land and Maritime Boundary between Cameroon and Nigeria (Cameroon* v. *Nigeria: Equatorial Guinea intervening)*, Judgment, 10 October 2002, ICJ Reports (2002), 303.

As the Court explained at the outset, the dispute between the parties as regards their land boundary fell 'within an historical framework marked initially, in the nineteenth and early twentieth centuries, by the actions of the European Powers with a view to the partitioning of Africa, followed by changes in the status of the relevant territories under the League of Nations mandate system, then the United Nations trusteeships, and finally by the territories' accession to independence'.[56] Indeed, while Nigeria had been a British colony for over half a century (1900–60), present-day Cameroon was initially a German colony. However, following Germany's defeat in World War I, the colony had been partitioned between the United Kingdom and France under a League of Nations mandate, with Britain's sector consisting of a strip bordering Nigeria from the sea to Lake Chad.

While the dispute might therefore be considered a classic case for the application of *uti possidetis* – the determination of a boundary between two former colonies belonging to the same metropolitan power – in fact, international treaties dating back to 1913 and the post-independence conduct of the parties were held to be the determining factors. Indeed the Court commented at the very outset that 'apart from the Anglo-German Agreements of 11 March and 12 April 1913 in so far as they refer to the endpoint of the land boundary on the coast, all the legal instruments concerning the maritime boundary between Cameroon and Nigeria post-date the independence of those two States'.[57]

After a detailed review of the arguments put forth by both parties,[58] the Court found that 'the Anglo-German Agreement of 11 March 1913 was valid and applicable in its entirety'[59] and that, as a result, it need not 'pronounce upon the arguments of *uti possidetis* advanced by the Parties in relation to Bakassi'.[60] Indeed, the Court concluded that the boundary between Cameroon and Nigeria in Bakassi was delimited by Articles XVIII–XX of the Anglo-German Agreement of 11 March 1913, and that consequently sovereignty over the peninsula lay with Cameroon.[61]

With respect to the delimitation of the maritime boundary between the parties, the Court declared that it was 'anchored' to the mainland in accordance with Articles XVIII and XXI of the said Agreement.[62] It then upheld the validity of the Declarations of Yaoundé II and Maroua, pursuant to which the Heads of State of Nigeria and Cameroon had in 1971 and 1975 agreed upon the maritime boundary between the two

[56] *Ibid.*, 330, para. 31. [57] *Ibid.*, 333, para. 38.
[58] *Ibid.*, 400–12, paras. 195–215. [59] *Ibid.*, 412, para. 217.
[60] *Ibid.* [61] *Ibid.*, 416, para. 225. [62] *Ibid.*, 429, para. 261.

countries from the mouth of the Akwayafe to a point G. As for the maritime boundary further out to sea, the Court essentially endorsed the delimitation method advocated by Nigeria.[63] It drew an equidistance line between Cameroon and Nigeria, declaring that in its view, such a line produced an equitable result. The Cameroon/Nigeria decision is therefore of interest only for the Court's refusal to equate respect for the provisions of an international treaty with the *uti possidetis* principle.

By a Notice of Arbitration dated 16 February 2004, Barbados initiated arbitration proceedings concerning its maritime boundary with the Republic of Trinidad and Tobago. No reference to the *uti possidetis* principle was made in any of the parties' pleadings or formal arguments, and it is also absent from the final award delivered on 11 April 2006.[64]

The maritime boundary between the two former British colonies was determined by the tribunal by reference to the equidistance/special circumstances rule. In arguing that the provisional equidistance line ought to be adjusted in the Caribbean sector, Barbados had relied upon three core factual submissions, including 'a centuries-old history of artisanal fishing in the waters off the northwest, north and northeast coasts of Tobago by Barbadian fisherfolk'.[65] In support of this contention, Barbados had adduced evidence showing that Barbadian fisherfolk had long-range boats and other equipment to enable them to fish off Tobago between the eighteenth and twentieth centuries.[66] The tribunal, however, ultimately ruled that the factual circumstances invoked by Barbados had not been proven[67] and consequently that the equidistance line ought not to be adjusted.

While it appears that there were no pre-existing maritime limits between the parties going back to colonial times which deserved consideration, *uti possidetis* might nonetheless have played a minor or supporting role. It is noteworthy that when invoking centuries-old artisanal fishing activities in the disputed sector, Barbados made no reference to British colonial administrative texts or *effectivités*. It may be that such colonial evidence was 'too fragmentary and ambiguous . . . for any firm conclusion to be based upon it' as the Court commented in its El Salvador/Honduras ruling.[68] Yet the complete absence of any reference to the *uti possidetis*

[63] Division for Ocean Affairs, *Digest*, 137.

[64] *Arbitration between Barbados and the Republic of Trinidad and Tobago, Relating to the Delimitation of the Exclusive Economic Zone and the Continental Shelf between Them*, Decision of 11 April 2006, Reports of International Arbitral Awards, 27 (2008), 147.

[65] *Ibid.*, 184, para. 125. [66] *Ibid.*, 185, para. 127. [67] *Ibid.*, 221, para 265.

[68] *Land, Island and Maritime Frontier Dispute (El Salvador/Honduras: Nicaragua intervening)*, 563, para. 341.

juris principle either by the parties or the tribunal appears to cast some doubt on the purported status of *uti possidetis juris* as a binding rule of customary international law.

On 8 October 2007, the International Court rendered its decision in the *Case concerning the Territorial and Maritime Dispute between Nicaragua and Honduras in the Caribbean Sea.*[69] The case concerned sovereignty over four islands beyond the territorial sea of the two parties and the delimitation of maritime areas between Nicaragua and Honduras in the Caribbean Sea.

The Court began by acknowledging that 'the principle of *uti possidetis* has kept its place among the most important legal principles' regarding territorial title and boundary delimitation at the moment of decolonisation.[70] This phrase and conclusion, borrowed from the *Burkina Faso/Mali* judgment, was then further emphasised by reproducing the key passage from that same case regarding the status of *uti possidetis* under international law: 'It is a general principle, which is logically connected with the phenomenon of obtaining of independence, wherever it occurs. Its obvious purpose is to prevent the independence and stability of new States being endangered by fratricidal struggles provoked by the challenging of frontiers following the withdrawal of the administering power.'[71] The Court also endorsed the Chamber's earlier finding that pre-eminence should be accorded to legal title over effective possession as a basis for sovereignty.[72] Finally, and quoting from the judgment in the *Land, Island and Maritime Frontier Dispute*, the Court stressed that '*uti possidetis juris* may, in principle, apply to offshore possessions and maritime spaces'.[73]

In deciding the question of sovereignty over the islands in dispute, the Court found that 'in order to apply the principle of *uti possidetis*

69 *Territorial and Maritime Dispute between Nicaragua and Honduras in the Caribbean Sea (Nicaragua* v. *Honduras)*, Judgment, 8 October 2007, ICJ Reports (2007), 659.

70 *Territorial and Maritime Dispute between Nicaragua and Honduras in the Caribbean Sea (Nicaragua* v. *Honduras)*, 706, para. 151, quoting *Frontier Dispute (Burkina Faso/Republic of Mali)*, 567, para. 26.

71 *Territorial and Maritime Dispute between Nicaragua and Honduras in the Caribbean Sea (Nicaragua* v. *Honduras)*, 706, para. 151, quoting *Frontier Dispute (Burkina Faso/Republic of Mali)*, 565, para. 20.

72 *Territorial and Maritime Dispute between Nicaragua and Honduras in the Caribbean Sea (Nicaragua* v. *Honduras)*, 706, para. 152, quoting *Frontier Dispute (Burkina Faso/Republic of Mali)*, 566, para. 23.

73 *Territorial and Maritime Dispute between Nicaragua and Honduras in the Caribbean Sea (Nicaragua* v. *Honduras)*, 707, para. 156, quoting *Land, Island and Maritime Frontier Dispute (El Salvador/Honduras: Nicaragua intervening)*, 558, para. 333 and 589, para. 386.

juris... it must be shown that the Spanish Crown had allocated them to one or the other of its colonial provinces'.[74] To underline this key point, the Court again quoted from the Chamber's judgment in the *Land, Island and Maritime Frontier Dispute*:

> It should be recalled that when the principle of *uti possidetis juris* is involved, the *jus* referred to is not international law but the constitutional or administrative law of the pre-independence sovereign, in this case Spanish colonial law; and it is perfectly possible that that law itself gave no clear and definitive answer to the appurtenance of marginal areas, or sparsely populated areas of minimal economic significance.[75]

This proved to be the case as the Court found that the parties had not produced documentary or other evidence from the pre-independence period which explicitly referred to the islands.[76] The Court therefore concluded that 'notwithstanding the historical and continuing importance of the *uti possidetis juris* principle so closely associated with Latin American decolonization, it [could] not in this case be said that the application of this principle to those small islands... would settle the issue of sovereignty over them'.[77] In fact, the Court was compelled to admit, despite its earlier sweeping endorsement, that 'the principle of *uti possidetis* affords inadequate assistance in determining sovereignty over these islands'.[78] The Court therefore ultimately had to rely on post-independence *effectivités* in awarding sovereignty over the disputed islands to Honduras.

As for the delimitation of the maritime areas, Honduras relied upon a Spanish Royal Decree dated 17 December 1760 which established that Spain's territorial waters extended for 6 nautical miles. It was Nicaragua's contention, however, that jurisdiction over the territorial sea fell to Spanish authorities in Madrid, not to local authorities. It insisted that the Spanish Crown's claim to a 6-nautical mile territorial sea said nothing with regard to the limit of this territorial sea between the Spanish provinces of Honduras and Nicaragua. And the Court agreed, stating:

> The Court further observes that Nicaragua and Honduras as new independent States were entitled by virtue of the *uti possidetis juris* principle to

[74] *Territorial and Maritime Dispute between Nicaragua and Honduras in the Caribbean Sea (Nicaragua* v. *Honduras)*, 707, para. 158.

[75] *Territorial and Maritime Dispute between Nicaragua and Honduras in the Caribbean Sea (Nicaragua* v. *Honduras)*, 708, para. 160, quoting *Land, Island and Maritime Frontier Dispute (El Salvador/Honduras: Nicaragua intervening)*, 558–9, para. 333.

[76] *Territorial and Maritime Dispute between Nicaragua and Honduras in the Caribbean Sea (Nicaragua* v. *Honduras)*, 708.

[77] *Ibid.*, 709, para. 163. [78] *Ibid.*, 710–11, para. 167.

> such mainland and insular territory and territorial seas which constituted their provinces at independence... It has not been shown however that the Spanish Crown divided its maritime jurisdiction between the colonial provinces of Nicaragua and Honduras even within the limits of the territorial sea. Although it may be accepted that all States gained their independence with an entitlement to a territorial sea, that legal fact does not determine where the maritime boundary between adjacent seas of neighbouring States will run.[79]

Having found that the *uti possidetis juris* principle did not provide a basis for an alleged 'traditional' maritime boundary along the fifteenth parallel[80] and in light of the difficulty in identifying base points along the parties' mainland coasts, the Court proceeded to rely on the bisector method to define a single maritime boundary.

On 6 December 2001, the Republic of Nicaragua instituted proceedings against the Republic of Colombia in respect of a dispute between the two States concerning title to territory and maritime delimitation in the western Caribbean. Nicaragua asked the Court to adjudge and declare that it had sovereignty over the islands of Providencia, San Andrés and Santa Catalina and all the appurtenant islands and keys and also over Roncador, Serrana, Serranilla and Quitasueño keys insofar as they were capable of appropriation. Secondly, and in the light of its determination as to title over the features specified, the Court was asked to determine the course of a single maritime boundary between the areas of continental shelf and exclusive economic zones (EEZ) appertaining respectively to Nicaragua and Colombia.

In a judgment dated 13 December 2007 regarding preliminary objections raised by Colombia,[81] the Court held that it had no jurisdiction in regards to Nicaragua's claim to sovereignty over the islands of Providencia, San Andrés and Santa Catalina. The Court ruled that this question had been determined by the Treaty concerning Territorial Questions at Issue between Colombia and Nicaragua signed at Managua on 24 March 1928, by which Nicaragua had recognised Colombian sovereignty over the three islands.[82]

In regard to the remaining features in dispute, the Court held in November 2012[83] that Albuquerque and East-Southeast Cays as well as

79 *Ibid.*, 729, para. 234. 80 *Ibid.*, 729, para. 236.

81 *Territorial and Maritime Dispute (Nicaragua* v. *Colombia)*, Preliminary Objections, Judgment, 13 December 2007, ICJ Reports (2007), 832.

82 *Ibid.*, 861, para. 90.

83 *Territorial and Maritime Dispute (Nicaragua* v. *Colombia)*, Merits, Judgment, 19 November 2012, ICJ Reports (2012).

Roncador, Serrana, Serranilla and Bajo Nuevo islands and one feature (QS 32) on Quitasueño were capable of appropriation.[84] It then considered the effect of the 1928 Barcenas-Esguerra Treaty and the *uti possidetis juris* principle invoked by the two parties as sources of their title.[85]

Article 1 of the 1928 Treaty provided:

> The Republic of Colombia recognises the full and entire sovereignty of the Republic of Nicaragua over the Mosquito Coast between Cape Gracias a Dios and the San Juan River, and over Mangle Grande and Mangle Chico Islands in the Atlantic Ocean (Great Corn Island and Little Corn Island). The Republic of Nicaragua recognises the full and entire sovereignty of the Republic of Colombia over the islands of San Andrés, Providencia and Santa Catalina and over the other islands, islets and reefs forming part of the San Andrés Archipelago.

The Court was therefore compelled to first establish what constituted the San Andrés Archipelago. Unable to make a precise determination on the basis of the geographical location of the maritime features in dispute or on the historical records relating to the composition of the San Andrés Archipelago referred to by the parties,[86] the Court turned to the second basis of sovereignty invoked by Nicaragua and Colombia in the course of their pleadings: *uti possidetis juris at the time of independence from Spain.*

Nicaragua claimed that the Captaincy-General of Guatemala (to which Nicaragua was a successor State) held jurisdiction over the disputed islands on the basis of the Royal Decree of 28 June 1568, confirmed in 1680 by Law VI, Title XV, Book II of the Compilation of the Indies, and later, the New Compilation of 1744, which signalled the limits of the *Audiencia de Guatemala* as including 'the islands adjacent to the coast'.[87] It contended that it held original and derivative rights of sovereignty over the Mosquito Coast and its appurtenant maritime features based on the *uti possidetis juris* at the moment of independence from Spain.[88] Although, as a result of the 1928 Treaty, it had ceded its sovereignty over the islands of Providencia, San Andrés and Santa Catalina, this did not affect sovereignty over the other maritime features appertaining to the Mosquito Coast.[89]

For its part, Colombia claimed that its sovereignty over the San Andrés Archipelago had its roots in the Royal Order of 1803, which

[84] *Ibid.*, 19, para. 27 and 22, para. 37.

[85] It should be noted that Colombia also invoked *effectivités* as a source of title over the maritime features in dispute.

[86] *Ibid.*, 25–6, para. 53. [87] *Ibid.*, 26, para. 58. [88] *Ibid.*, 27, para. 59. [89] *Ibid.*

placed the Archipelago under the jurisdiction of the Viceroyalty of Santa Fé (New Granada). Colombia therefore argued that it held original title over the San Andrés Archipelago based on the principle of *uti possidetis juris* supported by the effective administration of the Archipelago by the Viceroyalty of Santa Fé (New Granada) until the date of independence.[90]

The Court however was quick to point out that with regard to the claims of sovereignty asserted by both parties on the basis of the *uti possidetis juris* at the time of independence from Spain, 'none of the orders cited by either Party specifically mentions the maritime features in dispute'.[91] The Court then proceeded to quote paragraph 333 from its 1992 Judgment in the *Land, Island and Maritime Frontier Dispute* which, as we have seen, it also highlighted in its Nicaragua/Honduras decision:

> [W]hen the principle of the *uti possidetis juris* is involved, the *jus* referred to is not international law but the constitutional or administrative law of the pre-independence sovereign, in this case Spanish colonial law; and it is perfectly possible that that law itself gave no clear or definite answer to the appurtenance of marginal areas, or sparsely populated areas of minimal economic significance.[92]

In the light of this reality, the Court was compelled to admit that the *uti possidetis juris* principle was of precious little assistance in resolving the dispute between the parties:

> In light of the foregoing, the Court concludes that in the present case the principle of *uti possidetis juris* affords inadequate assistance in determining sovereignty over the maritime features in dispute between Nicaragua and Colombia because nothing clearly indicates whether these features were attributed to the colonial provinces of Nicaragua or of Colombia prior to or upon independence. The Court accordingly finds that neither Nicaragua nor Colombia has established that it had title to the disputed maritime features by virtue of *uti possidetis juris.*[93]

The Court ultimately awarded sovereignty over the disputed islands to Colombia on the basis of post-colonial *effectivités*: 'It has thus been established that for many decades Colombia continuously and consistently acted *à titre de souverain* in respect of the maritime features in dispute.'[94]

[90] *Ibid.*, 27, para. 60. [91] *Ibid.*, 28, para. 64.

[92] *Ibid.*, quoting *Land, Island and Maritime Frontier Dispute (El Salvador/Honduras: Nicaragua intervening)*, 559, para. 333.

[93] *Ibid.*, 28, para. 65. [94] *Ibid.*, 34, para. 84.

As for the determination of the single maritime boundary dividing the EEZs and continental shelves of the parties, the Court applied the three-part test it had developed in the *Black Sea* case.[95] Notwithstanding arguments by Nicaragua in favour of an alternative approach, the Court proceeded to draw a provisional median line, considered whether relevant circumstances militated in favour of an adjustment of that line, and finally tested the final result for any significant disproportionality.

C An assessment of the actual role of the colonial uti possidetis principle in the resolution of maritime boundary disputes

As a result of my review of relevant cases, it appears that, notwithstanding Judge Bedjaoui's compelling arguments in his dissenting opinion in the 1986 *Guinea Bissau/Senegal* case, international courts and arbitral tribunals have firmly established that '*uti possidetis juris* may, in principle, apply to offshore possession and maritime spaces'.[96] However, the precedents examined reveal the very real limitations of the *uti possidetis juris* principle. In fact, nearly all of the theoretical and practical difficulties which I identified in my thesis as hindering the effectiveness of *uti possidetis* for the determination of land boundaries between the former units of a single colonial power were also a factor in the maritime delimitations considered.

Certain theoretical uncertainties and contradictions continue to plague attempts to rely on the *uti possidetis juris* principle for the settlement of boundary disputes. For instance, in resolving the maritime dispute between Nicaragua and Colombia, the Court had first to establish a definitive meaning for the phrase '*uti possidetis juris* at the time of independence from Spain'. In the *Land, Island and Maritime Frontier Dispute*, despite recognising the '*uti possidetis of 1821* as the necessary starting-point for the determination of sovereignty over the disputed islands', the Chamber ruled that it had to take 'colonial *effectivités*' into account in reaching its decision. And yet, a consideration of actual and effective acts of possession is completely at odds with the task of establishing a formal right of

[95] *Maritime Delimitation in the Black Sea (Romania* v. *Ukraine)*, Judgment, 3 February 2009, ICJ Reports (2009), 61.

[96] *Land, Island and Maritime Frontier Dispute (El Salvador/Honduras: Nicaragua intervening)*, 558, para. 333 and 589, para. 386 and also *Territorial and Maritime Dispute between Nicaragua and Honduras in the Caribbean Sea (Nicaragua* v. *Honduras)*, 707, para. 156.

ownership between the parties on the basis of official colonial instruments. It is, in effect, to rely on effective occupation to determine sovereignty and therefore to espouse the *uti possidetis de facto* formula rather than the mainstream *uti possidetis juris* principle.

The principal conclusion however which flows from this brief analysis of the cases is that practical difficulties – incomplete knowledge, ambiguous historical records – continue to prevent the *uti possidetis juris* principle from exercising any real or effective influence on the determination of boundaries.

The lack of any allocation of maritime areas between the various colonial units in all of the cases examined, while not surprising, certainly highlights the limited impact the *uti possidetis* principle will likely have on the delimitation of maritime boundaries. Indeed, while the ICJ in the *Land, Island and Maritime Frontier Dispute* appears to have decided that the *uti possidetis juris* principle could determine the legal status of marine areas, displacing the traditional equidistant-special circumstances method and its recent adjunct, the proportionality test, the absence of pre-existing colonial lines at sea makes this little more than an interesting theoretical possibility.

The strongest confirmation of my earlier conclusions is provided by the cases when sovereignty over islands was at issue. Even in this supporting role, as a key mechanism for the determination of ownership of insular features capable of generating substantial maritime claims, the *uti possidetis juris* principle had little or no influence. Indeed, despite ringing endorsements of the principle as in the *Nicaragua/Honduras* case – 'the principle of *uti possidetis* has kept its place among the most important legal principles regarding ... boundary delimitation' – in practical terms, *uti possidetis* proved of little assistance to the courts and tribunals tasked with the peaceful settlement of the boundary disputes examined.

As McEwen notes: '[A] doctrine which attempts to crystallize, or maintain the *status quo* of, boundaries is little more than an abstract proposition unless there is a factual and tangible identification of the boundaries themselves.'[97] Therefore, and despite claims to the contrary, it appears fairly obvious that, in fact, *uti possidetis* as a means of establishing maritime boundaries has had and is likely to continue to have less than stellar success. Moore's assessment of the *uti possidetis* principle's influence remains as true today as when he wrote his influential article in 1944:

[97] McEwen, *International Boundaries of East Africa*, 28.

'It has not been so constantly invoked nor has its practical effect been by any means so important as writers and learned advocates have sometimes asserted.'[98]

[98] John Bassett Moore, 'Memorandum on *Uti Possidetis*: Costa Rica–Panama Arbitration 1911' in *The Collected Papers of John Bassett Moore*, 7 vols. (New Haven: Yale University Press, 1944), III, 344.

15

Room for 'State continuity' in international law? A constitutionalist perspective

INETA ZIEMELE

I am grateful to the editors for their idea and initiative to mark Professor Crawford's contribution to the discipline of international law in a book written by his former doctoral students. Crawford's analysis of the notions of State continuity and State succession was of particular importance for Estonia, Latvia and Lithuania when, following the demise of the USSR, they were formulating their claims to State continuity in view of the unlawful occupation of their territories by the Soviet Union since 1940. A book honouring James Crawford should carry an analysis of the notion of State continuity, which is therefore the purpose of this chapter.

Overview of reasons for scepticism over a distinction between State continuity and State succession

Professor Crawford has argued that international law:

> embodies a fundamental distinction between State continuity and State succession: that is to say, between cases where the 'same' State can be said to continue to exist despite sometimes drastic changes in its government, its territory or its people and cases where one State has replaced another with respect to a certain territory and people. The law of State succession is predicated on this distinction.[1]

Crawford recognises that the notion of 'State continuity' has been criticised by many scholars as a misleading and overly political concept. Ian Brownlie pointed out that 'the assumption of a neat distinction between categories of "continuity" and "state succession" only make a difficult

[1] See James Crawford, *The Creation of States in International Law*, 2nd edn (Oxford: Clarendon Press, 2006), 667–8.

subject more confused'.[2] Matthew Craven offers an insightful analysis of the critique of the distinction between continuity and succession, which had been already voiced by Professor O'Connell and later continued by Professor Schachter and others, observing and analysing the processes in Central and Eastern Europe at the beginning of the 1990s. This critique focused on the difficulty of placing legal personality in the centre of the distinction between continuity and succession.[3] Craven sums it up:

> If personality connoted nothing more than an undifferentiated 'legal capacity' it could not usefully be employed as a means of determining what rights and obligations a State might have as a consequence of a change in sovereignty, nor as a way of usefully separating the doctrine of succession from other forms of argument about legal change.[4]

I have argued elsewhere that a general category of 'legal personality' is not really helpful when dealing with specific questions that arise in relation to statehood and changes that might affect it. It is, in fact, not a function of 'legal personality'.[5] Legal personality demonstrates the recognition of a particular legal system and means that, in principle, the entity concerned has rights and obligations. It certainly does not point to differences that might distinguish one legal person from another in the sense of being useful for the purposes of separating cases of State succession and State continuity. This is the reason why Crawford proposed to distinguish between a 'general' concept of legal personality and a 'specific' concept of legal personality,[6] whereby the latter characterises a particular subject of law. Be that as it may, inquiry into the question of whether the State is the 'same' State does not raise the question whether it is the same legal personality, because irrespective of whether it is 'new' or 'old', the State as such has legal personality. Therefore the search into the 'new' or 'old' personality should be approached differently. According to Crawford this

2 See Ian Brownlie, *Principles of Public International Law*, 6th edn (Oxford University Press, 2003), 80. See also Martti Koskenniemi, 'Report of the Director of Studies of the English-speaking Section of the Centre' in Pierre M. Eisemann and Martti Koskenniemi (eds.), *La Succession d'états: la codification á l'éprouve des facts/State Succession: Codification Tested against the Facts* (The Hague: Martinus Nijhoff, 2000); Konrad Bühler, *State Succession and Membership in International Organizations: Legal Theories versus Political Pragmatism* (The Hague: Kluwer Law International, 2001).

3 See Matthew Craven, *The Decolonization of International Law: State Succession and the Law of Treaties* (Oxford: Clarendon Press, 2007), 216 *et seq.*

4 *Ibid.*

5 See Ineta Ziemele, *State Continuity and Nationality: The Baltic States and Russia* (Leiden: Martinus Nijhoff, 2005), 97–8.

6 Crawford, *The Creation of States in International Law*, 30.

essentially depends upon the view one takes of the role that international law plays concerning the creation of States. Legal personality is neither a solution to nor a problem for the questions of creation and change.

For Crawford, 'the determination of identity and continuity [is] dependent on the basic criteria for statehood. A State may be said to continue as such so long as an identified polity exists with respect to a significant part of a given territory and people.'[7] Thus Crawford clearly moved the debate from a legal personality paradigm, as understood by O'Connell, to an examination of the elements of statehood within the legal system. This fundamental shift entails ramifications and consequences which have not been fully explored. For example, the International Court of Justice in its Advisory Opinion on *Accordance with International Law of the Unilateral Declaration of Independence in Respect of Kosovo* did not engage in a broader analysis of the issues relevant to the question whether or not an independent State had been created in compliance with the relevant international law criteria of statehood.[8] For the purposes of this chapter, the practical follow-up to Crawford's theory of statehood will not be examined.[9] The aim of this chapter is to develop further a few aspects relating to his theory. I will adapt the thesis that the creation of States is not merely a matter of fact situated outside the realm of international law.[10] Like Crawford I take an opposite view. Where decisions on statehood are taken within the international legal system, it should be possible to determine the changes affecting States and raising questions as to their continuity by reference to, at least, some rules of international law.

To put it differently, one could say that there has always been a certain tension between what could be called private law and public law approaches to changes affecting States. According to the first approach, it is important that there is a legal entity upholding, inheriting or succeeding to the existing obligations, even if it is a different or new subject, since it is legal certainty that matters. According to the latter, the very

7 *Ibid.*, 671.

8 See *Accordance with International Law of the Unilateral Declaration of Independence in Respect of Kosovo*, Advisory Opinion, 22 July 2010, ICJ Reports (2010). Also Anne Peters, 'Statehood after 1989: "Effectivités" between Legality and Virtuality' in James Crawford and Sarah Nouwen (eds.), *Select Proceedings of the European Society of International Law III* (Oxford: Hart, 2010), 182–3.

9 Crawford relies on such authorities as Verzijl, Marek, etc., *The Creation of States in International Law*, 255.

10 E.g. a classical Anglo-Saxon approach to the creation of States is summed up by Brierly: 'Whether or not a new state has actually begun to exist is a pure question of fact.' See Andrew Clapham, *Brierly's Law of Nations*, 7th edn (Oxford University Press, 2012), 149.

existence of the 'same' subject, referring inter alia to the self-identification of the historical community, is of primary importance and the continuity or discontinuity of rights and obligations normally follow therefrom. As Crawford said: 'The rights are better referred to the entity than the entity to the rights.'[11] Certainly, where no change has taken place no difficulties as to legal certainty should arise since it is presumed that the same State will continue the same international obligations or, at least, as in the case of the Baltic States, this will be a presumption on the basis of which to develop new legal obligations.[12]

For the purposes of this chapter, the relevance of what could be broadly defined as a private *versus* public law divide in conceptualising State continuity in international law will be explored. I argue that James Crawford's view in *The Creation of States* appears to take a constitutionalist reading of the subject of the creation and disappearance of States. I would add that a constitutionalist reading sits more comfortably with the fact that rules such as the prohibition of the use of force and the right to self-determination may have an important impact on claims of statehood or State continuity, or State succession, as seen, for example, during the decolonisation process.[13]

The dissolution of States in Central and Eastern Europe in the early 1990s, while in many ways different from the decolonisation process, reaffirmed the importance of the question of identity of a 'new State', and not only in the case of the Baltic States.[14] With the benefit of hindsight, in view of the manner in which new democracies in Central and Eastern Europe have been able to deal with the challenges that they faced following the political change, a proposition emerges that relevant traditions and a clear identity of a particular polity are extremely important for a more successful functioning of that polity as a State. While the claim to identity in the 1990s of the Baltic States unlawfully occupied by the Soviet Union in 1940 was first and foremost a reaction based on a strong sense that the three States and the peoples concerned suffered from one of the most serious violations of international law, there was also another level of thinking which had to do with the need to go back to the origins

[11] Crawford, *The Creation of States in International Law*, 670.

[12] Ziemele, *State Continuity and Nationality*, 77–82.

[13] See Peters, 'Statehood after 1989', 175. More precisely Crawford's thinking would fit within the constitutionalist pluralist approach; see J. L. Cohen, 'Sovereignty in the Context of Globalization: A Constitutional Pluralist Perspective' in Samantha Besson and John Tasioulas (eds.), *The Philosophy of International Law* (Oxford University Press, 2010), 273.

[14] For a different view, see Craven, *The Decolonization of International Law*, 264–6.

or the original identity of these States. This explains the return to the pre-occupation with Constitutions and institutional settings within the States.[15] The steps undertaken to reunite with the historical origins of these States have proved to be the strength of the modern Baltic States as compared, perhaps, with the State-building processes in the neighbouring countries. Apart from the example of the Baltic States, all the cases of continuity or succession claims in Central and Eastern Europe are valuable examples for studying whether identity issues are important or not in the context of such claims. There is clearly a basis for suggesting that in situations which, like the decolonisation processes or the Baltic cases, derive from unlawfulness or injustice in international law, questions of identity are highly pertinent. It cannot be said that they lose their relevance in other more classical situations of State succession. In fact, the reunification of Germany and the creation of new States in the territory of the former Yugoslavia underline the importance of identity, which was both a motivating factor and the basis of often serious disputes.

Why is there a difference in the appreciation of the importance of the identity question in scholarly writings on State succession and State continuity? What is the possible ideological or theoretical divide?

Private law reading of State continuity

The wisdom and practicability of distinguishing between State continuity and State succession was strongly criticised in the 1960s by O'Connell who 'complained that legal doctrine on succession had been derailed by the predominance of Hegelian conceptions of the State, which, from the time of Bluntschli onwards, had placed the issue of identity at the forefront'.[16] In O'Connell's view the question should be whether existing obligations survive the change, and he considered that the nature and degree of change should be examined with a view to preserving obligations. To put it differently, he was persuaded that a minimal disturbance of existing legal situations is in the greater interest of humanity and that such an approach is consistent with the very nature of law.[17] Craven has summed up the essence of O'Connell's conviction as follows: 'Legal continuity thus preceded sovereignty, and sovereignty could only thus

[15] See Ziemele, *State Continuity and Nationality*, ch. 3; see also Yaël Ronen, *Transition from Illegal Regimes under International Law* (Cambridge University Press, 2011), 170–1.

[16] See Craven, *The Decolonization of International Law*, 75.

[17] On this and further explanations, see *ibid.*, 85 *et seq.*

mean a competence or right of decision in relation to the array of legal relations that were already in place.'[18]

One can indeed agree with O'Connell that succession does not take place in a legal vacuum and that a proper legal system certainly contains guidance as to the nature of change and the consequences. For the purposes of international law as a system, O'Connell's views have a considerable importance. It has to be noted, however, that O'Connell only refers to legal relations that are in place, and not the rules or criteria that may determine the subject of these relations. It has to be observed further that the criticism that O'Connell addresses to the central role given to liberty and sovereignty of States in international law follows the traditional critique mounted earlier in the British international law scholarship of Hersch Lauterpacht and James Brierly. Lauterpacht also argued in his *Private Law Sources and Analogies of International Law* that States should be kept to the same standards of behaviour as individuals, but that the Hegelian conception as concerns the status of a State as it had evolved in international law was the main barrier to such a development. Lauterpacht pointed out that:

> it will serve no useful purpose to deny that the modern science of international law follows closely the Hegelian conception of State and sovereignty. Accordingly, it will not be found surprising that its expounders did not view with sympathy any larger reception of private law. For private law suggests subordination to an objective rule.[19]

Lauterpacht's main argument was that even where States have not consented to some international rules, international law should nevertheless be applied by international judges since there are no gaps in the legal system.[20] In other words, there was at the time a very strong view, especially among the British and American schools of international law, that the concept of State sovereignty, as it had emerged following Emer de Vattel's *Droit de gens*, was highly problematic for the purposes of the proper development of an international legal system with autonomous rules binding States irrespective of their consent.[21] Scholars were

[18] *Ibid.*, 86.

[19] See Anthony Carty, 'Hersch Lauterpacht: A Powerful Eastern European Figure in International Law', *Baltic Yearbook of International Law*, 7 (2007), 93, 101.

[20] See Elihu Lauterpacht, *The Life of Hersch Lauterpacht* (Cambridge University Press, 2010), 56.

[21] For an excellent overview of the slow but progressive development of international law as a legal system and its basic concepts, see Emmanuelle Jouannet, *Le Droit international liberal-providence: une histoire du droit international* (Bruxelles: Bruylant, 2011).

dealing with this challenge in different ways, one of which was that of Hersch Lauterpacht, bringing back to the discourse State practice and private law analogies to show the effect of rules limiting States. O'Connell's view on change of sovereignty and international obligations falls clearly within this broader disagreement on the nature of international law as an autonomous legal system. Ever since, scholars have been bound to examine the notions of continuity and succession and to provide their views on the possibility and practicability of a definition in this respect; the differences of view have persisted depending on what theoretical or philosophical outlook one took on international law at large.

The question nevertheless remains whether the critique directed towards the role attributed to a State and the principles of State sovereignty and consent in international law, as introduced above, is fully justified.

Constitutionalist reading of State continuity

There are scholars who take a different view and State practice shows that one cannot completely ignore the issue of identity, which remains important for the political realities of the communities concerned.[22] It has been stated that:

> State sovereignty is valuable in international law and international relations for (at least) three interrelated reasons. First, it is part of a just answer to the question of personhood in international law (because it offers a technique for the people of any territory to participate in international relations in a way that is regulated and facilitated by international law). Secondly, state sovereignty is valuable in so far as there is value in national self-determination (the capacity of a nation to make decisions – good or bad – (within limits) for itself). Thirdly, the very substantial independence involved in state sovereignty is valuable.[23]

It was pointed out earlier in this chapter that, while having legal certainty in relations between the subjects of a legal system is an important value in itself, in a system where States as the main subjects of law are made up of individuals forming a community or a polity with a distinct sense of identity, sovereignty acquired through self-determination is also an important value. This is not limited to the decolonisation process. While the approach to State continuity and State succession as per a private law

22 See Carty, 'Hersch Lauterpacht', 77 (with reference to Koskenniemi's analysis).

23 See Timothy Endicott, 'The Logic of Freedom and Power' in Samantha Besson and John Tasioulas (eds.), *The Philosophy of International Law* (Oxford University Press, 2010), 255.

or even natural law reading would not address the nature of change in sovereignty as part of the analysis, the constitutionalist reading, I submit, is capable of and indeed requires such an analysis since 'sovereignty protects moral values and has normative value itself'.[24]

Anne Peters builds on Crawford's theory and underlines that '[f]rom a constitutionalist perspective . . . states – as international legal subjects – are constituted by international law'.[25] This is indeed the value of the proposition that international law contains certain criteria and rules that, if applied, are capable of leading to the determination of the existence of a State. In this regard, Peters observes that the fundamental requirement of effectiveness governing the definition of statehood for a long time has 'suffered some modifications'.[26] 'One discernible aspect of the constitutionalization of statehood is that the principle of effectiveness has been complemented and to some extent even substituted by the principle of international legality and legitimacy in international recognition practice.'[27] The dismemberment of the Socialist Federal Republic of Yugoslavia is likely to be the most striking example of modern State practice where Serbia was not given the 'legal and moral advantage' that would stem from the acceptance of its claim to State continuity in view of the particularly grave humanitarian situation that it created.[28]

It is certainly true that the post-1945 period has seen the growing role of rules of international law, such as the prohibition of the use of force and the prohibition of apartheid, which have prevented *de facto* effectiveness from acquiring expected legitimacy and legal consequences in international law. We have also seen the effect of these rules as concerns claims to State continuity or succession in the above-mentioned case of the Baltic States. These are processes and developments which give reason to argue in favour of the constitutionalisation of international law and thus a constitutional reading of the concept of State and related issues such as effects of changes in sovereignty. James Crawford argued in favour of

24 See Cohen, 'Sovereignty in the Context of Globalization', 279.

25 See Anne Peters, 'Membership in the Global Constitutional Community' in Jan Klabbers, Anne Peters and Geir Ulfstein (eds.), *The Constitutionalization of International Law* (Oxford University Press, 2009), 179.

26 *Ibid.*, 180. 27 *Ibid.*, 181.

28 Crawford, *The Creation of States in International Law*, 714. See also Ineta Ziemele, 'Is the Distinction between State Continuity and State Succession Reality or Fiction? The Russian Federation, the Federal Republic of Yugoslavia and Germany', *Baltic Yearbook of International Law*, 1 (2001), 208.

'a certain peremptory authority' of modern international law[29] in matters eminently political such as the creation of States a couple of decades before the fall of the Berlin wall.

However, apart from the debate on the effect of international rules on decisions relevant to the creation of States and their disappearance, I would argue that a constitutionalist reading of international law suggests at least a slightly different analysis of the distinction between State succession and State continuity since, as explained, the constitutionalisation perspective helps 'the right questions of fairness, justice, and effectiveness to be asked'.[30] Evidently, if the primary concern is the continuity of international obligations as per the private law paradigm, introduced earlier, some of the questions of justice are not always particularly helpful. Indeed most of the debate about the distinction between State succession and State continuity has focused on difficulties that continuity claims raise in terms of their extremely diverse character which, for example, gave ground to significant concern in Europe in the 1990s.[31] Craven correctly notes that for reasons of presumed difference from the decolonisation era and based on the understanding that international law itself does not require any dramatic change, the presumption of treaty continuity emerged as an appropriate policy response to the uncertainties of that time. He admits, however, that it would have been too radical to fully embrace O'Connell's position since differentiation between various categories 'of succession' could not be easily dismissed.[32] His summary of the main view of the events in Eastern and Central Europe in the 1990s is perfectly correct and goes as follows:

> So for those who were busy advocating the necessity of legal continuity in the turbulent changes that had enveloped Europe, there was also a sense that O'Connell's prescription really demanded too much. Change was also required, but it came in the form not of a law of succession as such, but in an apparently prior deliberation as to status.[33]

If it is accepted that international law constitutes States, it should also follow that it determines the character of changes affecting States, or at least

[29] E.g., Crawford's argument on the peremptory character of the prohibition of use of force and the effects of that in the Baltic cases, *The Creation of States in International Law*, 704.

[30] Peters, 'Conclusions' in 'Membership in the Global Constitutional Community', 344. For a particularly useful insight into the understanding of international law and processes within the constitutionalism discourse, see also Cohen, 'Sovereignty in the Context of Globalization', 278.

[31] Craven, *The Decolonization of International Law*, 228–9.

[32] *Ibid.*, 258. [33] *Ibid.*

contains a number of elements for such purposes. If one agrees with this proposition in principle, one needs to determine its meaning and importance. I think it is relevant to make a point with regard to the decolonisation era and contemporary challenges posed by it to international law. It should be recalled that in the decolonisation period of the 1960s and 1970s, the manner in which succession issues were addressed represented an attempt to depart from international law's colonial past.[34] The vindication of the principle of 'clean slate' in the Vienna Conventions on State Succession,[35] even if recognising a number of limitations, was seen as a proper functioning of self-determination and the sovereign equality of States, as reflected in the UN Charter.[36] Admittedly, this approach was seen as rather troubling to those advocating a more autonomous character for international law.

It is therefore no surprise that the majority of commentators on the events in the 1990s were engaged in a search for arguments that would support the least possible disruption in legal relations. Matthew Craven notes in this regard that '[a]ll were agreed that the "new events" were profoundly different from the past, and the sense of contestation that had underpinned discussions during decolonisation was almost entirely absent'.[37] It may well be that there was less contestation, or that at least it was different in nature as compared to the decolonisation era. Nevertheless, and as noted above, the need for change was clearly present in the 1990s and was recognised even if it was approached with great caution. The reasons might be very different but among them there was thinking similar to that present during the decolonisation process among the powerful States for whom legal certainty clearly was more important. The need for change in the 1990s too was in line with the principle of sovereign equality, which in its internal perspective means that the domestic legal order is supreme and determines the compatibility of external decisions with this order. This takes place, however, within the context of a growing constitutional quality of the international legal order.[38] It is

[34] See Anthony Anghie, 'The Evolution of International Law: Colonial and Postcolonial Realities', *Third World Quarterly*, 27 (2006), 739.

[35] See Vienna Convention on Succession of States in Respect of Treaties (Vienna, adopted 23 August 1978, entered into force 6 November 1996), reproduced in *International Legal Materials*, 17 (1978), 1488; Vienna Convention on Succession of States in Respect of State Property Archives and Debts (Vienna, adopted 8 April 1983, not yet in force), *International Legal Materials*, 22 (1983), 306.

[36] See Craven, *The Decolonization of International Law*, 263. [37] *Ibid.*, 264.

[38] See Cohen, 'Sovereignty in the Context of Globalization', 273–4.

therefore the case that the acceptance of the changes in statehood that do take place, and that may have consequences for the rights and obligations of the State concerned, does not automatically bring about a dramatic disruption in legal relations. The examination of, and decisions on, status belong to a constitutionalist perspective in international law, as does the process leading to a better identification of applicable rules to consequences of change. One does not conflict with the other. This brings me to some concluding remarks.

Conclusions

James Crawford offers three main reasons for the usefulness of the concept of continuity in international law. In short, they are as follows: first, continuity of a State presumes the continuity of its obligations certainly to a greater extent than in situations of State succession; secondly, there is usually a close relationship between the claim of continuity and the peoples' self-determination or self-awareness; and, thirdly, the issue of continuity or 'sameness' does not arise in general but only in relation to a specific legal question.[39]

These reasons continue to be perfectly valid and are reinforced by the previous analysis. On a more general level, I agree with Jean L. Cohen that it is not a feasible Utopia to abandon sovereignty in favour of a cosmopolitan world view and that sovereignty has a special role in protecting domestic democratic processes with global implications.[40] Within the constitutionalist pluralist vision, decisions on status in situations raising questions as to State continuity or State succession are very important since they are linked to internal processes taking place within a particular community. This does not mean that rules should not be further developed and changed at an international level, imposing greater responsibility and accountability on States and other international actors.[41] This is equally necessary in situations where such events arise that are likely to affect States and raise questions as to their identity and continuity. In other words, I would submit that if one takes a constitutionalist perspective on international law, including with respect to questions of State continuity and State succession, the confrontation between the views surveyed above is beside the point and in fact each view can have its valid

[39] Crawford, *The Creation of States in International Law*, 668.

[40] Cohen, 'Sovereignty in the Context of Globalization', 279.

[41] *Ibid.*, 278.

place in the constitutionalist debate. The notion of State continuity has its legitimate place within the international legal order since it provides the means for accepting valid and lawful claims of the community concerned and responds to important self-determination and self-awareness processes.

PART III

State responsibility

16

Law-making in complex processes

The World Court and the modern law of State responsibility

CHRISTIAN J. TAMS*

1 Introduction

State responsibility and the International Court of Justice (ICJ) have dominated much of James Crawford's activity during the last two decades. This chapter addresses a question situated at the intersection of these two themes: it evaluates the ICJ's (as well as the Permanent Court of International Justice's (PCIJ)) influence on the law of responsibility and asks to what extent has the current law of responsibility been shaped (or even 'made') by pronouncements of these two 'World Courts'? What has been the relative impact of ICJ and PCIJ – compared to other 'agencies of legal development',[1] and compared to their role in other fields of international law?[2] These are the two questions on which this chapter seeks to shed some light. As the topic is huge, the treatment is broad-brush rather than nuanced. But as much of our current debate about responsibility is perhaps too granular, it may be defensible to step back and offer some reflections 'from a distance'.

* This chapter, focusing on general questions of State responsibility, was completed before the publication of James Crawford's latest publication on the subject matter. See James Crawford, *State Responsibility: The General Part* (Cambridge University Press, 2013).

[1] The term is borrowed from Hersch Lauterpacht, *The Development of International Law by the International Court of Justice* (London: Stevens, 1958), ch. 1 ('The International Court as an Agency for Developing International Law'); and Hersch Lauterpacht, *The Development of International Law by the Permanent Court of International Justice* (London: Longmans Green and Company, 1934), 2.

[2] A recent attempt to provide a comparative account can be found in Christian J. Tams and James Sloan (eds.), *The Development of International Law by the International Court of Justice* (Oxford University Press, 2013).

The topic has been covered before, and there is no shortage of views. 'The law of responsibility has always been essentially judge-made', states Alain Pellet in a recent Festschrift contribution.[3] James Crawford admits a little more diversity; according to him, '[t]he rules of state responsibility have been derived from cases, from practice, and from often unarticulated instantiations of general legal ideas'.[4] And of course, though curiously missing from the two quotations, there is the United Nations International Law Commission (ILC), which rightly counts work on State responsibility among its major contributions to the codification and progressive development of international law. All these have contributed in some way to our understanding, and Patrick Daillier is no doubt right to emphasise the 'interdependence of the various sources of law in the complex process of the formulation of the law on international responsibility'.[5] But what are the respective roles played by the various 'sources' in the 'complex process', and where in particular has the PCIJ's and ICJ's jurisprudence made a difference? In order to address these questions, it is necessary to, first, demarcate the field of 'State responsibility' before tracing and assessing the two Courts' contributions to it.

2 State responsibility: three levels of normative decisions

The PCIJ's and ICJ's influence on the development of the law is best assessed by working backwards: by describing the status quo and then inquiring to what extent it can be traced back to judicial decisions. As the development of international law is no mechanical process, the assessment must always remain tentative, but influence can be gauged by analysing how judicial pronouncements have been received in the subsequent debate: have they become 'brigh[t] beacons' guiding arguments and widely referred to, or 'flicker[ed] and die[d] near-instant deaths'?[6]

[3] Alain Pellet, 'Some Remarks on the Recent Case Law of the International Court of Justice on Responsibility Issues' in Péter Kovács (ed.), *International Law: A Quiet Strength (Miscellanea in memoriam Géza Herczegh)* (Budapest: Pazmany Press, 2011), 112.

[4] James Crawford, 'The International Court of Justice and the Law of State Responsibility' in Christian J. Tams and James Sloan (eds.), *The Development of International Law by the International Court of Justice* (Oxford University Press, 2013), 81.

[5] Patrick Daillier, 'The Development of the Law of Responsibility through the Case Law' in James Crawford, Alain Pellet and Simon Olleson (eds.), *Handbook of International Responsibility* (Oxford University Press, 2010), 38.

[6] Jan Paulsson, 'International Arbitration and the Generation of Legal Norms: Treaty, Arbitration and International Law' in Albert Jan van den Berg (ed.), *ICCA Congress Series No. 13: International Arbitration 2006: Back to Basics?* (The Hague: Kluwer Law International, 2007), 879, 881.

In all that, it helps if the status quo can be identified with reasonable certainty, and in this respect, State responsibility offers distinct advantages. For although much detail remains disputed, most would consider the ILC's Articles on State Responsibility (ASR), adopted after second reading in 2001[7] and widely referred to in practice and jurisprudence, to be the obvious point of reference. If there exists, even only as a working hypothesis, an agreed status quo, then this is the result of an astonishingly successful exercise in clarifying international law through 'normative accretion': patient work towards consensus, based on the careful study of prior practice and jurisprudence (including that of PCIJ and ICJ), distilled by the Commission into general legal propositions and then affirmed or modified in a fairly inclusive and at times detailed debate. The ILC's text indeed (as James Crawford has observed) 'encode[s] the way in which we think about responsibility'[8] – but one needs to add that in 'encoding', the ILC has changed and shaped our thinking about the topic.[9] In fact, so completely have we internalised the ILC's approach that it has become quite a challenge to identify the choices made on the journey towards the ILC's 2001 text. If an attempt is made, perhaps our specific understanding of State responsibility could be described as the result of normative decisions on three levels:

(i) The *first*, most fundamental, decision concerns the concept of responsibility. Since the fundamental re-orientation of the early 1960s, responsibility has been posited as the key to debates about wrongfulness: a broad concept situated (as Philip Allott has put it) 'between illegality and liability'[10] and encompassing (in the ILC's words) 'the general conditions under international law for the State to be considered responsible for wrongful actions or omissions, and

[7] ILC Articles on Responsibility of States for Internationally Wrongful Acts, reproduced with commentaries in *ILC Yearbook*, 2(2) (2001), 26. (All future references to the ILC's text are to this source.)

[8] Crawford, 'The International Court of Justice and the Law of State Responsibility', 81.

[9] A quick glance at Ian Brownlie's *System of the Law of Nations: State Responsibility*, 1st edn (Oxford University Press, 1983) is sufficient to illustrate the point. Published barely three decades ago, the work – with its detailed exposition of causes of action, its focus on remedies and on protest etc. – feels very much 'out of sync' with contemporary understanding. The same is true for Philip Allott's 'State Responsibility and the Unmaking of International Law', *Harvard International Law Journal*, 29 (1988), 1 – notwithstanding his fantastic description of the ILC's approach ('generalizing about the effect of unlawful acts without talking too much about any particular wrongful acts', 7). Rereading these (and other) works is useful as it illustrates alternative approaches to responsibility. And at the same time, one appreciates how decisively international law has moved on.

[10] Allott, 'State Responsibility and the Unmaking of International Law', 6 (his footnote 18).

the legal consequences which flow therefrom'.[11] The concept is astonishingly ambitious in its scope of application (governing all forms of wrongfulness across the board, from 'minor breaches of a bilateral treaty... to the invasion of Belgium'[12]); and remarkable also in presuming that the international law of responsibility should be unitary, forgoing principled distinctions based on sources[13] or gravity.[14]

(ii) Key organising principles operationalising the broad notion of responsibility comprise the *second level* of normative decisions. They concern the substantive understanding of 'responsibility' as well as the ILC's delimitation between general aspects of the international regime (addressed in the ILC's text) and special rules. Among these organising principles, the following stand out:
- International responsibility is an objective concept (generally not dependent on fault or damage) and autonomous from domestic law. Responsibility is the result of conduct of persons/entities acting (or failing to act) for a State.
- Responsibility as a general concept covers forms of 'ancillary conduct' (notably complicity in the unlawful conduct of another State) as well as in a limited number of circumstances precluding the wrongfulness of conduct.

11 See para. 1 of the ILC's Introductory Commentary to the Articles on State Responsibility. Not expressly mentioned is the fact that the ASR should also set out modalities governing the invocation of responsibility. A remark by Rosalyn Higgins, made before the completion of even the first reading, captures the scope of the project very well: 'One can now begin to see why a topic that should on the face of it take one summer's work has taken forty years. It has been interpreted to cover not only issues of attributability to the state, but also the entire substantive law of obligations, and the entirety of international law relating to compensation'; see Rosalyn Higgins, *Problems and Process: International Law and How We Use It* (Oxford University Press, 1995), 148.

12 Crawford, 'The International Court of Justice and the Law of State Responsibility', 76.

13 See commentary to Art. 12 ASR, para. 5: 'there is no room in international law for a distinction, such as is drawn by some legal systems, between the regime of responsibility for breach of a treaty and for breach of some other rule, i.e. for responsibility arising *ex contractu* or *ex delicto*'.

14 See Part II, Chapter 3 (comprising Arts. 40, 41 ASR) for the ILC's attempt to rescue some form of 'special regime' for particularly egregious breaches. As the introductory commentary to that chapter (para. 7) makes clear, the chapter spells out certain special consequences, without reflecting a categorical distinction between 'classes' of breaches. This is in contrast to the Commission's initial scheme which – in draft Art. 19 of the first reading text – had divided wrongful conduct into two classes, viz. 'crimes' and 'delicts'. The appropriateness and usefulness of that categorical distinction have been much discussed: for a summary see James Crawford, *The International Law Commission's Articles on State Responsibility* (Cambridge University Press, 2002), Introduction, 16–20.

- Wrongful conduct gives rise to general duties of cessation and reparation (as 'the new legal relations that arise from the commission . . . of an internationally wrongful act'[15]) which seek to ensure a return to lawfulness and a re-establishment of the situation affected by the breach. Any attempt to enforce these duties must comply with certain general conditions governing the invocation of responsibility (the establishment of a 'title' to respond; prior notification, etc.).
- While applying to wrongful conduct across the board (irrespective of the nature of the 'victim'), the general law of responsibility only covers consequences of wrongfulness, and modalities of invocation, as between States.

(iii) Specific rules spelling out these organising principles make up the *third level* of normative decisions determining the current regime of State responsibility. This third level is typically reflected in the specific provisions of the ILC's text which give concrete meaning to the 'second level' principles. This is done, for example, by listing grounds of attribution[16] and circumstances precluding wrongfulness,[17] by formulating forms of reparation,[18] by spelling out the potential 'titles' permitting a State to invoke another State's responsibility[19] and so on. Many of these specific rules existed long before the ILC began its work on responsibility, but it is within that framework that we now perceive them.

3 Shaping the modern law of State responsibility

Even from this briefest, and no doubt schematic, sketch, it is clear that the making of the modern law of responsibility was a 'complex process'[20] involving different actors, and different levels of co-ordination. The subsequent sections trace the different roles played by the PCIJ and the ICJ, distinguishing between the different levels of decisions outlined above. However, before assessing the influence of the PCIJ and ICJ, it seems important to note that not all aspects of the contemporary regime of responsibility are 'essentially judge-made'.[21]

15 ASR, Introductory commentary, para. 3(f).

16 Arts. 4–11 ASR. 17 Arts. 20–7 ASR.

18 Arts. 31–9 ASR, as well as (for the special consequences triggered by serious breaches of *jus cogens* norms) Arts. 40–1.

19 See Arts. 42 and 48 ASR.

20 Daillier, 'The Development of the Law of Responsibility through the Case Law'.

21 *Cf.* above n. 2.

(a) The ILC's 'master plan'.

While the PCIJ and ICJ were influential in shaping general principles of responsibility and specific rules implementing them (the second and third levels of normative decisions mentioned in the preceding section), it is important to note that the conceptual decision to think of responsibility as an overarching category comprising the general conditions for, and consequences flowing from, wrongful conduct was taken by the ILC. Unlike other changes of direction in the law, the crucial decision can indeed be traced with relative precision: in 1963, having failed to agree on a regime of State responsibility for injuries to aliens, the Commission decided to change tack – in a rare attempt to bring a project 'back to life'[22] by moving from the specific to the general/abstract. After some debate, a subcommittee was set up to study ways of rescuing the Commission's work on the topic proposed to 'give priority to the codification of general rules governing the international responsibility of States'.[23] In retrospect, it seems clear that on the journey towards the current law of responsibility, this was the decisive fork in the road, and the Commission's subsequent endorsement of the subcommittee's recommendation – and its appointment of Roberto Ago, the key figure in the subcommittee's deliberations, as Special Rapporteur – was to change the legal landscape. For it was in the Commission's engagement with Ago's reports that, for better or worse, the contemporary notion of responsibility took shape, was 'encoded'.[24] And while many of the specific rules (level 3) and some of the organising principles (level 2) would be revisited at a later stage, the strategic decision to understand responsibility as the crucial concept 'between illegality and liability'[25] would stand. In that respect, developments since the early 1960s have followed the ILC's 'master plan'.

(b) Foundational decisions by the PCIJ

But of course, the Commission did not decide out of the blue to embark on its most ambitious codification project. In its subcommittee, the view

[22] Allott, 'State Responsibility and the Unmaking of International Law', 7. In James Crawford's words, 'Ago recognised that propositions about state responsibility would, curiously, be more stable than substantive rules, which are liable to change' in Christian J. Tams and James Sloan (eds.), *The Development of International Law by the International Court of Justice* (Oxford University Press, 2013), 6.

[23] As summarised in Roberto Ago, 'First Report on State Responsibility', *ILC Yearbook*, 2 (1969), 125, 139. The subcommittee's deliberations, summarised by Roberto Ago, and the working papers submitted to it, are reproduced in *ILC Yearbook*, 2 (1963), 227.

[24] See above n. 8.

[25] Allott, 'State Responsibility and the Unmaking of International Law', 6 (his footnote 18).

prevailed that responsibility could be approached from a general angle as questions of attribution, or consequences, were governed by common principles. Trying to persuade the ILC subcommittee to move away from the study of responsibility in particular areas (such as the treatment of aliens), Mustafa Kamil Yasseen suggested that 'the first step must be to define the general theory of responsibility. *That theory exists.*'[26] Not everyone agreed at the time; hence the continued attraction of 'going (or staying) sectoral'.[27] But Yasseen's view – that '[a general theory of responsibility] exists' and awaits codification, which the subcommittee adopted – certainly seemed plausible. In fact, with the benefit of hindsight, one wonders why it took so long to emerge: the trees were there; it was time to think of the forest.

In distilling general principles of responsibility (from which a 'general theory' could be deduced), the Permanent Court was highly influential. Alongside scholarship[28] and diplomatic and arbitral practice, its jurisprudence had established a number of fundamental propositions, on which the codification effort (embarked upon in the 1960s) would draw. Three of them stand out:

First, a string of PCIJ decisions had affirmed the autonomy of international responsibility from domestic laws. In fact, it may well be the principle most frequently affirmed by the Permanent Court. This is true for its two 'variations': (i) violations of constitutional law do not render conduct *internationally* wrongful;[29] and (ii) compliance with domestic

[26] Working Paper, reproduced in *ILC Yearbook*, 2 (1963), 251. The statement continued: '[C]ertain principles have a general scope transcending the particular case [i.e. field, CJT] of responsibility to which they are applied. State responsibility should therefore be considered as a whole.'

[27] In the subcommittee, this approach was, for example, favoured by Jiménez de Aréchaga and Modesto Paredes: see their working papers, reproduced in *ILC Yearbook*, 2 (1963), 237 and 244.

[28] In an annex to his working paper submitted in 1963 (*ILC Yearbook*, 2 (1963), 254), Ago listed a wealth of relevant works. Yet as Brownlie, *System of the Law of Nations: State Responsibility I*, 7 and 8, notes, much of the literature did not discuss State responsibility as a general concept: '[m]uch of the literature of the nineteenth century continued to ignore the issues of responsibility of states as such', whereas literature in the 'formative period (1898–1930) was varied' and focused on special issues, notably injury to aliens. As Brownlie goes on to note, some of the twentieth-century classics of British scholarship like Brierly's *Law of Nations* 'contain[ed] no discussion of state responsibility as a category' (*System of the Law of Nations: State Responsibility I*, 2) (which remains true for the most recent edition prepared by Clapham). One should add that where State responsibility was discussed as a category, the treatment often remained focused on injuries to aliens.

[29] *Treatment of Polish Nationals and Other Persons of Polish Origin or Speech in the Danzig Territory*, Advisory Opinion, 4 February 1932, PCIJ, Series A/B, No. 44, 24–5; *SS Lotus (France* v. *Turkey)*, Judgment No. 9, 7 September 1927, PCIJ, Series A, No. 10, 24.

law cannot justify violations of international law.[30] As regards the latter, more important, variation, the judgment in the *Polish Nationals* case contains the quintessential formulation; in it, the PCIJ affirmed that 'a State cannot adduce as against another State its own Constitution with a view to evading obligations incumbent upon it under international law or treaties in force'.[31] Seventy years later, that principle would be affirmed, with due reference to the PCIJ's formative jurisprudence, in Article 3 of the ILC's text.[32]

Secondly, the PCIJ's jurisprudence could be read to foreshadow the emergence of responsibility as a separate notion 'between illegality and liability' – a notion the relevance of which failed to convince Allott.[33] In *Phosphates in Morocco*, the Court referred to attribution and illegality as the two key conditions[34] and noted that where these conditions were met, 'international responsibility would be established immediately as between the two States'.[35] While this paved the way for appreciating responsibility as a notion combining conditions for, and consequences of, wrongfulness, the reference to 'two States' betrayed a bilateralist mindset[36] that

[30] In addition to the statement made in *Polish Nations* (referred to in the next footnote) see e.g. *SS 'Wimbledon' (United Kingdom* v. *Germany)*, Judgment, 17 August 1923, PCIJ, Series A, No. 1, 29–30; *Greco-Bulgarian 'Communities'*, Advisory Opinion, 31 August 1930, PCIJ, Series B, No. 17, 32; *Free Zones of Upper Savoy and the District of Gex*, Judgment, 7 June 1932, PCIJ, Series A/B, No. 46, 167.

[31] *Treatment of Polish Nationals and Other Persons of Polish Origin or Speech in the Danzig Territory*, 24.

[32] Art. 3 ASR provides as follows: 'The characterization of an act of a State as internationally wrongful is governed by international law. Such characterization is not affected by the characterization of the same act as lawful by internal law.'

[33] See above n. 10.

[34] It did so in the context of an alleged breach of treaty, stating that the purportedly wrongful conduct had to be 'attributable to the State and described as contrary to the treaty right of another State': *Phosphates in Morocco (Italy* v. *France)*, Judgment, 14 June 1938, PCIJ Series A/B, No. 74, 28.

[35] *Ibid.*

[36] For alternative approaches contrast the PCIJ's decisions in the *SS 'Wimbledon' (United Kingdom* v. *Germany)*, 20 (accepting a broad right of standing of applicant States that had 'a clear interest in the execution of the provisions relating to the Kiel Canal, since they all possess fleets and merchant vessels flying their respective flags); and *Interpretation of Statute of Memel Territory (UK, France, Italy and Japan* v. *Lithuania)*, Order of 24 June 1932, PCIJ Series A/B, No. 47 and No. 49 (recognising the standing of applicants whose 'only interest [was] to see that the Convention to which they are Parties is carried out by Lithuania' – as put by the British agent: see PCIJ, Series C, No. 59, 173). As the brief references suggest, the PCIJ could be surprisingly modern in determining whether claimant States had standing *in judicio*. In his separate opinion in the 1962 judgment in *South West Africa*, Judge Jessup drew on the PCIJ's jurisprudence to argue (persuasively)

reduced responsibility to reciprocal relations involving rights of claimants and corresponding duties of respondents – a restriction which haunts debates to this day.[37] Moreover, the Court's State-centred interpretation of diplomatic protection claims – by which a State was 'in reality asserting its own rights'[38] – would add a further restriction of lasting impact.[39]

Thirdly, in a much-cited passage, the PCIJ would formulate, in a general way, the most important automatic consequence 'immediately arising'[40] from responsibility. In *Factory*, it noted that a breach of international law 'involves an obligation to make reparation'; this was said to be 'a principle of international law, and even a general conception of law'.[41] In a later passage of the same case, the PCIJ then explored the content of the obligation:

> [to] wipe out all the consequences of the illegal act and reestablish the situation which would, in all probability, have existed if that act had not been committed.[42]

that '[i]nternational law has long recognised that States may have legal interests in matters which do not affect their financial, economic, or other "material", or, say, "physical" or "tangible" interests' (*South West Africa* cases *(Ethiopia* v. *South Africa*; *Liberia* v. *South Africa)*, Preliminary Objections, Judgment, 21 December 1962, ICJ Reports (1962), 425). The 1966 judgment in the same cases unfortunately would come to overshadow the PCIJ's earlier and more nuanced approach to legal standing. For more on these aspects see Christian J. Tams, *Enforcing Obligations Erga Omnes in International Law* (Cambridge University Press, 2005, rev. pbck edn 2010), 69–79.

37 For details see e.g. Bruno Simma, 'Bilateralism and Community Interest in the Law of State Responsibility' in Yoram Dinstein and Mala Tabory (eds.), *International Law in a Time of Perplexity: Essays in Honour of Shabtai Rosenne* (Dordrecht: Martinus Nijhoff, 1989), 821; James Crawford, 'Responsibilities for Breaches of Communitarian Norms: An Appraisal of Article 48 of the ILC Articles on Responsibility of States for Wrongful Acts' in Ulrich Fastenrath *et al.* (eds.), *From Bilateralism to Community Interest: Essays in Honour of Judge Bruno Simma* (Oxford University Press, 2011), 221. The author's own view is set out in Tams, *Enforcing Obligations Erga Omnes in International Law.*

38 *Mavrommatis Palestine Concessions (Greece* v. *Britain)*, Judgment, 30 August 1924, PCIJ Series A, No. 2 (1924), 12.

39 As diplomatic protection was subsequently 'spun off' into a separate topic (related to, but independent from, the modern notion of responsibility), the matter is not pursued in detail here. For a recent analysis see Kate Parlett, 'Diplomatic Protection and the International Court of Justice' in Christian J. Tams and James Sloan (eds.), *The Development of International Law by the International Court of Justice* (Oxford University Press, 2013), 87.

40 *Cf.* above n. 35.

41 *Factory at Chorzów (Germany* v. *Poland*) (Merits), Judgment, 13 September 1928, PCIJ Series A, No. 17 (1928), 29.

42 *Ibid.*, 47. This was said to be an 'essential principle contained in the actual notion of an illegal act'.

This was followed by a statement on the relationship between two potential forms of reparation:

> Restitution in kind, or, if this is not possible, payment of a sum corresponding to the value which a restitution in kind would bear; the award, if need be, of damages for loss sustained which would not be covered by restitution in kind or payment in place of it – such are the principles which should serve to determine the amount of compensation due for an act contrary to international law.[43]

The impact of these statements has been no less than remarkable. Hardly supported by argument, they have become cornerstones of the regime of consequences of responsibility: relied upon to support the existence of a general duty to make reparation[44] and the primacy of restitution over compensation.

Taken together, the three instances show the remarkable role of the PCIJ in preparing the ground for the emergence, and gradual formulation, of the modern law of State responsibility between the 1960s and 2001. The PCIJ was not the architect of the modern notion – as a judicial body deciding specific cases it had limited powers to design broad normative frameworks. However, the PCIJ's jurisprudence (partly drawing on earlier arbitral practice, partly relying on 'conceptualist reasoning')[45] recognised a number of important general principles that shape or influence the law of responsibility to this day and that, in the terminology introduced above, form part of the 'second level' of normative decisions.

[43] *Ibid.*

[44] See e.g. para. 1 of the ILC's commentary to Art. 31 ASR: 'The general principle of the consequences of the commission of an internationally wrongful act was stated by PCIJ in the *Factory at Chorzów* case.' As regards the primacy of restitution, the ILC's commentary pragmatically emphasises that '[o]f the various forms of reparation, compensation is perhaps the most commonly sought in international practice' (commentary to Art. 36, para 2). But Art. 36 ASR does accept (in the words of para. 3 of the commentary) 'primacy as a matter of legal principle'.

[45] The point was recently made by Akbar Rasulov: '[A]s even the briefest scrutiny of its case-law can confirm, the Court throughout its twenty-year career remained a very committed practitioner of conceptualist reasoning': it would identify, without much argument, the alleged 'objective meaning' of a principle and 'deduce from this principle by way of "objective" legal reasoning an entire juridical regime with numerous details and complicated normative and remedial structures'. See Akbar Rasulov, 'The Doctrine of Sources in the Discourse of the Permanent Court of International Justice' in Christian J. Tams and Malgosia Fitzmaurice (eds.), *Legacies of the Permanent Court of International Justice* (Leiden: Brill, 2013), 308–9.

(c) *The ICJ's continuing relevance*

The ICJ's work has been influential, too, but its impact has typically been at a different level. At least for the last four decades,[46] the World Court has decided responsibility cases against the backdrop of the ILC's work. And quite clearly, this has affected its impact on legal development.

(i) Operating within the ILC's master plan

With respect to the 'level' of normative decisions, the emergence on the scene of an ambitious Law Commission had a constraining influence: as the ILC's 'master plan' for responsibility began to unfold and as it was translated into the different organising principles of responsibility summarised in the preceding section (thus 'encod[ing] the way we think about responsibility'),[47] other actors were no longer as free to roam. This affected many potential agencies of legal development, including scholarship,[48] and also the ICJ. Rather than 'discovering' general principles of responsibility (which then would be drawn upon by others, as the PCIJ had done), the ICJ, from the 1970s onwards, operated within the ILC's framework. Its impact became more specific: in the terminology used in the preceding section, one might say it typically shifted to the (third) level of specific rules of responsibility.

(ii) 'Normative ping pong': the ILC and ICJ in concert

This shift should not be taken to mean that the ICJ became 'less powerful', or less influential; if anything, the reverse is true. In addressing specific normative propositions through its case law, the ICJ was highly influential, and the list of provisions of the ILC's text that in one way or the other owe their existence or formulation to some form of ICJ pronouncement is long. Of course, operating within the ILC's 'master plan', the ICJ would not single-handedly create new law but work in tandem with the ILC. However, over the years, the two institutions seemed

[46] As regards early ICJ pronouncements preceding the ILC's reconceptualisation see notably *Corfu Channel (United Kingdom* v. *Albania)*, Judgment, 9 April 1949, ICJ Reports (1949), 4 and 244. The *Reparations* opinion (*Reparation for Injuries Suffered in the Service of the United Nations*, Advisory Opinion, 11 April 1949, ICJ Reports (1949), 171) sets the stage for the subsequent development of a regime of responsibility of international organisations (ARIO 2011); as it does not concern State responsibility, it is left aside here.

[47] See above n. 8.

[48] See above n. 9 for comment on two alternative visions of responsibility that would be left to one side as the ILC's approach became dominant.

to develop an almost symbiotic relationship as 'partners in law-making'. The degree and character of the Court's influence within that symbiotic relationship vary, but three categories can be conveniently distinguished.

First, a number of ICJ cases raised 'responsibility issues' that were fairly novel and would be taken up in the ILC's work. Two examples may serve to illustrate the point.

In *Tehran Hostages*, the Court had to assess to what extent essentially 'private conduct' – the occupation of the US embassy by students and militants – was attributable to a State that, while not actively participating, endorsed it, and exploited it for its own purposes. In the view of the Court, approval, endorsement and 'exploitation' were sufficient to turn a private act into an attributable public act:

> The approval given to these facts by the Ayatollah Khomeini and other organs of the Iranian State, and the decision to perpetuate them, translated continuing occupation of the Embassy and detention of the hostages into acts of that State.[49]

The ILC's subsequent work essentially 'acknowledged and adopted' the ICJ's position: the *Hostages* case having been decided only in Ago's final year on the Commission, the matter would not be considered until the second reading when Special Rapporteur Crawford recommended[50] the addition of a provision inspired by the Court's judgment (while also indicating that it should be construed narrowly).[51] In line with that, Article 11 of the 2001 ASR effectively translates the ICJ's approach into a rule of attribution.

While it had a more chequered history, the famous '*erga omnes* dictum' from the *Barcelona Traction* case is another ICJ pronouncement that would, over time, morph into a provision of the modern law of responsibility. For a while, the Court's unnecessarily cryptic statement that

[49] *United States Diplomatic and Consular Staff in Tehran (United States of America* v. *Iran)*, Judgment, 24 May 1980, ICJ Reports (1980), 3, 35, para. 74.

[50] See James Crawford, 'First Report on State Responsibility', UN Doc. A/CN.4/490, Add. 5, paras. 281–6. In addition to the *Hostages* case, reliance was placed on the *Lighthouses* award, which had considered a similar situation in the context of State succession (*Lighthouses Arbitration (France* v. *Greece)* (18 April 1956), Reports of International Arbitral Awards, vol. 12, 155).

[51] See para. 6 of the ILC's commentary to Art. 11 ASR, explaining that, while the ICJ had spoken of 'approval' and 'endorsement', 'as a general matter, conduct will not be attributable to a State under article 11 where a State merely acknowledges the factual existence of conduct or expresses its verbal approval of it'; instead an official 'adoption' was required.

particularly important obligations should be owed 'towards the international community as a whole' would be relied upon to support the existence of 'international crimes' as a separate category of wrongful conduct. From the mid-1990s onwards, when 'crimes' fell out of fashion, the more mundane (but still ambitious) idea of 'public interest enforcement' persisted: pursuant to Article 48(1)(b) of the ILC's 2001 text, any State 'is entitled to invoke the responsibility of another State ... if the obligation breached is owed to the international community as a whole'. As the commentary acknowledges, this really 'intends to give effect to the statement by the ICJ in the *Barcelona Traction* case ... that ... "[i]n view of the importance of the rights involved, all States can be held to have a legal interest in th[e] protection ... of obligations *erga omnes*"'.[52]

Secondly, the ICJ has not always put forward propositions that the ILC has then taken up. As often, the order has been reversed, with the ICJ stabilising ILC provisions whose fate was, prior to the ICJ's *imprimatur*, at best uncertain. The gradual recognition of a defence of necessity is probably the most prominent example: adopted by the Commission in 1980 and featuring as draft Article 33 of the 1996 text, the provision was received cautiously as it seemed to invite abuse. The arbitral award in the *Rainbow Warrior* reflected the persisting doubts. The ILC's work, noted the tribunal sceptically, 'allegedly authorizes a State to take unlawful action invoking a state of necessity'; however this was considered 'controversial'.[53] In retrospect, it seems to have been the ICJ's *Gabčíkovo Nagymaros* judgment that settled matters.[54] Without too much concern, and referring to draft Article 33, the Court recognised:

> that the state of necessity is a ground recognized by customary international law for precluding the wrongfulness of an act not in conformity with an international obligation.[55]

This endorsement was enough to ensure the relatively smooth passage of the provision during the second reading. Since 2001, of course, Article 25 of the ILC's text has been much in demand: investment arbitration

[52] Commentary to Art. 48 ASR, para. 8, citing *Barcelona Traction, Light and Power Company, Limited (Belgium* v. *Spain)* (Second Phase), ICJ Reports (1970), 3, 32, para. 33.

[53] *Rainbow Warrior Arbitration (New Zealand* v. *France)* (30 April 1990), Reports of International Arbitration Awards, vol. XX (1990), 254.

[54] As put by James Crawford ('The International Court of Justice and the Law of State Responsibility', 80–1): 'At the time when the Court dealt with the argument of necessity, it was very much an open question whether it would be accepted.'

[55] *Gabčíkovo-Nagymaros Project (Hungary* v. *Slovakia)*, Judgment, 25 September 1997, ICJ Reports (1997), 40, para. 51.

of the last decade would not have been the same without it and while many questions remain (including whether it should apply to the Argentinean crisis of 2001), it now seems beyond doubt that international law recognises a defence of necessity.

Since the completion of the ILC's project, the ICJ has continued to lend its authority to some of the more ambitious provisions of the 2001 text. Article 41, spelling out special consequences of serious breaches of *jus cogens* rules (highly controversial at the time), was in essence applied in the *Wall* opinion, even if without reference to the ILC's text.[56] And three years later, in the *Genocide* case, the Court explicitly referred to Article 16 of the ILC's text, which – in one of the more remarkable instances of legal development – proposed a general rule against complicity in State responsibility.[57] The ICJ not only confirmed the provision in the most casual fashion,[58] but even extended it to a setting involving not two States, but one non-State entity and one State. And judging from the subsequent response, the combination of ILC provision and ICJ endorsement seems to have redrawn the map of shared responsibility.[59]

Finally, the ICJ's influence can also be felt at a more granular level: in many instances, ICJ pronouncements delivered clarity regarding the scope of provisions that everyone agreed would feature in the ILC's text but which required some clarification. The eventual formulation of the ILC's provisions on countermeasures provides an illustration: while many of the crucial questions had been addressed beforehand, the ICJ's *Gabčíkovo Nagymaros* judgment usefully added precision, for example by clarifying the relationship between countermeasures and treaty-law responses based on Article 60 of the Vienna Convention on the Law of Treaties (VCLT) or by introducing the notion of a 'commensurate' response.[60] Whereas

[56] *Legal Consequences of the Construction of a Wall in the Occupied Palestinian Territory*, Advisory Opinion, 9 July 2004, ICJ Reports (2004), 199–200, paras. 154–9.

[57] Art. 16 ASR provides as follows: 'A State which aids or assists another State in the commission of an internationally wrongful act by the latter is internationally responsible for doing so if: (*a*) that State does so with knowledge of the circumstances of the internationally wrongful act; and (*b*) the act would be internationally wrongful if committed by that State.'

[58] *The Application of the Convention on the Prevention and Punishment of the Crime of Genocide (Bosnia and Herzegovina* v. *Serbia and Montenegro)*, Judgment, 26 February 2007, ICJ Reports (2007), 217, para. 420.

[59] Many aspects are explored by SHARES, the research project on shared responsibility in international law, available at www.sharesproject.nl/.

[60] *Gabčíkovo-Nagymaros Project*, 55–7, paras. 82–7. For the ILC's reception of the judgment see e.g. commentary to Art. 49 ASR, paras. 2, 4 and Art. 51, para. 4; for a detailed comment on Art. 60 VCLT (including on the provision's relationship to countermeasures) see Bruno Simma and Christian J. Tams, 'Article 60' in Olivier Corten and Pierre Klein (eds.), *The*

this increased clarity, the ICJ's impact in other fields was more decisive. In relation to Article 8 of the ILC's text – governing the attribution of private conduct directed and/or controlled by a State – both the ICJ and ILC were robust in defending the relatively restrictive construction of that rule, as shaped by the *Nicaragua* case,[61] against the International Criminal Court for the Former Yugoslavia's (ICTY) more lenient *Tadić* test.[62] As the matter has been discussed in detail elsewhere,[63] it is sufficient to refer to the ICJ's judgment in the *(Bosnian) Genocide* case, in which – without much substantive argument, and despite the Court's willingness to take on board the ICTY's approach to issues of international criminal law – the *Tadić* test was dismissed out of hand.[64] As a result, it would seem far-fetched today to suggest that overall control is sufficient to justify attribution of private conduct – faced with dissent the ILC-ICJ has struck back.

4 Taking stock: the substantial impact of PCIJ and ICJ jurisprudence

The preceding considerations, though selective and cursory, suggest that in the complex process of shaping the contemporary law of State responsibility, the PCIJ and ICJ have been highly influential. To call the law of responsibility 'essentially judge-made'[65] may be an exaggeration; it ignores the ILC's essential role in devising a 'master plan' and in overseeing its gradual implementation. However, both Courts have been pivotal players: the PCIJ in setting the stage, the ICJ as the ILC's 'co-agent' of legal development. In fact, if one were to engage in a comparative exercise and 'rate' the PCIJ's and ICJ's impact on the development of different areas of law,[66] State responsibility would be in the top flight, alongside the

Vienna Conventions on the Law of Treaties: A Commentary (Oxford University Press, 2011), 1352.

61 *Military and Paramilitary Activities in and against Nicaragua (Nicaragua* v. *United States of America)*, Judgment, 27 June 1986, ICJ Reports (1986), 62 and 64–5, paras. 109 and 115 (requiring effective control of the specific wrongful acts).

62 *Prosecutor* v. *Tadić*, Case IT-94–1-A (1999), ICTY, Appeals Chamber, Judgment, 15 July 1999, ILM 38 (1999), 1541 *et seq.*

63 See e.g. André J. J. de Hoogh, 'Articles 4 and 8 of the 2001 ILC Articles on State Responsibility, the Tadić Case and Attribution of Acts of Bosnian Serb Authorities to the Federal Republic of Yugoslavia', *British Yearbook of International Law*, 72 (2001), 255.

64 *The Application of the Convention on the Prevention and Punishment of the Crime of Genocide (Bosnia and Herzegovina* v. *Serbia and Montenegro)*, 206–11, paras. 396–407.

65 *Cf.* above n. 2.

66 For an attempt see Christian J. Tams, 'The ICJ as a "Law-Formative Agency": Summary and Synthesis' in Christian J. Tams and James Sloan (eds.), *The Development of International Law by the International Court of Justice* (Oxford University Press, 2013), 377.

law of territory, diplomatic protection (to the extent that it is admitted as an autonomous area of international law) and, perhaps, the law of treaties. On all of these fields, the PCIJ and ICJ, over time, have exercised a substantial influence.

(a) Some comparative remarks

With respect to State responsibility, three aspects of this substantial influence stand out.

First, State responsibility has been a permanent feature of the PCIJ and ICJ caseload, and their jurisprudence has been a constant source of influence. The PCIJ's first contentious case (*Wimbledon*) involved questions of responsibility, as did *Corfu Channel*, the case of the ICJ; since then, questions of responsibility have been a regular feature of ICJ proceedings. Of the various branches and sections of public international law, the law of treaties (and perhaps the law of claims, unless it is viewed as part of responsibility) may be the only other with a similarly long-standing record of jurisprudence. Other areas have either come before the Court sporadically[67] or they have come and gone.[68] Responsibility has stayed and little suggests that this should change. This does not ensure influence on the development of the law but it is an enabling factor.

Secondly, whereas in many other areas of international law the PCIJ and ICJ have only pronounced on specific issues – such as maritime delimitation within the law of the sea,[69] or the relationship between human rights and general international law[70] – the Courts' jurisprudence on questions of responsibility has left footprints all over the field: from general

[67] This would, for example, be true for many of the substantive areas of international law: as Sir Franklin Berman points out, 'the occasional and adventitious nature of the ICJ's caseload has the almost automatic consequence that the Court is unlikely to be given the opportunity to revisit successively particular areas of substantive international law': 'The International Court of Justice as an "Agent" of Legal Development?' in Christian J. Tams and James Sloan (eds.), *The Development of International Law by the International Court of Justice* (Oxford University Press, 2013), 20.

[68] Proceedings relating to immunity would fall within the first category: the ICJ really only started to get involved in the last decade. Case law on minority rights belongs to the second category; it effectively stopped when the inter-war system of minority protection (in which the PCIJ played a crucial supervisory role) came to an end.

[69] For an exposition see Vaughan Lowe and Antonios Tzanakopoulos, 'The Development of the Law of the Sea by the International Court of Justice' in Tams and Sloan, Christian J. Tams and James Sloan (eds.), *The Development of International Law by the International Court of Justice* (Oxford University Press, 2013), 177.

[70] See e.g. Bruno Simma, 'Human Rights before the International Court of Justice: Community Interest Coming to Life?' in Christian J. Tams and James Sloan (eds.), *The Development*

principles formulated by the PCIJ to specific rules clarified by the ICJ, few parts of the contemporary law of responsibility have completely escaped judicial scrutiny. Whereas typically the PCIJ and ICJ address specific and selected issues of a given area of law, in the field of responsibility their jurisprudence has been a pervasive factor.

Thirdly, PCIJ and ICJ pronouncements on questions of responsibility have throughout been treated as authoritative. Binding only 'between the parties and in respect of that particular case',[71] PCIJ and ICJ decisions have to persuade to be relevant. And, while generally, the PCIJ and ICJ have been rather successful, persuasion often is a matter of degree: there are (rare) instances in which judgments have been overruled (such as *Lotus*) or deliberately bypassed,[72] and a number of decisions have remained highly controversial.[73] By contrast, the brief survey given above suggests that in the field of responsibility, jurisprudence is indeed accorded 'a truly astonishing deference'.[74] PCIJ statements continue to be seen as 'the law', and on more than one occasion, the ICJ has been recognised as the supreme arbiter deciding the fate of controversial ILC provisions. Despite the wealth of jurisprudence, and the sensitive character of some of the PCIJ and ICJ cases on questions of responsibility, it is hard to think of any equivalent to *Lotus* or *Fisheries*.[75] As a general matter, PCIJ and ICJ decisions have been 'bright beacons': rather than 'flicker[ing] and [dying] near-instant deaths',[76] they have been remarkably persistent.

(b) Three lessons

The development of the modern law of State responsibility in many respects displays unique features. However, it yields a number of general

of International Law by the International Court of Justice (Oxford University Press, 2013), 301.

71 See Art. 59 of the ICJ Statute.

72 The 'reversal' of the *Lotus* holding on port state jurisdiction over collisions on the high seas is the most prominent example of overruling, contrast the *Lotus case (SS Lotus (France* v. *Turkey)*, 27) to Art. 1 of the International Convention for the Unification of Certain Rules Relating to Penal Jurisdiction in Matters of Collision or Other Incidents of Collision ('1952 Brussels Convention') (Brussels, adopted 10 May 1952, entered into force 20 November 1955), 439 UNTS 233. As for bypassing, see e.g. *Fisheries Jurisdiction (UK* v. *Iceland)*, Judgment, 25 July 1974, ICJ Reports (1974), 3 and 175: the Court's comments on 'fisheries zones' would not be taken up; the EEZ was too attractive.

73 One need only think of consecutive ICJ pronouncements on the *jus ad bellum*.

74 As put by Daniel Patrick O'Connell, *International Law*, 2nd edn, 2 vols. (London: Stevens and Sons, 1970), I, 32.

75 See the references above n. 72. 76 *Cf.* above n. 6.

lessons about the role of international courts as 'law-formative agencies'.[77] In concluding, three such lessons merit being briefly spelled out.

First, the preceding survey suggests that the impact of PCIJ and ICJ pronouncements on the development of international law in a given area is a natural by-product of their dispute settlement activity. This sounds trite, but it may be worth stressing since much of the scholarship seeks to explain factors accounting for the precedential impact of judicial pronouncements, which is said to depend on the attitude of courts,[78] on the strength of their reasoning[79] or on the (essential or *obiter*) character of a particular pronouncement.[80] Experience in the field of State responsibility does not bear out these distinctions: it includes *ratio* and *dicta*,[81] well-reasoned statements, and mere assertions.[82] And who could say whether the PCIJ and ICJ, since the 1920s, have been 'activist' or 'restrained'? If the PCIJ and ICJ have been influential players in the development of State responsibility (unlike in other areas of international law), then this would primarily seem to reflect the fact that they have decided responsibility cases for nine decades. The first lesson can be formulated in refreshingly simple terms: 'The impact of international courts and tribunals on the evolution of international law largely depends upon how many cases are brought before them.'[83] This would explain the relatively high influence on the development of State responsibility.

Secondly, the substantial impact of PCIJ and ICJ pronouncements on State responsibility may also reflect the fact that the law of responsibility is particularly receptive to judicial development. It belongs to the core

[77] The term has been coined by O'Connell, *International Law*, 31.

[78] *Cf.* debates about judicial activism: for a recent account see e.g. Daniel Terris, Cesare P. R. Romano and Leigh Swigart, *The International Judge: An Introduction to the Men and Women Who Decide the World's Cases* (Oxford University Press, 2007), 121.

[79] See e.g. Georg Schwarzenberger, *International Law as Applied by International Courts and Tribunals*, 3rd edn (London: Stevens and Sons, 1957), 32; and similarly O'Connell, *International Law*, 32.

[80] See e.g. Robert Y. Jennings, 'The Judiciary, National and International, and the Development of International Law', *International and Comparative Law Quarterly*, 45 (1996), 6 *et seq.*; Mohamed Shahabuddeen, *Precedent in the World Court* (Cambridge University Press, 1996), 152–64.

[81] Among the latter, one could mention celebrated dicta decreeing the primacy of restitution over compensation (*Factory at Chorzów (Germany* v. *Poland)*, 47) and 'discovering' the concept of obligations *erga omnes* (*Barcelona Traction, Light and Power Company, Limited (Belgium* v. *Spain)* 32–3).

[82] E.g. there is a remarkable absence of legal argument in the successful rejection, by the ICJ and the ILC, of the ICTY's *Tadić* approach to attribution.

[83] Alan Boyle and Christine Chinkin, *The Making of International Law* (Oxford University Press, 2007), 269.

of general international law, on which the world's 'generalist' court is particularly trusted. It is based on organisational principles that require to be spelled out and applied – which are much better suited to be concretised in dispute settlement processes than, for example, specialised fields of law comprising vast numbers of specific provisions (such as the law of the sea, international humanitarian, or international environmental law). As importantly, as a field of law, State responsibility lacks specialised institutions to administer the application of the law – in the way human rights committees or Meetings of the Parties (MoPs) and Conferences of the Parties (CoPs) 'manage' their respective treaties, moulding them in a process of regular engagement and adaptation. What is more, as has been shown, the ILC, as the key institution overseeing the codification process, seemed to co-operate harmoniously with the Court. Experience in the field of State responsibility thus suggests that, in addition to numbers of cases, the impact of international courts on legal development may depend on the 'make-up' of the field, which can be receptive (such as State responsibility, but also diplomatic protection, or the law of treaties) or not.

Thirdly, the survey highlights how the role of courts as agencies of legal development can change over time. Where the PCIJ could lay down general principles, the ICJ would operate within the parameters of responsibility established by the ILC. Conversely, the ICJ retained an important role, as through its decisions it could engage with normative propositions and confirm or modify the legal status of specific draft articles. This markedly differs from the much more limited role of international courts that only become involved after the completion of a codification exercise – as happened, for instance, with respect to the law of the sea or international humanitarian law. A third lesson to be drawn from this brief survey is that international courts, as agencies of legal development, depend on the right circumstances or 'setting': they are influential during the formative stages of the law and during long-term and on-going codification attempts.

5 Conclusion

The making of the modern law of State responsibility has been a complex and long-standing process. Since the 1960s, the process has been led by the International Law Commission guided by its Special Rapporteurs. If the work – allegedly to be accomplished within a few summer months[84] – was

[84] *Cf.* above n. 11.

eventually completed then it is because, in implementing its 'master plan', the Commission could draw on the work of reliable agencies of legal development. Among these agencies, the PCIJ and ICJ were of crucial importance: their jurisprudence shaped many of the building blocks, and some of the cornerstones, of the eventual edifice. In retrospect, it seems clear that without the jurisprudence of the two World Courts the project could not have been completed.

17

Defending individual ships from pirates

Questions of State responsibility and immunity

DOUGLAS GUILFOYLE*

1 Introduction

Somali and, increasingly, West African piracy has captured international attention since 2008. A significant international law literature has followed, largely focused on the multinational naval deployment in the Gulf of Aden and Indian Ocean which is engaged in efforts to deter, prosecute and imprison pirates.[1] This neglects a key development: State and industry efforts to defend individual ships. The naval deployments, given limited resources, have focused on area protection: stationing ships to 'picket' areas of ocean or to protect vessels within a recommended transit corridor.[2] Obviously, this approach cannot guarantee the security of any one vessel.

The shipping industry has concluded that the best way to secure any given vessel against pirate attack is to 'harden' that individual vessel as a target. Initially, such measures consisted primarily of Best Management Practices, recommendations for the passive or non-lethal defence of vessels through measures such as barriers to boarding, converted fire-hose water-cannons and secure 'citadels'.[3] The more controversial development, discussed here, has been the turn to armed security. This may take two forms, both of which may implicate State responsibility.

* In 2009–13 the author worked closely with the legal issues working group of the Contact Group on Piracy off the Coast of Somalia.

[1] A useful survey can be found in Tullio Treves, 'Piracy and the International Law of the Sea' in Douglas Guilfoyle (ed.), *Modern Piracy: Legal Challenges and Responses* (London: Elgar, 2013), ch. 6, n. 1.

[2] House of Commons Foreign Affairs Committee, 'Tenth Report – Piracy off the Coast of Somalia', HC 1318 (5 January 2012), Evidence Annexe, Ev 14, available at www.parliament.uk/business/committees (hereinafter House of Commons Report).

[3] 'Best Management Practices for Protection against Somalia Based Piracy (Version 4 – August 2011)', annexed to IMO Doc. MSC.1/Circ.1339 (14 September 2011).

First, many in the industry have called for the deployment of marines, typically from the flag State's armed forces, aboard commercial vessels in Vessel Protection Detachments (VPDs).[4] The presumption was that such VPDs would clearly enjoy both authority to use force and sovereign immunity before national courts in the event of mistaken uses of force. However, the *Enrica Lexie* incident of February 2012, in which two Italian marines serving in a VPD allegedly killed two Indian fishermen, demonstrates that the questions involved are more complex. At time of writing, the case remains before Indian courts (although one marine has returned to Italy for medical treatment).

Secondly, recognising that military assets are finite, there has been a turn by an initially reluctant industry towards using Privately Contracted Armed Security Personnel (PCASP).[5] Novel questions arise regarding: (a) the duties of States to regulate the use of PCASP aboard their flag vessels where they are aware that such use is occurring; and (b) the consequences for States (if any) which may flow from permitting the use of PCASP. In particular, when may inadequate regulation and control of the use of force by PCASP become internationally wrongful? Further questions arise about the extent to which corporations, such as Private Maritime Security Companies (PMSCs) engaged in the employment and supply of PCASP, can commit international wrongs and whether States can be complicit in those wrongs.[6] These questions are addressed after a brief consideration of the international law applicable to the use of force against pirates.

2 Using force in countering piracy

This section does not review the rules governing the use of force in maritime policing operations in detail. It is sufficient to note that when a State attempts to capture a vessel and those aboard for law enforcement purposes, the use of force should be necessary (that is, used as a last resort) and proportionate.[7] The more pertinent question here is the

[4] House of Commons Report, para 25.

[5] On early reluctance, see e.g. 'Statement on International Piracy by Giles Noakes Chief Maritime Security Officer of BIMCO before the United States House of Representatives Committee on Transportation and Infrastructure Subcommittee on Coast Guard and Maritime Transportation' (February 2009), available at www.marad.dot.gov/documents/HOA_Testimony-Giles%20Noakes-BIMCO.pdf.

[6] e.g. Robert McCorquodale and Penelope Simons, 'Responsibility beyond Borders: State Responsibility for Extraterritorial Violations by Corporations of International Human Rights Law', *Modern Law Review*, 70 (2007), 599.

[7] *M/V 'Saiga' (No. 2) (Saint Vincent and the Grenadines* v. *Guinea)*, Judgment, ITLOS Reports (1999), 65, para. 155. Treaties sometimes use the term 'reasonable' rather than

difference between government counter-piracy operations and individual self-defence against pirates.

The UN Convention on the Law of the Sea 1982 (UNCLOS)[8] provides that warships or 'other duly authorized ships or aircraft clearly marked and identifiable as being on government service' (Article 107) have the right to 'seize a pirate ship . . . or a ship . . . under the control of pirates, and arrest' persons aboard (Article 105). This power is *not* exercisable by VPDs aboard private vessels, unless such vessels are both 'authorised' to conduct such operations and 'marked' as on 'government service'. What powers at international law does a VPD have, then, to repel pirates? They have the same power as private individuals: self-defence. The International Law Commission stated that the concept of 'seizure' of pirate craft (commenting on the equivalent provision in what became Article 19 of the Convention on the High Seas 1958[9]): '[c]learly . . . does not apply in the case of a merchant ship which has repulsed . . . [a pirate] attack . . . and, in exercising its right of self-defence, overpowers the pirate ship and subsequently hands it over to a warship' or coastal State authorities.[10] The presence of a State VPD or State-licensed but privately retained PCASP aboard a merchant vessel should not change this position. The important point is that self-defence by those aboard a merchant vessel against pirate attack is not an exercise of sovereign authority. The applicability of the basic right of individual self-defence on the high seas might be considered to follow from either a general principle of law common to all legal systems[11] or a simple application of the flag State's criminal law.

'proportionate': Art. 22(1)(f), Agreement for the Implementation of Provisions of the United Nations Convention on the Law of the Sea of 10 December 1982 Relating to the Conservation and Management of Straddling Fish Stocks and Highly Migratory Fish Stocks (New York, adopted 4 August 1995, entered into force 11 November 2001), 2167 UNTS 88; Art. 22, Agreement concerning Cooperation in Suppressing Illicit Maritime and Air Trafficking in Narcotic Drugs and Psychotropic Substances in the Caribbean Area (San José, adopted 10 April 2003, entered into force 18 September 2008) available at www.state.gov/s/l/2005/87198.htm; Art. 8bis(9), Protocol of 2005 to the Convention for the Suppression of Unlawful Acts against the Safety of Maritime Navigation (London, adopted 14 October 2005, entered into force 28 July 2010), IMO Doc. LEG/CONF.15/21.

8 UN Convention on the Law of the Sea (Montego Bay, adopted 10 December 1982, entered into force 16 November 1994), 1833 UNTS 3.

9 The Geneva High Seas Convention (HSC) (Geneva, adopted 29 April 1958, entered into force 30 September 1962), 450 UNTS 11.

10 Commentaries to the ILC Articles concerning the Law of the Sea, *ILC Yearbook*, 2 (1956), 283.

11 Art. 38(1)(c), Statute of the International Court of Justice, *American Journal of International Law Supplement*, 39 (1945), 215.

3 Vessel Protection Detachments and counter-piracy: questions of State responsibility and immunity

States including France, Spain, Israel and Italy have provided VPDs to some vessels flying their flags and transiting the so-called 'High Risk Area' for piracy (essentially the Gulf of Aden and Indian Ocean).[12] For example, French tuna trawlers operating out of the Seychelles have carried embarked marines since 2009.[13] Controversy can occur, however, when VPDs use force – especially if acting in mistaken self-defence.

The most controversial such case is the *Enrica Lexie* incident of 15 February 2012 in which two Italian marines allegedly fired upon a vessel mistaken for a pirate craft, killing two Indian fishermen.[14] The incident occurred outside India's territorial waters, but the *Enrica Lexie* subsequently entered port and the marines were arrested. There is no doubt that, as a unit of Italy's armed forces, the VPD was a State organ and Italy is responsible for its actions.[15] If the use of force in mistaken self-defence is an international wrong, Italy must obviously make reparation. Italy has already directly compensated the families of the dead fishermen,[16] but may further owe India satisfaction for mistakenly firing upon its fishing vessel.[17]

While the deaths are clearly attributable to the Italian State, the more difficult questions have been the jurisdiction of Indian courts and the immunity of Italian marines from that jurisdiction. The potential bases of Indian jurisdiction are straightforward. First, India could clearly rely on passive personality jurisdiction[18] or – by analogy with the territorial effects doctrine – jurisdiction over acts causing effects on its flag vessel.[19] India also invoked the Convention for the Suppression of Unlawful Acts

[12] House of Commons Report, Ev 14.

[13] 'French Marines Repel New Pirate Attack on Trawlers', *AFP*, 13 October 2009, available at www.google.com/hostednews/afp/article/ALeqM5jCiyLdxWAsMNAzPu-HCg5VCH7OuQ.

[14] 'Italy Challenges India in Supreme Court over Fishermen's Deaths', *Reuters*, 29 August 2012, http://timesofindia.indiatimes.com/india/Italy-challenges-India-in-Supreme-Court-over-fishermens-deaths/articleshow/15955783.cms.

[15] Art. 4 Articles on Responsibility of States for Internationally Wrongful Acts (Articles on State Responsibility), UN Doc. A/56/83 (2001).

[16] *Ibid.*, Art. 36 Articles on State Responsibility. Compare the duty of compensation in Art. 110(3) UNCLOS (though it is questionable if this duty applies directly where a State is not exercising its Art. 105 powers).

[17] *'Saiga' (No. 2)*, para. 176.

[18] Malcolm N. Shaw, *International Law*, 6th edn (Cambridge University Press, 2008), 644–6.

[19] *SS Lotus case (France* v. *Turkey)*, Judgment, 7 September 1927, PCIJ Series A, No. 10 (1927), 23.

against the Safety of Maritime Navigation 1988 (SUA Convention),[20] which obliges it to prosecute an 'act of violence against a person on board a ship if that act is likely to endanger the safe navigation of that ship',[21] and which upholds India's jurisdiction over such offences committed 'against or on board a ship flying [its] flag'.[22] However, Italy sought to rely on Article 97(1) UNCLOS, providing:

> In the event of a collision *or any other incident of navigation* concerning a ship on the high seas, involving the penal ... responsibility of the master or of *any other person in the service of the ship*, no penal ... proceedings may be instituted ... except before the judicial ... authorities either of the flag State or of the State of which such person is a national.[23]

While VPD members are arguably 'in the service of the ship', it is difficult to consider that firing upon another vessel is an 'incident of navigation'. The term 'incident of navigation' probably extends to cover 'maritime casualties' as defined in Article 221(2) UNCLOS, including:

> [any] collision of vessels, stranding or other incident of navigation, or other occurrence on board a vessel or external to it resulting in material damage or imminent threat of material damage to a vessel or cargo.[24]

Nothing in this wording prima facie encompasses death or injury to natural persons – though this was undoubtedly the intended effect. The inspiration for Article 97, the 1952 Brussels Convention rules on criminal jurisdiction over collisions, was originally introduced in response to Turkey's prosecution of a French national for negligent navigation occasioning a fatal high seas collision (as famously litigated in the *Lotus*

[20] Convention for the Suppression of Unlawful Acts against the Safety of Maritime Navigation (Rome, adopted 10 March 1988, entered into force on 1 March 1992), 1678 UNTS 221. On its invocation, see Duncan Hollis, 'The Case of *Enrica Lexie*: *Lotus* Redux?', Opinio Juris Blog, 17 June 2012, available at http://opiniojuris.org/2012/06/17/the-case-of-enrica-lexie-lotus-redux/; and note the Indian implementing legislation: Suppression of Unlawful Acts against Safety of Maritime Navigation and Fixed Platforms on Continental Shelf Act 2002 (Act No. 69 of 2002).

[21] Art. 3(1)(b) SUA Convention.

[22] *Ibid.*, Art. 6(1)(a) SUA Convention.

[23] Emphasis added. Earlier provisions to the same effect are found in Arts. 1 and 2 International Convention for the Unification of Certain Rules Relating to Penal Jurisdiction in matters of Collisions and Other Incidents of Navigation (Brussels, adopted 10 May 1952, entered into force 21 November 1959), 233 UNTS 439; Art. 11(1) Convention on the High Seas (Geneva, adopted 29 April 1958, entered into force 30 September 1962), 450 UNTS 11; on its history see Robin R. Churchill and Alan Vaughan Lowe, *The Law of the Sea*, 3rd edn (Manchester University Press, 1999), 208.

[24] Satya Nandan, Shabtai Rosenne, and Neal Grandy (eds.), *United Nations Convention on the Law of the Sea 1982: A Commentary*, 3rd edn (Dordrecht: Martinus Nijhoff, 1995), 168.

case).[25] However, the terms 'collision' and 'incident of navigation' appear to focus closely on the steering and management of the ship itself as an object capable of causing death or injury. Extending the provision to cover intentional acts by the crew in projecting force beyond the ship would appear a broad reading unsupported by the plain language.

If Indian courts therefore have jurisdiction, the question becomes one of functional immunity. Cases involving the shooting of nationals by foreign armed forces are invariably controversial, and the State practice is diverse. Identifying the relevant context is important. Different rules may apply to cases where foreign State organs are present by invitation in a State's territory (in which case their official acts will be held immune)[26] and those cases where they enter uninvited or commit espionage.[27] One 2011 case in the UK held that functional immunity cannot apply where a State official commits illegal acts within another State's territory.[28] However, the present scenario does not clearly fit such categories: the marines physically remained within Italian jurisdiction though their acts occasioned consequences within Indian jurisdiction. An analogy might be made with perimeter guard cases, dealing with the customary international law status of foreign bases. For example, in *In re Gilbert* a United States soldier had shot dead a Brazilian citizen who had repeatedly attempted to enter a US base. The Brazilian courts upheld immunity on the basis that the 'marine committed the offence in the exercise of his specific duty as a sentry'.[29] In a seemingly contrary case, *Japan* v. *Girard*, a Japanese court held (strictly, *obiter*) that a marine surrendered to Japanese justice after shooting a local woman for scavenging on an artillery range would have enjoyed no immunity.[30] The case turned, however, on a finding that the defendant acted to gratify his own sadistic whims by luring the deceased to a point where he was authorised to shoot her. Such flagrant abuse of authority was seen as severing the connection between his act and his State function. Similarly, in the present

25 See above n. 23; *Lotus* case, 4.

26 *Schooner Exchange* v. *McFaddon*, 11 US (7 Cranch) 116 (1813); *Wright* v. *Cantrell* (Supreme Court of New South Wales, 1943) 12 International Law Reports, 133.

27 As in the *Rainbow Warrior* incident (although notably France never directly invoked State immunity), see *Ruling of 6 July 1986 of the United Nations Secretary-General*, Reports of International Arbitral Awards, vol. XIX, 213.

28 *Khurts Bat* v. *The Investigating Judge of the German Federal Court* [2011] EWHC 2029 (Admin).

29 *In re Gilbert* (Brazil, Supreme Federal Court, 1944) 13 International Law Reports, 86, 88.

30 *Japan* v. *Girard* (Maebashi District Court, 1957) 26 International Law Reports, 203, 207.

case Indian courts have to date rejected any plea of immunity, a state High Court holding:

> [t]he shooting was 'cruel' and 'brutal' and hence it can be inferred that . . . [the naval guards acted] . . . on their own.[31]

The reasoning involved, denying immunity to objectively sovereign acts by reference to the actor's subjective motives, is dubious unless there is clear evidence of substantial departure from the scope of official duties.[32]

The Indian Supreme Court entertained an interlocutory appeal on jurisdiction in the case, delivering its judgment in January 2013.[33] The judgment holds that India may assert jurisdiction and that Article 97(1) UNCLOS is not applicable. The result is correct, but the Supreme Court's reasoning that Article 97(1) cannot cover criminal acts is almost certainly wrong.[34] It also, rather peculiarly, held that India could claim jurisdiction on the basis that while the relevant events occurred outside India's territorial sea they occurred within its contiguous zone and that the Indian Penal Code therefore applied as UNCLOS allows full criminal law enforcement jurisdiction in that zone out to 24 nautical miles from a State's baselines.[35] Quite simply, it does not.[36] The holding is puzzling as the Supreme Court otherwise acknowledged that beyond the territorial sea a coastal State enjoys only limited sovereign rights.[37] Most peculiarly, the Supreme Court did not directly confront the 'degree of immunity'

[31] 'Fishermen's Killing: Kerala High Court Dismisses Italy's Plea, Says Indian Courts Can Try Naval Guards', *Times of India* (29 May 2012), available at http://articles.timesofindia.indiatimes.com/2012–05–29/india/31886910_1_kollam-court-indian-courts-indian-fishermen.

[32] Douglas Guilfoyle, *Shipping Interdiction and the Law of the Sea* (Cambridge University Press, 2009), 318. On the 'substantial departure' standard see e.g. Facilities and Areas and the Status of United States Armed Forces in Korea Agreement (Agreed Minute re Article XXII) 9 July 1966, 17 UST 1677 and 1816; and Protocol to Amend Article XVII of the Administrative Agreement under Article III of the Security Treaty between the USA and Japan (Agreed Minute re Paragraph 3), 29 September 1953, 4 UST 1847 and 1851.

[33] *Republic of Italy and others* v. *Union of India and others*, Writ Petition (Civil) No. 135 of 2012, Supreme Court of India, 18 January 2013, available at http://judis.nic.in/supremecourt/imgs1.aspx?filename=39941.

[34] *Ibid.*, para. 95.

[35] *Ibid.*, para. 100. The reasoning in the separate opinion of Chelameswar J is far more nuanced on point.

[36] Art. 33(1) UNCLOS provides only authority to punish or prevent 'infringement of [the coastal State's] customs, fiscal, immigration or sanitary laws and regulations *within its territory or territorial sea*' (emphasis added). It does not extend the applicability of national criminal law to events occurring *only* in the contiguous zone.

[37] *Republic of Italy and others* v. *Union of India*, para. 99.

enjoyed by a State's armed forces for events occurring within a foreign State's jurisdiction.[38] It did, however, expressly state that questions of immunity could be re-agitated at the trial in the light of the evidence adduced.[39] The Supreme Court may, therefore, have implicitly accepted the submission that there was a dispute as to whether the marines' acts were not inherently sovereign acts (acts *jure imperii*) but rather were acts any person can perform (acts *jure gestionis*).[40] This would make the existence of immunity dependent on the trial court's characterisation of the facts. At the time of writing, the case had not yet come to trial.

One reason State immunity case law tends to become a wilderness of single instances is a lack of analytical clarity. Much municipal case law has regrettably tended to focus 'more upon the act than the actor' in determining which acts benefit from immunity.[41] However, this assumes all acts can neatly be divided into acts *jure imperii* or acts *jure gestionis*, a division for which there is no generally accepted test.[42] The deployment of marines as a VPD is clearly an act of sovereign authority, but defending a private vessel from pirates is an act any person could perform. As Crawford has pointed out, rather than searching for an elusive dividing line between sovereign and ordinary acts, it would be more logical (as numerous contemporary treaties and national statues do)[43] to treat state immunity as applying to all organs of state by virtue of their status as such (*ratione personae*) and then to define the acknowledged exceptions.[44] On this approach, the Italian VPD would be immune from Indian criminal jurisdiction until a relevant exception could be identified. One might think the issue could be resolved by the 'territorial tort' principle. For example, under section 5(a) of the UK State Immunity Act a foreign state 'is not immune as respects proceedings in respect of . . . death or personal injury . . . caused by an act or omission in the United Kingdom'; however, this provision has no application to criminal cases.[45] Similarly, the UN Convention on Jurisdictional Immunities of States and their Property,

38 Though see *ibid.*, para. 98 (raising but not answering the question).

39 *Ibid.*, para. 102.

40 *Ibid.*, para. 70.

41 Hazel Fox, *The Law of State Immunity*, 2nd edn (Oxford University Press, 2008), 6.

42 James Crawford, 'International Law and Foreign Sovereigns: Distinguishing Immune Transactions', *British Yearbook of International Law*, 54 (1983), 75–118.

43 European Convention on State Immunity (Basel, 6 May 1952, entered into force 11 June 1976), ILM, (1972) 11, 470; United Nations Convention on Jurisdictional Immunities of States and their Property, annexed to UNGA Res. 59/38, 2 December 2004 (not yet in force); State Immunity Act (United Kingdom) 1978, Chapter 33, ILM, (1978) 17, 1123; Foreign States Immunities Act 1985 (Australia) (No. 196 of 1985), ILM, (1986) 25, 715; State Immunity Act 1982 (Canada), 1980–3, c. 95; ILM, (1982) 21, 798.

44 Crawford, 'International Law and Foreign Sovereigns', 91.

45 See above n. 43.

despite containing a similar principle in Article 12, is understood to have no application in criminal cases.[46] The point, therefore, remains controversial.

4 PCASP: questions of State responsibility

4.1 State responsibility for non-State actors: the ordinary principles

The International Maritime Organisation (IMO) has, since 2009, issued 'interim' guidance to flag States and shipowners on the use of PCASP to protect vessels from pirate attack in the High Risk Area.[47] The embarkation of PCASP is increasingly common with up to 15–25 per cent of all vessels transits through the High Risk Area now carrying them.[48] This State practice clearly indicates that the use of PCASP does not per se violate international law.[49] PCASP have also proved extraordinarily effective; so far, no vessel with embarked PCASP has been taken by pirates.[50] However, as the *Enrica Lexie* incident shows, having armed persons defend a vessel can have tragic consequences. When, then, might flag States incur responsibility if PCASP are embarked upon their vessels?

First, the use of PCASP may *indirectly* implicate the responsibility of a flag State. States are generally not directly responsible for the acts of individuals unless they are State agents or an exceptional rule applies.[51] However, States may come under a duty to mitigate the risk that activities within their jurisdiction pose to other States (and their nationals). A State must take all 'necessary steps immediately' to prevent or mitigate injury to other States arising from dangers within its jurisdiction.[52] This suggests that when States know their flag vessels are using PSCAP they are subject to an international duty to take necessary steps to mitigate any

46 UNGA Res. 59/38, 2 December 2004, para. 2.

47 See most recently revised Interim Guidance to Shipowners, Ship Operators and Shipmasters on the Use of PCASP on Board Ships in the High Risk Area, IMO Doc. MSC.1/Circ. 1405/Rev. 2 (25 May 2012); Revised Interim Recommendations for Flag States regarding the Use of Privately Contracted Armed Security Personnel on board Ships in the High Risk Area, IMO Doc. MSC.1/Circ.1406/Rev.2 (25 May 2012).

48 House of Commons Report, para. 26.

49 Although the issuing of IMO Recommendations on PCASP is 'not intended to endorse or institutionalize their use' (see IMO documents cited above in n. 47).

50 House of Commons Report, para. 29. Though this may be more a question of 'luck rather than design': Sarah Percy, 'Private Security Companies: Regulating the Last War', *International Review of the Red Cross*, 94 (2012), 941, 957.

51 See generally, Arts. 4–11 Articles on State Responsibility.

52 *Corfu Channel case (UK* v. *Albania)* (Merits), Judgment, 9 April 1949, ICJ Reports (1949), 4, paras. 22–3.

risk to other States (and their nationals) arising from that use. Such a duty would not involve strict liability; at most it would be a standard of 'due diligence', the content of which depends upon relevant treaty obligations owed other States.[53] In exercising rights of freedom of navigation on the high seas States must, under UNCLOS, 'have due regard for the interests of other States in their exercise of the freedom of the high seas'.[54] This obligation alone could sustain a finding that a due diligence obligation exists regarding activities conducted aboard a vessel under a flag State's jurisdiction. Further, under the Convention every State must also 'effectively exercise its jurisdiction and control in administrative, technical and social matters over ships flying its flag'.[55] The term 'administrative, technical and social matters' is not defined elsewhere in the Convention.[56] It obviously extends, however, at least to such matters as are expressly provided for in the Convention concerning construction and seaworthiness, the crewing of vessels, and matters regarding communication and avoidance of collisions.[57] It should also be interpreted to include criminal jurisdiction generally, as a flag State must be able to effectively discipline seafarers in criminal cases involving 'incidents of navigation' (discussed above).[58]

Taken together, these basic duties under UNCLOS to exercise 'due regard' and to 'effectively exercise . . . jurisdiction' suggest that if PCASP embarked on a vessel wrongfully injure foreign nationals or a foreign vessel, the flag State may risk incurring international responsibility. As above, this would not be vicarious liability for the acts of the PCASP themselves. Nonetheless, liability could arise from a failure of 'due diligence', such as a failure to take the minimum necessary steps to have an adequate regulatory regime in place governing PCASP and their acts.

What would such a minimum regime look like? Percy notes that private security companies in general are 'poorly regulated' because 'they

[53] See, albeit in different contexts, *Pulp Mills on the River Uruguay (Argentina* v. *Uruguay)*, Judgment, 20 April 2010, ICJ Reports (2010), 14, para. 197; *Responsibilities and Obligations of States Sponsoring Persons and Entities with respect to Activities in the Area*, Advisory Opinion, Seabed Disputes Chamber of the International Tribunal for the Law of the Sea, 1 February 2011, paras. 110–16; *Asian Agricultural Products Ltd* v. *Sri Lanka*, Case No. ARB 87/3, (1991) 30 ILM 580.

[54] Art. 87(2) UNCLOS; *cf.* Art. 2 HSC (which refers to 'reasonable regard').

[55] Art. 94(1) UNCLOS; Art. 5(1) HSC.

[56] It was intended to recall 'suggestions made by the International Labour Office at the [1956] Preparatory Technical Maritime Conference': UNCLOS I, *Official Records* IV (1958), 10 and 61.

[57] Art. 94(3) UNCLOS. [58] Art. 97(1) UNCLOS.

are inherently difficult to regulate'.[59] At the international level, regulatory efforts tend to find difficulty in securing agreement on effective measures; and 'domestic regulation alone could never regulate an industry that operates almost entirely abroad'.[60] Further, the fast pace of industry change has meant that regulation tends to be backward-looking rather than focused on present challenges.[61] One might think such concerns were lessened where the activities in question, while still extraterritorial, are *not* extra-jurisdictional. Flag States should be in a relatively good position to regulate maritime PCASP through their direct jurisdictional control over their vessels on the high seas. Whether this theoretical advantage is borne out in practice depends, of course, on the nature of regulation and the capacity of the flag State. A principal forum for regulatory efforts regarding maritime PCASP has been the IMO.

In May 2012 the IMO issued Revised Interim Recommendations for Flag States regarding the use of Privately Contracted Armed Security Personnel in the High Risk Area.[62] These recommendations run only to two pages. Essentially, the IMO Recommendations note that the permissibility of PCASP aboard vessels 'is a matter for flag States', which may individually 'determine if and under which conditions [their use] will be authorized'.[63] Flag States are encouraged to consider whether PCASP 'would be an appropriate measure' in the High Risk Area,[64] taking into account 'the possible escalation of violence which could result from the use of firearms'.[65] Notably, flag States should also 'require the parties concerned to comply with all relevant requirements of flag, port and coastal States' as a vessel carrying PCASP may need to take those personnel (and their weapons) through a variety of jurisdictions.[66] If a flag State then decides to permit PCASP, the IMO recommends that any policy governing their use include consideration of:[67]

1. 'the minimum criteria or minimum requirements with which PCASP should comply', taking into account the relevant IMO guidance to shipowners on PCASP[68]
2. 'a process for authorizing the use of [those] PCASP' which meet with the flag State criteria

[59] Sarah Percy, *Regulating the Private Security Industry* (London: International Institute for Strategic Studies, 2006), 63.
[60] *Ibid.* [61] Percy, 'Private Security Companies', 957. [62] Above n. 47.
[63] *Ibid.*, para. 2. [64] *Ibid.*, para. 5.1. [65] *Ibid.*, para. 3. [66] *Ibid.*, para. 4.
[67] *Ibid.*, para. 5.2 with sub-subparagraphs as indicated.
[68] See Interim Guidance to Shipowners.

3. 'a process by which shipowners, ship operators or shipping companies may be authorized to use PCASP'
4. 'the terms and conditions under which the authorization is granted and the accountability for compliance associated with that authorization'
5. 'references to any directly applicable national legislation pertaining to the carriage and use of firearms by PCASP . . . and the relationship of PCASP with the Master while on board'
6. 'reporting and record-keeping requirements'.

The reference to the IMO Guidance to Shipowners does incorporate some further detail (as noted below).[69] Nonetheless, this IMO list of relevant considerations for flag States does more to highlight than to dispel the potential difficulties. First, while PCASP will have to comply with any flag State firearms regulation, the relevant port State laws will also apply. Where port States are hostile to weapons being carried aboard foreign ships, this may require that certain ports be avoided, or that weapons are 'bonded' aboard the vessel, or deposited at a government-run 'floating armoury',[70] or simply thrown overboard.[71] Secondly, there is the question of the 'relationship of PCASP with the Master'. The IMO Interim Guidance to Shipowners further recommend that a 'documented [PCASP] command and control structure should provide . . . a clear statement recognizing that at all times the Master remains in command and retains the overriding authority on board'.[72] Under international law, ultimate authority for decisions regarding safety aboard a merchant vessel rests with the master. For example, Regulation 8(a) of Chapter XI-2 of the SOLAS Convention provides: 'The master shall not be constrained by the Company, the charterer or any other person from taking or executing any decision which, in the professional judgement of the master, is necessary to maintain the safety and security of the ship.' The final, and perhaps most significant, difficulty in regulating the use of force by PCASP is in 'reporting and record-keeping requirements' and ensuring 'accountability for compliance' with relevant standards. The most important issue here is, obviously, standards governing the use of force and post-shooting incident inquiries. There may be real problems in conducting an adequate review of shooting incidents occurring far from the flag State's territory, let alone mounting a criminal investigation.

[69] *Ibid.*, especially paras. 5.6–5.19.

[70] 'Sri Lanka Launches Floating Armoury', *Lloyd's List* (26 September 2012), available at www.lss-sapu.com/index.php/piracynews/view/1027.

[71] House of Commons Report, para. 41.

[72] See above n. 47, para. 5.9.1.

Nonetheless, a flag State which fails to take adequate measures to prevent such abuses before the fact (through establishing an adequate regulatory framework) or to investigate them afterwards may incur responsibility towards the State whose nationals are injured. As regards the establishment of an adequate regulatory framework, Percy notes that the complexity of regulating the private security industry has tempted States generally to rely on industry self-regulation, such as the voluntary International Code of Conduct for Private Security Service Providers (ICoC) initiative convened by the Swiss government and the Geneva Centre for the Democratic Control of Armed Forces.[73] An International Standards Organisation (ISO) certification for PCASP is also being developed in consultation with the industry.[74] A completely 'hands-off' approach by States, simply relying on such third-party certification, would probably not satisfy due diligence obligations. Nonetheless, instruments such as the ICoC may provide evidence of the internationally accepted minimum standards for the conduct of PCASP on issues such as the use of force. Incorporating such third-party standards into national regulations would, however, likely be desirable.

States may already have national laws applicable to PCASP activities, even if they were not designed for such a purpose. For example, UK law does not require direct government approval of a decision to use PCASP, simply the submission of a 'counter-piracy plan'.[75] However, aboard a UK-flagged vessel a person in possession of a firearm will likely require a certificate under the Firearms Act 1968;[76] and any UK national 'supplying' or 'delivering' weapons across an international border will require a relevant trade licence (unless covered by an employer licence).[77] While this latter law was designed to regulate arms traders, it (unintentionally)

[73] Percy, 'Private Security Companies', 953–4. See further the ICoC website available at www.icoc-psp.org; and note the Security Association for the Maritime Industry (a self-regulation body), available at www.seasecurity.org/.

[74] ISO PAS 28007 Procedures for Private Maritime Security Companies.

[75] Department for Transport (UK), Interim Guidance to UK Flagged Shipping on the Use of Armed Guards to Defend against the Threat of Piracy in Exceptional Circumstances, version 1.1, June 2012, para. 5.6, available at http://assets.dft.gov.uk/publications/use-of-armed-guards-to-defend-against-piracy. This contrasts with an earlier policy that the UK government would not authorise the carriage of firearms aboard UK vessels: UK Maritime and Coastguard Agency Marine Guidance Note 298(M) (2005), para. 6.15.1, available at www.dft.gov.uk/mca/298–2.pdf.

[76] s. 1 Firearms Act 1968 (1968 c. 27).

[77] Art. 21, Export Control Order 2008 (No. 3231 of 2008). Small firearms are listed as controlled 'military goods' in Schedule 2.

also applies, for example, to persons carrying corporate-owned weapons who at the end of a voyage will return them to their employer.[78] Whether such laws are appropriately adapted for regulating PCASP or PMSCs is another question.

Of course, a State must not only enact PCASP regulations but also take action regarding 'accountability for compliance'. A key question will be accountability for the use of force. The question then arises as to the international standard for the use of force in self-defence by private individuals.[79] As regards the appropriate standard for the use of force by PCASP the IMO Interim Guidance to Shipowners states that:

> PMSC should require their personnel to take all reasonable steps to avoid the use of force . . . In no case should the use of force exceed what is strictly necessary and reasonable in the circumstances. Care should be taken to minimize damage and injury and preserve human life.
>
> PMSC should require that their personnel not use firearms against persons except in self-defence or defence of others.[80]

This language closely tracks the ICoC, which borrows much of its drafting from the UN Basic Principles on the Use of Force and Firearms by Law Enforcement Officials.[81] The UN Basic Principles are a soft-law instrument adopted by consensus by 127 States at the Eighth UN Congress on the Prevention of Crime and Treatment of Offenders in 1990.[82] The document is thus not binding but represents persuasive evidence of widespread State consensus (*opinio juris*) as to the applicable law. While the UN Basic Principles apply only to State officials, the replication of these standards in other instruments applicable to private individuals, such as the ICoC and IMO Recommendations, may also suggest that they are increasingly accepted as having broader application. Failure to make adequate efforts to ensure compliance with such basic standards through, *inter alia*, appropriate post-incident investigation might thus incur State responsibility.

[78] See further the flow chart in the House of Commons Report, Evidence Annexe, Ev 67.

[79] *Cf.* Art. 31(1)(c), Rome Statute of the International Criminal Court (Rome, adopted 17 July 1998, entered into force 1 July 2002), 2187 UNTS 90.

[80] See above n. 47, paras 5.14 and 5.15.

[81] Art. 9, Basic Principles on the Use of Force and Firearms by Law Enforcement Officials, UN Doc. A/CONF.144/28/Rev.1 (7 September 1990) ('[l]aw enforcement officials shall not use firearms against persons except in self-defence or defence of others against the imminent threat of death or serious injury, [or] to prevent the perpetration of a particularly serious crime involving grave threat to life . . . [and] only . . . when strictly unavoidable in order to protect life').

[82] See A/CONF.144/28/Rev.1, 269 (adoption) and 201 and 207 (participating States).

However, this is not to suggest that flag State implementation of international minimum standards suffices. The International Court of Justice and the International Tribunal for the Law of the Sea have defined 'an obligation to act with due diligence' as involving:

> an obligation which entails not only the adoption of appropriate rules and measures, but also a certain level of vigilance in their enforcement and the exercise of administrative control applicable to public and private operators, such as the monitoring of activities undertaken by such operators.[83]

This makes the obvious point that due diligence involves not only identifying the risks that may be posed by 'private operators' and taking appropriate steps (including implementing any relevant international minimum standards) but also monitoring those private operators with an appropriate degree of vigilance. In the present case the IMO Recommendations simply point the way towards States devising effective regulatory systems of their own. They represent little more than a bare minimum supplemented by industry self-regulation. As Percy observes: '[w]hether or not the bare minimum is sufficient to regulate an industry that has significant lethal potential is questionable'; and given that this is a sector dealing 'in lethal force' one may also question the appropriateness of relying on self-regulation.[84] Neither formal compliance with the IMO Recommendations nor reliance on self-regulation will likely be enough to discharge any duty of due diligence. The key will be effective monitoring and enforcement. Weaknesses of flag State supervision is an acknowledged reality in matters such as fisheries management, and, if oversight of PCASP is no better, this could be deeply worrying.

4.2 Responsibility for State 'complicity' with corporate human rights breaches

Even so, this is a relatively narrow field within which States might incur responsibility. A question arises as to whether a State might also incur responsibility under a broader standard of 'complicity' in corporate misconduct. Such an approach could be based on an extension of Article 16

[83] *Pulp Mills on the River Uruguay*, para. 197 as quoted in *Activities in the Responsibilities and obligations of States sponsoring persons and entities with respect to activities in the Area*, Advisory Opinion, 1 February 2011, ITLOS Case No. 17, para. 115.

[84] Percy, 'Private Security Companies', 955.

of the ILC Articles on State Responsibility dealing with situations where a State aids or assists another State's internationally wrongful act:

> A State which aids or assists another State in the commission of an internationally wrongful act by the latter is internationally responsible for doing so if: (a) that State does so with knowledge of the circumstances of the internationally wrongful act; and (b) the act would be internationally wrongful if committed by that State.

One may suggest that the same principle should cover situations where a State assists certain types of *corporate* misconduct breaching human rights or international criminal law. McCorquodale and Simons have argued for just such an approach:

> A home state may also be found to be complicit in the extraterritorial activities of corporations . . . and thus incur international responsibility . . . While the ILC's Articles deal only with the responsibility of states, they do not exclude the possibility of other actors . . . incurring responsibility. It is now established that individuals can incur international responsibility for . . . international crimes. Moreover, it has been convincingly argued that corporations . . . have obligations under international law not to commit international crimes and therefore can incur international responsibility for complicity in, and commission of . . . international crimes.[85]

McCorquodale and Simons argue that it follows that a State may incur international responsibility for complicity in corporate acts which 'if committed by that home state would constitute internationally wrongful acts . . . at least where the [state's] aid or assistance "contributed significantly to that act"'.[86] The argument remains, however, speculative. Certainly, the ILC Articles do not preclude the individual responsibility of natural persons for international crimes. The idea that corporations can incur 'international responsibility' for international crimes is less well established. Direct criminal responsibility for corporate actors was famously excluded from the jurisdiction of the International Criminal Court. Further, the possible extension of Article 16 to cover complicity in corporate conduct is, at present, at best a suggestion *de lege ferenda* unsupported by State practice.

To the extent the argument is limited to violations of human rights law one may question whether we really need an expanded concept of State complicity at all, given that a different standard of attribution may already

[85] McCorquodale and Simons, 'Responsibility beyond Borders', 613–14. [86] *Ibid.*, 614.

apply. Human rights bodies have long set a lower requirement for State responsibility for the actions of actors who are not State organs than the stringent test articulated by the ICJ.[87] That is, for the ICJ to find a State responsible for the acts of a non-State entity it requires either:[88]

(a) the exercise of *actual* or *complete* control by a State over a non-State entity (that control being based on a position of complete dependence of the entity on the State) or
(b) 'effective control' over the particular conduct alleged to give rise to State responsibility. Essentially, there is State responsibility 'if the person or group of persons is in fact acting on the instructions of, or under the direction or control of, that State' in a particular case.[89]

The European Court of Human Rights, by contrast, will find a State responsible for the actions of State-like entities where they are either under the 'decisive influence' of a State (as in the *Ilaşcu* case)[90] or which are *acting within* territory under the 'effective overall control' of a State (as in the *Loizidou* case where the governmental acts of the Turkish Republic of Northern Cyprus were held attributable to Turkey).[91] Neither is a particularly stringent standard, and the latter may seem particularly lax. Milanović cogently suggests that cases such as *Loizidou* are not, strictly speaking, about attribution at all.[92] Rather, they are about the circumstances in which a State has positive duties to secure or ensure human rights in territory under its control, for example the right to life. Thus, during an occupation, a State may incur international responsibility not only for wrongs committed by its own forces but also:

87 See generally, Stefan Talmon, 'Responsibility of Outside Powers for Acts of Secessionist Entities', *International and Comparative Law Quarterly*, 58 (2009), 493–517, discussing *Military and Paramilitary Activities in and against Nicaragua (Nicaragua* v. *USA)*, Judgment, 27 June 1986, ICJ Reports (1986), paras. 108–12, 114–16; and *Application of the Convention on the Prevention and Punishment of the Crime of Genocide (Bosnia and Herzegovina* v. *Serbia and Montenegro)*, Judgment, 26 February 2007, ICJ Reports (2007), paras. 241, 388, 391–4, 399; and *cf.* Marko Milanović, 'State Responsibility for Genocide: A Follow-Up', *European Journal of International Law*, 17 (2006), 576–7.

88 *Ibid.*, 502. 89 Art. 8 Articles on State Responsibility.

90 *Ilaşcu and others* v. *Moldova and Russia*, Application No. 48787/99, ECtHR, 8 July 2004, para. 392.

91 *Loizidou* v. *Turkey*, Application No. 40/1993/435/514, ECtHR, 23 February 1995; and see Talmon, 'Responsibility of Outside Powers for Acts of Secessionist Entities', 508–11.

92 Marko Milanović, *Extraterritorial Application of Human Rights Treaties: Law, Principles, and Policy* (Oxford University Press, 2011), 46–52.

> for any *lack of vigilance* in preventing violations of human rights . . . by other actors present in the occupied territory, including rebel groups.[93]

The suggestion in such cases is clearly that the State has a 'due diligence' obligation to take measures to prevent such violations. If this line of analysis is correct, human rights jurisprudence adds nothing unique to the present discussion. It simply provides a separate foundation for the same conclusion: States have an obligation to exercise due diligence to secure respect for human rights within spaces under their jurisdiction or control. This could readily extend to taking effective measures to minimise the risks of unlawful violence by PCASP or PMSCs operating from flag vessels.

5 Conclusions

We can expect the increasing use of PCASP and VPDs to implicate the law of State responsibility in one of two ways. Where VPDs are deployed as State organs to protect merchant vessels, the controversy will largely be one of State immunity. In such cases a more rational and predictable case law would follow from, as Crawford has suggested, shifting the focus from classifying the impugned act to identifying relevant exceptions to the immunity applicable prima facie. Where PCASP are permitted by flag States (or even used despite flag State policy) the question will be one of due diligence. While international standards are emerging,[94] the real question will be the extent to which States satisfy their duty of vigilance. The history of effective flag State control over vessels on the high seas, sadly, is not particularly encouraging in this regard.

[93] *Armed Activities on the Territory of the Congo (Congo* v. *Uganda)*, Judgment, 19 December 2005, ICJ Reports (2005), para. 179 (emphasis added).

[94] On calls for the 'establishment of a framework governing the use of' PCASP see UN Secretary-General, 'Remarks to Security Council Debate on Maritime Piracy as a Threat to International Peace and Security', 19 November 2012, available at www.un.org/apps/news/infocus/sgspeeches/statments_full.asp?statID=1702#.UKuWS4b4KWk.

18

Excessive collateral civilian casualties and military necessity

Awkward crossroads in international humanitarian law between State responsibility and individual criminal liability

YUTAKA ARAI-TAKAHASHI*

Introduction

When an attack is launched by an army against a military objective of the adverse party to an international armed conflict (IAC), causing incidental civilian casualties, the legal question that immediately arises is whether such 'collateral damage' is 'excessive' in relation to 'the concrete and direct military advantage anticipated' within the meaning of Articles 51(5)(b) and 57(2) of the 1977 Geneva Additional Protocol I (API).[1] These provisions embody the principle of proportionality, which is recognised as part of customary international law.[2] Assuming that the test of attribution is met, the responsibility of the attacking State can be engaged. Further, if such an attack has been carried out in the knowledge that the incidental loss 'would be clearly excessive in relation to the concrete and direct overall military advantage anticipated', then the question of individual criminal

* The author wishes to express special thanks to Prof. Andrea Bianchi for his comments on the earlier draft of this chapter.

[1] Protocol Additional to the Geneva Conventions of 12 August 1949, and Relating to the Protocol of Victims of International Armed Conflicts (Protocol I), 8 June 1977. The same language of proportionality appears also in the original 1980 Protocol on Prohibitions or Restrictions on the Use of Mines, Booby-traps and Other Devices annexed to the Convention on Prohibitions or Restrictions on the Use of Certain Conventional Weapons which May Be Deemed to Be Excessively Injurious or to Have Indiscriminate Effects, Art. 3(3)(c); and the amended Protocol of 3 May 1996, Art. 3(8)(c).

[2] *Prosecutor* v. *Galić*, Case No. IT-98–29-T, ICTY Trial Chamber, Judgment, 5 December 2003, para. 58. See also Jean-Marie Henckaerts and Louise Doswald-Beck, *Customary International Humanitarian Law* (Cambridge University Press, 2005), 46–62.

responsibility of the soldier involved in the attack may concurrently arise under Article 8(2)(b)(iv) of the Rome Statute of the International Criminal Court (ICC Statute). With respect to incidental casualties of civilians (and damage of civilian objects, and combination thereof), it is clear that Article 8(2)(b)(iv) ICC derives from the rules embodied under Articles 51(5)(b) and 57(2) API.

As Bianchi notes,[3] such duality of responsibility, and this without any hierarchy between them,[4] has been 'a constant feature of international law'.[5] That said, fundamental differences must be borne in mind. The law on State responsibility is an 'objective' regime,[6] which is not predicated on a 'fault' (*culpa*) or subjective element of the pertinent State's organ or agent, save for the primary rules that inherently incorporate a subjective element, such as those on genocide.[7] The responsibility of a State for the excessive collateral damage arises, even though perpetrators are judged as not having entertained the requisite degree of *mens rea*, as required under Article 30 ICC Statute, with respect to their conduct.

This chapter examines some salient issues that may arise with respect to the identification of State responsibility and individual criminal responsibility with respect to disproportionate collateral civilian casualties in the context of IAC. It is limited to examining incidental loss of civilian lives, excluding analyses of other protected legal interests contained in Article 8(2)(b)(iv) ICC Statute, namely, civilian objects, or a combination of civilians and civilian objects, and the environment. This chapter is nonetheless compelled to emphasise that while the literature tends to discuss these protected interests under the generic notion of 'collateral civilian damage' in ascertaining the proportionality equation, a clear

[3] Andrea Bianchi, 'State Responsibility and Criminal Liability of Individuals' in Antonio Cassese (ed.), *Oxford Companion of International Criminal Justice* (Oxford University Press, 2009), 23.

[4] *Prosecutor* v. *Delalić and others*, Case No. IT-96–21, ICTY Appeals Chamber, Judgment, 20 February 2001, para. 24.

[5] *Application of the Convention on the Prevention and Punishment of the Crime of Genocide (Bosnia Herzegovina* v. *Serbia and Montenegro)*, Judgment, 26 February 2007, para. 173. See also *Prosecutor* v. *Krstić*, Case No. IT-98–33, ICTY Appeals Chamber, Judgment, 19 April 2004.

[6] James Crawford, *The International Law Commission's Articles on State Responsibility: Introduction, Text and Commentaries* (Cambridge University Press, 2002), 81–2, para. 3, commentary to Art. 2.

[7] Brigitte Stern, 'The Elements of an Internationally Wrongful Act' in James Crawford, Alain Pellet and Simon Olleson (eds.), *The Law of International Responsibility* (Oxford University Press, 2010), 210.

line must be drawn between the incidental loss of civilian *lives* and the incidental loss of civilian *objects*. It should be obvious that a more stringent appraisal is required with respect to the balance between two 'incommensurable values' (lives of civilians and the military advantage) than in the case of weighing two less comparable elements (civilian objects and the military advantage).[8]

Implications of qualifying words in the material elements of the offence of collateral civilian casualties

On a closer inspection, there are some differences in relation to the material element of the two associated rules. The drafters of Article 8(2)(b)(iv) ICC Statute have appended the adverb 'clearly' before the adjective 'excessive',[9] whilst the word 'overall' has been added so as to create an expression that may appear an oxymoron, 'concrete and direct overall military advantage anticipated'.[10] In view of these, it may be argued that the drafters of the ICC Statute deliberately set a higher threshold for ascertaining the war crime of excessive collateral damage of attacks under Article 8(2)(b)(iv) ICC Statute. Such a move conforms to the declaration of interpretation made by many Western States with respect to the associated rules under API (Articles 51(5)(b) and 57(2)). According to their interpretation, the military advantage anticipated from the attack should be comprehended as the advantage considered as a whole and not from isolated or specific parts of the attack.[11]

[8] This does not, however, mean that long-term deleterious impacts of damage to civilian infrastructure on the health and lives of civilians should be discounted. See Paolo Benvenuti, 'The ICTY Prosecutor and the Review of the NATO Bombing Campaign against the Federal Republic of Yugoslavia', *European Journal of International Law*, 12 (2001), 508.

[9] Amichai Cohen and Yuval Shany, 'A Development of Modest Proportions: The Application of the Principle of Proportionality in the Targeted Killings Case', *Journal of International Criminal Justice*, 5 (2007), 319.

[10] Knut Dörmann, *Elements of War Crimes under the Rome Statute of the International Criminal Court: Sources and Commentary* (Cambridge University Press, 2003), 166 and 169.

[11] See the UK reservation (i) concerning Arts. 51 and 57 (2 July 2002). See also Henckaerts and Doswald-Beck, *Customary International Humanitarian Law*, 49, n. 27 (referring to the practice of Australia, Belgium, Canada, France, Germany, Italy, the Netherlands, New Zealand, Spain, United Kingdom, United States, as well as the non-Western State of Nigeria). The reservations and declarations are available at www.icrc.org/applic/ihl/ihl.nsf/States.

Some commentators voice a concern over modifying the existing proportionate equation embodied under the relevant provisions of API.[12] Under international humanitarian law (IHL), there have been debates over whether the 'extensive'[13] or 'severe'[14] nature of incidental casualties can be read in the expression 'excessiveness'.[15] Now there is a fear that the standard of 'clear excessiveness' introduced at the Rome Conference (1998) may remove the normative constraint further away from the reality of side effects of aerial bombardment on the ground, whose fall-out disproportionately affects children, women and the aged. Indeed, one expert comments that the insertion of those words 'does not fulfil its ostensible purpose, which was to clarify the crime, but simply raises the threshold and introduces greater uncertainty into the law in this area'.[16]

As is known, at Rome the Representative of the International Committee of the Red Cross and Crescent (ICRC) underscored that the introduction of the words 'clearly' and 'overall' under Article 8(2)(b)(iv) ICC Statute does not alter the existing rule under API and the customary law equivalent:

> The word 'overall' could give the impression that an extra unspecified element has been added to a formulation that was carefully negotiated during the 1974–1977 Diplomatic Conference that led to Additional Protocol I to the 1949 Geneva Conventions and this formulation is generally recognized as reflecting customary law. The intention of this additional word appears to be to indicate that a particular target can have an important military

[12] Louise Doswald-Beck and Sylvain Vité, 'International Humanitarian Law and Human Rights Law', *International Review of the Red Cross*, 293 (1993), 109; and Anthony E. Cassimatis, 'International Humanitarian Law, International Human Rights Law, and Fragmentation of International Law', *International and Comparative Law Quarterly*, 56 (2007), 629.

[13] Protocol Additional to the Geneva Conventions of 12 August 1949, and relating to the Protection of Victims of International Armed Conflicts (Protocol I), 8 June 1977. Commentary – Protection of the civilian population, 625–6, para. 1980, www.icrc.org/applic/ihl/ihl.nsf/Comment.xsp?viewComments=LookUpCOMART&articleUNID=4BEBD9920AE0AEAEC12563CD0051DC9E.

[14] W. J. Fenrick, 'The Rule of Proportionality and Protocol I in Conventional Warfare', *Military Law Review*, 98 (1982), 111.

[15] A. P. V. Rogers, *Law on the Battlefield*, 3rd edn (Manchester University Press, 2012), 25–6; Sandesh Sivakumaran, *The Law of Non-international Armed Conflict* (Oxford University Press, 2012), 350–1.

[16] Robert Cryer, 'Of Custom, Treaties, Scholars and the Gavel: The Influence of the International Criminal Tribunals on the ICRC Customary Law Study', *Journal of Conflict and Security Law*, 11 (2006), 259–60.

> advantage that can be felt over a lengthy period of time and affect military action in areas other than the vicinity of the target itself. As this meaning is included in the existing wording of Additional Protocol I, the inclusion of the word 'overall' is redundant.[17]

The outcomes revealed by the ICRC's Customary IHL Study[18] suggest that the insertion of the words 'clearly' and 'overall' under Article 8(2)(b)(iv) ICC Statute has not (yet) modified the standard of the affiliated rule under customary IHL. According to the *Study*, the material elements of the latter are found to remain consistent with those embodied in Articles 51(5)(b) and 57(2) API.[19]

Further, one might contend that the standard of ascertaining the war crime of disproportionate attack in the ICC Statute does not reflect customary law. According to this argument, such a higher threshold that appears to be introduced by the ICC Statute should be understood as delimiting the jurisdictional scope of the ICC rather than as providing the definitional elements of this war crime under customary law.[20]

Different thresholds for establishing State responsibility and individual criminal liability concerning collateral damage

This chapter duly heeds the *bona fide* concern expressed by the ICRC and publicists with respect to the possible elevation of the threshold for identifying a violation of the rule of proportionality under Article 8(2)(b)(iv) ICC Statute. It nevertheless argues that such a change in the construction, if any, relates solely to the question of individual criminal responsibility. Such a modification in the interpretation is recognisable,[21] without the law relating to war crimes entailing negative effects in shaping the corresponding IHL rule.

[17] UN Doc. A/CONF.183/INF/10 of 13 July 1998, available at ICC preparatory works; as cited in Dörmann, *Elements of War Crimes under the Rome Statute of the International Criminal Court*, 169–70.

[18] ICRC, *Customary International Humanitarian Law*, ed. Jean-Marie Henkaerts and Louise Doswald-Beck (Cambridge University Press, 2005).

[19] Henckaerts and Doswald-Beck, *Customary International Humanitarian Law*, 46–55.

[20] Sivakumaran, *The Law of Non-International Armed Conflict*, 80–1.

[21] Hermann von Hebel and Darryl Robinson, 'Crimes within the Jurisdiction of the Court' in Roy S. Lee (ed.), *The International Criminal Court: The Making of the Rome Statute – Issues, Negotiations, Results* (The Hague: Kluwer, 1999), 111; Roberta Arnold, 'War Crimes – para. 2(b)(IV)' in Otto Triffterer (ed.), *Commentary to the Rome Statute of the International Criminal Court: Observers' Notes, Article by Article*, 2nd edn (Munich: C. H. Beck, 2008), 339; Sivakumaran, *The Law of Non-international Armed Conflict*, 79–80.

Banal as it may sound, it is essential that the war crime rules be construed more narrowly and strictly to conform to the principle *nulla poena sine lege* than the equivalent rules of IHL.[22] It is precisely for this reason that some circumspection is needed for transposing the elements of international criminal law to the congenial rules of IHL.[23] With specific regard to the war crime of excessive collateral damage under Article 8(2)(b)(iv) ICC Statute, given the insertion of the qualifying words 'clearly' and 'overall', this is drafted in a narrower manner than the equivalent IHL rule.[24]

The different thresholds for establishing the two systems of responsibility should not be surprising, not least because war crimes relate only to a 'serious' violation of IHL.[25] 'Non-serious' breaches of IHL generate issues only of State responsibility. Conversely, for 'ordinary' breaches of IHL, even if the threshold of individual criminal responsibility is unattained, the requisite level for establishing State responsibility for violating the equivalent IHL rules may be reached.[26]

Trying perpetrators in the dock for war crimes cannot be determined solely by the 'objective' ascertainment of breaches of international obligations. Rather, identifying war crimes is contingent upon complex evaluations of many other factors such as the *mens rea*, grounds precluding individual criminal responsibility, mistakes of fact or mistake of law, superior order, the *nullum crimen sine lege* principle and the rights of fair trial of the accused.[27]

22 Michael Bothe, 'War Crimes' in Antonio Cassese, Paola Gaeta and John R. W. D. Jones (eds.), *The Rome Statute of the International Criminal Court: A Commentary*, 2 vols. (Oxford University Press, 2002), I, 381.

23 Sivakumaran, *The Law of Non-international Armed Conflict*, 79.

24 See also the introduction of the proportionate equation under Art. 8(2)(b)(iv) ICC Statute, the element that does not feature under the associated rules on the protection of environment under Arts. 35(3) and 55(1) API, and Art. 1 of the Convention on the Prohibition of Military or any Hostile Use of Environmental Modification Technique (New York, adopted 10 December 1976, entered into force 5 October 1978), 1108 UNTS 151.

25 Yoram Dinstein, *The Conduct of Hostilities under the Law of International Armed Conflict*, 2nd edn (Cambridge University Press, 2010), 266. See also *Prosecutor* v. *Delalić et al.*, Case No. IT-96–21-T, ICTY Trial Chamber, Judgment, 16 November 1998, para. 1154.

26 However, the converse is true, so that the identification of state responsibility for violations of IHL constitutes a 'precondition' for affirming individual criminal responsibility: Benvenuti, 'The ICTY Prosecutor and the Review of the NATO Bombing Campaign against the Federal Republic of Yugoslavia', 527.

27 See also Sivakumaran, *The Law of Non-international Armed Conflict*, 80.

Overcoming the 'binary analytical mindset'

This chapter's underlying premise is that our analysis must not be confined to the binary thinking that a conduct in armed conflict is either lawful or tantamount to a war crime.[28] There is a concern that the interpretive development of the latter body of law may depend too closely on the work of war crimes tribunals, such as the ICC.[29] Such a 'dichotomised mindset' may make us oblivious to breaches of IHL rules that stop short of amounting to war crimes, but for which State responsibility may remain. We should not ascertain elements of IHL rules exclusively through the lens of their 'secondary rules' (war crimes rules),[30] as if the latter 'freeze' or 'push' the development of corresponding rules of IHL.[31] In 2000, on the basis of the Report submitted by the Review Committee, the then ICTY Prosecutor decided not to open a criminal investigation into the aerial bombings undertaken by the North Atlantic Treaty Organization (NATO) on Serbia. The Review Committee's controversial report, albeit unintentionally, seems to have given the public impression that by finding no evidence of war crimes there was accordingly no State responsibility for this damage.[32] This has been the case even though it was outside the Review Committee's mandate to analyse issues of State responsibility. As discussed above, the absence of war crimes does not necessarily translate into the non-existence of State responsibility for the contested conduct.

[28] Marco Sassòli, 'The Implementation of International Humanitarian Law: Current and Inherent Challenges', *Yearbook of International Humanitarian Law*, 10 (2007), 54.

[29] Sivakumaran, *The Law of Non-international Armed Conflict*, 81. Such an unintended result is surely contemplated by Art. 10 ICC.

[30] The suggestion that international criminal law on war crimes constitutes the secondary rules in relation to the primary rules of IHL is accepted in the literature: Bothe, 'War Crimes', 381; and Sivakumaran, *The Law of Non-international Armed Conflict*, 77 and 478.

[31] W. J. Fenrick, 'The Law Applicable to Targeting and Proportionality after Operation Allied Force: A View from the Outside', *Yearbook of International Humanitarian Law*, 3 (2000), 79–80; David Turns, 'At the "Vanishing Point" of International Humanitarian Law: Methods and Means of Warfare in Non-International Armed Conflicts', *German Yearbook of International Law*, 45 (2002), 146–7.

[32] Benvenuti, 'The ICTY Prosecutor and the Review of the NATO Bombing Campaign against the Federal Republic of Yugoslavia', 527 (criticising that 'the [Review] Committee has done its best to deny the international responsibility of the state as such, in order to achieve an *a priori* exclusion of the role of the ICTY in evaluating the positions of individuals').

The concept of military necessity

Overview

One salient aspect that should be borne in mind when examining the relationship between the two systems of responsibility for collateral civilian casualties is the ramifications of the concept of military necessity. The following appraisals aim to address some of the confusion that may arise when the concept of military necessity is invoked as an attempt to deny responsibility for collateral civilian casualties on two levels (exculpation of criminal responsibility of a defendant; and/or exoneration of State responsibility).

The analysis starts with the thesis that the operational scope of this concept is confined to those specific IHL provisions that expressly or implicitly set it forth, so that any endeavour to plead for a further ambit of derogability to escape responsibility under the *general* context of IHL is futile. Next, the analysis turns to defending the argument that with the concept of military necessity already ingrained in the normative parameters of *all* IHL rules, reliance on it is excluded at the level of the secondary rules on State responsibility. The underlying assumption is that the principle of proportionality, which necessitates ascertaining the elements of military objective and military advantage, as well as the relative degree of 'excessiveness', is a specific form of the notion of military necessity.[33]

No room for the concept of military necessity save under the specific rules that incorporate it

The concept of military necessity in the present-day context of IHL is completely differentiated from its historical counterpart that was affiliated

[33] Myres S. McDougal and Florentino P. Feliciano, *The International Law of War: Transnational Coercion and World Public Order* (Dordrecht: Martinus Nijhoff, 1994), originally published as *Law and Minimum World Public Order: The Legal Regulation of International Coercion* (New Haven: Yale University Press, 1961), 72; William V. O'Brien, 'The Meaning of "Military Necessity" in International Law', *World Polity*, 1 (1957), 138, 148–9; Robert Kolb, 'La Nécessité militaire dans le droit des conflits armés: essai de clarification conceptuelle', *Colloque de Grenoble, La nécessité en droit international*, Société française pour le droit international (Paris: Pedone, 2007), 164–5 and 167–8; Robert D. Sloane, 'The Cost of Conflation: Preserving the Dualism of *Jus ad Bellum* and *Jus in Bello* in the Contemporary Law of War', *Yale Journal of International Law*, 34 (2009), 74; Gabriella Venturini, 'Necessity in the Law of Armed Conflict and in International Criminal Law', *Netherlands Yearbook of International Law*, 41 (2010), 73. See, however, Stefan Oeter, 'Methods and Means of Combat' in Dieter Fleck (ed.), *The Handbook of International Humanitarian Law*, 2nd edn (Oxford University Press, 2008), 135.

to the Prussian doctrine of *Kriegsraison geht vor Kriegsmanier*,[34] which was premised on the very wide interpretation of the right of self-preservation.[35] This concept does not have any place outside specific exceptional clauses that provide for it.[36] Conversely, the treaty provisions that do not contain such saving clauses must never allow any plea of military necessity.[37] Otherwise, the very express clauses or provisions that integrate this concept would be deemed superfluous.[38] Once there is a finding that specific IHL rules have been flouted, there is no room for the concept of military necessity to operate again to exonerate the recalcitrant State's responsibility,[39] as if this were an implied and overarching principle of IHL. Indeed, this chapter argues that in view of the close parallel development of customary law and conventional rules, there is no residual customary law that would allow the broader scope of application *ratione materiae* of the concept of military necessity beyond the clauses that incorporate it.[40]

This understanding has been fully established in the case law.[41] In the *Krupp* case, the United States Military Tribunal III-A at Nuremberg held that if the laws of war did not contain any escape valve of military necessity, then derogation was not permissible from those

34 See Julius Stone, *Legal Controls of International Conflict: A Treatise on the Dynamics of Disputes – and War-Law* (Sydney: Maitland, 1954), 352–3. See also Holland, The Hague, Special Criminal Court, 4 May 1948; and Special Court of Cassation, 12 January 1949, *In re Rauter*, International Law Reports, 16 (1949), 543 (rejecting this doctrine).

35 Kolb, 'La Nécessité militaire dans le droit des conflits armés', 168 and 170; Venturini, 'Necessity in the Law of Armed Conflict and in International Criminal Law', 51.

36 See, *inter alia*, Erik Castrén, *The Present Law of War and Neutrality* (Helsinki: Suomalaisen Tiedeakatemian Toimituksia, 1954), 66; Frits Kalshoven, *Belligerent Reprisals* (The Hague: Martinus Nijhoff, 1971), 366, (repr. Leiden: Martinus Nijhoff, 2005); ICRC Commentary to APs (1987), paras. 1389 and 1405; Henri Meyrowitz, 'The Principle of Superfluous Injury or Unnecessary Suffering: From the Declaration of St. Petersburg of 1868 to Additional Protocol I of 1977', *International Review of the Red Cross*, 299 (1994), 108; Dinstein, *The Conduct of Hostilities under the Law of International Armed Conflict*, 6–7; Robert Kolb, *Ius in Bello: le droit international des conflits armés*, 2nd edn (Basel: Helbing Lichtenhahn, 2009), 119. See also Georg Schwarzenberger, *International Law as Applied by International Courts and Tribunals*, II: *The Law of Armed Conflict* (London: Stevens and Sons, 1968), 135–6.

37 Venturini, 'Necessity in the Law of Armed Conflict and in International Criminal Law', 52; Marco Sassòli, 'State Responsibility for Violations of International Humanitarian Law', *International Review of the Red Cross*, 84 (2002), 416.

38 Kolb, 'La Nécessité militaire dans le droit des conflits armés', 168.

39 *Ibid.*, 158 and 168. 40 *Ibid.*, 170.

41 Apart from the *Krupp* case discussed here, see also *The Hostage Trial (Trial of Wilhelm List and others)*, Law Reports of Trials of War Criminals, 8 (1949), 35–6, 63–4 and 66–9.

rules.[42] Admittedly, despite the *Krupp* ruling, the Trial Chamber of the International Criminal Tribunal for the former Yugoslavia (ICTY) in some instances erred in reverting to the argument put forward by the defendants in the *Krupp* case, holding that '[t]argeting civilians is an offence when not justified by military necessity'.[43] This interpretation overlooks the non-derogable nature of the outlawing of a deliberate attack on civilians.[44] Such a construction has been duly rectified by the ICTY Appeals Chamber, which has reaffirmed that 'there is an absolute ban on targeting civilians in customary international law'.[45] Allowing States to plead a *general* and implicit concept of military necessity outside the expressly recognised rules to justify deviations from otherwise unqualified IHL rules 'would risk making the law . . . subservient to the exigencies of war'.[46]

No room for military necessity under Article 25(2)(a) Articles on Responsibility of States for Internationally Wrongful Acts (ARSIWA)

If we reach a conclusion under IHL (namely, on the level of the primary law) that the notion of military necessity does not justify a certain conduct or omission, on the level of the secondary law of State responsibility, this notion can no longer serve as a ground for precluding an internationally wrongful act within the meaning of Article 25(2)(a) ARSIWA. At first glance, the contention that the state of necessity under the law of peace cannot be invoked in the context of IHL that deals with much greater

42 *Trial of Alfred Felix Alwyn Krupp and eleven others (The Krupp Trial)*, Law Reports of Trials of War Criminals, 10 (1949), 138–9. See also Holland, The Hague, Special Criminal Court, 4 May 1948; and Special Court of Cassation, *In re Rauter*, 533 and 543.

43 *Prosecutor* v. *Tihomir Blaskić*, Case No. IT-95–14-T, ICTY Trial Chamber, Judgment, 3 March 2000, para. 180. See also *Prosecutor* v. *Dario Kordić and Mario Čerkez*, Case No. IT-95–14/2-T, ICTY Trial Chamber, Judgment, 26 February 2001, para. 328.

44 Christine Byron, 'International Humanitarian Law and Bombing Campaigns: Legitimate Military Objectives and Excessive Collateral Damage', *Yearbook of International Humanitarian Law*, 13 (2010), 188–9.

45 *Prosecutor* v. *Tihomir Blaskić*, Case No. IT-95–14-A, ICTY Appeals Chamber, Judgment, 29 July 2004, para. 109. See also *Prosecutor* v. *Dario Kordić and Mario Čerkez*, Case No. IT-95–14/2-A, ICTY Appeals Chamber, Judgment, 17 December 2004, para. 54; and *Legality of the Threat or Use of Nuclear Weapons*, Advisory Opinion, 8 July 1996, ICJ Reports (1996), para. 78.

46 Nobuo Hayashi, 'Requirements of Military Necessity in International Humanitarian Law and International Criminal Law', *Boston University International Law Journal*, 28 (2010), 55. See also Venturini, 'Necessity in the Law of Armed Conflict and in International Criminal Law', 65.

exigencies than other fields of international law seems paradoxical. Yet, when we grasp that IHL already takes into account such exigencies, and above all that '[i]l n'y a pas une seule norme du droit des conflits armés qui ne réponde à une mise en balance entre les intérêts humanitaires et les intérêts issus des nécessités de la situation de belligérance',[47] such a paradox should soon dissolve. Put succinctly, 'a balance between military necessity and humanitarian concerns has been made in advance'[48] on the level of primary rules. As a consequence, once violations of the IHL rules on proportionality are found, the State concerned is precluded from invoking the concept of military necessity under Article 25(2)(a) of the International Law Commission's (ILC) ARSIWA.[49]

Article 25(2)(a) ARSIWA assumes this line of thought. It stipulates the non-availability of the plea of necessity in case 'the international obligation [in the primary rule] in question excludes the possibility of invoking necessity'. The ILC commentary explains that:

> Paragraph (2)(a) [of Article 25] concerns cases where the international obligation in question explicitly or implicitly excludes reliance on necessity. Thus certain humanitarian conventions applicable to armed conflict expressly exclude reliance on military necessity. Others while not explicitly excluding necessity are intended to apply in abnormal situations of peril for the responsible State and plainly engage its essential interests. In such a case the non-availability of the plea of necessity emerges clearly from the object and the purpose of the rule.[50]

The third sentence of the above passage contemplates the specific IHL rules that contain the concept of military necessity expressly, such as Articles 23(1)(g) the Hague Regulations; Articles 33(2), 34 and 54 First Geneva Convention 1949 (GCI); Article 126(2) GCIII; and Articles 49(2)

[47] Kolb, 'La Nécessité militaire dans le droit des conflits armés', 158: 'there is not any single norm of the law of armed conflict that does not respond to the balancing between the humanitarian interests and the interests stemming from the necessity of the situation of belligerence' (English translation by the present author).

[48] Elies van Sliedregt, *The Criminal Responsibility of Individuals for Violations of International Humanitarian Law* (The Hague: T. M. C. Asser Press, 2003), 296.

[49] That said, the concept of military necessity can be invoked as 'a ground for excluding [*individual*] criminal responsibility other than those referred to in paragraph 1' under Art. 31(3) ICC Statute: Kolb, 'La Nécessité militaire dans le droit des conflits armés', 153–4; and William A. Schabas, *The International Criminal Court: A Commentary on the Rome Statute* (Oxford University Press, 2010), 493.

[50] Crawford, *The International Law Commission's Articles on State Responsibility*, 185, commentary to Art. 25, para. 19.

and 53 GCIV.[51] It also suggests that IHL rules deal essentially with emergency situations, and that such exigencies are already taken into account within the normative substance of the rules.[52]

Most crucially, the ILC commentary highlights what should be obvious: the concept of military necessity is relevant only in respect of the obligations under IHL, and this concept is not given another part to play in the sphere of the law on State responsibility.[53] In other words, the concept of military necessity works exclusively in relation to the primary rules (that is, the rules of IHL), which is separate from the '*general* (secondary) rule of necessity'[54] under the law on State responsibility. The ILC commentary observes that:

> As embodied in article 25, the plea of necessity is not intended to cover conduct which is in principle regulated by the primary obligations. This has a particular importance in relation to the rules relating... to the question

[51] See also the provisions with qualifying words: Art. 51 of the 1909 London Declaration Concerning the Laws of Naval War (London, adopted 26 February 1909; did not enter into force), 208 CTS 338; Arts. 8(3) and 34(2) GCI (Convention for the Amelioration of the Condition of the Wounded and Sick in Armed Forces in the Field) (Geneva, adopted 12 August 1949, entered into force 21 October 1950), 75 UNTS 31; Art. 53 GCIV (Convention Relative to the Protection of Civilian Persons in Time of War) (Geneva, adopted 12 August 1949, entered into force 21 October 1950), 75 UNTS 287; Art. 11(2) of the Convention for the Protection of Cultural Property in the Event of Armed Conflict (The Hague, adopted 14 May 1954, entered into force 7 August 1956), 249 UNTS 240. See also provisions suggesting this concept by way of 'soft' language ('as far as possible', 'if circumstances allow', 'to the fullest extent practicable', 'feasible'): Venturini, 'Necessity in the Law of Armed Conflict and in International Criminal Law', 53.

[52] David Kretzmer, 'The Advisory Opinion: The Light Treatment of International Humanitarian Law', *American Journal of International Law*, 99 (2005), 99; and Hayashi, 'Requirements of Military Necessity in International Humanitarian Law and International Criminal Law', 58.

[53] This understanding was already clarified in the ILC's earlier work. The Report of the ILC on its work of 32nd session noted that:

> The rules of humanitarian law relating to the conduct of military operations were adopted in full awareness of the fact that 'military necessity' was the very criterion of that conduct... States signing the Conventions undertook... not to try to find pretexts for evading it... It is true that some of these conventions on the humanitarian law of war contain clauses providing for an explicit exception to the duty to fulfill the obligations they impose... But these are provisions which apply only to the cases expressly provided for. Apart from these cases, it follows implicitly from the text of the conventions that they do not admit the possibility of invoking military necessity as a justification for State conduct not in conformity with the obligations they impose.

'Report of the International Law Commission on the Work of its Thirty-second Session', *ILC Yearbook*, 2(2) (1980), 46, para. 28.

[54] Robert D. Sloane, 'On the Use and Abuse of Necessity in the Law of State Responsibility', *American Journal of International Law*, 106 (2012), 497.

> of 'military necessity'... The same thing [that the legality of unilateral forcible humanitarian intervention is not covered by article 25] is true of the doctrine of 'military necessity' which is, in the first place, the underlying criterion for a series of substantive rules of the law of war and neutrality, as well as being included in terms in a number of treaty provisions in the field of international humanitarian law... while considerations akin to those underlying article 25 may have a role, they are taken into account in the context of the formulation and interpretation of the primary obligations.[55]

The ARSIWA furnish another clear indication that the notion of 'military necessity' under IHL is a normative species that should be distinguished from the concept of 'necessity' under Article 25. Subparagraph (1)(a) of that provision calls for the absence of any other alternative to invoke the concept of necessity, a stringent requirement that is unfamiliar to the intrinsically elusive notion of military necessity under IHL.[56]

Confusion as to the primary and secondary rules of necessity

The foregoing discussions notwithstanding, even the ICJ was once trapped in a confusion that suggests the 'double counting' of necessity on two levels: first, military necessity operating on the level of primary rules (IHL) and, secondly, the general or secondary concept of necessity deployed under the law of State responsibility.[57] The ICJ in its *Wall* Advisory Opinion ruled that:

> The Court has, however, considered whether Israel could rely on a state of necessity which would preclude the wrongfulness of the construction of the wall. In this regard the Court is bound to note that some of the conventions at issue in the present instance include qualifying clauses of the rights guaranteed or provisions for derogation [Article 53 GCIV, and derogations clause of HRL]. Since those treaties already address considerations of this kind ['military exigencies'] within their own provisions, it might be asked whether a state of necessity as recognized in customary international law could be invoked with regard to those treaties as a ground for precluding the wrongfulness of the measures or decisions being challenged.[58]

55 Crawford, *The International Law Commission's Articles on State Responsibility*, 185–6, para. 21, commentary to Art. 25, footnotes omitted.

56 ARSIWA, Art. 25(1)(a) ('the only way for the State to safeguard an essential interest against a grave and imminent peril'); Crawford, *The International Law Commission's Articles on State Responsibility*, 184, para. 15, commentary to Art. 25.

57 *Cf.* Kolb, 'La Nécessité militaire dans le droit des conflits armés', 158.

58 *Legal Consequences of the Construction of a Wall in the Occupied Palestinian Territory*, Advisory Opinion, 9 July 2004, ICJ Reports (2004), para. 140.

This reasoning would 'immunise' an act not justified by military necessity under a state of necessity codified under Article 25 ARSIWA. The Court's reasoning is incongruous as it itself acknowledges that the considerations of military exigencies are already inherent in the primary rules of IHL.[59] Venturini criticises that '[t]his method, which firstly applies international humanitarian law as *lex specialis* and subsequently goes back to *lex generalis* for further evaluation, tends to blur the traditional separation between *jus in bello* and *jus ad bellum*'.[60] Needless to say, such an approach would dilute the IHL's foundational idea that this body of law is 'agnostic' or 'eclectic' with respect to the moral or deontological rationales of the *casus belli*.[61]

The ICJ *Wall* opinion entails the effect of enabling Article 25 ARSIWA to 'give states "two bites at the apple" of necessity'.[62] The Court's dictum is at odds with the idea that IHL was crafted as a 'closed system', immune to all justifications, including any ground of necessity under the law on State responsibility.[63] The grounds of necessity codified under Article 25 ARSIWA are prevented from playing a 'role *de lege ferenda*' in allowing the introduction of 'new rules of exception over the normative threshold' into the primary rules of IHL.[64]

59 *Ibid.*, para. 142 ('the Court considers that Israel cannot rely . . . on a state of necessity in order to preclude the wrongfulness of the construction of the wall resulting from the considerations mentioned in paragraphs 122 ["severely" impeding the right to self-determination] and 137 above ["breaches by Israel of various of its obligations under the applicable international humanitarian law and human rights instruments"]').

60 Venturini, 'Necessity in the Law of Armed Conflict and in International Criminal Law', 63. See also *ibid.*, p. 74; Marco Sassòli, '*Ius ad Bellum* and *Ius in Bello* – The Separation between the Legality of the Use of Force and Humanitarian Rules to Be Respected in Warfare: Crucial or Outdated' in Michael N. Schmitt and Jelena Pejic (eds.), *International Law and Armed Conflict: Exploring the Faultlines – Essays in Honour of Yoram Dinstein* (Leiden: Martinus Nijhoff, 2007), 250–2.

61 See Sloane, 'The Cost of Conflation', 66, 69, 75 and 110. See also the Final Report of the Review Committee to the ICTY Prosecutor concerning the NATO bombardment, which interpreted the key concept of proportionality equation, 'concrete and direct military advantage anticipated', very broadly, as if this had coincided with the humanitarian objective of the NATO's overall military operation: *ibid.*

62 Sloane, 'On the Use and Abuse of Necessity in the Law of State Responsibility', 497. See also Kolb, 'La Nécessité militaire dans le droit des conflits armés', 158.

63 Gabriella Blum, 'The Laws of War and the "Lesser Evil"', *Yale Journal of International Law*, 35 (2010), 12. However, this observation must be qualified in that the relation between States cannot be governed exclusively by IHL, and that insofar as the laws of peace continue to operate in parallel, there is some scope of relying on a ground of necessity under Art. 25 ARSIWA: Kolb, 'La Nécessité militaire dans le droit des conflits armés', 159.

64 Sarah Heathcote, 'Circumstances Precluding Wrongfulness in the ILC Articles on State Responsibility: Necessity' in James Crawford, *The International Law Commission's Articles*

Conclusion

Despite the arguments presented earlier in this chapter, it is not excluded that the ICC, applying a *considerably more rigorous standard* of ascertaining the individual criminal responsibility for excessive collateral civilian casualties, may influence the interpretation of the corresponding IHL rules, making it more difficult to identify State responsibility for the violation of these rules. Because of a close liaison between violations of IHL and war crimes, or between the two systems of responsibility (individual and State), the strict interpretation of war crimes may bring about a 'spill-over effect' in circumscribing the normative substance and scope of the associated rules of IHL.[65] Such an effect, if any, is 'collateral' and inadvertent. The underlying tenet of this chapter is that the two systems of responsibility, albeit intimately connected and operative in parallel, are conceptually separate and not convergent.

The latter part of this chapter purports to dispel confusion surrounding the implications of the concept of military necessity on the interaction between primary rules (IHL) and secondary rules (the law on State responsibility). IHL rules on collateral civilian casualties, which are bound by the requirement of proportionality, are already reflective of the concept of military necessity. It should now be made clear that the finding that those rules have been transgressed on the level of IHL will obliterate the possibility of a State invoking a ground of necessity under the law of State responsibility to justify its impugned attack.

on State Responsibility: Introduction, Text and Commentaries (Cambridge University Press, 2002), 500–1 (discussing the ICSID cases that reveal the concept of 'financial necessity' in the primary rule, as influenced by the secondary rule of necessity).

65 Marco Sassòli, 'Humanitarian Law and International Criminal Law' in Antonio Cassese (ed.), *Oxford Companion to International Criminal Justice* (Oxford University Press, 2009), 117.

19

Third-party countermeasures

Observations on a controversial concept

MARTIN DAWIDOWICZ

I Introduction

It is a great honour to contribute to this *Liber Doctorandorum* for James Crawford. James is an inspirational figure in many ways, and not only in matters of international law. It is only at the end of a journey that you can truly reflect on the road travelled. In the words of T. S. Eliot, 'the end of all our exploring will be to arrive where we started . . . and know the place for the first time'.[1] I am forever indebted to James for his guidance throughout my journey of exploration.

This chapter addresses what James Crawford, as the International Law Commission's (ILC) last Special Rapporteur on State responsibility, rightly described as an 'extremely controversial' topic;[2] namely, the role of third-party countermeasures in international law. In 2000, as Special Rapporteur, he expressed his support for a regime of third-party countermeasures in the ILC Articles on State Responsibility (ASR), which were provisionally endorsed by the ILC in the same year.[3] But like the Grand Old Duke of York, having courageously and painstakingly marched his troops up to the top of the hill, he promptly marched them back down again – and for good reason.

The main explanation for this tactical retreat was the strong opposition of a handful of influential States. The pendulum ultimately swung from belief to agnosticism and a last-ditch compromise was found, expressed in the agnostic arrangement in Article 54 ASR. The sources of this controversy are manifold. This chapter briefly considers whether some

[1] T. S. Eliot, *Four Quartets* (Harcourt: New York, 1943).

[2] James Crawford, 'Fourth Report on State Responsibility', *ILC Yearbook*, 2(1) (2001), 73, para. 47.

[3] ILC Report (2000), UN Doc. A/55/10, 70–1.

of the most common criticisms of the concept are actually borne out in practice.

Perhaps the most common and potentially most effective critique is that countermeasures entail an inherent risk of abuse as their unilateral character tends to favour more powerful States. Already in 1850, the so-called *Don Pacifico* affair – involving a British naval blockade of the Greek port of Piraeus following Greece's refusal to compensate a British subject for injuries inflicted by a violent mob – provides a good example of so-called 'gunboat diplomacy' and the risk of abuse traditionally associated with unilateral coercive measures.[4] In a famous speech before the House of Commons, Lord Palmerston vigorously defended the action:

> [A]s the Roman, in days of old, held himself free from indignity, when he could say *Civis Romanus sum*; so also a British subject, in whatever land he may be, shall feel confident that the watchful eye and the strong arm of England, will protect him against injustice and wrong.[5]

No doubt with such examples in mind, Judge Padilla Nervo stated:

> The history of the responsibility of States in respect to the treatment of foreign nationals is the history of abuses, illegal interference in the domestic jurisdiction of weaker States, unjust claims, threats and even military aggression under the flag of exercising rights of protection, and the imposing of sanctions in order to oblige a government to make the reparations demanded.[6]

Several other late-nineteenth and early-twentieth-century examples of gunboat diplomacy by powerful Western States, notably against Latin American countries, could also be mentioned.[7] As ILC Special Rapporteur on diplomatic protection, Dugard observed that the institution had been 'greatly abused' as it had in practice 'provided a justification for military intervention or gunboat diplomacy' under the guise of protection.[8] As a consequence, '[i]nevitably diplomatic protection of this kind came

4 Wilhelm Georg Grewe, *The Epochs of International Law*, tr. Michael Byers (Berlin: Walter de Gruyter, 2000), 525–7.

5 House of Commons Debates, 25 June 1850, vol. 112 (3rd Ser.) c. 444 (statement of Lord Palmerston).

6 *Barcelona Traction, Light and Power Company Limited (Belgium* v. *Spain)*, Judgment, 5 February 1970, ICJ Reports (1970), 3, Sep. Op. Judge Padilla Nervo, 246.

7 For examples see Grewe, *The Epochs of International Law*, 525–7.

8 John Dugard, 'First Report on Diplomatic Protection', *ILC Yearbook*, 2(1) (2000), 212. See also Mohamed Bennouna, 'Preliminary Report on Diplomatic Protection', *ILC Yearbook* 2(1) (1998), 311 ('diplomatic protection has served as a pretext for intervention in the affairs of certain countries').

to be seen by developing nations, particularly in Latin America, as a discriminatory exercise of power rather than as a method of protecting the human rights of aliens'.[9]

By the turn of the last century, at the Second Hague Peace Conference, these concerns prompted the adoption of the 1907 Drago-Porter Convention.[10] Albeit limited in scope, this Convention proscribed the enforcement by armed reprisal of public debt obligations. Today, given the increasing importance attached to the notion of an international community as a repository of common values, and the evolving multilateral dimension of State responsibility, one could perhaps say that Lord Palmerston's jingoistic invocation of *Civis Romanus sum* has at least in part been replaced by a more cosmopolitan exclamation: '*Civis mundi sum!*' Indeed, around the time of Lord Palmerston's statement in the British Parliament, similar propositions had already been advanced by Heffter and Bluntschli. They both considered that, in response to a 'public danger', third States could act 'as representatives of mankind' and formally enforce obligations protecting the community interest as a way of promoting *Weltjustiz*.[11]

The basic controversy can thus be stated in simple terms: there is an inherent tension between the need for a more effective legal order notwithstanding decentralisation, and the risks of abuse relating to the allocation of enforcement authority to individual States, even if limited to the most serious illegalities. It is certainly true that the primary means of dealing with major international crises – at least when they impact on international peace and security – do not lie within the law of State responsibility. It is the main responsibility of competent international organisations, notably the United Nations (UN) and its principal political organs to deal with such matters.[12] But the primary function of the Security Council under the UN Charter (at least as originally conceived) is not to restore legal order but to restore public order. These are not necessarily identical: peace enforcement is distinct from law enforcement.[13] Still, the

[9] Dugard, 'First Report on Diplomatic Protection', 212.

[10] See Convention on the Limitation of Employment of Force for Recovery of Contract Debts (The Hague, adopted 18 October 1907, entered into force 26 January 1910), 205 CTS 250.

[11] August Wilhelm Heffter, *Das Europäische Völkerrecht der Gegenwart auf den bisherigen Grundlagen* (1844), 191, §110; Johann Caspar Bluntschli, *Das moderne Völkerrecht der civilisirten Staaten als Rechtsbuch dargestellt* (1868), 241, 263–4, §471–3 (translation supplied).

[12] James Crawford, 'Third Report on State Responsibility', *ILC Yearbook*, 2(1) (2000), 98, para. 372.

[13] See notably Hans Kelsen, *The Law of the United Nations* (Praeger: New York, 1950), 294.

practice of the Security Council under Chapter VII of the UN Charter (even in the post-Cold War era) indicates that it has not always taken enforcement action to restore international public order, let alone acted to restore international legality. On those numerous occasions where the Security Council has not taken enforcement action in response to serious breaches of international law, as, for instance, in the cases of Cambodia, Uganda, Rwanda, Burundi, Burma, Zimbabwe or Syria, States have traditionally only had the bilateral regime of State responsibility to fall back on in order to protect community interests in the absence of recourse to an effective treaty-mechanism. Special Rapporteur Crawford succinctly articulated the problem with the bilateral model of enforcement in the following terms:

> Older structures of bilateral State responsibility are plainly inadequate to deal with gross violations of human rights and humanitarian law, let alone situations threatening the survival of States and peoples.[14]

These concerns neatly encapsulate the basic reason for the gradual rejection of the strictly bilateral model of enforcement in modern international law.[15] At the same time, as some ILC members recognised, 'leaving it up to the... United Nations to react to breaches of obligations *erga omnes* bordered on cynicism'.[16] Others have suggested that to rely exclusively on institutional mechanisms would render the enforcement of *erga omnes* obligations a vacuous proposition.[17] For his part, Special Rapporteur Crawford recognised that, although the primary means of dealing with the most serious breaches of international law reside with the Security Council in the discharge of its responsibilities under Chapter VII, the law of State responsibility still had an important role to play.[18] The mere expectation that international organisations will be able to resolve the humanitarian or other crises that often arise from serious breaches of

[14] Crawford, 'Third Report on State Responsibility', 108, para. 411.

[15] See para. 4 of the commentary to Art. 1 ASR, ILC Report (2001), UN Doc. A/56/10, 33.

[16] *ILC Yearbook*, 1 (2000), 305, para. 31 (Mr Simma).

[17] See e.g. H. Fox, 'Reply of Lady Fox', *Annuaire de l'institut de droit international* 71(I) (Pedone, 2005), 158; Theodor Meron, 'International Law in the Age of Human Rights', *Recueil des Cours*, 301 (2003), 288; *ILC Yearbook*, 1 (2001), 107, para. 26 (Mr Pellet); Giorgio Gaja, 'Obligations *Erga Omnes*, International Crimes and *Jus Cogens*: A Tentative Analysis of Three Related Concepts' in Joseph Weiler, Antonio Cassese and Marina Spinedi (eds.), *International Crimes of State: A Critical Analysis of the ILC's Draft Article 19 on State Responsibility* (Berlin: Walter de Gruyter, 1989), 155–6; UN Doc. A/C.6/55/SR.17 (27 October 2000), 13, para. 76 (Austria).

[18] Crawford, 'Third Report on State Responsibility', 98, para. 372.

international law was plainly not enough.[19] The law of State responsibility should be able to operate independently of an ineffective Security Council by providing its own means of ensuring a more effective return to international legality in the case of serious illegalities.

Special Rapporteur Crawford also expressed the concern that, if third-party countermeasures were not allowed to enforce fundamental norms, there might be 'further pressure on States to intervene in other, perhaps less desirable ways'.[20] While there was no clear support for third-party countermeasures in international law, his conclusion was nevertheless clear:

> [I]nternational law should offer to States with a legitimate interest in compliance with such [fundamental] obligations, some means of securing compliance which does not involve the use of force [notably, humanitarian intervention] . . . The draft Articles should [therefore] allow collective countermeasures in response to a gross and well-attested breach.[21]

Other ILC members expressed support based on the same rationale:

> The Commission must not forget that it was devising a regime of non-forcible countermeasures which would help avoid situations where States claimed that they had exhausted all peaceful means and adopted the attitude which had been taken by the United Kingdom in the context of the collective measures adopted against Yugoslavia in 1998. If the Commission defined a feasible regime of pacific collective countermeasures, States would be less likely to adopt another course, such as the regrettable one taken in Kosovo.[22]

A similar line of reasoning can be traced back at least to Vattel and von Bulmerinq. For the latter, 'it has always been viewed as a main function of reprisals to prevent a greater evil, war'.[23]

These considerations have not made the concept of third-party countermeasures any less controversial. Critics maintain that the risk of abuse is simply too great. Several States emphasised this point during the lengthy debate on the ILC Articles in the Sixth Committee of the General

19 Crawford, 'Fourth Report on State Responsibility', 18, para. 74.

20 Crawford, 'Third Report on State Responsibility', 106, para. 405.

21 *Ibid.*, paras. 405–6. See also *ibid.*, paras. 396–7, 401.

22 *ILC Yearbook*, 1 (2000), 305, para. 33 (Mr Simma). See also *ILC Yearbook*, 1 (2001), 35, para. 4 (Mr Simma); ILC Report (2000), 60, para. 368.

23 August von Bulmerincq, 'Die Staatstreitigkeiten und ihre Entscheidung ohne Krieg' in F. von Holtzendorff, *Handbuch des Völkerrechts: auf Grundlage Europäischer Staatspraxis*: IV, *Die Staatsstreitigkeiten und ihre Entscheidung* (1889), 84–9; Emer de Vattel, *Le Droit des gens ou principes de la loi naturelle* (1758, English translation 1916), bk II, §354.

Assembly. As Bahrain stated, 'according to one view countermeasures were the prerogative of the more powerful State, and many small States regarded the concept as synonymous with aggression or intervention'.[24] Similarly, Ecuador observed that countermeasures 'were frequently used as an instrument of intervention or aggression'.[25] Likewise, Cuba opined that 'despite the stipulation that the regime of countermeasures would exclude the use of military force, it contained the seeds of aggression because . . . political coercion and economic pressure were as much forms of aggression as was military force'.[26] According to Botswana, third-party countermeasures were 'open to abuse by powerful States against a weaker State that they might particularly dislike for other reasons'.[27] For its part, Germany sounded a note of caution: 'there was a danger that disproportional unilateral acts, which in reality were not justified by the interest they sought to protect, might be disguised countermeasures. That would threaten the credibility of the concept.'[28] In sum, in the words of Tanzania, 'it could hardly be refuted that countermeasures were a threat to small and weak States'.[29]

Other States providing comments on the ILC Articles expressed concern that unilateral third-party countermeasures would have 'disruptive effects';[30] they would be 'potentially highly destabilizing of treaty relations . . . [in particular]by creating a parallel mechanism for responding to serious breaches which lacked the coordinated, balanced and collective features of existing mechanisms'.[31] Responsibility for dealing with the most serious breaches of international law was 'better left to the Security Council' as the law of State responsibility (including third-party countermeasures) was an 'inappropriate vehicle' for such matters.[32] Yet other

[24] UN Doc. A/C.6/47/SR.26 (3 November 1992), 6, para. 18 (Bahrain).

[25] UN Doc. A/C.6/47/SR.30 (6 November 1992), 12, para. 49 (Ecuador).

[26] UN Doc. A/C.6/47/SR.29 (5 November 1992), 14, para. 59 (Cuba). See also e.g. UN Doc. A/C.6/55/SR.22 (1 November 2000), 8–9, para. 52 (Libya).

[27] UN Doc. A/C.6/55/SR.15 (24 October 2000), 10, para. 63 (Botswana).

[28] UN Doc. A/C.6/55/SR.14 (23 October 2000), 10, para. 54 (Germany).

[29] *Ibid.*, 9, para. 46 (Tanzania). Contrast Mongolia's position whose delegation 'regretted, however, that the final draft omitted the provision in the former draft article 54 [2000] for a non-injured State to take countermeasures. As a small State, Mongolia believed that the option of . . . countermeasures should have been preserved in the draft articles' (UN Doc. A/C.6/56/SR.14 (1 November 2001), 9, para. 56).

[30] UN Doc. A/CN.4/515/Add.1 (3 April 2001), 9 (Mexico).

[31] UN Docs. A/CN.4/515 (19 March 2001), 89 (United Kingdom); A/C.6/55/SR.15 (24 October 2000), 4–5, paras. 24–5 (Israel).

[32] UN Doc. A/CN.4/515 (19 March 2001), 53 (United States). See also, e.g., *ILC Yearbook*, 1 (2001), 54, para. 26 (Mr Tomka).

States not only expressed their preference for the traditional role of the Security Council in the maintenance of international peace and security under Chapter VII as a matter of policy, but also opined that a regime of third-party countermeasures would be legally impermissible as it would amount to an 'encroachment on the authority of the Security Council under Chapter VII of the Charter'.[33]

The same criticisms were expressed in the ILC: a regime of third-party countermeasures 'sooner or later might extend to the use of force . . . [and] was incompatible with the [UN] Charter'.[34] Moreover, it was suggested that the concept of third-party countermeasures is but a 'neologism' – a category 'completely invented' *ex post facto* – based on the highly selective and extremely inconsistent practice of a small number of mainly Western States with no evidence of *opinio juris* – not least because that practice was not always even officially designated as relating to third-party countermeasures.[35] Worse still, recognition of third-party countermeasures would constitute a '*lex horrenda*' and be 'an invitation to chaos' serving only to legitimise 'mob-justice', 'vigilantism' and 'power politics'.[36] Put simply, 'under the banner of law, chaos and violence would come to reign among states'.[37] Against this background, on the initial proposal of the United Kingdom, and in order not to jeopardise the approval of the ILC Articles as a whole, Special Rapporteur Crawford introduced a

[33] UN Doc. A/C.6/55/SR.18 (27 October 2000), 4, para. 15 (Mexico). See also UN Docs. A/C.6/56/SR.16 (2 November 2001), 7, para. 40 (Colombia); A/C.6/55/SR.15 (24 October 2000), 3, para. 17 (Iran); A/C.6/55/SR.22 (1 November 2000), 8, para. 52 (Libya); OAS Res. I on the 'Serious Situation in the South Atlantic' (28 April 1982), op. para. 6, 21 ILM (1982), 670–1.

[34] See notably *ILC Yearbook*, 1 (2001), 35, para. 2 (Mr Brownlie). See also ILC Report (2001), 36, para. 54.

[35] *ILC Yearbook*, 1 (2001), 35, paras. 2 and 5 (Mr Brownlie). See also Crawford, 'Third Report on State Responsibility', 104, para. 396(c).

[36] *ILC Yearbook*, 1 (2001), 35, paras. 2 and 5 (Mr Brownlie); Stephen McCaffrey, '*Lex Lata* or the Continuum of State Responsibility' in Joseph Weiler, Antonio Cassese and Marina Spinedi (eds.), *International Crimes of State: A Critical Analysis of the ILC's Draft Article 19 on State Responsibility* (Berlin: Walter de Gruyter, 1989), 244; *ILC Yearbook*, 1 (1983), 143, paras. 27–8 (Mr McCaffrey); Krystyna Marek, 'Criminalizing State Responsibility', *Revue belge de droit international*, 14 (1978–9), 481; Eduardo Jimenez de Aréchaga, 'International Law in the Past Third of a Century', *Recueil des Cours*, 159 (1978-I), 275; Bernard Graefrath, 'Responsibility and Damages Caused: Relationship between Responsibility and Damages', *Recueil des Cours*, 185 (1984-II), 9, 68; UN Doc. A/CN.4/515 (19 March 2001), 69 (China).

[37] Prosper Weil, 'Le Droit international en quête de son identité', *Recueil des Cours* 237 (1992-VI), 9, 433.

compromise proposal that became the saving clause in Article 54 ASR.[38] A decade or so later, it now seems opportune to briefly consider whether these criticisms, as well as the great hopes and fears raised by the concept of third-party countermeasures, have been borne out in practice.

II Third-party countermeasures in practice: salient critiques and other issues

The above overview underlines the common perception that there are several major problems with the concept of third-party countermeasures. Broadly speaking, these can be summarised as follows: (1) third-party countermeasures are a neologism with no basis in international law or its progressive development; (2) third-party countermeasures are contrary to the UN Charter and, in any event, within an evolving regime, the Security Council can operate as an institutional safeguard for third-party countermeasures, the use of which is effectively constrained by the powers of the Council under Chapter VII; and (3) third-party countermeasures are inherently prone to abuse by more powerful States arising from the auto-interpretation of allegedly wrongful conduct making them a mere pretext for power politics, intervention and even aggression (in short, a *lex horrenda*). State practice in turn provides support for the three basic propositions below.

1 Practice may be somewhat obscure, but third-party countermeasures are nevertheless part of the reality of international law

The saving clause in Article 54 ASR was based in part on the conclusion that State practice on third-party countermeasures was limited, embryonic, selective and confined to only a small number of mainly Western States.[39] But the ILC underestimated the true extent, consistency and geographical spread of State practice. There is, in fact, a considerable amount of practice evidencing the gradual recognition of an entitlement of States to adopt third-party countermeasures in response to gross and

[38] See UN Doc. A/C.6/55/14 (23 October 2000), 7, para. 32 (United Kingdom); Crawford, 'Fourth Report on State Responsibility', 15, 18, paras. 60, 74; *ILC Yearbook*, 1 (2001), 110, 112–3, paras. 48 and 64–5 (Chairman of the Drafting Committee, Mr Tomka).

[39] See paras. 3 and 6 of the commentary to Art. 54 ASR, ILC Report (2001), 137, 139.

systematic breaches of communitarian norms.[40] No doubt a similar conclusion motivated the Institut de Droit International to endorse a decentralised regime of third-party countermeasures at its Krakow session in 2005.[41]

It is not the purpose of this chapter to revisit this (still very contentious) matter in any detail. It suffices here to point to the widespread support for the third-party countermeasures adopted by a large and remarkably diverse group of States against Syria in 2011. The adoption of these third-party countermeasures, which have included the freezing of internationally protected assets (such as those belonging to President Al-Assad and the Central Bank of Syria) and a prima facie unlawful membership suspension from the League of Arab States, underline their continuing relevance in the limited toolbox of communitarian law enforcement.[42]

[40] For a detailed assessment, see Martin Dawidowicz, 'Public Law Enforcement without Public Law Safeguards? An Analysis of State Practice on Third-party Countermeasures and their Relationship to the UN Security Council', *British Yearbook of International Law*, 77 (2006), 333–418; Christian Tams, *Enforcing Obligations Erga Omnes in International Law* (Cambridge University Press, 2005), 207–51. See also e.g. Giorgio Gaja, 'Second Report on Obligations and Rights *Erga Omnes* in International Law', 71(1) *Annuaire de l'institut de droit international* (Pedone, 2005), 199–200; Linos-Alexandre Sicilianos, 'Countermeasures in Response to Grave Violations of Obligations Owed to the International Community' in James Crawford, Alain Pellet and Simon Olleson (eds.), *The Law of International Responsibility* (Oxford University Press, 2010), 1145–8.

[41] See Art. 5 of the resolution entitled 'Obligations *Erga Omnes* in International Law', available at www.idi-iil.org.

[42] See e.g. 'Syria's Assad Hit by EU Sanctions', *The Guardian*, 23 May 2011, available at www.guardian.co.uk/world/2011/may/23/syria-assad-eu-sanctions; 'US to freeze assets of Syrian president Bashar al-Assad and senior officials', *The Guardian*, 18 May 2011, www.guardian.co.uk/world/2011/may/18/bashar-al-assad-syria-us-sanctions; 'Syria Suspended from Arab League', *The Guardian*, 12 November 2011, available at www.guardian.co.uk/world/2011/nov/12/syria-suspended-arab-league; 'Syria Isolated after Unprecedented Arab League Sanctions', *The Telegraph*, 27 November 2011, www.telegraph.co.uk/news/worldnews/middleeast/syria/8919029/Syria-isolated-after-unprecedented-Arab-League-sanctions.html; 'Turkey Imposes Sanctions on Syria', *The Guardian*, 30 November 2011, available at www.guardian.co.uk/world/2011/nov/30/turkey-imposes-sanctions-on-syria; 'Swiss Freeze $53 Million in Syrian Funds', *Reuters*, 23 December 2011, available at www.reuters.com/article/2011/12/23/swiss-banks-assad-idUSL6E7NN0IT20111223; Australian Department of Foreign Affairs and Trade, 'Australia's Autonomous Sanctions: Syria', 13 May 2011, available at www.dfat.gov.au/un/unsc_sanctions/syria_autonomous_sanctions.html; Canadian Department of Foreign Affairs, Trade and Development, 'Syria: Latest Developments', 24 May 2011, available at www.international.gc.ca/sanctions/syria-syrie.aspx; Ministry of Foreign Affairs of Japan, 'Implementation of Measures to Freeze the Assets of President Bashar Al-Assad and his Related Individuals and Entities in Syria', 9 September 2011, available at www.mofa.go.jp/announce/announce/2011/9/0909_02.html.

In February 2012, on the proposal of then French President Sarkozy, the so-called 'Group of Friends of the Syrian People' was created.[43] This is a large and diverse diplomatic coalition of States and international organisations, which was created as a direct response to the Security Council's inability to take resolute action on Syria.[44] In April 2012, the 'Friends of the Syrian People International Working Group on Sanctions' (The Working Group) was formed:

> in order to achieve greater effectiveness in the enforcement of the restrictive measures already put in force by states or international organizations including the measures [such as the freezing of assets of senior Syrian regime officials] stipulated in the Chairman's Conclusions of the first meeting of the Friends' Group.[45]

At a meeting in September 2012, sixty Member States of the Working Group 'welcomed the increasing pressure placed on the [Syrian] regime by the wide range of sanctions [e.g. the freezing of State and Head of State assets] adopted by different states and organisations' and observed that they had 'seriously affected the Syrian regime and have reduced its ability to crack down on the Syrian people'.[46] They added that 'the members of the Group have adopted effective, proportional and coordinated sanctions . . . [and] urge[d] other countries to follow suit'.[47] More specifically:

> [T]he Group called upon all states to take steps to harmonise national and regional sanctions regimes by imposing, at a minimum, an asset freeze on senior Syrian regime officials involved in the repression, as well as an asset freeze on and restrictions on transactions with the Central Bank of Syria, the Commercial Bank of Syria and the Syrian International Islamic Bank to ensure their isolation from the international financial system.[48]

43 See 'Sarkozy: France, Partners Plan Syria Crisis Group', *The Jerusalem Post*, 4 February 2012, available at www.jpost.com/Middle-East/Sarkozy-France-partners-plan-Syria-crisis-group.

44 See, however, SC Res. 2118, 27 September 2013.

45 See Chairman's Conclusions, 2nd Conference of the Group of Friends of the Syrian People (Istanbul, 1 April 2012), para. 18, available at www.mfa.gov.tr/chairman_s-conclusions-second-conference-of-the-group-of-friends-of-the-syrian-people_-1-april-2012_-istanbul.en.mfa; Chairman's Conclusions of the International Conference of the Group of Friends of the Syrian People (Tunis, 24 February 2012), available at www.state.gov/r/pa/prs/ps/2012/02/184642.htm.

46 See Statement by the Friends of the Syrian People International Working Group on Sanctions (The Hague, 20 September 2012), available at www.government.nl/documents-and-publications/reports.

47 *Ibid.* 48 *Ibid.*

The Working Group has reaffirmed the same point in several subsequent meetings.[49] As a minimum, these repeated statements, at least insofar as they relate to the freezing of assets belonging to President Al-Assad and the Central Bank of Syria, are indicative of a willingness of a very large number of States to adopt prima facie unlawful unilateral coercive measures for which the justification can seemingly only be explained in legal terms by the concept of third-party countermeasures.

A few comments about practice of a more general nature are also warranted. The evaluation of State practice on third-party countermeasures admittedly raises some difficult questions. One such difficulty concerns the relative obscurity of practice; the primary evidence in the form of statements from States is rarely conclusive. If a State often provides some form of explanation (however brief and perfunctory) for its adoption of a unilateral coercive measure it rarely provides a clear statement to explain which of the sometimes many possible unilateral coercive measures it actually relies upon in a given case to justify its action in legal terms. Then ILC member Opertti Badan alluded to this difficulty when he observed that the concept of third-party countermeasures belongs to 'an area in which the borderline between international law *per se* and foreign relations [is] fairly indistinct'.[50] It is true that relevant examples from practice were 'not always officially designated as [third-party] countermeasures'.[51] Indeed, as Special Rapporteur Crawford has observed, States appear to have an 'implied preference for other concepts'.[52] The fact that foreign policy considerations – and the concomitant sensitivities surrounding the use of non-forcible coercion by individual States – appear to play a prominent role in this area helps to explain the relative obscurity of practice on third-party countermeasures and the considerable complexities involved in assessing it. These complexities are evident in the apparent unwillingness of States to rely expressly on the concept of third-party countermeasures in practice; this is a factor that has significantly clouded the legal issues involved and sometimes led to confusion in the analysis of *opinio juris*.

These problems are compounded in those situations where States have strongly supported third-party countermeasures in their practice, yet opposed them in the Sixth Committee of the General Assembly

[49] See e.g. Communiqué by the Friends of the Syrian People International Working Group on Sanctions (Sofia, 26 February 2013), available at www.government.nl/documents-and-publications/publications.

[50] *ILC Yearbook*, 1 (2000), 296, para. 46 (Mr Opertti Badan).

[51] *ILC Yearbook*, 1 (2001), 35, para. 2 (Mr Brownlie).

[52] Crawford, 'Third Report on State Responsibility', 104, para. 396.

during the ILC's work on State responsibility. As an illustration, the United States and the United Kingdom opposed the concept of third-party countermeasures in the Sixth Committee as an 'inappropriate vehicle' and as a 'highly destabilizing' means of enforcing fundamental norms, yet they have both on numerous occasions resorted to third-party countermeasures in practice.[53] For its part, Tanzania opposed third-party countermeasures by asserting before the Sixth Committee that 'it could hardly be refuted that [third-party] countermeasures were a threat to small and weak States'.[54] And yet Tanzania has itself adopted third-party countermeasures against South Africa, Nigeria, Burundi and Zimbabwe.[55] Likewise, Botswana, another ardent critic in the Sixth Committee,[56] expressed support in the Security Council for the third-party countermeasures adopted against Burundi by certain African States which in that instance at least 'deserve[d] the commendation of the international community'.[57]

While some hesitation may be understandable in accepting the relevance of the mentioned practice to the development of the law on third-party countermeasures, this appears to be an inevitable consequence of the complex interplay between law and politics in this area. Special Rapporteur Riphagen may have been right to observe that 'the more serious the breach of an international obligation, the less likely it is to find an objective legal appraisal of the allowable responses to such a breach'.[58] Still, in the final analysis, as States have relied on the rationale of the concept and no other justifications have been available, the concept of third-party countermeasures is needed to explain the practice of States in legal terms.[59] In short, third-party countermeasures cannot be described as a 'neologism' – a category 'completely invented' by *ex post facto* rationalisations of practice.[60] If the matter was still in doubt a decade ago, third-party countermeasures are today part of the reality of international law.

[53] See UN Doc. A/CN.4/515 (19 March 2001), 53 and 89 (United States and United Kingdom).

[54] UN Doc. A/C.6/55/SR.14 (23 October 2000), 9, para. 46 (Tanzania).

[55] See Dawidowicz, 'Public Law Enforcement without Public Law Safeguards?', 352–4, 386–90, 394–6.

[56] See text above accompanying n. 27 above.

[57] UN Doc. S/PV.3692 (28 August 1996), 16–7 (Botswana).

[58] Willem Riphagen, 'Preliminary Report on State Responsibility', *ILC Yearbook*, 2(1) (1980), 128–9, para. 97.

[59] Dawidowicz, 'Public Law Enforcement without Public Law Safeguards?', 350, 414–5. See also to similar effect Antonios Tzanakopoulos, *Disobeying the Security Council: Countermeasures against Wrongful Sanctions* (Oxford University Press, 2011), 188.

[60] *ILC Yearbook*, 1 (2001), 35, paras. 2 and 5 (Mr Brownlie).

2 Third-party countermeasures and UN Charter Chapter VII enforcement measures are distinct and may operate in parallel

The influential view in the ILC and the Sixth Committee, already noted above, that a decentralised regime of third-party countermeasures would be contrary to the UN Charter as it would encroach on the powers of the Security Council under Chapter VII, does not withstand scrutiny. At least in part, it is a view initially informed by Special Rapporteur Ago's conclusion from the 1970s that, as a matter of *lex lata*, obligations *erga omnes* were not enforceable by a decentralised regime of third-party countermeasures; but by the organised international community, in the form of the competent organs of the UN, notably the Security Council.[61] From historical experience, in which countermeasures 'were frequently used as an instrument of intervention or aggression',[62] it was not possible to underestimate the risks of abuse involved in pressing recognition of the concept of unilateral third-party countermeasures and the introduction of another circumstance precluding wrongfulness, which 'sooner or later might extend to the use of force'.[63] During the debate on the ILC Articles in the Sixth Committee, several States insisted in categorical terms that third-party countermeasures could only be adopted within the UN framework.[64] Cameroon's position aptly sums up these concerns. It stated:

> [D]raft article 54 [2000] . . . might lead to the taking of multilateral or collective countermeasures simultaneously with other measures taken by the competent United Nations bodies; the [ILC] draft articles must not be allowed to create overlapping legal regimes that could weaken the Organization as a whole or marginalize the Security Council, particularly in the light of the recent and disturbing tendency of some States to take action, including armed intervention, without the Council's consent. The situations envisaged in draft article 54 [2000] were adequately dealt with under Articles 39 to 41 of the Charter of the United Nations, which was the best expression of the will of the community of States.[65]

61 Roberto Ago, 'Eighth Report on State Responsibility', *ILC Yearbook*, 2(1) (1979), 43, paras. 91–2. See also paras. 12–3 of the commentary to Art. 30 [1996], *ILC Yearbook*, 2(2) (1979), 118–9.

62 UN Doc. A/C.6/47/SR.30 (6 November 1992), 12, para. 49 (Ecuador).

63 *ILC Yearbook*, 1 (2001), 35, para. 2 (Mr. Brownlie).

64 See e.g. UN Docs. A/C.6/55/SR.15 (24 October 2000), 3, para. 17 (Iran); A/C.6/55/SR.22 (1 November 2000), 8, para. 52 (Libya); A/C.6/56/SR.16 (2 November 2001), 7, para. 40 (Colombia); A/CN.4/515/Add.1 (3 April 2001), 9–12 (Mexico); A/C.6/55/SR.18 (27 October 2000), 11, paras. 59–62 (Cuba).

65 UN Doc. A/C.6/55/SR.24 (3 November 2000), 11, para. 64 (Cameroon).

It was against the background of these concerns that much of the debate in the ILC and Sixth Committee on third-party countermeasures came to focus on the potential role of the Security Council as an institutional safeguard against abuse. But these concerns are not reflected in State practice; and in addition, they conflate the analytical distinction between enforcement measures under Chapter VII of the UN Charter and third-party countermeasures.

A striking feature of the very substantial amount of State practice in the UN period is that third-party countermeasures have largely been adopted without any intervention of the Security Council whatsoever. In fact, in several cases, such as those involving Argentina, Iraq, Burundi, Yugoslavia and Sudan, third-party countermeasures have even been adopted while the Security Council has been actively seized of these matters.[66] Likewise, the third-party countermeasures adopted against Syria in 2011 continue (without much controversy)[67] to operate in parallel with the action taken against it by the Security Council in September 2013.[68] The practice accumulated over several decades provides a strong indication that third-party countermeasures do not contradict the UN Charter, nor unduly encroach on the powers of the Security Council.

The preferred policy option of the Special Rapporteurs on first reading had nevertheless been to link the law of collective security to the law of State responsibility. As it happened, this approach, in its various forms,[69] was overwhelmingly rejected as incompatible with the existing powers of the Security Council under the UN Charter.[70] In any event, the ILC deemed such an institutional safeguard unnecessary given the likely involvement of the Security Council in addressing the most serious illegalities.[71] Ultimately, the complex relationship between

66 See Dawidowicz, 'Public Law Enforcement without Public Law Safeguards?', 368–74, 384–6, 389–91, 393–4.

67 For Russia's protest see e.g. UN Doc. S/PV/6627 (4 October 2011), 5 (Russia).

68 See above n. 44. Previous draft resolutions against Syria had been vetoed by China and Russia: see UN Docs. S/2011/612 (4 October 2011); S/2012/77 (4 February 2012).

69 Willem Riphagen, 'Fifth Report on State Responsibility', *ILC Yearbook*, 2(1) (1984), 3–4; Willem Riphagen, 'Sixth Report on State Responsibility', *ILC Yearbook*, 2(1) (1985), 5–8, 11, 13–14 (for his draft Arts. 5(e), 9 and 14(3)); Gaetano Arangio-Ruiz, 'Seventh Report on State Responsibility', *ILC Yearbook*, 2(1) (1995), 29–30 (for his draft Arts. 17 and 19).

70 See para. 9 of the commentary to Art. 40 ASR, ILC Report (2001), 113.

71 *Ibid.* Other last-minute proposals (compatible with the UN Charter) to subordinate the use of third-party countermeasures to action duly taken under Chapter VII of the UN Charter were not considered. See further Crawford, 'Fourth Report on State Responsibility', 18, para. 73; *ILC Yearbook*, 1 (2001), 40, para. 41 (Mr Economides); *ILC Yearbook*, 1 (2000), 328, para. 49 (Mr Opertti Badan); UN Doc. A/C.6/55/SR.17 (27 October 2000), 14, para. 85 (Greece); A/CN.4/515, 87 (the Netherlands). To similar effect: UN Docs.

third-party countermeasures and the Security Council is safeguarded by Article 59 ASR, which is based on what could perhaps be described as the principles of co-existence and co-ordination.

The principle of co-existence is based on the premise of two distinct spheres of application: the Security Council deals with the political aspects of maintaining or restoring international peace and security, whereas the law of State responsibility (including third-party countermeasures) deals with the legal aspects of serious breaches.[72] As Jordan explained before the Sixth Committee:

> [C]ountermeasures should not be interpreted as an encroachment on the authority of the Security Council under Chapter VII of the Charter. Draft article 59 should provide the necessary guarantees in that respect to those who considered that there was an overlap between the two regimes of measures. Countermeasures could in fact be necessary to ensure that the State committing the internationally wrongful act ceased its action and made reparation for the damage caused.[73]

The principle of co-existence, that is to say, the seemingly clear-cut distinction between the law of State responsibility and the law of collective security,[74] appears to have been the source of some confusion among a number of States in the ILC's work on State responsibility; almost by definition, the Security Council cannot resort to third-party countermeasures. As Spain emphasised before the Sixth Committee:

> [W]hile the Security Council is authorized to take 'enforcement action' under Chapter VII, such measures are not subordinated to the general regime of countermeasures, since they do not necessarily respond to the commission of internationally wrongful acts... [T]he Council is not a judicial body, but a political body ...[75]

A/C.6/55/SR.15 (24 October 2000), 3, para. 17 (Iran); A/C.6/56/SR.11 (29 October 2001), 7, para. 39 (Morocco).

72 See e.g. ILC Report (1998), UN Doc. A/53/10, 70–1, para. 286; Vera Gowlland-Debbas, 'Responsibility and the United Nations Charter' in James Crawford, Alain Pellet and Simon Olleson (eds.), *The Law of International Responsibility* (Oxford University Press, 2010), 116.

73 UN Doc. A/C.6/55/SR.18 (27 October 2000), 4, para. 15 (Jordan). See also the topical summary of governments' views, in UN Doc. A/CN.4/513 (15 February 2001), 35, para. 189.

74 See Kelsen, *The Law of the United Nations*, 294 ('the purpose of the enforcement action under Article 39 [of the UN Charter] is not to maintain or restore the law, but to maintain or restore peace, which is not necessarily identical with the law').

75 UN Doc. A/CN.4/515 (19 March 2001), 92 (Spain).

In the ILC debate, Simma observed that 'it seemed not entirely clear to some States' that third-party countermeasures and enforcement measures under Chapter VII of the UN Charter could not be assimilated.[76] Put simply, there is no *a priori* role for the Security Council in a regime of third-party countermeasures.

A reason for the apparent confusion could be found, as Special Rapporteur Crawford suggested, in what France termed the ILC's 'ambiguous'[77] definition of countermeasures on first reading.[78] It gave the unfortunate impression of including within its definition both institutional (that is, Chapter VII of the UN Charter) and decentralised forms of coercive measures, as opposed to clearly spelling out the critical distinction of a previous wrongful act that separates Chapter VII enforcement measures from countermeasures. As Crawford explained, 'collective responses of that sort were not countermeasures; they were measures authorized by a competent international organization and did not belong in the framework of article 30 [1996] [defining countermeasures on first reading]'.[79] France (followed by Crawford and Simma) indeed articulated the need for this issue to be clarified on second reading, but the matter was not taken further.[80] The ambiguity, then, essentially remains the same in Article 22 ASR.[81] Still, the basic point of distinction remains intact. Countermeasures are a separate genus from Security Council action; they perform different functions and can therefore, in principle, co-exist autonomously in response to the same wrongful conduct. Third-party countermeasures cannot be said to encroach on the (distinct) powers of the Security Council, let alone contravene the UN Charter in any *a priori* sense. That said, even where conceptual boundaries are clearly demarcated in theory, functional ones may not be in practice. This brings us to the more complex principle of co-ordination.

In reality, it is not uncommon for the Security Council – in the maintenance or restoration of international peace and security under Chapter VII of the UN Charter – to adopt enforcement measures aimed at ensuring the cessation of wrongful conduct and/or reparation for injury. In these

76 *ILC Yearbook*, 1 (1999), 162, para. 79 (Mr Simma).

77 See UN Doc. A/CN.4/488 (25 March 1998), 82 (France).

78 *ILC Yearbook*, 1 (1999), 161–2, para. 75 (Mr Crawford). See also *ibid.*, 161, para. 73 (Mr Tomka).

79 *ILC Yearbook*, 1 (1999), 139, para. 16 (Mr Crawford).

80 UN Doc. A/CN.4/488, 82 (France); *ILC Yearbook*, 1 (1999), 162, para. 75 (Mr Crawford); *ibid.*, 162, para. 79 (Mr Simma).

81 See para. 3 of the commentary to Art. 22 ASR, ILC Report (2001), 75.

situations, there is inevitably a point of convergence with the law of State responsibility and, in particular, with the law of countermeasures. The ILC recognised this fact by pointing out that at least '[cessation] is frequently demanded not only by States but also by . . . the Security Council in the face of serious breaches of international law'.[82] It follows that enforcement measures under Chapter VII of the UN Charter, such as various forms of asset freezes, embargoes or other suspensions of treaty rights – to the extent that they overlap with the law of State responsibility – may act either as a complement to the possible concurrent use of third-party countermeasures or operate to constrain such use in a given case.

The extent of the actual interplay or co-ordination between the law of State responsibility (including countermeasures) and the law of collective security raises questions of considerable complexity with no obvious answers from practice. As a general matter, it can be observed that the UN Charter is not a self-contained regime. It can therefore be argued that third-party countermeasures will remain available (subject to overall compliance with its safeguards regime, notably proportionality)[83] to the extent that the Security Council is ineffective; or their use has not been proscribed by the specific language of a given Security Council Resolution; or would otherwise contradict Charter obligations in the circumstances.

3 There is no requirement of a 'widely acknowledged breach', although in practice joint statements on alleged serious illegalities limit the risk of abuse

The major and potentially most effective criticism of countermeasures undoubtedly concerns the inherent risk of abuse associated with the auto-interpretation of allegedly wrongful conduct. It is a risk exacerbated by the factual inequalities between States. As the arbitral tribunal in the *Naulilaa* case was careful to emphasise, 'the first requirement – *sine qua non* – of the right to take reprisals is a motive furnished by an earlier act contrary to the law of nations'.[84] Likewise, the ILC stressed that the

[82] See para. 4 of the commentary to Art. 30 ASR, ILC Report (2001), 89.

[83] The safeguards regime is essentially analogous to the one applicable to bilateral countermeasures. See further Arts. 49–53 ASR, ILC Report (2001), 129–37; Art. 5 of the resolution 'Obligations and Rights *Erga Omnes* in International Law'.

[84] *Responsabilité de l'Allemagne a raison des dommages causés dans les colonies portugaises du sud de l'Afrique* (*Portugal* v. *Germany*) (*Naulilaa* case), Reports of International Arbitral Awards, vol. II (1928), 1027. See further Art. 49 ASR and the commentary thereto, ILC Report (2001), 129–31.

existence of a prior breach of international law entitling a State to invoke the responsibility of the wrongdoing State is a 'fundamental prerequisite' of any lawful countermeasure; its establishment 'presupposes an objective standard'.[85] A State that resorts to countermeasures in the erroneous belief that a breach has occurred does so at its own peril – *caveat actor*.[86] Still, in an essentially decentralised system, 'each State establishes for itself its legal situation vis-à-vis other States'.[87] This raises the spectre that any number of States could individually resort to third-party countermeasures contrary to the obligations incumbent upon them on the basis of the mere assertion or claim of wrongful conduct.

These concerns are understandable and help explain the 'extreme sensitivity'[88] of the topic. A decentralised regime of third-party countermeasures is an institution that affects the very foundations of international law; and, at least in theory, poses a threat of some seriousness to sovereignty and the freedom of action of States within the law (the *domaine réservé*). The fear that a future incarnation of Lord Palmerston might abusively exclaim '*Civis mundi sum!*' as mere pretext for 'power politics'[89] underlies the deep-rooted concern among some States (especially – but by no means limited to – developing States) that a regime of decentralised and self-assessed third-party countermeasures would be 'used as an instrument of intervention and aggression'.[90] In short, on this view, the concept of third-party countermeasures merely 'provided a superficial legitimacy for the bullying of small States on the *claim* that human rights must be respected'.[91]

The proposed solution favoured by the ILC Special Rapporteurs on first reading was therefore to involve the United Nations in the 'objective' prior determination of breach. For his part, Special Rapporteur Riphagen's proposal to involve the Security Council in this process was based on his belief that:

> [T]here is little chance that States generally will accept [a regime of third-party countermeasures] without a legal guarantee that they will not be charged by any or all other States of having committed an international crime, and be faced with demands and countermeasures of any or all other

85 See paras. 2 and 3 of the commentary to Art. 49 ASR, ILC Report (2001), 130.

86 *Ibid.*

87 *Air Services Agreement of 27 March 1946 (United States* v. *France)*, Reports of International Arbitral Awards, vol. XVIII, 416 (1979), 443, para. 81.

88 Crawford, 'Fourth Report on State Responsibility', 14, para. 55.

89 UN Doc. A/CN.4/515 (19 March 2001), 69 (China).

90 UN Doc. A/C.6/47/SR.30 (6 Nov. 1992), 12, para. 49 (Ecuador); James Crawford, 'Fourth Report on State Responsibility', 18, para. 71.

91 *ILC Yearbook*, 1 (2001), 35, para. 2 (Mr Brownlie) (emphasis added).

> States *without an independent and authoritative establishment of the facts and the applicable law.*[92]

In a similar vein, as already alluded to above, Special Rapporteur Arangio-Ruiz proposed a far more elaborate and ambitious institutional safeguards regime for third-party countermeasures informed by the 'indispensable role of international institutions'.[93] In essence, his scheme was based on a two-phase procedure in which the General Assembly or the Security Council would first make a political determination (under Chapter VI of the UN Charter), and the International Court of Justice (ICJ) would later make a decisive legal determination concerning the possible existence of a serious breach.[94] However, this regime was resoundingly rejected in both the ILC and Sixth Committee as inconsistent with the UN Charter; it was simply unrealistic – far removed from States' conception of international law as a decentralised system of law[95] – and, in any event, woefully ineffective. By the time the ICJ would finally authorise the use of individual third-party countermeasures any serious breach (such as genocide) would likely already have been consummated.[96]

On second reading, Special Rapporteur Crawford identified the risk of abuse posed by auto-interpretation as an important 'due process'[97] issue for the target State, but his proposed solution was more attuned to what remained a fundamentally decentralised system of international law enforcement. In the absence of a prior judicial determination of the existence of a previous wrongful act, it is often difficult to assess with confidence whether there has indeed been a violation of international law, let alone a serious violation. As Crawford explained:

> Exactly where the threshold should be set for countermeasures to be taken by individual States, acting not in their own but in the collective interest, is a difficult question. There is an issue of 'due process' so far as concerns

92 Willem Riphagen, 'Fourth Report on State Responsibility', *ILC Yearbook*, 2(1) (1983), 12, para. 65 (emphasis added).

93 Gaetano Arangio-Ruiz, 'Seventh Report on State Responsibility', *ILC Yearbook*, 2(1) (1995), 17, para. 70.

94 *Ibid.*, 17–29, paras. 70–138.

95 A particularly staunch critic dismissed the proposed regime as a 'castle in the sky', *ILC Yearbook*, 1 (1995), 113, para. 26 (Mr Rosenstock). See also ILC Report (1995), UN Doc. A/50/10, 47, 55–6, paras. 250, 305–7. For a summary of the (mostly) critical views expressed by governments in the 6th Committee debate, see UN Doc. A/CN.4/472/Add.1 (10 January 1996), 25–7, paras. 86–97.

96 See e.g. *ILC Yearbook*, 1 (1995), 97, paras. 8–9 (Mr Pellet); *ibid.*, 94, para. 51 (Mr Bowett); *ibid.*, 100–1, paras. 20 and 34 (Mr Mahiou); *ibid.*, 118–9, paras. 66–7 (Mr Thiam).

97 Crawford, 'Third Report on State Responsibility', 37, para. 115.

> the target State, since at the time collective countermeasures are taken, its responsibility for the breach may be merely asserted, not demonstrated, and issues of fact and possible justifications are likely to have been raised and left unresolved.[98]

He concluded that for decentralised third-party countermeasures to be permissible, 'some formula such as a "gross and reliably attested breach" was called for', alternatively formulated as 'gross and well-attested breach' or 'serious and manifest breach'.[99] Ultimately, the ILC left the formula for the prior ascertainment of breach open by the agnostic arrangement embodied in Article 54 ASR. Still, the ILC did make clear that an institutional procedure for the prior ascertainment of breach would contradict the UN Charter and, in any event, be unnecessary given the likely involvement of the main UN political organs in addressing serious breaches.[100]

Finally, in its Krakow Resolution of 2005, the Institut de Droit International proposed its solution to the problem of auto-interpretation. On Rapporteur Gaja's proposal, it concluded that:

> [C]ountermeasures may be taken by States other than those injured *only if there is widespread acknowledgment within the international community of the existence of a breach.*[101]

The Institut explained that 'the reference to the wide acknowledgment of the existence of a breach is designed to limit the risk of unilateral assessment . . . diminish the risk of abuses and ensure that States genuinely seek to protect an interest of the international community'.[102] Importantly, this position found support in practice on third-party countermeasures which has 'generally related to infringements of obligations *erga omnes* that were indeed widely acknowledged'.[103]

Indeed, resort to third-party countermeasures is often preceded by joint statements adopted by States as part of a process of multilateral diplomacy in international fora.[104] As part of this (often lengthy) diplomatic process, the responsible State will normally have been publicly requested in a joint statement to comply with its secondary obligations and will have

[98] *Ibid.* [99] *Ibid.*

[100] See para. 9 of the commentary to Art. 40 ASR, ILC Report (2001), 113.

[101] Giorgio Gaja, 'First Report on Obligations and Rights *Erga Omnes* in International Law', 71(I) *Annuaire de l'institut de droit international* (Pedone, 2005), 148 (emphasis added).

[102] *Ibid.*, 149, 199. [103] *Ibid.*, 200.

[104] See generally, Dawidowicz, 'Public Law Enforcement without Public Law Safeguards?', 333–418.

been notified of the possible imminent adoption of third-party countermeasures against it in the event that it does not promptly return to international legality. Still, practice does not seem to indicate that States have co-operated in this way out of a sense of legal obligation. Instead, these joint statements appear predominantly motivated by an overriding practical imperative: co-ordinating an effective response to the most serious breaches of international law. Two separate considerations appear to bear out this conclusion.

First, as the ILC itself has recognised, it is 'open to question'[105] whether general international law at present entails a positive duty of co-operation in response to serious breaches. The prevalence of the phenomenon of co-operation in response to serious breaches of community norms, especially in the context of international organisations, does not diminish the force of this conclusion. Quite simply, such co-operation is 'often the only way of providing for an effective remedy'.[106] Secondly, a duty of co-operation would seemingly be inconsistent with the instrumental function of countermeasures. As a minimum, States have an individual or autonomous entitlement to claim cessation of breaches of *erga omnes* obligations within the meaning of Article 48 ASR. A requirement of a joint statement, by which a breach must first be 'widely acknowledged', would be inconsistent with the autonomous entitlement of States to at least claim cessation for serious breaches under general international law, a claim *par excellence* enforced by third-party countermeasures. In the absence of clear *opinio juris* to the contrary, it can be presumed that practical considerations of effectiveness have predominantly influenced practice in this field. In principle, then, a State may lawfully resort to third-party countermeasures (assuming a relevant breach has actually occurred) even in those rare circumstances where the breach is not 'widely acknowledged'. Perhaps most importantly, practice also indicates that third-party countermeasures – whatever the mode of establishment of the individual breach – have overall not been adopted in an abusive manner but on the well-founded belief of a serious infringement of a community norm.

III Concluding observations

Third-party countermeasures may still be a controversial topic but they can neither be dismissed in simplistic terms as a '*lex horrenda*'[107] nor

[105] See para. 3 of the commentary to Art. 41 ASR, ILC Report (2001), 114. [106] *Ibid.*

[107] *ILC Yearbook*, 1 (2001), 35, para. 2 (Mr Brownlie).

hailed as a 'saving grace for international law'.[108] In reality, the use of third-party countermeasures has so far proved neither as abusive as many had feared nor as effective as many others had hoped. But the fact is that they are nevertheless an important tool in a limited international law enforcement toolbox. Third-party countermeasures are rarely adopted in isolation. They are almost invariably accompanied by other forms of coercive measures against the target State, such as diplomatic pressure (retorsion) or action by international organisations at both regional and universal levels. It is within the context of such concerted and deliberative action that the discrete and incremental role of third-party countermeasures in a fundamentally decentralised system of community law enforcement is best understood.

Third-party countermeasures are less decentralised than is often assumed. Though they are not legally required, the existence of a serious breach is almost always established and 'widely acknowledged' within international organisations prior to the concerted adoption of third-party countermeasures. States will not normally ascertain the existence of a breach of a community norm in splendid isolation but in concert with other States acting through a deliberative process of multilateral diplomacy. For example, the many serious breaches of international law that triggered the adoption of third-party countermeasures against Syria in 2011 have been 'widely acknowledged' on multiple occasions, including by the Security Council, the General Assembly, the Human Rights Council, the League of Arab States, the Organisation of Islamic Cooperation and the EU. Whatever reasons might justifiably exist to oppose an evolving regime of third-party countermeasures, the specific concern of 'auto-interpretation' appears to be one of limited significance in practice. Moreover, States are reluctant to openly rely on the concept and are more inclined to use it cautiously, being sensitive to accusations of vigilantism, intervention and excessive human rights policing. In fact, as Simma has observed, 'far from obsessively policing human rights violations across the world, the attitude of States towards human rights violations is all too often characterized by a remarkable lack of vigour to counter such breaches'.[109] In short, 'States have hardly shown the excessive human

108 David Bederman, 'Counterintuiting Countermeasures', *American Journal of International Law*, 96 (2002), 831.

109 Bruno Simma and Dirk Pulkowski, '*Leges speciales* and Self-contained Regimes' in James Crawford, Alain Pellet and Simon Olleson (eds.), *Handbook of International Responsibility* (Oxford University Press, 2010), 162.

rights "vigilantism" dreaded by some.'[110] These factors may help explain why third-party countermeasures have proved remarkably uncontroversial in international practice – including where issues pertaining to the legitimate powers of the Security Council under the UN Charter have been involved. As James Crawford concluded in his last report as Special Rapporteur:

> While it can be hoped that international organizations will be able to resolve the humanitarian or other crises that often arise from serious breaches of international law, States have not abdicated their powers of individual action.[111]

This appears to be so because States consider that third-party countermeasures perform an important function within a limited law enforcement toolbox and as such cautiously welcome them as a progressive development of international law.

[110] *Ibid.* For the same conclusion see also James Crawford, 'Responsibility for Breaches of Communitarian Norms: An Appraisal of Article 48 of the ILC Articles on Responsibility of States for Internationally Wrongful Acts' in Ulrich Fastenrath *et al.* (eds.), *From Bilateralism to Community Interest: Essays in Honour of Judge Bruno Simma* (Oxford University Press, 2011), 236; Gaja, 'First Report on Obligations and Rights *Erga Omnes* in International Law', 150–1.

[111] Crawford, 'Fourth Report on State Responsibility', 18, para. 74.

20

The Appellate Body's use of the Articles on State responsibility in *US – Anti-dumping and Countervailing Duties (China)*

ISABELLE VAN DAMME*

Introduction

In this chapter, I examine the World Trade Organization (WTO) Appellate Body's interpretation in its report *US – Anti-dumping and Countervailing Duties (China)*[1] of 'public body' in Article 1.1(a)(1) of the Agreement on Subsidies and Countervailing Measures (SCM Agreement).[2] Under this provision, a subsidy shall be deemed to exist if 'there is a financial contribution by a government or any public body within the territory of a Member (referred to in [the SCM Agreement] as "government")' and a benefit is thereby conferred. The Appellate Body was asked to review the Panel's interpretation of 'public body' so as to mean 'any entity controlled by a government' and the Panel's application of that interpretation to the facts at issue. In the appeal, James Crawford acted as counsel for China, the appellant on this issue. It was his first appearance before the Appellate Body.[3]

Before the Appellate Body, China complained that the Panel had not taken account of the defining characteristic of a 'public body', that is to

* I am grateful to the editors, Dr Holger Hestermeyer and an anonymous reviewer for the comments which I received on earlier drafts of this chapter. The views expressed in this chapter are personal and do not reflect the views of the institution at which I am employed.

1 Appellate Body Report, *United States – Definitive Anti-dumping and Countervailing Duties on Certain Products from China* WT/DS379/AB/R, adopted 25 March 2011.

2 The SCM Agreement forms part of Annex 1A (containing the multilateral agreements on trade in goods) to the WTO Agreement. See WTO, *The Legal Texts: The Results of the Uruguay Round of Multilateral Trade Negotiations* (Cambridge University Press, 1999).

3 I wrote my PhD thesis on treaty interpretation by the Appellate Body under the supervision of James Crawford. See Isabelle Van Damme, *Treaty Interpretation by the WTO Appellate Body* (Oxford University Press, 2009).

say the exercise of authority vested in that body by the government for the purposes of performing functions of a governmental character. On appeal, China sought to obtain an interpretation of the SCM Agreement that was fully consistent with the rules of attribution in the International Law Commission's (ILC) Articles on Responsibility of States for Internationally Wrongful Acts of 2001 (ILC Articles),[4] in particular Article 5 which concerns the attribution of conduct of persons or entities exercising elements of governmental authority.[5]

Unlike the Panel, the Appellate Body was receptive to using the ILC Articles in interpreting 'public body' by virtue of Article 31(3)(c) of the Vienna Convention on the Law of Treaties (Vienna Convention).[6] It was hesitant however to declare the customary international law status of Article 5 of the ILC Articles. It therefore first examined the substance of Article 5 and its relevance to the interpretation of Article 1.1(a)(1) of the SCM Agreement. Whilst the rules on attribution inspired the entire interpretive reasoning of the Appellate Body, it ultimately concluded that 'because the outcome of [its] analysis does not turn on Article 5, it is not necessary for [it] to resolve definitively the question of to what extent Article 5 of the ILC Articles reflects customary international law'.[7]

The focus of this chapter is on the interpretation of 'public body' in the light of the ILC Articles. The results of that interpretation raise significant challenges in terms of defining the applicable standard of review of investigating authorities and evidentiary standards but are not discussed here.[8]

[4] Articles on Responsibility of States for Internationally Wrongful Acts of 2001, Annexed to GA Res. 56/83, 12 December 2001.

[5] Art. 5 of the ILC Articles states: 'The conduct of a person or entity which is not an organ of the State under article 4 but which is empowered by the law of that State to exercise elements of the governmental authority shall be considered an act of the State under international law, provided the person or entity is acting in that capacity in the particular instance.'

[6] Vienna Convention on the Law of Treaties (Vienna, adopted 22 May 1969, entered into force 27 January 1980), 1155 UNTS 331.

[7] Appellate Body Report, *United States – Definitive Anti-dumping and Countervailing Duties (China)*, para. 316.

[8] On that standard of review, see e.g. Tegan Brink, 'What Is a "Public Body" for the Purpose of Determining a Subsidy after the Appellate Body Ruling in *US – AD/CVD*?', *Global Trade and Customs Journal*, 6 (2011), 313–15; Michel Cartland, Gérard Depayre and Jan Woznowski, 'Is Something Going Wrong in the WTO Dispute Settlement?', *Journal of World Trade*, 46 (2012), 1006, 1010–14.

The Panel's interpretation of 'public body'

A premise for several claims made by China was the issue of the qualification of an entity such as a State-owned enterprise (SOE) and a State-owned commercial bank (SOCB) as a 'public body' within the meaning of Article 1.1(a)(1) of the SCM Agreement. Article 1.1 of that agreement, entitled 'Definition of a subsidy', defines a subsidy; other provisions set out different obligations with regard to different types of subsidy. It states:

> For the purpose of this Agreement, a subsidy shall be deemed to exist if:
> (a)(1) there is a financial contribution by a government or any public body within the territory of a Member (referred to in this Agreement as "government"), i.e. where:
> (i) a government practice involves a direct transfer of funds (e.g. grants, loans, and equity infusion), potential direct transfers of funds or liabilities (e.g. loan guarantees);
> (ii) government revenue that is otherwise due is forgone or not collected (e.g. fiscal incentives such as tax credits);
> (iii) a government provides goods or services other than general infrastructure, or purchases goods;
> (iv) a government makes payments to a funding mechanism, or entrusts or directs a private body to carry out one or more of the type of functions illustrated in (i) to (iii) above which would normally be vested in the government and the practice, in no real sense, differs from practices normally followed by governments;
> or
> (a)(2) there is any form of income or price support in the sense of Article XVI of GATT 1994;
> and
> (b) a benefit is thereby conferred.

Based on the text of that provision, the Panel found that Article 1.1 identifies three types of actor that can convey government financial contributions within the meaning of the SCM Agreement, namely: (i) governments (Article 1.1(a)(1)); (ii) public bodies (Article 1.1(a)(1)); and (iii) private bodies that have been entrusted and directed by the government to make a financial contribution (Article 1.1(a)(1)(iv)).[9] The United States, in particular the United States Department of Commerce, had found that Chinese SOEs and SOCBs were public bodies. In the Panel's own words, the issue before it was 'whether wholly or majority government-owned

[9] Panel Report, *United States – Definitive Anti-dumping and Countervailing Duties (China)*, para. 8.54.

enterprises that produce and sell goods and services are more appropriately categorized' as one of the types of actor described in Article 1.1.[10] In particular, the question before it was whether the SOEs and SOCBs were private or public bodies. Depending on their proper characterisation, a separate test applied for defining a subsidy. In particular, entrustment or direction needed to be proven with regard to private bodies whilst that was not needed for government or public bodies.

According to the Panel, the three types of actors described in Article 1.1 encompassed 'the complete universe of all potential actors' and 'every entity (individual, corporation, association, agency, Ministry, etc.) must fall into one of these three categories'.[11] It followed that the SCM Agreement did 'not *a priori* rule out <u>any</u> entity from <u>potentially</u> coming within its scope'.[12]

The Panel found that the SCM Agreement defined neither the term 'government' nor the term 'public body'. It therefore used dictionary definitions of the terms in their three authentic languages,[13] whilst accepting that there existed no universally accepted definition or a uniform and narrowly drawn meaning of the latter term.[14] Those dictionary definitions appeared to suggest, without deciding the matter conclusively, that the meaning of 'public body' was wider than that suggested by China, namely 'government agency' or other entity vested with and exercising governmental authority.[15] The Panel then turned to the immediate context of 'any public body', which included the word 'government' and the disjunctive 'or', and took those contextual elements to suggest that the term had a separate and broader meaning than 'government' or 'government agency'.[16] Apart from those contextual elements, the Panel further considered the collective expression between brackets in the final part of Article 1.1(a)(1), '(referred to in this Agreement as "government")', but it refused to give substantive content to that expression. Rather, it was 'more likely that [its] use . . . [was] merely a device to simplify the drafting'.[17] With regard to the remaining phrase in that provision, 'within the territory of a Member', the Panel said that this phrase meant that 'in essence, . . . where the author of the financial contribution is either an executive organ of any level of government, or a public body of any kind at any level of government within the territory, the [SCM] Agreement considers the financial contribution to have been made by the

[10] *Ibid.*, para. 8.68. [11] *Ibid.* [12] *Ibid.* (original emphasis).
[13] *Ibid.*, paras. 8.57, 8.61 and 8.62. [14] *Ibid.*, paras. 8.59 and 8.60. [15] *Ibid.*, para. 8.63.
[16] *Ibid.*, para. 8.65. [17] *Ibid.*, para. 8.66.

"government" of that "Member" (directly)'.[18] That phrase thus appeared 'to connote a broad reading of the term "a government" to cover whatever forms and organs of government, be they national, provincial, municipal, etc., that may be present within the territory of a given Member'.[19]

However, according to the Panel, the most important contextual element for interpreting the terms 'government' and 'any public body' was the term 'private body' in Article 1.1(a)(iv).[20] At that stage in its analysis, it identified the issue before it as being whether the Chinese SOEs and SOCBs were private or public bodies and then focused on the definition of the term 'private body'. The Panel used the dictionary definitions of the terms 'private enterprise' and 'public sector' to understand the meaning of the term 'private body'; they suggested that the latter was 'an entity not controlled by the State, and that ownership is highly relevant to the question of control'.[21] The Panel refused to read the term 'public body' as meaning 'government agencies and other entities vested with and exercising governmental authority' and 'as presumptively excluding government-owned and/or government-controlled enterprises' because that would imply that government-owned and government-controlled enterprises would be private bodies and would result therefore in 'a complete reversal of the ordinary meaning of the term "private body"'.[22] Such an interpretation would also deprive the list of types of financial contribution in Article 1.1(a)(1)(i)–(iii) of its common-sense meaning and role.[23]

The Panel then provisionally concluded that the term 'public body' appeared to extend to 'entities controlled by governments, and [was] not limited to government agencies and other entities vested with and exercising governmental authority'.[24]

When next reading the relevant terms in the light of the object and purpose of the SCM Agreement, the Panel based its analysis on past case law of the Appellate Body and other panels. It found that Article 1.1(a)(1) should not be read as allowing 'avoidance of the SCM Agreement's disciplines by excluding whole categories of government non-commercial behaviour undertaken by government-controlled entities'.[25] That consideration was reinforced by the fact that the categorisation of an entity was just the first step in a multi-part analysis; that first step involved an inquiry into whether an entity undertaking a behaviour or measure was or was not the WTO Member, that is to say, an entity covered by the

[18] *Ibid.*, para. 8.67. [19] *Ibid.* [20] *Ibid.*, para. 8.68. [21] *Ibid.*, para. 8.69.
[22] *Ibid.*, para. 8.69. [23] *Ibid.*, para. 8.70. [24] *Ibid.*, para. 8.73. [25] *Ibid.*, para. 8.76.

WTO Agreement.[26] The Panel thus read 'any public body' as meaning 'any entity that is controlled by the government'.[27] A narrower interpretation would enable governments to hide behind the so-called private character of government-controlled entities whilst controlling them in a manner so as to deliberately provide trade-distorting subsidies.[28]

The final step in the Panel's interpretive analysis was to consider whether (i) the ILC Articles and (ii) the General Agreement on Trade in Services (GATS)[29] and its Annex on Financial Services showed, as China had argued, that the Panel should adopt a different (and, in fact, a narrower) interpretation.

Unlike the Appellate Body later on, the Panel first considered the status of the ILC Articles before addressing the substance of China's argument. According to the Panel, China had overstated the status accorded to the ILC Articles in WTO dispute settlement because in no previous panel or Appellate Body report had those articles been identified as 'relevant rules of international law applicable in the relations between the parties' within the meaning of Article 31(3)(c) of the Vienna Convention.[30] Rather, where they had been used, they offered 'conceptual guidance only to supplement or confirm, but not to replace, the analyses based on the ordinary meaning, context and objective and purpose of the relevant covered Agreements'.[31] That being the case, the Panel added that the ILC Articles themselves made it clear that they concerned whether or not a State is responsible for a given action that might constitute a substantive breach of an underlying international obligation. In that regard, the Panel found that Article 1.1 of the SCM Agreement was *lex specialis* in relation to the ILC Articles.[32] On the basis of these considerations, the ILC Articles could not be characterised as falling within the scope of Article 31(3)(c) of the Vienna Convention.[33] With regard to the use of the term 'public entity' in the Annex on Financial Services to the GATS, the Panel was relatively brief and found that that term and the term 'public body' in the SCM Agreement were very different terms used in separate agreements and there was no indication in either agreement of any conceptual or other link between them.[34]

[26] *Ibid.* [27] *Ibid.*, para. 8.79. [28] *Ibid.*, para. 8.82.

[29] The GATS is included as Annex 1B to the WTO Agreement. See WTO, *The Legal Texts: The Results of the Uruguay Round.*

[30] Panel Report, *United States – Definitive Anti-dumping and Countervailing Duties (China)*, para. 8.87.

[31] *Ibid.* [32] *Ibid.*, para. 8.90. [33] *Ibid.*, para. 8.91. [34] *Ibid.*, para. 8.92.

China appealed the Panel's interpretation of 'public body' in Article 1.1(a)(1) of the SCM Agreement, asking the Appellate Body to reverse that interpretation and to find that a public body is an entity that exercises authority vested in it by the government for the purposes of performing functions of a governmental character.[35]

The Appellate Body's interpretation of 'public body'

The Appellate Body reversed the Panel's interpretation of the term 'public body' in Article 1.1(a)(1) of the SCM Agreement. It first focused on the architecture and function of Article 1.1(a)(1). That provision in essence defines and identifies the governmental conduct that constitutes a financial contribution by identifying what conduct of what entities in what circumstances can be attributed to a WTO Member and therefore constitute governmental conduct.[36] Unlike the Panel, the Appellate Body identified only two categories of entity described in Article 1.1(a)(1) – that is to say, governmental bodies or 'a government or any public body' and 'private body'.[37] With regard to the former, it held that all their conduct constitutes a financial contribution to the extent that the conduct falls within subparagraphs (i)–(iii) and the first clause of subparagraph (iv), whereas for the latter an affirmative demonstration of the link between the government and the specific conduct was needed.[38]

Against that background, the Appellate Body interpreted the term 'public body'. It started its analysis with the dictionary definitions of the different terms used in Article 1.1(a)(1) and with how the terms 'government', 'public body' and 'private body' were used together in that provision. In that regard, it did not share the Panel's position that the phrase '(referred to in this Agreement as "government")' was merely a drafting tool and therefore irrelevant. The Panel had thus ignored the structure and the wording of the treaty.[39] The section of the report setting out the Appellate Body's position on the ordinary meaning and dictionary definitions concluded with a restatement of its report in *Canada – Dairy*, namely that 'the essence of government is that it enjoys the effective power to regulate, control, or supervise individuals, or otherwise restrain their conduct, through the exercise of lawful authority', adding that 'performance of governmental functions, or the fact of being vested with, and exercising, the

[35] Appellate Body Report, *United States – Definitive Anti-dumping and Countervailing Duties (China)*, para. 279 (referring to China's appellant's submission, para. 30).

[36] *Ibid.*, para. 284. [37] *Ibid.* [38] *Ibid.* [39] *Ibid.*, para. 289.

authority to perform such function appeared to be core commonalities between government and public body'.[40]

Next, the Appellate Body turned to context in order to refine its interpretation of 'public body' and of the core characteristics that such a body must share with government.[41] The first contextual element was the term 'private body' in Article 1.1(a)(1)(iv) of the SCM Agreement because it described a body that is not 'a government or any public body'.[42] In particular, Article 1.1(a)(1)(iv) foresees that a public body may 'entrust' or 'direct' a private body to carry out the type of functions or conduct listed in subparagraphs (i)–(iii).

The Appellate Body refused to accept the unqualified and unsupported statement of the Panel that certain acts listed in subparagraphs (i)–(iii) were in essence the core business of firms and corporations rather than of governments. It appeared to consider that this issue had no direct bearing on the constituent elements of a 'public body' within the meaning of Article 1.1(a)(1) of the SCM Agreement.[43] In fact, the functions described in (i)–(iii) appeared to support the idea that a 'public body' 'connote[d] an entity vested with certain governmental responsibilities, or exercising certain governmental authority'.[44] The remaining part of subparagraph (iv) also suggested that 'whether the functions or conduct are of a kind that are ordinarily classified as governmental in the legal order of the relevant Member may be a relevant consideration for determining whether or not a specific entity is a public body' and 'the classification and functions of entities within WTO Members generally may also bear on the question of what features are normally exhibited by public bodies'.[45]

The Appellate Body found that considerations regarding the object and purpose of the SCM Agreement were 'of limited use in delimiting the scope of the term "public body"'.[46] Whether an entity was a public body did not necessarily determine whether measures taken by that entity fell within the scope of the SCM Agreement.[47] That being so, the Appellate Body nonetheless faulted the Panel for not taking full account of the SCM Agreement's disciplines in interpreting the term 'public body' in the light of the object and purpose. The Panel had focused only on the consequences of interpreting the term too narrowly, whereas it should have taken into account also the risks of an overly broad interpretation because 'it could serve as a license for investigating authorities to dispense

[40] *Ibid.*, para. 290. [41] *Ibid.*, para. 291. [42] *Ibid.* [43] *Ibid.*, para. 296. [44] *Ibid.*
[45] *Ibid.*, para. 297. [46] *Ibid.*, para. 302. [47] *Ibid.*

with an analysis of entrustment and direction and instead find entities with any connection to government to be public bodies'.[48]

The Appellate Body then finally turned to China's argument that the rules of attribution in the ILC Articles reflected customary international law or general principles of law and should be taken into account under Article 31(3)(c) of the Vienna Convention as 'any relevant rules of international law applicable in the relations between the parties'. According to China, the rules of attribution in Articles 4, 5 and 8 closely resembled the attribution of financial contributions to WTO Members under the SCM Agreement when provided by a government, a public body or a private body entrusted or directed by a government or a public body. In particular, Article 5 encompassed the type of entity described as a 'public body' in Article 1.1(a)(1) of the SCM Agreement.

The Appellate Body first considered whether Article 31(3)(c) of the Vienna Convention applied to the particular provisions of the ILC Articles on which China relied. In its view, Article 31(3)(c) had three constituent elements: (i) the provisions must be 'rules of international law', (ii) the rules must be 'relevant' and (iii) those rules must be 'applicable in the relations between the parties'.[49] Applied to Articles 4, 5 and 8 of the ILC's Articles, this meant that, first, Article 31(3)(c) referred to the sources of international law in Article 38(1) of the Statute of the International Court of Justice which include customary international law and general principles of law recognised by civilised nations. Secondly, those provisions were 'relevant' to the extent that they concerned the same subject matter as Article 1.1(a)(1) of the SCM Agreement. Thirdly, insofar as Articles 4, 5 and 8 reflected customary international law or general principles of law, they were 'applicable in the relations between the parties'.[50]

Before turning to the issue of the status of Articles 4, 5 and 8 of the ILC Articles (which, if they were found to reflect customary international law, controlled the first and third elements of Article 31(3)(c) of the Vienna Convention), the Appellate Body considered the second element: the extent to which these rules provided guidance and thus were relevant to interpreting 'public body' in Article 1.1(a)(1) of the SCM Agreement.[51]

The Appellate Body accepted the commonality between those rules because they 'set out rules relating to the question of attribution of conduct to a State'.[52] Yet, there existed also differences: in the ILC Articles the connecting factor for attribution was the particular conduct, whereas

[48] *Ibid.*, para. 303. [49] *Ibid.*, para. 307. [50] *Ibid.*, para. 308.
[51] *Ibid.*, para. 309. [52] *Ibid.*

in Article 1.1(a)(1) the connecting factors were both the particular conduct and the type of entity. Despite those differences, the Appellate Body accepted that its interpretation of 'public body' coincided with the essence of Article 5 of the ILC Articles. This was especially so taking into account the commentary on Article 5 which stated that that provision 'refers to the true common feature of the entities covered by that provision, namely that they are empowered, if only to a limited extent or in a specific context, to exercise specified elements of governmental authority' and that greater or lesser State participation in its capital or ownership of its assets were not decisive criteria.[53] That consideration was based on the similarities in the core principles and functions of the ILC Articles and Article 1.1(a)(1) of the SCM Agreement and not on 'any details' or 'fine line distinctions' under Article 5 of the ILC Articles.[54]

At that stage, the Appellate Body in essence concluded that the fact that Article 5 supported, but did not control, its analysis meant that it did not need to consider whether, and possibly to what extent, Article 5 reflected customary international law. It said as follows:

> Yet, because the outcome of our analysis does not turn on Article 5, it is not necessary for us to resolve definitively the question of to what extent Article 5 of the ILC Articles reflects customary international law.[55]

Despite that conclusion, the Appellate Body then continued to address the Panel's statement that the ILC Articles had been cited in previous reports 'as conceptual guidance only to supplement or confirm, but not to replace, the analysis based on the ordinary meaning, context and objective and purpose of the relevant covered Agreements'.[56] In particular the fact that, as the Panel had observed, the ILC Articles had been cited as containing similar provisions as those in certain WTO agreements, whereas in other disputes those articles were cited by way of contrast with WTO provisions, showed that, in those previous reports, the ILC Articles had been 'taken into account' in the sense of Article 31(3)(c) of the Vienna Convention.[57]

The Appellate Body then turned to the Panel's position that, pursuant to Article 55 of the ILC Articles, Article 1.1(a)(1) of the SCM Agreement superseded Articles 4, 5 and 8 of the ILC Articles because it constituted

[53] *Ibid.*, para. 310. [54] *Ibid.*, para. 311.

[55] Appellate Body Report, *United States – Definitive Anti-dumping and Countervailing Duties (China)*, para. 311, adding in footnote 222 that 'with respect to Article 4 of the ILC Articles, the Panel in *US – Gambling* stated that the principle set out in Article 4 of the ILC Articles reflected customary international law concerning attribution'.

[56] *Ibid.*, para. 313. [57] *Ibid.*

lex specialis regarding attribution. Under Article 55, the ILC Articles 'do not apply where and to the extent that the conditions for the existence of an internationally wrongful act or the content or implementation of the international responsibility of a State are governed by special rules of international law'. To the Appellate Body, it was clear that Article 55 concerned solely the question of 'which rule to *apply* where there are multiple rules addressing the same subject matter'.[58] That was not the question being considered in the case under appeal. Rather, the question was 'whether, when interpreting the terms of Article 1.1(a)(1), the relevant provisions of the ILC Articles may be taken into account as one among several interpretative elements'.[59]

Assessment

Introduction

I do not consider this report to be a 'bad decision' as some have called it,[60] though it could have been clearer. The Appellate Body's use of the ILC Articles was hesitant but not necessarily incorrect.[61]

[58] *Ibid.*, para. 316. [59] *Ibid.*

[60] John D. Greenwald, 'A Comparison of WTO and CIT/CAFC Jurisprudence in Review of U.S. Commerce Department Decisions in Antidumping and Countervailing Duty Proceedings', available at www.cit.uscourts.gov/Judicial_Conferences/17th_Judicial_Conference/17th_Judicial_Conference_Papers/GreenwaldPaper.pdf.

[61] Other reports in which the ILC Articles were (positively) used include e.g. Appellate Body Report, *United States – Transitional Safeguard Measure on Combed Cotton Yarn from Pakistan* ('*US – Cotton Yarn*'), WT/DS192/AB/R, adopted 5 November 2001, DSR 2001:XII, 6027, para. 120; Appellate Body Report, *United States – Definitive Safeguard Measures on Imports of Circular Welded Carbon Quality Line Pipe from Korea* ('*US – Line Pipe*'), WT/DS202/AB/R, adopted 8 March 2002, DSR 2002:IV, 1403, para. 259; Appellate Body Report, *United States – Measures Relating to Zeroing and Sunset Reviews – Recourse to Article 21.5 of the DSU by Japan* ('*US – Zeroing (Japan) (Article 21.5 – Japan)*'), WT/DS322/AB/RW, adopted 31 August 2009, DSR 2009:VIII, 3441, para. 183 and footnote 466; Appellate Body Report, *United States – Continued Suspension of Obligations in the EC – Hormones Dispute* ('*US – Continued Suspension*'), WT/DS320/AB/R, adopted 14 November 2008, DSR 2008:X, 3507, para. 382; Panel Report, *United States – Measures Affecting the Cross-border Supply of Gambling and Betting Services* ('*US – Gambling*'), WT/DS285/R, adopted 20 April 2005, as modified by Appellate Body Report WT/DS285/AB/R, DSR 2005:XII, 5797 paras. 6.127–6.129; Panel Report, *Canada – Measures Affecting the Importation of Milk and the Exportation of Dairy Products* ('*Canada – Dairy*'), WT/DS103/R, WT/DS113/R, adopted 27 October 1999, as modified by Appellate Body Report WT/DS103/AB/R, WT/DS113/AB/R, DSR 1999:VI, 2097 para. 7.77, footnote 427; Panel Report, *Australia – Measures Affecting Importation of Salmon – Recourse to Article 21.5 of the DSU by Canada* ('*Australia – Salmon (Article 21.5 – Canada)*'),

Whilst the Appellate Body's interpretation of 'public body' corresponds with the head of attribution set out in Article 5 of the ILC Articles, it neglected to clarify how secondary rules (of State responsibility) are relevant to interpreting a provision which sets out the scope of primary rules, the breach of which results in a finding of State responsibility (but does not itself contain an obligation the breach of which might result in State responsibility). Nor did it convincingly establish the basis in the Vienna Convention for interpreting the term 'public body' against the background of Article 5 of the ILC Articles.

Article 31(3)(c) of the Vienna Convention sets forth three elements ('rules of international law', 'relevant' and 'applicable in the relations between the parties'). Yet the third element becomes obsolete if the rule is accepted as reflecting customary international law or a general principle of (international) law. In those circumstances, the rule evidently applies in the relations between the parties because of its general application (and irrespective of whether 'the parties' is held to mean 'the parties to the dispute' or 'the parties to the treaty being interpreted').[62]

WT/DS18/RW, adopted 20 March 2000, DSR 2000:IV, 2031, para. 7.12, footnote 146; Panel Report, *Korea – Measures Affecting Government Procurement* ('*Korea – Government Procurement*'), WT/DS163/R, adopted 19 June 2000, DSR 2000:VIII, 3541, para. 6.5, footnote 683; Decision by the Arbitrators, *Brazil – Export Financing Programme for Aircraft – Recourse to Arbitration by Brazil under Article 22.6 of the DSU and Article 4.11 of the SCM Agreement* ('*Brazil – Aircraft (Article 22.6 – Brazil)*'), WT/DS46/ARB, 28 August 2000, DSR 2002:I, 19 para. 3.44; Decision by the Arbitrator, *United States – Subsidies on Upland Cotton – Recourse to Arbitration by the United States under Article 22.6 of the DSU and Article 4.11 of the SCM Agreement* ('*US – Upland Cotton (Article 22.6 – US I)*'), WT/DS267/ARB/1, 31 August 2009, DSR 2009:IX, 3871 paras. 4.40 to 4.42. See also Alejandro Sánchez, 'What Trade Lawyers Should Know about the ILC Articles on State Responsibility', *Global Trade and Customs Journal*, 7 (2012), 292.

62 The meaning of that element of Art. 31(3)(c) VCLT has been widely documented and debated. See e.g. Van Damme, *Treaty Interpretation by the WTO Appellate Body*, 360–6 and 368–76; Richard Gardiner, *Treaty Interpretation* (Oxford University Press, 2008), chs. 7.3 and 7.4; Report of the ILC Study Group, Fragmentation of International Law: Difficulties Arising from the Diversification and Expansion of International Law – Finalized by Martti Koskenniemi and Draft Conclusions of the Work of the Study Group, Doc. A/CN.4/L.682 and Add.1 and Corr.1, 2 May 2006 [and taken note of by the UNGA 6th Committee, Doc. A/61/454, para III.4], paras. 470–2. In *EC and Certain Member States – Large Civil Aircraft*, the Appellate Body addressed the parties' disagreement on 'whether the reference is to all the parties to the treaty being interpreted, or a smaller sub-set of parties including, for instance, the parties to the dispute in which the interpretative issue arises'. Whilst the Appellate Body did not consider it necessary to take a final position on the meaning of 'the parties', it appeared to suggest that the term might be interpreted and applied differently depending on the context at issue or, as the Appellate Body put it, 'a delicate balance must be struck between, on the one hand, taking due account of an

Based on that consideration, the Appellate Body rightly focused on two elements: the status of the ILC Articles and their relevance to the question being considered. Logically, the Appellate Body first examined the second element because the issue of the status of the ILC Articles is inconsequential if those articles are found not to be relevant to the meaning of the term 'public body'.

Relevance of the ILC Articles

The Appellate Body defined relevance in function of the subject matter of both Article 1.1(a)(1) of the SCM Agreement and Articles 4, 5 and 8 of the ILC Articles: all set out rules relating to the attribution of conduct to a State.[63] Leaving aside conceptual distinctions between the character of each set of rules, the status of the ILC Articles and the extent to which each set was defined by reference to conduct and/or entity, it appears clear that the Appellate Body accepted the relevance of, in particular, Article 5 to interpreting the term 'public body' in Article 1.1(a)(1). Yet, despite the ILC Articles' relevance, the Appellate Body decided to forego determining the status of Article 5 as a matter of public international law because the outcome of its interpretive exercise did 'not turn on' it. That reasoning enabled the Appellate Body to avoid basing its analysis more firmly on Article 31(3)(c) of the Vienna Convention. In so doing, the Appellate Body injected a high standard of relevance into Article 31(3)(c) without explaining either the basis for that standard, or how to distinguish it from the normative weight that is to be given to a rule satisfying the conditions set out in Article 31(3)(c). Nor did it reflect upon how that standard affects the relationship between the general rule of interpretation in Article 31 of the Vienna Convention and that in Article 32. Those matters are discussed in the following section of this chapter.

Under the SCM Agreement, WTO Members can be held responsible for violating that agreement if they made a financial contribution, thereby

individual WTO Member's international obligations and, on the other hand, ensuring a consistent and harmonious approach to the interpretation of WTO law among all WTO Members'. In any event, the Appellate Body avoided taking a clearer position on the matter based on the consideration that the treaty at issue was not relevant to the specific question before it. Appellate Body Report, *European Communities and Certain Member States – Measures Affecting Trade in Large Civil Aircraft* ('*EC and Certain Member States – Large Civil Aircraft*'), WT/DS316/AB/R, adopted 1 June 2011, paras. 842–6 and 851.

[63] Appellate Body Report, *United States – Definitive Anti-dumping and Countervailing Duties (China)*, para. 309.

conferring a benefit, which is contrary to the substantive obligations set out in that agreement. Article 1 of the SCM Agreement defines a 'subsidy' by reference to (i) certain types of conduct, (ii) the entity performing the conduct and (iii) the conferral of a benefit as a result of that conduct. Under Article 1.1(a)(1), the types of conduct described in items (i)–(iv) all involve 'government' conduct for the purposes of the SCM Agreement. The use of the word 'government' in each of the items makes that plain. The meaning of that word is further explained in Article 1.1(a)(1) as meaning 'a government or any public body within the territory of a Member'. Evidently, Article 1 of the SCM Agreement forms part of the description of the scope of application of the obligations under the SCM Agreement the breach (or rather nullification or impairment) of which may entail the responsibility of the WTO Member awarding the subsidy. Those obligations apply to 'government' conduct as defined in items (i)–(iv) in Article 1.1(a)(1).

Thus, it appears undisputed that contributions that cannot be linked to a WTO Member cannot constitute a subsidy for which that Member can be held responsible because it violates the substantive obligations in the remainder of the SCM Agreement.[64] That required link is expressed in three different forms in Article 1.1 of the SCM Agreement: (i) the government itself, (ii) any public body within the territory of a Member and (iii) a private body entrusted or directed to carry out one or more of the functions illustrated in (i)–(iii) of Article 1.1(a)(1) of the SCM Agreement which would normally be vested in the government.[65] The first and second forms are collectively named 'government' in the SCM Agreement.

The Appellate Body appeared to take the same starting point: the measure defined under Article 1.1(a)(1) of the SCM Agreement is a subsidy only if it is attributable to a State. Thus, the element of attribution was

[64] The Appellate Body appears to have confirmed that principle when stating that 'situations involving exclusively private conduct – that is, conduct that is not in some way attributable to a government or public body – cannot constitute a "financial contribution" for purposes of determining the existence of a subsidy under the *SCM Agreement*'. Appellate Body Report, *United States – Countervailing Duty Investigation on Dynamic Random Access Memory Semiconductors (DRAMS) from Korea* ('*US – Countervailing Duty Investigation on DRAMS*'), WT/DS296/AB/R, adopted 20 July 2005, DSR 2005:XVI, 8131, para. 107.

[65] Situations listed in items (i)–(iii) describe financial contributions directly provided by the government. That listed in item (iv) refers to financial contributions indirectly provided, that is to say the situation where a private body is used as a proxy by the government. See Appellate Body Report, *US – Countervailing Duty Investigation on DRAMS*, para. 108.

treated as an intrinsic element of the definition. According to the Appellate Body, the connecting factor in the ILC Articles was conduct, whereas under Article 1.1(a)(1) of the SCM Agreement it was both the particular conduct and the type of entity.[66] It did not appear to recognise that, for example, the distinction made between Articles 4 and 5 of the ILC Articles is based also on the character of the entity performing the conduct, in particular whether or not that entity qualifies as an organ of State.[67] Nor did the Appellate Body take account of the separate functions of both types of rule – one being secondary norms and the other being primary rules (though of a type affecting the scope of application of an agreement). Whilst that distinction might be, as James has pointed out, somewhat artificial,[68] the respective functions of each type arguably cannot be ignored in determining whether one set is relevant to interpreting the other.

However, the Appellate Body was correct in characterising, albeit in an indirect manner, the matter under appeal as one regarding the attribution of conduct. Conduct that is not that of a WTO Member and, in particular, conduct that is not government conduct as defined in Article 1.1 cannot lead to consequences under the SCM Agreement. It is in this context that questions of attribution arise and that the ILC Articles' provisions on attribution became materially relevant. That context is not confined to

66 Appellate Body Report, *United States – Definitive Anti-dumping and Countervailing Duties (China)*, para. 309.

67 Art. 8 of the ILC Articles – also accepted as reflecting customary international law (see *Case concerning Application of the Convention on the Prevention and Punishment of the Crime of Genocide (Bosnia and Herzegovina* v. *Serbia and Montenegro)*, Judgment, ICJ Reports (2007), 43, para. 398) – foresees that conduct is attributed to a State 'if the person or group of persons is in fact acting on the instructions of, or under the direction or control of, that State in carrying out the conduct'. Its application depends on whether conduct can be attributed to the State on the basis of, among others, Arts. 4 and 5 of the ILC Articles. The commentary to Art. 8 expressly addresses the position of State-owned and -controlled companies or enterprises. The sole fact that a State established an enterprise is an insufficient basis for attributing conduct of that enterprise to that State. Instructions, direction or control must relate to the conduct that is allegedly an internationally wrongful act. 'Effective control' in that context has been interpreted by the ICJ to mean that 'the State's instructions were given, in respect of each operation in which the alleged violations occurred, not generally in respect of the overall actions taken by the persons or groups of persons having committed the violations' (*Application of the Convention on the Prevention and Punishment of the Crime of Genocide*, para. 400). See also James Crawford, *The International Law Commission's Articles on State Responsibility: Introduction, Text and Commentaries* (Cambridge University Press, 2002), 112 and 113.

68 See e.g. James Crawford, *Brownlie's Principles of Public International Law*, 8th edn (Oxford University Press, 2012), 540.

the issue of the scope of the SCM Agreement. In principle, attribution underlies most findings of inconsistency with WTO obligations because the latter are mostly obligations owed by WTO Members and in principle a nexus between a measure and a Member is required in order for those measures to be subject to dispute settlement proceedings.[69] However, Article 1.1(a)(1) of the SCM Agreement is distinct, though not unique, when compared to many other WTO provisions in that it expressly internalises attribution in defining the material scope of application of that agreement.[70] On that basis, the argument according to which the ILC Articles, and thus also the rules on attribution, become relevant only if something wrongful has happened lacks merit.[71] Indeed, the characterisation of a measure as a subsidy is separate from the determination of whether that measure is inconsistent with the substantive obligations set out in the SCM Agreement (that is, whether the subsidy is wrongful as a matter of WTO law). In the context of the SCM Agreement, the issue of attribution pertains to the former inquiry but not to the latter.

The Appellate Body has been criticised for using in this decision the ILC Articles that 'have nothing to do with international trade'.[72] That argument fails to acknowledge that the Appellate Body's reasoning reflects the logic that if WTO Members are to be held responsible for breaches

[69] See also e.g. Santiago M. Villalpando, 'Attribution of Conduct to the State: How the Rules of State Responsibility May Be Applied within the WTO Dispute Settlement System', *Journal of International Economic Law*, 5 (2002), 396–7. As regards that nexus, see e.g. Appellate Body Report, *United States – Sunset Review of Anti-Dumping Duties on Corrosion-Resistant Carbon Steel Flat Products from Japan* ('*US – Corrosion-Resistant Steel Sunset Review*'), WT/DS244/AB/R, adopted 9 January 2004, DSR 2004:I, 3, para. 81; Panel Report, *Canada – Certain Measures Affecting the Automotive Industry* ('*Canada – Autos*'), WT/DS139/R, WT/DS142/R, adopted 19 June 2000, as modified by Appellate Body Report WT/DS139/AB/R, WT/DS142/AB/R, DSR 2000:VII, 3043, para. 10.107; Panel Report, *Japan – Measures Affecting Consumer Photographic Film and Paper* ('*Japan – Film*'), WT/DS44/R, adopted 22 April 1998, DSR 1998:IV, 1179, para. 10.52.

[70] See also Luigi Condorelli and Claus Kress, 'The Rules of Attribution: General Considerations' in James Crawford, Alain Pellet and Simon Olleson (eds.), *The Law of International Responsibility* (Oxford University Press, 2010), 222.

[71] That argument was advanced in Cartland, Depayre and Woznowski, 'Is Something Going Wrong in the WTO Dispute Settlement?', 997, 999.

[72] Greenwald, 'A Comparison of WTO and CIT/CAFC Jurisprudence in Review of U.S. Commerce Department Decisions in Antidumping and Countervailing Duty Proceedings'. That author suspects that use of the ILC Articles was very much the doing of the Belgian member of the Appellate Body whom he describes as having 'an academic interest in injecting concepts taken from public international law into WTO agreements whether or not they lend themselves to practical application in laws specifically meant to regulate international trade'. He offers no support for that allegation, rendering it incredible.

of the treaties to which they consented to be bound, rules on attribution are indispensable for determining whose or what entity's conduct entails that responsibility. In that regard, WTO law is not distinct from public international law in general. In most cases decided before panels and the Appellate Body, that question of attribution is taken for granted because the measure at issue is obviously one that can be attributed to the State (usually because, on its face, it falls under the general rule of attribution set out in Article 4). Yet, with respect to certain provisions or agreements, such as the SCM Agreement, the issue of attribution is internalised in the terms defining the scope of (the obligations assumed under) the treaty.[73] In those circumstances, it becomes difficult to distinguish, in conceptual terms, the material scope of the primary rules the breach of which results possibly in State responsibility and the secondary rules offering the background against which to assess whether the conduct is that which can be attributed to the State.

Here, the Appellate Body thus accepted that attribution formed part of the material definition of a subsidy. However, whilst the SCM Agreement sets out the types of entity whose conduct, if corresponding with the forms of financial contribution listed in items (i)–(iii) and resulting in conferral of a benefit, can entail the responsibility of a WTO Member under that agreement when that conduct is inconsistent with the substantive obligations in the SCM Agreement, it did not define the terms 'government' and 'public body'.

The text of Article 1.1(a)(1) of the SCM Agreement, when read in isolation, can be interpreted in two ways. First, financial contributions made by a government, defined as encompassing both 'a government' and 'any public body within the territory of a Member', result in the responsibility of the WTO Member concerned for violating the SCM Agreement if found to be inconsistent with substantive obligations in that agreement independently from whether that 'government' was entrusted with the exercise of governmental authority. By contrast, financial contributions made by a 'private body' lead to the same result only if it was entrusted or directed to carry out a governmental function. However, that interpretation does not to distinguish 'government' from 'public body'. Nor does it

73 See e.g. under the Agreement on Technical Barriers to Trade ('TBT Agreement'), WTO Members have assumed certain obligations with regard to (for example) the preparation, adoption and application of technical regulations by non-governmental bodies, which are defined, in Annex 1(8) to that agreement, as bodies 'other than a central government body or a local government body, including a non-governmental body *which [have] legal power to enforce a technical regulation*' (emphasis added).

explain why collectively they are termed 'government' for the purpose of the SCM Agreement. Secondly, 'government' and 'any public body within the territory of a Member' can be read as having separate meanings (despite their collective denomination as 'government'), which are also distinct from those given to the term 'private' bodies described in Article 1.1(a)(iv). Whilst the text does not prescribe that public bodies must be directed or entrusted to perform certain functions in the same manner as private bodies, nor is their conduct or status as such sufficient to characterise them as belonging to the government. However, that interpretation does not resolve how to interpret the term 'public body' as meaning something different from the term 'government' as it first appears in Article 1.1(a)(1).

The Appellate Body opted for the second reading. It appears to have accepted that the first type of 'government' reflected the notion of the government in the strict sense or of those entities whose conduct is described in Article 4.1 of the ILC Articles – that is to say, 'conduct of any State organ shall be considered an act of that State under international law, whether the organ exercises legislative, executive, judicial or any other functions'. That provision 'defines the core cases of attribution'.[74] If the body is a State organ under internal law,[75] then its conduct is attributable to the State under Article 4.1. Under the most basic rule of attribution – which is accepted as reflecting customary international law[76] – that conduct must be exercised in official capacity.[77] The second type was read by the Appellate Body as broadly corresponding to the conduct described in Article 5, which applies only if the entity or person is not an organ of State under Article 4 and apparently has a legal personality separate from that of the State.[78]

[74] Crawford, *The International Law Commission's Articles on State Responsibility*, 94.

[75] Art. 4.2 of the ILC Articles.

[76] See e.g. *Difference Relating to Immunity From Legal Process of a Special Rapporteur of The Commission on Human Rights*, Advisory Opinion, 29 April 1999, ICJ Reports (1999) (I), 87, para. 62; *Application of the Convention on the Prevention and Punishment of the Crime of Genocide*, para. 385. In *US – Gambling Services*, the Panel accepted that Art. 4 reflects customary international law. Panel Report, *US – Gambling Services*, para. 6.128.

[77] Crawford, *Brownlie's Principles of Public International Law*, 94, 96, 99.

[78] See also Djamchid Momtaz, 'Attribution of Conduct to the State: State Organs and Entities Empowered to Exercise Elements of Governmental Authority' in James Crawford, Alain Pellet and Simon Olleson (eds.), *The Law of International Responsibility* (Oxford University Press, 2010), 244. Exceptionally, the conduct of *de facto* organs of State can be equated to that of organs of the State for purposes of international responsibility if they are deemed to have been completely dependent on the State. See *Application of the Convention on the Prevention and Punishment of the Crime of Genocide*, para. 393.

Article 5 of the ILC Articles applies to a person or entity that is 'empowered by the law of [a] State to exercise elements of the governmental authority . . . provided the person or entity is acting in that capacity in the particular instance'. The provision is intended to cover 'para-statal entities, which exercise elements of governmental authority in place of State organs . . . [and] situations where former State corporations have been privatized but retain certain public or regulatory functions'.[79] According to its commentary, such entities may include 'public corporations, semi-public entities, public agencies of various kinds and even, in special cases, private companies'.[80] In all circumstances, Article 5 applies solely if those entities are 'empowered by the law of the State to exercise functions of a public character . . . and the conduct of the entity relates to the exercise of the governmental authority concerned'.[81] It can cover conduct of private and public entities.[82] What constitutes 'governmental authority', according to the commentary, depends on 'the particular society, its history and traditions' and 'the content of the powers, but [also] the way they are conferred on an entity, the purposes for which they are to be exercised and the extent to which the entity is accountable to government to their exercise'.[83]

Leaving aside how the Appellate Body formally used the ILC Articles in order to interpret 'public body' in Article 1.1(a)(1) of the SCM Agreement and its focus on Article 5 of those articles, it thus appears to have read the terms 'government' (the first form) and 'public body' (the second form) as reflecting the distinction between the conduct described in Article 4.1 of the ILC Articles (conduct of State organs) and Article 5 of the same articles (conduct of persons and entities that are not State organs within the meaning of Article 4.1).

That leaves the question of how Article 1.1(a)(1)(iv) of the SCM Agreement (conduct of a private body entrusted or directed to carry out one or more of the type of functions illustrated in (i)–(iii) which would normally be vested in the government) fits in that structure. Article 5 of the ILC Articles makes no distinction between private and public entities. In principle, a private body can also be empowered by the law of a State to exercise elements of the governmental authority. In its report in *US – Countervailing Duty Investigation on DRAMS*, the Appellate Body

[79] Crawford, *The International Law Commission's Articles on State Responsibility*, 100; see also, for example, Crawford, *Brownlie's Principles of Public International Law*, 544.

[80] Crawford, *The International Law Commission's Articles on State Responsibility*, 100.

[81] *Ibid.* [82] *Ibid.* [83] *Ibid.*, 101.

accepted that position.[84] There, it held that '"entrustment" occurs where a government gives responsibility to a private body, and "direction" refers to situations where the government exercises its authority over a private body', and whether either form of instruction occurs 'will hinge on the particular facts of the case'.[85] At first glance, it thus would seem that Article 1.1(a)(1)(iv) of the SCM Agreement also describes heads of attribution which can be characterised as corresponding with that set out in Article 5 of the ILC Articles – at least on the understanding that transfer of authority resembles entrustment or direction. If that is indeed the consequence of reading together the Appellate Body's decisions in both cases, do the qualitative tests for attributing conduct of a 'public body' and a 'private body' differ?

That remains unclear. Whilst the Appellate Body in *US – Anti-dumping and Countervailing Duties (China)* considered what it called the juxtaposition of the collective term 'government' and 'private body', it did so to draw conclusions on the apparent 'nexus' between the term 'government' in the strict sense and the term 'public body'.[86] In that context, it did identify one distinction between a 'public body' and a 'private body' within the meaning of Article 1.1(a) of the SCM Agreement: a public body, just like 'government' in the strict sense, has 'the requisite attributions to be able to entrust or direct a private body, namely, authority in the case of direction and responsibility in the case of entrustment'[87] and this cannot be an attribute of a private body. The use of the term 'requisite' suggests that the governmental functions, which the public body must be authorised to exercise, must include this attribute. That might also indicate that (without having been expressly articulated by the Appellate Body in that manner) – in terms of heads of attribution – three different forms of government authority are reflected in the text of Article 1.1(a)(1) of the SCM Agreement and that the form relevant to the attribution of conduct by a public body is considerably stricter than those forms expressed in Article 1.1(a)(iv) and possibly stricter than that articulated in Article 5 of the ILC Articles. The first form, with respect to 'public body', appears to be wider than that described in Article 1.1(a)(iv) and includes also the attribute described above. Against that background, future controversies

[84] Appellate Body Report, *US – Countervailing Duty Investigation on DRAMS*, para. 112, footnote 179.

[85] *Ibid.*, para. 116.

[86] Appellate Body Report, *United States – Definitive Anti-dumping and Countervailing Duties (China)*, para. 288.

[87] *Ibid.*, para. 294.

will thus concern evidentiary standards for establishing each form and the applicable standard of review. Only then will it become clear what the proper standards are for determining whether an entity is a 'public body' or a 'private body' within the meaning of Article 1.1(a)(1) of the SCM Agreement.

Status of the ILC Articles

The Appellate Body's decision to forgo determining the status of in particular Article 5 of the ILC Articles is unhelpful but not surprising.[88] Had the outcome of the Appellate Body's interpretation of the term 'public body' turned on Article 5, it would have been necessary for it 'to resolve definitively' whether and to what extent Article 5 of the ILC Articles reflected customary international law.[89] That was the Appellate Body's explanation for not examining the legal status of Article 5: the provision, whatever its status, provided 'further support' for its analysis.[90]

This explanation is difficult to reconcile with the Appellate Body's so-called holistic approach to interpreting the covered agreements based on the ordinary meaning of their wording, context, object and other elements of interpretation included in the general rule in Article 31 of the Vienna Convention. It is also an unhelpful contribution to the wider debate about how to interpret those agreements against the background of international law and the incomplete case law addressing that question. By refusing to determine the status of Article 5, whilst accepting that that status of being a rule of international law is an essential element for applying Article 31(3)(c) of the Vienna Convention,[91] the Appellate Body thus accepted, albeit in an implicit manner, that it did not interpret on the basis of Article 31(3)(c) the term 'public body' against the background of Article 5 which, as is also apparent from its analysis, it nonetheless took to be relevant in that regard.[92]

[88] See also, with respect to the uncertainty resulting from the Appellate Body's position, Cartland, Depayre and Woznowski, Michel Cartland, Gérard Depayre and Jan Woznowski, 'Is Something Going Wrong in the WTO Dispute Settlement?', 998, 999.

[89] Appellate Body Report, *United States – Definitive Anti-dumping and Countervailing Duties (China)*, para. 311.

[90] *Ibid.*

[91] See also Cartland, Depayre and Woznowski, Michel Cartland, Gérard Depayre and Jan Woznowski, 'Is Something Going Wrong in the WTO Dispute Settlement?', 998.

[92] In that regard, see also Dukgeun Ahn, 'United States – Definitive Anti-dumping and Countervailing Duties on Certain Products from China', *American Journal of International Law*, 105 (2011), 761, arguing that 'this ruling needs further elaboration in future cases

What was then the basis for the Appellate Body's use of Article 5 of the ILC Articles? Possibly Article 32 of the Vienna Convention which provides for recourse to supplementary means of interpretation in order to, inter alia, 'confirm the meaning resulting from the application of article 31'. If that is, indeed, how the Appellate Body used Article 5 of the ILC Articles, then the interpretation of the covered agreements against the background of public international law:

(a) is subject to the conditions of Articles 31(3)(c) of the Vienna Convention only if the interpretation turns on, in the sense of depending on, those rules of public international law; but
(b) is subject to no conditions under Article 32 of the Vienna Convention if the interpretation is merely supported or confirmed by those rules of public international law.

The distinction between approaches (a) and (b) would then be based on the degree to which a rule of international law is accepted to be 'relevant'. The Appellate Body appears to read that term in Article 31(3)(c) of the Vienna Convention as implying a high standard so as to mean: pertinent to or bearing upon, or possibly decisively important to the meaning of, a term or phrase in the covered agreements. Yet, that reading of Article 31(3)(c) of the Vienna Convention is at odds with how the Appellate Body uses the different elements of interpretation in the general rule in Article 31. In general, its position has been that, for example, the ordinary meaning, the intent of the parties, the factual context and the circumstances surrounding the conclusion of the treaty are not 'rigid components', thus confirming the holistic approach towards treaty interpretation.[93] In principle, none of the elements is controlling even if the weight to be given to each element, with respect to a particular text, might not be the same. In that regard, the Appellate Body did not explain how its position on the meaning of 'relevant' in Article 31(3)(c) of the Vienna Convention can be reconciled with the distinction it made in *EC and Certain Member States – Large Civil Aircraft* between the three elements for applying

about what should suffice "taking into account" the relevant international law in legal interpretation of the WTO Agreements'.

[93] See e.g. Appellate Body Report, *European Communities – Customs Classification of Frozen Boneless Chicken Cuts* ('*EC – Chicken Cuts*'), WT/DS269/AB/R, WT/DS286/AB/R, adopted 27 September 2005, and Corr.1, DSR 2005:XIX, 9157, para. 176; also Appellate Body Report, *United States – Continued Existence and Application of Zeroing Methodology* ('*US – Continued Zeroing*'), WT/DS350/AB/R, adopted 19 February 2009, DSR 2009:III, 1291, paras. 268 and 273.

Article 31(3)(c) of the Vienna Convention and the normative weight to be ascribed to a rule satisfying those elements: the latter was controlled by the introductory phrase to Article 31(3) '[t]here shall be taken into account, together with the context'.[94]

But perhaps the Appellate Body did not intend its statement on the status and relevance of Article 5 of the ILC Articles to have such a wider implication on the meaning of Article 31(3)(c) of the Vienna Convention and the relationship between that provision and Article 32 of the Vienna Convention. Rather, the statement might need to be taken as an expression of the Appellate Body's reluctance to examine what constitutes customary international law. Where the status of a norm under international law is not definitely settled elsewhere, and in particular in the form of a pronouncement of the International Court of Justice, the Appellate Body is hesitant, if not defiant, to inquire itself into the evidence of that status.[95] So far, the Appellate Body has not exposed the theoretical underpinning for that position. An inquiry into evidence of the customary international law status of a rule requires an in-depth analysis of the material sources showing State practice and that the rule is accepted as international law (*opinio iuris*), involving possibly a considerable body of factual elements requiring sorting for determining their legal relevance.[96] That material evidence must be put before the Appellate Body and possibly be subject to a debate between parties that, so far, is usually lacking from submissions to interpret the WTO agreements against the background of customary international law by virtue of Article 31(3)(c) of the Vienna Convention. Jurisdictional limitations to the Appellate Body's inquiry in that regard do not appear to exist. If the Appellate Body is tasked to interpret the WTO agreements by using customary principles of treaty interpretation, including Articles 31–3 of the Vienna Convention, it must properly apply

[94] Appellate Body Report, *EC and Certain Member States – Large Civil Aircraft*, para. 841.

[95] A false example of the exercise of that type of inquiry is its position in *EC – Hormones* on the principle of *in dubio mitius*. See Van Damme, *Treaty Interpretation by the WTO Appellate Body*, 61–5. In that same decision, the Appellate Body considered that it was 'unnecessary, and probably imprudent', for it to take a position on the abstract question of whether the precautionary principle 'has been widely accepted by Members as a principle of *general* or *customary international law*'. In its view, the principle still awaited 'authoritative formulation'. Appellate Body Report, *EC Measures Concerning Meat and Meat Products (Hormones)* ('*EC – Hormones*'), WT/DS26/AB/R, adopted 13 February 1998, DSR 1998:I, 135, para. 123.

[96] Those material sources can include diplomatic correspondence, statements made by state organs or opinions of government legal advisers, and legislation. See, generally, Crawford, *Brownlie's Principles of Public International Law*, 24.

those principles, including the conditions set forth in Article 31(3)(c) of the Vienna Convention. Examining and taking a position on the evidence of the existence of a norm of customary international law are part of the judicial function upon which the Appellate Body acts in that context.

Putting aside those jurisdictional issues, the Appellate Body's avoidance of that type of inquiry could also be taken to signal a degree of judicial comity:[97] it prefers to defer to the judgment of other international courts and tribunals, in particular the International Court of Justice, on what is customary international law. That position might become difficult to sustain in the light of the growing body of dispute-settlement activity in the context of which material sources are examined and positions are taken on what constitutes customary international law. It is no longer possible or necessary to await, in relation to a particular rule, a pronouncement of the ICJ on that question.[98] Leaving aside the reasons of the Appellate Body for avoiding that inquiry, it should not ignore the question of whether a provision is a norm of customary international law or decide on the uncertainty regarding that status without at least appreciating the landscape of the available case law in that regard. Indeed, one Panel has suggested that the text of draft Article 7.2 'might be considered as reflecting customary international law'.[99] In particular with regard to the ILC Articles, there is a significant body of awards of arbitral tribunals in which the status of those provisions is considered. For example, the Iran–United States Claims Tribunal appears to consider that Part One of the ILC Articles, including Article 5, is an authoritative statement of current international law on State responsibility.[100] Other arbitral tribunals under

[97] See e.g. Daniel Terris, Cesare P. R. Romano and Leigh Swigart, *The International Judge: An Introduction to the Men and Women who Decide the World's Cases* (Oxford University Press, 2007), 121 quoting also an Appellate Body member admitting that 'I think we would never take on the ICJ. Whenever there is a reference, it is a reference as an authority.'

[98] Indeed, in the *Genocide* case, the ICJ expressly stated that it would leave it to another day to decide whether the ILC's Articles on attribution, other than Arts. 4 and 8, reflect customary international law (para. 414).

[99] Panel Report, *Canada – Dairy*, para. 7.77, footnote 427. Draft Art. 7(2) stated: 'The conduct of an organ of an entity which is not part of the formal structure of the State or of a territorial governmental entity, but which is empowered by the internal law of that State to exercise elements of the governmental authority, shall also be considered as an act of the State under international law, provided that organ was acting in that capacity in the case in question' (Report of the ILC on the Work of its 48th Session, General Assembly, Official Records, 51st Session, Supplement No. 1 (A/51/10), under Chapter III).

[100] See Iran – United States Claims Tribunal, *Rankin* v. *Islamic Republic of Iran*, Award No. 326–10913–2, 3 November 1987, 17 IRAN-US CTR 135, 141.

the ICSID Convention have accepted that Article 5 reflects a 'generally recognized rule' or established customary international law.[101] Without taking a position on its status, other international tribunals, courts or other bodies have also referred to Article 5.[102]

Whilst the Appellate Body's avoidance of inquiring itself into whether a rule or principle reflects customary international law (or a general principle of international law) might imply that a considerable body of normative activity and developments in international law are excluded from the scope of Article 31(3)(c) of the Vienna Convention (when used in the context of WTO dispute settlement), its interpretation of 'public body' in *US – Anti-dumping and Countervailing Duties (China)* shows that that formal impediment need not be an obstacle to using, for example, Article 5 provided that the latter is sufficiently relevant. Even if the Appellate Body's use of Article 5 in this case does not contribute to a better understanding of its position on the meaning of Article 31(3)(c) of the Vienna Convention, it nonetheless shows that, in the practice of WTO dispute settlement, the technical and often theoretical debate about the meaning of Article 31(3)(c) of the Vienna Convention increasingly is of little use. Instead, whether to use public international law and the weight to attribute to it (and possibly normatively relevant instruments that cannot (yet) be characterised as a source of public international law within the meaning of Article 38(1) of the ICJ Statute) depend, just like with all other elements of interpretation, on its relevance and the context in which it might be used.

Conclusion

Article 5 of the ILC Articles was undoubtedly relevant to the Appellate Body's interpretation of 'public body' in *US – Anti-dumping and Countervailing Duties (China)*. Yet it remains uncertain whether, and if so to what extent, there exists an analogy between the rules of attribution in the ILC

[101] See e.g. ICSID, *Noble Ventures, Inc.* v. *Romania*, Case No. ARB/01/11, Award, 12 October 2005, para. 70; ICSID, *Jan de Nul NV and Dredging International NV* v. *Arab Republic of Egypt*, Case No. ARB/04/13, Decision on Jurisdiction of 16 June 2006, para. 89.

[102] See UN General Assembly, Responsibility of States for Internationally Wrongful Acts – Compilation of Decisions of International Courts, Tribunals and Other Bodies – Report of the Secretary-General, A/62/62, 1 February 2007; and UN General Assembly, Responsibility of States for Internationally Wrongful Acts – Compilation of Decisions of International Courts, Tribunals and Other Bodies – Report of the Secretary-General, A/65/76, 30 April 2010. When compiling the decisions of international courts, tribunals and other bodies referring to the ILC, the UN Secretariat considered also the reports of the Appellate Body and GATT and WTO panels.

Articles and the three forms of attribution described in Article 1.1(a)(1) of the SCM Agreement. The Appellate Body dealt with, or rather avoided addressing, that question by defining the issue before it as regarding the interpretation of Article 1.1(a)(1) against the background of the ILC Articles rather than the application of special rules of attribution within the meaning of Article 55 of the ILC Articles.[103] However, when reading its interpretation of 'public body' in this case together with the meaning of 'private body', it becomes difficult to find a full correspondence between Article 1.1(a)(1) of the SCM Agreement and the ILC Articles, suggesting that the former is after all to some degree special and separate in relation to the latter. It is also in this context that the statement of the Appellate Body to the effect that its analysis did not turn on Article 5 of the ILC Articles becomes valid. However, it made that point for a different purpose, namely to justify its decision not to resolve the question of the extent to which Article 5 reflects customary international law. In that way, it implicitly appeared to inject a high standard of relevance for using, for interpretive purposes, other rules of international law on the basis of Article 31(3)(c) of the Vienna Convention. That decision might be explained on the basis of the particular sensitivity surrounding the Appellate Body's willingness, and WTO Members' perception of its competence, to analyse the material evidence regarding the status of a norm as customary international law. If that is the case, the need to show that a rule of international law is relevant insofar as it definitively resolved the interpretive question before a panel or the Appellate Body might not become a permanent feature of the use of Article 31(3)(c) of the Vienna Convention in treaty interpretation by the WTO dispute settlement bodies.

[103] Appellate Body Report, *United States – Definitive Anti-dumping and Countervailing Duties (China)*, para. 316.

21

The application of the rules on countermeasures in investment claims

Visions and realities of international law as an open system

KATE PARLETT*

1 Introduction

When the International Law Commission (ILC) was established in 1948, one of the first topics selected for codification was 'State responsibility'.[1] At that time it was assumed that the topic would cover the field of international responsibility: it was only in the 1949 Advisory Opinion in the *Reparations* case that it was definitively affirmed that inter-governmental organisations could be subjects of international law.[2] More than sixty years later, a very different picture of responsibility in the international legal system has emerged. It has long been accepted that international law may regulate relations between States and individuals, individuals and inter-governmental organisations, companies, States and so forth. The international legal system of today is not one concerned with bilateral and multilateral relations between States exclusively: it is rather a plurilateral system, in which many different actors have rights, responsibilities, opportunities to call other actors to account for breach of those rights and responsibilities, and opportunities to be called to account for their own actions. This change reflects the openness of the international legal system about which Professor Crawford spoke in 2002 (and published in his collection of selected essays under the title *International Law as*

* I am grateful to Anthea Roberts, Gebhard Buecheler, Ben Juratowitch, Ben Love and Liz Snodgrass for their comments on an earlier draft of this chapter. All errors and shortcomings remain the responsibility of the author.

1 *ILC Yearbook* (1949), 281.

2 *Reparations for Injuries Suffered in the Services of the United Nations*, Advisory Opinion, 11 April 1949, ICJ Reports (1949), 174.

an Open System).[3] Nevertheless, for historical reasons it remains the case that it is States on whom 'most obligations rest and on which the burden of compliance principally lies'.[4] It is therefore hardly surprising that it is in the context of State responsibility that modalities for invocation and implementation of responsibility are the most highly developed. As noted by Professor Crawford, 'State responsibility is, so far, the paradigm form of responsibility on the international plane.'[5]

While States remain the predominant *responsible actors* on the international level, States are no longer the predominant *claimants* on the international level. Today, the vast majority of international claims being brought to international tribunals are those in which State responsibility is invoked by a non-State actor. In 2012, no applications were filed with the International Court of Justice (ICJ) (although in 2011, three proceedings were instituted; and as at December 2013, three applications had been filed).[6] There was one inter-State proceeding commenced pursuant to the UN Convention on the Law of the Sea:[7] a claim by Argentina against Ghana concerning the *ARA Libertad*.[8] In contrast, there were fifty new claims by investors registered by the International Centre for the Settlement of Investment Disputes (ICSID)[9] and some twenty more administered by other institutions.[10] These investment cases involve a natural or legal person as claimant, and a State as respondent.

The extent to which the highly developed rules on State responsibility applicable to inter-State claims also apply to claims brought by non-State actors, and in particular to investment treaty claims, remains an open

[3] James Crawford, *International Law as an Open System: Selected Essays* (London: Cameron May, 2002), 17–38.

[4] James Crawford, 'The System of International Responsibility' in James Crawford, Alain Pellet and Simon Olleson (eds.), *The Law of International Responsibility* (Oxford University Press, 2010), 18.

[5] *Ibid.*

[6] See List of Pending Cases before the Court, available at www.icj-cij.org/docket/index.php?p1=3&p2=1.

[7] United Nations Convention on the Law of the Sea (Montego Bay, adopted 10 December 1982, entered into force 16 November 1994, 1833 UNTS 3.

[8] See *ARA Libertad case (Argentina* v. *Ghana)*, ITLOS Case No. 20, available at www.itlos.org/index.php?id=222 and www.pca-cpa.org/showpage.asp?pag_id=1526.

[9] ICSID, 'The ICSID Caseload – Statistics', Issue 2013–1, 22.

[10] See UNCTAD, 'IIA Issues Note: Recent Developments in Investor–State Dispute Settlement (ISDS)', May 2013; Arbitration Institute of the Stockholm Chamber of Commerce, 'The SCC in Numbers – 2012'.

question. The ILC Articles on State Responsibility[11] themselves provide some guidance: their provisions on their scope of application are discussed in section 2 below. Those provisions, however, lead one to conclude that it very much depends on the particular rule, and the particular treaty on which the claim is based. One area in which the application of a specific rule of State responsibility – that of a countermeasure as a circumstance precluding wrongfulness – has been examined by several tribunals constituted under the North American Free Trade Agreement (NAFTA), and is discussed in section 3 below. Some conclusions are drawn in section 4.

2 Applicability of the ILC Articles on State Responsibility to investment treaty claims

The ILC Articles themselves address their scope of application. In respect of investment treaty claims, there are two potentially relevant provisions – namely, provisions which might result in the exclusion or modification of the generally applicable rules of State responsibility: first, investment treaty claims could be seen as forming part of a *lex specialis* regime which may be excluded from the general rules; secondly, the rules may be excluded on the basis that the rules governing the invocation of responsibility set out in the ILC Articles on State Responsibility apply only when responsibility is invoked by another State, or the international community of States. Each of these possibilities will be examined in turn.

(a) *Lex Specialis* exclusion

Article 55 of the ILC Articles, entitled *Lex Specialis*, states:

> These articles do not apply where and to the extent that the conditions for the existence of an internationally wrongful act or the content or implementation of the international responsibility of a State are governed by special rules of international law.

Article 55 thus specifies that the Articles do not apply where special rules of international law govern the conditions for the existence of a wrongful act, or the content or implementation of international responsibility.

[11] International Law Commission, Articles on the Responsibility of States for Internationally Wrongful Acts, *ILC Yearbook*, 2(2) (2001), 26 (ILC Articles).

The commentary to Article 55 refers to the examples of the World Trade Organization Dispute Settlement Understanding and the European Convention on Human Rights as regimes that displace the rules contained in the ILC Articles.[12] However, Article 55 also makes clear that the Articles have a residual character, and that they apply to the extent that they are not excluded by a special rule.

To the extent that investment treaty arbitration could be said to form part of a *lex specialis* regime of international responsibility, containing separate rules governing State responsibility, according to Article 55, the general rules set out in the ILC Articles do not apply.

Investment treaty arbitration has been described as constituting a *lex specialis* regime in the context of the distinction between investment treaty arbitration from diplomatic protection. The ILC, in its Draft Articles on Diplomatic Protection, concluded that international investment arbitration constitutes a *lex specialis* regime and the rules applicable in the investment treaty context do not govern diplomatic protection claims or contribute to the development of customary rules generally applicable to diplomatic protection claims.[13] The same point was made by the ICJ in *Diallo* in 2007, distinguishing between direct claims by investors under ICSID and diplomatic protection claims.[14] This has also been acknowledged by investment tribunals and commentators.[15]

In general however, insofar as international responsibility is concerned, investment treaties do not prescribe their own rules for invocation of responsibility. Certainly, they do prescribe procedural rules governing the invocation of responsibility. For example, an investment treaty may allow an investor to commence ICSID proceedings, in which the ICSID arbitration rules govern the procedure of the arbitration. However, these

[12] ILC commentary to Art. 55, para 3. For example, the WTO regime prescribes its own rules for the taking of countermeasures. See WTO Dispute Settlement Understanding, Art. 22.3. See generally Yang Guohua, Bryan Mercurio and Li Youngjie, *WTO Dispute Settlement Understanding: A Detailed Interpretation* (The Hague: Kluwer Law International, 2005), 251–79. See also Zachary Douglas, *The International Law of Investment Claims* (Cambridge University Press, 2009), 97.

[13] International Law Commission, Report of International Law Commission, 58th Session, UN Doc. A/CN.4/L.684 (2006), Art. 17.

[14] *Case concerning Ahmadou Sadio Diallo (Republic of Guinea* v. *Democratic Republic of the Congo)* (Preliminary Objections), 24 May 2007, ICJ Reports (2007), para. 88.

[15] See e.g. *Camuzzi International SA* v. *Argentine Republic*, ICSID Case No. ARB/03/2, Decision on Objections to Jurisdiction, 11 May 2005, para. 145; Cristoph H. Schreuer *et al.*, *The ICSID Convention: A Commentary*, 2nd edn (Cambridge University Press, 2009), 417, paras. 27–9. *Cf.* Stephen Schwebel, 'The Influence of Bilateral Investment Treaties on Customary International Law', *ASIL Proceedings*, 98 (2004), 27.

procedural issues are not matters which are governed by the ILC Articles on State Responsibility. In contrast, investment treaties do not ordinarily specify the basis on which conduct is to be attributable to the respondent State. In the absence of specific rules in the treaty, Article 55 of the ILC Articles would not preclude the application of the rules on attribution set out in the Articles themselves.

If an investment treaty excludes or modifies the general rules of State responsibility, Article 55 preserves the applicability of the special rule set out in the investment treaty as the governing rule. An example may be found in the expropriation provision in a multitude of investment treaties, which provides in practice for the payment of compensation for lawful expropriation. That specific rule would, according to Article 55, apply to the exclusion of the general rule under international law, according to which restitution is a primary remedy.[16]

The relevant question is whether and to what extent the applicable bilateral investment treaty (BIT) sets out rules governing responsibility that differ from the generally applicable rules. This will require an examination of the applicable BIT. In the absence of specific rules governing the existence of an internationally wrongful act, or the content or implementation of international responsibility, investment claims cannot be said to form part of a *lex specialis* regime which excludes, pursuant to Article 55, the applicability of the general rules.

(b) Exclusion of application of legal consequences according to Article 33(2)

Part Two of the ILC Articles on State Responsibility addresses the legal consequences for an internationally wrongful act. These include the obligation to make reparation (restitution, compensation, satisfaction) and specific consequences arising from breaches of peremptory norms, such as the obligation not to recognise such a situation as lawful, nor to render aid or assistance in maintaining such situation. Article 33, entitled 'Scope of international obligations set out in this Part' provides:

1. The obligations of the responsible State set out in this Part may be owed to another State, to several States, or to the international community as a whole, depending in particular on the character and

[16] But see further, below, on the applicability of Part Two of the ILC Articles to investment treaty claims.

content of the international obligation and on the circumstances of the breach.
2. This Part is without prejudice to any right, arising from the international responsibility of a State, which may accrue directly to any person or entity other than a State.[17]

Thus Article 33(1) purports to limit the scope of application of the rules governing consequences of an internationally wrongful act to situations in which the obligations of the responsible State are owed to other States or to the international community as a whole; arguably the consequences may be different when the responsible State breaches an obligation owed to other actors.[18] At the same time, Article 33(2) expressly recognises and preserves the possibility of a State's responsibility towards a non-State actor under international law.

Article 33(2) appears clear in its terms: the provisions of Part Two, which include the obligation to make reparation, do not necessarily apply in respect of rights granted to persons or entities other than States. As noted by the commentary, '[t]he articles do not deal with the possibility of the invocation of responsibility by persons and entities other than States, and paragraph 2 makes this clear'.[19] However, this exclusion is not a general one: it applies only to rules governing invocation of responsibility, dealt with in Part Two and in parts of Part Three of the ILC Articles.[20]

3 Applying the ILC Articles on State Responsibility in practice: the invocation of countermeasures in an investment treaty claim

An interesting practical example of the application of rules governing State responsibility to investment claims concerns the plea of countermeasures,

17 ILC Articles, Art. 33(2).

18 See also ILC commentary to Part Three, Chapter I, para. (1), noting that Part Three of the Articles (on the implementation of international responsibility of a State) 'is concerned with . . . the entitlement of other States to invoke the international responsibility of the responsible State and with certain modalities of such invocation. The rights that other persons or entities may have arising from a breach of an international obligation are preserved by article 33(2).'

19 ILC commentary to Art. 33, para. 4, 210.

20 Part Three of the Articles on The Implementation of the International Responsibility of the State 'giv[es] effect to the obligations of cessation and reparation which arise for a responsible State under Part Two by virtue of its commission of an internationally wrongful act'.

as a circumstance precluding wrongfulness, in defence to an investment treaty claim.

(a) *Countermeasures as a circumstance precluding wrongfulness*

International law permits an injured State to take non-forcible countermeasures in response to an internationally wrongful act by another State, provided that certain conditions are met. Countermeasures have been described as 'a feature of a decentralised system by which injured States may seek to vindicate their rights and to restore the legal relationship with the responsible State which has been ruptured by the internationally wrongful act'.[21] The origins of countermeasures may be traced to the practice of 'reprisals', traditionally used to denote otherwise unlawful measures of self-help.[22]

In codifying the rules on non-forcible countermeasures, the ILC Articles on State Responsibility provide that wrongfulness of the measure taken by the injured State is precluded, if and to the extent that it constitutes a countermeasure. This general rule is codified in Article 22:

> The wrongfulness of an act of a State not in conformity with an international obligation towards another State is precluded if and to the extent that the act constitutes a countermeasure taken against the latter State in accordance with Chapter II of Part Three.

Chapter II of Part Three (Articles 49–54) of the ILC Articles sets out conditions and limitations on the taking of countermeasures by an injured State and addresses the conditions of the implementation of countermeasures. The objects and limits of countermeasures are elaborated in Article 49, which provides:

1. An injured State may only take countermeasures against a State which is responsible for an internationally wrongful act in order to induce that State to comply with its obligations under Part Two.
2. Countermeasures are limited to the non-performance for the time being of international obligations of the State taking the measures towards the responsible State.

[21] ILC commentary, 281.

[22] See generally Evelyn Speyer Colbert, *Retaliation in International Law* (New York: King's Crown, 1948), 60–103; and also James Crawford, *State Responsibility: The General Part* (Cambridge University Press, 2013), 684–5.

3. Countermeasures shall, as far as possible, be taken in such a way as to permit the resumption of performance of the obligations in question.

(b) Countermeasures and third parties

Article 49 makes clear that countermeasures must be directed against the State committing the prior wrongful act – the responsible State. The wrongfulness of a measure taken as against a third State is not precluded. The ILC commentary to Article 49 states:

> A second essential element of countermeasures is that they 'must be directed against' a State which has committed an internationally wrongful act and which has not complied with its obligations of cessation and reparation under Part Two of the present articles. The word 'only' in paragraph 1 applies equally to the target of the countermeasures as to their purpose and is intended to convey that countermeasures may only be adopted against a State which is the author of the internationally wrongful act. Countermeasures may not be directed against States other than the responsible State. In a situation where a third State is owed an international obligation by the State taking countermeasures and that obligation is breached by the countermeasure, the wrongfulness of the measure is not precluded as against the third State. In that sense the effect of the countermeasures in precluding wrongfulness is relative. It concerns the legal relations between the injured State and the responsible State.[23]

While this paragraph of the commentary refers only to the rights of third States, the following paragraph elaborates with respect to the effects of countermeasures as against third States and refers in that context to other parties, contemplating that countermeasures may not preclude the wrongfulness of acts taken in violation of rights of third parties other than States:

[23] See ILC commentary to Art. 49, para. 4, 285. This general principle was stated by an arbitral tribunal in 1930, adjudging Germany's responsibility for damage to certain Portuguese interests before Portugal entered the First World War.

> [L]es représailles, consistent en un acte en principe contraire, ne peuvent se justifier qu'autant qu'elles ont été *provoquées* par un autre acte également contraire à ce droit. *Les représailles ne sont admissible que contre l'État provocateur.* Il se peut, il est vrai, que des représailles légitimes, exercées contre un État offenseur, atteignent des ressortissants d'un État innocent. Mais il s'agira là d'une conséquence indirecte, involontaire, que l'État offense s'efforcera, en pratique, toujours d'éviter ou de limiter autant que possible [Cyne (Responsibility of Germany for acts committed subsequent to 31 July 1914 and before Portugal entered the war) (*Portugal* v. *Germany*) (1930), Reports of International Arbitral Awards, vol. II, 1035, 1056–7 (original emphasis)].

> This does not mean that countermeasures may not incidentally affect the position of third States or indeed other third parties. For example, if the injured State suspends transit rights with the responsible State in accordance with this Chapter, other parties, including third States, may be affected thereby. If they have no individual rights in the matter they cannot complain. Similarly if, as a consequence of the suspension of a trade agreement, trade with the responsible State is affected and one or more companies lose business or even go bankrupt. Such indirect or collateral effects cannot be entirely avoided.[24]

The commentary therefore implies that the effect of Article 49(1) is that the wrongfulness of a countermeasure is not precluded as against third parties, where those third parties have *individual rights* which are affected by the measure. That is to say, a countermeasure may affect the position or interests of third parties. However, it may not affect the rights of third parties.

(c) Countermeasures in practice: a trio of NAFTA awards

In three NAFTA cases, Mexico invoked countermeasures as a circumstance precluding the wrongfulness of any breach of its obligations under NAFTA vis-à-vis the investor. In all three cases, Mexico's invocation of countermeasures was rejected.

The facts relevant to the pleas of countermeasures were materially identical in all three cases, as they all concerned the same measure imposed by Mexico. The proceedings were initiated against Mexico by American agricultural companies, relating to the imposition of a 20 per cent tax by Mexico on soft drink bottlers using the sweetener High Fructose Corn Syrup (HFCS). In response to its alleged violation of the national treatment standard in Article 1102 of NAFTA, Mexico argued that it had imposed the tax as a countermeasure against two violations of NAFTA by the United States. The alleged breaches of NAFTA by the US related to access of Mexico's surplus sugar produce to the US market.[25] All three NAFTA tribunals have issued redacted awards.[26]

[24] ILC commentary to Art. 49, para. 5, 285.

[25] There has been a long-running trade dispute between the US and Mexico covering the same subject-matter: see WTO Panel Report, 'Mexico Tax Measures on Soft Drinks and Other Beverages', 7 October 2005, WTO Doc. WT/DS308/R; WTO Appellate Body, *Mexico – Tax Measures on Soft Drinks and Other Beverages* (Mexico – Taxes on Soft Drinks), WTO Doc. WT/DS308/AB/R, adopted 6 March 2006.

[26] *Corn Products International, Inc.* v. *United Mexican States*, ICSID Case No. ARB(AF)/04/01, Decision on Responsibility, 15 January 2008 (Professor Christopher Greenwood (President), Professor Andreas F. Lowenfeld and Licenciado Josh Alfonso Serrano de la Vega)

(i) *ADM* v. *Mexico*

The tribunal in *ADM* v. *Mexico* rejected Mexico's countermeasures plea because it concluded that (a) the measure was not adopted to induce compliance with NAFTA by the US and (b) it did not meet the proportionality requirements for a valid countermeasure under customary international law.[27] However, the tribunal considered that countermeasures could, in principle, operate as a defence to a Chapter XI claim. In this regard, the tribunal concluded that investors derived only a procedural right to arbitrate from NAFTA and that the remaining rights (including substantive rights of protection) were inter-State rights against which a valid countermeasure could be taken.[28]

The tribunal noted that there were '[d]ifferent doctrinal theories regarding the nature of investors' rights under international investment agreements'.[29] It referred to the derivative theory, according to which obligations of treatment are owed to the investor's national State and, in case of breach of those obligations, 'the investor may bring the host State to an international arbitration in order to request compensation, but the investor will be in reality stepping into the shoes and asserting the rights of the home State'.[30] The tribunal also noted that international law may confer direct rights on individuals, who may have a significant role in asserting State responsibility before international dispute settlement bodies.[31] The tribunal considered that investors did not have substantive rights under investment treaties. It noted that Chapter XI of NAFTA provides two separate sets of obligations: Section A establishes substantive protection obligations regarding investments; and Section B establishes a procedural obligation to submit a dispute to investor-to-State arbitration,

(*CPI* Award); *Archer Daniels Midland Company and Tate & Lyle Ingredients Americas, Inc.* v. *United Mexican States*, ICSID Case No. ARB(AF)/04/05, Award, 21 November 2007 (Mr Bernado M. Cremades (President), Mr Arthur W. Rovine and Mr Eduardo T. Siqueiros) (*ADM* Award); and *Cargill, Inc.* v. *United Mexican States*, ICSID Case No. ARB(AF)05/2, Award, 18 September 2009 (Dr Michael C. Pryles (presiding), Professor David D. Caron and Professor Donald M. McRae) (*Cargill* Award).

27 *ADM* Award, para. 180. In an earlier part of its decision, the tribunal addressed the question of whether it had jurisdiction to determine the countermeasures defence, since it would involve determining whether the US had breached NAFTA. The tribunal expressly stated that it had 'no jurisdiction to decide whether the United States committed an internationally wrongful act which justified a countermeasure' (see *ADM* Award, para. 131). As this would be a precondition for a valid countermeasure, it is difficult to see how the tribunal could have concluded that Mexico's countermeasure precluded the wrongfulness of its acts, even if it considered that all other requirements had been met.

28 *ADM* Award, paras. 161 *et seq.* 29 *Ibid.*, 169. 30 *Ibid.* 31 *Ibid.*, 170.

in which the host State's conduct will be decided in accordance with the standards set out in Section A. The tribunal considered that obligations imposed in Section A were inter-State obligations. It stated:

> In the Tribunal's view, the obligations under Section A remain inter-state, providing the standards by which the conduct of the NAFTA Party towards the investor will be assessed in the arbitration. All investors have under Section B is a procedural right to trigger arbitration against the host State. What Section B does is to set up the investor's exceptional right of action through arbitration that would not otherwise exist under international law, when another NAFTA Party has breached the obligations of Section A.[32]

In contrast to the obligations in Section A, the tribunal considered that the procedural obligation under Section B of Chapter XI 'is owed directly to the beneficiary of the obligation, in this case the investors'.[33] Thus investors hold a procedural right to bring international arbitral proceedings under Section B. The arbitral tribunal considered that the countermeasures did not impair the claimant's procedural right to bring a claim against Mexico, since the measure was not related to the Respondent's offer to submit the dispute to arbitration.[34]

(ii) *CPI* v. *Mexico*

The tribunal in *CPI* v. *Mexico* concluded that countermeasures as a circumstance precluding wrongfulness are not applicable to Chapter XI claims under NAFTA, because NAFTA confers upon investors substantive rights separate and distinct from those of the State of which they are nationals, and countermeasures cannot affect the rights of third parties. It followed that any countermeasure would not preclude the wrongfulness of the measure as against the investor.

Referring to the ILC commentary to Article 49, the tribunal noted that a countermeasure must be directed against the State which committed the prior wrongful act, and if it entailed action inconsistent with obligations owed to 'another party', the countermeasures doctrine does not preclude the wrongfulness of the measure as against that other party.[35] The tribunal noted that a countermeasure cannot, therefore, 'extinguish or otherwise affect the *rights* of a party other than the State responsible for prior

[32] *Ibid.*, 173. On this point, Arthur W. Rovine disagreed with the tribunal; see Concurring Opinion of Arthur W. Rovine, Issues of Independent Investor Rights, Diplomatic Protection and Countermeasures, paras. 14, 47 and 82–3.

[33] *ADM* Award, para. 177. [34] *Ibid.*, 180. [35] *CPI* Award, para. 163.

wrongdoing', although it could affect their *interests*.[36] Thus the tribunal framed the central question as whether an investor within the meaning of Article 1101 of NAFTA 'has rights of its own, distinct from those of the State of its nationality, or merely interests'.[37] If an investor has rights, then countermeasures will not preclude the wrongfulness of the act against CPI, even though it might preclude the wrongfulness of acts as against the US.

The tribunal noted that, in the current state of international law, individuals and corporations may possess direct rights. It framed the relevant test as one of intention derived from the text of the treaty.[38] It concluded that the intention of the parties to NAFTA was to confer substantive rights directly upon investors:

> In the case of Chapter XI of NAFTA, the Tribunal considers that the intention of the Parties was to confer substantive rights directly upon investors. That follows from the language used and is confirmed by the fact that Chapter XI confers procedural rights upon them. The notion that Chapter XI conferred upon investors a right, in their own name and for their own benefit, to institute proceedings to enforce rights which were not theirs but were solely the property of the State of their nationality is counterintuitive.[39]

Thus the tribunal concluded that a countermeasure taken by Mexico against the US could not deprive a US investor of its rights – what is at stake are the *rights* of the investor, not only its *interests*. Thus '[e]ven if the doctrine of countermeasures could operate to preclude the wrongfulness of the HFCS tax vis-à-vis the United States (and . . . the Tribunal makes no comment on that question), they cannot do so vis-à-vis CPI'.[40]

[36] *Ibid.*, 164 (original emphasis). [37] *Ibid.*, 165. [38] *Ibid.*, 168.

[39] *Ibid.*, 168–9. In his separate opinion, Andreas Lowenfeld agreed with the tribunal's conclusion on this point but argued that aspects of its discussion 'blur[red] the message' about the essence of investor–State arbitration (see *CPI* Award, Separate Opinion, para. 5).

[40] *CPI* Award, para.176. The tribunal also noted that it had no jurisdiction to determine breaches of any of the other provisions of the NAFTA (apart from Chapter XI) or to rule on the conduct of the US which was not a party to the proceedings, and that these jurisdictional limits gave rise to 'serious difficulties' in addressing Mexico's defence. It considered that the requirement of a prior violation of international law was an 'absolute precondition' of the right to take countermeasures, and it was not open to the tribunal to dispense with a fundamental prerequisite of this kind. The tribunal therefore concluded that even if countermeasures were applicable to Chapter XI proceedings (which the tribunal did not accept), Mexico's defence would inevitably fail because Mexico could not establish that its countermeasure was taken in response to a prior breach of international law by another State. See *CPI* Award, paras. 181–7. For discussion of the structural

(iii) *Cargill* v. *Mexico*

In the third decision, the tribunal in *Cargill* also rejected Mexico's countermeasures defence, ostensibly on the basis that investors possess rights under NAFTA against which a countermeasure, directed to an allegedly wrongful act committed by the US, could not be taken. The tribunal noted that 'countermeasures may operate only to preclude the wrongfulness of an act that is not in conformity with an obligation owed to the offending State'[41] and they would 'not necessarily have any such effect in regard to specific obligations owed to *nationals* of the offending State, rather than to the offending State itself'.[42] The tribunal noted that the parties 'have characterized the issue before the Tribunal as whether NAFTA Chapter XI investors possess not only procedural rights of access, but also substantive rights'.[43] The tribunal indicated its view that investors held rights under Chapter XI which were not 'mere procedural rights of access'.[44]

However, the tribunal subsequently rejected the significance of the distinction between substantive and procedural rights, stating:

> It is not fruitful, in the Tribunal's view, to characterize the issue as whether the rights conferred upon the investor are substantive or merely procedural. The fact is that it is the investor that institutes the claim, that calls a tribunal into existence, and that is the named party in all respects to the resulting proceedings and award.[45]

Thus the tribunal appears to have disagreed with the way the parties framed the issue – that is, as to whether Chapter XI of NAFTA gives investors substantive and not merely procedural rights. The tribunal rather placed emphasis on procedural characterisations – whether the investor institutes a claim, has functional control of the claim and is the named party in the proceedings and in the award.

The tribunal's apparent emphasis on the importance of the claims process – rather than the substantive rights/obligations – is also reflected in its treatment of Mexico's argument that the rejecting of a countermeasures defence would lead to absurd results. Mexico suggested that the resulting situation would be such that countermeasures could preclude the

problems raised by the defence of countermeasures, and the difficulties in addressing the *Monetary Gold* principle, see Martins Paparinskis, 'Equivalent Primary Rules and Differential Secondary Rules: Countermeasures in WTO and Investment Protection Law' in Tomer Broude and Yuval Shany (eds.), *Multi-sourced Equivalent Norms in International Law* (Oxford: Hart, 2011).

41 *Cargill* Award, para. 422. 42 *Ibid.* 43 *Ibid.*, para. 423.

44 *Ibid.*, paras. 424, 426. 45 *Ibid.*, para. 426.

wrongfulness of its act vis-à-vis the US generally, but those countermeasures would be 'nullified' by the fact that they would not have a similar effect on the claims of US nationals under Chapter XI. The tribunal saw no absurdity here, stating:

> To the degree that the existence of claims under Chapter 11 would limit the effectiveness of the countermeasures, then it need be recalled that there is always a range of possible countermeasures to be adopted. Moreover, customary international law itself prohibits certain countermeasures. There is no reason that the range of countermeasures might be further limited – either by direct exclusion in a treaty of certain measures or by the creation of a claims process placed directly in the hands of individuals – that limits the effectiveness of certain measures in whole or in part.[46]

Since countermeasures are not directly excluded by NAFTA, the tribunal seems to have characterised the relevant circumstance as being 'the creation of a claims process placed directly in the hands of individuals' – suggesting that an investor's procedural rights would be sufficient to prevent the invocation of a countermeasures defence. The tribunal did not make reference to any authorities on the ambit of application – or disapplication – of the countermeasures defence, and its reasoning on the defence, in merely eleven paragraphs, leaves the reader somewhat confused as to the precise reasoning underlying the tribunal's decision.

This confusion is somewhat exacerbated by the tribunal's statement on the countermeasures defence in its section entitled 'Final Disposition of the Tribunal', in the concluding paragraphs of its award. This states:

> The Tribunal finally holds that the wrongfulness of these breaches of Respondent's obligations under NAFTA Chapter 11 is not precluded by Respondent's assertion that its actions were lawful countermeasures. The Tribunal determines that countermeasures operate only to preclude the wrongfulness of an act that is not in conformity with an obligation owed to the offending state, not in regard to obligations owed to a third state nor those, as here, owed to the nationals of the offending state. The Tribunal further determines that, under the NAFTA, investors have both substantive and procedural rights, and investors are therefore protected under Chapter 11 from measures taken by a host state directly against them. This is true even if the same action might constitute valid countermeasures if taken instead against the offending state, and even despite the fact that such valid countermeasures may in fact result in secondary effects on the nationals of the offending state.[47]

[46] *Ibid.*, para. 428. [47] *Ibid.*, para. 553.

Here the tribunal has expressly recorded that NAFTA confers substantive rights on investors, a statement which is not recorded in the earlier reasoning.

Nevertheless, when read as a whole, the tribunal's decision seems to be to the effect that countermeasures could not preclude the wrongfulness of Mexico's acts vis-à-vis investors because those investors derive rights from NAFTA.

(iv) Assessment

All three NAFTA Tribunals referred to the rules governing countermeasures as a circumstance precluding wrongfulness. It appears not to have been argued before any of the three Tribunals that these rules were not applicable to investment treaty claims under NAFTA, either on the basis of the *lex specialis* exclusion in Article 55 or because Parts Two and Three of the ILC Articles, governing the legal consequences of responsibility and implementation of that responsibility, are not applicable to such claims, on the basis of Article 33(2). (It was of course argued that the rules are not applicable where rights of investors are involved.) Although it appears that there is little basis to contend that there is a *lex specialis* rule in NAFTA precluding the application of countermeasures as a defence in an investment treaty claim, Douglas considers that some weight ought to be given to the exclusion of the rule on the basis of the disapplication of Parts Two and Three of the ILC Articles, even though the general rule on countermeasures is codified in Part One, in Article 22. He argues:

> [A] measure taken by the host State that causes prejudice to a foreign State might not be internationally wrongful vis-à-vis the national State of the investor because it is a lawful countermeasure directed against a breach of an international obligation by the national State of the investor. The investor might nevertheless argue that the prejudice caused to its private interests by the countermeasures is both justiciable before an ICSID tribunal and liable to attract a remedy in damages. The investor would argue that an investment treaty obligation is owed to the investor directly and any rule precluding wrongfulness as between the host State and the national State of the investor is *res inter alios acta*.[48]

Indeed, the conclusion reached by Douglas is identical to that reached by two of the three tribunals (*CPI* and *Cargill*), but not on the basis

[48] Zachary Douglas, 'Specific Regimes of Responsibility: Investment Treaty Arbitration' in James Crawford, Alain Pellet and Simon Olleson (eds.), *The Law of International Responsibility* (Oxford University Press, 2010), 821.

of non-applicability of the rules governing countermeasures as a circumstance precluding wrongfulness, but on the basis that the rules themselves did not preclude the wrongfulness of the measure vis-à-vis the investor. Moreover, all three Tribunals considered that the rule governing inter-State responsibility was applicable to an investment treaty claim; all three also concluded that the requisite elements to invoke the circumstance precluding wrongfulness (either proportionality or non-impact on third parties' rights) were not present.

A brief note is warranted concerning the effectiveness of countermeasures. If one accepts the position taken by the Tribunals in *CPI* and *Cargill* that investors derive rights under investment treaties which cannot be affected by countermeasures taken against their State of nationality, a further question arises as to the utility of taking countermeasures at all. An attempt by a victim State to apply a countermeasure against a wrongdoing State, in response to the wrongdoing State's breach of its obligations, may be futile in practice if the victim State is then compelled to compensate nationals of the wrongdoing State for the impact of the countermeasure. This may naturally follow from the opening of the international legal system to a plurality of actors, but there is no immediately obvious answer to it, and one might therefore expect countermeasures to become increasingly ineffective as a means to procure compliance of wrongdoing States with their international obligations.

4 Conclusions

In the modern reality of an international legal system which engages a multiplicity of actors, with a multiplicity of claims being brought by investors invoking the international responsibility of States before international tribunals, in numbers which dwarf inter-State claims concerning State responsibility, it is unsurprising that difficult questions arise concerning the application of rules of responsibility formulated on the assumption that both claimant and respondent in an international claim are States. The ILC Articles on State Responsibility contain two technical rules which shed some light on their scope of application and, in general terms, caution against the wholesale and uncritical application of the rules set out in the Articles to claims brought by non-State actors. Indeed, as a general principle, this approach must be right: an investment tribunal should not uncritically apply all of the rules formulated in the context of inter-State responsibility to a treaty claim brought by an investor against a State. Nevertheless, it is also apparent that a highly individualised subsystem of rules on State responsibility applicable to investment claims is unwarranted.

The decisions of the NAFTA Tribunals on countermeasures do not contain much analysis of the principled application of the rules on countermeasures to NAFTA claims. Of course, the Tribunals are likely to have been guided by the way in which the arguments were put by the claimants. In any event, for the reasons explained in section 3 above, all three Tribunals rejected Mexico's pleas of countermeasures, on the basis that the requisite elements for invocation of countermeasures were not present. Nevertheless, it is arguable that a more nuanced approach is warranted in applying the ILC Articles on State Responsibility to investment treaty claims.

When Professor Crawford wrote of the 'openness' of the modern international legal system, he also emphasised that the foundations of the system have endured:

> [I]n principle, the foundations do not appear to have changed (statehood, treaty, custom, consent, acquiescence . . .). Thus we have the apparent paradox of rapidly expanding horizons and a simple, not to say elemental, set of underpinnings. Our system is one which international lawyers of four generations ago would have no particular difficulty in recognising or working with, once they got over its bulk.[49]

This observation is apt to describe the matters discussed in this chapter; indeed, the occasionally complex issues which investment tribunals must address in the context of determining State responsibility can be usefully informed by the long history of experience which has led to the highly developed rules of State responsibility in the context of inter-State claims. The challenge is in reasoning their application – or disapplication – in the particular circumstances.

[49] Crawford, *International Law as an Open System*, 17.

22

The external relations of the European Union and its Member States

Lessons from recent developments in the economic sphere

DAMIEN GERADIN

Introduction

Since the creation of the European project, the external relations of the European Union (EU) and its Member States have been central to their development at the international level. A striking feature of international relations today is the increasing number of international organisations and international agreements, as well as the increasingly wide range of matters they touch upon. This naturally leads the EU and its Member States to make active use of their external powers. If the EU has been granted many external powers – through the treaties and case law – the Member States may still pursue autonomous actions provided they do not infringe EU law.

In this context, it became necessary to clarify the rules regulating these powers in order to determine with more certainty whether it was for the Union or for the Member States to act in a particular situation. The Lisbon Treaty brought such clarification, but it did not solve all the problems raised by the conclusion of international agreements and the participation in international organisations. The competence may differ depending upon the matters concerned leading sometimes to the participation of both the EU and the Member States. And even in situations where the EU has exclusive competence, it may be that, in practical terms, it is impossible for the EU institutions to fulfil their role. In such a situation, the Member States will have to take over, complying however with the position defended by the Union. The complexity of the rules regarding the conclusion of international agreements reflects a lack of clarity which, in turns, impacts upon the ability of the Union to speak with one voice and the transparency of its position. Despite such complexity, the EU and the Member States still have to negotiate and conclude agreements with third countries or international organisations on a regular basis. It is all the more complicated in sectors which present strategic importance for the Member States and the EU and which therefore are already subject to heavy national and/or EU regulation.

External relations of the EU and the allocation of competences

Article 47 of the Treaty on the European Union (TEU) provides that the Union has legal personality. Despite a lack of reference in the treaties to the Union's international personality, the Court of Justice of the European Union (CJEU or the Court) already recognised it in its famous *AETR* judgment which states that 'in its external relations the [Union] enjoys the capacity to establish contractual links with third countries over the whole field of objectives [of the Treaties]'.[1] The treaties contain various legal bases for the conclusion by the EU of international agreements with third countries and international organisations. However, the ability of the EU to conclude international agreements is complicated first by the rules regulating the allocation of competences between the Union and its Member States, and by the remaining power of the latter to conclude such agreements.

The exclusive competence of the Commission to conclude international agreements

The Lisbon Treaty, for the first time, lists the exclusive competences of the Union. Article 3(2) TFEU indicates that the EU has an exclusive competence for the conclusion of international agreements. Article 216 TFEU reiterates the exclusive competence of the Union to 'conclude agreements with one or more third countries or international organisations where the Treaties so provide or where the conclusion of an agreement is necessary in order to achieve, within the framework of the Union's policies, one of the objectives referred to in the Treaties, or is provided for in a legally binding Union act or is likely to affect common rules or alter their scope'. Such agreements are binding upon the institutions of the Union and on its Member States.

[1] Case 22/70, *Commission* v. *Council – (AETR)* [1971] ECR 263, para. 14.

When a legislative act of the Union expressly provides for the exclusive competence of the Union – such as for the Common Commercial policy[2] – this competence exists 'even if the specific matters covered by those agreements are not yet, or are only very partially, the subject of rules at [the EU] level'.[3]

In addition to these express competences, Article 216 also foresees a competence to act arising from its internal competence. Such a possibility flows from the *AETR* judgment, in which the CJEU held that, even if the EU Treaties did not expressly confer a competence upon the EU to conclude an international agreement in a particular field, such a competence could also flow from other provisions of the Treaties and from measures adopted by the EU institutions. The Court, considering that the attainment of the objective pursued by those rules and the objectives of the Treaties themselves would be compromised if Member States were free to adopt international agreements affecting EU rules,[4] held that 'each time the [EU], with a view to implementing a common policy envisaged by the Treaty, adopts provisions laying down common rules, whatever form these may take, the Member States no longer have the right, acting individually or even collectively, to undertake obligations with third countries which affect those rules'.[5] This judgment establishes a parallelism between the internal and external competences of the EU insofar as the EU institutions have exercised their competence at the internal level by adopting common rules to implement a common policy. This condition has been given a broad interpretation as it also includes the adoption of rules outside the scope of a specific common policy. In Opinion 2/91, the Court stressed that the authority of the *AETR* decision 'cannot be restricted to instances where the [Union] has adopted [EU] rules within the framework of a common policy. In all areas corresponding to the objectives of the Treaty, Article [4(3) TEU] requires Member States to facilitate the achievement of the [Union]'s tasks and to abstain from any measure which could jeopardise the attainment of the objectives of the Treaty.'[6]

However in Opinion 1/94,[7] the Court adopted a more restrictive view requiring that the policy area in question be fully harmonised at EU level

[2] Art. 207 Treaty of the Functioning of the European Union (TFEU) (ex-Art. 133 TEC), [2010] OJ C83/49.

[3] Case C-459/03, *Commission* v. *Ireland* [2006] ECR I-4635, paras. 94–5.

[4] Case C-266/03, *Commission* v. *Luxembourg* [2005] ECR I-4805, para. 41.

[5] *AETR*, para. 17. [6] Opinion 2/91 [1993] ECR I-1061, paras. 10–1.

[7] Opinion 1/94 – WTO Agreement [1994] ECR I-5267.

for it to become an exclusive competence. But subsequently the Court held that the exclusive competence of the EU institutions could flow from the fact that an international agreement fell into an area largely covered by EU rules, in particular in 'areas where there are harmonising measures'.[8]

Even where the EU has adopted such common rules, it will only benefit from an exclusive competence to conclude international agreements if a Member State's action 'might affect those rules or alter their scope'.[9] In Opinion 2/91, the Court adopted an extensive interpretation of this condition, considering it is fulfilled when the commitments arising from an international agreement were merely liable to affect EU rules even though there was no contradiction between the international agreement and the Directives at stake.[10] The Court went even further when it ruled that a mere proposal submitted by Greece to the International Maritime Organisation (IMO), which initiated a procedure potentially leading to the adoption by the IMO of new rules, had an effect on EU rules. According to the Court, Greece 'took an initiative likely to affect the provisions of the Regulation'.[11]

The ability of the Member States to enter into international agreements

Article 2(1) TFEU provides that '[w]hen the Treaties confer on the Union exclusive competence in a specific area, only the Union may legislate and adopt legally binding acts, the Member States being able to do so themselves only if so empowered by the Union or for the implementation of Union acts'. Such exclusivity means that the competence has been entirely transferred by the Member States to the Union. Any action by a Member State in the same area is *a priori* in conflict with EU law. Yet, EU Member States have continued to conclude international agreements in their own name with or without the Union. Although they may appear extraneous to EU law, such agreements are still relevant for the Union.[12]

Article 4(2) provides a non-exhaustive list of areas in which the Union does not hold an exclusive competence, but shares its competence with the Member States, including, *inter alia*, the internal market, environmental

[8] Opinion 1/03 – Lugano Convention [2006] ECR I–1145, para. 118.

[9] *AETR*, para.17.

[10] Opinion 2/91, paras. 9, 25–6.

[11] Case C-45/07, *Commission* v. *Greece* [2009] ECR I-00701, paras. 21–3.

[12] Allan Rosas, 'The Status in EU Law of International Agreements Concluded by EU Member States', *Fordham International Law Journal*, 34 (2011), 1310.

protection, transport and energy. Regarding the external relations of the EU, when a specific field falls within a shared competence, it is likely to lead to the conclusion of a mixed agreement signed by the Union and the Member States on the one hand and third parties on the other. The category of shared external competence is broad and encompasses different situations. This may result from an explicit provision in the treaty or from the fact that the agreement covers different matters falling both within EU and Member States competences. In these areas, Member States may only exercise their power to the extent that the Union has not exercised – or ceased to exercise – its competence. A Protocol on the exercise of shared competences annexed to the Lisbon Treaty specified that 'when the Union has taken action in a certain area, the scope of this exercise of competence only covers those elements governed by the Union act in question and therefore does not cover the whole area'.[13] This leaves a certain margin for Member States' intervention.

Agreements concluded by the Member States without the participation of the Union cover a broad range of situations, such as when agreements were concluded by the Member States before they adhered to the Union and when agreements concern a matter falling outside the competence of the EU. Such agreements are generally not binding on the EU and the CJEU has no jurisdiction to give rulings on their interpretation. However, the Union is bound by them whenever they are integrated into the EU legal order through an express '*renvoi*' or when the EU has taken over the powers formally vested in the Member States.[14] Moreover, in a situation where the Union itself is not bound by an agreement but all the Member States are, the Court indicated that the latter fact is 'liable to have consequences for the interpretation of . . . the provisions of secondary law which fall within the field of application of [the international agreement]'.[15] This finding is based on 'the customary principle of good faith, which forms part of general international law, and of Article [4(3) TEU]' considering that it was 'incumbent upon the Court to interpret those provisions taking account of [the international agreement concerned]'.[16]

Even where an agreement concerns a matter falling within the exclusive competence of the EU, Member States may still act, provided

[13] Protocol (No. 25) on the Exercise of Shared Competence [2010] OJ C83/307.

[14] See e.g. Case C-439/01, *Libor Cipra and Vlastimil Kvasnicka* v. *Bezirkshauptmannschaf Mistelbach* [2003] ECR I-745, para. 24.

[15] Case C-308/06, *The Queen, on the application of International Association of Independent Tanker Owner (Intertanko) and others* v. *Secretary of State for Transport* [2008] ECR I-4057, para. 52.

[16] *Ibid.*, para. 52.

that they obtain an authorisation from the EU.[17] Such an authorisation will, for instance, be granted when the EU is not formally represented within an international organisation, or cannot itself negotiate and conclude an agreement because the international body reserves the right to adhere to States, excluding regional integration organisations such as the EU. The Court has acknowledged the fact that the International Labour Organisation was not open to EU adherence and that, therefore, Union competence 'may, if necessary, be exercised through the medium of the Member States acting jointly in the [Union]'s interest'.[18] In this situation, the Council adopts a decision expressly authorising the Member States to conclude an agreement or a general framework of regulations establishing the procedure to be followed by the Member States.[19]

External relations of the EU and their practical implications

Position of the EU in international organisations

The possibility for the EU to negotiate and conclude international agreements has been recognised by the treaties but the question of its participation in international organisations or bodies has not been entirely dealt with.[20] Yet, in practice, it is sometimes difficult for the EU to express its opinion and to maintain a strong and credible position at the international level.

No provision directly relates to the participation of the EU in international organisations. Article 211 TFEU provides that 'the Union and the Member States shall cooperate with third countries and with the competent international organisations'. Article 218(9) lays down the rules applicable in establishing 'the positions to be adopted on the Union's behalf in a body set up by an agreement, when that body is called upon to adopt acts having legal effects'. This Article arguably does not apply to the discussions and negotiations within these organisations.

As a general matter, the founding treaties of international organisations do not foresee the adherence of regional organisations such as the EU.

[17] See e.g. Regulation No. 662/2009 of 13 July 2009 Establishing a Procedure for the Negotiation and Conclusion of Agreements between Member States and Third Countries on Particular Matters Concerning the Law Applicable to Contractual and Non-contractual Obligations [2009] OJ L 200/25.

[18] Opinion 2/91, paras. 5 and 37.

[19] Regulation No. 847/2004 on the Negotiation and Implementation of Air Service Agreements between Member States and Third Countries [2004] OJ L 157/7.

[20] Alan Hervé, 'The Participation of the European Union in Global Economic Governance Fora', *European Law Journal*, 18 (2012), 145.

Therefore, the status of the Union depends not only on the allocation of competences within the EU but also, and most importantly, on the rules of the organisations in question. The EU has full membership in a limited number of organisations including, for instance, the Food and Agricultural Organisation (FAO). Within the World Trade Organization (WTO) the Union holds a special status similar to full membership except for the voting rights.[21] The Member States are often also members of other organisations so that many competences are shared between them and the EU. The EU may also be granted an observer status which implies that it 'can attend meetings of a body or an organisation, but without voting rights'.[22] This is, for instance, the case within agencies of the United Nations (UN). Such a status entails important limitations, such as the fact that the EU's presence may be limited to formal meetings or an intervention coming after all of the other interventions.

The representation of the EU

Whether it can directly participate in international organisations or in the negotiation of international agreements or not, the question of the representation of the Union and its Member States matters. Article 218 TFEU lays down the rules generally applicable to the negotiation and conclusion of agreements between the Union and third countries or international organisations. The Treaties confirm the essential role played by the Commission. Article 17(1) TEU provides that '[w]ith the exception of the common foreign and security policy, and other cases provided for in the Treaties, [the Commission] shall ensure the Union's external representation'.

Despite this clear statement, the issue of the representation of the Union is not entirely solved. The situation is complicated when – and this is most often the case – the matter discussed is of concern for both the EU and the Member States, and the Union has been granted a mere observer status. In such a case, the EU is generally represented by both the Commission and the Member State holding the presidency of the Union.[23] This

[21] This flows from the fact that the Community was already a *de facto* member of the GATT.

[22] Knud Erik Jørgensen and Ramses A. Wessel, 'The Position of the European Union in (other) International Organizations: Confronting Legal and Political Approaches' in Panos Koutrakos (ed.), *European Foreign Policy: Legal and Political Perspectives* (Cheltenham: Edward Elgar Publishers, 2011), 269.

[23] Hervé, 'The Participation of the European Union in Global Economic Governance Fora', 150.

system is however not optimal as it creates confusion for third countries and requires careful discussions and statements by each party taking the floor.

One of the most interesting situations is when the EU has an exclusive competence in a given area but is not a member of the international organisation concerned, or cannot therefore conclude an agreement itself. According to Article 4(3) TFEU, 'pursuant to the principle of sincere cooperation, the Union and the Member States shall, in full mutual respect, assist each other in carrying out tasks which flow from the Treaties' and further facilitate the achievement of the Union's tasks, refraining from 'any measure which could jeopardise the attainment of the Union's objectives'. It follows that when the Union has competences that are at least exclusive and cannot be a member of an international organisation, the Member States must defend the EU's interests.[24]

The need for co-ordination

When Member States conclude international agreements, they must co-operate with each other as well as with the Union. For instance, the Court stated that 'where it is apparent that the subject-matter of an agreement or convention falls in part within the competence of the [EU] and in part within that of the Member States, it is essential to ensure close cooperation between the Member States and the [EU] institutions, both in the process of negotiation and conclusion and in the fulfilment of the commitments entered into. That obligation to cooperate flows from the requirement of unity in the international representation of the [EU].'[25]

When an international agreement is to be negotiated solely by the Member States, a common position must be reached. In *AETR*, the Court indicated that the Council and the Commission should 'reach agreement . . . on the appropriate methods of cooperation with a view to enduring most effectively the defence of the interests of the Union'.[26] In Opinion 2/91, the Court emphasised that co-operation was 'all the more necessary' since the Union could not conclude the agreement by itself. It added that '[i]t is therefore for the [Union] institutions and the Member States to take all the measures necessary so as best to ensure such cooperation both in the procedure of submission to the competent authority and ratification of Convention No 170 and in the implementation of commitments resulting from that Convention'.[27]

[24] Opinion 2/91. [25] Opinion 1/94, para. 108.
[26] *AETR*, para. 87. [27] Opinion 2/91, paras. 37–8.

Compliance with EU law by the Member States

When entering into international agreements, Member States are not totally free to exercise their powers as they wish. The duty of sincere co-operation imposes on them to 'exercise their international powers without detracting from Union law or from its effectiveness'[28] and requires them to facilitate the achievement of the Union's tasks, as well as to abstain from any measure which could jeopardise the attainment of the objectives of the Treaty. For instance, the Court held that in relation to a bilateral agreement regarding a matter falling within the competence of the Member States, 'the latter may not disregard [EU] rules but must exercise their powers in a manner consistent with [EU] law'. It added that 'when giving effect to commitments assumed under international agreements, be it an agreement between Member States or an agreement between a Member State and one or more non-member countries, Member States are required . . . to comply with the obligations that [EU] law imposes on them'.[29]

In *Commission* v. *Greece*, the Court further clarified that '[t]he mere fact that the [Union] is not a member of an international organisation in no way authorises a Member State, acting individually in the context of its participation in an international organisation, to assume obligations likely to affect [Union] rules promulgated for the attainment of the objectives of the Treaty'.[30] The duty of co-operation is therefore applicable to both the Commission and the Member States. The Court went further in deciding that even if the Commission had not entirely fulfilled its duty of co-operation – the Commission could arguably have done more to reach a common position – it does not entitle a Member State to 'unilaterally adopt, on its own authority, corrective or protective measures designed to obviate any breach by an institution of rules of [EU] law'.[31]

The Court confirmed that this duty is of general application and does not depend either on whether the Union competence was exclusive, or on any right of the Member States to enter into obligations towards third countries.[32] Where an EU Member State fails to comply with EU law, the Commission has powers to bring the infringement to an end and, where necessary, may refer the case to the ECJ under Article 258 TFEU

[28] K. Lenaerts and P. Van Nuffel, *European Union Law* (Sweet & Maxwell, 2011), 874.

[29] Case C-55/00, *Elide Gottardo* v. *Istituto nazionale della previdenza sociale (INPS)* [2002] ECR I-413, paras. 32, 3.

[30] *Commission* v. *Greece*, paras. 30–1. [31] *Ibid.*, para. 26.

[32] See e.g. *Commission* v. *Luxembourg*, para. 58.

for failure of the Member State to fulfil its obligations under EU law. Not only are Member States not allowed to conclude an agreement that would expressly violate EU rules, but they must also implement their international obligations in such a way as to take account of their EU obligations.[33]

Illustration of the complexity of the allocation of competences between the EU and its Member States through international negotiations in two specific sectors

The complexity of the principles and rules described in Sections I and II tends to create a lack of clarity and of certainty, which can be illustrated through two recent examples of negotiations in strategic sectors for the EU and its Member States.

1 Postal services: the Universal Postal Convention[34]

The Universal Postal Union (UPU) is an inter-governmental organisation acting as the primary forum for co-operation between postal sector players. In 2012, the UPU Congress, bringing together all the member countries, met to define the future world postal strategy and to review the Universal Postal Convention, including the system of terminal dues. Terminal dues correspond to the remuneration for the costs of handling and delivering cross-border mail in the country of destination. They are an important source of revenue for postal operators, in particular for those in transition economies and developing nations. The proposal made in view of the 2012 UPU Congress was trying to bring terminal dues closer to costs, which, in practice, would still be far from the actual costs of handling international mail.

The review of the terminal dues system raised two issues of considerable importance for the EU and its Member States. First, in application of the EU Treaties and the case law on the allocation of competences between the EU and the Member States, it appears that terminal dues is a subject matter that falls within the exclusive competence of the EU for two reasons.

[33] See e.g. Joined Cases C-176/97 and C-177/97, *Commission* v. *Belgium and Luxembourg* [1998] ECR I 3557.

[34] See Damien Geradin, 'Legal Opinion on the Compatibility of the Proposed Target System for Terminal Dues with EU Law' (29 April 2012), available at http://jcampbell.com/ref_upu_doha/eu/20120429_Legal%20Opinion%20-%20UPU%20System%20Terminal%20Dues.pdf.

First, the regulation of terminal dues falls *a priori* within the scope of the Common Commercial Policy. Secondly, the *AETR* doctrine seems to be applicable as the EU has developed a policy aiming to complete the internal market for postal services and has adopted common rules regulating the provision of postal services, including terminal dues – such as the Postal Directive. Besides, any action of the Member States might affect those rules or alter their scope. Therefore, the question can be raised as to whether, by participating in the 2012 Universal Postal Convention and voting on the proposed system of terminal dues, the Member States would infringe EU rules on the repartition of competence.

As the EU is not a member of the UPU, Member States were thus to co-ordinate their position in order to negotiate and conclude the agreement on its behalf. In the past, efforts have been made towards co-ordination between Member States and the EU. In 2004, the Commission adopted a Communication reaffirming the importance of ensuring 'that the Commission participates to the fullest extent possible in work in the UN system which concerns issues for which it is responsible within the EU'.[35] The Commission called for a common EU position during the negotiations and co-ordination among the Member States and with the Commission.[36] Despite the Council Resolution that followed, the Member States showed 'little apparent coordination' in the 2004 and 2008 Congresses, submitting individual proposals, sometimes inconsistent with each other.[37] Yet, the Commission clarified in the above-mentioned Communication that, whether the EU has exclusive competence or not, all Member States are obliged to somehow co-ordinate their positions.[38] Although this goal was reiterated by the Council in 2008, no common position was found.[39]

The second issue raised by these negotiations was linked to the compatibility of the proposed system of terminal dues with EU law. The UPU Target System of Terminal Dues seems to diverge not only from the Postal Directive[40] but also from the EU Treaties, and more specifically from its

[35] Commission Communication, The Universal Postal Union Congress 2004, COM(2004) 398 final, para. 14.

[36] *Ibid.*, para. 51.

[37] See James Campell *et al.*, 'Study for the European Commission, Study on the External Dimension of the EU Postal Acquis' (WIK Consult: November 2010), 151.

[38] *Ibid.*, 149. [39] 'Common Understanding Paper', Council, Document 11860/08.

[40] Directive 97/67/EC of 15 December 1997 on Common Rules for the Development of the Internal Market of Community Postal Services and the Improvement of Quality of Service, OJ L 15, as amended by Directive 2002/39/EC of 10 June 2002, OJ L 176; and Directive 2008/6/EC of 20 February 2008, OJ L 52.

competition rules. However, the case law has clearly stated that, when entering into an international agreement, Member States cannot infringe EU rules. This principle, based notably on the duty of sincere co-operation, may be considered as being even stronger when the Member States are acting on behalf and in the interests of the Union. In view of the 2012 UPU Congress, the Commission stated that it was essential to ensure compatibility between the UPU system and the EU framework and that it was 'necessary to ensure that the rules and the positions taken by the Member States in the coming UPU Congress are compatible, complementary and coherent with [EU] legislation in particular with that included in [the Postal Directive]'.[41]

To conclude, the Member States started the negotiations with divergent views – most probably due to divergent economic incentives – despite the necessity for them to defend the EU position. The situation was further complicated by the impossibility for the Union to directly participate in the negotiation and in the conclusion of the agreement. Generally speaking, the decision-making process at the UPU is problematic.

2 Telecommunications: the International Telecommunications Regulations

Telecommunications is subject to heavy regulation at the national as well as the European level. It was therefore logical for the EU and the Member States to react actively to the decision to hold a World Conference on International Telecommunications (WCIT or the Conference) in Dubai in December 2012, with the aim to revise the International Telecommunications Regulations (ITRs). The International Telecommunication Union (ITU) is a specialised agency of the UN which is responsible for information and communication technologies. It currently has a membership of 193 countries. The ITRs define the general principles for the provision and operation of international telecommunications. The Conference had been tasked with reviewing and updating ITRs that had remained unchanged since 1988. The new regulations would reflect the changes that the internet and new forms of communications have had on telecoms.

The main concern of the EU – and the US – was the position defended by countries such as Russia or China to increase regulation and strengthen control of the information spread on the internet. As only ITU members are full participants with the right to vote – other ITU members, including telecommunications operators and regional organisations, having an

[41] Directive 97/67/EC, para. 41.

observer status – the EU and its Member States had to co-ordinate their position. Contrary to the negotiations on terminal dues in the postal sector, the Member States managed here to agree on a common position, consisting of maintaining the current status and avoiding heavier regulation. Reaching a common position was essential for the EU and the Member States in order to defend their position with credibility.

Discussions took place between the EU institutions, the Member States, telecommunications operators and other bodies. In August 2012, the Commission submitted a proposal for a common EU position to submit for discussion in the Council.[42] It was proposed that, in relation to matters falling within its competence, Member States should ensure that any changes to the ITRs would be compatible with EU law and would not restrict future developments of the EU *acquis*. As regards matters falling outside of the EU competence, Member States were required to adopt common positions. This was underlined by the Cypriot president, who warned that any changes that might restrain future developments in the area of telecommunications and the internet were precluded.[43]

Beyond the substantial issues raised by these negotiations, the role of the Commission in drafting the common position was questioned. An issue was raised as to whether the Commission – which was not formally represented at the ITU – had the legal right to draft a position that was binding on EU governments. Normally, the Commission is mandated to negotiate on behalf of the EU in areas where the Union holds an exclusive competence. A motion for a Resolution submitted to the European Parliament proposed for the Council to negotiate on behalf of the EU. The Parliament amended it and proposed for the Commission to carry out such negotiations.[44] In October 2012, the legal service of the Council of the EU indicated that the Commission has the ability to speak on behalf of the Member States on matters where the latter have transferred their lawmaking power to the EU. But the fact that the Commission is not formally represented remained problematic. If it is considered that the

[42] Proposal for a Council Decision Establishing the EU Position for the Review of the International Telecommunications Regulations to Be Taken at the World Conference on International Telecommunications or its Preparatory Instances of 2 August 2012, COM(2012) 430 final.

[43] Speech by Loucas Louca at the European Parliament's plenary session of 20 November 2012.

[44] European Parliament Resolution of 22 November 2012 on the forthcoming World Conference on International Telecommunications (WCIT-12) of the International Telecommunication Union, and the possible expansion of the scope of international telecommunication regulations. *Cf.* the Motion for a resolution of 19 November 2012.

EU holds an exclusive competence in the field of telecommunications, a difficulty arises from the fact that the Commission – and more generally the Union – does not have a formal seat at the ITU but holds an 'observer member' status. The Union requested the admission of the Commission as an 'observer in an advisory capacity' which would not allow it to negotiate on behalf of the EU but would allow officials from the EU executive to ask for the floor and provide advice to Member State delegations on points relating to the EU position. This approach was finally approved.[45]

The proposal for a Common Position put forward by the Commission was adopted by the Council in November 2012. Despite these minor disagreements regarding the role of the Commission, the EU was able – for the first time in the ITU framework – to agree on a position before going to the Conference. This most probably sent an important signal to third countries. When preparing these negotiations, the long-term interests of the EU were carefully balanced in order to allow the Member States and the Union to defend their positions in future negotiations.

Finally, a proposal made in the final discussions introduced elements that were unacceptable to EU Member States including a possible extension of the ITRs to cover internet issues. EU Member States, alongside the United States, did not agree on these proposals. In the opinion of EU participants, the final text risked threatening the future of the open internet and internet freedoms, as well as having the potential to undermine future economic growth. The EU was concerned about this possible harm not only within the EU, but globally, including in developing countries.

Conclusion

The rules regarding the external relations of the EU and its Member States have been progressively developed over time. The EU has been granted more powers and the rules on the allocation of competences have been clarified. However, this evolution does not mean that there is no role to be played by the Member States. On the contrary, they remain essential in two regards. Member States are still entering into international agreements in their own interests – either on their own or next to the EU (mixed agreements). In addition, the EU also needs the Member States to negotiate and conclude agreements on its behalf

[45] See Transcript of WCIT Dubai, United Arab Emirates, 3 December 2012, Plenary 1.

either for political or legal reasons, such as when international law prohibits it from acting directly. This results in complex situations where both the Member States and the EU institutions may attend an international conference without third countries – and probably the Member States and the EU – knowing who represents whom. If efforts have been made with the Lisbon Treaty to clarify the various external competences of the EU, what remains to be dealt with is the above-mentioned situation. The system would benefit from a review of the rules on the representation of the EU at the international level. But one difficulty lies in the fact that sometimes the Member States prefer to defend their own position, where, as members of the Union, they should try to reach an agreement for the benefit of all them, and to defend such a position. When sitting at the negotiating table, the EU and the Member States should act as one, as any contradiction or disorganisation – even if only apparent – would weaken their position. They would then lose credibility towards third countries and international organisations.

It is therefore claimed that the rules on the representation of the Union should be reviewed in order to strengthen the position and the credibility of the EU at the international level. However, it has been argued that what really matters is not so much the extensive external competence of the EU, the consolidation of its formal representation or an enhanced co-ordination.[46] What matters is rather the field concerned and the willingness of the EU and its Member States to reach a common position, as illustrated by the differences between negotiations in the postal and the telecommunications sectors.

[46] Jørgensen and Wessel, 'The Position of the European Union in (other) International Organizations', 285–6.

23

Invoking, establishing and remedying State responsibility in mixed multi-party disputes

Lessons from Eurotunnel

FREYA BAETENS*

International disputes involving multiple claimants or respondents, or both, that are of mixed State/non-State nature seem to be arising with increasing frequency, as the circle of responsibility gradually widens to include, for example, international organisations. In a number of recent cases, issues of shared responsibility of States providing peacekeeping contingents, and of the organisation to which they are provided, have emerged.[1] These and similar envisaged contingencies raise difficult questions of substance and procedure which were only partially addressed by the International Law Commission (ILC) in its Articles on the Responsibility of States for Internationally Wrongful Acts (ILC Articles on State Responsibility).[2] Remaining issues are being grappled with by international adjudicatory bodies and scholars.

The present chapter draws from a wider research project on shared responsibility in mixed multi-party disputes, involving States and non-State entities as claimants as well as respondents. One specific case (the

* The author has previously worked for the Permanent Court of Arbitration but the opinions expressed here are solely her own and do not represent the position of the PCA or any of the parties to the mentioned disputes. She is grateful for the feedback of Maurizio Brunetti, Christine Chinkin, Brooks Daly, Yseult Marique, André Nollkaemper and Andrea Varga. Regarding potential errors or omissions, the usual disclaimer applies.

1 See e.g. *Behrami and Behrami* v. *France*, Application No. 71412/01 and *Saramati* v. *France, Germany and Norway*, Application No. 78166/01, ECtHR, Decision Court (GC), 2 May 2007; *Al-Jedda* v. *UK*, Application No. 27021/08, ECtHR, Judgment (Merits and Just Satisfaction) Court (GC), 7 July 2011; *The Netherlands* v. *Hasan Nuhanović* (12/03324 LZ/TT), Supreme Court of The Netherlands, Judgment (First Chamber), 6 September 2013.

2 UNILC, Draft Articles on Responsibility of States for Internationally Wrongful Acts (2001), GAOR 56th Session Supp 10, 43.

Eurotunnel arbitration)[3] is examined in terms of its ramifications on invoking, establishing and remedying State responsibility. This choice was inspired by two considerations: *Eurotunnel* provides a prime example of a mixed dispute likely to increasingly occur due to ever more complex joint ventures between States and non-State entities. Moreover, an analysis of *Eurotunnel* seemed a fitting contribution to this book as the arbitral tribunal that decided the case was presided over by the honouree of this work: Professor James Crawford.

The starting point of this chapter is that, although in principle there is no general rule in international law allowing for joint and several responsibility,[4] such a rule can be created by means of specific treaty provisions. The legal difficulty lies in applying and interpreting such a *lex specialis* rule within an appropriate procedural framework which allows for mixed disputes. This chapter is structured as follows: after setting out the facts, background and legal claims of *Eurotunnel* (section I), the Partial Award is analysed (section II) so as to identify the relevance of this case for future shared responsibility disputes between mixed parties (section III).

I The *Eurotunnel* dispute

A Facts and background

In 1985, the French and United Kingdom governments issued an invitation calling for tenders to develop, finance, construct and operate a 'Fixed Link' across the Channel between France and the UK, to be financed

[3] *The Channel Tunnel Group Limited and France-Manche S.A.* v. *The Secretary of State for Transport of the Government of the United Kingdom of Great Britain and Northern Ireland and Le Ministre de l'Équipement, des Transports, de l'Aménagement du Territoire, du Tourisme et de la Mer du Gouvernement de la République Française*, Partial Award, Permanent Court of Arbitration (PCA) (30 January 2007), 132 ILR 1 (*Eurotunnel* Partial Award). For an analysis of the entire case, see e.g. M. Audit, 'Un arbitrage aux confins du droit international public: observations sur la sentence du 30 janvier 2007 opposant le Groupe Eurotunnel au Royaume-Uni et à la République française', *Revue de L'Arbitrage*, 3 (2007), 445 ; Jean-Marc Thouvenin, 'L'arbitrage Eurotunnel', *Annuaire français de droit international*, 52 (2006), 199.

[4] As confirmed by James Crawford, *State Responsibility: The General Part* (Cambridge University Press, 2013), 328–32; to the contrary: Alexander Orakhelashvili, 'Division of Reparation between Responsible Entities' in James Crawford, Alain Pellet and Simon Olleson (eds.), *The Law of International Responsibility* (Oxford University Press, 2010), 647–65.

entirely by private investment.[5] France-Manche S.A. and The Channel Tunnel Group Ltd submitted a joint response[6] and on 20 January 1986, the French president and the British prime minister announced that they had been selected as the Concessionaires of the Fixed Link.[7] The Treaty concerning the Construction and Operation by Private Concessionaires of a Channel Fixed Link between the UK and France (Treaty of Canterbury) sets out the international legal framework to permit the construction and operation of this project.[8] Pursuant to its Article 1(2), the Fixed Link includes the tunnels themselves and associated terminal areas and freight facilities.

Article 10(1) establishes an Intergovernmental Commission (IGC) 'to supervise, in the name and on behalf of the two Governments, all matters concerning the construction and operation of the Fixed Link'. Subsequently, a Concession Agreement was signed on 14 March 1986 by the *ministre de l'équipement, du transport et de l'habitat* for France and the Secretary for Transport for the UK, on the one hand, and France-Manche S.A. and The Channel Tunnel Group Ltd, on the other, which granted both companies a concession to develop, finance, construct and operate the Fixed Link for a term of fifty-five years.[9] This period was extended to ninety-nine years by the Concession Extension Agreement of 13 February 1998.

The Fixed Link consists of 'a fixed twin-bored tunnel rail link under the English Channel, a service tunnel and terminal areas at Coquelles in the French Département du Pas de Calais and Cheriton in the County of Kent'.[10] Since its opening in 1994, it has accommodated the transport of road vehicles through trains and shuttles, at the time said to be the largest privately financed infrastructure project in history. The Coquelles terminal has a kilometres-long perimeter fence, supplemented by additional fencing, and is situated in a rural area, approximately 3 km from the town of Calais. The Partial Award includes a map of the region (see Figure 23.1).

[5] *Eurotunnel* Partial Award, para. 48.

[6] *Ibid.*, para. 46. France-Manche S.A. and The Channel Tunnel Group Ltd formed a *société en participation* under French law and a partnership under English law (agreement concluded on 31 August 1996).

[7] *Ibid.*, para. 49.

[8] France–UK, Treaty concerning the Construction and Operation by Private Concessionaires of a Channel Fixed Link (Canterbury, adopted 12 February 1986, entered into force 24 July 1987), 1497 UNTS 334.

[9] Clause 2 of the Concession Agreement.

[10] *Eurotunnel* Partial Award, paras. 55–7.

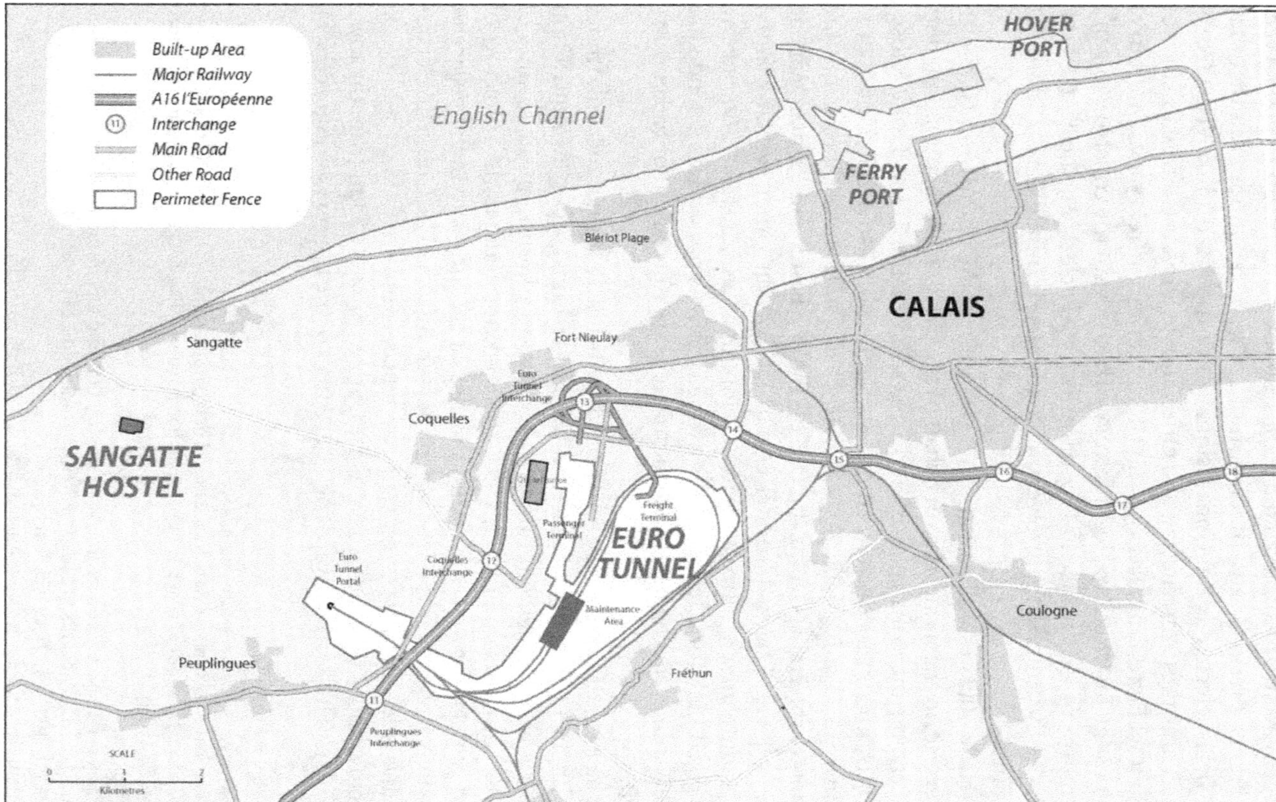

Figure 23.1 Map of the Calais Region

B Legal claims: Sangatte and SeaFrance

By a Notice of a Request for Arbitration dated 17 December 2003, the Channel Tunnel Group Ltd and France-Manche S.A. initiated arbitral proceedings against the UK and France under the auspices of the Permanent Court of Arbitration (PCA). Their two main claims related to (1) the allegedly inadequate protection of the Fixed Link against disruptions by clandestine migrants at Sangatte, linked to a complaint about the UK's civil penalty regime, and (2) the allegedly improper financial support to the SeaFrance sea link. Although both claims were brought against both respondents, the tribunal later held that there was no dispute between the Concessionaires and the UK as concerned the SeaFrance claim so, to the extent that this claim was directed against the UK, the case was dismissed entirely for want of jurisdiction.[11] Analysis of the SeaFrance claim hence provides no further relevance to the present discussion concerning shared responsibility.

With regard to the Sangatte claim, the Concessionaires asserted that the Fixed Link was inadequately protected against interference by clandestine migrants based at the Sangatte Hostel, especially from 1999 to 2003. Thousands of migrants from Kosovo, Afghanistan, Iraq and Somalia broke into the perimeter of the terminal site at Coquelles, hoping to smuggle themselves into shuttle trains destined for the UK. The claimants alleged that 'this caused significant disruption to the operation of the Fixed Link and cost a great deal in additional protective measures'.[12]

Linked was a complaint concerning the UK's civil penalty regime, introduced in April 2000 pursuant to Part II of the Immigration and Asylum Act (the 1999 Act),[13] under which persons or companies responsible for transporting clandestine migrants into the UK were subjected to a system of penalties. At first this regime applied only to road transport vehicles, but in 2001 it was extended to the claimants. Close to £400,000 in penalty charges were imposed on the Concessionaires, which were all subsequently remitted, up to the point where the UK entirely exempted claimants from the system in 2002. Later that same year, the UK amended the 1999 Act so as to re-render operators of freight shuttle trains liable for carrying clandestine migrants to the UK, but at the time of the Partial Award, no penalties had been imposed upon the Concessionaires under the amended 1999 Act.

[11] *Ibid.*, para. 143. [12] *Ibid.*, paras. 58–64. [13] *Ibid.*, paras. 66–9.

The UK also imposed liability on the claimants under the Immigration Act 1971, as modified by the Channel Tunnel (International Arrangement) Order (the 1993 Order), which incorporated the Sangatte Protocol into English law,[14] for the costs of detention and removal of clandestine migrants arriving in the UK via the Fixed Link. The Partial Award refers to an amount of over £100,000 paid by the claimants on this account.

II The *Eurotunnel* partial award

On 30 January 2007, an arbitral panel composed of Maître L. Yves Fortier, Judge Gilbert Guillaume, Lord Millett and Mr Jan Paulsson, chaired by Professor James Crawford, issued a Partial Award in the *Eurotunnel* arbitration.

A Applicable law and jurisdiction

The law to be applied by the tribunal consisted of the relevant provisions of the Treaty and the Concession Agreement, supplemented by English and French law insofar as necessary for the implementation of particular obligations. Furthermore, recourse could be had to 'the relevant principles of international law and, if the parties in dispute agree, to the principles of equity'.[15]

In order to establish the scope of its jurisdiction,[16] the tribunal distinguished three questions:

> (1) Was there a 'dispute' between the Claimants and either or both Respondents which existed at the time of the Request?
> (2) As to any such dispute, have the Claimants presented claims falling within the scope of Clause 40.1 of the Concession Agreement?
> (3) Does the fact that certain proceedings were or could have been brought before another forum pursuant to Clause 41.4 of the Concession Agreement affect the present Tribunal's capacity to deal with the claims?[17]

[14] The Treaty of Canterbury was supplemented by later agreements between the two States, including the Protocol concerning Frontier Controls and Policing, Cooperation in Criminal Justice, Public Safety and Mutual Assistance Relating to the Channel Fixed Link, Sangatte, 25 November 1991 (Sangatte Protocol).

[15] Clause 40.4 of the Concession Agreement.

[16] *Ibid.*, Clause 40.1.

[17] *Eurotunnel* Partial Award, para. 135.

The tribunal identified the source of its competence to determine the parties' respective rights and obligations as the Treaty ('but only insofar as it is given effect to by the Concession Agreement') and the Concession Agreement ('whether or not it goes beyond merely giving effect to the Treaty').[18]

B Findings on joint and several responsibility

Chapter V of the *Eurotunnel* Partial Award specifically deals with the claimants' thesis of 'Joint and Several Responsibility'. The Treaty of Canterbury, the Concession Agreement and their implementation were, at least in part, acts of the French and UK governments, so one contentious issue concerned 'the basis on which the Respondents may be held responsible'.[19] The question was whether the claimants needed to show precisely the degree to which any breach of obligations owed to them was specifically due to one or other government, or whether they could invoke some principle of solidary or collective responsibility.

1 Position of the claimants

The claimants argued that the conduct regarding the Sangatte claim (inadequate protection of the Fixed Link against clandestine migrants) was attributable to France and the UK, individually and collectively:[20]

> Any violation caused by the Governments' respective acts and omissions in the context of policing, security and frontier controls should, in addition to engaging the specific responsibilities of the relevant Government, also be attributable to both Governments jointly since these actions are manifestations of the Governments' joint failure to co-operate and co-ordinate their actions in making appropriate provision in relation to policing, security and frontier controls.[21]

Emphasising that both governments were jointly obliged with regard to security and frontier controls under the applicable rules, the claimants asked the tribunal to hold France and the UK 'liable in respect of all claims, either on the basis of their own acts or omissions, and/or on the basis of their failure to protect the claimants from the acts or omissions

[18] *Ibid.*, para. 153. [19] *Ibid.*, para. 162. [20] *Ibid.*, paras. 163–7.

[21] Claimants' Memorial, para. 262 – as cited in *Eurotunnel* Partial Award, para. 163 (original Memorial not publicly available).

of the other Government'.[22] Although accepting that joint responsibility does not generally exist under international law, the claimants pointed out that Article 47 of the ILC Articles on State Responsibility provides for the possibility of an agreement to the contrary between the States concerned. In the present case, this would imply that some form of 'joint liability flows from the fact that the [relevant] Instruments contemplate the Governments cooperating and coordinating their actions in making appropriate provisions in those fields'.[23]

This joint liability would be additional to the governments' individual liability. Thus, regardless of whether the relevant instruments gave rise to joint liability, the Concessionaires could still assert independent claims against both governments in those fields. The claimants further specified that such individual liability arose at two levels: first, 'each Government's liability for disregarding its specific responsibilities in relation to policing, security and frontier controls'; and second, 'each Government's failure to cooperate, coordinate and consult so as to prevent the other Government's breach'.[24]

The claimants asserted that accepting the concept of joint responsibility as outlined would not raise any complications at the compensation stage because 'each Government would be liable for the entirety of the damage to the Concessionaires' bearing in mind that '[t]he Concessionaires would not, of course, receive the same compensation twice over'.[25] The manner in which the governments' liabilities were subsequently to be apportioned between themselves was of no concern to the Concessionaires.

2 Position of the respondents

With reference to the closing of the Sangatte Hostel, France accepted that the two governments had assumed joint and several responsibilities. However, this solely concerned the execution of the Agreement so, in addition, each government retained 'its own onus of responsibility, which is the case for any obligations relative to public order which depend upon the

[22] Letter from Matthew Weiniger to Brooks Daly dated 26 April 2005, Bundle G, 3883 at point 3 – as cited in *Eurotunnel* Partial Award, para. 164 (original Letter not publicly available).

[23] Claimants' Reply, para. 136 – as cited in *Eurotunnel* Partial Award, para. 165 (original Reply not publicly available).

[24] *Ibid.*, para. 137 – as cited in *Eurotunnel* Partial Award, para. 166.

[25] *Ibid.*, para. 141 – as cited in *Eurotunnel* Partial Award, para. 167.

responsibility inherent to each State'.[26] How exactly the former (execution of the Agreement) was to be separated from the latter (public order obligations) was not clarified.[27] Moreover, France asserted that Clause 41.4 of the Concession Agreement granted national courts exclusive jurisdiction to address joint and several responsibility issues as it would be impossible for a tribunal to distinguish between breaches of France and those of the UK.

Unlike France, the UK maintained that it was unclear whether acts and omissions attributable to 'one or both of the Governments' entailed individual liability, joint liability or joint and several liability. In its view, 'Claimants must establish the specific responsibility of the United Kingdom for any alleged breach.'[28] Furthermore, the UK rejected the claimants' allegation that both governments had failed to co-operate, co-ordinate and consult so as to prevent the other government's breach, as such obligation of result was not stipulated in either the Concession Agreement or in any source of international law.[29] Whether it could instead potentially be construed as an obligation of conduct was not explored by either of the respondent parties.[30]

3 The tribunal's analysis

The tribunal commenced its investigation by examining Article 47 of the ILC Articles on State Responsibility (Plurality of responsible States) which provides:

1. Where several States are responsible for the same internationally wrongful act, the responsibility of each State may be invoked in relation to that act.
2. Paragraph 1:
   (a) does not permit any injured State to recover, by way of compensation, more than the damage it has suffered;

[26] Transcript, Day 9, 34 (translation of the original French version, Day 9, 30–1) Reply – as cited in *Eurotunnel* Partial Award, para. 169 (original Transcript not publicly available).

[27] Insofar as this can be derived from the Partial Award as the original Memorials are not publicly available.

[28] United Kingdom Counter-Memorial, para. 3.81 and Transcript, Day 4, 122–3 – as cited in *Eurotunnel* Partial Award, para. 171 (original Counter-Memorial and Transcript not publicly available).

[29] *Eurotunnel* Partial Award, para. 172.

[30] Insofar as this can be derived from the Partial Award as the original Memorials are not publicly available.

(b) is without prejudice to any right of recourse against the other responsible States.

The ILC stated in the commentary to this Article that:

> The general rule in international law is that of separate responsibility of a State for its own wrongful acts and paragraph 1 reflects this general rule. Paragraph 1 neither recognizes a general rule of joint and several or solidary responsibility, nor does it exclude the possibility that two or more States will be responsible for the same internationally wrongful act. Whether this is so will depend on the circumstances and on the international obligations of each of the States concerned.[31]

Applying this statement, the tribunal questioned 'whether the provisions of the Treaty of Canterbury as given effect to by the Concession Agreement and the Concession Agreement establish or imply any general principle of solidary responsibility for breaches of obligation'.[32] Although Clause 20 of the Concession Agreement established a system of joint and several liability of the Concessionaires to the Principals, there is no equivalent provision vice versa.

Thus the question became whether 'the Concession Agreement provided or at least assumed that an obligation of the Principals was a joint obligation of both or individual obligations of each'.[33] The claimants' argument that such obligation was included in the reference in the Concession Agreement to the French Minister for Transport and the British Secretary of State 'of the one part' and to the British and French companies 'of the other part', was rejected by the tribunal as it is a usual formulation which does not necessarily entail any form of joint and several responsibility.[34] More significance was attached to the conduct of the IGC, a joint supervisory organ created to supervise 'in the name and on behalf of the two Governments, all matters concerning the construction and operation of the Fixed Link'.[35] Its decisions require the assent of both States-Principals – a violation of the Concession Agreement by an act of the IGC could thus entail joint responsibility of France and the UK.[36] The claimants, however, were complaining not about an act, but an omission on the part of the IGC – which gave rise to the question of whether this

[31] Commentary to Art. 47 of the ILC Articles on State Responsibility, para. 6.

[32] *Eurotunnel* Partial Award, para. 175. [33] *Ibid.*, para. 177. [34] *Ibid.*, para. 178.

[35] Arts. 10(1) and 10(3)(c) of the Treaty of Canterbury.

[36] The Partial Award hereby refers to the ILC Articles on State Responsibility which envisage the situation of 'a single entity which is a joint organ of several States': commentary to Art. 6, para. 3; commentary to Art. 47, para. 2.

'failure to take action' entailed the joint liability of both Principals or the individual liability of each.[37]

This led the tribunal to examine the Invitation to Promoters, more specifically, the undertaking not to terminate the promoters' right to operate the Fixed Link.[38] This Invitation provided that the Treaty would lay down 'the conditions for the allocation of responsibility as between the States'.[39] Where a breach of such undertaking falls under the responsibility of both States, or where the responsibility is disputed, the issue is to be decided by arbitration on the basis of international law. The Treaty in general does not require any joint action – the one express reference being Article 5(4) on measures necessary for the defence and security of the Fixed Link, which states that:

> The Concessionaires shall, if required by the two Governments, take measures necessary for the defence and security of the Fixed Link. Save in exceptional circumstances of the kind envisaged in Article 6, the two Governments shall consult each other before requiring the Concessionaires to take such measures, and shall act jointly.

As Article 6 deals with natural disasters, acts of terrorism and armed conflicts, the tribunal concluded that the defence and security of the Fixed Link must be a wider concept. Furthermore, Article 15 on Compensation of Concessionaries states that:

> (3) . . . In those cases where *both States are liable* under this provision and where the Concessionaires make a claim for compensation against both States, *they may not receive from each State more than half of the amount of compensation payable* in accordance with the law of that State.
>
> (4) Each State shall bear the cost of the payment of the compensation to the Concessionaires *in proportion to its responsibility*, if any, in accordance with international law.[40]

The Treaty contains many provisions for consultation and co-operation between the two governments,[41] while in other respects proceeding on the basis that the implementation of the Fixed Link is a matter for one government or the other, depending on where the tasks are to be carried

[37] *Eurotunnel* Partial Award, paras. 179–80. [38] *Ibid.*, para. 181.
[39] Invitation to Promoters, para. 11.5. [40] Emphasis added.
[41] *Eurotunnel* Partial Award, para. 184.

out.[42] So, the tribunal scrutinised all provisions of the Concession Agreement which envisage joint or co-operative action by the Principals as well as action by each of them on its own responsibility.[43]

However, the tribunal found that 'there is no equivalent so far as the Principals are concerned of the joint and several responsibility and mutual guarantees exacted from the Concessionaires'.[44] As a result, to the extent that the claims relied on joint and several responsibility, defined as 'the *per se* responsibility of one State for the acts of the other', they failed. What was required was close co-operation between the two governments, in particular through their joint organs (the IGC and the Safety Committee); the Concession Agreement set out core commitments towards the Concessionaires, in particular to facilitate the construction and to permit the uninterrupted operation of the Fixed Link. Subsequently, the tribunal embarked upon an extensive analysis of the alleged breaches of the Concession Agreement resulting from the fault of one or other, or both, States – whereof the findings on the Sangatte claim are most relevant to the present discussion.

C Findings on the Sangatte claim

The Sangatte claim consisted of two allegations which were brought jointly against both respondents: (1) failure to protect the Coquelles site against clandestine migrant incursions and (2) favouring the *Société Nationale des Chemins de Fer Français* (French Railways National Society or SNCF) Terminal and Port of Calais to the detriment of the Fixed Link.

1 Failure to protect against incursions

Starting with the failure to protect the Coquelles site against incursions, the tribunal identified four applicable legal standards. First, the clauses placing the burden of the assumption of risk upon the Concessionaires do not apply in this case as these clauses concern external hazards – such as risks arising from acts of third parties or the state of the economy – as opposed to governmental non-compliance with commitments under the Concession Agreement.[45] Secondly, the legal standard against which the respondents' conduct had to be measured consisted of obligations to allow the Concessionaires freely to determine their commercial policy,

[42] *Ibid.*, para. 185.
[43] *Ibid.*, para. 186.
[44] *Ibid.*, para. 187.
[45] *Ibid.*, paras. 279–82.

not to intervene in the operation of the Fixed Link and not to interrupt its operation.[46] Thirdly, the respondents' conduct had to be examined in the light of the clauses relating to frontier controls.[47] The fourth and final legal standard was the claimants' primary reliance on certain systematic obligations of the Principals, acting in consultation and through the IGC, to maintain the basic conditions under which the Fixed Link could be constructed and operate.[48]

Applying these standards, the tribunal recognised that the opening of the Sangatte Hostel fell within the margin of appreciation of the French authorities but by January 2001, it should have been sufficiently clear to the Principals and the IGC that it was being used 'as a base for criminal activity'.[49] This led the tribunal to hold that '[u]nder Clauses 2.1 and 27.1 of the Concession Agreement, the IGC should have taken the necessary steps to ensure the orderly operation of the Fixed Link' but yet 'at crucial periods, the IGC sought to shift the whole burden of security on to Eurotunnel'.[50] Even though 'issues of policing outside the control zone were exclusively a matter for France, the overall responsibility for the security of the Fixed Link was shared and not divided'.[51]

It was not that the UK was responsible for the security of the Fixed Link on its side of the boundary, while France was responsible on the Continental side. Rather, both States shared that responsibility and under Clause 27.7 had agreed to ensure that the IGC took the necessary steps to facilitate the implementation of the entire Agreement. The tribunal concluded that:

> in the circumstances of the clandestine migrant problem . . . , it was incumbent on the Principals, acting through the IGC and otherwise, to maintain conditions of normal security and public order in and around the Coquelles terminal; that they failed to take appropriate steps in this regard, and thereby breached Clauses 2.1 and 27.7 of the Concession Agreement, and that the Claimants are entitled to recover the losses directly flowing from this breach.[52]

This finding was not considered inequitable vis-à-vis the UK because all measures to secure the Coquelles terminal were taken to benefit the integrity of UK immigration laws. Moreover, the IGC record did not show 'consistent and conscientious opposition by the United Kingdom to a unilateral French policy, such that the United Kingdom could argue that it did everything within its power to bring a clearly

[46] *Ibid.*, paras. 279–89. [47] *Ibid.*, paras. 290–4. [48] *Ibid.*, paras. 295–302.
[49] *Ibid.*, paras. 306–9. [50] *Ibid.*, para. 309. [51] *Ibid.*, para. 317. [52] *Ibid.*, para. 319.

unsatisfactory situation promptly to an end'.[53] As a result, the tribunal held the UK co-responsible with France for the damages caused to the claimants.

2 Favouring the SNCF Terminal and Port of Calais

Subsequently, the tribunal moved to examine the discrimination claim brought against the respondents, namely the allegation that both governments had favoured the SNCF Terminal and Port of Calais to the detriment of the Fixed Link. Although this could in principle have resulted in a shared responsibility finding, the tribunal held that there was 'no general obligation on the Principals under the Concession Agreement to observe the principle of non-discrimination between different cross-Channel operators in respect of operational requirements such as security and safety'.[54] Hence, as there was no general obligation, there could be no general breach either, resulting in a finding of shared responsibility.[55]

3 The extent of responsibility as between the respondents

In sum, only one ground for shared responsibility was accepted by the tribunal: the failure to prevent incursions on the Coquelles site. Regarding the apportionment of the established shared responsibility and the division of compensation obligations, as between the UK and France, the tribunal referred to the second phase of the proceedings, in which the quantum of the claimants' loss would be determined and apportioned.

The tribunal in the *Eurotunnel* Partial Award held that it had jurisdiction over the Sangatte claim in relation to both respondents. Furthermore, in the circumstances of the examined clandestine migrant problem, 'it was incumbent on the Principals, acting through the IGC and otherwise, to maintain conditions of normal security and public order in and around the Coquelles terminal'.[56] In failing to take appropriate steps in this regard, the tribunal decided with a 4:1 majority (with Lord Millett dissenting) that the Principals had breached Clauses 2.1 and 27.7 of the Concession Agreement. As a result, the claimants were entitled to recover the losses directly flowing from this breach, to be assessed in a separate phase.[57] This next phase, the proceedings on damages, terminated when the

[53] *Ibid.*, para. 318. [54] *Ibid.*, para. 324.
[55] *Ibid.*, paras. 325–35. [56] *Ibid.*, para. 395. [57] *Ibid.*

parties reached a settlement, the precise terms of which are not available to the public.[58]

The reasoning underlying the majority decision on liability can be summarised as follows: (1) both governments bore the responsibility for security maintenance under the Concession Agreement; (2) both governments were liable for damages suffered by the Concessionaires based on the fact that the Channel Tunnel required close co-operation between the two governments and through their joint organ, the IGC; (3) as a result, what the IGC as a joint organ failed to do (protect the French terminal against intrusions of clandestine migrants), the governments in whose name and on whose behalf it acted, equally failed to do.

III Relevance of the *Eurotunnel* award for shared responsibility

A Reciprocity of joint and several responsibility?

Arguably, Clause 20, which establishes a system of joint and several liability of the Concessionaires vis-à-vis the Principals but not vice versa, may seem prima facie 'unfair' as it contradicts the reciprocity of contractual obligations, creating a potential imbalance in the relationship between the contracting parties. However, although the fact of private corporations being joint and severally liable in the absence of a similar liability as between the States may seem to lack symmetry, there is a clear reason why enterprises which run commercial ventures are often assumed to be joint and severally liable while governments are not.[59] Under private law, the system of joint and several liability aims at strengthening the position of the creditor, extending the assets available for recovery in case the debtor goes bankrupt. The traditional position is that States and public bodies, even when engaging in commercial activities, cannot be equated with private corporations because, amongst other things, they cannot go bankrupt. In case of contractual breach, the creditor will still be able to obtain a (financial) remedy,[60] which could explain the position taken when the Eurotunnel Concession Agreement was signed. Although the current financial crisis may weaken this argument, it remains

58 Correspondence with the UK Foreign and Commonwealth Office, on file with author.

59 See e.g. Scott L. Hoffman, *The Law and Business of International Project Finance*, 3rd edn (Cambridge University Press, 2008), 158–63.

60 *Ibid.*

indisputable that States cannot simply be equated with private companies in the anticipation of bankruptcy.

B The Eurotunnel *case as a precedent for determining shared responsibility*

1 The Partial Award: dividing the allocation of responsibility

When it comes to providing guidance as to the allocation of responsibility or reparation in shared responsibility cases, the approach taken by the *Eurotunnel* tribunal can be seen as rather careful – for very good reasons. The caution in the liability award hardly comes as a surprise, if one considers that the chair of the arbitral tribunal in the *Eurotunnel* dispute (Professor James Crawford) was also the ILC Special Rapporteur under whose charge the ILC Articles on State Responsibility – which are equally non-committal with regard to shared responsibility – were finalised. What the *Eurotunnel* case does teach us is the importance of the specific terms of the agreement upon which the jurisdiction of the adjudicatory body is to be based. Does this agreement, as *lex specialis*, prescribe any particular form of shared responsibility? More specifically, has a system of joint and several liability been stipulated? Has the issue of implementation of any such responsibility been devised, particularly when it comes to remedies, or should recourse be made to national law?

This is where arbitration as a procedural means to an end – settling shared responsibility claims – might have an edge over international and domestic litigation, as it allows for *ad hoc* solutions via the conclusion of an arbitration agreement. Moreover, arbitration also allows for the participation of a variety of actors – as seen in the *Eurotunnel* case in which two companies successfully invoked the shared responsibility of the two States involved. The decision adopted in *Eurotunnel* was to divide the allocation of responsibility between France and the UK rather than holding them jointly and severally responsible, with the concrete determination and allocation of the compensation to be made in a subsequent phase. Nothing in the procedural toolbox of arbitration, however, predetermines this division of the allocation of responsibility to be repeated in similar future proceedings.

2 The Millett dissent: with no power comes no responsibility

Lord Millett's dissent has a certain straightforward, practical charm: why would a State be held responsible for omissions if it was not in a position to act? Why would the UK have to pay damages for lack of maintenance of public order if it did not have the competence to authorise any actions on French soil? The answer, as found in the majority opinion, is that this was exactly what the parties had agreed to in the Concession agreement: the creation of a legal fiction, whereby two States could indeed be held jointly responsible on an abstract level, whereas only the actions of one of them could have prevented the breach in practice. Legally, it is a logical and common set-up to hold someone liable for damages due to failure to act, even if their own conduct did not contribute to the damages – for the sole reason that this was a joint operation.

Although Lord Millett agreed that the UK shared France's understanding of their legal obligations in this matter, he maintained that the respondents' authorisation of the IGC's conduct did not form a breach of the Concession Agreement in itself, but at most 'some encouragement to France'.[61] As a result, France – and only France – violated the Concession Agreement. Concluding that Clause 27 does not add anything to Clause 2.1[62] is an illustration of circular reasoning, effectively leaving Clause 27 devoid of legal meaning. Furthermore, it is rather unfair to the majority to state that:

> [t]he key proposition on which the majority base their finding against the United Kingdom is that it did not 'do everything within its power to bring an unsatisfactory situation promptly to an end' . . . This is, with respect, an abbreviated version of the truth, omitting as it does a crucial qualification. The true position is that the United Kingdom did not do everything within its power to bring an unsatisfactory situation promptly to an end *by getting France to perform its obligations.*[63]

The majority did *not* include the latter finding (either explicitly or implicitly) in its award. The most straightforward explanation is that this was not included because it was not part of the majority's position. The dissent seems to read an obligation of result into what is phrased as an obligation of conduct. Taken at face value, the award states exactly what it was in all likelihood meant to state: the UK could have undertaken certain actions to try to induce France to comply with the obligations resting upon both respondents, but the UK failed to do this. The reason is quite simple: the UK was labouring under the same understanding of these obligations as France was, thereby encouraging France to continue acting accordingly.

Had the UK, however, adopted the correct – the tribunal's – understanding of the Principals' obligations and done everything in its power

[61] Dissent Lord Millett, para. 16. [62] *Ibid.*, para. 18.
[63] *Ibid.*, para. 23 (emphasis in original).

to convince France to change course, but failed in achieving that goal, the discussion would presumably have run a different course. The facts being as they are, the majority rightly concluded that the shared responsibility of both respondent States had been established. Particularly as to the IGC's conduct, the majority decision concurs with the line of reasoning followed by the International Court of Justice (ICJ) in its decision in *Certain Phosphate Lands in Nauru* relating to the shared responsibility of Australia, the UK and New Zealand for their joint organ, the Administrative Council[64] – incidentally also the first ICJ case in which the chair of the *Eurotunnel* arbitration and honouree of this work appeared as counsel.

This is not to imply that Lord Millett's dissent should be discarded: particularly relevant remains his analysis of the consequences of primary as opposed to secondary responsibility and, more precisely, the consequences pertaining to the different nature of the internationally wrongful act committed by the UK.[65] The majority award could be criticised not so much for the injustice of holding the UK liable, but for reducing France's liability to any extent, as 'ultimately the cause of the United Kingdom's supposed liability is that France failed to discharge its obligations under the Concession Agreement'.[66] Indeed, if France on its own had adopted the correct understanding of the Principals' obligations under the Concession Agreement and had satisfactorily discharged such obligations, there would have been no dispute, regardless of the UK's understanding. Thus, in such case, even if the UK had maintained its present incorrect understanding that no action was required, this would not have entailed a shared responsibility finding as there would have been no injury and ensuing cause for damages.

Even if one accepts that the UK and France jointly committed the same internationally wrongful act, the responsibility of one involved State (France) cannot be reduced due to the existence of a co-perpetrator (the UK). To what extent this may influence the allocation of the damages is a different matter.[67]

[64] *Certain Phosphate Lands in Nauru (Nauru* v. *Australia)*, Judgment on Preliminary Objections, 26 June 1992 ICJ Reports (1992), 240, 258–9, para. 48; see also Christian Dominicé, 'Attribution of Conduct to Multiple States and the Implication of a State in the Act of Another State' in James Crawford, Allain Pellet, Simon Olleson (eds.), *The Law of International Responsibility* (Oxford University Press, 2010), 281–4.

[65] This option was cursorily mentioned by Lord Millett in para. 19 of his Dissent: '[e]ven if [the conduct of the UK] did [constitute a breach of the Concession Agreement], it would not be the same wrong but a wrong of a very different order'.

[66] *Ibid.*, para. 24.

[67] *Certain Phosphate Lands in Nauru (Nauru* v. *Australia)*, Separate Opinion of Judge Shahabuddeen, 283–5; Commentary to the Art. 47 of the ILC Articles on State Responsibility

C Determining damages

Regarding the precise division of the damages flowing from the establishment of shared responsibility in the confidential settlement of the *Eurotunnel* case, one can only resort to speculative guesswork. Inasmuch as the IGC's conduct is concerned, it is most likely that the responsibility of the States involved has been divided on a fifty-fifty basis. Such estimation is based on the formulation of the Concession Agreement, and more precisely the stipulations under Clause 27 which give both Principals an equal role in the Agreement's implementation and the functioning of the IGC and the Safety Authority. Resulting from such equal power to drive the IGC's actions, and in the absence of evidence to the contrary, it would appear that each State should bear an equal measure of responsibility if and when the IGC fails to act to an extent that such omission is found to be in breach of the Agreement.

However, the same reasoning will not necessarily have been applied concerning the determination of the compensation for breaches due to acts or omissions of the respondents directly (as opposed to through the IGC). The tribunal held that 'it was incumbent on the Principals, acting through the IGC *and otherwise*, to maintain conditions of normal security and public order in and around the Coquelles terminal'.[68] The liability for the Principals' actions covered by the term 'and otherwise' is where the distinction between the consequences of primary versus secondary liability could come into play, because the settlement may have, as expressed in Lord Millett's words, treated 'the United Kingdom liable to the Claimants . . . in a very small amount'.[69] It is impossible to establish whether UK protests against French conduct would have had any effect. Hence, in the absence of any information on actual UK actions that have effectively contributed to the damage, it could even be possible that the UK share of reparation for this part of the Sangatte shared responsibility claim (as opposed to the IGC-related part) remained limited to some form of satisfaction, rather than actual compensation.

IV Conclusion

When it comes to providing guidance as to the allocation of responsibility or reparation in shared responsibility cases, the approach taken by the

for Internationally Wrongful Acts, para. 11; see also, Orakhelashvili, 'Division of Reparation between Responsible Entities', 647–65.

68 *Eurotunnel* Partial Award, para. 395 (emphasis added).

69 Dissent Lord Millett, para. 24.

Eurotunnel tribunal can be seen as quite cautious; a significant contribution to alleviate the under-theorisation and under-exploration in this field has not been realised due to the confidential settlement reached by the parties to the dispute. What the Partial Award in the *Eurotunnel* case does teach us is the importance of the specific terms of the treaty upon which the jurisdiction of the adjudicatory body is to be based. Does this *lex specialis* prescribe any particular form of shared responsibility? More specifically, has a system of joint and several liability been provided? Has the implementation of such responsibility been regulated, particularly concerning remedies, or should recourse be made to general law?

The solution advocated in this chapter is to anticipate shared responsibility claims that may arise in the future and address their implementation already in the treaty or contract which contains the primary obligations – as a *lex specialis* to the limited provisions in the ILC Articles on State Responsibility. A subsidiary solution, if there is no primary treaty or contract, or if it does not regulate shared responsibility claims, would be that parties to an existing dispute try to reach an agreement *in abstracto* on the implementation of shared responsibility, incorporate this in their arbitration agreement and then let an arbitral tribunal decide, first, whether the primary obligation has been breached, and, secondly, how the shared responsibility regulations have to be applied in the case at hand.

Including a 'division formula' in a treaty is not entirely uncommon, an illustration being the 1976 Convention on the Protection of the Rhine from Pollution by Chlorides and its 1991 Additional Protocol, which allocate the clean-up costs for the pollution of the Rhine among the riparian States according to a predetermined formula.[70] Evidently, the contributory payment under this treaty and protocol formed the primary obligation and not a secondary one resulting from previous internationally wrongful conduct but States, international organisations and non-State entities could similarly work out a formula for existing or future shared responsibility claims.

Arbitration as a procedural means to an end – settling shared responsibility claims – has an edge over international and domestic

[70] Agreement for the Protection of the Rhine against Chemical Pollution (Bonn, signed 3 December 1976, entered into force 1 February 1979), 1124 UNTS 406; *Case concerning the Audit of Accounts between the Netherlands and France in Application of the Protocol of 25 September 1991 Additional to the Convention for the Protection of the Rhine from Pollution by Chlorides of 3 December 1976 (Netherlands* v. *France)*, Award, 12 March 2004, United Nations Reports of International Arbitral Awards, vol. XXV, 267–344.

litigation, as it allows for *ad hoc* solutions to be created via the conclusion of an arbitration agreement. Moreover, and just as important, arbitration also allows for the participation of a variety of actors – an option which is not limited to allowing companies to bring claims against States, as seen in the *Eurotunnel* case – but could be extended to include, as claimants or respondents, various combinations of States, international organisations, companies, peoples and individuals. In this manner, a just sharing of responsibility among all accountable actors becomes less of an unattainable ideal and more of an achievable reality.

INDEX

Abbas, Mahmoud, 241–2
Abkhazia, Republic of, ICJ extraterritoriality cases and, 56–8, 63–5
Aboriginal customary law, Crawford and, xvii–xviii
accessibility, polar sovereignty and issues of, 111–14
accountability, of non-state actors, 84
acquis communautaire, state recognition and, 205–6
Act of Free Choice
  analysis of, 221–7
  historical background concerning, 209–10
  Indonesian incorporation of West Papua under, 219–20
  New York Agreement and, 217–19
administrative law, investment treaty case law and, 105–8
admiralty jurisdiction, Crawford's work in, xvii
ADM v. *Mexico*, 398n27, 399
aerial bombardment, collateral civilian damage and, 327–9
AETR doctrine, EU external relations and, 407–11, 413, 415–17
Afghanistan, European state actors in, 67–70
Africa, *uti possidetis* principle and decolonisation in, 250–2, 255–6n32, 257n33, 258, 262–4
African Charter on Human and Peoples' Rights (ACHPR)
  extraterritoriality and, 54–8
  jurisdictional issues and, 63–5
African National Congress (ANC), 238n43
African Union, 169–70
  responsibility to protect and, 29–30
Ago, Roberto, 292n21–22, 293n28, 297–301, 352–6
Agreement on Subsidies and Countervailing Measures (SCM Agreement), 363–4
  International Law Commission relevance in, 375–83
  'public body' concept interpreted by, 365–9
  World Trade Organisation (WTO) Appellate Body's interpretation of 'public body' concept, 369–73
Ahtisaari Plan, 161–6
Al-Adsani case, 187–8
Albania
  Corfu Channel case and, 47–8
  Kosovo Albanians and, 161–6
Albright, Madeleine, 26–27n16
Alexandre (President), 166–70
Algeria, 157–61, 165n66
Allot, Philip, 288–9n9, 291, 292–6
Al-Skeini case, 'exceptional' nature of territoriality in, 65–7
Althusius, Johannes, 172
American Convention on Human Rights
  extraterritoriality and, 54–6
  jurisdiction in, 60–5
American Law Institute (ALI)
  on disclaimers in recognition of states, 205–6
  'Manifestation of Intention to Recognize', 202–4

Restatement (1965) on state recognition, 198–202
Amis, Martin, 3
Anastasiou case, 177–9
Anglo-German Agreements of 1913, Cameroon-Nigerian boundary dispute and, 262–4
Annan, Kofi, 26–7, 32–3, 157–61
Antarctica, polar sovereignty issues and, 110–11
Antarctic continental shelf, sovereignty issues concerning, 116–17
Antarctic sovereignty, 114–17
Antarctic Treaty (1959), 110–11, 114–17, 124–5
Antarctic Treaty System (ATS), 114–17
Anzilotti, Dionisio, 144–5, 151–2
Arab League
Syrian and suspension from, 348–51
UN Security Council Resolution 1973 and, 37–8
Arangio-Ruiz, Gaetano, 356–60
Arctic Maritime Shipping Assessment (AMSA) Report, 118–21
Arctic sovereignty, 110–11, 118n45, 121
Arctic Water Pollution Prevention Act, 118–21
Arendt, Hannah, 4–5
Argentina
Antarctic sovereignty and, 121–4
ARA Libertad case and, 389–91
Beagle Channel arbitration and, 259–60
Eichmann extradition and, 47–8
investment treaty claims in, 90–3
polar sovereignty and, 111–14
State responsibility principles in, 297–301
third party countermeasures and, 352–6
Aristide, Jean-Bertrand, 166–70
Armed Activities on the Territory of Congo, ICJ opinion on, 204–5
arms shipments, PCASP guidelines and, 315–21
Articles on State Responsibility (ASR)
countermeasures of investment treaty claims and, 395–6
Eurotunnel dispute and, 427–8, 429–32, 436
military necessity limits in, 334–7
mixed multi-party disputes and, 421–2
normative principles in, 288–90n11, 291
primary and secondary rules of military necessity and, 337–8
State complicity with corporate human rights breaches and, 321–4
third party countermeasures and, 340–1, 347–51
U.S. – Antidumping and Countervailing Duties (China) and, 363–4
Articles on State Responsibility (ILC), 47–8, 173–82, 188–90
Asian sovereignty. *See* East Asia
Assad, Bashar al-, 37–8, 44–6, 347–51
assumption of risk, in Eurotunnel dispute, 432–4
attribution, test of
collateral civilian casualties and, 327–9
U.S.-Antidumping and Countervailing Duties (China) and, 363–4
Audencia de Guatemala, 267–70
Australia
Antarctic sovereignty and, 114–17, 121–4
investment treaty claims and, 90–3
polar sovereignty issues and, 110–11
Australian Antarctic Territory (AAT), 114–17
Australian Courts of Law, xvi
Australian Law Reform Commission, xvi
auto-interpretation, third party countermeasures and problem of, 356–60

Badan, Opertti, 350
Badinter Commission, 192–6
uti possidetis principle and, 248–52

Bahrain, third party countermeasures and, 343–7
Baker, James, 157–61
Baker Plan (Framework Agreement) (2001), 157–61
Baltic States, state continuity and succession in, 273–7
Banković case
  'exceptional' nature of territoriality in, 65–7
  'legal space' concept in, 67–70
Barbados, maritime boundary dispute in, 265
Barcelona Traction opinion, 297–301
Barcenas-Esguerra Treaty, 267–70
Barry, Elizabeth, 6–7
Basten, Henry, xiv
Beagle Channel arbitration, 259–60
Beckett, Samuel, 14, 15–17, 21
Bedjaoui, Judge, 249–50, 270–2
Beer, Gillian, 5
Belgium, Palestine statehood supported by, 239–42
Bellinger, John B. III, 46
Best Management Practices, piracy defence in shipping industry, 307–8
Bianchi Andrea, 325–7
bilateral investment treaties (BITs)
  constitutional legitimacy of, 90–3
  investment treaty case law and, 105–8
  lex specialis principle and, 391–3
bilateral recognition, objective statehood principle and, 231–4
binary analytic mindset, collateral damage and, 331
Black, Eugene R., 20–1
Black Sea case, *uti possidetis* principle and, 270
Blair, Tony, 23, 30–1, 40
Bluntschli, 277–9, 342–3
Bolivia
  investment treaty claims by, 90–3
  uti possidetis/uti possidetis juris principle and, 254n24
Bosnia-Herzegovina
  humanitarian crisis in, 25–6, 43
  international recognition of, 196–8, 202–4
Bosnian Genocide case, 297–301
Botswana, third party countermeasures and, 343–7, 350–1
boundary disputes
  Barbado boundary dispute, 265
  Cameroon-Nigerian boundary dispute, 262–4
  Colombian-Nicaraguan boundary dispute, 267–70
  during colonialisation, 252–8
  Gulf of Fonseca maritime boundary dispute, 258–9, 260–2
  Honduran-Nicaraguan boundary dispute, 265–7
  maritime boundaries, *uti possidetis* principle in, 258–70
  uti possidetis juris principle and, 248–52
Brazil
  functional immunity in perimeter guard case in, 310–15
  uti possidetis de facto formula in, 252–4n24, 258
Bricker Amendment, non-self-executing treaties and, 95–9
Brierly, James, 277–9
Briggs, Herbert, 233n16, 231–4, 234n22
Brown, Jethro, xv
Brownlie, Ian, xv–xvi, 289n9, 293n28
Brownlie's Principles of International Law (Crawford), xxi
Brownlie's Principles of Public International Law, 198–202
Brussels Convention, rules on criminal jurisdiction over collisions, 310–15
Bulgaria, neutrality concerning Palestinian statehood, 241–2
Bunker, Ellsworth, 217–19
Burkina Faso/Mali case, 249–50
  state recognition in, 198–202
  uti possidetis principle and, 255–8, 260–2, 265–7

Burundi, third party countermeasures and, 350–1, 352–6

Cairo Declaration, Senkaku/Diaoyudao Islands dispute and, 128–30
California Alien Land Law, international law and, 95–9
California Supreme Court, UN Charter and rulings by, 95–9
Cambridge University, Crawford's presence at, xx–xxv
Cameroon, Republic of
  boundary dispute with Nigeria, 262–4
  third party countermeasures and, 352–6
Canada
  Arctic sovereignty issues and, 121–4
  Arctic sovereignty issues in, 118–21
  EU asbestos dispute and, 81
  investment treaty claims and, 90–3
  Palestinian statehood supported by, 239–42
  polar sovereignty issues and, 110–11
  Quebec separatism in, 248
  United Postal Service of America Inc (UPS) v. *Canada* and, 179–82
Canada-Dairy case, WTO Appellate Body's interpretation of 'public body' concept and, 369–73, 386n99
carbon markets
  Forest Carbon Partnership Facility (World Bank), 81, 81n56
  normative conflicts over establishment of, 71–3
  regime interaction and, 81
Cargill v. *Mexico*, 401–3
casus belli, primary and secondary rules of military necessity and, 337–8
Central American Court of Justice
  Gulf of Fonseca boundary dispute and, 258–9
  Land, Island and Maritime Frontier Dispute, 260–2
Central Bank of Nigeria, restrictive immunity doctrine and, 186–7
Central Europe, state continuity and succession in, 273–7
Centre for the Democratic Control of Armed Forces, 315–21
Channel Tunnel Group Ltd., 422–3
  Sangatte migrants and, 425–6
Channel Tunnel (International Arrangement) Order, 425–6
The Charkieh ruling, 182–8
Charlesworth, Hilary, 15–17
Chatterjee, Partha, 18–20
Chesterman, Simon, 47–8
Chile
  Beagle Channel arbitration and, 259–60
  polar sovereignty and, 111–14
China, People's Republic of
  critique of Senkaku/Diaoyudao Islands claims, 134–6
  East Asian sovereignty and, 126–43
  history of Senkaku/Diaoyudao Islands ownership and, 128–30
  overview of Senkaku/Diaoyudao claims, 129–130n16, 131–3
  polar sovereignty issues and, 110–11
  Senkaku/Diaoyudao Islands dispute with Japan and, 126–8
  state-owned enterprises and state-owned commercial banks in, 365–9
  Syria and, 44–6
  U.S.-Antidumping and Countervailing Duties (China) and, 363–88
  U.S. relations with, 126–8
Churkin, Vitaly, 36–7
Cicero, 250–2
civil law, restrictive immunity doctrine and, 187–8
civil rights litigation (U.S.)
  human rights treaties and, 90–3
  international law and, 95–9
Civis Romanus sum, third party countermeasures and, 342–3
'clean slate' principle, state continuity and succession and, 279–83

'clear excessiveness' standard, collateral civilian damage and, 327–9
clichés
  historical origins of, 6–7
  in international law, 7–14
  rousing of, 15–21
  terminology of, 4–7
climate change
  international regime for, 73–8
  polar sovereignty issues and, 118n45, 121, 124–5
coastal State rights, *Enrica Lexie* incident and, 310–15
Cobbett, Pitt, xviii
coexistence principle, third party countermeasures and, 352–6
Cohen, Jean L., 283–4
Cold War
  Indonesian independence and, 217–19
  polar sovereignty issues and, 110–11
  regime change ideology in wake of, 166–70
  responsibility to protect and end of, 41–2
collateral damage
  binary analytic mindset concerning, 331
  international law concerning, 325–7
  military necessity concept and, 332
  qualifying words pertaining to offence of, 327–9
  state *vs.* individual responsibility thresholds for, 329–30
collective recognition, of Palestinian statehood, in UNGA Resolution 67/19, 234–42
Colombia
  investment treaty claims by, 90–3
  Nicaraguan boundary dispute with, 267–70
  uti possidetis/ *uti possidetis juris* principle and, 254n24
Colonial Declaration, *uti possidetis* principle and, 255–8
colonialisation. *See also* decolonisation; independence
  Act of Free Choice in West Papua and, 209–10
  Crawford's Admiralty work and, xvii
  'legal space' concept and, 67–70
  uti possidetis principle and, 252–8, 270–2
  Western Sahara territorial disposition and, 157–61
  West New Guinea under, 213–15
Commission on the Limits of the Continental Shelf (CLCS)
  Antarctic sovereignty issues and, 116–17
  Arctic sovereignty issues and, 118–21
  contemporary challenges involving, 121–4
  polar sovereignty issues and, 110–11
Commission v. *Greece*, 414–15
Common Commercial Policy, EU competences concerning, 407–9
communitarian law enforcement, third party measures and, 347–51
comparative public law analysis, investment treaty case law, 105–8
Comprehensive Peace Agreement (CPA) between the Government of The Republic of Sudan and the Sudan People's Liberation Movement/ Sudan People's Liberation Army 2005, 159n26
compulsory jurisdiction, legal characteristics of states and, 145–7
conceptual clichés, 10
Concession Agreement, in Eurotunnel dispute, 426–7, 429–32
conduct of states. *See* State responsibility
  conduct of persons empowered by, 364n5
  countermeasures in investment treaty claims and, 395–6
  in Eurotunnel dispute, 432–4

normative principles of State responsibility and, 288–91
third party countermeasures and, 356–60
WTO Appellate Body's interpretation of 'public body' concept and, 369–73, 377n67

Conferences of the Parties (CoPs), State responsibility law and, 304–5

Confucianism, territorial sovereignty and principles of, 139–41

I Congreso case, 182–8

constitutionality issues
European Community legal order and, 99–105
international law and, 95–9, 292–6
investment treaty claims and, 90–3
state continuity and succession, 279–83

Constitution of the United States, international law and, 95–9

Constitutive Act of the African Union, 29–30

constructive possession, *uti possidetis* principle and, 252–8

contiguity principle, polar sovereignty and, 111–14

continental shelf claims
Antarctic sovereignty issues concerning, 116–17
Arctic sovereignty issues and, 118–21
Colombian-Nicaraguan boundary dispute and, 267–70
polar sovereignty issues and, 110–11
Senkaku/Diaoyudao Islands dispute and, 128–30

Convention Against Torture and Other Cruel, Inhuman or Degrading Treatment or Punishment (CAT)
extraterritoriality and, 54–7
jurisdiction in, 60–3
law of state responsibility and, 179–82
U.S. ratification of, 95–9

Convention for the Suppression of Unlawful Acts Against the Safetey of Maritime Navigation, 310–15

Convention on the Elimination of All Forms of Discrimination Against Women (CEDAW), 54–6

Convention on the Elimination of All Forms of Racial Discrimination (CERD), 54–8
extraterritoriality and, 63–5

Convention on the International Trade of Endangered Species (CITES)
accountability to sovereign states of, 84
experts' role in, 82–3
regime interaction and, 80

Convention on the Prevention and Punishment of Genocide, 95–9

Convention on the Rights of the Child (CRC)
Democratic Republic of Congo v. *Uganda* and, 63–5
extraterritoriality and, 54–8
jurisdiction in, 60–3

Convention on the Settlement of Investment Disputes (ICSID)
'Exit' and 'Voice' dichotomy in, 93–5
investment claim countermeasures and, 389–91
investment treaty compatibility with, 90–3
lex specialis principle and, 391–3
state recognition and, 203–4

coordination principle, third party countermeasures and, 352–6

Corfu Channel Case, 47–8, 302–3

corporate misconduct, State complicity with corporate human rights breaches and, 321–4

Costa Rica, Palestinian statehood supported by, 239–42

Côte d'Ivoire, regime change in, 169–70

Council of the League of Nations, 147–9

'counter-limits' (*controlimiti*), European Community legal order and, 99–105
countermeasures
  in investment treaty claims, 389–405
  by third parties, 340–1, 362
counter-terrorist politics
  Kosovo and, 161–6
  state immunity and, 182–8
  Western Sahara territorial disposition and, 157–61
Court of Appeal of England and Wales, 177–9
Court of Justice of the European Union (CJEU), 407–11
  EU Member States' international agreements and, 409–11
  need for EU coordination and, 413
  Opinion 1/94 of, 408–9
  Opinion 2/91, 413
Covenant of the League of Nations, 147–9
CPI v. *Mexico*, 399–401n40
Craven, Matthew, 273–83
Crawford, James
  The Creation of States in International Law and, xv–xvi, xxi, 144–7, 273–7
  'The Creation of the State of Palestine: Too Much Too Soon,' 229–31
  'Democracy in International Law' lecture, 93–5
  democratisation of international law, quest for, 93–5
  early life and career, xi–xix
  Eurotunnel partial award and, 426, 436
  on evolution of international law, 88–9
  human rights laws and, 51–4
  investment claim countermeasures and, 389–91, 405
  legacy of, xx–xxv, 51–4
  on legal characteristics of states, 144–5, 151–2
  mixed multi-party disputes and work of, 421–2
  on Palestinian statehood, 229–31
  on presumption of sovereignty, 80n51
  on regime interaction, 83–4
  on sector theory, 111–14
  on state continuity and succession, 273–7, 283–4
  on statehood, 155–6, 172
  on state immunity, 173–7, 310–15
  on State responsibility, 287–8, 291–292n21, 297–301
  on third party countermeasures, 340–1, 343–7
  third party countermeasures and, 352–60
  U.S.-Antidumping and Countervailing Duties (China) and, 363–4
  uti posssidetis principle and work of, 248–72
Crawford, James Allen, xiii
Crawford, Josephine Margaret, xiii
Crimes at Sea Act, xvii
Croatia, international recognition of, 196–8
Cuba
  Palestinian statehood supported by, 242–3
  third party countermeasures and, 343–7
customary international law. *See* international law
Cyprus
  Anastasiou case and, 177–9
  international recognition of, 205–6
  Turkish occupation of, 67–70
Cyprus v. *Turkey*, 177–9

Declaration of Maroua, 262–4
Declaration of Yaoundé II, 262–4
decolonisation
  self-determination and, 210–13, 221–7
  state continuity and succession and, 279–83

statehood recognition and, 232n11
uti possidetis principle and, 250–2
Decolonising International Law (Pahuja), 20–1
deep sea technologies, *uti possidetis* principle, marine space territorialisation, 250–2
degeneration, cliché as expression of, 4–5
de jure recognition of states, 198n30, 202, 204–5
de lege ferenda, State complicity with corporate human rights breaches and, 321–4
Democratic Republic of Congo v. *Uganda*, 51–4, 56–8
  extraterritorial applicability in, 63–5
  International Covenant on Civil and Political Rights applicability in, 60–3
  'legal space' concept in, 67–70
Democratic Republic of Congo (DRC)
  'legal space' concept and law of occupation and, 67–70
  separation barrier with Uganda, 56–8
Democratic Republic of Vietnam, 202–4
democratisation
  in international law, 93–5
  regime change and, 166–70
Demopoulos case, 177–9
Denmark, Arctic sovereignty issues and, 118–24
Denning (Lord), 177–9
developing countries, Kosovo air strikes opposed by, 26–7
'Diaoyu Dao, an Inherent Territory of China', 131–3
Dictionary of Received Ideas, 6–7
Diplock, Lord, 182–8
diplomatic protection
  investment treaty claims and, 391–3
  State responsibility and, 295n39
direct effect doctrine, European Community legal order and, 99–105
disclaimers, in law of recognition, 205–6
dispute settlement, PCIJ and ICJ activities concerning, 304
domestic courts, extraterritoriality in rulings by, 56–7
domestic law
  autonomy of international responsibility from, 292–6
  'Exit' and 'Voice' dichotomy and, 109
  international law and rule of irrelevance of, 93–5
  investment treaty case law and, 105–8
  sovereignty and regime interaction and, 80n50
  State immunity cases and, 310–15
  US civil rights litigation and international law and, 95–9
Dominican Republic, Haitian regime change and, 166–70
Don Pacifico affair, 341
Douglas, Zachary, 401–3
Drago-Porter Convention, 342–3
Droit de gens, 277–9
dualism, statehood dynamics and, 174–5
dubio mitius principle, 385n95
due diligence
  State complicity with corporate human rights breaches and, 321–4
  State responsibility and PCASP protection, 315–21
due process
  investment treaties and, 90–3
  third party countermeasures and, 356–60
Dugard, John, 231–2n11, 234, 341–2
Dumbarton Oaks Conference, law of recognition and, 192–6
Dutch East Indies, 213–15
  decolonisation and, 221–2
duty of cooperation
  Member States' compliance with EU laws and, 414–15

duty of cooperation (*cont.*)
  USU Target System of Terminal Dues and, 415–17

East Asia
  Chinese Senkaku/Diaoyudao claims and traditional law in, 141–3
  palimpestic aspects of sovereignty in, 138–41
  palimpsestic reconstruction of sovereignty in, 139–41
  Senkaku/Diaoyudao dispute and sovereignty concepts in, 131–3
  sovereignty issues in, 126–43
  traditional regional order in, Chinese Senkaku/Diaoyudao claims and, 134–6
Eastern Carelia opinion, 147–9
Eastern Europe, state continuity and succession in, 273–7
Eastern Greenland case, 124–5
  polar sovereignty and, 111–14
East Timor, Indonesian invasion of, 227–8
East Timor Case (Portugal v. *Australia)*, 227–8
EC-Hormones case, 385n95
Economic Community of West African States (ECOWAS)
  intervention in Côte d'Ivoire, 169–70
  interventions in Liberia and Sierra Leone by, 47–8
Ecuador
  investment treaty claims and, 90–3
  third party countermeasures and, 343–7
effects test, investment treaty case law and, 105–8
Eichmann, Adolf, 4–5, 47–8
Eliot, T. S., 14
El Salvador, Gulf of Fonseca boundary dispute and, 258–9, 260–2
Enrica Lexie incident, 307–8, 310–21
environmental institutions, regime interaction and, 73–8, 81
Environment Protection and Biodiversity Conservation Act 1999 (EPBC Act) (Australia), 114–17
epistemic communities, international relations scholarship on, 73–8
equality of states, Chinese Senkaku/Diaoyudao claims and, 134–6
equal protection clause (U.S. Constitution), international law and, 95–9
erga omnes dictum
  State responsibility and, 297–301
  third party countermeasures and, 343–7, 356–60
ethnic identity, self-determination and, 221
EULEX, Kosovo independence and, 161–6
European Community (EC)
  'Exit' and 'Voice' dichotomy in law of, 93–5, 99–105
  integration of, constitutional implications for, 99–105
  investment treaties and law of, 90–3
European Convention on Human Rights (ECHR)
  extraterritoriality and, 54–6
  human rights obligations in non-sovereign territory of treaty parties, 67–70
  jurisdiction 'triggers' and, 58–63
  State responsibility concerning investment treaty claims and, 391–3
European Court of Human Rights, 56–7
  'exceptional' nature of extraterritoriality and, 65–7
  extraterritoriality in cases of, 65–7
  human rights obligations in non-sovereign territory of treaty parties, 67–70
  law of state responsibility and, 177–9
  Namibia exception and, 177–9
  recognition as intentional act under, 198–202
  restrictive immunity doctrine and, 187–8
  State complicity with corporate human rights breaches and, 321–4

state immunity principles and, 182–7n52, 188
Turkish occupation of Cyprus and, 67–70
European Court of Justice
European Community legal order and, 99–105
law of recognition and, 177–9
national courts and, 90–3
European Union
allocation of competences and external relations of, 407–11
Anastasiou case and, 177–9
Canadian asbestos dispute and, 81
disclaimers in state recognition by, 205–6
Eritrea recognition by, 192–6
exclusive competence regarding international agreements, 407–9
external relations of, 406–20
future challenges in external relations of, 419–20
international organisations and position of, 411–12
investment treaty claims and, 90–3
Kosovo intervention and, 161–6
Member States' compliance with law of, 414–15
Member States' international agreements and, 409–11
need for coordination in, 413
postal services in, 415–17
recognition of Kosovo by, 192–6
recognition of South Sudan by, 196–8
representation of, in international institutions, 412–13
telecommunications regulations in, 417–19
USU Target System of Terminal Dues and, 415–17
Eurotunnel dispute
applicable law and jurisdiction in, 426–7
claimants' position in, 427–8
damage determination in, 439
facts and background on, 422–3
failure to protect against incursions in, 432–4
favouritism towards SNCF and Port of Calais in, 434
Invitation to Promoters in, 429–32
joint and several responsibility findings in, 427–32
legacy of, 439–41
legal claims in, 425–6
Millett dissent in, 436–8
partial award in, 426–36, 439
respondents' position in, 428
Sangatte claim findings in, 432–5
shared responsibility in, 434–5, 436–8
Tribunal's analysis in, 429–32
EU-US Transatlantic Trade and Investment Partnership, 90–3
Evans, Gareth, 40
Exclusive Economic Zones (EEZs)
Colombian-Nicaraguan boundary dispute and, 267–70
Senkaku/Diaoyudao Islands dispute and, 128–30
'Exit' and 'Voice' dichotomy
case law on investment treaties, comparative law perspective, 105–8
comparative law approach and, 109
European Community legal order and, 99–105
in investment treaties, 93–5
U.S. civil rights litigation and international law and, 95–9
experts, enhanced role of, regime interaction and, 82–3
extraterritoriality
'exceptional' nature of in human rights law, 65–7
of free-standing obligations in treaties, ICJ affirmation of, 63–5
human rights law in context of, 51–4
of jurisdiction, ICJ ruling on, 60–3
'legal space' concept and, 67–70
treaty law framework on, 54–6

Factory at Chorzów case, State responsibility in, 292–6, 296n44
factual exceptionalism
 Banković case and, 65–7
 third party countermeasures and, 356–60
failed states
 UN Security Council intervention in, 155–6
 Western Sahara territorial disposition states and concept of, 161
Fayt, Carlos, 90–3
Federal Court of Australia, 114–17
Federal Republic of Yugoslavia (FRY), 161–6
 recognition of Bosnia-Herzegovina by, 196–8
 state continuity and succession and dismantling of, 279–83
Federated States of Micronesia, 155–6
Finland, Palestine statehood supported by, 239–42
Firearms Act of 1968 (United Kingdom), 315–21
fisheries law
 Arctic sovereignty issues and, 118–21
 Barbados maritime boundary dispute and, 265
 comparison of ICJ/PCIJ jurisprudence on, 302–3
 regime interaction and, 71–3, 77, 88–9
 Senkaku/Diaoyudao Islands dispute and, 128–30
 State responsibility and, 303n72
flag States
 firearms regulations, privately contracted armed security personnel compliance with, 315–21
 responsibilities, PCASP protection and, 315–21
Food and Agriculture Organisation (FAO)
 accountability to sovereign states of, 84
 EU membership in, 411–12
 experts' role in, 82–3
 regime interaction and, 80
forceful intervention. *See also* responsibility to protect (R2P); unilateral intervention
 in Kosovo, 161–6
 regime change and, 166–70
 third party countermeasures and, 341, 360–2
 Western Sahara territorial disposition states and issue of, 161
foreign policy issues, third party countermeasures and, 350
foreign state immunity, Crawford's work on, xvi–xvii
Forest Carbon Partnership Facility (World Bank), 81, 81n56
Fortier, L. Yves, 426
fourteenth amendment (U.S. Constitution), international law and, 95–9
Fragd decision, European Community legal order and, 99–105
fragmentation of international law
 norm conflicts and, 71–3
 regime interaction and, 71–89
France
 Antarctic sovereignty and, 114–17
 European Community legal order and, 99–105
 Eurotunnel dispute and, 421–41
 Geneva Agreements of 20 July 1954 and, 202–4
 intervention in Côte d'Ivoire and, 169–70
 partition of Cameroon and, 262–4
 recognition of Serbia by, 192–6
 SS Lotus Case (France v. *Turkey)* and, 80n51
 Syrian chemical weapons attack and, 38–9, 347–51
 Syrian weapons shipments and, 44–6
 third party countermeasures and, 352–6

Turkish negligent navigation prosecution against, 310–15
Vessel Protection Detachments for piracy defence from, 310–15
Western Sahara territorial disposition states and, 161
France-Manche S.A., 422–3
Sangatte migrants and, 425–6
Frente Polisario, 157–61
"Friends of the Syrian People International Working Group on Sanctions", 347–51
frontier controls, in Eurotunnel dispute, 432–4
Frontini case, European Community legal order and, 99–105
functional immunity, piracy defence and issues of, 310–15

Gabčíkovo Nagymaros judgment, 297–301
Gaddafi, Muammar, 34–5n51, 36
Gaelic language protections, European Community legal order and, 99–105
Gbagbo Laurent (President), 169–70
General Agreement on Trade and Services (GATS), 365–9
Geneva Additional Protocol I
collateral damage in, 325–7
qualifying words pertaining to collateral civilian damage in, 327–9
Geneva Agreements of 20 July 1954, 202–4
geopolitics, UN Security Council and, 155–6
Georgia, Palestinian statehood supported by, 236–9
Georgia, Russian invasion of, 31n34, 51–4, 56–8
Georgia v. *Russia*, 51–4
'free-standing' approach in, 63–5
'legal space' concept and, 67–70
German classical school, statehood theory and, 172
Germany
colonisation of Cameroon by, 262–4
European Community legal order and, 99–105
investment treaty claims in, 396n23
neutrality concerning Palestinian statehood, 241–2
third party countermeasures and, 343–7
The Wimbeldon case, 149–50
Germany v. *Italy* case, 187–8
Ghana, *ARA Libertad* case and, 389–91
Gladstone, W. E., xiv
global environmental issues, normative conflicts over, 71–3
globalisation, sovereignty demands and, 78–84
Goff, Lord, 182–8
good faith obligation, in public law, 107–8
governmental authority
law of immunity and test of, 188–90
law of state responsibility and, 179–82
Palestinian statehood and principle of, 236–9
public body concept and, 365–9, 381–3
restrictive immunity doctrine and, 182–8
statehood dynamics and, 173–7, 188–90
governmental liability doctrine, European Community legal order and, 99–105
Granital decision, European Community legal order and, 99–105
Greece
Don Pacifico affair in, 341
EU compliance by, 414–15
International Maritime Organization and, 409
recognition of Macedonia by, 196–8
'Green March' (Morocco), 157–61
Groener decision, European Community legal order and, 99–105

Grotius, Hugo, 172
Group of 77, Kosovo air strikes opposed by, 26–7
Group of 77 states
  international legal order and, 141–3
  opposition to humanitarian intervention among, 26–7
'Group of Friends of the Syrian People', 347–51
Guantanamo Bay detentions, legal black hole cliché and, 18–20
The Guardian, 45–6
  investment treaty claims in, 90–3
Guatemala, *uti possidetis/uti possidetis juris* principle and, 254n24
Guilfoyle, Douglas, 307–24
Guillaume, Gilbert, 426
Guinea Bissau/Senegal case, 249–50, 257n33, 270–2
Gulf of Fonseca, maritime boundary dispute concerning, 258–9, 260–2
Gumplowicz, Ludwig, 175–6
'gunboat diplomacy', third party countermeasures and, 341

Hague, William, 44–5
The Hague Academy, Crawford's courses at, xxi–xxii
The Hague Agreement, 213–15
The Hague Regulations of 1907, responsibility to protect and, 34–6
Haiti, UN Security Council intervention in, 166–70
Hale, Brenda Lady, 63–5
Haltern, Ulrich, 105
Hammerskjöld, Åke, 149
Han-key Lee, 141–3
Hans Island, Arctic sovereignty issues over, 118–21
Happy Days, 14, 17–18
Heard Island (Australia), 114–17
Hegelian philosophy
  East Asian sovereignty in context of, 139–41
  state continuity and succession and, 277–9
Henkin, Louis, 17
Hesperides case, 177–9
High Risk Area
  Privately Contracted Armed Security Personnel protection in, 315–21
'hinterland' principle, polar sovereignty and, 111–14
historic title principle
  Chinese position on Senkaku/Diaoyudao dispute and, 131–3
  critique of Chinese claims in Senkaku/Diaoyudao Islands claim based on, 134–6
  Japanese position in Senkaku/Diaoyudao Islands claims and, 133–4
Hollande, François, 39
Holtzendorff, E. von, 344
Holy See, statehood status for, 241–2
Honduras
  Gulf of Fonseca boundary dispute and, 258–9, 260–2
  Nicaraguan boundary dispute with, 265–7
Horn of Africa, piracy cases and 'legal space' concept and, 67–70
Huber, Max, 111–14, 144–5, 149
Humane Society International (HSI), 114–17
Human Rights Advisory Panel, Kosovo human rights violations and, 161–6
human rights law
  'exceptional' nature of exterritoriality and, 65–7
  extraterritoriality and, 51–4
  investment treaties and, 90–3
  Kosovo violations of, 161–6
  'legal space' concept in, 67–70
  NGO involvement in, 73–8
  nonratification by U.S. of human rights treaties, 90–3, 95–9
  normative conflicts over, 71–3
  State complicity with corporate human rights breaches and, 321–4
  territorial control and, 58–60

UN Security Council powers concerning, 24–5

Ilaşcu case, State complicity with corporate human rights breaches and, 321–4
Ilulissat Declaration, 121–4
immigrant issues, Eurotunnel dispute and, 425–6
Imperial Map of Native and Foreign Lands *(Huangchao Zhongwai Yitong Yutu)*, 131–3
imputation theory, statehood dynamics and, 173–7
inclusio unius, exclusio alterius principle, self-determination in West Papua and, 224–7
independence
Kosovo intervention and establishment of, 161–6
legal characteristics of states and, 145–7
Permanent Court of International Justice and, 147–9
self-determination in West Papua and, 210–13, 224–7
uti possidetis principle in Africa and, 252–8, 262–4
India
Enrica Lexie incident and, 307–8, 310–15
recognition of South Sudan by, 196–8
Indian Penal Code, *Enrica Lexie* incident and, 310–15
indigenous rights
legal framework for, 88
regime interaction with institutions for, 73–8
West New Guinea decolonisation and, 213–15
individual criminal responsibility
collateral civilian casualties and, 325–7
threshold for, in collateral damage rulings, 329–30
individual liability, Eurotunnel dispute and, 427–8
Indonesia
independence of, 213–15
invasion of East Timor by, 227–8
Soviet arms shipments to, 217–19
West Papua incorporation into, 209–28
West Papua nationalism and, 215–16
Indonesian Communist Party, 217–19
in dubio pro libertate principle, independence *vs.* sovereignty and, 147–9
'inherent territory' principle, Chinese position on Senkaku/Diaoyudao dispute and, 131–3
In Larger Freedom (Annan), 32–3
In re Gilbert, 310–15
Institut de Droit International, 198–202, 204–5
Crawford's presence at, xviii, xx–xxv
third party countermeasures and, 347–51, 356–60
insult, cliché as expression of, 4–5
integration, self-determination in West Papua and, 224–7
intent
in piracy defence, State responsibility and immunity and, 310–15
state recognition and element of, 198–202
Inter-American Commission on Human Rights
'exceptionalism' of extraterritoriality and, 65–7
extraterritoriality and, 54–7
Haitian intervention and, 166–70
jurisdiction in, 60–5
Inter-American Declaration of the Rights and Duties of Man
extraterritoriality and, 54–6
jurisdiction in, 60–5
Intergovernmental Commission (IGC), in Eurotunnel dispute, 422–3, 429–34

inter-governmental organisations (IGOs)
  accountability and assessment of, 84
  regime interaction and, 73–8, 81–2
Interim Accord of 13 September 1995, 196–8
Interim Agreement between Israel and the PLO, 239–42
international armed conflict collateral civilian casualties and, 325–7
International Association of Machinists and Aerospace Workers v. *OPEC*, 182–8
International Coalition for the Responsibility to Protect, 49n110
International Code of Conduct for Private Security Services Providers (ICoC), 315–21
International Commission on Intervention and State Sovereignty (ICISS)
  Constitutive Act of the African Union and, 29–30
  responsibility to protect and, 28–9, 32–3, 41–2, 48–50
International Committee of the Red Cross
  Customary IHL Study, 327–9
International Committee of the Red Cross and Crescent (CRC), collateral civilian damage qualifications and, 327–9
International Committee on Economic, Social and Cultural Rights (ICESCR)
  'exceptional' nature of extraterritoriality and, 65–7
  Wall Advisory Opinion and, 63–5
International Court of Justice (ICJ)
  Accordance with International Law of the Unilateral Declaration of Independence in Respect of Kosovo opinion, 273–7
  affirmation of extraterritorial 'jurisdiction' by, 60–3
  Case Concerning the land and maritime boundary between Cameroon and Nigeria, Equatorial Guinea Intervening, 262–4
  comparison of Permanent Court of International Justice with, 302–3
  Corfu Channel Case, 47–8
  East Timor self-determination opinions and, 227–8
  'exceptional' nature of exterritoriality in human rights law and, 65–7
  extraterritoriality applicability in rulings by, 56–8, 59–60n22
  free-standing obligations in treaties, extraterritoriality in, 63–5
  human rights cases before, 51–4
  ICL collaboration with, on State responsibility, 297–301
  impact on international human rights law of, 70
  implied powers of international institutions and, 81–2
  investment claim countermeasures and, 389–91
  investment treaty law and, 107–8
  Kosovo independence and, 161–6
  Land, Island and Maritime Frontier Dispute, 260–2
  Namibia Advisory Opinion, 58–60, 177–9
  Nicaragua Case, 40n72, 41–2
  normative principles of State responsibility and, 288–91
  Nuclear Weapons opinion of, 147–9
  on-going codification by, 305
  polar sovereignty issues and, 110–11
  primary and secondary rules of military necessity and, 337–8
  regime theory and practices of, 73–8
  restrictive immunity doctrine and, 187–8
  State actors in non-sovereign territory of treaty parties, treaty obligations in, 67–70

statehood recognition and, 192–6
state recognition in opinions of, 198–202, 204–5
State responsibility and jurisprudence of, 287–8, 297–305
State responsibility in piracy defence and, 315–21
third party countermeasures and, 356–60
treaty law framework for extraterritoriality and, 54–6
uti possidetis principle and, 249–50, 255–8, 270–2
Western Sahara territorial disposition and, 157–61
WTO Appellate Body's interpretation of 'public body' concept and, 369–73

International Covenant on Civil and Political Rights (ICCPR)
'exceptional' nature of extraterritoriality and, 65–7
extraterritoriality and, 54–8, 60–3
U.S. ratification of, 95–9

International Covenant on Economic, Social and Cultural Rights (ICESCR), 54–6, 60–5

International Criminal Court (ICC)
collateral civilian casualties and, 325–7, 339
Palestinian statehood and, 242–6
qualifying words pertaining to collateral civilian damage and, 327–9
state *vs.* individual responsibility thresholds for collateral damage and, 329–30

international criminal law
Brussels Convention rules on criminal jurisdiction over collisions and, 310–15
collateral civilian casualties and, 325–7
State responsibility and, 297–301
state *vs.* individual responsibility thresholds for collateral damage and, 329–30

International Criminal Tribunal for the Former Yugoslavia, 33–34n45, 297–301
binary analytic mindset concerning collateral damage in, 331
military necessity principle and, 332–7

international criminal tribunals, national legal systems and, 161–6

international humanitarian law
binary analytic mindset concerning, 331
collateral civilian casualties and, 339
collateral civilian damage and, 327–9
military necessity principle and, 332
primary and secondary rules of military necessity and, 337–8
specific rules of military necessity and, 332–7
state *vs.* individual responsibility thresholds for collateral damage and, 329–30

international human rights instruments
extraterritoriality and, 54–6, 63–5
ICJ rulings and, 60–3

international institutions
EU position in, 411–12
implied powers of, 81–2
investment treaties and, 90–3
legal framework for, 84
observer status for, 80
Palestinian statehood question and admission to, 245–6
regime interaction and, 73–8
'regimes' of, 73–5n14, 78
representation of EU in, 412–13
third party countermeasures and, 342–3

International Labour Organisation, EU Member States' international agreements and, 409–11

international law. *See also* treaty law
Chinese ascendancy and, 137–8, 141–3

international law (*cont.*)
Chinese claims in Senkaku/Diaoyudao Islands dispute and, 134–6, 139–141n46
clichés in, 7–14
collateral damage in, 325–7
Crawford's democratisation efforts in, 93–5
Crawford/s influence in, xx–xxv
in Eurotunnel dispute, 426–7
evolution and adaptation of, 88–9
extraterritorial applications of human rights law and, 51–4
fragmentation of, 71–89
independence principle in, 147–9
investment claim countermeasures and, 389–91
investment treaties and, 90–3
Japanese Senkaku/Diaoyudao Islands claims and, 136–7, 139–141n46
law of recognition and, 192–6, 204–5
legal characteristics of states in, 145–7
Palestinian statehood and, 229–31
palimpsestic reconstruction in, 139–41
Permanent Court of International Justice rulings and, 151–2
piracy and, 307–8
polar sovereignty and, 121–4
privately contracted armed security personnel protection and, 315–21
'regimes' of, 73–5n14, 78
regime theory and, 73–8
responsibility to protect and, 23–50
rise of China in, 126–8
rousing of clichés in, 15–21
rules on interpretation of UNGA resolutions and, 234–42
safety on merchant vessels and, 315–21
self-determination in, 210–13
sovereignty demands and, 79–80, 84
state continuity and succession and, 273–84
statehood dynamics and, 173–7
state immunity in, 182–8
State responsibility and, 288–9n9, 291, 302n67
territorial disposition by UN Security Council and, 156–66
third party countermeasures and, 343–51, 356–60
uti possidetis principle and, 248–52
visual clichés in, 9–10, 20–1
West Papuan self-determination and violations of, 227–8
International Law as an Open System (Crawford), 389–91
International Law Commission (ILC)
Articles on Responsibility of States for Internationally Wrongful Acts limits on military necessity and, 334–7
Articles on State Responsibility, 47–8, 173–82, 188–90, 288–91
consequences of breach of State responsibility, 393–4
defence against piracy and, 308–9
Draft Articles on Diplomatic Protection, 391–3
fragmentation of international law and, 71–3
Guiding Principles on statehood and, 234–42
on humanitarian law, 336n53
ICJ collaboration with, on State responsibility, 297–301, 304–5
investment claim countermeasures and, 389–91
law of recognition and opinions of, 198–202, 203, 204–5
'master plan' for State responsibility of, 292, 297
mixed multi-party disputes and, 421–2
Namibia exception and, 177–9
public body concept and, 365–9
relevance to SCM Agreement of, 375–83
'special regimes' concept and, 73–8
on State responsibility, 287–8

State responsibility to investment treaty claims and, 391–4
status of articles on 'public body', 383–7
third party countermeasures and, 340–1, 343–7, 352–60, 396–7
U.S.-Antidumping and Countervailing Duties (China) and, 363–4
WTO Appellate Body's interpretation of 'public body' concept and, 369–73
International Law Commission Commentary, Articles on Responsibility of States for Internationally Wrongful Acts limits on military necessity and, 334–7
international legal system, responsibility to protect and, 48–50
International Maritime Organization (IMO)
Court of Justice of the European Union and, 409
Guidance to Shipowners by, 315–21
guidelines for PCASP from, 315–21
international relations scholarship
on Chinese-U.S. relations, 126–8
European Union external relationships and, 406–7
Palestinian statehood and, 229n3
regime interaction in, 73–8
rise of China in, 126–8
Senkaku/Diaoyudao Islands dispute and, 139–41
international responsibility, investment treaty claims and, 391–4
international security, Western Sahara territorial disposition states and concept of, 161
International Standards Organisation (ISO), PCASP certification and, 315–21
International Telecommunications Regulations (EU), 417–19
International Telecommunication Union (ITU), 417–19
international terrorism
definitions of, 162n46
Kosovo and, 161–6
Western Sahara territorial disposition and, 157–61
international trade
human rights institutions and, 73–8
regime for, 73–8
International Tribunal for the Law of the Sea, State responsibility in piracy defence and, 315–21
internet, International Telecommunication Regulations and, 417–19
inter-regime scrutiny, regime interaction and, 84
inter-State proceedings
ADM v. *Mexico* investment claims and, 398–9
investment claim countermeasures and, 389–91
intervention. *See* forceful intervention
intra-regime interaction, institutional organisations and, 73–8
investment arbitration tribunals, investment treaty case law and, 105–8
investment treaties
case law, comparative law perspective on, 105–8
countermeasures in investment claims and, 394–404
exit/voice dichotomy in, 93–5
ICSID Convention and, 90–3
legitimacy of, 90–109
NAFTA-based investment treaty claims and, 397–404
State responsibility concerning claims, ILC applicability in, 391–4
third party countermeasures in claims against, 396–7
Ionesco, Eugene, 14
Iran–US Claims Tribunal, investment treaty law and, 107–8
Iraq, third party countermeasures and, 352–6

Iraq War, responsibility to protect and, 30–1
Ireland, European Community legal order and Gaelic language protection in, 99–105
Island of Palmas Arbitration, 111–14, 139–141n46
Israel
  Eichmann trial and, 47–8
  ICJ on jurisdiction of, 60–3
  'legal space' concept and Palestinian occupation, 67–70
  military necessity claims and collateral damage by, 338n59
  occupation of Palestinian Territories by, 56–8, 60–3
  Palestinian statehood resolutions and, 233–234n16, 236–9
  rejection of extraterritoriality rulings by, 56–8
  Vessel Protection Detachments for piracy defence from, 310–15
  Wall Advisory Opinion and, 63–5
Italian Constitutional Court, European Community legal order and, 99–105
Italy
  Enrica Lexie incident and, 307–8, 310–15
  European Community legal order and, 99–105
  Palestinian statehood supported by, 244n72
  Vessel Protection Detachments for piracy defence from, 310–15

Jamaica, Palestine statehood opposed by, 241–2
Japan
  Antarctic sovereignty and, 114–17
  European law and Senkaku/Diaoyudao Islands claims, 141–3
  functional immunity case against U.S. in, 310–15
  history of Senkaku/Diaoyudao Islands ownership and, 128–30
  overview of Senkaku/Diaoyudao claims, 133–4
  Palestinian statehood supported by, 239–42
  polar sovereignty issues and, 110–11
  postwar economic and financial rise of, 141–3
  recognition of South Sudan by, 196–8
  Senkaku/Diaoyudao Islands dispute with China and, 126–8
Japan v. *Girard*, 310–15
Jellinek, Georg, 172
Jennings, Robert (Sir), 198–202
Jessup, Philip, 174–5
Johns, Fleur, 18–20
Johnson, D. H. N., xviii
'Joint and Several Responsibility'
  Eurotunnel dispute and, 427–32
  reciprocity in, 435–6
joint liability, Eurotunnel dispute and, 427–8
joint statements, third party countermeasures and, 356–60
Jones and Others v. *UK*, 187n52, 188
Jordan, third party countermeasures and, 352–6
Joyce, James, 14
jure gestionis, maritime law and piracy defence and, 310–15
jure imperii
  maritime law and piracy defence and, 310–15
  state immunity and, 188–90
jurisdiction
  in ECHR, 58–60
  in Eurotunnel dispute, 426–7
  'exceptional' nature of, 65–7
  extraterritoriality and, 54–6, 58, 60–3
  free-standing obligations in treaties, ICJ affirmation of, 63–5
  'legal space' concept and, 67–70
  in *Namibia* Advisory Opinion, 58–60
Jurisdiction of Courts of Danzig opinion, 151–2

jus ad bellum, primary and secondary rules of military necessity and, 337–8
jus cogens principle
 responsibility to protect and, 40–50
 State responsiblity and, 297–301
 weapons shipments and, 45–6
jus in bello, primary and secondary rules of military necessity and, 337–8
justice, visual clichés of, 10

Kelsen, Hans, 173–7, 231–4
Kennedy, David, 17–18
Kerry, John (Secretary of State), 39
Kibris Turk Hava Yollari v. *Secretary of State for Transport*, 177–9
Kirby, Michael, xvi
Kissinger, Henry, 126–8
Kompetenz-Kompetenz problem, European Community legal order and, 99–105
Korean War, UN Security Council powers during, 24–5
Koskenniemi, Martti, 71–3, 90–3
Kosovo
 humanitarian crisis in, 26–7n16, 27n17
 international recognition of, 198–202, 206–7
 regime change and crisis in, 166–70
 state continuity and succession in, 273–7
 statehood recognition and advisory proceedings on, 192–6
 territorial disposition in, 161–6
Kosovo Advisory Opinion, 198–202
Krabbe, Hugo, 173–7
Kriegsraison geht vor Kriegsmanier doctrine, military necessity principle and, 332–7
Krupp case, military necessity principle and, 332–7
Kuwait Air Co. case, 182–90
Kuwali, Dan, 29–30
Kyodo Senpaku Kaisha, 114–17

Laband, Paul, 172
la conscience juridique, Schachter's concept of, 15
LaGrand opinion, 151–2
Land, Island and Maritime Frontier Dispute, 260–2, 265, 267–72
Latin America
 competing colonial interpretations *uti possidetis* in, 252–8
 early maritime boundary disputes in, 258–70
 Honduran-Nicaraguan boundary dispute and decolonisation in, 265–7
 origins of *uti possidetis* principle in, 250–2
 third party countermeasures in, 341
Lauterpacht, Hersch, 277–9
Lauterpacht Research Centre on International Law, 51–4
 Crawford at, xx–xxv
Lavrov, Sergey, 31n34
law of collective security, third party countermeasures and, 352–6
law of countermeasures, third party countermeasures and, 352–6
law of occupation, 'legal space' concept and, 67–70
law of the sea
 international regime for, 73–8
 uti possidetis principle and maritime boundary disputes, 248–52
League of Arab States, Syrian suspension from, 347–51
legal black hole, cliché of, 18–20
legal characteristics of states, 144–52
 basic principles, 145–7
 independence *vs.* sovereignty and, 147–9
 international/national divide concerning, 151–2
 Permanent Court of International Justice sovereignty rulings and, 149–50
 statehood dynamics and, 173–7
Legal Counsel of the UN, 157–61
legal fictions, statehood dynamics and, 173–7

legal personality principle, state continuity and succession and, 273–7
legal sovereignty, statehood dynamics and, 173–7
'legal space' concept, human rights obligations and, 67–70
legitimacy
  of European Community legal order, 99–105
  'Exit' and 'Voice' dichotomy in investment treaties and, 93–5
  of investment treaties, 90–109
  of non-state actors, sovereignty demands and, 84
Leigh, Monroe, 90–3
lex generalis, primary and secondary rules of military necessity and, 337–8
lex horrenda principle, third party countermeasures and, 343–7
lex specialis
  Eurotunnel dispute and, 436
  mixed multi-party disputes and, 421–2
  NAFTA investment treaty claims and, 397–404
  primary and secondary rules of military necessity and, 337–8
  public body concept and, 365–9, 371–3
  regime theory and, 73–8
  State responsibility concerning investment treaty claims and, 391–3
Liberia, ECOWAS intervention in, 47–8
Libya
  arms embargo in, 43–4
  humanitarian crisis in, 34–6, 36n56
  no-fly zone established in, 37–8
Lisbon Treaty
  EU Member States' international agreements and, 409–11
  European Union external relationships and, 406–7
Loizidou case, State complicity with corporate human rights breaches and, 321–4
loss, cliché as expression of, 4–5
The Lotus case, 147–9, 302–3, 303n72
  piracy defence and rulings of, 310–15

Maastricht judgment (German Constitutional Court), European Community legal order and, 99–105
Mabo case, xvii–xviii
Macedonia, international recognition of, 196–8, 205–6
Macquarie Island (Australia), 114–17
Maine, Henry Sir, 173–7
Malay Indonesians, rights of, 213–15
Mali, Western Sahara territorial disposition states and, 161
maritime law
  Arctic sovereignty issues and, 118–21
  Barbados maritime boundary dispute and, 265
  Beagle Channel arbitration, 259–60
  Brussels Convention rules on criminal jurisdiction over collisions and, 310–15
  Cameroon-Nigerian boundary dispute and, 262–4
  Colombian-Nicaraguan boundary dispute and, 267–70
  Gulf of Fonseca boundary dispute and, 258–9
  Honduran-Nicaraguan boundary dispute and, 265–7
  piracy defence and, 310–15
  polar sovereignty and, 124–5
  State responsibility under, 315–24
  uti possidetis principle in maritime boundary dispute resolution, 255–8, 270–2
Martin, Paul, 31–2
Mawson, Douglas (Sir), 114–17
McCorquodale, Robert, 321–4
McDonald Island (Australia), 114–17
McEwen, A. C., 256n32, 271

McLuhan, Marshall, 13–14
Mediterranean high seas,
migration-related cases and 'legal space' concept and, 67–70
Meetings of the Parties (MoPs), State responsibility law and, 304–5
Medhi, Rostane, 250–2
Melanesian West Papuans, rights of, 213–15
mens rea, collateral civilian casualties and, 325–7
metaphors, clichés and, 12–13
Mexico, NAFTA investment treaty claim countermeasures and, 397–404
migration-related cases, 'legal space' concept and, 67–70
military necessity
  Articles on Responsibility of States for Internationally Wrongful Acts limits on, 334–7
  collateral damage and concept of, 332
  primary and secondary rules of, 337–8
  special rules for incorporation of, 332–7
Millett, Lord, 426, 436–8
Milošević, Slobodan, 162n47
Ming Dynasty, history of Senkaku/Diaoyudao Islands ownership and, 128–30
minimum regime concept, State responsibility and PCASP protection and, 315–21
MINURSO, 157–61. *See* United Nations Mission for the Referendum in Western Sahara
MINUSTAH, 166–70. *See* United Nations Stabilisation Mission in Haiti
mistaken of self-defence, piracy protection and, 310–15
mitigation, responsibility to protect role in, 47–8
mixed multi-party disputes, State responsibility in, 421–41
modern laws, of State responsibility, 291–301
Mongolia, third party countermeasures and, 345n29
monism, statehood dynamics and, 174–5
monopolies of rights and representation, regime interaction and, 83–4
Montevideo Convention, recognition of states under, 198–202
Morocco, 'Green March' into Western Sahara by, 157–61
multilateral treaties. *See also* treaty law
  impact on internal law of, 95–9
  UN General Assembly resolutions and, 242–6
multinational naval deployment, piracy and, 307–8
Musil, Robert, 9–10
musyawarah practices, 224n59, 227
  West Papua self-determination and, 218, 219–20

Namba v. *McCourt*, 95–9
Namibia Advisory Opinion, 51–4
  law of recognition and, 177–9
  legacy for human rights law of, 70
  South African obligations in, 56–8
  spatial and territorial definitions in, 60–3
  territorial control *vs.* sovereignty in, 58–60
Nansei Shoto Islands, Japanese Senkaku/Diaoyudao claims and, 136–7
National Aeronautics and Space Administration (NASA), black holes explained by, 18–20
national constitutional standards, international law and, 93–5
nationalism, growth in West Papua of, 215–16
Nationality Decrees opinion, 147–9
national law
  European Community legal order and, 105
  in Eurotunnel dispute, 426–7

national law (*cont.*)
  international law and, 93–5
  international law and rule of irrelevance of, 161–6
  legal characteristics of states and, 145–7
  Permanent Court of International Justice rulings and, 151–2
  pre-emption interpretation of, 99–105
  restrictive immunity doctrine and, 182–8
  rule of irrelevance and, 93–5
  sovereignty and regime interaction and, 80n50
  statehood recognition and, 192–6
  U.S. civil rights litigation and international law and, 95–9
Naulilaa case, 356–60
nemo dat principle, *uti possidetis* principle and, 255–8
neo-liberal capitalism, democratisation and, 166–70
Nervo, Padilla, 341
Nesi, Giuseppe, 250–2
Netherlands
  Indonesian independence and, 217–19, 221–7
  West New Guinea decolonisation and, 213–14n14, 215–16
Netherlands School of Human Rights research, 15–17
New York Agreement on West Papua, 217–19, 221–7
New York Times, 45–6
New Zealand
  Antarctic sovereignty and, 114–17, 121–4
  Palestine statehood supported by, 239–42
Ng, Angie, 213–15
Nicaragua
  Colombian boundary dispute with, 267–70
  Gulf of Fonseca boundary dispute and, 258–9, 260–2
  Honduran boundary dispute with, 265–7
Nicaragua Case, 40n72, 41–2
Nigeria
  Cameroon boundary dispute with, 262–4
  restrictive immunity doctrine and, 186–7
  third party countermeasures and, 350–1
non-forcible countermeasures, investment treaty claims and, 395–6
nongovernmental organisations (NGOs)
  accountability and assessment of, 84
  Antarctic sovereignty and, 114–17
  legal framework for, 84
  regime interaction and, 73–8
non-intervention principle, Permanent Court of International Justice and, 147–9
non-member observer state status in UN, Palestinian statehood and, 236–9, 242
non-recognition of states, obligations concerning, 207–8
non-self-executing treaties, Bricker Amendment for, 95–9
non-self-governing territories, decolonisation and, 221–2n50, 227
non-state entities
  governmental authority test and, 188–90
  investment claim countermeasures and, 389–91
  law of state responsibility and, 179–82
  legal framework for, 84
  Permanent Court of International Justice rulings and, 151–2
  regime interaction and, 73–8
  sovereignty demands and, 78–84
  State responsibility for, 315–21
normative principles
  Chinese Senkaku/Diaoyudao claims and, 134–6, 138–9

fragmentation of international law and, 71–3
ILC/ICJ collaboration on State responsibility and, 297–301
Japanese Senkaku/Diaoyudao claims and, 136–7
legal framework for non-state actors and, 84
regime interaction and, 73–8
in Senkaku/Diaoyudao dispute, 131–3
State responsibility and, 288–91
territorial claims and, 138–9
third party countermeasures and, 343–7
norm entrepreneurship, responsibility to protect and, 23, 40, 48–50
North African states, migration-related cases and 'legal space' concept and, 67–70
North American Free Trade Agreement (NAFTA)
Chapter 11 investment protections in, 90–3
investment claim countermeasures and, 389–91, 397–404, 405
United Postal Service of America Inc (UPS) v. *Canada* and, 179–82
North Atlantic Treaty Organiztaion (NATO)
Banković case and, 65–7
Bosnian air strikes and, 25–6
Kosovo air strikes and, 26–7, 161–6
Libyan campaign of, 36–40
post-Cold War spending reductions and, 41–2
Serbian air strikes by, 331, 338n61
Northern Sea Route, Arctic sovereignty issues and, 118–21
Northwest Passage
Arctic sovereignty issues and, 118n45, 121
polar sovereignty issues and, 110–11, 118–21
Norway
Arctic sovereignty issues and, 118–24
law of recognition and, 192–6
Nuclear Tests cases, state recognition in, 198–202
nuclear weapons legality, implied powers rulings concerning, 81–2
Nuclear Weapons opinion, 147–9
nulla poena sine lege, state *vs.* individual responsibility thresholds for collateral damage and, 329–30
nullum crimen sine lege principle, 329–30

Obama, Barack, Syrian policies of, 44–6
objective statehood principle
collateral civilian casualties and, 325–7
Palestinian statehood and, 231–4
observer status
of European Union, 412–13
state consent to non-member observer status, 80
O'Connell, D. P., xv
Okinawa Revision Agreement, 129–130n16
Olbrechts-Tyteca, Lucie, 13–14
Operation Uphold Democracy (Haiti), 166–70
opinio juris sive necessitates
responsibility to protect and, 41–2
State responsibility in piracy defence and, 315–21
third party countermeasures and, 343–7, 350, 356–60
weapons shipments and, 45–6
Optional Protocol to the Convention on the Rights of the Child on the Involvement of Children in Armed Conflict of 2000, 54–6
Oregon Alien Land Law, international law and, 95–9
Organisasi Papua Merdaka ('Free Papua Movement') (OPM), 219–20
Organisation of African Unity (OAU), 29–30, 157–61
Orwell, George, 6–7, 11–12, 21
Ouattara, Alassane (President), 169–70
Oyama v. *California*, 95–9

Pahuja, Sundhya, 20–1
Palestine Liberation Organisation (PLO), 236–9, 240, 242–6
Palestinian Authority (PA), 236–9
Palestinian Territories
 collective recognition of statehood under UN General Assembly Resolution 67/19, 234–42
 consequences of Resolution 67/19 for statehood in, 242–6
 Israeli occupation of, 56–8, 60–5
 legacy of UN General Assembly Resolution 67/19 for, 246–7
 'legal space' concept and Israeli occupation of, 67–70
 objective statehood principle and, 231–4
 'permanent two-State solution' and, 236–9
 state recognition for, 229–47
 textual interpretation of Resolution 67/19 concerning statehood for, 236–9
 votes for statehood adoption, circumstances and explanations, 239–42
palimpsestic reconstruction
 Chinese reascendancy and, 137–8
 East Asian territorial sovereignty and, 126–8, 138–43
 in Senkaku/Diaoyu Islands dispute, 139–41
Palmerston (Lord), 341, 356–60
Paraguay, *uti possidetis/uti possidetis juris* principle and, 254n24
Paris Peace Conference of 1919, 221
Partridge, Eric, 4–5, 8
Paulsson, Jan, 426
peaceful coexistence principle, Chinese ascendancy and, 141–3
Peace Plan for Self-Determination of Western Sahara, 157–61
Pellet, Alain, 198–202, 287–8
Pemex case, 182–8
People's Daily (Chinese Communist Party newspaper), 133–4
Percy, Sarah, 315–21
Perelman, Chaim, 13–14
perimeter guard cases, functional immunity in, 310–15
Permanent Court of Arbitration (PCA), Eurotunnel dispute and, 425–6
Permanent Court of International Justice (PCIJ)
 Arctic sovereignty rulings and, 118–21
 comparison with ICJ, 302–3
 Eastern Greenland ruling, 111–14
 foundational decisions on State responsibility by, 292–6
 founding argument for sovereignty by, 80n51
 independence and, 147–9
 international/national divide and, 151–2
 legal characteristics of states and rulings by, 144–52
 normative principles of State responsibility and, 288–91
 on-going codification by, 305
 sovereignty principles and, 80n51, 149–50
 State responsibility and jurisprudence of, 287–8, 294–295n36, 301–5
'permanent two-State solution', Palestinian statehood and, 236–9
Peru, *uti possidetis/uti possidetis juris* principle and, 254n24
Peters, Anne, 279–83
The Philippine Admiral Case, xvi–xvii
Phillimore, Robert (Sir), 182–8
Phillipson, Coleman, xv
Phosphates in Morocco case, 292–6
Pinochet case, restrictive immunity doctrine and, 187–8
piracy
 defences against, 307–24
 future challenges in defence against, 324
 state responsibility and immunity issues and, 310–15
 use of force against, 308–9

plenary competence, legal characteristics of states and, 145–7
Poland
  investment treaty law and, 105–8
  Permanent Court of International Justice rulings and, 151–2
  Rolimpex case and, 186–7
  state recognition of, 202–4
polar sovereignty
  Antarctic sovereignty, 114–17
  Arctic sovereignty, 118–21
  basic principles of, 111–14
  contemporary challenges to, 121–4
  current issues in, 110–25
Polish Nationals case, 292–6
'political question' doctrine, non-self-executing treaties and, 95–9
political will
  investment treaties and, 90–3
  responsibility to protect and, 33–4
'Politics and the English Language' (Orwell), 11–12, 21
Portugal, investment treaty claims in Germany and, 396n23
power
  shared responsibility Eurotunnel dispute and, 436–8
  statehood dynamics and use of, 173–7
pre-modern legal practices, Chinese Senkaku/Diaoyudao claims based on, 137–9, 139n45
private bodies
  as government proxies, 376n65
  WTO Appellate Body's interpretation of 'public body' concept and, 369–73
private enterprise, public body concept and, 365–9
private international law
  Namibia exception and, 177–9
  state continuity and succession in, 277–9
Private Law Sources and Analogies of International Law (Lauterpacht), 277–9
private legal regimes, sovereignty issues and, 73–8
Privately Contracted Armed Security Personnel (PCASP), 307–9, 315–24
Private Maritime Security Companies (PMSCs), 307–8
private military companies (PMC)
  arms regulations and, 315–21
  increased use of, 324
  law of state responsibility and, 179–82
  restrictive immunity doctrine and, 188–90
private security
  minimum regime concept and, 315–21
  piracy defence and, 307–8
  private military companies and, 179–82, 188–90
Privy Council (United Kingdom), state recognition and, 202–4
property rights, law of recognition and, 177–9
proportionality test
  applications of, 325n1
  Articles on Responsibility of States for Internationally Wrongful Acts limits on military necessity and, 334–7
  collateral civilian casualties and, 327–9
  investment treaty case law and, 105–8
  proportionality equation and, 330n24, 338n61
  state *vs.* individual responsibility thresholds for collateral damage and, 329–30
'public body' concept. *See also* private bodies
  international legal interpretations of, 365–9
  legal implications of, 373–5
  relevance of International Law Commission articles to, 375–83
  status of International Law Commission articles on, 383–7

proportionality test (*cont.*)
U.S.-Antidumping and Countervailing Duties (China) and, 363–4
WTO Appellate Body's interpretation of, 369–73
public law
good faith obligation in, 107–8
investment treaty law, comparative analysis of, 105–8
law of recognition and, 177–9
statehood dynamics and, 173–7
public sector, public body concept and, 365–9

'Q&A on the Senkaku Islands', 133–4
Qing dynasty, history of Senkaku/Diaoyudao Islands ownership and, 128–30
Quéneudec, 255–8
Quigley, John, 229n3

racial discrimination
exterritoriality and cases of, 63–5
U.S. civil rights litigation and international law and, 95–9
Rainbow Warrior arbitration, 297–301
Rasulov, Akbar, 296n45
ratio decidendi principle, *Land, Island and Maritime Frontier Dispute*, 260–2
rationae materiae concept, military necessity principle and, 332–7
rationae personae status, state immunity and, 310–15
rebel forces, responsibility to protect and support for, 41n73, 42
reciprocal recognition of states, examples of, 196–8
reciprocity, in Eurotunnel dispute, 435–6
recognition, law of
categories of acts and intention to recognise, 202–4
circumstance of statement of conduct and, 207
collective recognition of statehood under UNGA Resolution 67/19, 234–42
constitutive approach to, 229–31
declaratory approach to, 229–31
disclaimers in, 205–6
express indication of, 196–8
identifying factors in, 204
intentional act under, 198–202
mechanisms and procedures, 192–6
non-recognition of states and, 207–8
non-state entities and, 188–90
organs or agents acting toward entity, 204
Palestinian state, 229–47
statehood and, 177–9
third party statements concerning, 206–7
Redfern, Walter, 4–5, 8, 12
reduced emissions from deforestation and forest degradation ('REDD') programs
experts' role concerning, 82–3
indigenous and forest-dwelling communities and, 88
normative conflicts over, 71–3
regime interaction for, 81
regime change
in Côte d'Ivoire, 169–70
in Haiti, 169–70
in Kosovo, 161–6
UN Security Council and, 166–70
regime interaction
experts' role in, 82–3
fragmentation of international law and, 71–89
impact on sovereignty of, 78–80n50, 84
of international laws and institutions, 73–8
legal framework for, 84
normative conflicts and, 71–3
reparations, State responsibility and, 292–6
Reparations case, 81–2
Republic of Korea, objective statehood principle and, 231–4
Republic of the Marshall Islands and Palau, 155–6
responsibility, legal concepts of, 288–91

responsibility to protect (R2P). *See also* forceful intervention; unilateral intervention
arms shipments and, 44–6
Bosnian humanitarian crisis and, 25–6, 43
Constitutive Act of the African Union and, 29–30
development of, 24–40
International Commission on Intervention and State Sovereignty and, 28–9
international law and, 23–50
international legal system and, 48–50
Iraq War and, 30–1
Kosovo humanitarian crisis and, 26–7n16-17
legal status of, 40–8
Libyan humanitarian crisis and Security Council Resolution 1973, 34–6
mitigation role of, 47–8
norm entrepreneurship and, 23
post-Libya consequences for, 36–40
rebel support and, 41n73, 42
regime change and, 166–70
Russian invasion of Georgia and, 31n34
Rwandan genocide and, 26
in Somalia (1992–1993), 25
threats, challenges and changes to, 31–2
UN Secretary-General's report and World Summit Outcome Document, 32–3
UN Security Council Resolution 1674, 33–4
restrictive immunity doctrine
law of state immunity and, 182–8
'separate entity' principle and, 188–90
Richards Lord Justice, 177–9
Ricks, Christopher, 11–12, 21
Riphagen, Willem, 350–1, 356–60
Roberts, Hugh, 37n59
Rolimpex case, 186–7
Roma Rights case, 63–5
Rome Conference (1998), collateral civilian damage and, 327–9
Rome Statute, collateral civilian casualties and, 325–7
Rosatti, Horacio, 90–3
Round Table negotiations on Indonesia, 213–15
rousing, international legal clichés and, 15–21
Rowe, A. P., xiv
rule-systems, normative conflicts over, 71–3
Russia
Arctic sovereignty issues and, 118–24
ICJ on jurisdiction against, 60–3
invasion of Georgia by, 31n34, 51–4, 56–8
polar sovereignty issues and, 110–11
rejection of extraterritoriality rulings by, 56–8
Syria and, 44–6
Rwanda, responsibility to protect and genocide in, 26

Saar Papier v. *Poland* case, 105–8
Saharawi people, Western Sahara territorial disposition and, 157–61
St. Domingo, British recognition of, 202–4
Salmond, John, xv
San Francisco Peace Treaty (1951), 128–30
Sangatte Hostel
claimants' position in, 427–8
clandestine migrants at, Eurotunnel dispute and, 425–6
Tribunal findings on, 432–5
Sarkozy, Nicholas, 347–51
Sayre, Paul, 95–9
Schachter, Oscar, 15, 273–7
SeaFrance, Eurotunnel dispute and, 425–6
sea ice melting, Arctic sovereignty issues and, 118–21
Second Hague Peace Conference, 342–3

sector theory claims, polar sovereignty and, 111–14
Sei Fujii v. *State of California*, 95–9
self-determination
in East Timor, 227–8
ethnic identity and, 221
in international law, 210–13
uti possidetis principle and, 255–8
Western Sahara territorial disposition and, 157–61
West Papua and, 210–13, 221–7
Senkaku/Diaoyudao Islands dispute
Chinese position concerning, 131–3
critique of Chinese position in, 134–6
East Asian sovereignty and, 126–43
historical overview, 128–30
Japanese position concerning, 133–4
'the name follows its owner' *(mingcongzhuren)* principle and, 139–41
'separate entity' principle, dynamics of statehood and, 188–90
September 11, 2001 attacks, regime change and, 166–70
Serbia
Banković decision on air strikes in, 65–7
Bosnian atrocities committed by, 43
ethnic cleansing in Kosovo by, 26–7, 162n47
NATO air strikes in, 25–6
recognition of Kosovo and, 192–6, 206–7
state continuity and succession and, 279–83
UN intervention in, 161–6
Settlement Plan for Western Sahara, 157–61
Seychelles, Vessel Protection Detachments for piracy defence in, 310–15
shared institutional practices
EU Member States' international agreements and, 409–11
normative conflicts over, 71–3
shared responsibility, in Eurotunnel dispute, 434–5, 436–8
Shaw, LJ, 111–14, 198–202
Shelley v. *Kraemer*, 95–9
shibboleths, clichés and, 5
shipping industry
Arctic sovereignty issues and, 118–21
guidelines for PCASP for, 315–21
piracy and defence of, 307–8
Short, Dr. Augustus, xiv
Sierra Leone, ECOWAS intervention in, 47–8
Simma, Bruno, 352–6
Simons, Penelope, 321–4
Singapore
Palestine statehood opposed by, 241–2
recognition of Taiwan by, 198–202
Sino-centric ideology, East Asian sovereignty and, 139–41
Sino-Japanese War, 128–30
Sivakumaran, Sandesh, 59–60n22
sleeping metaphors, clichés and, 13–14
Slovenia, international recognition of, 196–8
Smith, Anthony L., 213–15
socialist states, law of state immunity and, 182–8
Société Nationale des Chemins de Fer Français (French Railways National Society) (SNCF), in Eurotunnel dispute, 434
soft law instruments, PCASP guidelines and, 315–21
Solange I doctrine, European Community legal order and, 99–105
Solange II doctrine, European Community legal order and, 99–105
Somalia
humanitarian crises in, 25
piracy from, 307–8
Sorel, Jean-Marc, 250–2
South Africa
African National Congress and, 238n43

Namibia Advisory Opinion and role of, 58–60, 177–9
third party countermeasures and, 350–1
Southern Rhodesia, UN Security Council powers concerning, 24–5
South Ossetia, Republic of, 56–8
ICJ extraterritoriality cases and, 56–8, 63–5
South Sudan, Republic of
creation of, 159n26
international recognition of, 196–8
sovereignty. *See also* legal sovereignty
activity and decision-making limits for, 182–8
Antarctic sovereignty, 114–17
Arctic sovereignty, 118–21
Beagle Channel arbitration concerning, 259–60
challenges to, 88–9
Chinese reliance on, in Senkaku/Diaoyudao claims, 138–9
clichés about, 17
demands and presumptions of, 78–84
in East Asia, 126–43
European Community legal order and issues of, 99–105
human rights obligations in non-sovereign territory of treaty parties, 67–70
independence *vs.*, 147–9
investment treaties and, 90–3
law of state immunity and, 182–8
legal characteristics of states and, 145–7
legal framework for regime interaction and, 88
Permanent Court of International Justice founding argument for, 80n51, 149–50
polar sovereignty, 110–25
private international law and, 277–9
regime interaction and, 73–8
statehood and, 172, 188–90
state immunity and, 173–7
third party countermeasures and, 356–60
West New Guinea decolonisation and, 213–15
Soviet Union
Antarctic sovereignty and, 114–17
arms shipments to Indonesia by, 217–19
impact on international law of, 141–3
polar sovereignty issues and, 110–11
Spain
third party countermeasures and, 352–6
Vessel Protection Detachments for piracy defence from, 310–15
spatial applicability. *See* extraterritoriality
specialisation, regime interaction and, 73–8
'special regime' principle, State responsibility and, 290n14
'spheres of influence' doctrine, polar sovereignty and, 111–14
Srebrenica massacre, 25–6
SS Lotus Case (France v. *Turkey)*, 80n51
SS *Manhattan* voyage, Arctic sovereignty issues and, 118–21
SS Wimbledon. *See* The Wimbledon opinion
Stahn, Carsten, 33n43
Stanford v. *Kentucky*, 95–9, 99n44
State consent
legal characteristics of states and, 145–7
observer status and, 80
state continuity and succession
constitutionalist reading of, 279–83
international law and, 273–84
private law reading of, 277–9
scepticism concerning, 273–7
statehood
decolonisation and recognition of, 232n11
dynamic aspect of, 173–7

statehood (*cont.*)
future challenges for, 190–1
historical evolution of, 172, 174–5, 175n12
International Criminal Court rulings on, 242–6
Kosovo independence and, 161–6
law of recognition and, 177–9, 192–208
mechanisms and procedures, 192–6
objective statehood principle, 231–4
Palestine State recognition and, 229–47
regime change and, 166–70
territorial disposition by UN Security Council and, 156–66
textual interpretations of Palestinian UNGA state resolutions and, 236–9
UN Security Council and concepts of, 155–71
Western Sahara case study, 157–61
state immunity, law of
non-state entities and, 188–90
piracy defence, Vessel Protection Detachments, 310–15
primary and secondary rules of military necessity and, 337–8
statehood dynamics and, 173–7, 182–8
State responsibility and, 302n68
state-owned commercial banks (SOCB), public body concept and, 365–9
state-owned enterprises (SOEs), public body concept and, 365–9
state-owned natural resources, state immunity law and, 182–8
State responsibility. *See* legal characteristics of states
collateral civilian casualties and, 325–7
common intentions of state parties and, 71–3
comparison of ICJ/PCIJ jurisprudence on, 302–3
complicity with corporate human rights breaches and, 321–4
conduct of persons empowered by, 364n5
countermeasures in investment treaty claims and, 394–404
dispute settlement activity and, 304
in Eurotunnel dispute, 432–5
extraterritoriality and, 54–8
ILC/ICJ collaboration on norms for, 297–301
ILC 'master plan' for, 292, 297
international law and, 288–9n9, 291, 302n67
investment claim countermeasures and, 389–91, 404–5
investment treaties and, 391–4
judicial development concerning, 304–5
law of, 179–82
in mixed multi-party disputes, 421–41
modern laws of, 291–301
Namibia Advisory Opinion and role of, 58–60
in non-sovereign territory of treaty parties, obligations involving, 67–70
for non-state actors, 315–21
non-state entities and, 188–90
normative principles and, 88
PCIJ and ICJ jurisprudence and, 301–5
PCIJ foundational decisions on, 292–6
piracy defence, Vessel Protection Detachments, 310–15
Privately Contracted Armed Security Personnel and, 315–24
recognition on basis of, 196–8
regime theory and, 73–8
sovereignty demands and, 78–84
third party countermeasures and, 342–7, 352–60, 396–7
threshold for, in collateral damage rulings, 329–30
U.S.-Antidumping and Countervailing Duties (China), 363–88
Stavropoulos, Constantin, 221–2

Stephenson Lord Justice, 186–7
stereotypes, clichés and, 5–6
Steyn, Johan (Lord), 18–20, 63–5
Stone, Julius, xviii
Strasbourg Court. *See* European Court of Human Rights
'strategic' trust territories, 155–6
'strict status neutrality' principle, third-party recognition of states, 206–7
structural congruence *(strukturelle Kongruenz)*, European Community legal order and, 99–105
subsidies
  definitions of, 365–9
  U.S.-Antidumping and Countervailing Duties (China) and, 363–4
substantial departure standard, state immunity and, 313, 313n32
Sudan
  Palestine statehood opposed by, 241–2
  third-party countermeasures and, 352–6
suffrage rights violations, in West Papua, 224–7
Suharto (President), 227–8
Sukarno (President), 213–16
Supremacy Clause (U.S. Constitution), 95–9
supremacy of EC law, 'Exit' and 'Voice' dichotomy and, 99–105
Supreme Court (U.S.), civil rights litigation and international law and, 95–9
Switzerland
  arms exports suspension by, 44–6
  International Code of Conduct for Private Security Services Providers and, 315–21
  Palestinian statehood supported by, 239–40n49, 242
Syrian war
  Arab League and, 37–8
  arms shipments during, 44–6
  chemical weapons attack in, 38–9
  responsibility to protect and, 36–40
  third party countermeasures and, 347–51, 352–6, 360–2

tabula rasa, in East Asian sovereignty, 126–8
Tadić Case, 33–34n45
Taiwan
  international recognition of, 205–6
  Singapore's recognition of, 198–202
Tanzania, third party countermeasures and, 343–7, 350–1
'technicalisation of international affairs', regime interaction and, 82–3
technology
  polar sovereignty and impact of, 111–14
  power of, regime interaction and, 82–3
Tecmed v. *Mexico*, investment treaty law and, 107–8
Tehran Hostages case, 297–301
terra nullius principle
  Chinese Senkaku/Diaoyudao claims and, 131–3
  Crawford's work in, xvii–xviii
  Japanese Senkaku/Diaoyudao Island claims and, 133–4, 136–7, 139–41
  Senkaku/Diaoyudao Islands dispute and, 128–30
territorial claims
  Chinese position concerning Senkaku/Diaoyudao Islands dispute, 131–3, 134–6
  East Asian sovereignty and principle of, 126–43
  European law concerning, 141–3
  Japanese position concerning, 133–4
  polar sovereignty and, 111–14
  uti possidetis principle and, 255–8
territorial control, principle of
  in ICJ rulings, 56–8
  in *Namibia* Advisory Opinion, 58–60
  polar sovereignty and, 110–25

territorial disposition
  in Kosovo, 161–6
  UN Security Council authority concerning, 156–66
  Western Sahara case study, 157–61
'territorial' space. *See* 'legal space' concept
Teubner, Gunter, 87
'the name follows its owner' *(mingcongzhuren)* principle, Senkaku/Diaoyu Islands dispute and, 139–41
third parties
  EU position in international organisations and, 411–12
  recognition of states by, 206–7
third party countermeasures
  future challenges for, 360–2
  international law and, 347–51
  investment treaty claims, 396n23, 397
  joint statements of alleged abuse and, 356–60
  obscurity of, 350
  overview of, 343–7
  in practice, 347–60
  UN Charter Chapter VII enforcement parallel operation and, 352–6
Thompson v. *Oklahoma*, 99n44
tobacco lobbies, World Health Organisation and, 84
Tobago, Barbados maritime boundary dispute and, 265
torture
  restrictive immunity doctrine and, 188–90
  state use of, 34–6, 41n75
Total v. *Argentina*, 107–8
Toto v. *Lebanon*, 107–8
transnational institutions, regime interactions and, 73–8
transnational law
  legal framework for regime interaction and, 88
  normative conflicts and, 71–3
Treaty concerning Territorial Questions at Issue between Colombia and Nicaragua, 267–70
treaty law
  Antarctic sovereignty and, 114–17
  Bricker Amendment and, 95–9
  EU allocation of competences and external relations and, 407–11
  EU exclusive competences in, 407–9
  EU Member States' international agreements and, 409–11
  European Community legal order and, 99–105
  in Eurotunnel dispute, 426–7
  'Exit' and 'Voice' dichotomy in, 93–5
  extraterritoriality in framework of, 54–6, 63–5
  of free-standing obligations in, ICJ affirmation of, 63–5
  investment treaty claims and, 90–3
  legal characteristics of states and, 145–7
  'legal space' concept and, 67–70
  maritime law and, 308–309n7
  need for EU coordination and, 413
  nonratification by U.S. of human rights treaties, 90–3, 95–9
  non-self-executing treaties and, 95–9
  recognition of states in, 196–8, 204–5
  representation of EU in, 412–13
  responsibility to protect and, 24–40
Treaty of Canterbury, 422–3, 426n14, 427–32
Treaty of Peace, Friendship, Commerce and Navigation (1855), 259–60
Treaty on the European Union (TEU), 407–11
  EU Member States' international agreements and, 409–11
  EU position in international organisations and, 411–12
  exclusive competence regarding international agreements in, 407–9
  Member States' compliance with law of, 414–15
  representation of EU in, 412–13
Trendtex case, 186–7
'triggers' of jurisdiction

extraterritoriality and, 54–6, 58, 60–3
in *Namibia* Advisory Opinion, 58–60
Trusteeship Agreement, 155–6
Turkey
'legal space' concept and invasion of Cyprus by, 67–70
negligent navigation prosecution against France, 310–15
Palestinian statehood supported by, 236–42
SS Lotus Case (France v. *Turkey)* and, 80n51
U.S. arms shipments to, 45–6
Turkish Republic of Northern Cyprus (TRNC), 177–9
international recognition of, 205–6
State complicity with corporate human rights breaches in, 321–4

Uganda
ICJ on jurisdiction against, 60–3
'legal space' concept and law of occupation and, 67–70
rejection of extraterritoriality rulings by, 56–8
separation barrier with DRC, 56–8
unilateral intervention, responsibility to protect and, 30–1
UN Interim Administration in Kosovo (UNMIK), 161–6
United Arab Emirates, Swiss arms exports to, 44–6
United Kingdom
Antarctic sovereignty and, 114–17, 121–4
Corfu Channel Case, 47–8
Don Pacifico affair and, 341
Eurotunnel dispute and, 421–41
functional immunity cases in, 310–15
Immigration and Asylum Act (1999), 425–6
Indonesian incorporation of West Papua and, 219–20
investment treaty claims and, 90–3
Kosovo air strikes and, 26–7, 38–9
law of recognition in, 177–9
Palestine statehood opposed by, 241–2
partition of Cameroon and, 262–4
PCASP approval in, 315–21
recognition of Serbia by, 192–6
Roma Rights case and, 63–5
state continuity in laws of, 275n10, 277–9
State Immunity Act of, 182–8
state immunity legislation in, 310–15
Syrian chemical weapons attack and, 38–9
Syrian weapons shipments and, 44–6
third party countermeasures and, 343–7, 350–1
United Nations
EU external relations in, 411–12
law of recognition and, 192–6
Palestinian membership in, 229–31
Reparations case and, 81–2
third party countermeasures and involvement of, 356–60
United Nations Basic Principles on the Use of Force and Firearms by Law Enforcement Officials, 315–21
United Nations Charter
Article 41, 161–6
Chapter VII enforcement parallel operation with third party countermeasures, 352–6
legal characteristics of states and, 145–7
responsibility to protect and principles of, 24–40
self-determination in, 210–13
third party countermeasures and, 342–3, 356–60
U.S. civil rights law and, 95–9
uti possidetis principle and, 255–8
United Nations Commission on Indonesia, 213–15
United Nations Committee on the Rights of the Child, 56–7
United Nations Congress on the Prevention of Crime and Treatment of Offenders, 315–21

United Nations Convention on the Law of the Sea (UNCLOS), 73–8
Antarctic sovereignty and, 116–17
Arctic sovereignty issues and, 118–21
investment claim countermeasures and, 389–91
polar sovereignty issues and, 121–4
State responsibility and PCASP protection under, 315–21
use of force against piracy and, 308–9
Vessel Protection Detachments against piracy and, 310–15
United Nations Economic, Social and Cultural Organization (UNESCO), Palestinian membership in, 229–31, 239–42, 245
United Nations Economic Commission for Asia, 128–30
United Nations Framework Convention on Climate Change (UNFCCC), Conferences of Parties to, 73–8
United Nations General Assembly
Antarctic Treaty and, 114–17
decolonisation and self-determination resolutions of, 210–13
Decolonisation Committee, 155–6
'Friendly Relations Resolution', 41–2
objective statehood principle and resolutions of, 232n14, 231–3, 234
Resolution 43/177, 229–31
Resolution 67/19, 229–31, 234–46
Resolution 181, 241–2
Resolution 1514, 155–6, 210–13, 221–7
Resolution 1541, 155–6, 210–13, 221–7
Resolution 1803, 182–8
Resolution 2504, 219–20
responsibility to protect (R2P) debate in, 31–2
rules on interpretation of resolutions by, 234–42
territorial disposition and, 155–6
textual interpretation of Resolution 67/19 and, 236–9
third party countermeasures and, 350–1
'Uniting for Peace' resolution of, 28–9
votes for Palestinian statehood adoption, circumstances and explanations, 239–42
West New Guinea draft resolutions and, 213–15
United Nations High-Level Panel on Threats, Challenges and Change, responsibility to protect and, 31–2
United Nations Human Rights Committee
'exceptionalism' of extraterritoriality and, 65–7
jurisdiction in Views of, 60–3
Views and General Comments by, 56–8
United Nations Human Rights Council, 157–61
United Nations Mission for the Referendum in Western Sahara (MINURSO), 157–61
United Nations Protection Force (UNPROFOR), 25–6
United Nations Security Council
Bosnian crisis (1992–1995), 25–6
global politics and role of, 170–1
Kosovo air strikes and, 26–7, 161–6
Post war expansion of powers and scope, 155–6
regime change and, 166–70
Resolution 221, 24–5
Resolution 836, 25–6
Resolution 1244, 161–6
Resolution 1674, 33–4, 47–8
Resolution 1970, 43–4
Resolution 1973, 34–6n56, 40
responsibility to protect and, 24–40
rules of interpretation for resolutions of, 234–42

Rwandan genocide and, 26
Somalian humanitarian crises and, 25
statehood concepts and, 155–71
territorial disposition and, 156–66
third party countermeasures and, 342–3, 352–6
Western Sahara territorial disposition and, 157–61
United Nations Stabilisation Mission in Haiti (MINUSTAH), 166–70
United Nations Temporary Executive Authority (UNTEA), administration of West Papua by, 217–19
United Postal Service of America Inc (UPS) v. *Canada*, 179–82, 188–90
United States
Antarctic sovereignty and, 114–17
Arctic sovereignty issues and, 118–24
arms shipments by, 45–6
China relations with, 126–8
functional immunity in perimeter guard case in Brazil and, 310–15
Haitian regime change and, 166–70
historical evolution of, 175n12
human rights treaties and civil rights litigation in, 90–3
Indonesian independence and, 217–19
international law and civil rights litigation in, 95–9
International Telecommunication Regulations and, 417–19
investment treaty claims and, 90–3
Kosovo intervention and, 26–7, 161–6
law of recognition, 192–6
military forces and Somalian humanitarian crises, 25
Nicaragua Case, 41–2
Palestine statehood opposed by, 239–42
polar sovereignty issues and, 110–11
recognition of new states by, 196–8
Senkaku/Diaoyudao islands dispute and, 128–30, 130n16
Syrian chemical weapons attack and, 38–9
third party countermeasures and, 350–1
United Postal Service of America Inc (UPS) v. *Canada* and, 179–82
UN Security Council and dominance of, 170–1
U.S.-Antidumping and Countervailing Duties (China) and, 363–88
Western Sahara territorial disposition states and, 161
United States Military Tribunal III-A (Nuremberg), 332–7
Universal Declaration of Human Rights, U.S. civil rights law and, 95–9
Universal Postal Union (UPU), 415–17
University of Adelaide, Crawford's attendance at, xi–xix
UN-led peacekeeping forces, Somalian humanitarian crises and, 25
UN Mission in Haiti (UNMIH), 166–70
UN Operation in Côte d'Ivoire (UNOCI), 169–70
U.S.–Antidumping and Countervailing Duties (China), 363–88
U.S. – Countervailing Duty Investigation on DRAMS, 381–3
use of force
guidelines for PCASP concerning, 315–21
law of state responsibility and, 179–82
piracy defence and, 308–9
statehood dynamics and, 173–7
US-Shrimp dispute, environmental regimes and, 81
USU Target System of Terminal Dues, EU treaties and, 415–17
uti possidetis/uti possidetis juris principle
African decolonisation and, 250–2, 255–8

uti possidetis/uti possidetis juris principle (*cont.*)
Barbados maritime boundary dispute and, 265
Beagle Channel arbitration and, 259–60
Cameroon-Nigerian boundary dispute and, 262–4
categories of, 252–4n24, 258
Colombian-Nicaraguan boundary dispute and, 267–70
Gulf of Fonseca boundary dispute and, 258–9
Honduran-Nicaraguan boundary dispute and, 265–7
Land, Island and Maritime Frontier Dispute, 260–2
Latin American colonisation and, 252–8
maritime boundary dispute resolution, 258–70

Vattel, Emer de, 277–9
Venezuela, *uti possidetis/uti possidetis juris* principle and, 254n24
Verhoeven, Joe, 198–202
verticality principle, international law in opposition to, 134–6
Vessel Protection Detachments (VPDs)
increased use of, 324
piracy defence and, 307–8
state responsibility and immunity issues and, 310–15
Vielleicht ('Maybe') decision, European Community legal order and, 99–105
Vienna Convention on the Law of Treaties (VCLT)
Palestinian statehood and, 234–42
public body concept and, 365–9, 374–375n62, 383
recognition of states in, 204–5
sovereignty demands and, 79–80
U.S.-Antidumping and Countervailing Duties (China) and, 363–4
WTO Appellate Body's interpretation of 'public body' concept and, 369–73
Vienna Conventions on State Succession, 279–83
'visible college' cliché, in international law, 15–17
visual clichés, in international law, 9–10, 20–1
'Voice'. *See* 'Exit' and 'Voice' dichotomy
von Bulmerinq, August, 343–7
von Holtzendorff, F., 227–8

Waiting for Godot, 15–17
Wall Advisory Opinion, 51–4, 56–8
'exceptional' nature of extraterritoriality in, 65–7
extraterritoriality of free-standing obligations in treaties, ICJ affirmation of, 63–5
ICCPR applicability in, 60–3
'legal space' concept in, 67–70
primary and secondary rules of military necessity and, 337–8
State responsibility in, 297–301
Wang Tieya, 139–41
war crime rules
binary analytic mindset concerning, 331
state *vs.* individual responsibility thresholds for collateral damage and, 329–30
Warsaw Pact nations, responsibility to protect and, 41–2
Watts, Arthur (Sir), 41–2
weapons shipments, responsibility to protect and, 43, 44–6
Weber, Max, 175–6
Weiler, Joseph, 93–5, 105
Western Sahara
Kosovo case compared with, 165–6
territorial disposition in, 157n17, 161, 165n66
West New Guinea, postwar status of, 213–15
West New Guinea Council, 215–16
West Papua

analysis of Act of Choice impact on, 221–7
historical background of, 209–10
Indonesian administration and incorporation of, 219–20
nationalism in, 215–16
New York Agreement concerning, 217–19
Whale Sanctuary (Australia), 110–11, 114–17
whaling industry, Antarctic sovereignty and, 114–17
Wilberforce (Lord), 176–7, 182–8
Williams, Paul, 29–30
Wilson, Woodrow, 221
Wimbeldon opinion case, 149–50, 294–295n36, 302–3
World Bank
experts' role at, 82–3
Forest Carbon Partnership Facility, 81, 81n56
World Conference on International Telecommunications (WCIT), 417–19
World Court, State responsibility laws and, 287–306
World Health Organisation (WHO)
Framework Convention on Tobacco Control, 84
implied powers rulings concerning, 81–2
statehood recognition by, 242–6
World Summit Outcome Report (2005) (UN), 33n43
responsibility to protect and, 32–3, 47–8
UN Security Resolution 1973 and, 34–6
World Trade Organisation (WTO)
Appellate Body's interpretation of 'public body' concept, 369–73, 374–375n62, 376n64, 378n72, 383
Dispute Settement Understanding of, 205–6, 391–3
environmental regimes and, 81
EU membership in, 411–12
international trade regime and, 73–8
investment treaties and, 90–3, 392n12
non-governmental bodies and, 379n73
observer status for, 80
standards established for, 84
status of ILC articles to 'public body' interpretations and, 383–7
U.S.-Antidumping and Countervailing Duties (China) and, 363–88
Vienna Convention on Law of Treaties Article 3(3)(c) ruling by, 79–80
wrongful conduct
countermeasures in investment treaty claims and, 395–6
NAFTA investment treaty claims and, 397–404
normative principles of State responsibility and, 288–91

Xingxing Daguo Guanxi (Chinese power theory), 126–8

Yan Shusen, 139–41
Yasseen, Mustafa Kamil, 292–6
Yudhoyono President, 209–10
Yugoslavia Arbitration Commission, 248–52

Zhongguo Guojifa Shijianyu Anli (International Law in China: Cases and Practice), 129–130n16, 131–3
Zimbabwe, third party countermeasures and, 350–1

For EU product safety concerns, contact us at Calle de José Abascal, 56–1°, 28003 Madrid, Spain or eugpsr@cambridge.org.

www.ingramcontent.com/pod-product-compliance
Lightning Source LLC
LaVergne TN
LVHW020326220926
848484LV00001BB/246

* 9 7 8 1 1 0 7 0 4 4 2 5 8 *